Autodesk 3ds Max 2020: A Detailed Guide to Modeling, Texturing, Lighting, and Rendering

Pradeep Mamgain

PADEXI

Autodesk 3ds Max 2020:
A Detailed Guide to Modeling, Texturing, Lighting, and Rendering

Book Code: PDX016P

ISBN: 9781095759141

*For information about the books, eBooks, and video courses published by PADEXI ACADEMY, visit our website: **www.padexi.academy***

Contents

Acknowledgments

I would like to express my gratitude to the many people who saw me through this book; to all those who provided support, offered comments, and assisted in the editing, proofreading, and design.

Thanks to:

Parents, family, and friends.

Teachers and mentors: Thank you for your wisdom and whip-cracking--they have helped me immensely.

I am grateful to my many students at the organizations where I've taught. Many of them taught me things I did not know about computer graphics.

Everyone at Autodesk [**www.autodesk.com**].

Finally, thank you for picking up the book.

About the Author

I'll keep this short, I am a digital artist, teacher, consultant, and founder of Padexi Academy [**www.padexi.academy**]. I am self-taught in computer graphics, Internet has been the best source of training for me [thanks to those amazing artists, who share the knowledge for free on YouTube]. I have worked with several companies dealing with animation and VFX. I love helping young aspiring 3D artists to become professional 3D artists. I helped my students to achieve rewarding careers in 3D animation and visual effects industry.

I have more than ten years of experience in CGI. I am passionate about computer graphics that helped me building skills in particles, fluids, cloth, RBD, pyrotechnics simulations, and post-production techniques. The core software applications that I use are: Maya, 3ds Max, CINEMA 4D, Photoshop, Nuke, After Effects, and Fusion. In addition to the computer graphics, I have keen interest in web design/development, digital marketing, and search engine optimization.

You can contact me by sending an e-mail to **pradeepmamgain@gmail.com.**

This page is intentionally left blank

Introduction

The **Autodesk 3ds Max 2020: A Detailed Guide to Modeling, Texturing, Lighting, and Rendering** book is perfect for both beginners and intermediate users of 3ds Max and for those moving from other software to 3ds Max. This brilliant guide takes you step-by-step through the whole process of modeling, texturing, UV mapping, lighting, and rendering. You will learn important concepts and techniques about 3ds Max which you can utilize to create your 3ds Max projects. This book also cover the Arnold renderer.

Using a structured and pragmatic approach, this guide begins with basics of modeling, then builds on this knowledge using practical examples to enhance your modeling, texturing, lighting, and rendering skills. Each unit builds on the knowledge gained in the previous unit, showing you all the essentials of 3ds Max 2020. As you go from hands-on exercise to hands-on exercise, you'll develop a strong arsenal of skills that combined will form a complete end to end process to create high quality renders using 3ds Max 2020.

This book shares tips, tricks, notes, and cautions throughout, that will help you become a better 3ds Max artist and you will be able to speed up your workflow. This book is aimed to be a solid teaching resource for learning 3ds Max. It avoids any jargon and explains concepts and techniques in an easy-to-understand manner. The first page of the every unit summarizes the topics that will be covered in the unit. Hands-on exercises in this book instruct users how things can be done in 3ds Max step-by-step.

Practicing is one of the best ways to improve skills. This book contains practice activities which you are highly encouraged to complete and gain confidence for real-world projects. By completing these activities, you will be able to master the powerful capabilities of 3ds Max. By the time you're done, you'll be ready to model, texture, and render any scene in 3ds Max.

If you buy this book, you'll also get access to all 3ds Max files, texture files, and any other resource used in the book. You are free to use these resources in your own projects personal or commercial. These working files allow you to follow along with the author throughout the units.

What are the key features of the book?

- Covers 3ds Max's updated user interface, navigation, tools, functions, and commands.
- Explains the polygon, subdivision, and spline modeling techniques.
- Covers all modifiers.
- Covers Standard materials and lights.
- Covers UV mapping techniques.
- Covers Arnold lights, shaders, and rendering techniques.
- Detailed coverage of tools and features.
- Features **75** hands-on exercises – complete with before and after files.
- Features practice activities to test the knowledge gained.
- Additional guidance is provided in the form of tips, notes, and cautions.
- Important terms are in bold face so that you never miss them.
- The content under **"What just happened?"** heading explains the working of the instructions.
- The content under **"What next?"** heading tells you about the procedure you will follow after completing a step(s).
- Includes an ePub file that contains the color images of the screenshots/ illustrations used in the textbook. These color images will help you in the learning process. This ePub file is included with the resources.
- Tech support from the author.
- Access to each exercise's initial and final states along with the resources used in hands-on exercises.
- Quiz to assess the knowledge.
- Bonus hands-on exercises.

Who this book is for?
- Beginners and intermediate users of 3ds Max
- Digital artists
- Motion graphics artists
- Indie game developers
- And anyone who wants to learn 3ds Max

Prerequisites
- Before you start this book, you should have 3ds Max 2020 installed on your system
- You should have the desire to learn
- Willingness to be awesome

What you will learn?
- Polygon, subdivision, and spline modeling techniques
- Texturing, lighting, and rendering techniques
- Edit geometry using modifiers
- Speedup your workflow
- Create cool looking renders

How this book is structured?

This book is divided into following units:

Unit DM1: Introduction to 3ds Max -I, introduces the 3ds Max interface as well as the tools that allow you to transform objects in the viewport.

Unit DM2: Introduction to 3ds Max -II, covers the tools and procedures that will help you immensely during the modeling process. You will know about various explorers as well as various precision tools that 3ds Max offers.

Unit DM3: Geometric Primitives and Architectural Objects, explains the **Standard** and **Extended** primitives and how you can use them to create some basic models. This unit also covers AEC objects.

Unit DM4: Polygon Modeling, introduces you to the polygon modeling tools, concepts, and techniques. This unit talks about polygons components, selection tools, polygons structure tools, and modeling objects.

Unit DM5: Graphite Modeling Tools, describes the tools available in the **Ribbon** and how you can use them to improve your modeling workflow.

Unit DM6: Spline Modeling, introduces you to the spline modeling tools, concepts, and techniques.

Unit DM7: Modifiers, walks you through the various modifiers available in 3ds Max that you can use to sculpt or edit the objects without changing its base structure.

Unit DMB: Bonus Hands-on Exercises [Modeling], contains bonus hands-on exercises.

Unit DMP: Practice Activities [Modeling], contains practice activities which you are highly encouraged to complete.

Unit DT1: Material Editors, introduces you to **Compact Material Editor** and **Slate Material Editor**.

Unit DT2: Standard Materials and Maps, explains the **General/Scanline** materials and maps.

Unit DT3: Physical and Autodesk Materials, covers the **Physical** material and Autodesk materials.

Unit DTB: Bonus Hands-on Exercises [Texturing], contains bonus hands-on exercises.

Unit DL1: Standard Lighting, introduces you to the standard lighting available in 3ds Max. You will know about basic lighting concepts and light linking.

Unit DL2: Photometric Lights, describes about photometric lights that 3ds Max offers.

Unit DL3: Sunlight and Daylight Systems, covers the **Sunlight** and **Daylight** systems, **Sun Positioner** and **Physical Sky.**

Unit DA1: Introduction to Arnold, introduces you to the Arnold renderer. You will also learn about the sampling and ray depth settings.

Unit DA2: Arnold Lights, introduces you to Arnold Lights, Light Filters, Fog Shader, and Atmospheric Volume shader.

Unit DA3: Arnold Shaders and Materials, explains Arnold materials and shaders.

Unit DAP: Practice Activities [Arnold], contains practice activities which you are highly encouraged to complete.

Appendix DMA: Quiz Answers [Modeling], contains quiz answers.
Appendix DTA: Quiz Answers [Texturing], contains quiz answers.
Appendix DLA: Quiz Answers [Lighting], contains quiz answers.
Appendix DAA: Quiz Answers [Arnold], contains quiz answers.

Conventions
Icons Used in This Book

Icon	Description
	Tip: A tip tells you about an alternate method for a procedure. It also show a shortcut, a workaround, or some other kind of helpful information.
	Note: This icon draws your attention to a specific point(s) that you may want to commit to the memory.
	Caution: Pay particular attention when you see the caution icon in the book. It tells you about possible side-effects you might encounter when following a particular procedure.
	What just happened?: This icons draws your attention to working of instructions in a hands-on exercise.

Icon	Description
	What next?: This icons tells you about the procedure you will follow after completing a step(s).
	Parameter: This icons draws your attention to working of a parameter used in a hands-on exercise.

Given below are some examples with these icons:

Note: The editable poly objects vs editable mesh objects
The editable poly object is similar to the edit mesh object with the only difference is that the edit mesh object comprises of triangular faces whereas the editable poly object comprises of polygons with any number of vertices.

Tip: Dragging a modifier to an object
*To drag a modifier form one object to another object in the scene, select an object that already has a modifier. To copy a modifier without instancing it, drag the modifier name from the stack display to the target object in the scene. If you want to create an instance, **Ctrl**+drag the modifier's name.*

Caution: Preserving the parametric nature of a primitive
*When you convert an object to an editable poly object, you loose all of its creation parameters. If you want to retain the creation parameters, use the **Edit Poly** modifier.*

Parameter: Turbidity
*This parameter determines the amount of aerosol content [dust, moisture, ice, and fog] of the air. This value [range **1** to **10**] affects the color of the Sun and sky. Given below is a quick rundown of the values you can use:*

__2:__ Produces a very clear, arctic–like sky.
__3:__ A clear sky in a temperature climate [default value].
__6:__ A sky on a warm–moist day.
__10:__ A slightly hazy day.

What just happened?
*The **Detach** tool separates the selected sub-objects and associated polygons as new object or element[s]. When you click **Detach**, the **Detach** dialog box appears. Type the name of the new object in the **Detach as** text box and click **OK** to create the new object with the specified name. The selection is removed from the original object. You can turn on **Detach To Element** to make the detached*

sub-object selection part of the original object but it becomes a new element. Select **Detach as Clone** *to detach the selection as copy of the original selection; the selection remains intact with the original object.*

 What next?
Now, we will create a sphere and then conform the splines to the sphere.

Important Words

Important words such as menu name, tools' name, name of the dialog boxes/windows, button names, and so on are in bold face. For example:

In the **Create** panel, click **Geometry**, and then choose **Standard Primitives** from the drop-down list located below **Geometry**. In the **Object Type** rollout, click **Tube**. Create a tube in the **Top** viewport. Place the tube at the origin. Switch to the **Modify** panel and then in the **Parameters** rollout, change **Radius 1** to **30**, **Radius 2** to **50**, **Height** to **15**, **Height Segments** to **1**, **Cap Segments to 2**, and **Sides** to **24**.

Unit Numbers

Following terminology is used for the unit numbers and appendix:

Unit(s)	Description
DM1 ... DM7	DM stands for 3(**d**)s Max (**M**)odeling
DMB	DMB stands for 3(**d**)s Max (**M**)odeling (**B**)onus Hands-On Exercises
DMP	DMP stands for 3(**d**)s Max (**M**)odeling (**P**)ractice Activities
DMA	DMA stands for 3(**d**)s Max (**M**)odeling (**A**)ppendix
DT1 ... DT3	DT stands for 3(**d**)s Max (**T**)extuing
DTB	DTB stands for 3(**d**)s Max (**T**)extuing (**B**)onus Hands-On Exercises
DTA	DTA stands for 3(**d**)s Max (**T**)extuing (**A**)ppendix
DL1 ... DL3	DL stands for 3(**d**)s Max (**L**)igting
DLA	DLA stands for 3(**d**)s Max (**L**)igting (**A**)ppendix
DA1 ... DA3	DA stands for 3(**d**)s Max (**A**)rnold
DAA	DAA stands for 3(**d**)s Max (**A**)rnold (**A**)ppendix

This approach helps us better organize the units when multiple modules are included in a textbook. For example, animation units will be numbered as **DAN1, DAN2, DAN3**, and so on; dynamics units will be numbered as **DD1, DD2**, and so on.

Figure Numbers

In theory, figure numbers are in the following sequence **Fig. 1, Fig. 2**, and so on. In exercises, the sequence is as follows: **Fig. E1, Fig. E2**, and so on. In exercises, the sequence restarts from the number **E1** for each hands-on exercise.

LMB, MMB, and RMB

These acronyms stand for left mouse button, middle mouse button, and right mouse button.

Tool

If you click an item in a palette, toolbar, manager, or window and a command is invoked to create/edit an object or perform some action then that item is termed as tool. For example: **Align** tool, **Mirror** tool, **Select and Move** tool.

Quad Menus

The right-click menus or quad menus [see Fig. 1] are the contextual menus in 3ds Max that provide quick access to the commands/functions/tools related to the currently selected entities.

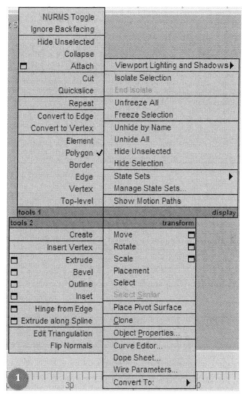

Check Box

A small box [labelled as 1 in Fig. 2] that, when selected by the user, shows that a particular feature has been enabled or a particular option chosen.

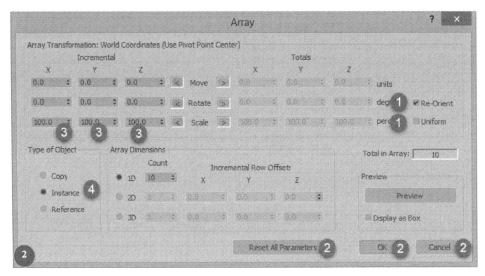

Button

The term button [sometimes known as a command button or push button] refers to any graphical control element [labelled as 2 in Fig. 2] that provides the user a simple way to trigger an event, like searching for a query, or to interact with dialog boxes, like confirming an action.

Dialog Box or Dialog

An area on screen in which the user is prompted to provide information or select commands. Fig. 2 shows the **Array** dialog box.

Spinner

Spinners [labelled as 3 in Fig. 2] are controllers that you will touch on regular basis. They allow you to quickly amend numerical values with ease. To change the value in a spinner, click the up or down arrow on the right of the spinner. To change values quickly, click and drag the arrows. You can also type a value directly in the spinner's field.

Radio Button

A radio button [labelled as 4 in Fig. 2] is the one in which a set of options, only one of which can be selected at any time.

Drop-down

A drop-down [abbreviated drop-down list; also known as a drop-down menu, drop menu, pull-down list, picklist] is a graphical control element, similar to a list box, that allows the user to select one value from a list. Fig. 3 shows the **Workspaces** drop-down list.

Window

A window is a separate viewing area on a computer display screen in a system that allows multiple viewing areas as part of a graphical user interface (GUI). Fig. 4 shows the **Render Setup** window.

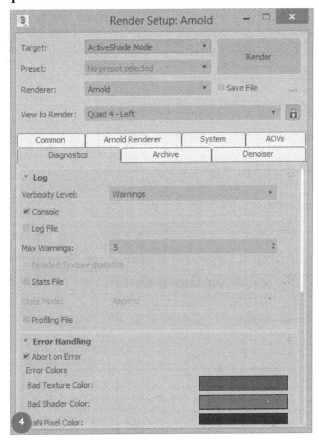

Trademarks

Windows is the registered trademarks of **Microsoft Inc. 3ds Max** is the registered trademarks of **Autodesk Inc.**

Access to Electronic Files

This book is sold via multiple sales channels. If you don't have access to the resources used in this book, you can place a request for the resources by visiting the following link: *http://www.padexi.academy/contact*. Fill the form under the **Book Resources [Electronic Files]** section and submit your request.

Tech Support

At **PADEXI Academy,** our technical team is always ready to take care of your technical queries. If you are facing any problem with the technical aspect of the textbook, please send an email to author at the following address: **pradeepmamgain@gmail.com**

Errata

We have made every effort to ensure the accuracy of this book and its companion content. If you find any error, please report it to us so that we can improve the quality of the book. If you find any errata, please report them by visiting the following link: *http://www.padexi.academy/errata*.

This will help the other readers from frustration. Once your errata is verified, it will appear in the errata section of the book's online page.

- Understanding workspaces
- Navigating the workspace
- Customizing the interface
- Understanding various UI components
- Working with the file management commands
- Setting preferences for 3ds Max
- Working with viewports
- Setting preferences for the viewports
- Creating objects in the scene
- Selecting objects
- Using the navigational gizmos
- Moving, rotating, and scaling objects
- Getting help
- Per-view Preferences, Asset Library, and Game Exporter

Unit DM1: Introduction to 3ds Max - I

Welcome to the latest version [2020] of **3ds Max**. In any 3D computer graphics application, the first thing you see is interface. Interface is where you view and work with your scene. 3ds Max's interface is intuitive and highly customizable. You can make changes to the interface and then save multiple 3ds Max User Interface [UI] settings using the **Workspaces** feature. You can create multiple workspaces and switch between them easily.

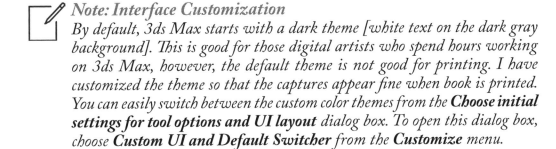

Note: Interface Customization
By default, 3ds Max starts with a dark theme [white text on the dark gray background]. This is good for those digital artists who spend hours working on 3ds Max, however, the default theme is not good for printing. I have customized the theme so that the captures appear fine when book is printed. You can easily switch between the custom color themes from the ***Choose initial settings for tool options and UI layout*** *dialog box. To open this dialog box, choose* ***Custom UI and Default Switcher*** *from the* ***Customize*** *menu.*

When you first time open 3ds Max, you will see the **Welcome Screen**. This screen hosts a slide show designed to inspire as well as provide new users some basic information to get them started.

Close **Welcome Screen** to view the default UI of 3ds Max [refer Fig. 1]. Notice, I have marked different components of the UI with numbers to make the learning process easier. In 3ds Max, commands and tools are arranged in groups so that you can find them easily. For example, all viewport navigation tools are grouped together on the bottom-right corner of the interface [marked as I in Fig. 1].

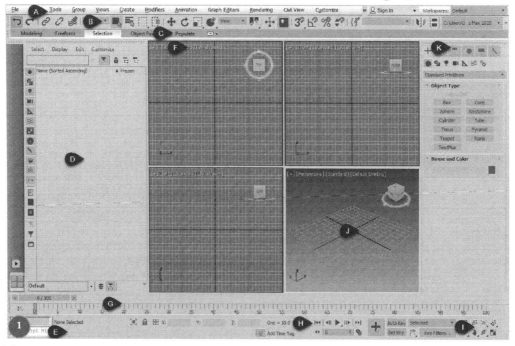

The 3ds Max interface can be divided into 11 sections. I have marked those sections in Fig. 3. Table 1 summarizes the numbers and the sections of the UI they represent.

No.	Item	Description
Table 1: 3ds Max interface overview		
A	Menubar	The menubar provides access to command and tools.
B	Main toolbar	This toolbar consists of many commonly used tools.
C	Ribbon	**Ribbon** contains many tools for modeling and painting in the scene. Also, here you will find tools for adding people to populate a scene.
D	Scene Explorer	The **Scene Explorer** lets you view, sort, filter, and select objects in a scene. You can also use it to rename, delete, hide, and freeze objects. It is also used to create and amend object hierarchies.

E	Status Bar	The **Status Bar** contains the prompt and status information about the scene. The **Coordinate Transform Type-In** boxes in the **Status Bar** let you transform the objects manually.
F	Viewport Label Menus	These menus let you change the shading style for the viewport. They also contain other viewport related commands and features.
G	Time Slider	Allows you to navigate along the timeline.
H	Create and Play Back Animation	These controls affect the animation. This area also contains buttons to playback animation in the viewports.
I	Viewport Navigation	These buttons allow you to navigate your scene [Active Viewport].
J	Viewports	Viewports let you view your scene from multiple angles. They also allow you to preview lighting, shading, shadows, and other effects.
K	Command panel	The **Command** panel is the nerve center of 3ds Max. It contains six panels that you can use to create and modify objects in 3ds Max.

There are some other elements of the interface that are not visible in the default UI. These elements appear when you run a command from the **Main** toolbar or menu, or choose an option from the **RMB** click menu. Here's is the quick rundown to those elements:

■ **Toolbars**: There are quite a few toolbars available in 3ds Max. To access these toolbars, **RMB** click on an empty gray area on the **Main** toolbar to open a context menu [see Fig. 2] containing the options for invoking the toolbars. When I chose **MassFx Toolbar** from the context menu, the **Mass FX Toolbar** appeared [see Fig. 3].

■ **Quad Menus**: Whenever you **RMB** click in an active viewport [except on a viewport label], 3ds Max opens a **Quad** menu at the location of the mouse pointer. The **Quad** menu can display up to four quadrants [see Fig. 4] with various commands and allows you to work efficiently because the commands in the menu are context-sensitive. The **Quad** menu is the quickest way to find commands. Fig. 6 shows a **Quad** menu which appeared when I **RMB** clicked on an **Editable Poly** object in the viewport.

■ **Caddy Controls**: A caddy control in 3ds Max can be described as **"in-canvas"** interface that comprises a dynamic label and an array of buttons superimposed over a viewport. You can use the standard mouse operations such as clicking and dragging to change the values in the spinners. The changes you made are immediately updated in the viewport. The **Chamfer** caddy control shown in Fig. 5 appeared when I selected edges of a box and then clicked **Chamfer**'s settings button in the **Command** panel.

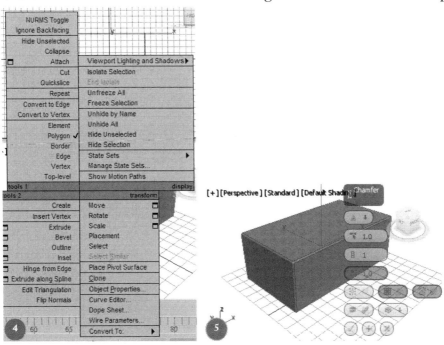

■ **Dialogs, Windows, and Editors**: Some of the commands in 3ds Max opens dialog boxes, editors, and windows. Some of these elements have their own menu bars and toolbars. Fig. 6 shows **Slate Material Editor**. You can use the **M** hot key to open this editor.

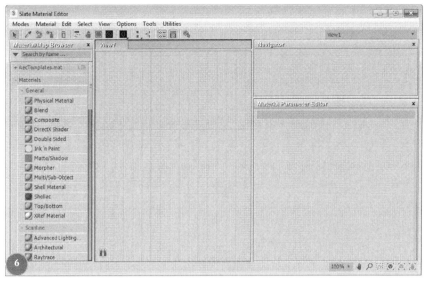

Note: Spinners

Spinners *are found everywhere in 3ds Max [I have marked **U** and **V** spinners with black rectangle in Fig. 7]. Spinners are controllers that you will touch on regular basis. They allow you to quickly amend numerical values with ease. To change the value in a spinner, click the up or down arrow on the right of the spinner. To change values quickly, click and drag the arrows. You can also type a value directly in the spinner's field.*

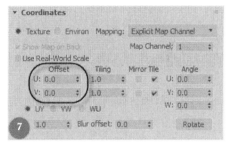

Tip: Fast and slow scroll rate in a spinner

*Press and hold **Alt** and then click–drag the spinner's up or down arrow for a slower numerical scroll rate. Hold **Ctrl** for the faster scroll rate. **RMB** click on a spinner to set it to its default value.*

Note: Numerical Expression Evaluator

*If the type cursor is located inside a spinner and you press **Ctrl+N**, the **Numerical Expression Evaluator** appears [see Fig. 8]. This evaluator lets you calculate the value for the spinner using an expression. For example, if you type* **30+50** *in this evaluator's field and click **Paste**, **80** appears in the associated spinner.*

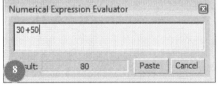

*Quite a few dialog boxes in 3ds Max are modeless meaning the dialog box doesn't need to be closed in order to work on other elements of the interface. A good example of modeless dialog box is **Slate Material Editor**. You can minimize the editor and continue working on the scene. Other modeless dialog boxes that you would frequently use are **Transform Type-In** dialog boxes, **Caddy** controls, **Render Scene** dialog box, and so on.*

Tip: Toggling the visibility of all open dialog boxes
*You can toggle visibility of all open dialog boxes by using the **Ctrl+~** hotkeys.*

UI Components

You can easily customize the workspace by floating and docking the window, panels, toolbars, and so on. You can dock any element of the interface that has a handle. A handle can be at the left or top of the element [see Fig. 9]. To float an element, click drag the handle. As you move around the handle, target dock locations will be highlighted in blue. Drop the element on the blue highlight if you want to dock element in the interface.

Caution: Toolbars
Toolbars can be docked only on the outer edge of the interface.

Caution: Resize Elements
When you move around elements, some of the elements may not automatically resize. In such cases, you will have to resize elements manually.

Note: Docking floating windows
*You can dock a floating window by **RMB** clicking on the title bar or handle of the window and then choosing **Dock** from the context menu. Then, you can select available location from the menu displayed.*

Once you are happy with the arrangement of the elements in the interface, you can save the arrangement using the **Workspaces** feature. This feature is available on the right of the menubar. Different 3ds Max UI components are discussed next.

Caption Bar

The **Caption** bar is another name for the **Title** bar. It is the topmost element in the 3ds Max UI. The **Title** bar displays the name of the current 3ds Max file.

Menubar

The menubar is located below the **Caption** bar. The menus in the menubar gives you access to various commands and tools.

What is the function of the Reset command?
This command clears all data as well as resets 3ds Max settings such as viewport configuration, snap settings, Material Editor, background image, and so on. If you have done some customization during the current session of the 3ds Max, and you execute the **Reset** *command, all startup defaults will be restored according to the setting stored in the* **maxstrat.max** *file. The* **Reset** *command is available in the* **File** *menu.*

How can I use maxstart.max?
You can use this file to make the changes you would like to see at the startup. Start 3ds Max and make the adjustments. Then, save file in the **scenes** *folder with the name* **maxstrat.max**.

Note: Templates
If you reset the scene, it will also affect the template that you had used to open the scene. The template will be reset back to its default settings.

How can I change the undo levels?
You can change it from the **Preferences** *dialog box. By default, 3ds Max allows only* **20** *levels for the undo operations. To change it, choose* **Preferences** *from the* **Customize** *menu. In the* **General** *panel of the dialog box, you can set* **Levels** *from the* **Scene Undo** *group.*

What is the use of the Preferences dialog box?
The **Preferences** *dialog box contains options that 3ds Max offers for its operations. 3ds Max behaves according to the options you set in the* **Preferences** *dialog box. You have just seen an example how you can change the undo levels. If you increase the number of levels, you force 3ds Max to obey that setting. The* **Preferences** *dialog box comprises many panels with many options that you can use.*

Tip: The Preferences dialog box
You can also open the **Preferences** *dialog box by selecting* **Preferences** *from the* **File** *menu.*

Can I undo all commands in 3ds Max?
*No. You cannot undo some commands such as saving a file or using the **Collapse** utility. If you know an action cannot be undone, first hold you scene by choosing **Hold** from the **Edit** menu [Hotkeys: **Ctrl+H**]. When you want to recall, choose **Fetch** from the **Edit** menu [Hotkeys: **Alt+Ctrl+F**].*

Why do I need a project folder?
*When you work on a project, you have to deal with many scenes, texture files, third party data, rendering, material libraries, and so on. If you don't organize the data for the project, it would be very difficult for you to manage the assets for the project. The project folder allows you to organize all your files in a folder for a particular project. You can set a project by using the options available in the **File** > **Project** menu.*

How to use the Workspaces feature?
*This feature allows you to quickly switch between the different arrangement of panels, toolbars, menus, viewports, and other interface elements. Choose **Reset To Default State** from the **Workspaces** drop-down list to rest the workspace to the saved settings of the active workspace. On selecting the **Manage Workspaces** option from the **Workspaces** drop-down list, the **Manage Workspaces** dialog box appears from where you can switch, add, edit, and delete workspaces.*

The menu system follows the standard **Windows** conventions. When you click on a menu item on the menu bar, a pulldown menu appears. You can also open a pulldown menu by pressing the associated menu hot key with **Alt**. When you hold **Alt**, the hot key is denoted by an underline in the name of the menu. For example, if you want to open the **Edit** menu, press **Alt+E**. Similarly, for the **Customize** menu, press **Alt+U**.

If a hot key is available for a command, it will appear in the menu next to the command name. You can use these hot keys to execute the command without invoking the menu. For example, to select all objects in a scene, you can press **Ctrl+A**. To execute this command from the menubar, you have to choose **Select All** from the **Edit** menu.

Not all the commands are available all the time, some commands are context-sensitive. If a black triangle appears [for example, the **Selection Region** command in the **Edit** menu] on the next to a menu command, it indicates that a sub-menu exists. Place the mouse pointer on the command to view the sub-menu.

Viewports

In 3ds Max, you will be doing most of the work in the viewports. Viewports are openings into 3D space you work. A viewport represents 3D space using the **Cartesian** coordinates system. The coordinate are expressed using three numbers such as **[10, 10, 20]**. These number represent points in 3D space. The origin is always at **[0, 0, 0]**.

By default, 3ds Max displays a four viewport arrangement: **Top, Front, Left,** and **Perspective.** The **Top, Front,** and **Left** are known as orthographic views. 3ds Max provides many options to change the viewport as well as the layout. Using multiple viewports can help you visualize the scene better.

What do you mean by an Orthographic View?
Most of the 3D designs created using computer relies on the 2D representation of the designs. Some examples of the 2D representations are maps, elevations, and plans. Even to create a character model, you first design it on paper [front, side, and back views] [see Fig. 10] and then create 3D model using these designs.

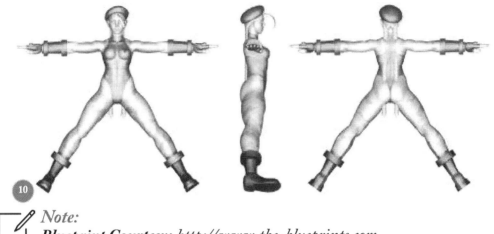

Note:
Blueprint Courtesy: *http://www.the-blueprints.com*

In laymen terms, you can think of the orthographic views as flat, or straight on. The orthographic views are two dimensional views. Each dimension is defined by two world coordinate axes. Combination of these two axes produce three sets of orthographic views: **Top and Bottom, Front and Back,** and **Left and Right.** Fig. 11 shows a model in three orthographic views [**Top, Right,** and **Left**] and in the **Perspective** view.

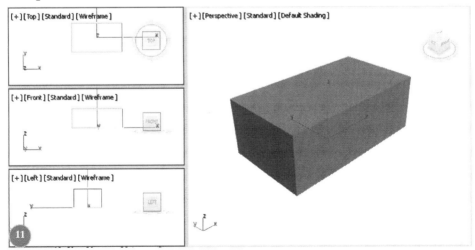

You can change a viewport to various orthographic views using the options available in the **Point-Of-View (POV)** viewport label menu. The **Perspective** view on the other hand closely resembles with the human view. In 3ds Max, there are three ways to create a perspective view: **Perspective** view, camera view, and light view.

 Can you tell me little bit more about Viewport Label menus and how can I change a viewport to the orthographic views?
*Notice on top-left corner of a viewport, there are four labels. Fig. 12 shows labels on the **Perspective** viewport. Each label is clickable [click or **RMB** click]. When you click on any of the labels, a popup menu appears.*

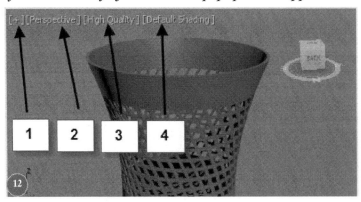

The left most menu is the **General Viewport** label menu [marked as 1], in the middle is the **Point-Of-View [POV]** viewport label menu [marked as 2], and on the right is **Lights and Shadows** viewport label menu [marked as 3]. The right most menu is the **Shading** viewport label menu [marked as 4]. The **General Viewport** label menu comprises of options for overall viewport display or activation. It also gives you access to the **Viewport Configuration** dialog box. The **POV Viewport** label menu provides options mainly for changing the viewports. To switch a viewport, for example, to change the **Top** viewport into the **Bottom** viewport, make sure the **Top** viewport is active and then click or **RMB** click on the **POV Viewport** label menu. Now, choose **Bottom** from the menu. You can also use the hot key **B**. Table 2 summarizes the hot keys that you can use to change the viewports.

Table 2: The hot keys for switching the viewports	
View	**Hotkey**
Top	T
Bottom	B
Front	F
Left	L
Camera	C
Orthographic	U
Perspective	P

The **Shading Viewport** menu lets you control how objects are displayed in the viewport. I will discuss the options in this menu later in the unit. The **Lighting and Shadows** option lets you adjust the behavior of the lights and shadows in the viewport. You can also adjust quality settings from this menu.

What is an active viewport?
*An active viewport is where all actions take place in 3ds Max. One viewport is always active in 3ds Max marked with a highlighted border. To switch the active viewport, you can use any of the three mouse buttons. It is recommended that you use the **MMB** for making a viewport active as **LMB** and **RMB** clicks are also associated with other command in 3ds Max.*

When viewports are not maximized, you can press the **Windows** key and **Shift** on the keyboard to cycle the active viewport. When one of the view is maximized, pressing **Windows** key and **Shift** displays the available viewports [see Fig. 13] and then you can press **Shift** repeatedly with the **Windows** key held down to cycle among viewports. When you release the keys, the chosen viewport becomes the maximized viewport.

How can I change the viewport configuration like the one shown in Fig. 11?
*The **Viewport Layouts** bar lets you quickly switch among different types of viewport layouts. This bar generally docked on the left of the viewports [see Fig. 14]. If it is not visible, **RMB** click on the empty area of the **Main** toolbar and then choose **Viewport Layout Tabs**. To change the layout, click on the arrow on the bar to open a flyout and then click on the desired layout to make it active.*

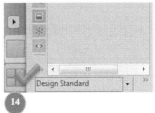

You can also change the layout using the **General Viewport** label menu. Click on the label and then choose **Configure Viewports**. The **Viewport Configuration** dialog box appears [see Fig. 15]. Select the **Layout** panel and then choose the desired layout. Now, click **OK** to accept the changes.

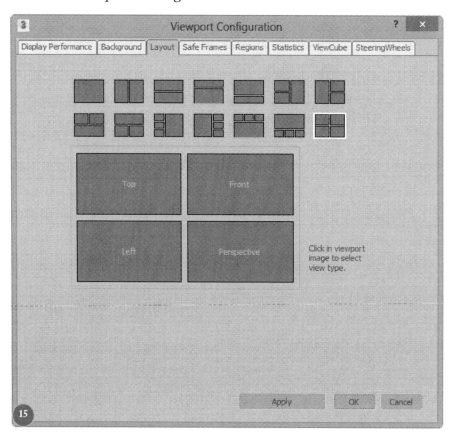

 I can see a grid in each viewport, how can I use it?
The grid you see in each viewport is one of the three planes [along the X, Y, and Z axes] that intersects at the right angles to each other at a common point called origin [X=0, Y=0, and Z=0]. The three planes based on the world coordinate axes are called home grid. To help you easily position objects on the grid, one plane of the home grid is visible in each viewport. The grid acts as a construction plane when you create objects on it.

 Tip: Turning off the grid
*You can turn off the grid in the active viewport by pressing the **G** hot key.*

Command Panel

The **Command** panel is the nerve center of 3ds Max. It comprises of six panels that give you access to most of the modeling tools, animation features, display choices, and utilities. Table 3 summarizes the panels in the **Command** panel.

Table 3: Different panels in the **Command** panel	
Panel	**Description**
Create	Contains options for creating object such as geometry, lights, cameras, and so on.
Modify	Contains options for editing objects as well as for applying modifiers to the objects.
Hierarchy	Contains options for managing links in the hierarchy, joints, and inverse kinematics.
Motion	Contains options for animation controllers and trajectories.
Display	Contains options that lets you hide/unhide objects. It also contains display options.
Utilities	Contains different utility programs.

Rollouts

Most of the parameters in the **Command** panel live inside rollouts. A rollout is a group of parameters, a section of the **Command** panel that shows parameters of the selected object. You can collapse the rollouts. When you collapse them, only the title bar of the rollout appears. Fig. 16 shows the **Parameters** rollout of the **Box** primitive in the **Modify** panel of the **Command** panel.

Once you create a box in the viewport, you can modify its parameters such as **Length** and **Width** using the **Parameters** rollout. Each rollout has a title bar that you can click to collapse or expand the rollout. You can also change the default position of the rollout by dragging the dots located on the right of the title and dropping on another place when a blue line appears [see Fig. 17].

By default, the rollout occupies a single column space in UI. However, you can increase the numbers of columns by dragging the left most edge of the panel. You can create as many columns as you want [see Fig. 17] as long as the screen real state is available. Multiple columns are helpful when you are working with an object with which many rollouts are associated.

If you **RMB** click on a rollout [on the empty gray area], a context menu appears [see Fig. 18]. This menu allows you to open or close all rollouts at once, or close the rollout on which you **RMB** clicked. In the bottom section of the context menu, you will see a list of rollouts available for the selected object. No tick appears for the collapsed rollouts.

If you have changed order of the rollouts, you can reset the order by choosing **Reset Rollout Order** from the bottom of the menu [see Fig. 19]. If you have expanded the **Command** panel to more than one column and you **RMB** click on a rollout, only those rollouts appear on the context menu that are in the column.

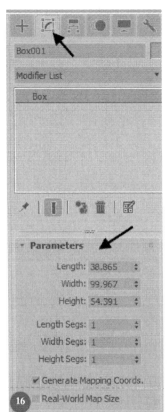

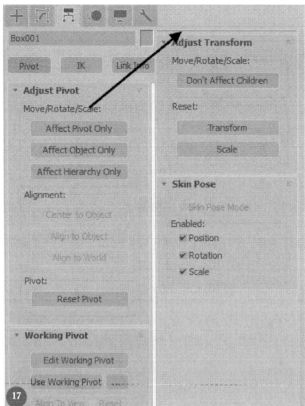

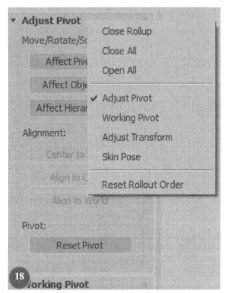

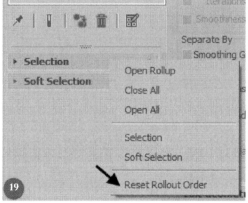

Tip: The default value for the spinners

The nature of the spinners in 3ds Max is persistence meaning that value specified for the spinners remains set for the current spinners. For example, if you created a **Sphere** primitive with **64** segments. When you create the next sphere, the value **64** will be default for it. To reset spinners to their default values, choose **Reset** from the **File** menu.

Main Toolbar

The **Main** toolbar comprises commonly used tools. Table 4 summarizes the tools available in the **Main** toolbar.

Item	Icon	Description
Undo/Redo		**Undo** reverses the last command. **Redo** reverses the last undo command.
Select and Link		Defines the hierarchical relationship [links] between two objects.
Unlink Selection		Removes the hierarchical relationship between two objects.
Bind to Space Warp		Attaches the current selection to a space warp or vice versa.
Selection Filter List	All ▼ / All / Geometry / Shapes / Lights / Cameras / Helpers / Warps / Combos... / Bone / IK Chain Object / Point / CAT Bone	Limits the selection to specific types and combinations of objects.
Select Object		Selects objects and sub-objects. Hotkey: **Q**.
Select by Name		Allows you to select specific objects from a list of objects using the **Select From Scene** dialog box. Hotkey: **H**.
Selection Region Flyout		Allows you to select objects within a region using different methods. You can create different marquee shapes using the options available in this flyout.
Window/Crossing Selection Toggle		Switches between the window and crossing methods for selection.
Select and Move		Selects and moves objects. Hotkey: **W**.

Table 4: The **Main** toolbar interface overview

Table 4: The **Main** toolbar interface overview		
Item	**Icon**	**Description**
Select and Rotate		Selects and rotates objects. Hotkey: **E**.
Select and Scale		Selects and scales objects. Hotkey: **R** to cycle.
Select and Place Flyout		Position an object accurately on the surface of another object.
Reference Coordinate System	Local ▼ View Screen World Parent Local Gimbal Grid Working Local Aligned Pick	Specifies the coordinate system used for a transformation (Move, Rotate, and Scale).
Use Center Flyout		Specifies geometric centers for the scale and rotate transformations.
Select and Manipulate		Selects objects and allows editing of the parameters for certain objects, modifiers, and controllers by dragging "manipulators" in the viewports.
Keyboard Shortcut Override Toggle		Allows you to toggle between using only the "Main User Interface" hotkeys or using both the main hotkeys and hotkeys for groups such as **Edit/Editable Mesh**, **Track View**, **NURBS**, and so on.

Item	Icon	Description
2D Snap, 2.5D Snap, 3D Snap		These options specify the snap types. Hotkey: **S** to cycle.
Angle Snap Toggle		Enables angle increment snap for rotation. It allows you to snap rotations to certain angles. Hotkey: **A**.
Percent Snap Toggle		Toggles increment scaling of objects by the specified percentage. Hotkeys: **Shift+Ctrl+P**.
Spinner Snap Toggle		Sets the single-click increment or the decrement value for all of the spinners in 3ds Max.
Manage Selection Sets		Displays the **Named Selections Sets** dialog box, letting you manage named selection sets of sub-objects
Named Selection Sets	Create Selection Se ▾	Allows you to name a selection set and recall the selection for later use.
Mirror		Enables you to move and clone selected objects while reflecting their orientation.
Align Flyout		Gives you access to six different tools for alignment. Hotkeys: **Align [Alt+A]**, and **Normal Align [Alt+N]**.
Toggle Scene Explorer		Toggles the **Scene Explorer**.
Toggle Layer Explorer		Toggles the **Layer Explorer**.
Toggle Ribbon		Expands or collapses the **Ribbon**.
Curve Editor		Opens the **Track View - Curve Editor**.

Table 4: The **Main** toolbar interface overview

Table 4: The **Main** toolbar interface overview		
Item	**Icon**	**Description**
Schematic View		Opens the **Schematic View** window.
Material Editor flyout		Opens the material editor that provides functions to create and edit materials and maps.
Render Setup		Opens the **Render Setup** window. Hotkey: **F10**.
Rendered Frame Window		Opens the **Rendered Frame Window** that displays rendered output.
Render Production		Renders the scene using the current production render settings without opening the **Render Setup** window.
Render in the Cloud		Opens a dialog box for setting up cloud rendering with Autodesk A360.
Open Autodesk A360 Gallery		Opens the default browser that displays the home page of the Autodesk A360 image library.

Main Toolbar Flyouts

You might have noticed a small triangle on the lower-right corner of some icons on the **Main** toolbar. Click and hold on such icons to expand a flyout with additional icons. Fig. 20 shows the **Selection Region** flyout.

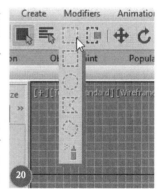

Ribbon

The **Ribbon** [see Fig. 21], is available below the **Main** toolbar. The **Ribbon** appears in the collapsed state by default. To expand it, double-click on it. You can toggle the display of the **Ribbon** by clicking **Toggle Ribbon** in the **Main** toolbar.

It contains many tabs. The content in these tabs is depended on the context. The items displayed may vary according to the selected sub-objects. I will cover the **Ribbon** in later units. Most of the tools are only visible in the **Ribbon** when you are editing a poly object.

Animation and Time Controls

The animation controls are found on the left of the **Viewport Navigation** controls [see Fig. 22]. Two other controls that are vital to animation are **Time Slider** and **Track Bar** [see Fig. 23]. These controls are available below the viewports. The **Time Slider** works with the **Track Bar** to allow you to view and edit animation. The sliders shows the current frame and the total number of frames in the range. The **Track Bar** shows the frame numbers and allows you to move, copy, and delete keys.

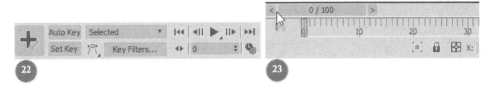

Table 5 summarizes the animation controls.

Table 5: The animation controls		
Item	**Icon**	**Description**
Auto Key Set Key Set Keys		**Auto Key** toggles the automatic key mode. Hotkey: **N** **Set Keys** allows you to create keys for selected object's individual tracks using a combination of the **Set Keys** button and **Key Filters**. Hotkey: **'**
Selection List		Provides quick access to **Named Selection Sets** and track sets.
Default In/Out Tangents for New Keys		This flyout provides a quick way to set a default tangent type for new animation keys.
Key Filters		Opens the **Set Key Filters** dialog box where you can specify the tracks on which keys are created.
Go To Start		Moves the time slider to the first frame of the active time segment. Hotkey: **Home**
Previous Frame/Key		Moves the time slider back one frame. Hotkey: **,**
Play Animation Stop Animation		The **Play Animation** button plays the animation in the active viewport. You can stop the playback by clicking on the button again. Hotkey: **/**
Next Frame/Key		Moves the time slider ahead one frame. Hotkey: **.**

Table 5: The animation controls

Item	Icon	Description
Go To End	▶▶|	Moves the time slider to the last frame of the active time segment. Hotkey: **End**
Current Frame (Go To Frame)	38 ⬍	Displays the number or time of the current frame, indicating the position of the time slider.
Key Mode	◀▶	Allows you jump directly between keyframes in your animation.
Time Configuration	⚙	Opens the **Time Configuration** dialog box that allows you to specify the settings for the animation.

Viewport Navigational Controls

The **Viewport Navigation Controls** are located at the right end of the **Status Bar** [see Fig. 24]. The controls in the **Viewport Navigational Controls** depend on the type of viewport [**Perspective**, orthographic, camera, or light] active. Some of the buttons have a little black triangle at the right bottom corner. The arrow indicates that there are some hidden buttons exist. To view them, press and hold the **LMB** on the button. When a button is active, it is highlighted, to deactivate it, press **ESC**, choose another tool, or **RMB** click in a viewport.

Table 6 shows the controls available for all viewports. Table 7 shows the controls available for the **Perspective** and orthographic views. Table 8 shows the controls available for the camera views. Table 9 shows the controls available for the light views.

Table 6: The viewport navigational controls available for all viewports

Item	Icon	Description
Zoom Extents All / Zoom Extents All Selected	🔳	Allow you to zoom selected objects or all objects to their extent in the viewport.
Maximize Viewport Toggle	🔳	It switches any active viewport between its normal size and full-screen size. Hotkeys: **Alt+W**.

Table 7: The viewport navigational controls available for **Perspective** and orthographic views

Item	Icon	Description
Zoom	🔍	Allows you to change the magnification by dragging in a **Perspective** or orthographic viewport. Hot keys: **Alt+Z**. You can also use the bracket keys, [and].

Table 7: The viewport navigational controls available for **Perspective** and orthographic views

Item	Icon	Description
Zoom All		Allows you to adjust view magnification in all perspective and orthographic viewports at the same time.
Zoom Extents, Zoom Extents Selected		**Zoom Extents** centers all visible objects in an active perspective or orthographic viewport until it fills the viewport. Hotkeys: **Ctrl+Alt+Z**. **Zoom Extents Selected** centers a selected object, or set of objects. Hotkey:**Z**.
Field-of-View		**Field-of-View** adjusts the area of the scene that is visible in a viewport. It's only available in the **Perspective** viewport. Hotkeys: **Ctrl+W**. **Zoom Region** magnifies a rectangular area you drag within a viewport.
Pan View		**Pan View** moves the view parallel to the current viewport plane. Hotkeys: **Ctrl+P**.
Walk Through		Allows you to move through a viewport by pressing arrow keys. Hot key: **Up Arrow**.
Orbit, Orbit Selected, Orbit Sub-Object		**Orbit** rotates the viewport and uses the view center as the center of rotation. Hotkeys: **Ctrl+R**. **Orbit Selected** uses the center of the current selection as the center of rotation. **Orbit Sub-object** uses the center of the current sub-object selection as the center of rotation.

Table 8: The viewport navigational controls available for camera views

Item	Icon	Description
Dolly Camera, Target, or Both		This flyout replaces the **Zoom** button when the **Camera** viewport is active. Use these tools to move camera and/or its target along the camera main axis.
Perspective		It performs a combination of FOV and Dolly for target cameras and free cameras.
Roll Camera		Rotates a free camera around its local z-axis.
Field-of-View		Adjusts the amount of the scene that is visible in a viewport
Truck Camera		Moves the camera parallel to the view plane.

Table 8: The viewport navigational controls available for camera views

Item	Icon	Description
Walk Through		Allows you to move through a viewport by pressing a set of shortcut keys.
Orbit/Pan Camera		**Orbit Camera** rotates a camera about the target. **Pan Camera** rotates the target about the camera.

Table 9: The viewport navigational controls available for light views

Item	Icon	Description
Dolly Light, Target, or Both		Moves the light or its target or both along the light's main axis, toward, or away from what the light is pointing at.
Light Hotspot		Allows you adjust the angle of a light's hotspot.
Roll Light		**Roll Light** rotates the light about its own line of sight (the light's local Z axis).
Light Falloff		Adjusts the angle of a light's falloff.
Truck Light		Moves a target light and its target parallel to the light view, and moves a free light in its XY plane.
Orbit/Pan Light		Rotates a light about the target. **Pan Light** rotates the target about the light.

Interaction Mode Preferences

If you are an **Autodesk Maya** user then it's good news for you that you can change the interaction mode to **Maya**. The **Interaction Mode** panel of the **Preferences** dialog box [see Fig. 25] allows you to set the mouse and keyboard shortcuts according to **3ds Max** or **Maya**.

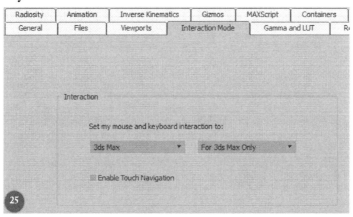

When you set **Interaction Mode** to **Maya,** most of the hotkeys and mouse operations behave as they do in **Autodesk Maya**. Here's the list:

- Pressing **Spacebar** maximizes the viewport that is beneath the mouse pointer.
- **Shift+Click** adds or removes from the selection. **Ctrl+Click** removes from the selection.
- The **Orbit** tools are not available in the orthographic views.
- **Alt+Home** switches to the default **Perspective** view.
- **Alt+LMB** drag rotates the view. **Alt+MMB** drag pans the view. **Alt+RMB** drag zooms in or out in the view.

Table 10 shows a comparison between the **3ds Max** and **Maya** hotkeys.

Table 10: The comparison between 3ds Max and Maya hotkeys		
Function	**3ds Max**	**Maya**
Maximize Viewport Toggle	Alt+W	Spacebar
Zoom Extents Selected	Z	F
Zoom Extents All	Shift+Ctrl+Z	A
Undo Viewport Operation	Shift+Z	Alt+Z
Redo Viewport Operation	Shift+Y	Alt+Y
Play Animation	/	Alt+V
Set Key	K	S
Group	None	Ctrl+G
Editable Poly > Repeat Last Operation	;	G

Getting Around in 3ds Max

In the previous section, you have seen various components of the 3ds Max's UI. Don't get hung up on all the buttons, commands, menus, and options. It was a quick tour of the interface to get your feet wet. The more time you spent on **Unit DM1** and **Unit DM2**, easier it will be for you to understand rest of the units.

Creating Objects in the Scene

You can't do much with a blank scene. You need some objects in the scene in order to work on them. 3ds Max offers a wide range of standard objects. Let's start with creating some geometry in the scene.

Start 3ds Max, if not already running. Choose **Reset** from the **File** menu to open the **3ds Max** message box. Click **Yes** to reset the scene. Notice there are several panels in the **Command** panel: **Create**, **Modify**, **Hierarchy**, **Motion**, **Display**, and **Utilities**. Position the mouse pointer on a panel's icon; a tooltip appears showing the name of the panel. The **Create** panel comprises of the following basic categories: **Geometry**, **Shapes**, **Lights**, **Cameras**, **Helpers**, **Space Warps**, and **Systems**. Each category is farther divided into sub-categories.

Notice in [see Fig. 26] the **Create** panel [marked as 1], the **Geometry** button [marked as 2] is active. Below that button you will see a drop-down list [marked as 3] that contains the **Geometry** sub-categories 3ds Max offers. Notice the **Standard Primitives** is selected by default in the drop-down list.

Below the drop-down list there is the **Object Type** rollout [marked as 4]. There are eleven buttons in this rollout. When you click on one of the buttons, the corresponding tool gets active and then you can create the corresponding object in the scene interactively using the mouse or by entering precise values using the keyboard.

Let's create an object from the **Standard Primitive** sub-category. Ensure you are in the **Command** panel > **Create** panel > **Geometry** category > **Standard Primitives**. Now, click on **Box** in the **Object Type** rollout. Notice four rollouts appears in the **Create** panel: **Name and Color**, **Creation Method**, **Keyboard Entry**, and **Parameters**.

The **Keyboard Entry** rollout is collapsed whereas the other two are in the expanded state. Expand the **Keyboard Entry** rollout by clicking on the title bar of the rollout. Change **Length** to **50**, **Width** to **50**, and **Height** to **10**. Click **Create**. You need to press **Enter** or **Tab** after typing the values. Congratulations, you have created your first object in 3ds Max [see Fig. 27].

You have not changed values of the **X**, **Y**, and **Z** parameters in the **Keyboard Entry** rollout. As a result, the box is created at the origin of the home grid [0, 0, 0].

Also, notice the name of the object [**Box001**] in the **Name and Color** rollout. Every time you create an object, 3ds Max assigns it a default name. Collapse the **Keyboard Entry** rollout. In the **Parameters** rollout, change **Length** and **Width** to **100** each.

Notice the box in the viewports resizes as per the new dimensions we have set for the **Length** and **Width** parameters. The change occurs because still **Box** is active in the **Object Type** rollout. If you select any other tool, then you would not be able to modify values from the **Create** panel.

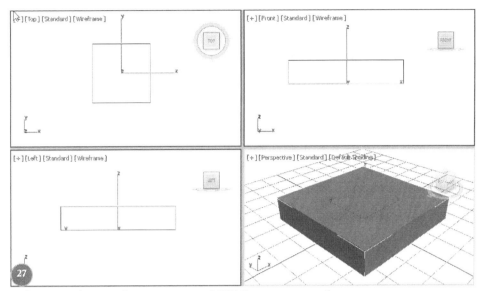

Then, how to change the parameters? Well, once you select any other tool, you can change values for parameters from the **Modify** panel [panel available on the right of the **Create** panel]. Click the **Modify** panel [see Fig. 28] and notice the **Parameters** rollout appears there. Change **Height** to **20**.

Change **Length Segs**, **Width Segs**, and **Height Segs** to **2** each. Notice the change is reflected on the object in the viewport.

Notice the white brackets around the box in the **Perspective** viewport. These are selection brackets that show the bounding box of the object. I am not a big fan of the selection brackets and don't find them very useful. Press **J** to get rid of the selection brackets. In order to change values for parameters of an object from the **Parameters** rollout, the object must be selected in the viewport. I will cover selection methods later in the unit.

Click the **General Viewport** label in the **Perspective** viewport and choose **Configure Viewports** from the popup menu. In the **Viewport Configuration** dialog box that appears, choose the **Layout** tab and then click on the layout button highlighted with white borders in Fig. 29. Now, click **OK** to change the viewport layout [see Fig. 30].

You have just changed the viewport layout. The **Top, Front,** and **Left** viewports are stacked over each other on the left and on the right you will see enlarged **Perspective** viewport.

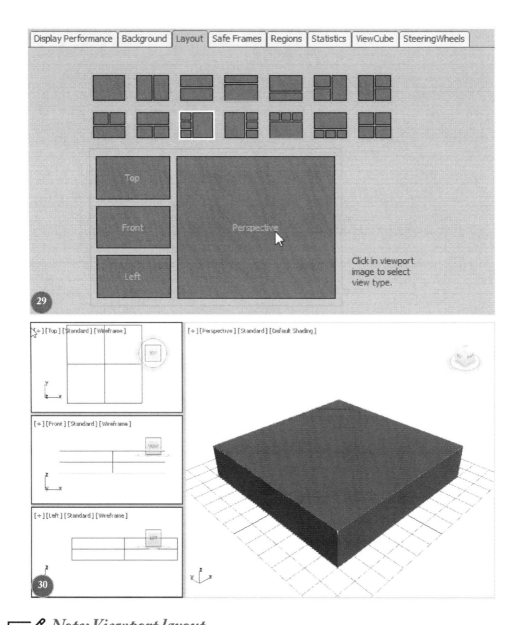

✐ Note: Viewport layout

I frequently change viewport layouts as per my needs. In hands-on exercises, if you find a different viewport layout in captures, this is the place from where you can change it. I have not written this process in hands-on exercises.

MMB click on the **Left** viewport to make it active. Press **B** to change it to the **Bottom** viewport. Press **L** to change it to the **Left** viewport. As discussed earlier, the options for changing the viewport are available in the **Point-Of-View [POV]** viewport label menu. Now onwards, I will refer **Point-Of-View [POV]** viewport label menu as **POV** viewport label menu.

Notice the text for the **Shading Viewport** label reads **Default Shading**. Click on the **Shading Viewport** label to display the **Shading Viewport** label menu. The options in this menu allow you to define the shading style for the viewport. Choose **Clay** from the menu to display object in the **Clay** shading mode. The **Edged Faces** modes allows you to view object subdivisions in the viewports. **Hidden Line** hides the faces and vertices whose normals are pointing away from the viewport. Shadows are unavailable in this mode.

Wireframe Override displays objects in the wireframe mode. The hotkey for toggling the **Wireframe** mode is **F3**. **Bounding Box** displays the edges of the bounding box of the geometry. **Clay** displays geometry in an uniform terracotta color. Fig. 31 shows the teapot in the **Hidden Line**, **Wireframe**, **Bounding Box**, and **Clay** modes, respectively. My favorite shading mode for modeling is **Clay** with **Edges Faces** and I have extensively used it in this book.

Press **Ctrl+S** to open the **Save File As** dialog box and then type the name of the file in the **File name** text box and click **Save** to save the file. Now, if you want to open this file later, choose **Open** from the **File** menu or press **Ctrl+O** to open the **Open File** dialog box. Navigate to the file and then click **Open** to open the file. If you want to save an already saved file with different name, choose **Save As** from the **File** menu.

You can also save a copy to the previous version of 3ds Max, choose **Save As** from the **File** menu to open the **Save File As** dialog box. In this dialog box, choose the appropriate option from the **Save as type** drop-down list [see Fig. 32]. Click **Save** to save the file.

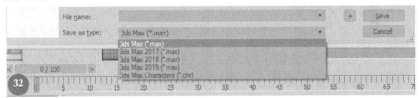

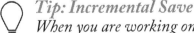

Tip: Incremental Save
*When you are working on a file, I highly recommend that you save different versions of it. If the current version gets corrupt, you can always fall back to a previous version of the file. 3ds Max allows you to save the file incrementally. In the **Save File As** dialog box, click + at the left of **Save** to save the file with a name ending in a number greater than the current number displayed with the file name. For example, if the current name is **x1.max**, clicking + will save file with the name **x02.max**.*

Selecting Objects

Selecting objects is an important process before you perform any action on an object or objects. Selection in 3ds Max works on the noun-verb terminology. You first select the object (**the noun**) and then execute a command (**the verb**). 3ds Max provides a wide variety of tools for selecting objects.

The **Selection** commands and functions are found in the following areas of interface:

- Main toolbar
- Edit menu
- Quad menu
- Tools menu
- Track View
- Display panel
- Modify panel
- Ribbon
- Schematic View
- Scene Explorer

Selecting Objects using Main Toolbar Selection Buttons

The buttons available on the **Main** toolbar provides direct means of selection. These buttons are: **Select Object, Select by Name, Select and Move, Select and Rotate, Select and Scale,** and **Select and Manipulate.** To select an object, click on one of the selection buttons on the **Main** toolbar. Position the mouse pointer on the object that you want to select. The shape of the pointer changes to a small cross if the object is eligible for the selection. Click on the object to select it or de-select any selected object.

 Note: Valid surface for selection
*The valid selection zone for the surface depends on the type of the object you are selecting and shading mode of the viewport in which you are selecting the object. In the **Shaded** mode, any visible area of the surface is valid selection zone whereas in the **Wireframe** mode any edge or segment of the object is valid including the hidden lines.*

Adding and Removing Objects from the Current Selection

To extend a selection [adds objects to the existing selection], press and hold **Ctrl** while you make selections. For example, if you have selected two objects and you want to add third object to the selection, press and hold **Ctrl** and click on the third object to add it to the selection. To remove an object from selection, press and hold **Alt** and click on the object that you want to remove from the selection.

Inverting Selection

To invert the selection, choose **Select Invert** from the **Edit** menu. The hot keys for this operation are **Ctrl+I**. For example, if you have total five objects in the scene and three of them are selected. Now, to select the remaining two objects and terminating the current selection, press **Ctrl+I**.

Selecting All Objects

To select all objects, choose **Select All** from the **Edit** menu or press **Ctrl+A**.

Locking the Selection

When the selection is locked, you can click-drag mouse anywhere in the viewport without losing the selection. To lock a selection, click **Selection Lock Toggle** [see Fig. 33] from the **Status Bar** or press **Spacebar**. Press **Spacebar** again to unlock the selection.

Deselecting an Object

To deselect an object, click on another object, or click on an empty area of the viewport. To deselect all objects in a scene, choose **Select None** from the **Edit** menu or press **Ctrl+D**.

Selecting by Region

The region selection tools in 3ds Max allow you to select one more objects by defining a selection region using mouse. By default, a rectangular region is created when you drag the mouse. You can change the region by picking a region type from the **Region** flyout [see Fig. 34] from the **Main** toolbar.

Note: Using Ctrl and Alt

*If you draw a selection region with the **Ctrl** held down, the affected objects are added to the selection. Conversely, if you hold down **Alt**, the affected objects are removed from the selection.*

Table 11 lists the types of region selection. Fig. 35 shows the rectangular, circular, fence, lasso, and paint marquee selections, respectively.

Table 11: The region selection types	
Type	Description
Rectangular	Allows you select objects using the rectangular selection region.
Circular	Allows you select objects using the circular selection region.
Fence	Allows you to draw an irregular selection region.
Lasso	Allows you to draw an irregular selection region with single mouse operation.
Paint	Activates a brush. Paint on the objects to add them to the selection.

Note: Changing the Brush Size

*You can change the brush size from the **Preferences** dialog box. **RMB** on **Paint Selection Region** to open the dialog box. In the **General** panel > **Scene Selection** area, you can set the brush size by specifying a value for the **Paint Selection Brush Size** parameter. The default value for this parameter is **20**.*

Specifying Region Inclusion

The **Window/Crossing** button on the right of the **Region Selection** flyout is a toggle button. It allows you to specify whether to include objects touched by the region border. This button affects all region selection methods I have described above. The default state of the button is **Crossing**. It selects all objects that are within the region and crossing the boundary of the region [see Fig. 36]. The other state of the button is **Window**. It selects only those objects that are completely within the region [see Fig. 37].

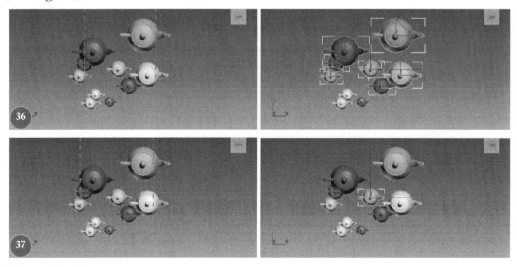

Select By Name

On clicking the **Select By Name** button on the **Main** toolbar, the **Select From Scene** dialog box appears [see Fig. 38]. It allows you to select objects by their assigned names.

To select objects by name, click **Select By Name** on the **Main** toolbar or press **H** to open the **Select From Scene** dialog box. It lists all the objects in the scene. Click on the names of one or more objects to select them and then click **OK** to select the object(s), close the dialog box, and select the highlighted objects. Use **Ctrl**+click to highlight more than one entry in this dialog box.

 Tip: Quickly selecting an object
*To select a single object, double-click on its name to select it and close the **Select By Name** dialog box.*

Named Selection Sets

You can name a selection in 3ds Max and then recall the selection by choosing their name from a list. To assign a name to the selection, select one or more objects or sub-objects in the scene. Click on the **Named Selection** field [see Fig. 39] on the **Main** toolbar to activate a text box and then type a name for your selection set. Press **Enter** to complete the operation.

 Caution: Case sensitive names
The names you enter for the selection are case-sensitive.

To retrieve a named selection set, click the **Named Selection Sets** list's arrow. Choose the desired name from the list. The corresponding objects are selected in the viewport. You can also select the selection sets from the **Named Selection Sets** dialog box [see Fig. 40]. To open this dialog box, click **Edit Named Selection Sets** from the **Main** toolbar. Highlight the name of the set in this dialog box and then click **Select Objects in Set** from the **Named Selection Sets** dialog box's toolbar.

Using the Selection Filters

You can use the **Selection Filter** list [see Fig. 41] to deactivate selection of all but a specific category by choosing category from this list. For example, if you select **Lights** from this list, you would be only select the light objects in the scene. To remove filtering, select **All** from this list.

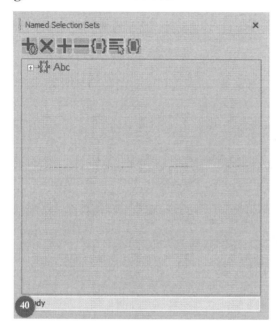

Using the Navigation Controls

3ds Max provides two controls to navigate a viewport: **ViewCube** and **SteeringWheels**. These semi-transparent controls appear on the upper right corner of a viewport and allow you to change the view without using any menu, command, or keyboard.

ViewCube

This gizmo [see Fig. 42] provides a visual feedback to you about the orientation of the viewport. It also lets you quickly switch between the standard and orthographic views. The **ViewCube** does not appear in the camera, light, or shape viewport as well as in the special type of views such as **ActiveShade** or **Schematic**. When the **ViewCube** is inactive, the primary function

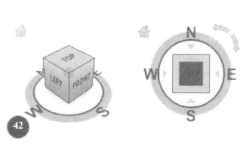

of the **ViewCube** is to show the orientation of the model based on the north direction of the model. The inactive **ViewCube** remains in the semi-transparent state. When you position the mouse pointer on it, it becomes active.

If you hover the mouse pointer on top of the **ViewCube**, you will notice that faces, edges, and corners of the cube are highlighted. Click on the highlighted part of the cube; 3ds Max animates the viewport and orients it according to the clicked part of the cube. Click on the home icon on the **ViewCube** to switch to the default viewport orientation. You can also click and drag the ring to spin model around its current orientation.

To change the **ViewCube's** settings, **RMB** click on the **ViewCube** and choose **Configure** from the context menu to open the **Viewport Configuration** dialog box with the **ViewCube** panel active. From this panel, you can change various settings of the **ViewCube**.

Table 12 lists the other option available in the context menu.

Table 12: The options available for **ViewCube** in the context menu	
Option	**Description**
Home	Restores the home view.
Orthographic	Changes the current orientation to the orthographic projection.
Perspective	Changes the current orientation to the perspective projection.
Set Current View as Home	Defines the home view based on the current orientation.
Set Current View as Front	Defines the front projection based on the current projection.
Reset Front	Resets the front projection to its default view.
Configure	Opens the **Viewport Configuration** dialog box.
Help	Launches the online help system and navigate to the **ViewCube's** documentation.

SteeringWheels
The **SteeringWheels** gizmo [see Fig. 43] allows you to access different 2D and 3D navigation tools from a single tool. When you first start 3ds max, the **SteeringWheels** gizmo is not available. To enable this gizmo press **Shift+W**. When the wheel is displayed, you can activate it by clicking on one of its wedges. If you click drag a wedge, the current view changes. The navigation tools listed in Table 13 support click action.

Table 13: The navigation tools

Tool	Function
Zoom	Adjust the magnification of the view.
Center	Centers the view based on the position of the mouse pointer.
Rewind	Restores the previous view.
Forward	Increases the magnification of the view.

To close a wheel, you can use one of the following methods:

1. Press **Esc**.
2. Press **Shift+W** to toggle the wheel.
3. Click the small **x** button at the upper right area of the wheel.
4. **RMB** click on the wheel.

 Tip: Changing wheel's settings
*You can change the **SteeringWheels'** settings from the **SteeringWheels** panel of the **Viewport Configuration** dialog box.*

There are other versions of the wheels available that you can activate from the **Wheel** menu. To open the menu, click on the down arrow on the bottom-right corner of the wheel. Table 14 lists those options.

Table 14: The options available in the **Wheel** menu.

Option	Function
Mini View Object Wheel	Displays the mini version of the **View Object** wheel [see the first image in Fig. 44].
Mini Tour Building Wheel	Displays the mini version of the **Tour Building** wheel [see the second image in Fig. 44].
Mini Full Navigation Wheel	Displays the mini version of the **Full Navigation** wheel [see the third image in Fig. 44].
Full Navigation Wheel	Displays the big version of the **Full Navigation** wheel [see the fourth image in Fig. 44].
Basic Wheels	Displays the big versions of the **View Object** or **Tour Building** wheel [Fig. 45].
Go Home	Restores the **Home** view.
Restore Original Center	Pans the view to the origin.
Increase Walk Speed	Doubles the walk speed used by the **Walk** tool.
Decrease Walk Speed	Cuts the walk speed by half used by the **Walk** tool.
Help	Navigates you to the online documentation of the steering wheels.

Table 14: The options available in the **Wheel** menu.	
Option	**Function**
Configure	Opens the **Viewport Configuration** dialog box that allows you set preferences for the wheel.

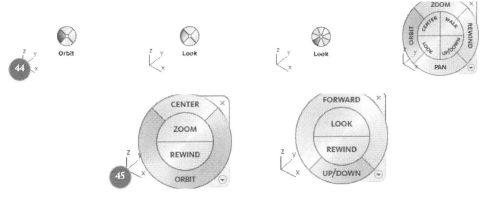

Zooming, Panning, and Orbiting Views using Mouse Scroll

To zoom in and out in the viewport, scroll the mouse wheel. It zooms in or out in steps and is equivalent to using bracket keys, [and]. If you want to gradually zoom, drag the wheel with the **Ctrl+Alt** held down. Press and hold **MMB** and then drag the mouse pointer to pan the view. You can pan the viewport in any direction. To rotate the viewport press and hold **Alt+MMB** and then drag the mouse pointer.

Moving, Rotating, and Scaling Objects

The transformation tools in 3ds Max allow you to move, rotate, and scale an object[s]. A transformation is the adjustment of position, orientation, and scale relative to the 3D space you are working in. 3ds Max provides four tools that allow you to transform the object: **Select and Move**, **Select and Rotate**, **Select and Scale**, and **Select and Place**. The **Select and Move**, **Select and Rotate**, and **Select and Scale** tools are generally referred to as **Move**, **Rotate**, and **Scale** tools. Now onward, I will use these names.

To transform an object, click the **Move**, **Rotate**, or **Scale** button from the **Main** toolbar. Position the mouse pointer on the object[s]. If the object[s] is already selected, the shape of the cursor changes to indicate transform. If object[s] is not selected, the shape of the mouse pointer changes to a cross hair. Now, drag the mouse pointer to apply the transform. You can restrict the motion to one or two axes by using the transform gizmos. The transform gizmos are the icons displayed in the viewport. Fig. 46 shows the **Move**, **Rotate**, and **Scale** gizmos, respectively.

Tip: Changing size of the gizmos
You can change the size of the gizmos by using the – and = keys on the main keyboard.

When no transform tool is active and you select objects, an axis tripod appears in the viewports [see Fig. 47]. Each axis tripod consists of three lines labeled as **X**, **Y**, and **Z**. The orientation of the tripod indicates the orientation of the current reference coordinate system.

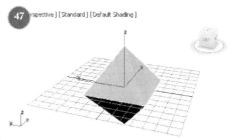

The point where the three lines meet indicates the current transform center and the highlighted red axis lines show the current axis constraints. Each gizmo indicates axes by using three colors: **X** is red, **Y** is green, and **Z** is blue. You can use any of the axes handles to constrain transformation to that axis.

The transform commands are also available from the **Quad** menu. To transform an object using the **Quad** menu, **RMB** click on the selected object[s], choose the transform command from the **Quad** menu and then drag the object to apply the transform.

Tip: Cancelling transform
*To cancel a transform, **RMB** click while dragging the mouse.*

Using the Transform Type-In dialog box

You can use the **Transform Type-In** dialog box to precisely enter the transformation values. To transform objects using this dialog box, make sure the **Move, Rotate**, or **Scale** tool is active, and then press **F12** to open the dialog box. You can also choose **Transform Type-In** from the **Edit** menu to open the associated **Transform Type-In** dialog box. Fig. 48 shows the **Move Transform Type-In, Rotate Transform Type-In**, and **Scale Transform Type-In** dialog boxes, respectively. You can enter both the absolute and relative transformation values in this dialog box.

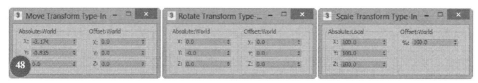

Tip: Transform Type-In dialog box
*You can also open this dialog box by **RMB** clicking on the tool's button on the **Main** toolbar.*

The parameters in this dialog box are also replicated in the **Status Bar**. You can use these **Transform Type-In** boxes in the **Status Bar** to transform the object. To switch between the absolute and relative transform modes, click the **Relative/Absolute Transform Type-In** button in the **Status Bar** [see Fig. 49].

Getting Help

Autodesk provides rock solid documentation for 3ds Max. There are several places in the UI from where you can access different forms of help. The help options are listed in the **Help** menu [see Fig. 50]. Click **Autodesk 3ds Max Help** from the **Help** menu to open the online documentation for 3ds Max. You can also download offline help from the Autodesk website and install on your computer. If you have a slow internet connection, you can download the offline help and use it. To access offline help, download and install it on your system. Press **Alt+U+P** hot keys to open the **Preferences** dialog box [refer Fig. 51].

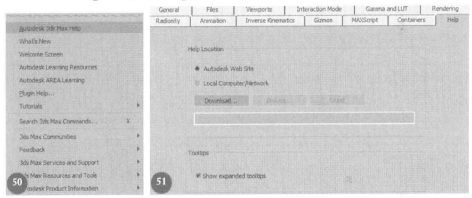

To use offline help, choose the **Help** panel from the dialog box. Next, click on the **Download** button to open the **Download** and **Install 3ds Max Product Help** page in your browser. Download help files from this page and install it. Now, click **Browse** to open the **Choose Local Help Folder** dialog box. In this dialog box, navigate to the directory where you installed help and then click **Select Folder** to close the dialog box. Click **OK** from the **Preferences** dialog box to close it. Now, when you press **F1**, 3ds Max will navigate you to the offline help.

Search Command

This feature helps you finding a specific command. For example, if you are looking for the **Sunlight** tool but not sure where it is on the interface. Press **X** to open the **Search Command** text box and then type **Sun; SunLight** System appears in a list. Click on it, 3ds Max takes you to **Systems** category of the **Create** panel in the **Command** panel.

Explore More

Per-view Preferences and Presets

We can define display quality settings for each viewport. For example, you can specify the rendering level [**Basic, Advanced**, and **DX**], Lighting and Shadow settings, ambient occlusion settings, and so on. The Per-view Preferences and Presets can be accessed from the **Viewport Setting and Preference** dialog box [see Fig. 52]. To open this dialog box, choose **Per-View Presets** from the third viewport label menu or **Per-View Preference** from the fourth viewport label menu.

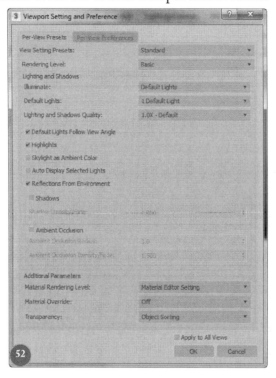

3ds Max Asset Library

To open the library, choose **Launch 3ds Max Asset Library** from the **Content** menu; 3ds Max opens the **https://apps.autodesk.com/en** page in the default browser. Choose **3ds Max** from the **Product Stores** column on the page and then download the desired app from this browser.

Game Exporter Utility

This utility [see Fig. 53] allows you to export the models and animations clips in **FBX** format to your game engine in a streamlined fashion.

This utility is specifically designed for game users to export game assets more efficiently. This utility uses minimal amount of settings, as a result, you can easily export the model without changing too many settings. It also supports animation clips thus allows you to export multiple clips as a single FBX file or as multiple files.

You can open this utility from the **File** menu or **Utilities** panel:

- **Utilities** panel > **Utilities** rollout > **More** button > **Utilities** dialog box > **Game Exporter** option
- **File** menu > **Export** > **Game Exporter**

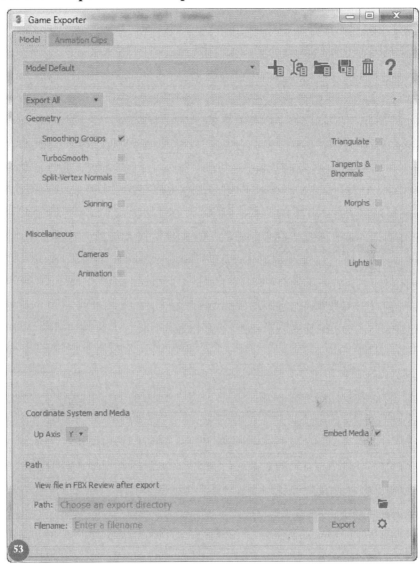

Hands-on Exercise

Before you start the exercise, let's first create a project folder for the hands-on exercise of this unit. You can proceed without creating a project folder but I highly recommend that you create one. The project folder allows you to keep your file organized.

Open **Windows Explorer** and create a new directory with the name **max2020projects** in the **C** drive of your system. Start 3ds Max. From the **File** menu, choose **Reset**. Click **Yes** from the dialog box that opens. From the **File** menu, choose **Project** > **Create Default** to open the **Choose a folder** dialog box. In this dialog box, navigate to the **3dsmax2020projects** directory and then click **New Folder** and then rename the folder as **unit-dm1**. Select the folder and then click **Select Folder** to create the project folder. Now, if you navigate to the **\max2020projects\unit-dm1** directory, you will see a number of sub-directories [see Fig. E1].

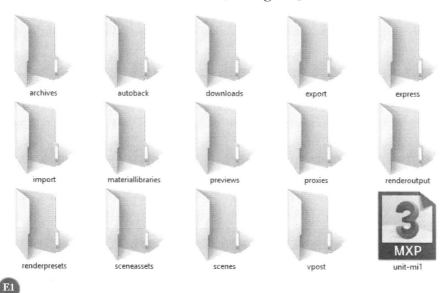

E1

What just happened?
*Here, I have set a project folder for the hands-on exercise of this unit. When you set a project folder for a scene, 3ds Max creates a series of folders such as **scenes**, **sceneassets**, and so on. These folders are default locations for certain types of operations in 3ds Max. For example, the **scenes** folder is used when 3ds Max opens or saves scene files.*

Tip: Resetting Scene
*It is a good idea to reset the scene before you start new work because the **Open** command defaults to the folder where the previous scene was saved. After the **Reset** operation, the **Open** command defaults to the **scenes** folder of the current project folder.*

Exercise 1: Creating Simple Model of a House
OK, now it is time to work on the first exercise of the book. In this exercise, we will create a simple model of a house using **Standard Primitives** [see Fig. E2].

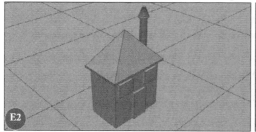

E2

Table E1 summarizes the exercise:

Table E1	
Skill level	Beginner
Time to complete	20 Minutes
Resources folder	**unit-dm1**
Final file	**house-finish.max**

1. Start 3ds Max. Choose **Reset** from the **File** menu. Click **Yes** on the **3ds Max** message box to reset the settings. Choose **Unit Setup** from the **Customize** menu to open the **Units Setup** dialog box. Ensure that **Generic Units** is selected in this dialog box and then click **OK** to close the dialog box.

2. Click **Box** in the **Object Type** rollout in the **Command** panel and then click-drag in the **Perspective** viewport to define the length and width of the box. Release the mouse button to define the length and width of the box. Release the **LMB** and then drag upward to define the height. Click to specify the height.

3. Press **J** to turn off the selection brackets and **F4** to turn on the **Edged Faces** mode. Now, click on the **Shading Viewport** label and choose **Clay** from the popup menu.

4. Press **G** To turn off the grid. Press **G** again to turn it on. Drag the mouse pointer with the **MMB+Alt** held down to rotate the view. Drag the mouse pointer with the **MMB** held down to pan the view. Drag the mouse pointer with the **Ctrl+Alt+MMB** held down to zoom in or out of the view. You need to place the mouse pointer on the area for which you want to change the magnification. Next, you will use the brackets keys to change the settings.

5. Place the mouse pointer on the area for which you want to change the magnification settings and then use the bracket keys [and] to change the level of magnification. **MMB** click on the **Perspective** viewport to make it active, if not already active. Press **Alt+W** to maximize the viewport. Click on the **Home** icon on the **ViewCube** to restore the home view. Alternatively, you can **RMB** click on the **ViewCube** and then choose **Home** from the **ViewCube's** menu.

6. Press **Alt+W** again to restore the four viewport arrangement. Click drag the compass ring of the **ViewCube** to change the orientation of the viewport. Now, click-drag edges, corners, or faces of the **ViewCube** and experiment with various possibilities that **ViewCube** offers. When done, click on the **Home** icon to restore the view.

7. Press **Shift+Z** repeatedly to undo the scene view changes. Press **Shift+Y** to redo the scene view changes. Click on the **ViewCube's Home** icon to restore the home view.

8. Press **Ctrl+P** to activate the **Pan View** tool and then drag in the viewport to pan the view. Now, press **Ctrl+R** to activate the **Orbit** tool and drag in the viewport to rotate the view. Press **Q** to deactivate the **Orbit** tool and activate the **Select** tool. Press **Shift+W** to activate **StreeringWheels**. Click-drag the **ZOOM** wedge to change the magnification level. Similarly, experiment with other wedges of the wheel. Press **Esc** to deactivate **SteeringWheels**.

9. Make sure **Box001** is selected in the viewport and then **RMB** click on the **Move** tool to open the **Move Transform Type-In** dialog box. In the **Absolute:World** group of the dialog box, **RMB** click on the spinners' arrows to set them to their default values which is **0**. You will notice that the box is now placed at the origin in the viewports. The **Move Transform Type-In** dialog box is a modeless dialog box. You don't have to close it in order to work on the model we are creating in this exercise.

10. Choose the **Modify** panel in the **Command** panel. In the **Parameters** rollout, change **Length**, **Width**, and **Height** to **80**, **50**, and **70**, respectively, to change the size of the box. Press **Ctr+Shift+Z** to zoom the box to its extents in all viewports [see Fig. E3]. If you press **Z** the box will be zoomed in the active viewport only.

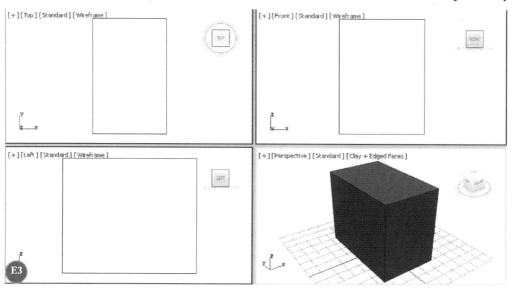

11. Now, let's create door and windows of the house. Create another box in the **Perspective** viewport and then set its **Length**, **Width**, and **Height** to **23**, **6**, and **40**, respectively [see Fig. E4]. Ensure **Box002** as well as the **Move** tool is selected and then enter **-25**, **-2.3**, and **-0.03** in the **Transform Type-In** boxes in the **Status Bar** [see Fig. E5].

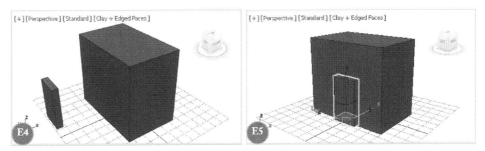

12. Create two windows using the **Box** primitive. Use the values **23**, **6**, and **18** for the **Length**, **Width**, and **Height** spinners, respectively. Now, align the boxes [see Fig. E6]. Ensure the **Box** tool is active and then select the **AutoGrid** check box from the **Object Type** rollout. Position the mouse pointer on the **Box001**, an axis tripod shows up [see Fig. E7]. Create a box on the **Box001**.

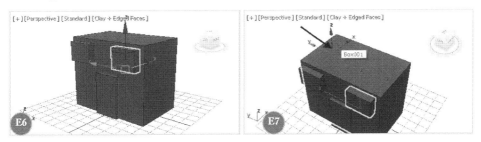

13. Ensure **Box005** is selected and then click **Align** in the **Main** toolbar. Now, click **Box001** in the **Perspective** viewport to open the **Align Selection** dialog box. In this dialog box, set the values as shown in Fig. E8 and click **OK** to align the boxes.

14. Ensure **Box005** is selected and then choose the **Modify** panel. In the **Parameters** rollout, change **Length**, **Width**, and **Height** to **91**, **60**, and **2**, respectively [see Fig. E9]. Choose the **Create** panel and ensure **Auto Grid** is on. Click **Pyramid** in the **Object Type** rollout and then create a pyramid on **Box005**. Align **Pyramid001** with **Box005** using the **Align** tool. Ensure **Pyramid001** is selected and then in the **Modify** panel > **Parameters** rollout, set **Width**, **Depth**, and **Height** to **60**, **90**, and **46**, respectively [see Fig. E10].

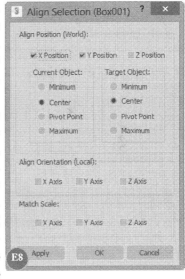

15. Now, let's create a chimney for the house. In the **Create** panel, choose **Cylinder** from the **Object Type** rollout and create a cylinder in the **Perspective** viewport. In the **Modify** panel > **Parameters** rollout, set **Radius** and **Height** to **5** and **60**, respectively. Now, place **Cylinder001** on the roof using the **Move** tool [see Fig. E11]. In the **Create** panel, choose **Cone** from the **Object Type** rollout and ensure **AutoGrid** is on. Create a cone on **Cylinder001**. Align **Cone001** and **Cylinder001**.

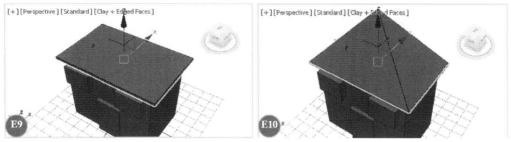

16. In the **Modify** panel > **Parameters** rollout, set **Radius 1, Radius 2,** and **Height** to **7.5, 2,** and **13,** respectively [see Fig. E12].

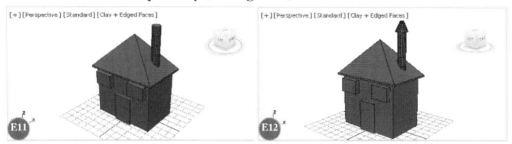

17. Choose **Select All** from the **Edit** menu to select all objects in the scene. Choose **Group** from the **Group** menu to open the **Group** dialog box. In this dialog box, type **House** in the **Group name** field and click **OK** to create a group. Press **Ctrl+S** to open the **Save File As** dialog box. In this dialog box, navigate to the location where you want to save the file. Type the name of the file in the **File name** text box and then click **Save** to save the file.

Quiz

Evaluate your skills to see how many questions you can answer correctly.

Multiple Choice
Answer the following questions:

1. Which the following keys is used for slower scroll rate in a spinner?

   [A] Alt   [B] Ctrl
   [C] Alt+Ctrl   [D] Shift

2. Which of the following keys is used to invoke the **Select Object** tool?

   [A] S   [B] Q
   [C] W   [D] R

3. Which of the following keys is used to switch any active viewport between its normal size and full-screen size?

[A] Alt+X   [B] Alt+M
[C] Alt+G   [D] Alt+W

4. Which the following keys is used to lock and unlock the selection?

[A] Spacebar   [B] L
[C] Alt+L   [D] Ctrl+L

5. Which of the following hot keys are used to invoke the **SteeringWheel** gizmo?

[A] Shift+S   [B] Shift+W
[C] Shift+A   [D] Shift+X

Fill in the Blanks
Fill in the blanks in each of the following statements:

1. Press _____ to open the **Numeric Expression Evaluator** for a spinner.

2. _____ click on a spinner to set it to its default value.

3. The _____ command is used to reset 3ds Max default settings.

4. The _____ hotkeys are used to hold the scene. To recall the scene you can press _____.

5. To select all objects in a scene press _____.

6. The _____, _____, and _____ hotkeys are used to invoke **Select and Move, Select and Rotate**, and **Select and Scale** tools.

7. The _____ hotkeys are used to switch to the default **Perspective** view angle.

8. To deselect all objects in a scene press _____.

9. You can change the size of the transform gizmos using the _____ and _____ keys on the main keyboard.

10. Press _____ to turn off the selection brackets.

11. Press _____ to toggle the wireframe mode.

12. Press _____ to toggle the edges face mode.

True of False
State whether each of the following is true or false:

1. You can use the **Ctrl** key for faster scroll rate in a spinner.

2. Press **Ctrl+~** to toggle the visibility of all open dialogs in 3ds Max.

3. Toolbars can only be docked on the outer edge of the interface.

4. You can press **H** to turn off the grid in the active viewport.

5. The **S** key is used to cycle through snap options.

6. You can press **Ctrl+I** to invert the current selection.

7. The **Shift+Z** and **Shift+Y** hot keys are used to undo and redo the scene view changes, respectively. [T/F]

Summary
The unit covered the following topics:

- Understanding workspaces
- Navigating the workspace
- Customizing the interface
- Understanding various UI components
- Working with the file management commands
- Setting preferences for 3ds Max
- Working with viewports
- Setting preferences for the viewports
- Creating objects in the scene
- Selecting objects
- Using the navigational gizmos
- Moving, rotating, and scaling objects
- Getting help
- Per-view Preferences, Asset Library, and Game Exporter

- Creating clones and duplicates
- Understanding hierarchies
- Working with the **Scene** and **Layer** Explorers
- Understanding the **Mirror**, **Select and Place**, and **Select and Manipulate** tools
- Working with the **Align** and **Array** tools
- Working with precision and drawing aids
- Understanding modifiers, and normals

Unit DM2: Introduction to 3ds Max - II

In the previous unit, I covered the interface as well as the tools that allow you to transform objects in the viewport. In this unit, I will cover the tools and procedures that will help you immensely during the modeling process. You will know about various explorers as well as various precision tools that 3ds Max offers. I have also covered the procedures for creating clones and duplicates.

Creating Copies, Clones, and References

The general terms used for duplicating objects is cloning. To create a duplicate, clone, or reference, transform [move, rotate, or scale] the object with **Shift** held down. This process is generally called **Shift+Transform**. There are some other tools such as the **Mirror** tool available in 3ds Max that allows you to create clones.

 What's is the difference between Copy, Instance, and Reference?
*There are three methods available in 3ds Max to clone the objects: **Copy**, **Instance**, and **Reference**. At geometry level, clones created using any method are identical. However, they behave differently when used with the modifiers such as **Bend** or **Twist**.*

*The **Copy** method allows you to create a completely different copy of the original object. If you modify the original object, it will have no effect on the other. The **Instance** method creates a completely interchangeable clone of the original. If you modify the original or the instance, the change will be replicated in both objects.*

The **Reference** method creates a clone dependent on the original upto the point when the object was created. If you apply a new modifier to the referenced object, it will affect only that object. Depending on the method used, the cloned objects are called copies, instances, or references.

Cloning Techniques

3ds Max provides several techniques for creating clones. You can use any of these techniques on any selection. Here's the list:

* Clone
* Shift+Clone
* Snapshot
* **Array** tool
* **Mirror** tool
* **Spacing** tool
* **Clone and Align** tool
* Copy/Paste (**Scene Explorer**)

Table 1 summarizes these techniques:

Table 1: The list of cloning techniques	
Technique	Description
Clone	The easiest method for creating clones is to use the **Clone** command. To create clone using this command, select the object[s] that you want to clone and then choose **Clone** from the **Edit** menu or press **Ctrl+V**. The **Clone Options** dialog box appears. Choose the method you want to use from the **Object** group of the dialog box and then specify a name for the cloned object using **Name** text box and then click **OK** to create a clone. The clone will be superimposed on the original object at the same location. Use the **Move** tool to separate the two.
Shift+Drag	You can use this technique to clone objects while transforming them. This technique is most used technique for cloning objects. To clone and transform objects, click **Move**, **Rotate**, or **Scale** in the **Main** toolbar and then select an object, multiple objects, group, or sub-objects in a viewport. Hold down **Shift** and then drag the selection. As you drag the selection, a clone is created and transformed. Now, release **Shift** and mouse button to open the **Clone Options** dialog box. Change the settings and click **OK** to create a clone.
Snapshot	You can use this feature to create an animated object over time. You can create a single clone on any frame or you can create clones on multiple frames along the animation path. The spacing between the clones is a uniform time interval.

Table 1: The list of cloning techniques	
Technique	**Description**
Array	You can use the **Array** tool to create repeating design patterns for example, legs of a round coffee table, blades of a jet engine, text on the dial of a watch, and so on. The **Array** command allows you to precisely control the transformations in the 3D space.
Mirror	**Mirror** allows you to create a symmetrical copy along any combination of axes. This tool also provides an option "**No Clone**" that allows you to perform a mirror operation without creating a clone.
Spacing tool	This tool distributes objects along a path defined by a spline. You can control the spacing between the objects.
Clone and Align tool	This tool allows you to distribute the source objects to a selection of destination objects. This tool is very useful when you work on an imported CAD file that contains lots of symbols. For example, you can replace the chair symbols in the CAD file with the actual chair geometry en masse.
Copy/Paste (Scene Explorer)	You can use the **Scene Explorer**'s **Edit** menu command to copy paste nodes. The **Scene Explorer** should be in **Sort By Hierarchy** mode.

Working with the Mirror Tool

On clicking **Mirror** in the **Main** toolbar, the **Mirror** dialog box appears [see Fig. 1]. The parameters in this dialog box allow you to mirror the current selection about the center of the current coordinate system. You can also create a clone while mirroring a selection. To mirror an object, make a selection in a viewport. Click **Mirror** in the **Main** toolbar or choose **Mirror** from the **Tools** menu. In the **Mirror** dialog box that appears, set the parameters and click **OK** [refer to Fig. 2]. In Fig. 2, I first selected the left leg of the robot and then used the **Mirror** dialog box to create his right leg.

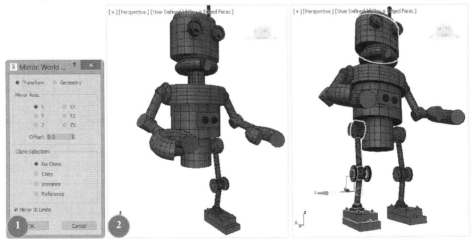

Notice in the **Mirror** dialog box, there are two options at the top: **Transform** and **Geometry**. These options control how the **Mirror** tool treats the reflected geometry. **Transform** uses the legacy mirror method. This method mirrors any word-space-modifiers [WSM] effect. **Geometry** applies a **Mirror** modifier to the object and does not mirror any **WSM** effect.

Tip: Mirrored arrays
*You can create mirrored arrays using the **Mirror** and **Array** tools in succession.*

Tip: Animating the mirror operation
*To animate the mirror operation, enable **Auto Key** and then set a target frame for the transition to end. Now, mirror the object using the **Mirror** tool. The object will appear flatten and then will reshape itself during the transition.*

Tip: Coordinate system
*The title bar of the **Mirror** dialog box shows the current coordinate system in use.*

Working with the Array Tool

The **Array** tool allows you to create an array of objects based on the current selection in the viewport. The **Array** button is not visible in the **Main** toolbar by default. The **Array** button is part of the **Extras** toolbar which is not visible by default.

To make it visible, **RMB** click on the empty gray area of **Main** **Toolbar** and then choose **Extras** from the popup to display the **Extras** toolbar [see Fig. 3].

Tip: Array command
*The **Array** command is also available in the **Tools** menu.*

Tip: Real-time update
*Click **Preview** in the **Array** dialog box to view the changes in the viewport as you change settings in the dialog box.*

To understand the functioning of this tool, reset 3ds Max, and create a teapot in the scene. Ensure teapot is selected in a viewport and then choose **Array** from the **Tools** menu to open the **Array** dialog box. Now, click **Preview** and set other parameters as shown in Fig. 4. Notice in Fig. 4, 3ds Max creates **4** copies of the teapot with **60** units distance between each copy.

Notice total distance is now **300** units, as shown in **Totals** group of the dialog box indicating that **5** copies of the teapot are taking up **300** units space along the **X** direction.

Now, if you want to distribute these teapots over a distance of say **400** units, click >
on the right of the **Move** label and then set **X** to **400** [see Fig. 5]; the teapots are
now spread over a distance of **400** units. Similarly, you can create an array using the
Rotate and **Scale** transformations. Settings in Figs. 6 and 7 show how you can create
a 2D or a 3D array using the **Array** dialog box.

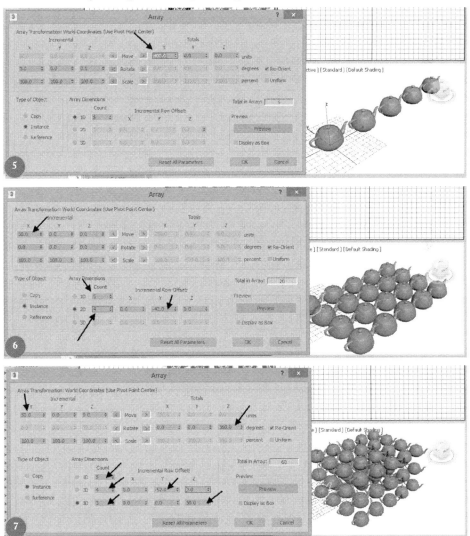

You can also create a **360** degree array using the **Array** dialog box. Reset 3ds Max and then create a **Teapot** primitive with radius **10** at the top edge of the grid [see Fig. 8]. From the **Main** toolbar > **User Center** flyout, choose **Use Transform Coordinate Center** [see Fig. 9]. Choose **Array** from the **Tools** menu to open the **Array** dialog box. Now, specify the settings, as shown in Fig. 10 to create 12 teapots in a full circle [360 degrees].

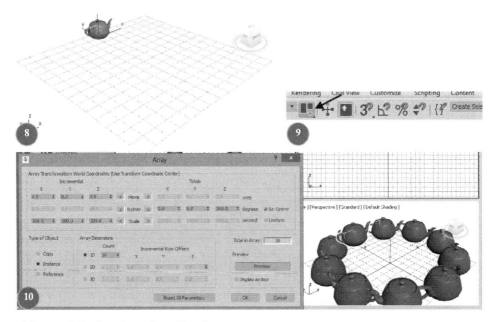

Working with the Spacing Tool

This tool allows you to distribute the selected objects along a spline or along the distance specified by the two points. You can also control the spacing between two objects. This tool can be activated by choosing **Tools > Align > Spacing Tool** from the menu bar or choosing **Spacing Tool** from the **Array** flyout. Alternatively, you can press **Shift+I**.

To distribute objects along a path, select the objects in the scene and then activate the **Spacing Tool** to open the **Spacing Tool** dialog box [see Fig. 11]. This dialog box provides you two methods for selecting path: **Pick Path** and **Pick Points**.

To use the **Pick Path** method, place a cursor on a spline in the view and click to select the spline as path. Now, specify the number of objects you want to distribute and then choose a distribution algorithm from the drop-down list available in the **Parameters** group [see Fig. 12]. Select **Follow**, if you want to align the pivot points of the object along the tangents of the spline [see Fig. 13].

If you click **Pick Points** from the **Spacing Tool** dialog box, you can specify the path by clicking on two places in the viewport. When you are done with the tool, 3ds Max deletes the spline.

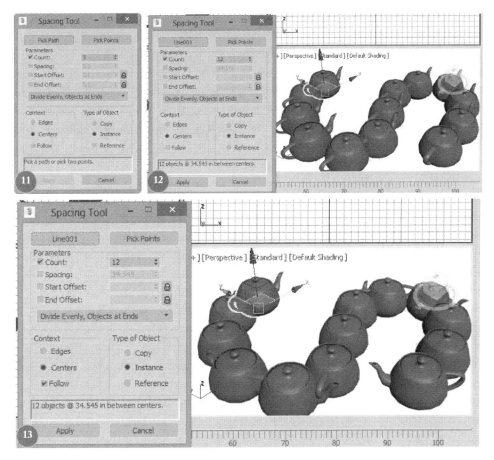

Working with Clone and Align Tool

This tool lets you distribute the source objects based on the current selection to a selection of the target objects. You can activate this tool by choosing **Align > Clone and Align** from the **Tools** menu. Alternatively, choose **Clone and Align** tool from the **Array** flyout.

To use the **Clone and Align** tool, create four teapots and a cone in the viewport [see Fig. 14]. Select cone in a viewport and then choose **Align > Clone and Align** from the **Tools** menu to open the **Clone and Align** dialog box.

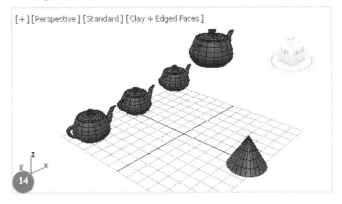

In this dialog box, click **Pick** and then click on each teapot to align the cone with the teapots [see Fig. 15]. If you want to pick multiple destination objects at once, click **Pick List** to open the **Pick Destination Objects** dialog box. In this dialog box, select the objects and then click **Pick**. This tool is very useful when you work on the CAD files. For example, you can replace the chair symbols in the CAD file with the actual chair geometry en masse using this tool.

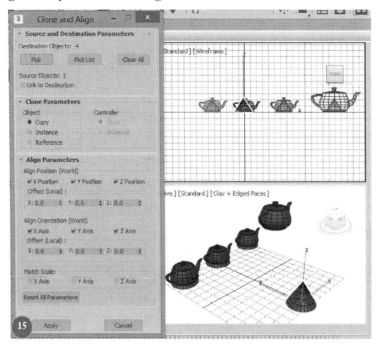

Working With the Select and Place Tool

This tool is cousin of the **AutoGrid** option found in the **Object Type** rollout. However, you can use it any time in your scene not just when you are creating an object. This tool can be activated by using one of the following four methods:

- Click the **Select and Place** icon in the **Main** toolbar.
- Choose **Placement** from the **Edit** menu.
- Press **Y** on the keyboard.
- **RMB** click on an object and then choose **Placement** from the **Transform** quadrant [see Fig. 16].

To place an object, you don't have to select it first. Pick the **Select and Place** tool, click-drag to place on another object [see Fig. 17].

As you drag the object, the orientation of the object changes based on the normals of the target object and object's **Up Axis** settings. The contact position of the target surface will be the object's pivot. To change the **Up Axis** settings, **RMB** click on the **Select and Place** tool in the **Main** toolbar to open the **Placement Settings** dialog box [see Fig. 18] and then select the axis from the **Object Up Axis** button array.

When **Rotate** is active in the **Placement Settings** dialog box, the translation of the object is prevented and object rotates around the local axis specified using the **Object Up Axis** settings. **Use Base as Pivot** is useful in those cases when the pivot is not already located in the base of the object. **Pillow Mode** is very useful when you are trying to place an object on a target whose surface is uneven. This option prevents the intersection of the objects. When **Autoparent** is active, the placed object automatically becomes the child of the other object. This is a quick way to make a parent-child relationship.

> *Note: Select and Rotate tool*
> *If you just want to rotate the object, you can use the **Select and Rotate** tool from the **Main** toolbar.*

There are some more goodies associated with this tool:

- You can clone an object while dragging it by pressing **Shift**.
- Hold **Ctrl** and then drag to position an object vertically along the **Up Axis**.
- You can prevent an object from rotating while you place it by holding **Alt**.

You can also place several objects at one go. You can either select the desired objects before picking the **Select and Place** tool or you can select additional objects using **Ctrl** when this tool is active. Each object will move according to its own pivot, unless objects are linked together.

Working With the Select and Manipulate Tool

The **Select and Manipulate** tool allows you to interactively edit the parameters of certain objects by dragging the manipulators in the viewports. The state of this tool is non-exclusive. You can manipulate objects as long as any of the select mode or one of the transform modes is active but if you want to select a manipulator helper, you must deactivate the **Select and Manipulate** tool. All those primitives with a **Radius** parameter have a built-in manipulator for the radius value. Let's see how it works:

Create a **Teapot** primitive in the scene. Pick the **Select and Manipulate** tool from the **Main** toolbar. A green ring appears beneath the teapot [see Fig. 19]. Click drag the ring to interactively change the radius of the teapot. Click on **Select and Manipulate** on the **Main** toolbar to deactivate the tool. There are three types of custom manipulators available in 3ds Max: cone angle manipulator, plane angle manipulator, and slider manipulator. The cone angle manipulator is used by a spot light's **Hotspot** and **Falloff** parameters. To create a cone angle manipulator, choose **Create** panel > **Helpers** > **Manipulators** and then click **Cone Angle**. Click drag in the viewport to create the helper [see Fig. 20]. To change its parameters, go to the **Modify** panel and change the values.

19   20

Now, let's work on a spot light to see this manipulator in action:

Create a **Teapot** primitive in the scene. Now, create a spot light and place it as shown in Fig. 21. Ensure the spot light is selected and then click **Select and Manipulate** from the **Main** toolbar. Three rings appear on the spot light [see Fig. 22].

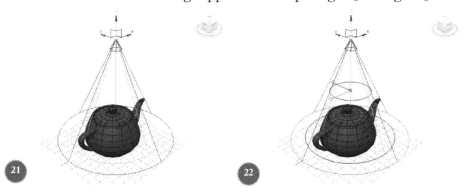

21   22

The bottom inner ring controls **Hotspot** whereas the outer rings controls **Falloff**. The center blue ring represents the roll angle. Using the **Select and Manipulate** tool, click drag on these rings to interactively change parameters.

The plane angle manipulator allows you to create a lever or joystick type shape. You can use its **Angle** parameter to create a custom control. You can use this control to drive parameter of another objects. Let's see how it works.

Choose **Create** panel > **Helpers** > **Manipulators** and then click **Plane Angle**. In the **Front** viewport, click drag to create a shape [see Fig. 23]. The **Plane Angle** manipulator always created vertically along the **Y** axis of the viewport in which you are creating it. Create a **Teapot** in the **Perspective** viewport. Ensure the **Select and Manipulate** tool is not active and manipulator is selected. Choose **Wire Parameters** > **Wire Parameters** from the **Animation** menu. In the popup that appears, choose **Object (Plane Angle Manipulator)** > **Angle** [Fig. 24]. A rubber band line appears. Click on the **Teapot**. In the popup that appears, choose **Object (Teapot)** > **Radius** [see Fig. 25].

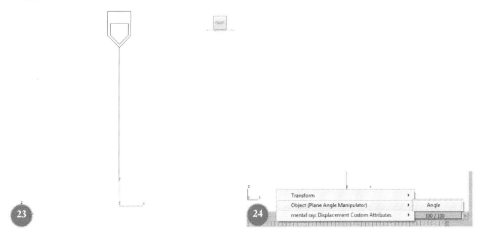

In the **Parameter Wiring** dialog box, click **One-way connection** button and then the **Connect** button [see Fig. 26] to make the connection. Now, close the dialog box. Pick the **Select and Manipulate** tool and drag the manipulator in a circular motion to interactively change the radius of the **Teapot**.

The third type of manipulator, **Slider**, which creates a graphic control in the viewport. You can wire its value to a parameter of another object within the scene. Here's how:

Create a **Slider** manipulator in the **Front** viewport. Create a **Teapot** in the **Perspective** viewport [see Fig. 27]. Wire the **value** parameter to the **Radius** of the **Teapot** as described above. Change the controls such as **Label**, **Minimum**, and **Maximum** values in the **Modify** panel [see Fig. 28]. Pick the **Select and Manipulate** tool and drag the manipulator's **Adjust** control to interactively change the shape of the teapot. Fig. 29 shows the components of a **Slider** control [**1.** Label, **2.** Value, **3.** Move, **4.** Show/hide, **5.** Slider bar, **6.** Adjust value, and **7.** Change width].

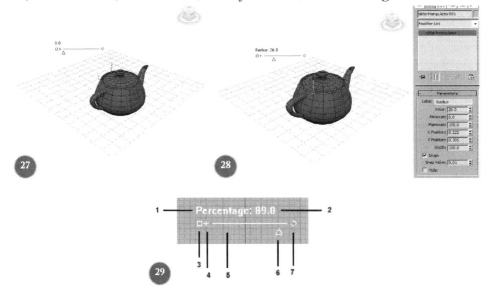

Scene Explorer

The **Scene Explorer** [see Fig. 30] is a modeless dialog box in 3ds Max that you can use to view, sort, filter, and select objects. In addition, you can rename, delete, hide, and freeze objects. You can also modify and edit object properties en masse. Each workspace in 3ds Max comes with a different **Scene Explorer** with the same name as its workspace. The **Scene Explorer** is docked to the left of the viewports.

Several explorers in 3ds Max are different versions of the **Scene Explorer**. These includes: **Layer Explorer, Container Explorer, MassFX Explorer**, and **Material Explorer**. The **Scene Explorer** comes with many toolbars [see Fig. 30]. Table 2 summarizes various toolbars available.

Table 2: The Scene Explorer toolbars	
Flag	**Toolbar**
1	Selection toolbar
4	View toolbar
5	Display toolbar

Table 2: The **Scene Explorer** toolbars	
Flag	**Toolbar**
6	Find toolbar
7	Tools toolbar

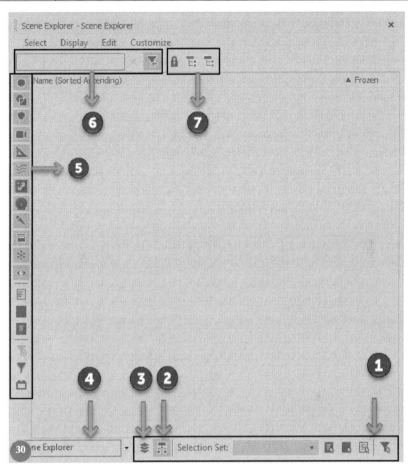

Selection Toolbar

The **Scene Explorer** comes with two sorting modes: **Sort By Layer** mode and **Sort By Hierarchy** mode. You can use the **Sort by Hierarchy** or **Sort By Layer** button on the **Selection** toolbar [marked as 1 in Fig. 30] to use these modes. The **Sort By Layer** button [marked as 3 in Fig. 30] sets the **Scene Explorer** to **Sort By Layer** mode. In this mode, you can use drag and drop feature for editing layers. Some other options are also available in this mode. The **Sort By Hierarchy** [marked as 2 in Fig. 30] button allows you to edit hierarchies using drag and drop functionality.

If you click on an object in the **Scene Explorer**, the object is selected and the associated row in the explorer gets highlighted. To select multiple objects, click on objects with **Ctrl** held down. Press **Ctrl+A** to select all objects, **Ctrl+I** to invert the selection, and **Ctrl+D** to deselect. These commands are also available at the right of the **Selection** toolbar [marked as 1 in Figure 30]. The **Selection Set** drop-down list in the **Selection** toolbar lets you select objects using **Named Selection Sets**.

Tools Toolbar

The tools available in this toolbar [marked as 7 in Fig. 30] are dependent on whether the **Sort By Hierarchy** mode or the **Sort By Layer** mode is active. When **Lock Cell Editing** is active, you cannot change any name or settings. The **Pick Parent** button is only available in the **Sort By Hierarchy** mode. It allows you to change the parent. To make an object parent, select one or more objects and then click **Pick Parent**. Now, select the object that you want parent of the selected object.

The **Create New Layer** button is available in the **Sort By Layer** mode. When you click **Create New Layer**, a new layer is created and the selection is automatically added to this layer. The new layer you create becomes the active layer and any subsequent objects you create are added to this layer automatically. If an existing layer is selected, and you click **Create New Layer**, the new layer becomes child of the selected layer. **Add to Active Layer** is available in the **Sort By Layer** mode only. When you click on this button, all selected objects and layers are assigned to the active layer. **Select Children** allows you to select all child objects and layers of the selected items.

 Tip: Selecting children
Double-clicking on a parent layer or object selects the parent and all its children.

The **Make Selected Layer Active** button is available in the **Sort By Layer** mode only. When you click on this button, 3ds Max makes the selected layer the active layer. Alternatively, click on the layer icon to make it the layer active.

Display Toolbar

The **Display** toolbar allows you to control the display various objects in the **Scene Explorer**. It controls the type of objects that appear in the **Scene Explorer**'s listing. You can also solo the category by clicking on one of the category buttons with **Alt** held down. You can also turn on or off the categories by choosing **Display > Object Types** from the **Scene Explorer**'s menu bar.

View Toolbar

The **View** toolbar is located at the bottom-left corner of the **Scene Explorer**. This toolbar shows the name of the current **Scene Explorer**. When you click on the black triangle located in this toolbar, a menu appears. This menu gives access to all the local and global explorers.

Local and Global Scene Explorers

3ds Max comes with different **Scene Explorer** configurations. These configurations are available to every scene you create in 3ds Max. Therefore, they are referred to as **Global Scene Explorers**. On the other hand, the **Local Scene Explorers** live within a single scene and saved/loaded with the scene. The options to make a **Local** explorer **Global** are available in the menu located on the **View** toolbar [see Fig. 31].

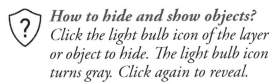

How to delete objects?
*To delete one or more objects in the **Scene Explorer**, select them and then press **Delete** or **RMB** click on the list and then choose **Delete** from the **Quad** menu.*

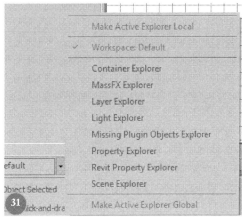

How to hide and show objects?
Click the light bulb icon of the layer or object to hide. The light bulb icon turns gray. Click again to reveal.

How to create hierarchies in the Sort By Hierarchy mode?
*To make a parent, drag and drop the child objects' name or icon onto the object that you want to act as parent. To restore the child objects to the top level, drag them to an empty area of the **Scene Explorer**. Alternatively, you can **RMB** click on them and then choose **Unlink** from the **Quad** menu. You can use the same techniques on the layers as well.*

How to freeze objects?
*To freeze objects, click on the **Frozen** column of the object. Click again to unfreeze. If you want to freeze many objects, select them and then click on the **Frozen** column of any selected objects.*

How to change object properties?
*To change the object properties, select one or more objects in the **Scene Explorer** and then **RMB**. Choose **Properties** from the **Quad** menu to open the **Object Properties** dialog box. You can use this dialog box to change the properties of the selected objects.*

How to rename an object?
*Select the object and then **RMB** click. Choose **Rename** from the **Quad** menu and then type a new name for the object.*

Tip: Renaming objects
*Slowly triple-click on the object name to rename the object if you don't want to use the **Quad** menu.*

Can I add more columns next to the Frozen column?
Yes, you can. **RMB** *click on any of the column head and then choose* **Configure Columns** *[see Fig. 32] from the context menu. The* **Configure Column** *window appears [see Fig. 33]. Click on the name of the column in this window that you want to add. Fig. 34 shows the* **Has Material** *column. A tick will appear in this column if a material has been assigned to the object.*

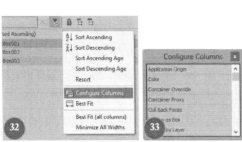

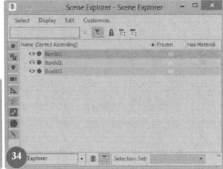

 Can I search object by names?
Yes, you can search object by using the search text box available in the **Find** *toolbar. Type the search string and then press* **Enter***. For example, if you have many teapots in the scene and all have default names. Entering* **tea** *in the search field and then pressing* **Enter** *will select all teapots in the scene. You can also use the wild card characters such as* **?** *and* ***** *to create a broader search criteria.*

Working with the Precision Tools

3ds Max comes with several tools and objects that allow you to position and align objects efficiently. Two of the tools [**Select and Place** tool, and **Select and Manipulate** tool] I have already discussed that let you align and position objects. You have also seen the use of some helpers that are used with the **Select and Manipulate** tool.

Using Units

Units define the measurement system for the scene. The default unit system in 3ds Max is **Generic Units**. Besides **Generic Units**, you can also use feet and inches both decimal and fractional. The **Metric** system allows you to specify units from millimeters to kilometers. You can specify the unit system from the **Units Setup** dialog box [see Fig. 35].

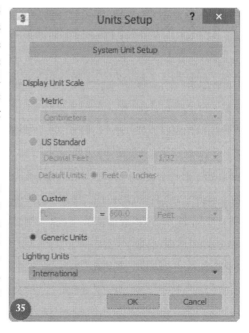

You can open this dialog box by choosing **Units Setup** from the **Customize** menu. On clicking **System Unit Setup** in this dialog box, the **System Unit Setup** dialog box appears from where you can specify the **System** units.

What is the difference between the Scene and System units?
The system units only affect how geometry appears in the viewports whereas the system units control the actual scale of the geometry.

Caution: System units
The system units should only be changed before you create your scene or import a **unitless** *file. Do not change the system units in the current scene.*

If you change units for a scene, 3ds Max automatically changes the values for the parameters. For example, if you are using **Centimeters** and value in a spinner is **30** cm, when you change units to **Decimal Inches**; 3ds Max will change the value to **11.811** inches. Now, if you type **50cm** in the spinner and press **Enter**, 3ds Max changes value to **19.685** inches. Similarly, if you type **2'** in the spinner, the value changes to **24.0** inches.

Using Grids

Grids are two dimensional arrays that you can use to position the objects accurately. You can use grids to visualize space, scale, and distance. You can use it as construction plane for creating objects as well use it for snapping objects using the snap feature. I will discuss about snap features later in this unit. 3ds Max provides two types of grids: **Home** grid and **Grid** objects.

Home Grid

The **Home** grid is defined by three intersecting planes along the world **X**, **Y**, and **Z** axes. These planes intersect at the origin defined by **0,0,0**. The **Home** grid is fixed, you cannot move or rotate it.

Tip: Home Grid
Press **G** *to toggle the visibility of the* **Home** *grid.*

Grid Object

The **Grid** object [see Fig. 36] is a helper object that you can use to create a reference grid as per your needs. You can create as many **Grid** objects as you want in a scene. However, only one **Grid** object will be active at a time. When a **Grid** object is active, it replaces the **Home** grid in all viewports. You can rename and delete the **Grid** objects like any other object. The **Grid** object is available in the **Helpers** category in the **Create** panel.

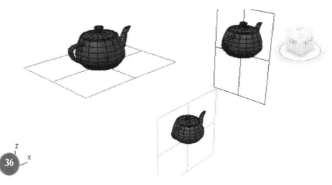

💡 *Tip: Activating the Home grid and the Grid object*
*You can activate the **Home** grid by choosing **Grids and Snaps** > **Activate Home Grid** from the **Tools** menu. When you choose this command, it activates the **Home** grid in all viewports and deactivates the current active **Grid** object. Similarly, you can activate a **Grid** object by choosing **Grids and Snaps** > **Activate Grid Object** from the **Tools** menu.*

💡 *Tip: Aligning a Grid object to the view*
*To align a **Grid** object with the current view, make sure it is selected and then choose **Grids and Snaps** > **Activate Grid Object** from the **Tools** menu. The **Grid** object is aligned and will be coplanar with the current view.*

Auto Grid

The **Auto Grid** feature lets you create objects on the surface of other objects. The **Auto Grid** option is available in the **Object Type** rollout of any category. It is also available in the **Extras** toolbar. When you activate this option and drag the cursor on the surface of an object, a construction plane is created temporarily on the surface of object.

💡 *Tip: Select and Place tool*
*The **Select and Place** tool discussed earlier provides a similar mechanism to align the objects.*

Aligning Objects

3ds Max provides six different tools for aligning the objects in a scene. These tools are available in the **Align** flyout on the **Main** toolbar.

Using with Align Tool

The **Align** tool in 3ds Max allows you to align the current selection to a target selection. You can pick the **Align** tool from the **Align** flyout in the **Main** toolbar. You can also activate this tool by choosing **Align** > **Align** from the **Tools** menu or by pressing **Alt+A**. Using this tool, you can align the position and orientation of the bounding box of a source object to the bounding box of a target object. A bounding box is a smallest box that encloses the extents (maximum dimensions) of an object.

A bounding box appears when you set a viewport to a non-wireframe mode. Fig. 37 shows the extents of a teapot model.

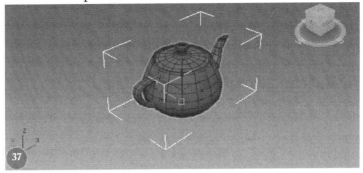

To toggle the display of the bounding box, select the object and then press **J**. You can also enable the display of the bounding boxes by turning on **Selection Brackets** from the **Viewport Setting and Preference** dialog box > **Per-View Preferences** panel [see Fig. 38]. Refer to **Explore More** section of **Unit DM1** for more information on **Viewport Setting and Preference** dialog box.

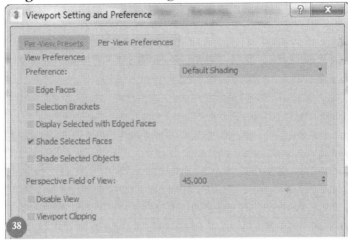

Let's dive in and align some objects. Create three boxes and assign them red, green, and blue colors [see Fig. 39]. Use the following dimensions:

Red Box: Length=52, Width=61, and Height=32
Green Box: Length=35, Width=40, and Height=12
Blue Box: Length=50, Width=40, and Height=30

RMB click on the red box and choose **Object Properties** from the **Quad** menu. In the **General** panel > **Display Properties** group, select **See-Through** and click OK;this will help you better see the alignment process. Now let's center align the red and blue boxes along the **X** and **Y** axes. Make sure the red box is selected and then pick the **Align** tool from the **Main** toolbar. Click the blue box. In the **Align Selection** dialog box > **Align Position (World)** group, select **X Position** and **Y Position**. Turn off **Z Position**. Make sure **Center** is selected in the **Current Object** and **Target Object** groups. You will see that both the objects are center aligned [see Fig. 40]. Click **OK** to accept changes.

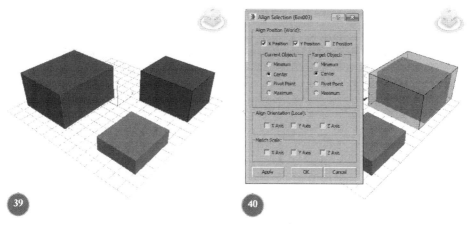

39   40

Now, let's see how to place blue box on the top of the red box.

Select the blue box and then pick the **Align** tool from the **Main** toolbar. Click red box. We have already performed alignment along the **X** and **Y** axes. Therefore, turn off **X Position** and **Y Position** and select **Z Position**. You will see that now the blue box is at the center of the red box. Select **Maximum** from the **Target Object** group. Notice the blue box's center is aligned to the center of the red box [see Fig. 41]. Now, select **Pivot Point** from the **Current Object** group. The blue box sits on the top of the red box [see Fig. 42]. Click **OK** to accept changes.

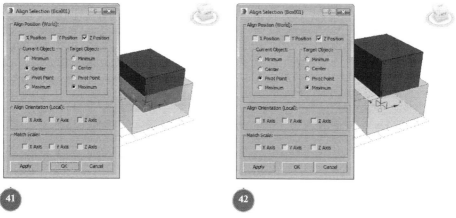

41   42

Now, let's align one corner of the green box with blue box.

Select the green box and then pick the **Align** tool from the **Main** toolbar. Click the blue box. Select **X Position**, **Y Position**, and **Z Position**. Select **Minimum** from the **Current Object** and **Target Object** groups [see Fig. 43]. Click **OK** to accept changes. With the green box selected, click the blue box using the **Align** tool. Now, select **Z Position** and turn off **X Position** and **Y Position**. Select **Maximum** from the **Target Object** group and click **OK**. The boxes are now stacked over each other [see Fig. 44].

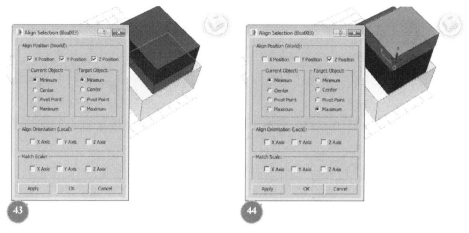

Using the Quick Align Tool

The **Quick Align** tool instantly aligns an object with the target object. The hotkeys associated with this tool are **Shift+A**. To align an object, select the source object and press **Shift+A** to activate the tool. Now, click on the target object to align two objects [see Fig. 45]. If the current selection contains a single object, this tool uses the pivot points of the two objects for alignment. If multiple objects are selected, the selection center of the source objects is aligned with the pivot of the target objects.

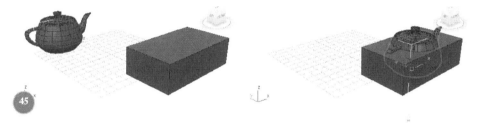

Using the Normal Align Tool

This tool allows you to align the two objects based on the directions of the normals of the selected faces. The hotkeys associated with this tool are **Alt+N**. To understand functioning of this tool, create a sphere and teapot in the scene [see Fig. 46]. Select the teapot, the source object in this case. Press **Alt+N** to activate the tool and then drag across the surface of the teapot, a blue arrow indicates the location of the current normal [see Fig. 47]. Keep dragging on the surface until you find the normal you are looking for. Now, click and drag on the surface of the sphere until you find the normal to which you want to align the source object. Release the mouse button; the teapot gets aligned with the sphere [see Fig. 48] and the **Normal Align** dialog box opens. Using the parameters available in this dialog box, you can offset the position and orientation of the teapot.

What are normals?

*A normal is a vector that defines the inner and outer surfaces of a face in a mesh. The direction of the vector indicates the front [outer] surface of a face or vertex. Sometimes, normals are flipped during the modeling process. To fix this issue, you can use the **Normal** modifier to flip or unify normals. Fig. 49 shows the vertex and face normals, respectively.*

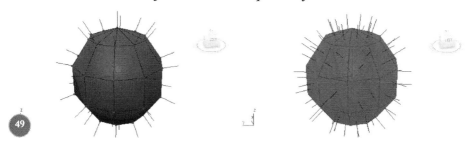

Using the Place Highlight Tool

You can use this tool to align an object or light to another object so that its highlight [reflection] can be precisely positioned. To position a light to highlight a face, make sure the viewport that you want to render is active. Choose **Place Highlight** from the **Align** flyout and drag the mouse pointer on the object to place the highlight. Now, release the mouse button when the normal indicates the face on which you want to place the highlight [see Fig. 50].

Note: Light type and highlights

With the omni, free spot, or directional light, 3ds Max displays face normal. With a target spotlight, 3ds Max displays target of the light and base of it's cone.

Using the Align Camera Tool

This tool lets you align the camera to a selected face normal. This tool works similar to the **Place Highlight** tool but it does not change the camera position interactively. You need to release the mouse button and then 3ds Max aligns the camera with the selected face.

Using the Align View Tool

When this tool is picked from the **Align** flyout, it opens the **Align to View** dialog box that lets you align the local axis of the selection or sub-object selection with the current viewport [see Fig. 51]. To use this tool, select the objects or sub-objects to align and then choose **Align to View** from the **Align** flyout. 3ds Max opens the **Align to View** dialog box. Choose the options from the dialog box as desired. If you want to flip the direction of alignment, select **Flip** in this dialog box.

Drawing Assistants

3ds Max provides several tools and utilities that help you in drawing objects with precession. Let's have a look.

Measuring Distances

The **Measure Distance** tool allows you to quickly calculate distance between two points. The calculated distance appears in the **Status Bar** in scene [display] units. To measure distance, choose **Measure Distance** from the **Tools** menu. Now, click on the point in the viewport from where you want to measure the distance. Click again in the viewport where you want to measure to. The distance between the two points is displayed in the **Status Bar**.

The **Measure** utility available in the **Utilities** panel displays the measurement of a selected object or spline. To display measurement of an object, select the object and then on the **Utilities** panel, click **Measure**. The measurements are displayed in the **Measure** rollout [see Fig. 52].

There is one more utility called **Rescale World Units** that you can use to rescale the word units. You can scale the entire scene or the selected objects. To rescale an object, select it and then on the **Utilities** panel click **More** to open the **Utilities** dialog box. Select **Rescale World Units** from the dialog box and then click **OK**. The **Rescale World Units** rollout appears in the **Utilities** panel. Click **Rescale** from this rollout to open the **Rescale World Units** dialog box [see Fig. 53].

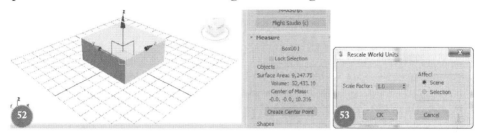

Set **Scale Factor** in this dialog box and then select **Scene** or **Selection** from the **Affect** group. Click **OK** to apply the scale factor to the selected object or to entire scene. For example, you specify **Scale Factor** as **2** and select **Selection** from the dialog box, the selected object will be scaled to double of its current size.

Using Snaps

The Snap tools in 3ds Max allow you to precisely control the dimensions and placement of the objects when you create or transform them. You can invoke these tools using the **Snap** buttons available on the **Main** toolbar. You can also invoke these tools by choosing **Grids and Snaps** from the **Tools** menu.

2D Snap, 2.5 Snap, and 3D Snap

The hotkey for activating snap is **S**. The **2D Snap** tool snaps the cursor to the active construction grid including the geometry on the plane of the grid. The **Z** axis is ignored by this tool. The **2.5D Snap** tool snaps the cursor to the vertices or edges of the projection of an object onto the active grid. The **3D snap** is the default tool. It snaps the cursor directly to any geometry in the 3D space. **RMB** click on snap toggle button to open the **Grid and Snap Settings** dialog box [see Fig. 54].

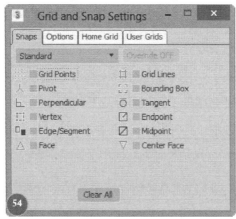

You can specify which type of snap of you want active from the **Snaps** panel of this dialog box. For example, if you want the cursor to snap to the pivot or vertices of the object, select **Pivot** and **Vertex** from this panel. To see snap in action, select **Pivot** and **Vertex** from the **Grid and Snap Settings** dialog box. Now, create a box and teapot in the viewport [see of Fig. 55]. Pick the **Move** tool from the **Main** toolbar and move the teapot to one of the vertex of the box or its pivot [see Fig. 56].

Angle Snap Toggle

You can use **Angle Snap Toggle** to rotate an object around a given axis in the increment you set. This snap toggle also works with the **Pan/Orbit** camera controls, **FOV** and **Roll** camera settings, and **Hotspot/Falloff** spotlight angles. The hotkey for invoking this tool is **A**.

To rotate an object, click **Angle Snap Toggle** in the **Main** toolbar and then rotate the object using the **Rotate** tool. By default, the rotation takes place in five degree increments. You can change this default value by specifying a value for the **Angle** parameter in the **Options** panel of the **Grid and Snap Settings** dialog box.

Percent Snap Toggle

% The **Percent Snap Toggle** lets you control the increments of scaling by the specified percentage. The hotkey for invoking this tool is **Shift+Ctrl+P**. The default percentage value is **10**. You can change this default value by specifying a value for the **Percent** parameter in the **Options** panel of the **Grid and Snap Settings** dialog box.

Spinner Snap Toggle

This toggle allows you to set single-increment or decrement value for all the spinners in 3ds Max. The default value is **1**. To change this value, **RMB** click on **Spinner Snap Toggle** on the **Main** toolbar to open the **Preferences Settings** dialog box. In the **Spinners** group of the **General** panel, specify a value for the **Snap** parameter.

Modifiers

The modifiers in 3ds Max provide a way to edit and sculpt objects. You can change shape of an object using the modifier's properties. Fig. 57 shows the original box [first image] and the modified geometry after applying the **Bend, Twist,** and **Taper** modifiers, respectively.

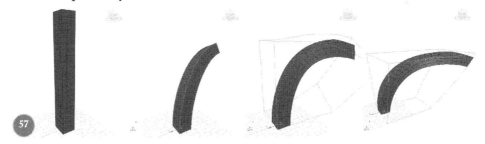

You can apply modifiers from the **Modifier** drop-down list available in the **Modify** panel of the **Command** panel [see Fig. 58]. The modifiers you apply to an object are stored in a stack called modifier stack. Modifiers are described in detail in a later unit.

Quiz

Evaluate your skills to see how many questions you can answer correctly.

Multiple Choice
Answer the following questions:

1. Which of the following keys is used to invoke the **Select and Place** tool?

    [A] X   [B] S
    [C] Y   [D] P

2. Which of the followings systems is the default unit system in 3ds Max?

    [A] Generic Units   [B] Metric
    [C] Imperial   [D] Custom

3. Which of the following keys is used to toggle the visibility of the home grid?

    [A] H   [B] Shift+H
    [C] G   [D] Alt+G

4. Which of the following key is used to invoke the **Align** tool?

    [A] Alt+T   [B] Alt+A
    [C] Ctrl+T   [D] Ctrl+A

Fill in the Blanks
Fill in the blanks in each of the following statements:

1. To create a clone, select the object[s] that you want to clone and then choose _____ from the _____ menu or press_____.

2. The _____ is used to distribute objects along a path or between two points.

3. The _____ method in the **Clone Options** dialog box allows you to create a clone dependent on the original upto the point when the object was created.

4. The _____ tool allows you to interactively edit the parameters of certain objects by dragging the manipulators in the viewports.

5. Press _____ to invoke the **Quick Align** tool.

6. A _____ is a vector that defines the inner and outer surfaces of a face in a mesh.

True of False

State whether each of the following is true or false:

1. The **Mirror** tool can be used to just create a mirror reflection.

2. The **Transform** option in the **Mirror** dialog box allows you to mirror any word-space-modifiers [WSM] effect.

3. You can not animate the mirror operation.

4. The **Clone and Align** tool lets you distribute the source objects based on the current selection to a selection of the target objects.

5. Double-clicking on a parent layer or object in the **Scene Explorer** selects the parent and all its children.

6. The system units only affect how geometry appears in the viewports whereas the system units control the actual scale of the geometry.

Summary

The unit covered the following topics:

- Creating clones and duplicates
- Understanding hierarchies
- Working with the **Scene** and **Layer** Explorers
- Understanding the **Mirror, Select and Place**, and **Select and Manipulate** tools
- Working with the **Align** and **Array** tools
- Working with precision and drawing aids
- Understanding modifiers, and normals

- Creating and modifying the **Standard** Primitives
- Creating and modifying the **Extended** Primitives
- Working with the **Architectural** objects
- Setting the project folder
- Using the **Align** and **Mirror** tools
- Creating clones
- Using the **Scene Explorer**
- Creating a group
- Setting grid spacings
- Using the **Transform Type-In** dialog box
- Using the **Array** dialog box
- Specifying the units for the scene

Unit DM3: Geometric Primitives and Architectural Objects

The 3D objects in the scene and the objects that are used to create them are known as geometries. Most of the 3D applications offer basic building blocks for creating geometries called geometric primitives. You can use these primitives and some modifiers to create basic models. In this unit, you will work with the **Standard** and **Extended** primitives as well as the **Architectural** objects.

You can edit these geometric primitives at sub-object levels to create complex models. This process is known as surface modeling that I've covered in the next unit. In this unit, I will explain **Standard** and **Extended** primitives and how you can use them to create some basic models. Geometric primitives in 3ds Max are divided into two categories: **Standard** primitives and **Extended** primitives. Let's first start exploring the **Standard** primitives.

Standard Primitives

3ds Max offers eleven standard primitives, see Fig. 1. You can combine **Standard** primitives into more complex objects. You can then further refine them by using modifiers. You can interactively create primitives in the viewport using the mouse. Primitives can also be created by entering precise values using the keyboard. You can specify the parameters before creating the primitives and as well as modify them later from the **Parameters** rollout in the **Modify** panel. Let's take a look at different **Standard** primitives.

Box

Box is the simplest of the primitives. You can use it to create rectangular as well as cubical geometries [see Fig. 2]. To create a **Box** primitive, in the **Create** panel, click **Geometry**, and then in the **Object Type** rollout, click **Box**.

To create a box, click and drag in a viewport to specify the length and width of the box. Now, release the mouse button and drag the mouse up or down [without holding any button] to specify the height of the box and then click to complete the process.

Whenever you choose a tool from the **Object Type** rollout, the **Name and Color**, **Creation Method**, **Keyboard Entry**, and **Parameters** rollouts appear on the **Command** panel. You can use these rollouts to specify the initial properties of the objects.

> *Tip: Navigating between the steps*
> *If you are creating a primitive that requires two or more steps [for example* **Cylinder** *or* **Torus**], *you can pan and orbit the viewport between the steps. To pan the viewport,* **MMB** *drag. To orbit, hold* **Alt** *and then* **MMB** *drag.*

Name and Color Rollout

The parameters in the **Name and Color** rollout allow you to rename the objects and change their colors. Whenever you create an object, 3ds Max assigns it a default name and color. For example, if you reset the scene and create a box in the viewport, 3ds Max assigns it the name **Box001**. To change the name of the object, type a new name in the text box available in the **Name and Color** rollout. The color swatch to the right of the text box lets you change the color of the object.

On clicking the color swatch, the **Object Color** dialog box appears. You can click on one of the color swatches and then click **OK** to assign the color to the object. If you want to specify a custom color, select a color swatch associated with the **Custom Colors** parameter and then click **Add Custom Colors**. In the **Color Selector : Add Color** dialog box that appears, specify a color and then click **Add Color** to add the chosen color to the selected swatch in the **Object Color** dialog box. Now, click **OK** to close the dialog box and apply selected color to the object.

Tip: Scene Explorer
*As discussed in Unit DM2, you can easily rename objects using the **Scene Explorer**.*

Creation Method Rollout

There are two parameters available in this rollout: **Cube** and **Box**. **Box** creates a standard box primitive with different settings for length, width, and height. **Cube** creates a cube with equal width, height, and length. Creating a cube is one step operation. Click and drag the mouse pointer in the viewport to create a cube.

Parameters Rollout

The default settings in this rollout produce a box with one segment on each side. Table 1 summarizes the controls in the **Parameters** rollout.

Table 1: The parameters in the **Box**'s **Parameters** rollout	
Parameters	**Description**
Length, Width, Height	The **Length, Width,** and **Height** parameters set the length, width, and height of the box, respectively. These controls also act as readouts when you interactively create a box.
Length Segs, Width Segs, Height Segs	The **Length Segs, Width Segs,** and **Height Segs** parameters set the number of segments [divisions] along each axis of the object. You can set these parameters before and after the creation of the box. The default value for these parameters is **1, 1, 1.**
Generate Mapping Coords	The **Generate Mapping Coords** check box is on by default for most objects. It generates coordinates for applying material to the box.
Real-World Map Size	The **Real-World Map Size** check box lets you create a material and specify the actual width and height of a 2D texture map in the material editor. The scaling values are controlled from the maps's [for example the **Diffuse** map] **Coordinates** rollout.

 Note: Default values
Whatever values you specify for these parameters become default for the current session.

 Tip: Resolution
*If you are planning to use the modifiers such as **Bend** on a primitive object, increase the values for the **Length Segs**, **Width Segs**, and **Height Segs** parameters to get some extra resolution on the objects. The higher the resolution, the smoother the bend will be.*

Keyboard Entry Rollout

You can use the parameters in this rollout to define both the size of the box as well as its position in 3D space in a single operation. The method for creating objects through keyboard is generally same for all primitives; differences might occur in the type and number of parameters. The **X**, **Y**, and **Z** parameters define the position of the object. The default value is **0, 0, 0** which is center of the active grid.

Cone

You can use this primitive to create round upward or inverted cones [see Fig. 3]. To create a cone, click **Cone** in the **Object Type** rollout. In the viewport, drag to define the base of the cone and then release the mouse button. Now, move the mouse pointer up or down in the viewport to define the height.

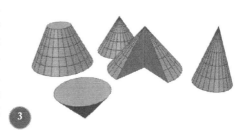

The height can be negative or positive. Click to set the height. Move the mouse pointer to define the radius of the other end of the cone. If you want to create a pointed cone, set this radius to zero.

Creation Method Rollout

Two creation methods are available for the **Cone** primitive: **Edge** and **Center**. **Edge** draws a cone from edge to edge. **Center** draws from the center out.

Parameters Rollout

The default settings in this rollout produce a smooth cone with 24 sides, one cap segment, and five height segments. Table 2 summarizes the parameters in the **Parameters** rollout.

Table 2: The parameters in the **Cone's Parameters** rollout	
Parameters	**Description**
Radius 1, Radius 2	**Radius 1** and **Radius 2** define the first and second radii of the cone. You can use these two parameters to create pointed or flat-topped cones.
Height	**Height** sets the dimension of the cone along the central axis. If you set a negative value, the cone will be created below the construction plane.
Height Segments	**Height Segments** parameter sets the number of divisions along the major axis of the cone.
Cap Segments	**Cap Segments** sets the number of concentric divisions in the top or bottom of the cone.
Sides	**Sides** determines the number of sides around the cone.
Smooth	**Smooth** is on by default. It blends the faces of the cone on rendering therefore producing smooth looking renders.

Table 2: The parameters in the **Cone**'s **Parameters** rollout	
Parameters	**Description**
Slice From, Slice To	You can use the **Slice From** and **Slice To** parameters to slice the cone. These two parameters set the number of degrees around the local Z axis. To activate these two parameters, select **Slice On**.

 Caution: Minimum and negative values
*If you specify negative values for **Radius 1** and **Radius 2**, these values will be converted to **0**. The minimum values for these parameters is **0**.*

 Note: Same value for Radius 1 and Radius 2
*If you specify a same value for **Radius 1** and **Radius 2**, a cylinder will be created. If these two values are close in size, an object is created which resembles the effect as if a **Taper** modifier is applied to a cylinder.*

 Tip: Pointed cones
For improved rendering on smooth pointed cones, increase the number of height segments.

Sphere

You can use the **Sphere** primitive to create a full sphere, a hemisphere, slice of the sphere, or some part of a sphere [see Fig. 4]. To create a sphere, in the **Create** panel, click **Geometry**, and then in the **Object Type** rollout, click **Sphere**.

In the viewport, drag the mouse pointer to define the radius of the sphere, release mouse button to set the radius. To create a hemisphere, create the desired sphere of the desired radius and then set **Hemisphere** to **0.5** in the **Parameters** rollout.

Creation Method Rollout
There are two methods available for creating a sphere: **Edge** and **Center**. **Edge** draws the sphere from edge to edge. **Center** draws a sphere from center out.

Parameters Rollout
The default values in the rollout produce a smooth sphere with **32** divisions. Table 3 summarizes the parameters in the **Parameters** rollout.

Table 3: The parameters in the **Sphere**'s **Parameters** rollout	
Parameter	**Description**
Radius	**Radius** specifies the radius of the sphere.
Segments	**Segments** defines the number of segments for the sphere.

Table 3: The parameters in the **Sphere**'s **Parameters** rollout	
Parameter	**Description**
Hemisphere	**Hemisphere** lets you create a hemisphere. It cuts off the sphere to create a partial sphere. You can use this parameter to create an animation in which the sphere will be cut off starting from its base to top.
Chop, Squash	**Chop** and **Squash** determine the number of vertices and faces when you create a hemisphere. **Chop** reduces the number of vertices and faces by chopping them out whereas **Squash** maintains the number of vertices and faces by squashing the geometry toward the top of the sphere. Fig. 5 shows the effect of **Chop** [left] and **Squash** [right] on a hemisphere with **16** segments.
Base To Pivot	If you select **Base to Pivot**, the sphere moves upward along its local Z axis and places the pivot point at its base. Fig. 6 shows the pivot at the center [left], which is default, and at the base of the sphere [right].

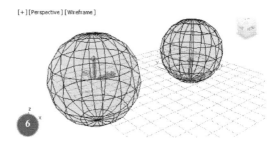

[+][Perspective][Wireframe]

GeoSphere

You can use the **GeoSphere** primitive to create spheres and geo-hemispheres based on three classes of polyhedrons: **Tetra**, **Octa**, and **Icosa** [see Fig. 7].

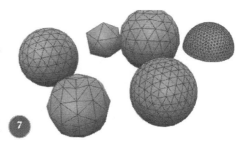

The **GeoSphere** primitive produces more regular shape than the **Sphere** primitive. Unlike the **Sphere** primitive, the geometry produced by the **GeoSphere** primitive has no poles which is an advantage is in certain modeling scenarios. Also, they appear slightly smoother than the standard sphere when rendered. To create a **GeoSphere**, in the **Create** panel, click **Geometry**, and then in the **Object Type** rollout, click **GeoSphere**. In the viewport, drag the mouse pointer to define the radius of the sphere, release mouse button to set the radius. To create a hemisphere, create the desired sphere of the desired radius and then select the **Hemisphere** check box in the **Parameters** rollout.

Creation Method rollout

There are two methods available for creating a geosphere: **Diameter** and **Center**. **Diameter** draws the geosphere from edge to edge whereas **Center** draws from the center out.

Parameters Rollout

Table 4 summarizes the parameters in the **Parameters** rollout.

Table 4: The parameters in the **GeoSphere**'s **Parameters** rollout	
Parameters	**Description**
Radius	**Radius** sets the radius of the geosphere.
Segments	**Segments** defines the number of faces in the geosphere.
Tetra, Octa, Icosa	The parameters in the **Geodesic Base Type** group let you choose one of the regular polyhedrons for geosphere geometry. **Tetra** creates a four-sided tetrahedron. The facets can vary in shape and size. The geosphere can be divided into four equal segments. **Octa** creates an eight-sided tetrahedron. The facets can vary in shape and size. The geosphere can be divided into eight equal segments. **Icosa** creates a 20-sided tetrahedron. The facets are equal in size. The geosphere can be divided into any number of equal segments.

Cylinder

Cylinder creates a cylinder that can be sliced along its major axis [see Fig. 8]. To create a cylinder, in the **Create** panel, click **Geometry**, and then in the **Object Type** rollout, click **Cylinder**. In the viewport, drag the mouse pointer to define the radius, release the mouse button to set the radius. Now, move the mouse pointer up or down to define the height, click to set it.

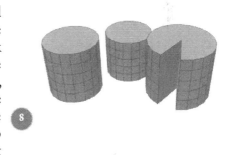

8

Parameters Rollout

The default parameters in the **Parameters** rollout produce an **18** sided smooth cylinder with the **5** height segments, **1** cap segment, and the pivot point at its base. Table 5 summarizes the parameters in the **Parameters** rollout.

Table 5: The parameters in the **Cylinder**'s **Parameters** rollout	
Parameter	**Description**
Radius	**Radius** sets the radius of the cylinder.
Height	**Height** defines the height of the cylinder along the cylinder's major axis.
Height Segments	**Height Segments** defines the number of divisions along the cylinder's major axis.
Sides	**Sides** sets the sides around the cylinder.
Cap Segments	**Cap Segments** sets the number of concentric divisions around the top and bottom of the cylinder.

Tip: Resolution
*If you are going to use the cylinder with a modifier such as **Bend**, increase the number of height segments. If you are planning to modify the end of the cylinder, increase the number of cap segments.*

Tube

The **Tube** primitive produces a cylinder with a hole in it [see Fig. 9]. You can use this primitive to use both round and prismatic tubes. To create a **Tube**, in the **Create** panel, click **Geometry**, and then in the **Object Type** rollout, click **Tube**. In the viewport, drag the mouse pointer to define the first radius, which can be either the inner or the outer radius of the tube,

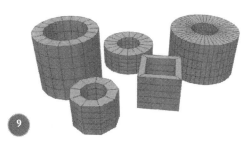

release the mouse button to set the first radius. Move the mouse pointer to create the second radius, and then click to set it. Move the pointer up or down to create the height [positive or negative] and then click to set the height of the tube.

Tip: Prismatic Tube
*To create a prismatic tube, set the number of **Sides** according to the type of the prismatic tube you want to create. Clear the **Smooth** check box and then create the tube.*

Parameters Rollout

Radius 1 and **Radius 2** are used to specify the inside and outside radii of the tube. The larger among the two values defines the outside radius of the tube.

Torus

You can use the **Torus** primitive to create a doughnut like shape which is ring with the circular cross section [see Fig. 10]. To create a torus, in the **Create** panel, click **Geometry**, and then in the **Object Type** rollout, click **Torus**. In the viewport, drag the mouse pointer to define a torus; the torus emerges from its center. Release the mouse button to set the radius of the torus

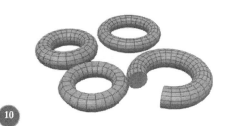

ring. Now, move the mouse pointer to define the radius of the cross section, and click to complete the creation process.

Parameters Rollout

The default values in this rollout produce a smooth torus with **12** sides and **24** segments. The pivot point of the torus is located at the center of the torus on the plane which cuts through the center of the torus. **Rotation** sets the degree of rotation.

The vertices are uniformly rotated about the circle running through the center of the torus ring. **Twist** defines the degree of twist. 3ds Max twists the cross sections about the circle running through the center of the torus.

Caution: Twisting a close torus
*Twisting a close torus will create a constriction in the first segment. To overcome this, you can either twist the torus in the increments of **360** or select **Slice** and then set both **Slice From** and **Slice To** to **0**.*

The parameters in the **Smooth** group control the level of smoothing. The default **All** parameter produces smoothing on all surfaces of the torus. **Sides** smooths the edges between the adjacent segments thus producing smooth bands which run around the torus. **None** turns off the smoothing and produces prism-like facets on the torus. **Segments** smooths each segment individually and produces ring-like segments.

Pyramid

The **Pyramid** primitive is used to create a pyramid like shape with the square or rectangle face and triangular sides [see Fig. 11]. To create a pyramid, in the **Create** panel, click **Geometry**, and then in the **Object Type** rollout, click **Pyramid**. In the viewport, drag the mouse pointer to define the base of the pyramid. Click to set it and then drag the mouse pointer up to define the height.

Tip: Constrain the base of the pyramid to a square
*To constrain the base of the pyramid to a square, drag with the **Ctrl** key held down.*

Plane

The **Plane** primitive creates a flat plane that you can enlarge to any size [see Fig. 12]. To create a **Plane**, in the **Create** panel, click **Geometry**, and then in the **Object Type** rollout, click **Plane**. In the viewport, drag the mouse pointer to create a plane.

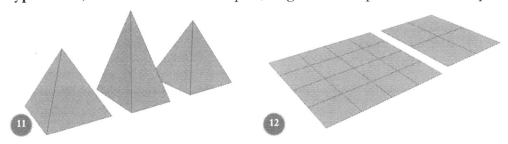

Parameters Rollout

The parameters in the **Render Multipliers** group are used to set the multipliers at the render time. You can use **Scale** to specify the factor by which both length and width will be multiplied at the render time. **Density** specifies a factor by which the number of segments in both length and width are multiplied at the render time.

Teapot

The **Teapot** primitive is used to create a parametric teapot object [see Fig. 12A]. This object is comprised of a lid, body, handle, and spout. You can create the whole teapot [which is default] or combination of the parts. You can even control which parts to display after creation. To create a **Teapot**, in the **Create** panel, click **Geometry**, and then in the **Object Type** rollout, click **Teapot**. In the viewport, click and drag to define the radius. Release the mouse button to set the radius and create teapot. You can control which part of the teapot you want to create by turning on the required parameters from the **Teapot Parts** group of the **Parameters** rollout.

TextPlus

The **TextPlus** primitive is used to create all-in-one text object. You can use this primitive to create an spline outline as well as solid, extruded beveled geometry. It allows you to apply different fonts and styles on a per-character basis and add animation and special effects. It is a very useful tool for producing motion graphics elements. To create the text, in the **Create** panel, click **Geometry**, and then in the **Object Type** rollout, click **TextPlus**. Click on the viewport to create the **TextPlus** object. If you want to create a region of text, click-drag in the viewport to define the region.

Layout Rollout

From this rollout, you can define the plane onto which you will type the text. The default option is **Auto**. Also, you can set whether you want to create a region of text or text just starting from a point [see Fig. 13].

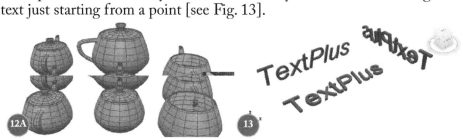

Parameters Rollout

From this rollout, you can set the font and other global parameters such as tracking and leading for the text. If you click on **Open Large Text Window**, the **Enter Text** window appears [see Fig. 14]. This window lets you easily type and format text. If you want to interactively change global parameters in the viewport, click **Manipulate Text**, some symbols appear on the text in the viewport [see Fig. 15]. You can use these symbols to manipulate the global parameters. When you are manipulating the text, you can you use the following:

- To select more than one letter, use **Ctrl**+click.
- If you click a letter with **Shift** held down, the clicked letter will be selected, all other previously selected letters will be de-selected.
- The tracking symbols only appear when you select more than one letter.
- You can change font and font type for individual characters.
- When you select letters in the **Text** field, letters are also selected in the viewport [see Fig. 16].

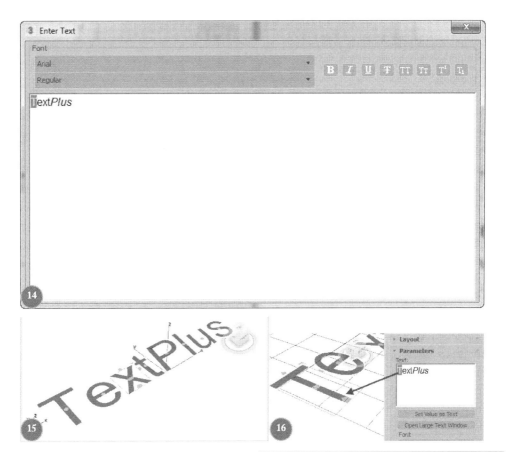

To reset the parameters, click **Reset Parameters**, the **Reset Text** dialog box appears [see Fig. 17]. Select the options that you want to reset and then click **Reset**.

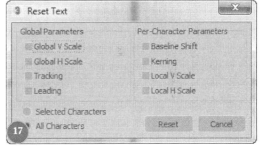

Geometry Rollout

The parameters in this rollout allow you to create depth using the **Extrude** and **Bevel** functions.

Values As Strings

You can also use the **TextPlus** object to display value of a object's parameter in the viewport. You can also show any value that can be returned from a script or expression. The value will dynamically update in the viewport when it changes. To see this feature in action, create a **TextPlus** object in a viewport and then type **radius:** in the **Text** field of the **Parameters** rollout. Create a sphere in a viewport. In the **Parameters** rollout of the **TextPlus** object, click **Set Value as Text** to open the **Edit Value As Text** dialog box. In this dialog box, select **Script** from the **Value Options** group [see Fig. 18] and then click **Pick Value From Scene**. Now, click on the sphere and then choose **Object (Sphere) > Radius** from the popup [see Fig. 19] to make the connection.

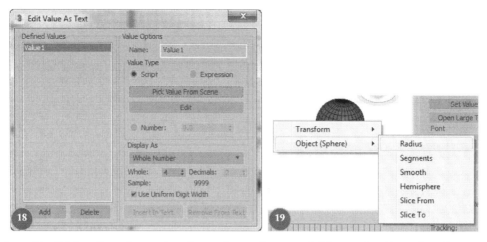

Select **Real Number** from the drop-down list available in the **Display As** group and then set **Decimals** to **2**. Now, put the cursor at the end of the text typed in the **Text** field and click **Insert In Text** from the **Edit Value As Text** dialog box. Close the dialog box. The string **%[Value1]** is appended in the **Text** field [see Fig. 20]. Now, if you change the value of the **Radius** parameter, the value will be dynamically updated in the **TextPlus** object.

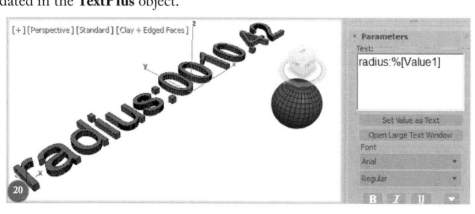

Extended Primitives

Extended primitives are little complex than the **Standard** primitives. 3ds Max offers thirteen extended primitives, see Fig. 21. You can combine the **Extended** primitives with the **Standard** primitives and modifiers to create refined models. You can interactively create **Extended** primitives in the viewport using the mouse and most of the primitives can be generated  by entering precise values using the keyboard. You can specify the parameters before creating the **Extended** primitives as well as modify them later from the **Parameters**

rollout in the **Modify** panel. Let's take a look at the commonly used **Extended** primitives. Experiment with the primitives that are not covered in this section. They are straight forward and you can easily understand their parameters by changing them from the **Parameters** rollout.

Hedra

You can use this primitive to create different type of polyhedra objects [see Fig. 22]. Table 6 summarizes the controls in the **Parameters** rollout.

Table 6: The parameters in the Hedra's Parameters rollout	
Group	**Description**
Family Group	The parameters in this group allow you to choose the type of polyhedral you want to create. **Tetra** creates a tetrahedron. **Cube/Octa** creates a cubic or octahedral polyhedron. **Dodec/Icos** creates a dodecahedron or icosahedron. **Star 1** and **Star 2** create two different star-shaped polyhedron.
Family Parameters Group	The **P** and **Q** parameters in this group change the geometry back and forth between the vertices and faces. In Fig. 23, the left polyhedron has **P** and **Q** values set to **0** each whereas the polyhedron on the right has the **P** and **Q** values set to **0.3** each. The combined value of **P** and **Q** can be equal to or less than **1**.
Axis Scaling Group	The **P, Q,** and **R** parameters in this group allow you to push or pull the corresponding facets in or out. The polyhedron at the left in Fig. 24 is created with the default parameters. For the polyhedron at the right, I have changed the **Q** and **R** values to **120** and **150**, respectively. On clicking **Reset**, the axes return to their default values.
Vertices Group	The parameters in this group determine the internal geometry of each facet of the polyhedron.
Radius	Sets the radius of the polyhedron.

> ✎ *Note: Creating Extended primitives*
> *To save some space, I am not writing the process to create the **Extended** primitives. You can easily create them using the standard click-drag methods as done in the **Standard Primitives** group.*

ChamferBox

You can use this primitive to create a box with beveled or round edges [see Fig. 25]. Most of the parameters in the **Parameters** rollout are similar to that of the **Box** primitive. Table 7 lists the parameters that are unique to **ChamferBox**.

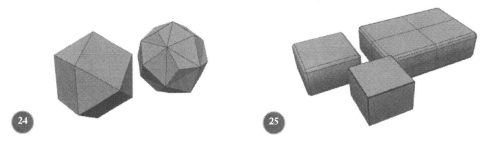

Table 7: The parameters in the **ChamferBox**'s **Parameters** rollout

Parameter	Description
Fillet	Slices the edges of the box. Higher the value you specify, more refined fillet you will get.
Fillet Segs	Determines the number of segments in the filleted edges.
Smooth	Blends the display of faces of the box. As a result, when rendered, box appears smooth in the rendered results.

ChamferCylinder

This primitive creates a cylinder with beveled or rounded cap edges [see Fig. 26].

Most of the parameters in the **Parameters** rollout are similar to that of the **Cylinder** primitive. Table 8 lists the parameters that are unique to **ChamferCylinder**.

Table 8: The parameters in the **Chamfer Cylinder**'s **Parameters** rollout

Parameter	Description
Fillet	It chamfers the top and bottom cap edges of the cylinder. The higher the value you specify, the more refined fillet will be.
Fillet Segs	Determines the number of segments in the filleted edges of the cylinder.

Architectural Objects

3ds Max provides several architectural objects that you can use as a basic building blocks for architectural models such as home, offices, and so on. Table 9 summaries the architectural objects that 3ds Max offers.

Table 9: The architectural objects	
Types	**Objects**
AEC Extended Objects	**Foliage, Railing,** and **Wall**
Stairs	**L-Type Stair, Spiral Stair, Straight Stair,** and **U-Type Stair**
Doors	**Pivot, Bifold,** and **Sliding**
Windows	**Awning, Casement, Fixed, Pivoted, Projected,** and **Sliding**

You can access all **AEC** objects from the **AEC Objects** sub-menu of the **Create** menu. You can also access these objects from the **Create** panel. Let's explore these objects.

Doors

The door objects allow you to quickly create a door. You can also set the door to be partially open even you can animate the opening. 3ds Max offers three types of doors. Table 10 summarizes these types.

Table 10: The door types	
Type	**Description**
Pivot	This door is hinged on one side only [see Fig. 27]. You can also make the door double-door, each hinged on its outer edge.
Bifold	This door is hinged in the middle as well as in the side. You can use this object to model a set of double doors [see Fig. 28].
Sliding	This type of door has a fixed half and a sliding half [see Fig. 29].

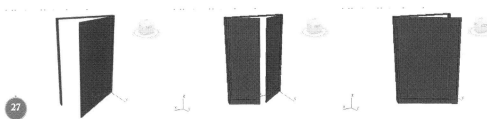

(27)

💡 *Tip: Navigating Viewport*
*If while creating **AEC** objects, you need to navigate the interface between clicks, drag the **MMB** to pan the viewport, **Alt+MMB** drag to orbit the viewport, and **Alt+Ctrl+Scroll** to zoom the viewport.*

To create a door, click **Command** panel > **Create** panel > **Geometry** and then choose **Doors** from the drop-down list. In the **Object Type** rollout, choose the type of the door you want to create and then set the desired create options from the rollouts. Drag the mouse in the viewport to create first two points to define the width and angle of the base of the door. Now, release the mouse button and drag to define the depth of the door and click to set. Drag the mouse to define the height of the door and then click to finish.

Assigning Material to Doors

By default, 3ds Max assigns five different IDs to the door you create. The default **Door-Template Multi-Subobject** material is found in the **Ace Templates.mat** material library. Fig. 30 shows the ID numbers and their associated parts in the door. 3ds Max does not assign a material to the door object. If you want to use the default material, you need to open the library in the material editor and then assign material to your object. Table 11 summarizes the material IDs assigned to doors.

Table 11: The material IDs	
ID	**Component**
1	Font
2	Back

Table 11: The material IDs	
ID	**Component**
3	Inner Bevel. This ID is used for glazing when you set **Panels** to **Glass** or **Beveled**.
4	Frame
5	Inner Door

 Tip: The Ace Template.mat library
You can find this library at the following location:
C:\Program Files\Autodesk\3ds Max 2020\materiallibraries.

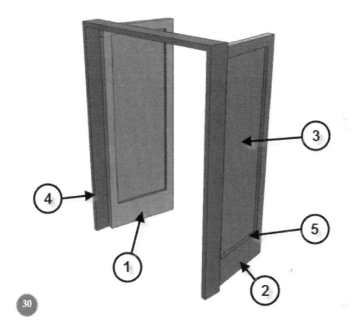

Windows

The window objects in 3ds Max allow you to create the appearance of a window. You can also set the window to be partially open even you can animate the opening. 3ds Max offers six types of windows. Table 12 summarizes the window types.

Table 12: The window types	
Type	**Description**
Casement	Two door like sashes arrangement that can swing inward or outward [see Fig. 31].
Pivoted	It pivots vertically or horizontally at the center of its sash [see Fig. 32].
Projected	It has three sashes two of which open like awning in opposite directions [see Fig. 33].

Table 12: The window types	
Type	**Description**
Sliding	It has two sashes one of which slides vertically or horizontally [see Fig. 34].
Fixed	It does not open [see Fig. 35].
Awning	It has a sash that is hinged at the top [see Fig. 36].

To create a window, click **Command** panel > **Create** panel > **Geometry** and then choose **Windows** from the drop-down list. In the **Object Type** rollout, choose the type of the window you want to create and then create the window in the viewport using click-drag operations.

Assigning Material to Windows

By default, 3ds Max assigns five different IDs to the window you create. The default **Window-Template Multi-Subobject** material is found in the **Ace Templates.mat** material library. Fig. 37 shows the ID numbers and their associated parts in a window. 3ds Max does not assign a material to the window object. If you want to use the default material, you need to open the library in the material editor and then assign material to your object. Table 13 summarizes the material IDs assigned to windows.

Table 13: The material IDs	
ID	**Component**
1	Front Rails
2	Back Rails
3	Panels. The Opacity is set to 50%.
4	Front Frame
5	Back Frame

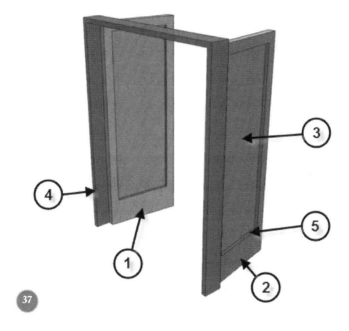

37

Stairs

3ds Max allows you to create four different types of stairs. The following table summarizes the types of stairs.

Table 14: The stairs types	
Type	**Description**
Spiral Stair	It allows you to create spiral staircase. You can specify radius and number of revolutions. You can also add stringers, center pole, and more to the stairs [see Fig. 38].

Table 14: The stairs types	
Type	**Description**
Straight Stair	It allows you to create simple straight stairs [see Fig. 39].
L-Type Stair	It lets you create the L-Type stairs [see Fig. 40].
U-Type Stair	It lets you create the U-Type stairs [see Fig. 41].

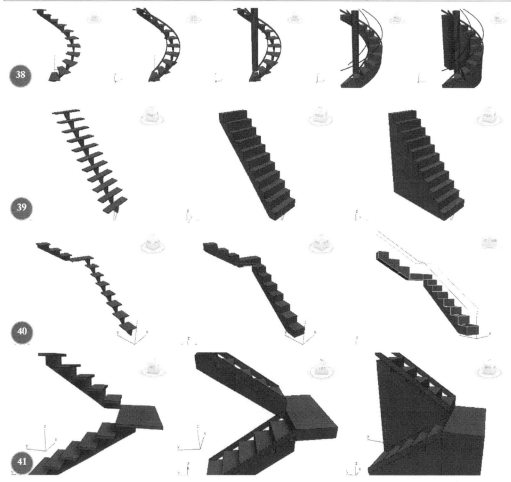

To create a stair, click **Command** panel > **Create** panel > **Geometry** and then choose **Stairs** from the drop-down list. In the **Object Type** rollout, choose the type of the stair you want to create and then create the stair in the viewport using click-drag operations.

Assigning Material to Stairs

By default, 3ds Max assigns five different IDs to the stairs you create. The default **Stairs-Template Multi-Subobject** material is found in the **Ace Templates.mat** material library. 3ds Max does not assign a material to the stairs object. If you want to use the default material, you need to open the library in the material editor and then assign material to your object. Table 15 summarizes the material IDs assigned to stairs.

Table 15: The material IDs	
ID	**Component**
1	Treads of the stairs.
2	Front riser of the stairs.
3	Bottom, back, and sides of the risers of the stairs.
4	Center pole of the stairs.
5	Handrails of the stairs.
6	Carriage of the stairs.
7	Stringers of the stairs.

AEC Extended Objects

AEC stands for **Architecture Engineer Construction**. These objects are designed to for use in the architectural, engineering, and construction field. To create an **AEC** object, click **Command** panel > **Create** panel > **Geometry** and then choose **AEC Extended** from the drop-down list. In the **Object Type** rollout, choose the type of the object you want to create and then create the object in the viewport using click-drag operations.

Railing

This tool allows you to create railings in a 3ds Max scene. The railing object includes rails, posts, and fencing [see Fig. 42]. You can create railing by specifying the orientation and height. You can also use a spline object to create railing along it. If you edit the spline, the railing object updates to follow the path. You can use railing object with the stair object to create a complete stair.

To create a railing, click **Command** panel > **Create** panel > **Geometry** and then choose **AEC Extended** from the drop-down list. In the **Object Type** rollout, click **Railing** and then create the railing in the viewport using click-drag operations.

Assigning Material to Railings

By default, 3ds Max assigns five different IDs to the railings you create. The default **Rail-Template Multi-Subobject** material is found in the **Ace Templates.mat** material library. 3ds Max does not assign a material to the railing objects. If you want to use the default material, you need to open the library in the material editor and then assign material to your object. Table 16 summarizes the material IDs assigned to railings.

Table 16: The material IDs	
ID	**Component**
1	Lower rails
2	Posts of the railing
3	Solid fill of the railing
4	Top of the railing
5	Pickets of the railing

Foliage

You can use this tool to place various kinds of tree species in a scene [see Figs. 43 and 44]. This tool can produce good looking trees efficiently. You can define height, density, pruning, seed, canopy display, and level of detail for the **Foliage** object.

To create a tree, click **Command** panel > **Create** panel > **Geometry** and then choose **AEC Extended** from the drop-down list. In the **Object Type** rollout, click **Foliage.** In the **Favorite Plants** rollout, either drag a tree to add to the scene or select the plant and then click on the viewport to place it. You can also double-click on a plant in the **Favorite Plants** rollout.

Tip: Placing plants in the scene
*You can use the **Spacing** tool to place plants along a path.*

Wall

The **Wall** tool is used to create walls [see Fig. 45] in 3ds Max. The wall object is made up of three sub-object types: **Vertex, Segment,** and **Profile** that you can use to edit it.

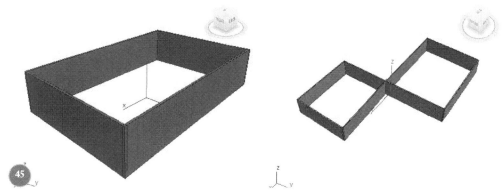

You can create wall in any viewport but for vertical walls you should use a **Perspective**, **Camera**, or **Top** viewport. To create a wall, set the **Width** and **Height** parameters and then click in a viewport. Now, release the mouse button and then drag to specify the length, click again.

If you want to create a single wall component, **RMB** click, else continue clicking. To finish creating a room, click on an end segment; 3ds Max displays the **Weld Point** dialog box. You can use the options in this dialog box to either weld the two end vertices into a single vertex or you can keep the two end vertices distinct. **RMB** click to finish the wall.

Assigning Material to Walls

By default, 3ds Max assigns five different IDs to the walls you create. The default **Wall-Template Multi-Subobject** material is found in the **Ace Templates.mat** material library. 3ds Max does not assign a material to the wall object. If you want to use the default material, you need to open the library in the material editor and then assign material to your object.

Table 17 summarizes the material IDs assigned to the walls.

Table 17: The material IDs assigned to the walls	
ID	**Component**
1	Vertical ends of the wall.
2	Outside of the wall.
3	Inside of the wall.
4	Top of the wall, including any edges cut out of the wall.
5	Bottom of the wall.

Note: ID 2 and 3
The definitions of ID 2 and 3 is interchangeable because the inside and outside of the wall depend on your point-of-view and how you created the wall object.

Note: Inserting doors and windows in a wall
3ds Max automatically makes opening for doors and windows in a wall object. It also makes the linked doors and windows children of the wall object. To do this, directly create doors and windows on the wall by snapping to its faces, vertices, or edges.

Tip: Making opening using Boolean operations
*You can also make openings in a wall using the **Boolean** operations. Single wall with many doors and windows can slow down you system. To speed up, use multiple walls instead of a single wall. You can also collapse the stack to speed up the performance of your system.*

Hands-on Exercises

Exercise 1: Creating a Sofa
In this exercise, we will model a sofa using the **Box** primitive [see Fig. E1]. Table E1 summarizes the exercise.

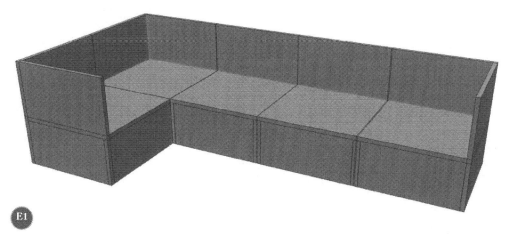

E1

Table E1	
Skill level	Beginner
Time to complete	30 Minutes
Topics	• Specifying the Units for the Exercise • Creating One Seat Section of the Sofa • Creating Corner Section of the Sofa
Resources folder	**unit-dm3**
Units	**US Standard – Decimal Inches**
Final file	**sofa-finish.max**

Specifying the Units for the Exercise
Follow these steps:

1. From the **Customize** menu choose **Units Setup**. In the **Units Setup** dialog box that appears, select **US Standard** from the **Display Unit Scale** group. Next, choose **Decimal Inches** from the drop-down list located below **US Standard** [see Fig. E2] and then click **OK** to accept the change.

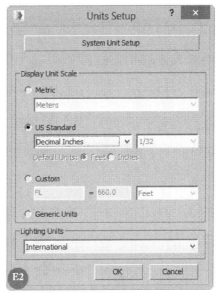

What just happened?
Here, we have set the display units for the scene. The units that you set here are used to measure geometry in the scene. You can also set the lighting units using this dialog box. Apart from the display units, you can also set the system units that 3ds Max uses for the internal mechanism. To view parameters available for changing system units, click **System Unit Setup** *in the* **Units Setup** *dialog box.*

Note: Units
It is important to understand the difference between the system and display units. The scene units only affect how geometry is displayed in the viewports whereas the system units control the actual scale of the geometry.

Caution: System Units
The system units should only be changed before you create your scene or import a **unitless** *file. Do not change the system units in the current scene.*

2. **RMB** click on any snap toggle button in the **Main** toolbar. In the **Grid and Snap Settings** dialog box that opens, choose the **Home Grid** panel and then set **Grid Spacing** to **3**, **Major Lines every Nth Grid Line** to **4**, and **Perspective View Grid Extent** to **10**. Close the **Grid and Snap Settings** dialog box.

What Just Happened?
The home grid provides a visual reference to the user. It helps in visualizing space, scale, and distance. Here, I have set **Grid Spacing** *to* **3***, the size of the smallest square of the grid. In the previous step, I have set the units to inches therefore the size of one grid space is equal to* **3** *inches. For example, if you create a box with width set to* **24** *inches, it will take* **8** *grid boxes.*

*The home grid displays heavier or "major" lines to mark groups of grid squares. Here, I've set the **Major Lines every Nth Grid Line** to **4**. As a result, the major grid divisions represent one feet. The **Perspective View Grid Extent** parameter sets the size of the home grid in the **Perspective** viewport. The **Perspective View Grid Extent** value represents the length of half the grid along an axis. Here, this means that **Grid Spacing=3** and **Perspective View Grid Extent=10**, will result in **60x60** units grid size.*

3. From the **File** menu, choose **Save** to open the **Save File As** dialog box. In the **File name** text box type **sofa-finish.max** and then click **Save** to save the file.

> *Note: Saving Files*
> *I highly recommend that you save your work regularly by pressing **Ctrl+S**.*

Creating One Seat Section of the Sofa
Follow these steps:

1. In the **Create** panel ⊞, click **Geometry** ◯, and then in the **Object Type** rollout, click **Box**. In the **Perspective** viewport, drag out a box of any size. Go to the **Modify** panel ⬚ and then in the **Parameters** rollout, set **Length** to **25.591**, **Width** to **25.591**, and **Height** to **1**.

2. **RMB** click on the **Select and Move** tool ✛ in the **Main** toolbar to open the **Move Transform Type-In** dialog box and then set **X** to **0**, **Y** to **0**, and **Z** to **11.42** in the **Absolute:World** group. Close the dialog box. Click **Zoom Extents All** ⊡ to zoom on **Box001** in all viewports [see Fig. E3].

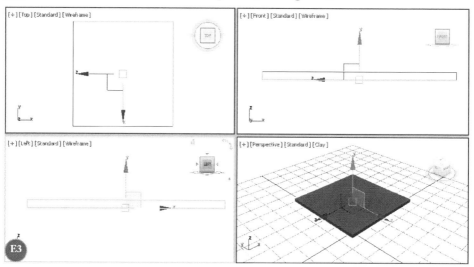

What just happened?
Here, I have set the position of the box using the **Move Transform Type-In** dialog box. This dialog box allows you to enter precise values for move, rotate, and scale transforms. To open this dialog box, **RMB** click on the **Select and Move** ✛, **Select and Rotate** ↻, or **Select and Scale** ▦ tool in the **Main** toolbar. You can also press **F12** while one of the aforesaid tools is active to open the dialog box.

Tip: Transform Type-In boxes
You can also use the **Transform Type-In** boxes in the **Status Bar**. To transform objects, ensure they are selected. Type the values in the **Transform Type-In** boxes and then press **Enter**. You can toggle between the absolute transform and relative transform by clicking the button available to the right of the **Selection Lock Toggle** button.

3. In the **Create** panel, click **Geometry**, and then in the **Object Type** rollout, click **Box**. Activate the **Top** viewport. Expand the **Keyboard Entry** rollout, and set **Length** to **25.591**, **Width** to **1**, and **Height** to **11.417**. Click **Create**. Click **Align** ▤ on the **Main** toolbar. Now, click **Box001**. In the **Align Selection** dialog box that opens, set the parameters shown in Fig. E4. Click **OK** to accept the changes made [see Fig. E5].

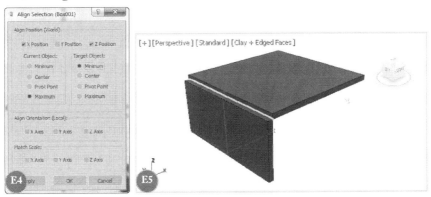

4. Align **Box001** and **Box002** using **Select and Move** [see Fig. E6]. Click **Mirror** ⚟ on the **Main** toolbar to open the **Mirror** dialog box. In this dialog box, make sure X is selected in the **Mirror Axis** group. Select **Copy** from the **Clone Selection** group and then set **Offset** to **24.591**. Click **OK** to accept the changes made and create a mirror copy of **Box002** [see Fig. E7].

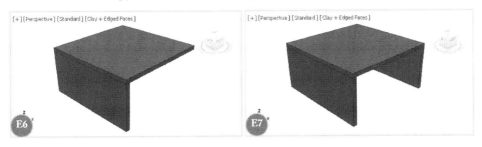

5. Activate the **Top** viewport. In the **Create** panel, click **Geometry**, and then in the **Object Type** rollout, click **Box**. Expand the **Keyboard Entry** rollout and then set **Length** to **1**, **Width** to **25.591**, and **Height** to **25.984**. Click **Create** to create a box with the name **Box004**. Make sure **Box004** is selected.

6. Activate the **Top** viewport. Click **Align** ▣ on the **Main** toolbar and then click **Box001**. In the **Align Selection** dialog box that opens, set the parameters shown in Fig. E8 and click **OK** to align the objects [see Fig. E9].

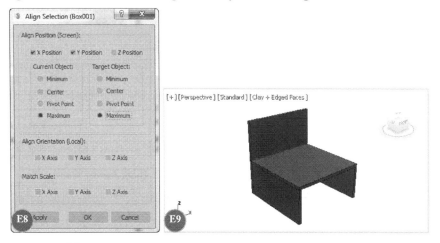

7. Activate the **Top** viewport. In the **Create** panel, click **Geometry**, and then in the **Object Type** rollout, click **Box**. Expand the **Keyboard Entry** rollout and then set **Length** to **1**, **Width** to **23.591**, and **Height** to **11.417**. Click **Create** to create a box with the name **Box005**. Next, align it as shown in Fig. E10.

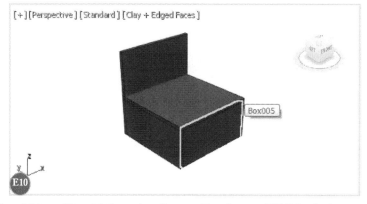

8. Select **Box001** to **Box005** in the **Scene Explorer**. RMB click on the selection to open a **Quad** menu. Choose **Add Selected To > New Group** from the menu. In the **Group** dialog box that opens, type the group name as **oneSeat** and click **OK**.

Creating Corner Section of the Sofa
Follow these steps:

1. Collapse **oneSeat** in the **Scene Explorer**, if no already collapsed, **RMB** click on it and select **Clone** from the **Quad** menu. In the **Clone Options** dialog box that opens, select **Copy** from the **Object** group. Change the **Name** to **cornerSeat** and click **OK**.

2. In the **Perspective** viewport, move the **cornerSeat** to the right of **oneSeat**. Select **cornerSeat** in the **Scene Explorer**, from the **Group** menu, select **Open**. Select the right-most box. Go to the **Modify** panel, and then on the **Parameters** rollout, set **Height** to **25.984**. From the **Group** menu, select **Close**. Fig. E11 shows the **cornerSeat** and **oneSeat**. Now, make various combinations of **oneSeat** and **cornerSeat** by making copies of them [see Fig. E12]. Press **CTRL+S** to save the file.

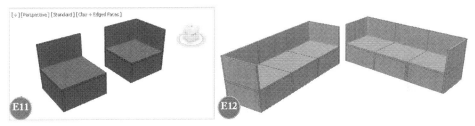

Exercise 2: Creating a Coffee Table
In this exercise, we will model a coffee table using the **Cylinder** and **Torus** primitives [see Fig. E1]. Table E2 summarizes the exercise.

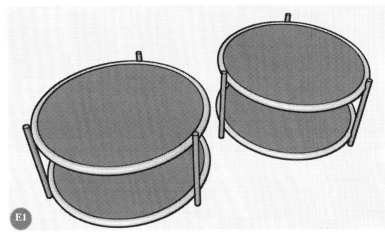

Table E2	
Skill level	Beginner
Time to complete	20 Minutes
Topics	• Specifying the Units for the Exercise • Creating the Coffee Table

Table E2	
Resources folder	**unit-dm3**
Units	**Metric - Centimeters**
Final file	**coffee-table-finish.max**

Specifying the Units for the Exercise
Follow these steps:

1. Reset 3ds Max. From the **Customize** menu choose **Units Setup**. In the **Units Setup** dialog box that opens, select **Metric** from the **Display Unit Scale** group. Next, select **Centimeters** from the drop-down list located below **Metric**, if already not selected. Click **OK** to accept the change. **RMB** click on any snap toggle button in the **Main** toolbar.

2. In the **Grid and Snap Settings** dialog box that opens, choose the **Home Grid** panel and then set **Grid Spacing** to **3**, **Major Lines every Nth Grid Line** to **4**, and **Perspective View Grid Extent** to **10**. Close the **Grid and Snap Settings** dialog box. From the **File menu**, choose **Save** to open the **Save File As** dialog box. In the **File name** text box type **coffee-table-finish.max** and click **Save** to save the file.

Creating the Coffee Table
Follow these steps:

1. In the **Create** panel, click **Geometry**, and then in the **Object Type** rollout, click **Cylinder**. Activate the **Top** viewport. Expand the **Keyboard Entry** rollout, and set **Radius** to **37.5** and **Height** to **2**. In the **Parameters** layout, set **Height Segments** to **1**, **Cap Segments** to **1**, and **Sides** to **64**. Click **Create** from the **Keyboard Entry** rollout.

2. In the **Create** panel, click **Geometry**, and then in the **Object Type** rollout, click **Torus**. Create a torus in the **Top** viewport. Go to the **Modify** panel and then in the **Parameters** rollout set **Radius 1** to **37.5**, **Radius 2** to **1.581**, **Segments** to **100**, and **Sides** to **12**. Now, click **Select and Place** [icon] tool on the **Main** toolbar and then drag torus onto the cylinder to align the two objects [see Fig. E2]. If required, use the **Move** tool to align the two objects. Place the two objects at the origin as discussed earlier.

3. Select the **Torus** and the **Cylinder001** and then activate the **Front** viewport by **MMB** clicking on it. Click **Select and Move** in the **Main** toolbar and then press **Shift**, move the selection down by **30** units along the negative **Y** direction. In the **Clone Options** dialog box that appears, choose **Copy** from the **Object** group and click **OK** to create a copy of the selected objects [see Fig. E3].

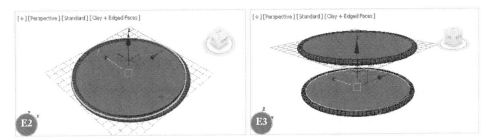

4. In the **Create** panel, click **Geometry**, and then in the **Object Type** rollout, click **Cylinder**. Create a cylinder in the **Top** viewport. Go to the **Modify** panel and then in the **Parameters** rollout, set **Radius** to **1.2**, **Height** to **41**, **Height Segments** to **1**, and **Sides** to **18**.

5. Make sure that **Select and Move** tool is active and then in the **Status Bar**, enter **-40.246, 0**, and **-35.352** in the **Transform Type-In** boxes to place the cylinder [see Fig. E4].

6. In the **Hierarchy** panel of the **Command** panel, click **Use Working Pivot** from the **Working Pivot** rollout. Choose **Array** from the **Tools** menu. Set the parameters in the **Array** dialog box, as shown in Fig. E5 and click **OK** to create two more copies of the cylinder [see Fig. E6].

7. Select all objects from the **Scene Explorer** and then choose **Group** from the **Group** menu. Name the group **coffeeTable**. Press **CTRL+S** to save the file.

Exercise 3: Creating a Foot Stool

In this exercise, we will model a foot stool using the **ChamferBox** and **OilTank** extended primitives [see Fig. E1]. Table E3 summarizes the exercise.

Table E3	
Skill level	Beginner
Time to complete	20 Minutes
Topics	• Specifying the Units for the Exercise • Creating the Stool
Resources folder	**unit-dm3**
Units	**US Standard – Decimal Inches**
Final file	**foot-stool-finish.max**

Specifying the Units for the Exercise

Follow these steps:

1. Reset 3ds Max. From the **Customize** menu choose **Units Setup**. In the **Units Setup** dialog box that opens, select the **US standard** option from the **Display Unit Scale** group. Next, select **Decimal Inches** from the drop-down list located below the **US Standard** option, if already not selected. Click **OK** to accept the change.

2. **RMB** click on any snap toggle button on the **Main** toolbar. In the **Grid and Snap Settings** dialog box that opens, choose the **Home Grid** panel and then set **Grid Spacing** to **3**, **Major Lines every Nth Grid Line** to **4**, and **Perspective View Grid Extent** to **10**. Close the **Grid and Snap Settings** dialog box.

Creating the Stool

Follow these steps:

1. In the **Create** panel, click **Geometry**, and then select **Extended Primitives** from the drop-down list located below **Geometry**. In the **Object Type** rollout, click **ChamferBox**. Create a chamfer box in the **Top** viewport.

2. Go to the **Modify** panel and then in the **Parameters** rollout set **Length** to **24.8**, **Width** to **31.5**, **Height** to **5**, **Fillet** to **1.2**, and **Fillet Segs** to **5**. Rename the chamfer box to **baseGeo**.

3. Click **Select and Move** in the **Main** toolbar and then enter **0** in all **Transform Type-In** boxes to place the box at the origin. Press **Shift+Ctrl+Z** to zoom the chamfer box to its extents. In the **Perspective** viewport, press **Shift** and drag **baseGeo** along the +**Z** axis about **5** units.

4. In the **Clone Option** dialog box that appears, make sure **Copy** is selected from the **Object** group. Type **seatGeo** in the name text box and click **OK**. Go to the **Modify** panel and then in the **Parameters** rollout set **Height** to **8**, **Fillet** to **0.72** and **Fillet Segs** to **3**. Align the boxes [see Fig. E2].

5. In the **Create** panel, click **Geometry**, and then select **Extended Primitives** from the drop-down list located below **Geometry**. In the **Object Type** rollout, click **OilTank**. Create an oil tank in the **Top** viewport. Go to the **Modify** panel and then in the **Parameters** rollout set **Radius** to **1.1**, **Height** to **5**, **Sides** to **25**, and **Cap Height** to **0.9**. Rename oil tank as **legGeo** and then align it [see Fig. E3]. Create three more copies of legGeo and align it viewports [see Fig. E4].

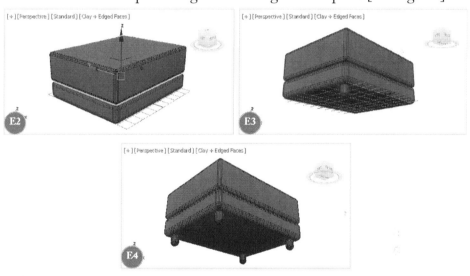

Exercise 4: Creating a Bar Table

In this exercise, we will model a bar table using the **ChamferBox** and **ChamferCyl** extended primitives [see Fig. E1]. Table E4 summarizes the exercise.

Table E4	
Skill level	Beginner
Time to complete	40 Minutes
Topics	• Specifying the Units for the Exercise • Creating the Bar Table
Resources folder	**unit-dm3**
Units	**US Standard – Decimal Inches**
Final file	**bar-table-finish.max**

Specifying the Units for the Exercise
Follow these steps:

1. Reset 3ds Max. From the **Customize** menu choose **Units Setup**. In the **Units Setup** dialog box that opens, select the **US standard** option from the **Display Unit Scale** group. Next, select **Decimal Inches** from the drop-down list located below the **US Standard** option, if already not selected. Click **OK** to accept the change.

2. **RMB** click on any snap toggle button on the **Main** toolbar. In the **Grid and Snap Settings** dialog box that opens, choose the **Home Grid** panel and then set **Grid Spacing** to 3, **Major Lines every Nth Grid Line** to 4, and **Perspective View Grid Extent** to 10. Close the **Grid and Snap Settings** dialog box.

Creating the Bar Table
Follow these steps:

1. In the **Create** panel, click **Geometry**, and then select **Extended Primitives** from the drop-down list located below **Geometry**. In the **Object Type** rollout, click **ChamferCyl**.

2. Create a cylinder in the **Top** viewport. Go to the **Modify** panel and then in the **Parameters** rollout set **Radius** to **13.78**, **Height** to **1.5**, **Fillet** to **0.15**, **Fillet Segs** to **5**, and **Sides** to **50**. Rename the cylinder as **topGeo**.

3. Click **Select and Move** in the **Main** toolbar and then enter **0** in all **Transform Type-In** boxes to place **topGeo** at the origin. Create another chamfer cylinder in the **Top** viewport and rename it as **supportGeo**.

4. Go to the **Modify** panel and then in the **Parameters** rollout set **Radius** to **1.3**, **Height** to **38**, **Fillet** to **0**, **Fillet Segs** to **1**, and **Sides** to **18**. Now, align **topGeo** and **supportGeo** in viewports [see Fig. E2].

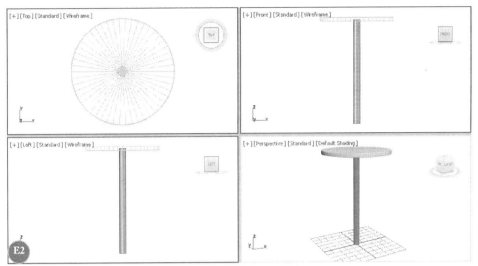

5. In the **Create** panel, click **Geometry**, and then choose **Standard Primitives** from the drop-down list located below **Geometry**. In the **Object Type** rollout, click **Tube**. Create a tube in the **Top** viewport. Place the tube, as shown in Fig. E3. Go to the **Modify** panel and then in the **Parameters** rollout set **Radius 1** to **4**, **Radius 2** to **1.3**, **Height** to **2**, and **Sides** to **50**. Rename tube as **tubeGeo** [see Fig. E3].

6. In the **Create** panel, click **Geometry**, and then select **Extended Primitives** from the drop-down list located below **Geometry**. In the **Object Type** rollout, click **ChamferBox**. Create a box in the **Top** viewport. Go to the **Modify** panel and then in the **Parameters** rollout set **Length** to **2.1**, **Width** to **12.8**, **Height** to **1.6**, **Fillet** to **0.1** and **Fillet Segs** to **6**. Rename the box as **legGeo**.

7. From the **Object-Space Modifiers** section of the **Modifier** list, select **Taper**. In the **Parameters** layout, set **Amount** to **-0.64**. Set **Primary** to X in the **Taper Axis** area. Now, aline **legGeo** with **tubeGeo** [see Fig. E4].

8. Create another chamfer box in the **Top** viewport. Go to the **Modify** panel and then in the **Parameters** rollout set **Length** to **1.57**, **Width** to **5.6**, **Height** to **0.64**, **Fillet** to **0.07**, **Width Segs** to **32**, and **Fillet Segs** to **3**.

9. From the **Object-Space Modifiers** section of the **Modifier** list, select **Bend**. In the **Parameters** layout, set **Angle** to **213**. Select X radio button in the **Bend Axis** area [see Fig. E5].

10. Create a chamfer cylinder in the **Top** viewport. Go to the **Modify** panel and then in the **Parameters** rollout set **Radius** to **1.362**, **Height** to **1.72**, **Fillet** to **0.1**,

Fillet Segs to **5**, and **Sides** to **50**. Align the cylinder with the box and then group them with the name **grpRoller**. Align **grpRoller** with **legGeo** [see Fig. E6] and then group them as **grpLeg**.

11. Ensure **grpLeg** is selected and activate the **Top** viewport. Select **Use Transform Coordinate Center** from the **Use Center** flyout the **Main** toolbar. Choose **Array** from the **Tools** menu. Now, set the values in the **Array** dialog box, as shown in Fig. E7, and then click **OK** to create **3** more copies [see Fig. E8].

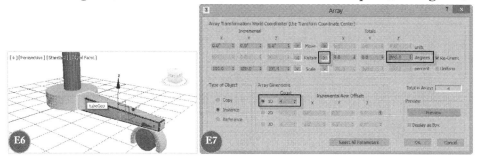

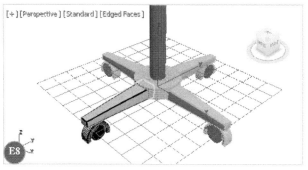

Quiz

Evaluate your skills to see how many questions you can answer correctly.

Fill in the Blanks
Fill in the blanks in each of the following statements:

1. You can use the **GeoSphere** primitive to create spheres and geo-hemispheres based on three classes of polyhedrons: _____, _____, and _____.

2. To constrain the base of the pyramid to a square, drag with the _____ key held down.

3. The default **Window-Template Multi-Subobject** material is found in the _____ material library.

True of False
State whether each of the following is true or false:

1. You can change the name of an object from the **Name and Color** rollout.

2. You can create a cube object using the **Box** tool.

3. The **GeoSphere** tool produces smooth shape than the **Sphere** tool.

Summary
The unit covered the following topics:

*   Creating and modifying the **Standard** Primitives
*   Creating and modifying the **Extended** Primitives
*   Working with the **Architectural** objects
*   Setting the project folder
*   Using the **Align** and **Mirror** tools
*   Creating clones
*   Using the **Scene Explorer**
*   Creating a group
*   Setting grid spacings
*   Using the **Transform Type-In** dialog box
*   Using the **Array** dialog box
*   Specifying the units for the scene

This page is intentionally left blank

- Working with the polygon modeling tools
- Using the polygon modeling techniques
- Selecting polygon sub-objects
- Transforming sub-objects
- Soft selecting sub-objects

Unit DM4: Polygon Modeling

In Unit DM3, we have modeled objects using the parametric modeling techniques. In parametric modeling, you create primitives from the **Create** panel and modify them using the creation parameters. Then, you transform the primitives using the transformation tools to create shape of the models. The **Parametric** modeling is powerful and easy but it has some limitations when it comes to creating complex models. The **Surface** modeling on the other hand is more flexible and allows you to create any object that you can imagine. Once you convert an object to an editable object such as an editable poly, editable mesh, editable patch, or NURBS object; 3ds Max provides specialized toolset to create the models.

Editable Poly Object

The editable poly object is an editable object with five sub-object levels: **Vertex**, **Edge**, **Border**, **Polygon**, and **Element**. Sub-objects such as vertices and edges are the basic building blocks of an object. Vertices are points in 3D space. They define the structure for other sub-objects such as edges and polygons. An edge is a line connecting two vertices. The connection forms one side of the polygon. An edge cannot be shared by more than two polygons. Also, normals of the two polygons should be adjacent. When three or more edges combine together, they form a polygon. **Elements** are groups of contiguous polygons. A border can be described as the edge of a hole in the object. Fig. 1 shows various sub-object levels available for the editable poly object.

> *Note: The editable poly objects vs editable mesh objects*
> *The editable poly object is similar to the edit mesh object with the only difference is that the edit mesh object comprises of triangular faces whereas the editable poly object comprises of polygons with any number of vertices.*

You can convert an object to an editable poly object by using one of the following methods:

1. Select an object in a viewport and then go to the **Modify** panel. Next, **RMB** click on the object entry in the stack display and then choose **Editable Poly** from the pop up menu displayed [see Fig. 2].
2. Select the object in a viewport and then **RMB** click. Choose **transform** quadrant> **Convert To:** > **Convert to Editable Poly** [see Fig. 3].
3. Apply a modifier to a parametric object that makes the object a poly object. For example, the **Turn to Poly** modifier.
4. Apply the **Edit Poly** modifier.

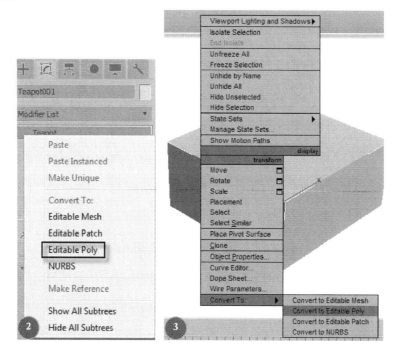

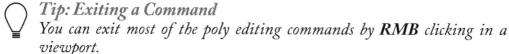

Tip: Exiting a Command
You can exit most of the poly editing commands by **RMB** *clicking in a viewport.*

Caution: Preserving the parametric nature of a primitive
When you convert an object to an editable poly, you loose all of its creation parameters. If you want to retain the creation parameters, use the **Edit Poly** *modifier.*

Caution: Limitations of the Edit Poly modifier
The **Edit Poly** *modifier offers most of the capabilities of the* **Editable Poly** *object except the* **Vertex Color Information***, the* **Subdivision Surface** *rollout, the* **Weight** *and* **Crease** *settings, and the* **Subdivision Displacement** *rollout.*

Note: Graphite modeling tools
The option to convert an object to an editable poly is also available in the **Graphite Modeling Tools**. *You will learn about these tools in a later unit.*

Selecting Sub-objects
You can select sub-objects using one of the following ways:

1. Expand the object's hierarchy [by clicking the triangle] from the stack display and then choose a sub-object level [see Fig. 4]. The selected sub-object will be highlighted in the stack display.
2. Click a selection button from the **Selection** rollout [see Fig. 5].
3. **RMB** click on an object in a viewport and then choose the sub-object level from the upper left quadrant [**tools 1**] of the **Quad** menu [see Fig. 6].
4. Choose a selection or transform tool and then click on the sub-objects in a viewport using the standard selection techniques.

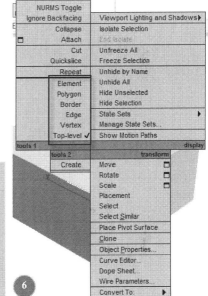

Note: Adding and removing from the selection
To select a vertex, edge, polygon, or element, click it. To add to the sub-object selection, press and hold **Ctrl** *and click. You can also drag a selection region to select a group of sub-objects. To subtract from the sub-object selection, press and hold* **Alt** *and click. You can also drag a selection region to deselect a group of sub-objects.*

Tip: Locking selection
Once you make the sub-object selection, you can lock the selection by pressing **Spacebar**. *Locking the selection helps in unintentionally selecting other sub-objects. To release the lock, press* **Spacebar** *again.*

Tip: Keyboard shortcuts
*You can use the numeric keys from **1** to **5** to activate the **Vertex**, **Edge**, **Border**,*
***Polygon**, and **Element** sub-object levels, respectively. Press **6** to return to the*
***Object** level.*

Creating and Modifying Selections

The parameters available in the **Selection** and **Soft Selection** rollouts let you access different sub-object levels as well as they give you ability to create and modify selections. Let's have a look at the tools available in these two rollouts.

Selection Rollout

There are five buttons at the top of the **Selection** rollout. These buttons allow you to select the sub-object levels. Table 1 summarizes function of these buttons:

Table 1: The sub-object buttons		
Button	**Icon**	**Description**
Vertex		Activates the **Vertex** sub-object level. Allows you to select the vertex beneath the mouse pointer. Draw a region selection to select the vertices within the region.
Edge		Activates the **Edge** sub-object level. Allows you to select the edge beneath the mouse pointer. Draw a region selection to select the edges within the region.
Border		Activates the **Border** sub-object level. Allows you to select a set of edges that borders a hole in the geometry. In other words, you can select the edges that are on the border.
Polygon		Activates the **Polygon** sub-object level. Allows you to select the polygon beneath the mouse pointer. Draw a region selection to select the polygons within the region.
Element		Activates the **Element** sub-object level. Allows you to select all contiguous polygons. Draw a region selection to select multiple elements within the region.

 Note: Border edges
*If the concept of border edges is not clear to you, I would recommend a simple exercise. Create a **Cylinder** primitive in the scene and then convert it to **Editable Poly**. Select the **Polygon** sub-object level and then click on the top face of the cylinder to select it. Press **Delete** to delete the top face. Now, activate the **Border** sub-object level, and click on the border to select the border element [see Fig. 7]. There is now only one border edge in the geometry that borders a hole in the cylinder.*

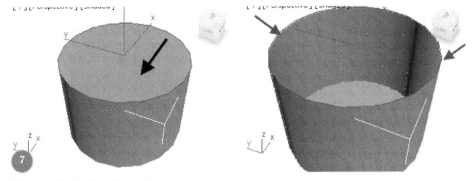

Working with Selection Sets

The **Named Selection Sets** list allows you to name a selection set [both at the object level as well as at the sub-object level] that you can recall later during the modeling process. For example, if you are modeling a face, you might want to select different sub-objects for various parts of the face. In such a case, you can create a selection set for a particular area of the face [nose, for example] and recall it later. It will save you lot of time as you do not have to recreate the selection later during the modeling process.

> *Caution: Selection Set Names*
> *The selection set names are case-sensitive.*

Keep the following in mind while working with the named selection sets:

- You can transfer sub-objects selection from one modifier to another. You can also transfer the sub-object selection from one level to another in the modifier stack.
- You can transfer named selection sets only between the same types of sub-objects. For example, you cannot transfer a **Vertex** selection to a **Face** selection.
- You are only allowed to transfer selection sets between the modifiers that work on the same geometry type. For example, you cannot transfer a selection set from an **Edit Spline** modifier to **Edit Poly** modifier.
- You can copy and paste selection sets between two modifiers assigned to two different objects. However, both modifiers should handle the same types of geometry.

> *Caution: Changing Topology*
> *If you modify the topology of the object, you might get unpredictable results when you use the named selection set.*

To create a named selection set, select the objects or sub-objects that you want part of the set and then type the name of the selection set in the **Named Selection Sets** field [see Fig. 8] in the **Main** toolbar. Press **Enter** to create the selection set.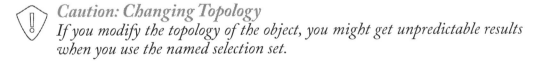

To recall a selection, select the name from the **Named Selection Sets** list. If you want to select more than one selection sets from the list, press **Ctrl** while selecting names. To remove name from the selection, press and hold **Alt** and then click the name in the list.

Once you make a sub-object selection, you can perform the following tasks:

- You can move, rotate, and scale sub-objects using the standard transformation tools.
- You can apply the object-space modifiers.
- You can bind a space warp to the selection.
- If you have made the polygon selection, you can use the **Align, Normal Align**, and **Align To View** tools from the **Align** flyout of the **Main** toolbar.

Transforming a Sub-object Selection

If you are working with an editable object such as mesh, poly, patch, or spline, you can directly manipulate the selection using the transformations tools. However, if you are using a selection modifier such as **Mesh Select** or **Spline Select**, you need to use an **XFrom Modifier** to transform the selection.

Here's how it works:

1. Create a polygon primitive such as **Box** and then convert to an **Editable Poly** object.
2. Make a sub-object selection and move it using the **Select and Move** tool. You will notice that you can easily move the selection [see Fig. 9]. Press **Ctrl+Z** to undo the last operation. Now, deselect everything. You can also press **6** on the main keyboard.
3. Apply the **Mesh Select** modifier [see Fig. 10] and then make a selection. Notice that the transformation tools are inactive on the **Main** toolbar.
4. Apply the **XFrom** modifier to the object. Expand the **XFrom** modifier in the stack display and select **Gizmo** [see Fig. 11]. Now, you can move the selection as required.

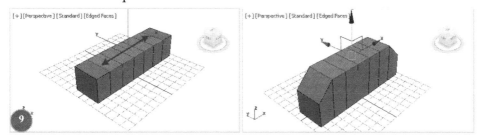

Cloning Sub-objects

When you **SHIFT**+transform [move, scale, or rotate] a sub-object selection, the **Clone Part of Mesh** dialog box appears [see Fig. 12]. This dialog box gives you two options: **Clone to Object** and **Clone to Element**. When you select **Clone To Object**, 3ds Max creates a separate object comprises of the selected sub-objects. If you select **Clone to Element**, the selection is cloned and it becomes an element of the current object.

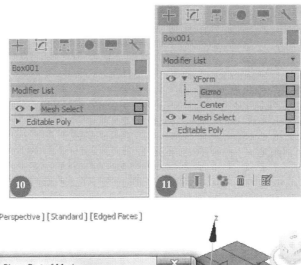

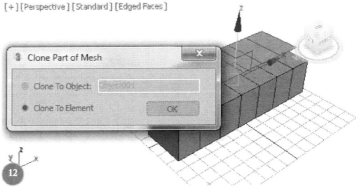

Converting Sub-Object Selections

If you make a sub-object selection, for example, a vertex selection, you can convert it to a different sub-object selection such as edge or face using the **Ctrl** and **Shift** keys:

- To convert a selection to a different sub-object selection, click on the sub-object level button in the **Selection** rollout with **Ctrl** held down [see Fig. 13].
- If you press **Ctrl+Shift** while clicking the sub-object level button, only those sub-objects will be selected whose source components were originally selected [see Fig. 14].
- If you press **Shift** while clicking the sub-object level button, only those sub-objects will be selected that border the selection [see Fig. 15].

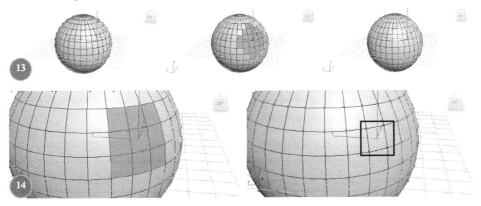

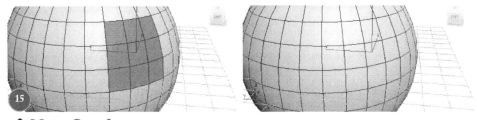

Note: Quad menu

The conversion commands are also available from the **Quad** *menu. To convert a selection,* **RMB** *click and then choose the desired option from the upper left quadrant of the* **Quad** *menu with* **Ctrl**, **Shift**, *or* **Ctrl+Shift** *held down.*

Now, let's explore the other options available in the **Selection** rollout. When **By Vertex** is selected, you can select the sub-objects that share the clicked vertex [see Fig. 16]. When **Ignore Backfacing** is selected, you can only select those sub-objects that are facing you. When off, you can select any sub-object beneath the mouse pointer.

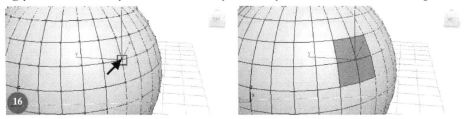

When **By Angle** is selected and you select a polygon, all neighboring polygons are also selected based on the angle value specified by the spinner to the right of **By Angle** [see Fig. 17].

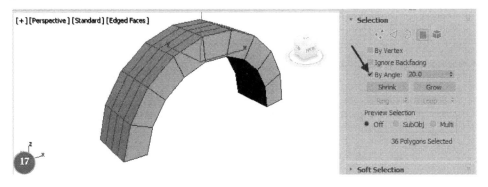

Shrink reduces the selection area by deselecting the outermost sub-objects [see Fig. 18]. On the other hand, **Grow** expands the selection in all possible directions [see Fig. 19].

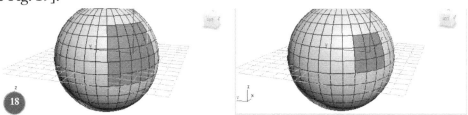

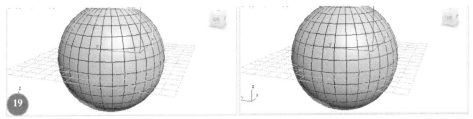

Ring lets you select an edge selection by selecting all edges parallel to the selected edges. To select an edge ring, select an edge[s] and then click **Ring** to select edges parallel to the selected edges [see Fig. 20].

💡 *Tip: Quickly selecting a ring/loop*
*Select an edge and then hover over another edge with **Shift** held down. This edge should be directly next to the previous selection (a consecutive edge). A yellow highlight will show the ring or loop to be selected. Now, click on the neighboring edge to select a ring.*

The spinner next to **Ring** allows you to move the selection in the either direction to other edges in the same ring. The left image in Fig. 21 shows the two edges selected. When I clicked on the up arrow of the spinner the selection moved, as shown in the right image of Fig. 21. This feature works with only the **Edge** and **Border** sub-object types.

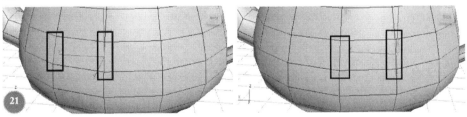

💡 *Tip: Loop*
If you have selected a loop, you can use the spinner to select the neighboring loop.

Loop allows you to expand edge selection as far as possible. The selection only propagates through four-way junctions. To select a loop, select and edge and then click **Loop** [see Fig. 22].

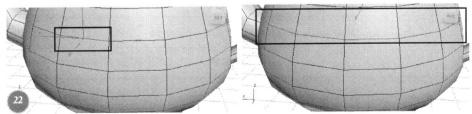

Tip: Loop selection shortcut
You can quickly select a loop by double-clicking on an edge.

The spinner to the right of **Loop** allows you to move the selection in either direction to other edges in the same loop. If you have selected a ring, it allows you to move the ring selection. This feature works with the **Edge** and **Border** sub-objects.

The parameters in the **Preview Selection** group allow you to preview a selection before actually selecting. When **Off** is selected, no preview will be available. When **SubObj** is selected, you can preview the selection at the current sub-object level. The preview appears in yellow color [see Fig. 23].

When **Multi** is selected, you can switch between various sub-object levels. For example, you can place the mouse pointer on an edge, the edge highlights, and clicking on the edge activates the **Edge** sub-object level and selects the edge. To select multiple sub-objects at current level, press and hold **Ctrl** and move [do not click] to add highlighted sub-objects to the preview. Now, to make the selection, click.

To remove sub-objects from the current sub-object level, press and hold **Ctrl+Alt**. Now, move the mouse to highlight more sub-objects, and then click a selected sub-object. This action deselects all highlighted sub-objects. The area below these parameters shows the information about the selected or highlighted polygons [see Fig. 24].

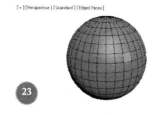
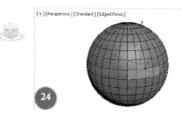

Soft Selection Rollout

The parameters in the **Soft Selection** rollout let you partially select the sub-objects in the vicinity of the selected sub-objects. As you transform the sub-objects, the sub-objects in the vicinity will be transformed smoothly [see Fig. 25]. The fall off appears in the viewport as a color spectrum [**ROYGB**: red, orange, yellow, green, and blue]. The sub-objects that you explicitly select coded in red color.

When **Edge Distance** is selected, 3ds Max limits the selection to a certain number of edges specified by the spinner to the right of **Edge Distance**. Fig. 26 shows the selection with **Edge Distance** value set to **1** and **7**, respectively.

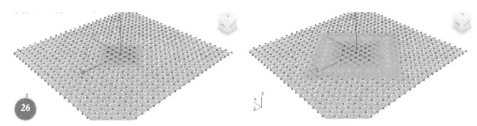

When **Affect Backfacing** is selected, those deselected faces whose normals face in the opposite direction to the average normal of the selected sub-objects are affected by the soft-selection. **Falloff** defines the distance in current units from the center to the edge of a sphere that defines the region of influence. The fall off curve appears below **Bubble**. **Pinch** affects the top point of the curve. **Bubble** lets you expand or shrink the falloff curve along the vertical axis. Experiment with these settings to get a better understanding of how these parameters affect the falloff curve. **Shaded Face Toggle** displays a color gradient in the viewport [see Fig. 27].

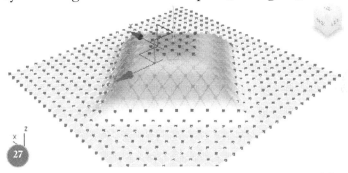

The gradient represents the weight on the faces of the geometry. This feature is only available when you are working with the editable poly or patch objects. **Lock Soft Selection** locks the soft selection to prevent any changes in the procedural selection.

The parameters in the **Paint Soft Selection** group, let you paint soft selection on the object using a brush. Click **Paint** and then drag the mouse pointer on the surface to paint the selection. **Blur** lets you soften the edges of the selection whereas **Revert** reverses the selection.

Object Level

When no sub-object level is active, you are at the **Object** level. The parameters available at the **Object** level are also available at all sub-object levels.

Edit Geometry Rollout

The **Edit Geometry** rollout provides global parameters for modifying a poly object. Let's have a look at these parameters:

Repeat Last

When clicked, 3ds Max repeats the most recently used command. For example, if you apply a command such as **Bevel** to some polygons and then want to apply the same settings to other set of polygons, select them, and then click **Repeat Last**. The same bevel settings will be applied to the last selected polygons.

Caution: Which commands are repeated?
Repeat Last *does not repeat all commands, for example, transformations. To check which command in 3ds Max will repeat, hover the mouse pointer on* **Repeat Last**. *A tooltip appears indicating which command will be repeated when you click this button [see Fig. 28].*

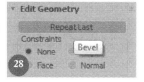

Tip: Keyboard Shortcut
You can also use the keyboard shortcuts to repeat the last command. If you are using the **3ds Max** *mode, press semicolon (;) and if you are using the* **Maya** *mode, press* **G**.

Constraints

The parameters in this rollout let you constrain the sub-objects transformations to edges, faces, or normals of the existing geometry. Table 2 summarizes the types of constraints.

Table 2: The **Constrains** types

Type	Description
None	This is the default option. No constraints will be applied.
Edge	It constrains transformations to the edge boundaries [see Fig. 29].
Face	It constrains transformations to the face boundaries.
Normal	It allows the transformations along the normals.

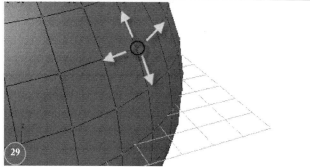

Preserve UVs

When **Preserve UVs** is selected, 3ds Max allows you to edit the sub-objects without affecting the UV mapping. The image at the left of Fig. 30 is the original vertex position. The middle image shows the result when **Preserve UVs** is selected. I scaled the selected vertices inward to show the function of **Preserve UVs**. The image at right of Fig. 30 shows the result when **Preserve UVs** is off.

Create

Allows you to create new geometry in the scene. The result produced by **Create** depends on which sub-object level is active. Table 3 summarizes the behavior of this command.

Table 3: Creating new geometry	
Level	**Description**
Object, Polygon, Element	Adds polygons by clicking existing or new vertices.
Vertex	Adds vertices.
Edge, Border	Adds edges between the pairs of the non-adjacent vertices on the same polygon.

To create geometry, activate a sub-object level and then click **Create**. Now, in the active viewport click to create the geometry [see Fig. 31]. **RMB** click or press **Esc** to exit the tool.

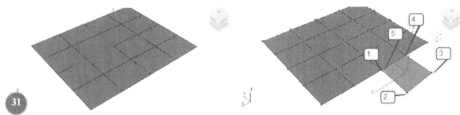

Collapse

It allows you to collapse contiguous selection of the vertices, edges, borders, or polygons by welding their vertices to a vertex. The welded vertex is placed at the center of the selection [see Figs. 32 and 33].

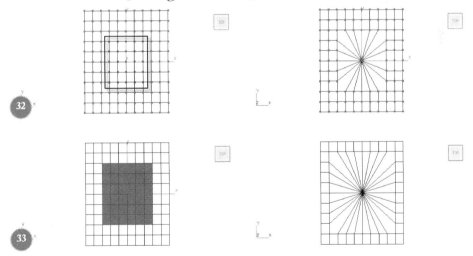

Attach

Attach allows you to attach other geometries to the selected poly object. To attach the objects, select a poly object and then click **Attach**. Now, click on the object that you want to attach; the **Attach** command remains active. If required, keep clicking on other objects to attach them to the selected object. **RMB** click or click **Attach** again to terminate the command.

You can also attach splines, patch objects, and NURBS surfaces to a poly object. If you attach a non-mesh object it is converted to an editable format. It becomes an element of the poly object [see Fig. 34].

On clicking **Attach List** available to the right of **Attach**, opens the **Attach List** dialog box. You can use this dialog box to attach multiple objects to the selected poly object.

Detach

Detach allows you to separate the selected sub-objects and corresponding polygons to an object or element. To detach sub-objects, select them and then click **Detach**. In the **Detach** dialog box that appears, type the name of the object in the **Detach as** field and then click **OK**.

There are two parameters in the **Detach** dialog box that let you detach sub-objects as an element or a clone. These parameters are **Detach To Element** and **Detach As Clone**. Select the required parameter and then click **OK**.

Slice Plane

This option is available at the sub-objects levels only. The parameters in the group are known as knife tools. These tools subdivide along a poly plane [slice] or in a specific area [cut]. When you click **Slice Plane**, a gizmo appears in viewports. Also, **Slice** and **Reset Plane** parameter become active in the rollout.

Transform the **Gizmo** in a viewport and then click **Slice** to create the edges where the gizmo intersects the edges [see Fig. 35]. Click **Slice Plane** to deactivate the command. Click **Reset Plane** to reset the position of the gizmo.

If you select **Split**, 3ds Max creates double sets of vertices that allows you to create hole in the geometry [see Fig. 36].

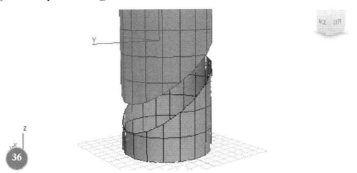

QuickSlice

QuickSlice allows you to quickly sub-divide a geometry without making adjustments to the gizmo. To slice a geometry, make a selection and then click **QuickSlice**. Now, drag the cursor in a viewport to create a slicing line. Release the mouse button to slice the selection [see Fig. 37]. You can continue slicing the geometry or **RMB** click to exit the command.

You can use **QuickSlice** in any viewport including **Perspective** and camera. 3ds Max also shows you the preview of the slice before you commit the command.

Caution: Polygons and Elements
*If you are at the **Polygon** or **Element** level, only selected sub-objects are sliced. If you want to slice entire object, use any sub-object level other than **Polygon** or **Element**.*

Cut

Cut allows you to subdivide polygons by creating edges from one polygon to another or within the polygons. It is available at the object level as well as at all sub-object levels. To create edges, click **Cut** and then click at the start point. Move the mouse pointer and then click on another point to create connected edges [see Fig. 38]. You can continue moving and clicking to create the edges. **RMB** click to exit the command.

Tip: Mouse pointer
The shape of the mouse pointer shows the type of sub-object it's over. Fig. 39 shows the shape of the mouse pointer when you are cutting to a vertex, edge, or polygon, respectively.

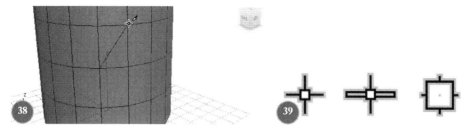

MSmooth

Applies smoothing to the selected area of the poly object [see Fig. 40]. Click **Settings** to the right of **MSmooth** to open the **MeshSmooth** caddy control [see Fig. 41] that allows you to adjust the settings used by the **MSmooth** command. Table 4 summarizes the **MeshSmooth** caddy control.

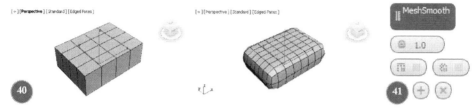

Table 4: The **MeshSmooth** caddy control	
Control	**Description**
Smoothness	Smoothness in a poly mesh is created by adding polygons to it. **Smoothness** determines how sharp the corners of the mesh are. A value of **1** adds polygons to all vertices of the mesh. If you set **Smoothness** to **0**, no polygons will be created.
Separate by Smoothing Groups	When on, the polygons are created at the edges that share atleast one smoothing group.
Separate by Materials ID	When on, the polygons are created at the edges that share the material IDs.

Tessellate

It subdivides the polygons based on the tessellate settings that can be accessed by clicking **Settings** on the right of **Tessellate**. Fig. 42 shows the **Tessellate** caddy control. Table 5 summarizes the **Tessellate** caddy control.

Table 5: The **Tessellate** caddy control	
Control	**Description**
Type	There are two tessellation types available: **Edge** and **Face**. When **Edge** is selected, 3ds Max inserts vertices at the center of each edge and then connect them. The polygons created are the number of sides of the original polygon [see Fig. 43]. On selecting the **Face** type, a vertex is created at the center of each polygon and then that vertex is connected to the original vertices. The number of polygons created are equal to the number of sides of the original polygon [see Fig. 44].
Tension	It is available for only for the **Edge** type. It determines the edge tension value. A positive value pulls the edges outward whereas a negative value pulls them inward [see Fig. 45].

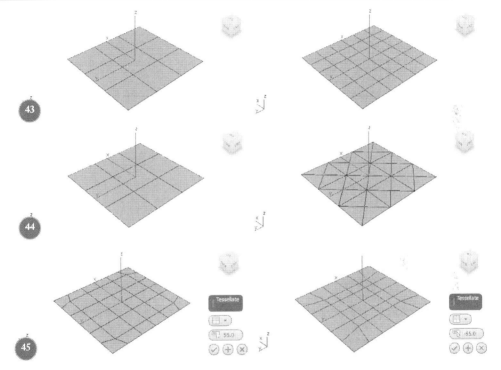

Make Planar

Makes all selected sub-objects to be coplanar. The sub-objects are forced to be coplanar along the average surface normal of the selection [see Fig. 46]. If you are at the **Object** level, all vertices of the object will be forced to be coplanar. The **X**, **Y**, and **Z** buttons let you to align the plane with the local coordinate system of the object. For example, if you click **Z**, the selection will be aligned according to the local **XY** axis [see Fig. 47].

View Align

It aligns all vertices of the object to the plane of the active viewport. It affects vertices only.

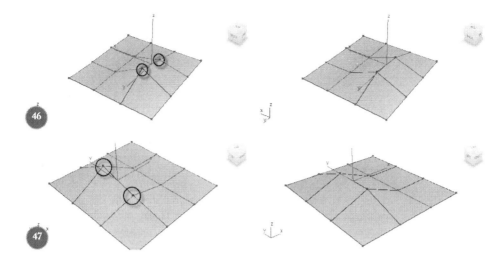

Grid Align

It aligns all vertices to the construction plane of the current view. Also, it moves them to that plane. If a **Perspective** or a camera viewport is active, this command aligns vertices to the home grid [see Fig. 48] otherwise the current construction plane is the active grid. For example, if you make the **Front** viewport active before clicking **Grid Align**, the **XZ** plane will be used for aligning process. If you are using a grid object, the current plane will be the active grid object.

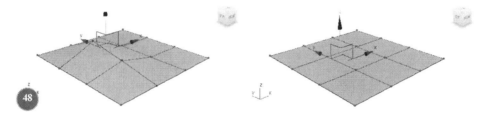

Relax

It relaxes [normalizes mesh spacing] the current selection by moving each vertex towards the average location of its neighboring vertices [see Fig. 49]. If you are at the **Object** level, 3ds Max applies smoothing to whole mesh otherwise the **Relax** function is applied to current sub-object selection.

The settings for the **Relax** command can be accessed by clicking **Settings** on the right of **Relax**. The **Relax** caddy control appears. Table 6 summarizes the **Relax** caddy control.

Table 6: The **Relax** caddy control	
Control	**Description**
Amount	Determines how far the vertex moves each iteration relax function. It defines a percentage of the distance from the original location to the average location of the neighbors.
Iterations	Determines how many times you want to repeat the **Relax** operation.
Relax Hold Boundary Points	When on [default], determines whether vertices at the edges of open meshes are moved or not.
Relax Hold Outer Points	When on, 3ds Max preserves the original position of the vertices that are farthest away from the center of the object. Fig. 50 shows a mesh when **Hold Outer Points** is off.

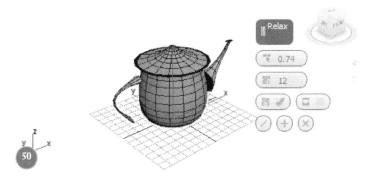

Hide Selected, Unhide All, Hide Unselected

These parameters are available at the **Vertex, Polygon,** and **Element** sub-object levels. Table 7 summarizes the functions of these parameters.

Table 7: The sub-object visibility	
Parameter	**Description**
Hide Selected	Hides the selected sub-objects.
Unhide All	Unhides the hidden sub-objects.
Hide Unselected	Hides unselected sub-objects.

Copy, Paste

These parameters allow you to copy and paste named selection sets from one object to another. These commands use sub-object IDs. Therefore if there is some difference between the source and target meshes, on pasting, the selection may comprises of different sub-object selected. To understand the working of these two parameters, create two **Teapot** primitives and then convert them to **Editable Poly**. Make the **Polygon** mode active and select some polygons on the source object. Type the name for the selection set in the **Named Selection Sets** drop-down list. Click **Copy** to open the **Copy Names Selection** dialog box, select name and then click **OK** to copy the selection set. Now, activate the **Polygon** selection level for the second teapot and click **Paste**. The polygons will be highlighted.

Delete Isolated Vertices

It is selected by default. As a result, when you delete a selection of contiguous sub-objects, the isolated vertices are deleted. If off, deleting sub-object selection leaves the vertices intact.

Full Interactivity

Allows you to toggle feedback on and off for dialog boxes and caddies as well as for the **Quick Slice** and **Cut** parameters. When on, 3ds Max updates the viewports in real-time as you use mouse in the viewport or change values numerically using keyboard.

Vertex Level

Edges and **Polygons** make a poly object. Vertices are the basic building blocks for edges and polygons. You can manipulate vertices at the **Vertex** sub-object level. The parameters available for modifying the geometry at the **Vertex** level are found in the **Edit Vertices** and **Vertex Properties** rollouts.

Edit Vertices Rollout

Let's discuss the controls available in this rollout.

Remove: Remove lets you delete selected vertices. The polygons that are using these vertices are combined [see the middle image of Fig. 51]. The keyboard shortcut for the **Remove** function is **Backspace**.

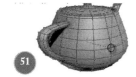  

Caution: Using Delete
*If you use the **Delete** key instead of **Backspace**, 3ds Max can create holes in the poly mesh [see the image at the right of Fig. 51].*

Break: Creates a new vertex for each connected polygon to the original selection that allows you to move the corners of polygons [see Fig. 52].

 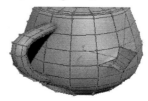

Extrude: You can use this parameter to extrude the vertices along a normal. 3ds Max creates new polygons that forms the sides of the extrusion [see Fig. 53]. The number of polygons in the extrusion will be equal to the number of polygons that were associated with the selected vertex. To extrude a vertex, select it and then click **Extrude**. Drag the selected vertex vertically to set the extent of the extrusion. Drag horizontally to set the size of the base. If you have selected multiple vertices, all are affected in the same way by the **Extrude** function. **RMB** click to end the **Extrude** operation.

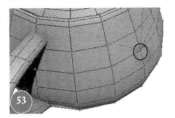 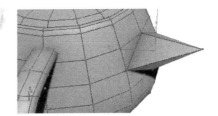

Clicking **Settings** on the right of **Extrude** opens the **Extrude** caddy control. Table 8 summarizes the **Extrude** caddy control.

Table 8: The **Extrude Vertices** caddy control	
Parameter	**Description**
Height	Determines the extent of the extrusion in scene units.
Width	Determines the size of the base of the extrusion.

Weld: This parameter lets you combine the contiguous selected vertices that fall within a threshold specified using the **Weld** caddy control. To weld vertices, make a selection and then click **Settings** on the right of **Weld** to open the **Weld Vertices** caddy control. Set **Weld Threshold** and then click **OK** to weld the vertices [see Fig. 54].

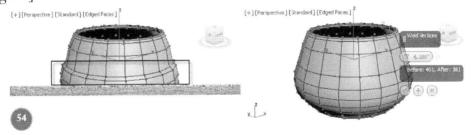

Chamfer: This parameter allows you to chamfer the vertices. To chamfer a vertex, select it and then click **Chamfer**. Now, drag the vertex in a viewport to apply chamfering. If you have selected multiple vertices, all vertices will be chamfered identically [see the middle image in Fig. 55]. Clicking **Settings** on the right of **Chamfer** opens the **Chamfer** caddy control. Table 9 summarizes the **Chamfer** caddy control.

Table 9: The **Chamfer** caddy control	
Parameter	**Description**
Vertex Chamfer Amount	Determines the extent of chamfer.

Table 9: The **Chamfer** caddy control	
Parameter	**Description**
Open Chamfer	When on, you can create open space around the chamfered vertices [see the last image in Fig. 56]

Target Weld: It allows you to select a vertex and then weld it to a contiguous target vertex. This tool works on those vertices that are connected with a single edge. Also, this parameter does not allow to cross newly created edges.

To weld a vertex, select it, and then click **Target Weld**. When you hover the mouse pointer over the vertex, the shape of the mouse pointer changes to a plus shape. Click and drag on the vertex, a rubber band line gets attached to the mouse pointer. Now, position the mouse pointer on the neighboring vertex and when shape of the mouse changes to a plus sign, click to weld the vertices [see Fig. 56].

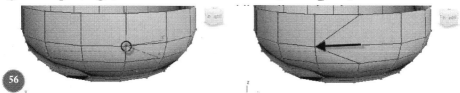

Remove Isolated Vertices: It deletes all vertices that do not belong to any polygon of the selected object.

Remove Unused Map Verts: If there are some unused map vertices that are appearing in the **Unwrap UVW** editor but cannot be used for mapping, click this parameter to remove them.

Weight: You can use this parameter to assign weight to the selected vertices. The specified weight is used by the **NURMS** subdivision function and the **MeshSmooth** modifier. The vertices with larger weights pull the smoothened result towards them.

Crease: It sets the crease value for the selected vertices. This value is used by the **OpenSubdiv** and **CreaseSet** modifiers. On increasing the crease weight, 3ds Max pulls the smoothened result towards the vertices and creates a sharp point.

Vertex Properties Rollout
The parameters in this rollout are only available for the **Editable Poly** object. They are unavailable for the **Edit Poly** modifier.

Edit Vertex Colors Group: The parameters in this group allow you to set the color and illumination color of the selected vertices. Click the **Color** swatch to change their color. **Illumination** allows you to change the illumination color of the vertices without changing their color. The **Alpha** parameter lets you set the alpha values for the vertices. These values are used when you export the data containing full RGBA set for the color values.

Select Vertices By Group: You can select **Color** or **Illumination** from this group to determine whether to select vertices by using the vertex color or vertex illumination values. You can also specify a custom color for selecting vertices by using the color swatch available in this group. On clicking **Select**, 3ds Max selects the vertices depending on the selection parameter that you had turned on. The **Range** parameter allows you to specify a range for the color match.

Edge Level
The edge connects two vertices. This section covers the parameters available at the **Edge** sub-object level. These parameters are available in the **Edit Edges** rollout.

Insert Vertex
It allows you to subdivide the edges. To insert a vertex, click **Insert Vertex** and then click on an edge [see Fig. 57]. You can continue adding vertices as long as the command is active. **RMB** click to exit the command.

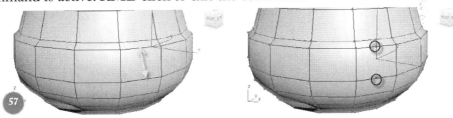

Remove
Removes the selected edges and combines the polygons [see Fig. 58]. The keyboard shortcut is **Backspace**. When you remove edges, the vertices remain intact [see the left image in Fig. 59]. To remove the corresponding vertices, press and hold **Ctrl** when you click **Remove** [see the right image in Fig. 59].

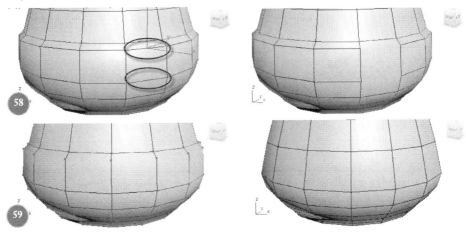

Split

It divides the mesh along the selected edges [see Fig. 60].

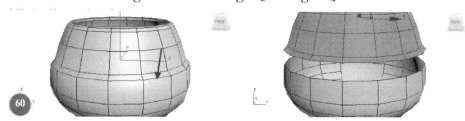

Extrude

This parameter allows you to extrude the edges manually or using the precise values. The precise values can be entered using the **Extrude Edges** caddy control. The parameters in the **Extrude Edges** caddy control are similar to that of the **Extrude Vertices** caddy at **Vertex** level, refer to Table 8.

To extrude an edge, select it and then click **Extrude**. Drag the selected edge vertically to set the extent of the extrusion. Drag horizontally to set the size of the base [see Fig. 61]. If you have selected multiple edges, all are affected in the same way by the **Extrude** function. **RMB** click to end the extrude operation.

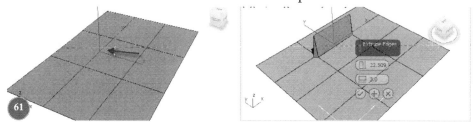

Weld, Target Weld

Refer to the **Vertex Level** group for understanding the functioning of these parameters. You need to select edge instead of vertex when dealing with edge welding.

Chamfer

This parameter allows you to chamfer an edge creating two or more edges for each chamfered edge. 3ds Max provides two types of chamfering: **Standard Chamfer** and **Quad Chamfer**. For **Standard Chamfer**, refer to the **Vertex Level** group. The **Quad Chamfer** type is discussed next.

Quad Chamfer

When you use the **Standard Chamfer** type, 3ds Max generates quadrilaterals and triangles [see the middle image in Fig. 62]. The **Quad Chamfer** type generates quadrilaterals only [see the right image in Fig. 62]. The area providing support to the chamfered region might contain triangles.

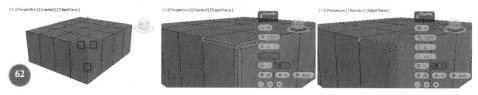

When you click on **Settings** on the right of **Chamfer**, the **Chamfer** caddy control appears. Table 10 summarizes the **Chamfer** caddy control.

Table 10: The **Chamfer** caddy control	
Parameter	**Description**
Edge Chamfer Amount	Determines the amount of chamfer in scene units.
Connect Edge Segments	Adds number of polygons over the region of chamfer.
Edge Tension	Determines the angle between the new polygons. At the value of **1**, all polygons will be coplanar. Fig. 63 shows the chamfered edges with **Edge Tension** set to **0, 0.5**, and **1**, respectively.
Open Chamfer	Deletes the faces created after the chamfer operation.
Invert Open	This option is available for **Quad Chamfer** only. Also, **Open Chamfer** should be on. When **Invert Open** is selected, 3ds Max deletes all faces except those created by the chamfering operation.
Smooth	When on, it applies smoothing groups after chamfering. Also, it enables the **Smooth Type** function.
Smooth Type	There are two types of smoothing methods available. **Smooth Entire Object** applies smoothing groups to the entire object. **Smooth Chamfers Only** applies smoothing groups to the newly created polygons.
Quad Intersections	This option defines how corners are affected when multiple edges connect to the same vertex.

Bridge

You can use the **Bridge** parameter to bridge the border edges to create a polygon bridge between them. Keep in mind that **Bridge** only connects the borders edges. To create bridge between the edges, select two or more border edges, and then click **Bridge**. A bridge will be created using the existing **Bridge** settings [see Fig. 64]. To set **Bridge** settings, click **Settings** on the right of **Bridge**; the **Bridge Edges** caddy control appears. Table 11 summarizes the **Bridge Edges** caddy control.

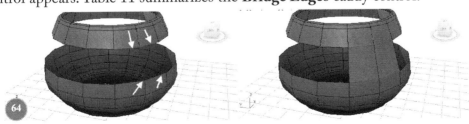

Table 11: The **Bridge Edges** caddy control	
Parameters	**Description**
Segments	Specifies the number of polygons along the length of the bridge.
Smooth	Sets the maximum angle for smoothing to occur.
Bridge Adjacent	Controls the minimum angle between the adjacent edges across which bridging can occur. The edges that are at less than this angle will not be bridged.
Reverse Triangulation	When you are bridging two borders, each of which contains different numbers of edges, you can use this parameter to define the method of triangulation. Fig. 65 shows the bridge when **Reverse Triangulation** is **On** and **Off**, respectively.
Use Edge Selection	It allows you to choose between two methods. Either you can use the existing selection or you can choose the edges using the caddy control. When you choose **Use Specific Edges**, the **Pick Edge 1**, and **Pick Edge 2** parameters become available.
Pick Edge 1, Pick Edge 2	Click **Pick Edge 1** and then click a border edge in a viewport. Select the other border edge using **Pick Edge 2**, the bridge will be created between the two border edges.

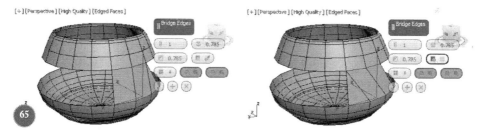

Connect

Allows you to refine selected edges by creating new edges between them. To create new edges, select the edges of the active object that you want to connect and then click **Connect** [see Fig. 66].

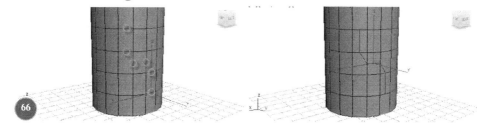

Caution: Connecting edges
*You can connect edges on the same polygon. The **Connect** command will stop the new edges to cross. For example, if you select all edges of a polygon face and apply this function, only neighboring edges are connected. The new edges will not cross each other [see Fig. 67].*

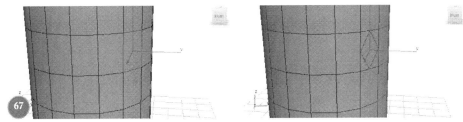

67

Clicking on the **Settings** on the right of **Connect** opens the **Connect Edges** caddy control that allows you to change settings for the **Connect** command and also preview the changes before committing them [see Fig. 68].

68

Table 12 summarizes the **Connect Edges** caddy control.

Table 12: The **Connect Edges** caddy control	
Parameter	**Description**
Segments	Defines the number of new edges between each adjacent pair of selected edges.
Pinch	The relative spacing between the new and connecting edges.
Slide	The relative positioning of the new edges.

Create Shape from Selection

This parameter allows you to create a shape [spline] from the selected edges. The pivot of the shape will be created at the geometric center of the poly object. To create a shape, select the edges of the active object, and then click **Create Shape from Selection** to open the **Create Shape** dialog box. Type the new name in the **Curve Name** field and then choose **Shape Type**. Next, click **OK** to create the shape [see Fig. 69].

69

Edit Tri

This parameter gives you ability to modify the triangulation for the polygons. To enable triangulation, click **Edit Tri**. The hidden edges appear on the object [see left image in Fig. 70]. Now, to change the triangulation for a polygon, click a vertex; a rubber band line appears attached to the mouse pointer. Now, click on an adjacent vertex to create a new triangulation [see the right image in Fig. 70].

Turn

It allows you to modify polygon triangulation by clicking on the diagonals. To change triangulation, click **Turn**. The current triangulation appear on the object. Click on the diagonals to change the triangulation.

Border Level

A border can be described as the edge [boundary] of a hole. As discussed earlier, if you create a cylinder and delete its caps, the adjacent row of edges form a border. You can manipulate borders using the parameters available in the **Edit Borders** rollout. Most of the parameters are similar to that of the edge and vertex controls. Select border edges and experiment with these parameters. One additional parameter appears in the **Edit Borders** rollout called **Cap**. It caps an entire border loop with a polygon. You can use it to fill holes in an object.

Polygon/Element Level

A polygon is formed by connecting three or more edges. Polygons form a surface that you can render. At the **Polygon** sub-object level, you can select polygons and then apply various polygon modeling functions to them. At the **Element** sub-object level, you can edit groups of contiguous polygons.

> *Tip: Highlighting polygons*
> *When you select a polygon, it is highlighted in red in the viewport. You can toggle this feature by pressing the **F2** key.*

You can edit polygons and elements using the parameters available in the **Edit Polygons** and **Edit Elements** rollouts, respectively.

Edit Polygons Rollout
Let's first explore the tools available in the **Edit Polygons** rollout.

Insert Vertex
Allows you to subdivide a polygon manually. It also works at the **Element** sub-object level. To subdivide the polygon, click **Insert Vertex** and then click on a polygon to subdivide it. You can continue subdividing the polygons as the command remains active until you **RMB** click [see Fig. 71].

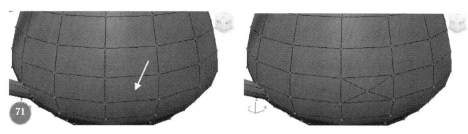

Extrude

Extruding is a process in which polygons move along a normal and new polygons are created. This command lets you extrude the polygons. To extrude the polygons, select them in a viewport and then click **Extrude**. Position the mouse pointer on the polygons. The shape of the cursor changes to the **Extrude** cursor. Drag the cursor vertically to specify the extent of extrusion and horizontally to set the base [see Fig. 72]. On clicking **Settings** on the right of **Extrude**, the **Extrude Polygons** caddy control appears that allows you to specify settings for extrusion. Table 13 summarizes the **Extrude Polygons** caddy control.

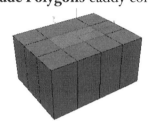

Table 13: The **Extrude Polygons** caddy control	
Parameter	**Description**
Extrusion Type	This drop-down list provides three methods for extrusion: **Group**, **Local Normal**, and **By Polygon**. On selecting **Group**, 3ds Max extrudes polygons along the average normal of each contiguous group of polygons [see the left image in Fig. 73]. When **Normal** is selected, the extrusion takes place along each normal of the selected polygon [see the middle image in Fig. 73]. On selecting **By Polygon**, 3ds Max extrudes each polygon individually [see the right image in Fig. 73].
Extrusion Height	Determines the amount of extrusion in scene units.

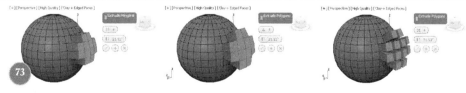

Outline

This command lets you increase or decrease the outside edge of each group of contiguous polygons. It does not scale, it just changes the size of the outside edge of the selected polygons. To change the size of the outside edge of polygons, select a group of contiguous of polygons and then click **Outline**. Now, position the mouse pointer on the selected polygons and drag the pointer to outline the polygons [see Fig. 74]. Notice in Fig. 74 that the inner polygons are not affected by the **Outline** operation. If you want to manually specify the outline amount, then click **Settings** on the right of the **Outline** to open the **Outline** caddy control and specify the value using the **Amount** parameter.

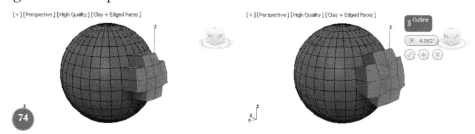

Bevel
It allows you to perform bevel function on a group of contiguous selected polygons. To bevel the polygons, select them in a viewport and then click **Bevel**. Position the mouse pointer on the polygons; the shape of the cursor changes to the **Bevel** cursor. Drag the cursor vertically to define the height and horizontally to define the outline amount [see Fig. 75].

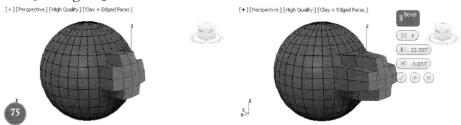

On clicking **Settings** on the right of **Bevel**, the **Bevel** caddy control appears that allows you to specify settings for extrusion. Table 14 summarizes the **Bevel** caddy control.

Table 14: The **Bevel** caddy control	
Parameter	**Description**
Bevel Type	This drop-down list provides three methods for beveling: **Group**, **Local Normal**, and **By Polygon**. On selecting **Group**, 3ds Max bevels polygons along the average normal of each contiguous group of polygons. When **Normal** is selected, the beveling takes place along each normal of the selected polygon. On selecting **By Polygon**, 3ds Max bevels each polygon individually.
Height	Determines the amount of extrusion in scene units.
Outline	Lets you make the outer border of the selection bigger or smaller.

Inset
This command performs a bevel with no height. To inset polygons, select them and then click **Inset**, position the cursor over the polygons and the drag to define the **Inset** amount [see Fig. 76].

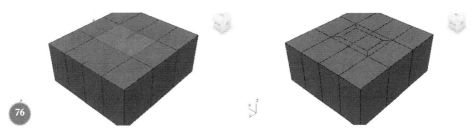

On clicking **Settings** on the right of **Inset**, the **Inset** caddy control appears that allows you to specify settings for extrusion. Table 15 summarizes the **Inset** caddy control.

Table 15: The **Inset** caddy control	
Parameter	**Description**
Inset Type	This drop-down list provides two methods for insetting: **Group**, and **By Polygon**. On selecting **Group**, 3ds Max insets polygons across each selection of multiple, contiguous polygons. On selecting **By Polygon**, 3ds Max insets each polygon individually.
Amount	Determines the extent of inset in scene units.

Bridge

You have seen how we have applied the **Bridge** function on the edges. It works similarly at the **Polygon** sub-object level. Here, you have to select polygons instead of edges [see Fig. 77]. Fig. 77 shows an external bridge [right] as well as internal bridge [left].

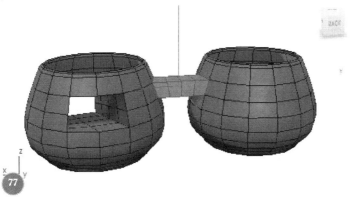

To specify settings for the **Bridge** function, click **Settings** on the right of **Bridge** to open the **Bridge Polygons** caddy control. Table 16 summarizes the **Bridge Polygons** caddy control.

Table 16: The **Bridge Polygons** caddy control	
Parameter	**Description**
Segments	Determines the number of polygons along the length of the bridge.

Table 16: The **Bridge Polygons** caddy control	
Parameter	**Description**
Taper	Allows you to taper the bridge length towards its center. Negative values make bridge center smaller whereas the positive values make center bigger.
Bias	Defines the location of the maximum taper amount.
Smooth	Sets the angle for smoothing.
Twist 1, Twist 2	Allow you to twist each end of the bridge.
Use Specific Polygons, Use Polygon Selection	It allows you to choose between two methods. Either you can use the existing selection or you can choose the polygons using caddy control. When you choose **Use Specific Polygons**, the **Pick Polygon 1** and **Pick Polygon 2** parameters become available.
Pick Polygon 1, Pick Polygon 2	Click **Pick Polygon 1** and then click a polygon in a viewport. Select the other polygon using **Pick Polygon 2**, the bridge will be created between the two border edges.

Flip
Allows you to reverse the direction of normals on the selected polygons.

Hinge From Edge
This command allows you to perform a hinge operation in the viewport. Make a polygon selection in a viewport and then click **Hinge From Edge**. Now, drag on an edge to hinge the selection [see Fig. 78]. On clicking **Settings** on the right of **Hinge From Edge**, the **Hinge From Edge** caddy control appears that allows you to specify settings for extrusion. Table 17 summarizes the **Hinge From Edge** caddy control.

Table 17: The **Hinge From Edge** caddy control	
Parameter	**Description**
Angle	Sets the rotation angle around the hinge [see Fig. 79].
Segments	Specifies the number of polygons along the extruded side.
Pick Hinge	Click it and then click on an edge to specify the hinge edge.

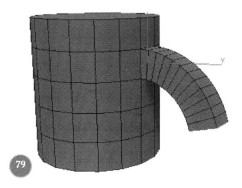

Extrude Along Spline

Allows you to extrude a selection along a spline. To extrude, create a spline and then select the polygons that you want to extrude. Click **Extrude Along Spline** and then click the spline in a viewport to extrude the polygons [see Fig. 80].

On clicking **Settings** on the right of **Extrude Along Spline**, the **Extrude Along Spline** caddy control appears that allows you to specify settings for extrusion. Table 18 summarizes the **Extrude Along Spline** caddy control.

Parameter	Description
Table 18: The **Extrude Along Spline** caddy control	
Segments	Determines the number of polygons along the extrusion [see Fig. 81].
Taper Amount	Sets the taper amount for the extrusion.
Taper Curve	Defines the rate at which tapering occurs.
Twist	Applies a twist along the length of taper.
Extrude Along Spline Align	Aligns the extrusion along the face normal [see Fig. 82].
Rotation	Sets the rotation of extrusion.
Pick Spline	Allows you to pick a spline along which the extrusion will occur.

Edit Triangulation/Turn

Refer to the **Edge Level** group for understanding the functioning of these parameters.

Retriangulate

When clicked, 3ds Max automatically performs best triangulation on the selected polygon[s].

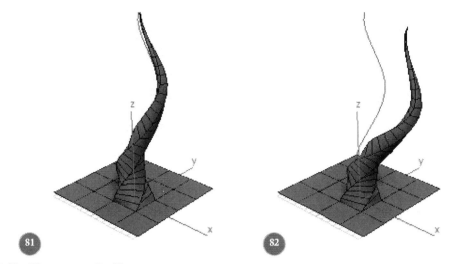

81   82

Edit Elements Rollout
Refer to **Edit Polygons** rollout for the parameters available in this rollout.

Hands-on Exercises

Exercise 1: Creating a Circular Hole in the Geometry
In this exercise, we will learn to create a perfect circular hole in a geometry [see Fig. E1]. Table E1 summarizes the exercise.

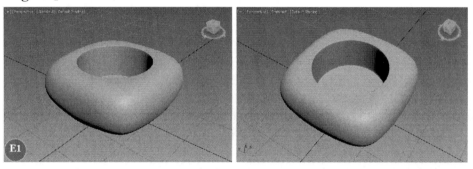

E1

Table E1	
Skill level	Beginner
Time to complete	40 Minutes
Topics	• Specifying the Units for the Exercise • Creating the Hole
Resources folder	**unit-dm4**
Units	**Generic**
Final file	**hole-finish.max**

Specifying the Units for the Exercise
Follow these steps:

1. From the **Customize** menu choose **Units Setup**. In the **Units Setup** dialog box that appears, select **Generic Units** from the **Units Setup** dialog box. Click **OK** to accept the changes made.

2. From the **File** menu, choose **Save** to open the **Save File As** dialog box. In the **File name** text box type **hole-finish.max** and then click **Save** to save the file.

Creating the Hole
Follow these steps:

1. In the **Create** panel, click **Geometry**, and then in the **Object Type** rollout, click **Plane**. In the **Perspective** viewport, create a plane. Switch to the **Modify** panel and then in the **Parameters** rollout, change **Length** to **50**, **Width** to **50**, **Height Length Segs** to **2**, and **Width Segs** to **2**. Place the plane at the origin.

2. **RMB** click on the sphere and then choose **transform** quadrant > **Convert To:** > **Convert to Editable Poly**. In the **Modify** panel > **Selection** rollout, click **Vertex** to activate the vertex sub-object level.

3. Select the vertices, as shown in Fig. E2 and then in the **Modify** panel > **Edit Vertices** rollout, click **Connect** [see Fig. E3]. Similarly, connect the other vertices diagonally [see Fig. E4].

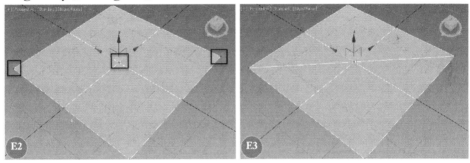

4. Select the center vertex and then in the **Modify** panel > **Edit Vertices** rollout, click **Chamfer** > **Settings** to open the **Chamfer** caddy control. Change **Vertex Chamfer Amount** to **10** and then click **OK** [see Fig. E5].

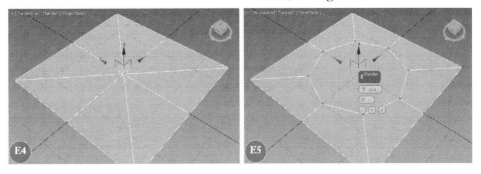

5. In the **Modify** panel > **Selection** rollout, click **Polygon** to activate the polygon sub-object level. Select the center polygon and then delete it [see Fig. E6]. In the **Modify** panel > **Selection** rollout, click **Border** to activate the border sub-object level. Select the border, as shown in Fig. E7.

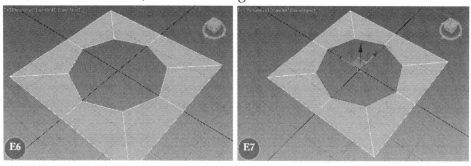

6. Invoke the **Move** tool and then drag the border along to -**Z** axis to create the extrusion [see Fig. E8]. Invoke the **Scale** tool and then scale border inwards using the **Scale** tool and the **Shift** key [see Fig. E9].

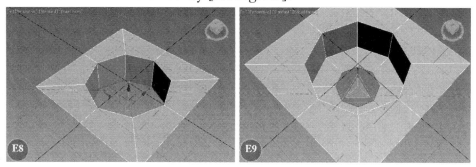

7. In the **Modify** panel > **Selection** rollout, **Ctrl**+click on **Vertex** to convert selection to vertices. Now, in the **Modify** panel > **Edit Geometry** rollout, click **Collapse** [see Fig. E10]. Select the edges [see Fig. E11] and then in the **Modify** panel > **Selection** rollout, click **Loop**.

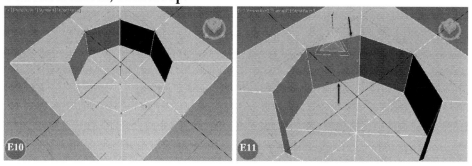

8. In the **Edit Edges** rollout, click **Chamfer** > **Settings** to open the **Chamfer** caddy control. Change **Edge Chamfer Amount** to **0.3** and **Connect Edge Segments** to **2**. Now, click **OK** [see Fig. E12].

9. Invoke the **Move** tool and then double-click on the outer edge to select the loop. Now, hold down **Shift** and then drag the loop along **-Z** axis to create the extrusion [see Fig. E13].

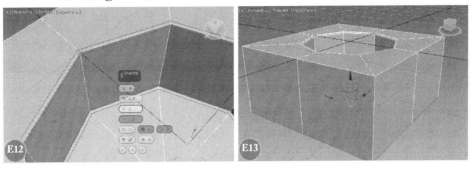

10. In the **Modify** panel > **Selection** rollout, click **Border** to activate the border sub-object level. Now, in the **Edit Borders** rollout, click **Cap** [see Fig. 14].

11. From the **Object-Space Modifiers** section of the **Modifier** list, select **MeshSmooth**. In the **Subdivision Amount** rollout, change **Iterations** to 3 [see Fig. E15].

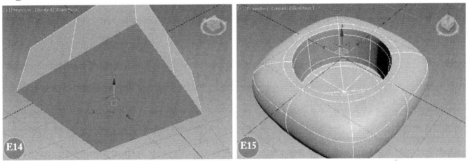

Exercise 2: Creating a Circular Hole in a Cube

In this exercise, we will learn to create hole in a cube [see Fig. E1]. Table E2 summarizes the exercise.

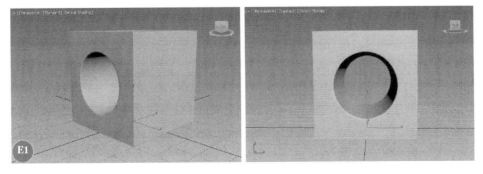

Table E2	
Skill level	Beginner
Time to complete	40 Minutes
Topics	• Specifying the Units for the Exercise • Creating the Hole
Resources folder	**unit-dm4**
Units	**Generic Units**
Final file	**hole-cube-finish.max**

Specifying the Units for the Exercise
Follow these steps:

1. From the **Customize** menu choose **Units Setup**. In the **Units Setup** dialog box that appears, select **Generic Units** from the **Units Setup** dialog box. Click **OK** to accept the changes made.

2. From the **File** menu, choose **Save** to open the **Save File As** dialog box. In the **File name** text box type **hole-cube-finish.max** and then click **Save** to save the file.

Creating the Hole
Follow these steps:

1. In the **Create** panel, click **Geometry**, and then in the **Object Type** rollout, click **Box**. In the **Perspective** viewport, create a box. Switch to the **Modify** panel and on the **Parameters** rollout, change **Length** to **40**, **Width** to **40**, and **Height** to **40**. Change **Length Segs**, **Width Segs**, and **Height Segs** to **2** each [see Fig. E2].

2. **RMB** click on the sphere and then choose **transform** quadrant > **Convert To:** > **Convert to Editable Poly**. Now, create holes in the opposite faces of the box, as done in the previous exercise [see Fig. E3].

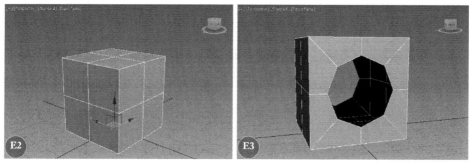

3. In the **Modify** panel > **Selection** rollout, click **Border** to activate the border sub-object level. Select the border edges, refer to Fig. E4. Now, in the **Edit Edges** rollout, click **Bridge** to connect the edges [see Fig. E5].

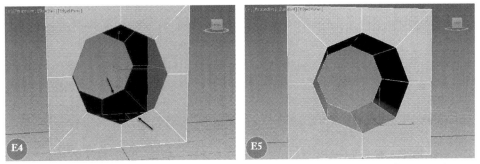

4. Chamfer all the border edges and then apply the **MeshSmooth** modifier.

Exercise 3: Creating a Solid Model

In this exercise, we will create a solid model [see Fig. E1].

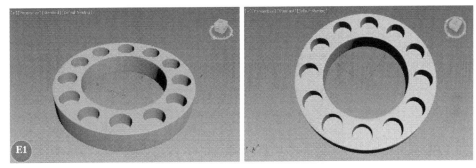

Table E3 summarizes the exercise.

Table E3	
Skill level	Beginner
Time to complete	30 Minutes
Topics	• Specifying the Units for the Exercise • Creating the Model
Resources folder	**unit-dm4**
Units	**Generic Units**
Final file	**solid-1-finish.max**

Specifying the Units for the Exercise

Follow these steps:

1. From the **Customize** menu choose **Units Setup**. In the **Units Setup** dialog box that appears, select **Generic Units** from the **Units Setup** dialog box. Click **OK** to accept the changes made.

2. From the **File** menu, choose **Save** to open the **Save File As** dialog box. In the **File name** text box type **solid-1-finish.max** and then click **Save** to save the file.

Creating the Model

Follow these steps:

1. In the **Create** panel, click **Geometry**, and then choose **Standard Primitives** from the drop-down list located below **Geometry**. In the **Object Type** rollout, click **Tube**. Create a tube in the **Top** viewport. Place the tube at the origin. Switch to the **Modify** panel and then in the **Parameters** rollout, change **Radius 1** to **30**, **Radius 2** to **50**, **Height** to **15**, **Height Segments** to **1**, **Cap Segments to 2**, and **Sides** to **24** [see Fig. E2].

2. **RMB** click on the tube and then choose **transform** quadrant > **Convert To:** > **Convert to Editable Poly**. In the **Modify** panel > **Selection** rollout, click **Polygon** to activate the polygon sub-object level. Select the polygons, as shown in Fig. E3. Press **Ctrl+I** to invert the selection and then press **Delete** to delete the polygons [see Fig. E4].

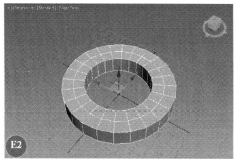
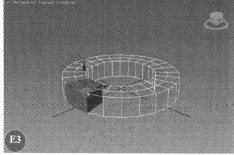

3. In the **Modify** panel > **Selection** rollout, click **Vertex** to activate the vertex sub-object level. Select the center vertex and then in the **Modify** panel > **Edit Vertices** rollout, click **Chamfer** > **Settings** to open the **Chamfer** caddy control. Change **Vertex Chamfer Amount** to **7.5** and then click **OK** [see Fig. E5].

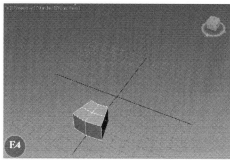
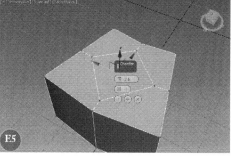

4. In the **Modify** panel > **Selection** rollout, click **Edge** to activate the edge sub-object level. Now, connect the newly created edges [see Fig. E6]. In the **Modify** panel > **Edit Geometry** rollout, click **Cut** and then create edges, as shown in Fig. E7.

5. In the **Modify** panel > **Selection** rollout, click **Polygon** to activate the polygon sub-object level. Select the polygons, as shown in Fig. E8 and then press **Delete**. In the **Modify** panel > **Selection** rollout, click **Vertex** to activate the vertex sub-object level. Now, select the vertices as shown in Fig. E9 and then scale them using the **Scale** tool [see Fig E10].

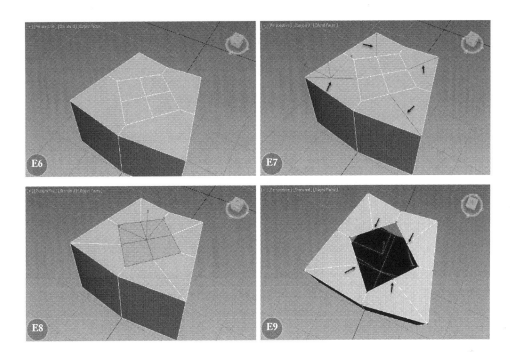

6. Select all vertices associated with the hole and then from the **Object-Space Modifiers** section of the **Modifier** list, select **Spherify** [see Fig. E11]. **RMB** click on the mesh and then choose **transform** quadrant > **Convert To:** > **Convert to Editable Poly**. Now, create rest of the hole, as done earlier [see Fig. E12].

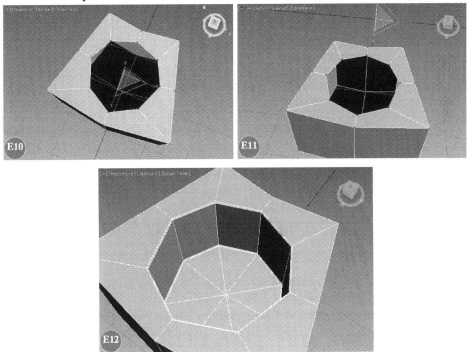

Caution: Chamfer
*Use the **Quad Chamfer** type to avoid distortions in the mesh. It will help you to get the clean geometry when you will smooth the mesh.*

7. Make sure mesh is selected and you are in the **Object** mode and then choose **Array** from the **Tools** menu to open the **Array** dialog box. Set the values in the dialog box, as shown in Fig. E13 and then click **OK** [see Fig. 14].

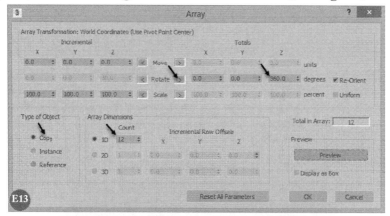

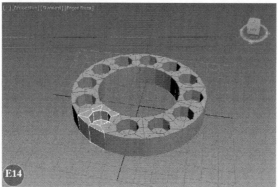

8. In the **Modify** panel > **Edit Geometry** rollout, click **Attach** > **Settings** to open the **Attach List** dialog box. Now, select all objects and click **Attach**.

9. In the **Modify** panel > **Selection** rollout, click **Vertex** to activate the vertex sub-object level. Select all boundary vertices, as shown in Fig. E15. In the **Modify** panel > **Edit Vertices** rollout, click **Weld**.

10. In the **Modify** panel > **Selection** rollout, click **Edge** to activate the edge sub-object level. Select all border edges, as shown in Fig. E16. Now, chamfer these edges [see Fig. E17]. From the **Object-Space Modifiers** section of the **Modifier** list, select **MeshSmooth**. In the **Subdivision Amount** rollout, change **Iterations** to 3 [see Fig. E18].

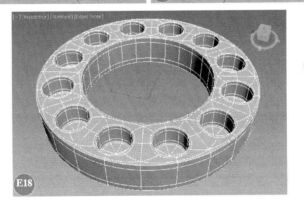

Exercise 4: Creating a Solid Model

In this exercise, we will create a solid model [see Fig. E1]. Table E4 summarizes the exercise.

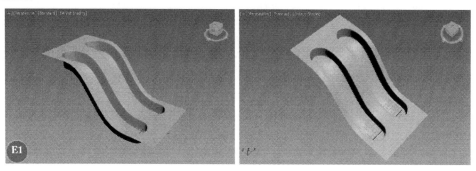

Table E4	
Skill level	Beginner
Time to complete	30 Minutes
Topics	• Specifying the Units for the Exercise • Creating the Model
Resources folder	**unit-dm4**
Units	**Generic Units**
Final file	**solid-2-finish.max**

Specifying the Units for the Exercise
Follow these steps:

1. From the **Customize** menu choose **Units Setup**. In the **Units Setup** dialog box that appears, select **Generic Units** from the **Units Setup** dialog box. Click **OK** to accept the changes made.

2. From the **File** menu, choose **Save** to open the **Save File As** dialog box. In the **File name** text box type **solid-2-finish.max** and then click **Save** to save the file.

Creating the Model
Follow these steps:

1. In the **Create** panel, click **Geometry**, then click **Plane**. In the **Top** viewport, create a plane. In the **Modify** panel > **Parameters** rollout, change **Length** to **150** and **Width** to **200**. Also, change **Length Segs** and **Width Segs** to **1** each. Place the plane at the origin.

2. **RMB** click on the sphere and then choose **transform** quadrant > **Convert To:** > **Convert to Editable Poly**. In the **Modify** panel > **Selection** rollout, click **Edge** to activate the edge sub-object level. Select the edge, as shown in Fig. E2 and then extrude the edge using **Shift** [see Fig. E3]. Again, extrude the edge, as shown in Fig. E4.

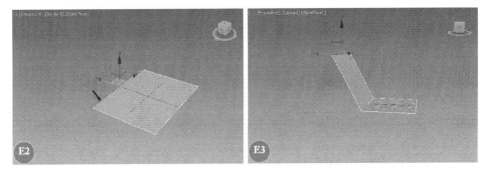

3. Select the edge ring, as shown in Fig. E5 and then in the **Modify** panel > **Edit Edges** rollout, click **Connect** > **Settings** to open the **Connect Edges** caddy control. Now, change **Segments** to **2** and **Pinch** to **80** [see Fig. E6].

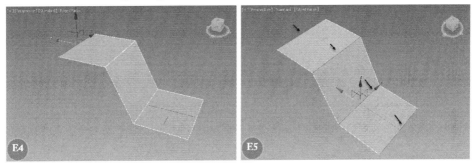

4. Select the edge ring, as shown in Fig. E7 and then in the **Modify** panel > **Edit Edges** rollout, click **Connect** > **Settings** to open the **Connect Edges** caddy control. Now, change **Segments** to **2** and **Pinch** to **-16** [see Fig. E8].

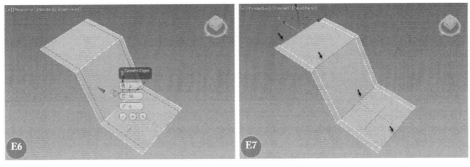

5. Select the edge rings as shown in Fig. E9 and then in the **Modify** panel > **Edit Edges** rollout, click **Connect** > **Settings** to open the **Connect Edges** caddy control. Now, change **Segments** to **1** and **Pinch** to **0** [see Fig. E10].

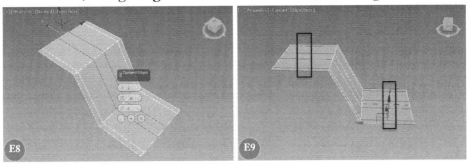

6. Select the edges, as shown in Fig. E11 and then in the **Modify** panel > **Edit Edges** rollout, click **Connect** > **Settings** to open the **Connect Edges** caddy control. Now, change **Segments** to **6** and **Pinch** to **0** [see Fig. E12].

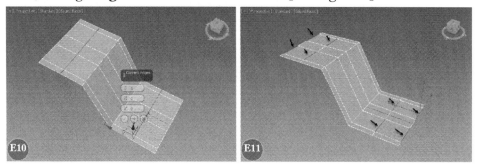

7. In the **Modify** panel > **Selection** rollout, click **Edge** to activate the edge sub-object level and then using the **Move** tool, create shape, as shown in Fig. E13. In the **Modify** panel > **Selection** rollout, click **Polygon** to activate the polygon sub-object level and then select polygons, as shown in Fig. E14.

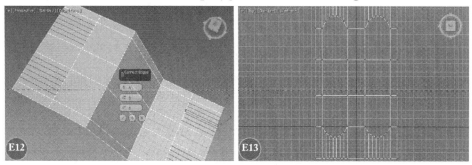

8. In the **Modify** panel > **Edit Polygons** rollout, click **Extrude** > **Settings** to open the **Extrude Polygons** caddy control. In the caddy control, change extrusion type to **Local Normal**, and **Height** to **-35** [see Fig. E15].

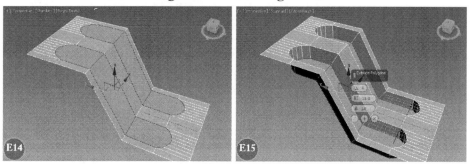

9. In the **Modify** panel > **Selection** rollout, click **Edge** to activate the edge sub-object level and then select the edges, as shown in Fig. E16. In the **Modify** panel > **Edit Edges** rollout, click **Chamfer** > **Settings** to open the **Chamfer** caddy control. In the caddy control, change **Chamfer type** to **Quad Chamfer, Amount** to **1.5** and then click **OK** [see Fig. E17]. From the **Object-Space Modifiers** section of the **Modifier** list, select **MeshSmooth**. In the **Subdivision Amount** rollout, change **Iterations** to **3** [see Fig. E18].

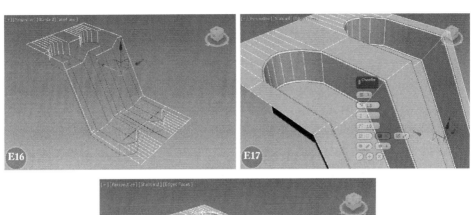

Exercise 5: Creating a Solid Model

In this exercise, we will create a solid model [see Fig. E1].

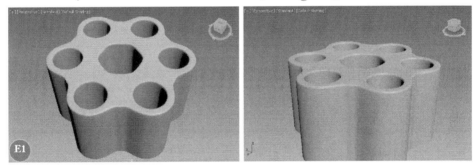

Table E5 summarizes the exercise.

Table E5	
Skill level	Beginner
Time to complete	30 Minutes
Topics	• Specifying the Units for the Exercise • Creating the Model
Resources folder	**unit-dm4**
Units	**Generic Units**
Final file	**solid-3-finish.max**

Specifying the Units for the Exercise

Follow these steps:

1. From the **Customize** menu choose **Units Setup**. In the **Units Setup** dialog box that appears, select **Generic Units** from the **Units Setup** dialog box. Click **OK** to accept the changes made.

2. From the **File** menu, choose **Save** to open the **Save File As** dialog box. In the **File name** text box type **solid-3-finish.max** and then click **Save** to save the file.

Creating the Model

Follow these steps:

1. In the **Create** panel, click **Geometry**, and then choose **Standard Primitives** from the drop-down list located below **Geometry**. In the **Object Type** rollout, click **Tube**. Create a tube in the **Top** viewport. Switch to the **Modify** panel and then in the **Parameters** rollout, change **Radius 1** to **20**, **Radius 2** to **30**, **Height** to **0**, **Height Segments** to **1**, **Cap Segments to 1**, **Sides** to **8**, and **Height** to **2**.

2. **RMB** click the **Move** tool to open the **Move Transform Type-In** dialog box. In the **Absolute:World** group of the dialog box, change **X**, **Y**, and **Z** to **0**, **65**, and **0**, respectively. **RMB** click and then choose **transform** quadrant > **Convert To:** > **Convert to Editable Poly**. In the **Modify** panel > **Selection** rollout, click **Polygon** to activate the polygon sub-object level. Select all polygon except the top polygons [see Fig. E2] and then press **Delete** to delete selected polygons [see Fig. 3].

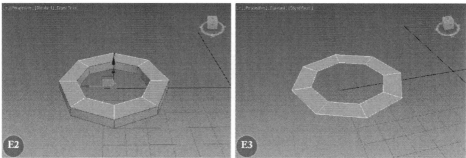

3. Press **6** to switch to the **Object** mode. Select **Use Transform Coordinate Center** from the **Use Center** flyout. Make sure mesh is selected and then choose **Array** from the **Tools** menu to open the **Array** dialog box. Set the values in the dialog box, as shown in Fig. E4 and then click **OK** [see Fig. E5]. Select **Pivot Point Center** from the **Use Center** flyout.

4. In the **Modify** panel > **Edit Geometry** rollout, click **Attach** > **Settings** to open the **Attach List** dialog box. Now, select all objects and click **Attach**.

5. Select the edges, as shown in Fig. E6 and then in the **Modify** panel > **Edit Edges** rollout, click **Bridge** to bridge the edges [see Fig. E7]. Similarly, connect all edges [see Fig. E8].

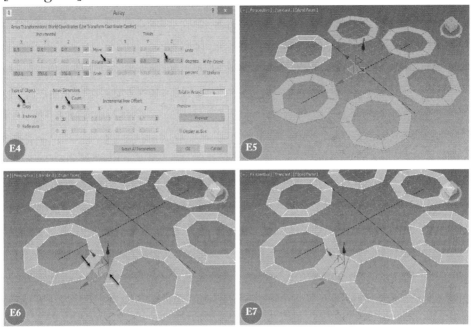

6. Select the edges, as shown in Fig. E9 and then in the **Modify** panel > **Edit Edges** rollout, click **Connect** [see Fig. E10]. Similarly, connect all edges [see Fig. E11].

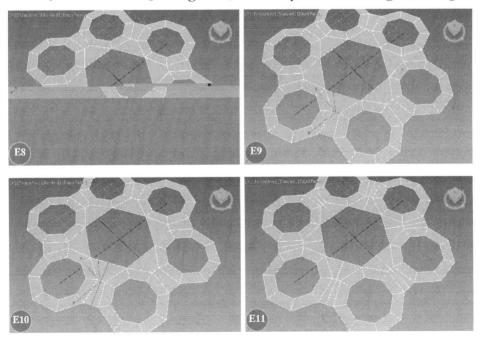

7. In the **Modify** panel > **Selection** rollout, click **Vertex** to activate the vertex sub-object level. Select the vertices, as shown in Fig. E12 and then uniformly scale them using the **Scale** tool [see Fig. E13].

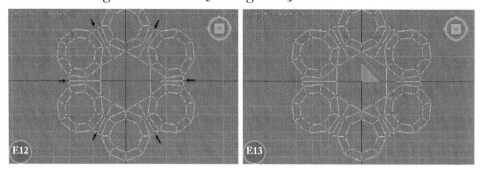

8. In the **Modify** panel > **Selection** rollout, click **Border** to activate the border sub-object level and then select the border, as shown in Fig. E14. Extrude the border using the **Scale** tool and **Shift** [see Fig. E15].

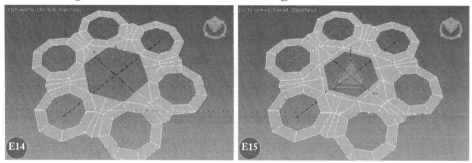

9. Select the borders, as shown in Fig. E16 and then type **Borders** in the **Named Selection Sets** drop-down list in the **Main** toolbar [see Fig. 17]. Extrude selected borders downwards using the **Move** tool and **Shift** [see Fig. E18].

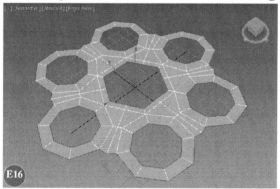

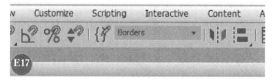

10. Select **Borders** from the **Named Selection Sets** drop-down list. In the **Modify** panel > **Edit Edges** rollout, click **Chamfer** > **Settings** to open the **Chamfer** caddy control. In the caddy control, change **Chamfer type** to **Quad Chamfer**, **Amount** to **1.5** and then click **OK** [see Fig. E19].

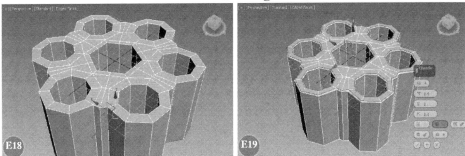

11. From the **Object-Space Modifiers** section of the **Modifier** list, select **MeshSmooth**. In the **Subdivision Amount** rollout, change **Iterations** to **3** [see Fig. E20].

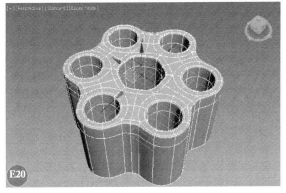

Exercise 6: Creating a Serving Bowl

In this exercise, we will create model of a bowl [see Fig. E1].

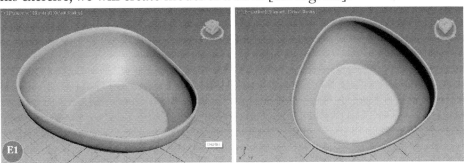

Table E6 summarizes the exercise.

Table E6	
Skill level	Beginner
Time to complete	20 Minutes

Table E6	
Topics	• Specifying the Units for the Exercise • Creating the Bowl
Resources folder	**unit-dm4**
Units	**Metric - Centimeters**
Final file	**bowl-finish.max**

Specifying the Units for the Exercise
Follow these steps:

1. From the **Customize** menu choose **Units Setup**. In the **Units Setup** dialog box that opens, select **Metric** from the **Display Unit Scale** group. Next, select **Centimeters** from the drop-down list located below **Metric**, if already not selected. Click **OK**.

2. In the **Create** panel, click **Helpers** and then in the **Object Type** rollout, click **Grid**. Create a grid on the **Top** viewport. Set the **Transform Type-In** boxes in the **Status Bar** to **0** to place the grid at the origin. Go to the **Modify** panel and then in the **Parameters** rollout, set **Length, Width,** and **Grid** to **60, 60,** and **5,** respectively. Press **X** to open the **3ds Max Commands** list and type **Activate** in the **Search All Actions** field.

3. Select **Activate Grid Object** from the list to hide the **Home** grid and activate the grid that we just created [see Fig. E2].

 What just happened?
*Here, I've created a **Grid** object that will act as a construction plane for the objects. A **Grid** object is a parametric object. You can create any number of grid objects in the scene. They are saved with the scene. When you select **Activate Grid Object** command, the **Home** grid is deactivated and the selected **Grid** object becomes the active construction plane. Here, I have created a **60x60** cm grid and each grid square represents size of the smallest square in the grid [5 cm].*

4. From the **File** menu, choose **Save** to open the **Save File As** dialog box. In the **File name** text box type **bowl-finish.max** and then click **Save** to save the file.

Creating the Bowl
Follow these steps:

1. In the **Create** panel, click **Geometry**, select **Standard Primitives** from the drop-down list, and then in the **Object Type** rollout, click **Cylinder**. Create a cylinder in the **Top** viewport. Go to the **Modify** panel and then in the **Parameters** rollout, set **Radius** to **25.591, Height** to **13, Sides** to **36,** and **Height Segments** to **2**. Set the **Transform Type-In** boxes in the **Status Bar** to **0** to place the cylinder at the origin [see Fig. E3]. Now, rename the cylinder as **bowlGeo**.

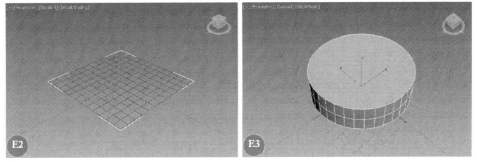

2. **RMB** click on **bowlGeo**. In the **transform** quadrant of the **Quad** menu that appears, choose **Convert To: Convert to Editable Poly**. Click **Polygon** in the **Modify** panel > **Selection** rollout and then select the top polygon of **bowlGeo**. Press **Delete** to remove the polygon.

3. Click **Select and Uniform Scale** on the **Main** toolbar. Select the bottom set of vertices and uniformly scale them down about **70%** [see Fig. E4]. You can use the **Scale Transform Type-In** dialog box to precisely enter the scale value.

> 💡 *Tip: Percent Snap Toggle*
> *You can activate **Percent Snap Toggle** [Hotkey: **Shift+Ctrl+P**] from the **Main** toolbar to increment the scale values by an increment of **10%** [default value]. You can change the percentage value from the **Grid and Snap Settings** dialog box.*

4. Select the bottom polygon and then press **Delete** to delete it [see Fig. E5]. Now, select the edges, as shown in Fig. E6 and then in the **Modify** panel > **Edit Edges** rollout, click **Bridge** to bridge the edges [see Fig. E7].

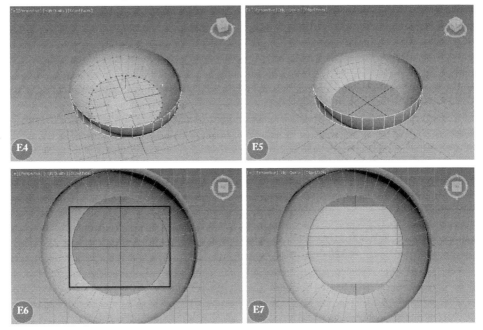

5. Select the edge ring, as shown in Fig. E8 and then in the **Modify** panel > **Edit Edges** rollout, click **Connect** > **Settings** to open the **Connect Edges** caddy control. Now, change **Segments** to **7** [see Fig. E9]. Now, bridge the edges [see Fig. E10].

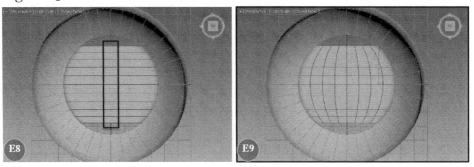

6. Press **3** to activate the border sub-object level and then select the borders [see Fig. E11]. In the **Modify** panel > **Edit Borders** rollout, click **Cap** [see Fig. E12].

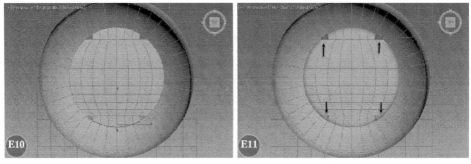

7. Select the edge ring, as shown in Fig. E13 and then in the **Modify** panel > **Edit Edges** rollout, click **Connect** > **Settings** to open the **Connect Edges** caddy control. Now, change **Segments** to **1** [see Fig. E14]. Similarly, connect the edges on the opposite side [see Fig. E15].

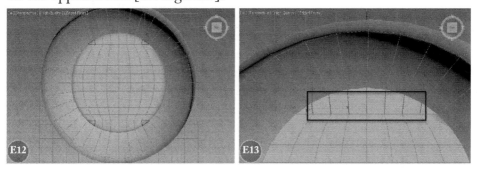

8. Select the vertices, as shown in Fig. E16 and then scale them in to maintain the topology [see Fig. E17]. Select newly created polygons and then click **Settings** on the right of **Extrude** in the **Modify** panel > **Edit Polygons** rollout. In the **Extrude's** caddy, set **Height** to **1** and click **OK** [see Fig. E18].

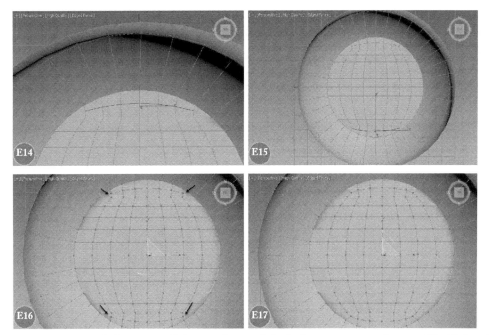

9. From the **Modifier** list > **Object-Space Modifiers** section, choose **Shell**. In the **Parameters** rollout, set **Outer Amount** to **0.5**.

10. From the **Modifier** list > **Object-Space Modifiers** section, choose **CreaseSet**. Similarly, add the **OpenSubdiv** modifier. In the **Modify** panel > **General Controls** rollout, set **Iterations** to **2**.

> *What just happened?*
> *Here, I've added the **OpenSubdiv** modifier. This modifier performs subdivision and smoothing operations on a mesh object. It can read the crease values from underlying stack entities [creases defined using the **CreaseSet** modifier] and applies them to the smooth mesh. The **Iterations** parameter controls the number of times a mesh is subdivided.*

11. Expand the **CreaseSet** modifier in the modifier stack and select **Edge**. Now, select the top two loops using **Ctrl** double-clicking [see Fig. E19].

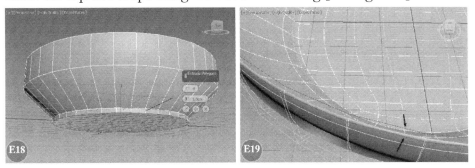

12. In the **Modify** panel > **Crease Sets** rollout, type name as **top_crease** and then click **Create Set** to create a new crease set [see Fig. E20]. Now, enter **0.5** in the spinner besides **top_crease** to round the edges [see Fig. E21].

 What just happened?
*Here, I have used the **CreaseSet** modifier to create a crease set. This modifier provides various tools for creating and managing creases in conjunction with the **OpenSubdiv** modifier. A crease set is a collection of edges and vertices having the same crease value.*

13. Similarly, create crease sets for the bottom and inner edges [see Figs. E22 and E23].

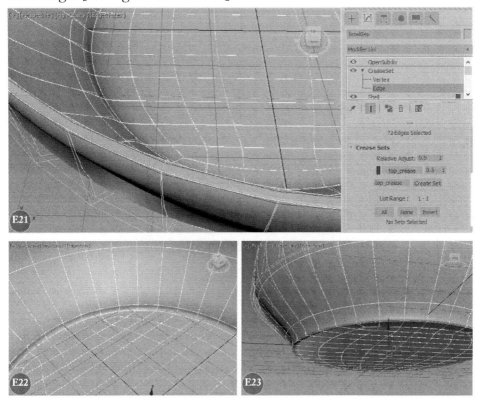

14. From the **Modifier** list > **Object-Space Modifiers** section, choose **Edit Poly**. From the **Modifier** list > **Object-Space Modifiers** section, choose **Taper**. In the modifier stack display, expand **Taper** and click on **Gizmo** sub-object. Click **Select and Uniform Scale** on the **Main** toolbar and then scale down the gizmo [see Fig. E24]. Exit **Taper's** sub-object level.

15. In the **Parameters** rollout, set **Amount** to **0.26** and **Curve** to **-0.93**. Also, set **Primary** to **X** and **Effect** to **Y** [see Fig. E25].

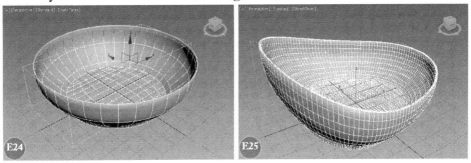

 What just happened?
*I have applied the **Taper** modifier to change the shape of the bowl. This modifier produces a tapered contour by scaling the ends of the geometry. The **Taper's** gizmo allows you to manipulate the result. **Amount** defines the extent of scaling. The parameters in the **Primary** group define the central axis for taper. **Effect** determines the direction of taper.*

Exercise 7: Creating a Kitchen Cabinet
In this exercise, we will create model of a kitchen cabinet [see Fig. E1].

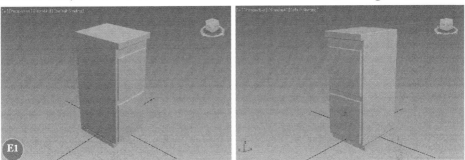

Table E7 summarizes the exercise.

Table E7	
Skill level	Beginner
Time to complete	20 Minutes
Topics	• Specifying the Units for the Exercise • Creating the Kitchen Cabinet
Resources folder	**unit-dm4**
Units	**Metric - Centimeters**
Final file	**kitchen-cabinet-finish.max**

Specifying the Units for the Exercise
Follow these steps:

1. From the **Customize** menu choose **Units Setup**. In the **Units Setup** dialog box that opens, select **Metric** from the **Display Unit Scale** group. Next, select **Centimeters** from the drop-down list located below **Metric**, if already not selected. Click **OK**.

2. From the **File** menu, choose **Save** to open the **Save File As** dialog box. In the **File name** text box type **kitchen-cabinet-finish.max** and then click **Save** to save the file.

Creating the Cabinet
Follow these steps:

1. In the **Create** panel, click **Geometry** and then in the **Object Type** rollout, click **Box**. Create a box in the **Top** viewport. Go to the **Modify** panel and then in the **Parameters** rollout, set **Length** to **38**, **Width** to **45**, and **Height** to **76**. Set the **Transform Type-In** boxes in the **Status Bar** to **0** to place the box at the origin [see Fig. E2].

2. Convert the **Box001** to the **Editable Poly** object. Select the top and bottom polygons of the box [see Fig. E3] and then click **Detach** from the **Modify** panel > **Edit Geometry** rollout. Click **OK** in the **Detach** dialog box to create a new object from the selected polygons with the name **Object001**.

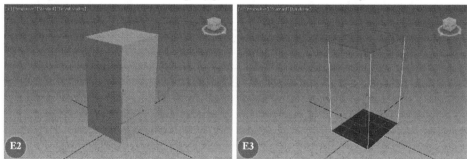

3. Select **Object001** from the **Scene Explorer** and activate the **Polygon** sub-object level. Now, select top and bottom polygons of **Object001**. Click **Settings** on the right of **Extrude** in the **Modify panel** > **Edit Polygons** rollout. In the **Extude's** caddy, set **Height** to **5** and click **OK** [see Fig. E4]. Select the polygon, as shown in Fig. E5 and then move it by **3** units in the positive **X** direction [see Fig. E6].

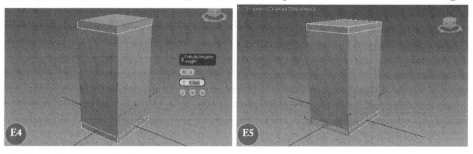

4. Select the top polygon and then click **Settings** on the right of **Extrude** in the **Modify** panel > **Edit Polygons** rollout. In the **Extude's** caddy, set **Height** to **5** and click **OK** [see Fig. E7].

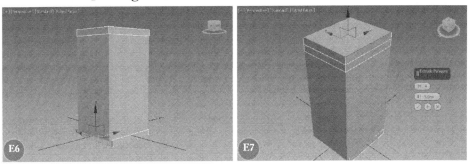

5. Similarly, extrude the front polygon by **3** units [refer Fig. E8]. Select **Box001** from the **Scene Explorer** and then activate the **Edge** sub-object level. Select the edges, as shown in Fig. E9.

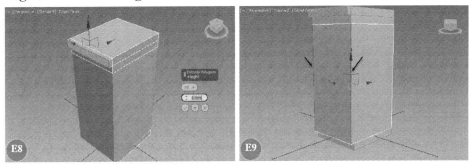

6. Click **Connect** in the **Modify** panel > **Edit Edges** rollout to connect the selected edges [see Fig. E10]. Select the polygons as shown in Fig. E11 and then click **Settings** on the right of **Inset** in the **Modify** panel > **Edit Polygons** rollout.

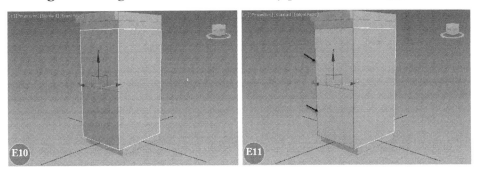

7. In the **Inset's** caddy, set **Inset Type** to **By Polygon, Amount** to **2,** and then click **OK** [see Fig. E12]. Click **Settings** on the right of **Extrude** in the **Modify** panel > **Edit Polygons** rollout. In the **Extrude's** caddy, set **Extrusion Type** to **By Polygon** and **Height** to **1.5** and click **OK** [see Fig. E13].

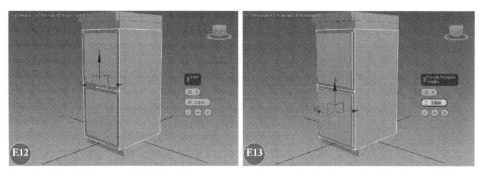

8. In the **Modify** panel > **Edit Geometry** rollout, click **Attach**. Click on **Object001** in a viewport to attach the two objects. Now, rename the resulting mesh as **cabinetGeo**. Activate the **Edge** sub-object and then select the outside edges of the drawers [see Fig. E14].

9. In the **Modify** panel > **Edit Edges** rollout, click **Chamfer** > **Settings** to open the **Chamfer** caddy control. In the caddy control, change **Chamfer type** to **Quad Chamfer**, **Amount** to **0.3**, and then click **OK** [see Fig. E15].

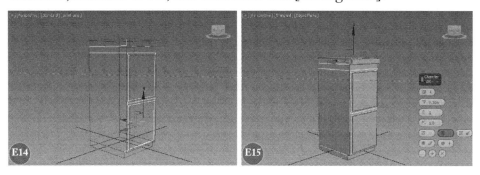

Exercise 8: Creating a Book

In this exercise, we will create model of a book [see Fig. E1]. Table E8 summarizes the exercise.

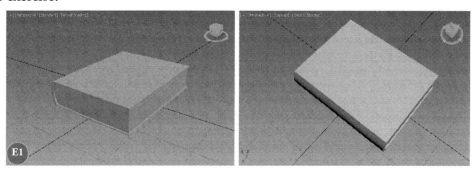

Table E8	
Skill level	Beginner
Time to complete	20 Minutes

Table E8	
Topics	• Specifying the Units for the Exercise • Creating the Book
Resources folder	**unit-dm4**
Units	**US Standard – Decimal Inches**
Final file	**book-finish.max**

Specifying the Units for the Exercise

Follow these steps:

1. From the **Customize** menu choose **Units Setup**. In the **Units Setup** dialog box that opens, select **US Standard** from the **Display Unit Scale** group. Next, select **Decimal Inches** from the drop-down list located below **US Standard** and then click **OK** to accept the change.

2. From the **File** menu, choose **Save** to open the **Save File As** dialog box. In the **File name** text box type **book-finish.max** and then click **Save** to save the file.

Creating the Book

Follow these steps:

1. In the **Create** panel, click **Geometry** and then in the **Object Type** rollout, click **Box**. Create a box in the **Top** viewport. Go to the **Modify** panel, and in the **Parameters** rollout, set **Length** to **7.44**, **Width** to **9.69**, and **Height** to **2**. Set the **Transform Type-In** boxes in the **Status Bar** to **0** to place the box at the origin. Now, rename the box as **bookGeo**.

2. **RMB** click on **bookGeo**. In the **transform** quadrant of the **Quad** menu that appears, choose **Convert To: Convert to Editable Poly**. Click **Edge** in the **Modify** panel > **Selection** rollout and then select the edge shown in Fig. E2. Click **Ring** to select the edge ring [see Fig. E3].

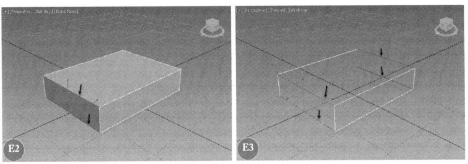

3. Click **Settings** on the right of **Connect** in the **Edit Edges** rollout. In the **Connect's** caddy, set **Slide** to **95** [see Fig. E4] and then click **OK** to connect the selected edges. Similarly, add four edge loops [**Segments: 4, Slide: 0**] to the part of the book that will make up the pages [see Fig. E5].

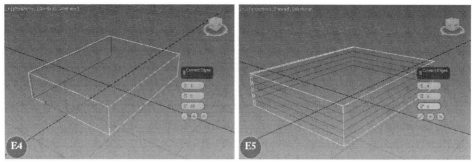

4. Click **Polygon** in the **Modify** panel > **Selection** rollout and then select the polygons shown in Fig. E6. Click **Settings** on the right of **Inset** in the **Edit Polygons** rollout. In the **Inset's** caddy, set **Amount** to **0.08** [see Fig. E7] and then click **OK** to inset the polygons.

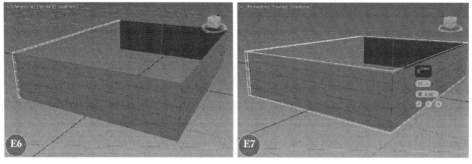

5. Click **Settings** on the right of **Extrude** in the **Edit Polygons** rollout. In the **Extrude's** caddy, set **Group** to **Local Normal** and **Height** to **-0.129** [see Fig. E8] and then click **OK** to extrude the polygons. Click **Edge** in the **Modify** panel > **Selection** rollout and then select all outer edges of the cover shown in Fig. E9.

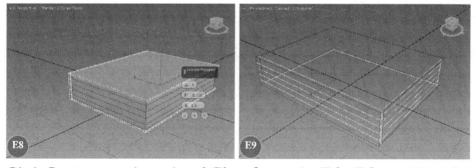

6. Click **Settings** on the right of **Chamfer** in the **Edit Edges** rollout. In the **Chamfer's** caddy, set **Chamfer Type** to **Quad Chamfer**, **Edge Chamfer Amount** to **0.01** and **Connect Edge Segments** to **2** [see Fig. E10] and then click **OK** to chamfer the edges. Click **Vertex** in the **Modify** panel > **Selection** rollout and then select the vertices in the **Left** viewport, as shown in Fig. E11.

7. Invoke the **Select** tool from the **Main** toolbar and then adjust the vertices in the **Left** viewport to modify the shape of the book [see Fig. E12].

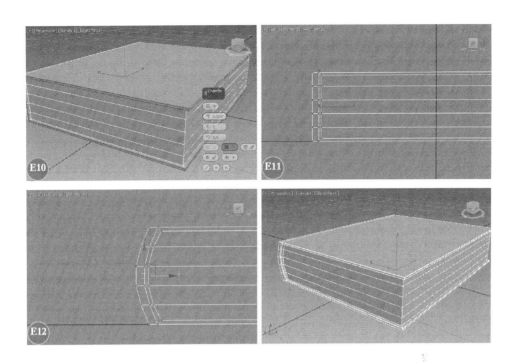

Quiz

Evaluate your skills to see how many questions you can answer correctly.

Multiple Choice
Answer the following questions:

1. Which the following keys is used to add to the sub-object selection of a polygonal object?

   [A] Alt   [B] Ctrl
   [C] Alt+Ctrl   [D] Shift

2. Which the following keys is used to remove from the sub-object selection of a polygonal object?

   [A] Alt   [B] Ctrl
   [C] Alt+Ctrl   [D] Shift

3. Which the following keys is used to repeat the last command?

   [A] '   [B] .
   [C] >   [D] ;

4. Which of the following keys is used to enable polygon selection highlighting?

   [A] F3   [B] F2
   [C] F9   [D] F8

Fill in the Blanks
Fill in the blanks in each of the following statements:

1. The editable poly object is an editable object with five sub-object levels: _____, _____, _____, _____, and _____.

2. The editable poly object is similar to the edit mesh object with the only difference is that the edit mesh object comprises of _____ faces whereas the editable poly object comprises of polygons with any number of vertices.

3. When you convert an object to an editable poly object, you loose all of its creation parameters. If you want to retain the creation parameters, use the _____ modifier.

4. You can use the numeric keys from _____ to _____ to activate the **Vertex, Edge, Border, Polygon**, and **Element** sub-object levels, respectively. Press _____ to return to the Object level.

5. The _____ command allows you to attach other geometries to the selected poly object.

6. If a face is selected and you use the _____ key instead of _____, 3ds Max can create holes in the poly mesh.

True of False
State whether each of the following is true or false:

1. You can lock a sub-object selection by pressing **Spacebar**.

2. If you are working with an editable object such as mesh, poly, patch, or spline, you can directly manipulate the selection using the transformations tools.

3. When you **Shift**+Transform [move, scale, or rotate] a sub-object selection, the **Clone of Mesh** dialog box appears.

Summary

The unit covered the following topics:

- Working with the polygon modeling tools
- Using the polygon modeling techniques
- Selecting polygon sub-objects
- Transforming sub-objects
- Soft selecting sub-objects

- Working with the **Graphite Modeling Tools**
- Selecting sub-objects
- Creating models using the tools available in the **Ribbon**

Unit DM5: Graphite Modeling Tools

In the previous unit, I covered everything you need to know about modeling with polygons. You created geometric primitives and converted them into editable poly objects and then used the tools and commands available in the **Command** panel to create the models. 3ds Max provides another workflow for creating and editing polygons based on the **Ribbon** interface. If you have worked with any other Autodesk product such as products from the **Revit** family, you might be aware of the **Ribbon** interface. In this unit, I describe the tools available in the **Ribbon** interface and how you can use them to improve your modeling workflow.

The Ribbon

The **Graphite Modeling** tools are available in the **Ribbon**. These tools offer vide variety of features for editing polygons. The **Ribbon** comprises all standard **Editable Poly** tools and some additional tools for creating, selecting, and editing geometries. By default, **Ribbon** sits on top of the viewports in the collapsed state [see Fig. 1].

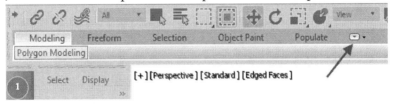

To expand **Ribbon,** either double-click on the empty gray area of the **Ribbon** or click **Show Full Ribbon** [marked with an arrow in Fig. 1]. The **Ribbon** with the **Modeling** tab appears [see Fig. 2].

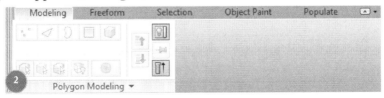

Tip: Toggling display of Ribbon
If **Ribbon** is not visible, click the **Show Ribbon** button on the **Main** toolbar or choose **Show UI** > **Show Ribbon** from the **Customize** menu.

 Tip: Docking Ribbon to the right
You can doc the **Ribbon** on the left or right of the interface [see Fig. 3].

Each tab in **Ribbon** comprises various panels such as the **Polygon Modeling** panel in the **Modeling** tab [marked with an arrow in Fig. 4]. The display of panel in the tab is context sensitive. To view other panels in the tab, create a primitive in a viewport, and then covert it to **Editable Poly**.

When you click on the arrow on the right of the panel's name, the panel expands revealing the tools and commands available in that panel. Fig. 4 shows the expanded **Polygon Modeling** panel. Click on **Polygon Modeling** to collapse the panel [marked with an arrow in Fig. 4].

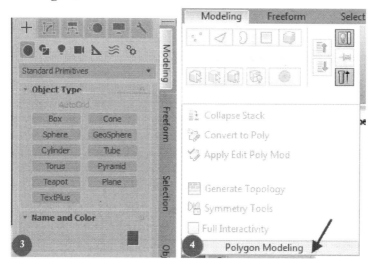

Table 1 summarizes the tabs available in the **Ribbon**.

Table 1: The tabs available in the **Ribbon**	
Tab	**Description**
Modeling	The tools in this tab are mainly used for polygon modeling. These tools are organized in different panels for easy access.
Freeform	This tab contains tools for creating and modifying geometry by painting on the surface of a geometry. You can also specify settings for paint brushes from this tab.
Selection	The special tools in this tab allow you to make sub-object selection in a unique way. For example, select sub-objects from a concave or convex area, and select sub-objects that face the viewport.

Table 1: The tabs available in the **Ribbon**	
Tab	**Description**
Object Paint	The tools available in this tab allow you to freehand paint objects anywhere in the scene.
Populate	This tab provides tools for adding animated pedestrians and idlers in the scene.

Tip: Tools help
*3ds Max provides extended tooltip for the tools available in the **Ribbon**. Position the mouse pointer on a tool; 3ds Max displays a smaller tooltip. If you place the mouse pointer on a tool for little longer, 3ds Max expands the tooltip and sometimes you will also see an illustration in the tooltip. Fig. 5 shows an expanded tooltip when mouse pointer was placed on the **Ring** tool.*

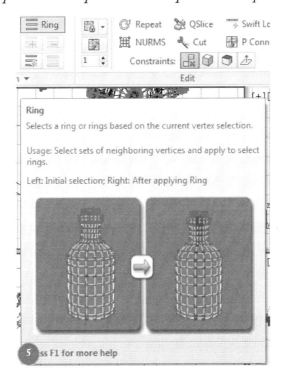

Modeling Tab

The **Modeling** tab contains the tools that you will use with the polygon models. These tools are organized in separate panels for easy access. Most of the tools in this tab are clones of the polygon editing tools found in the **Command** panel. The best way to understand these tools is to practice them. You will use these tools in the hands-on exercises of this unit.

Freeform Tab

The **Freeform** tab [see Fig. 6] provides tools for creating and modifying geometry by painting on the surface of a geometry. This tab contains three panels: **PolyDraw**, **Paint Deform**, and **Defaults**. These panels are discussed next.

PolyDraw Panel

The tools in this panel allow you to quickly sketch or edit a mesh in the main grid. You can also sketch on the surface of another object or on the object itself. This panel also provides tools for molding one object to the shape of another object. Before we explore the tools, let's understand the **Conform Options** panel which is always displayed when a conform brush tool is active.

Conform Options Panel

The options in this panel [see Fig. 7] let you specify the settings for modifying tool's effects. When any conform brush tool other than the **Conform Brush** is active, the panel is named **Transform Conform Options**. Also, an additional toggle appears with the name **Offset Relative**.

Here's the quick rundown to the options available in the **Conform Options** panel.

Full Strength: Defines the size of the center area represented by a white circle in the brush [see Fig. 8]. The **Strength %** setting [see Fig. 7] is fully applied in this area. To adjust the brush size interactively, **Shift**+drag.

Falloff: Falloff is represented by the bigger black circle [see Fig. 8]. The **Strength** in this circle decreases from full strength to zero. To adjust the brush size interactively, **Ctrl**+drag.

Conform: It defines the rate at which the **Conform** brush deforms the painted object. The higher the values you specify for this option, the instant will be the conforming effect.

 Mirror: When **Mirror** is active, the tool's effect is applied equally to both sides [see Fig. 9] across the mirror axis defined by the **Mirror Axis** parameter.

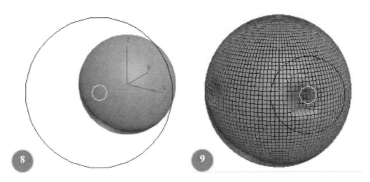

View/ **Vertex Normals:** These two options [see Fig. 10] control the direction in which the **Conform** brush moves the vertices. **View** pushes vertices away from the screen therefore it is dependent on the view angle of the scene. **Vertex Normals** pushes the vertices along their own normal toward the target.

Offset Relative: This brush is only available when you use one of the transform conform brushes. When on, it helps you in retaining the original shape of the object.

Strength %: This option defines the overall rate at which a brush deforms an object. To interactive change the value for this option, **Shift+Alt**+drag.

Use Selected Verts: When on, deform tools only affect the selected vertices. When off, it affects all vertices of the object.

Ignore Backfacing: When on, the tools affects vertices facing you.

Mirror Axis X/Y/Z: Allow you to choose the axis across which the conform action will be mirrored.

Freeze Axis X/Y/Z: When any **Freeze Axis** button is active, the tool is prevented from moving vertices on the corresponding axis of the object. To limit the effect to a particular axis, select **Freeze Axis** for other two axes.

Freeze Selected Edges X/Y/Z: When any **Freeze Selected Edges** button is active, the tool is prevented from moving edges on the corresponding axis of the object. The un-selected edges move freely. These options apply to all sub-objects levels.

PolyDraw Panel - Drag and Conform Tools

The tools in this panel [see Fig. 11] produce different effects depending on which combination keys [**Ctrl, Alt,** and **Shift**] you press. Although, **PolyDraw** tools do not require you to select any sub-object level, however, it is recommended that you use these tools at the **Vertex** sub-object level for better results.

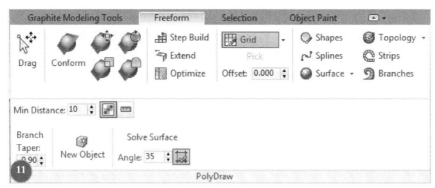

The **Min Distance** parameter allow you to specify a distance you need to drag the mouse before the next step in the tool is taken. There are two buttons available on the right of the **Min Distance** parameter: **in Pixels** and **in Units**. You can use these buttons to specify the minimum distance in pixels and world units, respectively.

The **Branch Taper** parameter allows you to specify the amount by which the branches taper as you draw them. On clicking the **New Object** button, 3ds Max creates a new empty editable object, activates the **Vertex** sub-object level, and keeps the current **PolyDraw** tool active. Now, you can use the **PolyDraw** tools to add geometry.

On clicking the **Solve Surface** button, 3ds Max attempts to create a workable mesh composed of mostly quads. You can use this tool to clean up the mesh after using tools such as **Draw Polygon Shapes**.

Drag: You can use the **Drag** tool to move sub-objects on a surface or grid. Table 2 summarizes the functions available with this tool.

Table 2: Functions of the **Drag** tool	
Function	**Description**
Normal	Without any modifier keys this tool moves vertices by dragging them.
Shift	Moves edges.
Ctrl+Drag	Moves polygons.
Shift+Ctrl+Drag	Moves edge loops.
Shift+Ctrl+Alt+Drag	Moves elements.

You can also use this tool to move the sub-objects in screen space [perpendicular to the current view selection]. Table 3 shows these functions.

Table 3: Functions of the **Drag** tool in the screen space	
Function	**Description**
Alt+Drag	Moves vertices.
Alt+Shift+Drag	Moves edges.
Alt+Ctrl+Drag	Moves polygons.

Conform Brush: The **Conform** brushes move the conform object's vertices towards the target to mold a conform object into the shape of the target object. You can use these brushes in variety of modeling scenarios such as painting a road on a hilly terrain or painting a mask on the face of a character.

To conform an object to the target object. Select the object that you want to conform. Activate the **Vertex** sub-object level for better control. Select **Draw On: Surface** from the **Draw On** drop-down list [Surface] on the **PolyDraw** panel. Click **Pick** and then click the target object in a viewport. The name of the object appears on the **Pick** [Pick] button. Click **Conform**, adjust brush size and strength, and then drag the object toward the target using the **Conform** brush. The selected object takes shape of the target object. In Fig. 12, I have conformed a **Plane** primitive to a **Sphere** primitive.

Apart from the basic **Conform** brush that is described above, 3ds Max also provides four transformed based variants: **Move Conform Brush**, **Rotate Conform Brush**, **Scale Conform Brush**, and **Relax Conform Brush**. The **Relax Conform Brush** applies a relax effect to the vertices within a spherical volume.

PolyDraw Panel - Add Geometry and Optimize Tools

Step Build: This tool works at the **Object** level as well as the sub-objects level. You can use this tool to build a surface vertex by vertex or polygon by polygon. Table 4 summarizes the functions of this tool.

Function	Description
Table 4: Functions of the **Step Build** tool	
Normal	Click to place vertices on the grid or surface.
Shift+Drag	Drag over the floating vertices to fill the gaps with quad polygons.
Ctrl+Click	Click on a polygon to delete it.
Alt+Click	Click on a vertex to remove it.
Ctrl+Alt+Click	Click on an edge to remove it.
Ctrl+Shift+Click	Click to place and select vertices. You can also select the existing vertices.
Shift+Alt	Move the mouse pointer [do not drag] over the vertices to select them.
Ctrl+Shift+Alt	Drag mouse pointer to move a vertex on a grid or surface.

Caution: Vertex Ticks
*When the **Step Build** tool is active, vertex ticks are not always visible in the viewport. If you don't see the ticks at levels other than the **Vertex** level, change the display of the object to **By Object** in the object's display properties.*

 Extend Tool: You can use this tool with the open edges that are on the border of the surface that have only one polygon attached. Table 5 summarizes the functions of this tool.

Table 5: Functions of the **Extend** tool

Function	Description
Normal	Drag a border vertex to create a polygon.
Shift+Drag	Drag a border edge to create a polygon.
Ctrl+Shift+Drag	Drag an edge to extend its entire loop.
Ctrl+Alt+Drag	Drag between two edges to create a polygon.
Ctrl+Click	Click to delete a polygon and associated isolated vertices.
Ctrl+Shift+Alt+Drag	Drag a vertex to move it on the surface or grid.
Alt+Drag (Screen Space)	Drag a border to create a polygon.
Alt+Shift+ Drag (Screen Space)	Drag a border edge to create a polygon.

Optimize Tool: This tool is used to remove the details from the model by drawing on it. Table 6 shows the functions of this tool.

Table 6: Functions of the **Optimize** tool

Function	Description
Normal	Click on the edges to collapse. It merges two vertices into one.
Shift+Drag	Drag from one vertex to another to weld them.
Ctrl+Drag	Drag between the vertices to connect them.
Alt+Click	Click to remove a vertex.
Shift+Ctrl+Click	Click to remove an edge loop.
Shift+Alt+Click	Click to remove a ring.
Ctrl+Alt+Click	Click on an edge to remove it.
Shift+Ctrl+Alt+Drag	Drag on a vertex to move it.

Draw On: The options in this drop-down list allow you to choose the entity type on which you want to draw. The **Grid** ⊞ option creates geometry on the grid of the active viewport. This option works well with the orthographic views, however, you can also use it in the **Perspective** viewport. The **Surface** ⊘ option allows you to draw on another object that you specify. The **Selection** option lets you create geometry on the selected object.

Pick: This button lets you pick an object to draw on. To pick object, select **Surface** from the **Draw On** drop-down list and then click **Pick**. Now, click on the object to draw on.

Offset: It specifies the distance that **PolyDraw** uses for creating the geometry.

PolyDraw Panel - Create Geometry Tools

Shapes: You can use this tool to draw polygons on a surface or grid. Click **Solve Surface** after creating the polygon to generate a workable mesh. The **Solve Surface** option will be displayed when you expand the **PolyDraw** panel [see Fig. 13].

When **Shapes** is active, you can delete a polygon by clicking on it with the **Ctrl** held down. To move a polygon, drag the mouse pointer with **Ctrl+Shift+Alt** held down.

Topology: This tool is used to create quad polygons by drawing lines in a viewport. As you draw the quads using this tool, 3ds Max fills them with a polygon. To draw the mesh, pick **Topology** and then draw lines in a viewport. When you are done with the lines, **RMB** click to complete the operation [see Fig. 14].

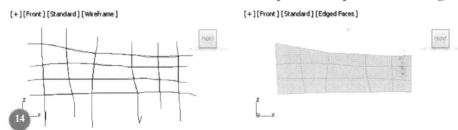

The drop-down list associated with **Topology** contains an option, **Auto Weld**. When **Auto Weld** is selected, 3ds Max automatically attaches the mesh to the selected object and weld their border vertices. If **Auto Weld** is off, **Topology** always creates a new mesh. The **Minimum Distance** parameter available in the expanded **PolyDraw** panel defines the resolution of the lines. The default value for this control is **10** which works well in most of the cases. When **Topology** is active, you can **Shift**+Drag to continue a line from the closest endpoint. To delete a line, click on it with **Ctrl** held down.

Splines: This tool draws a spline on a surface or grid. The splines created using this tool are renderable. Select the desired option from the **Draw On** drop-down list and then draw to create splines. All splines are combined into single [separate] object. When **Splines** is active, you can delete a spline by clicking on it with the **Ctrl** held down. You can also move a spline to the closest splines by dragging it with **Ctrl+Shift+Alt** held down.

Strips: This tool can be used to quickly layout the topology foundation for a mesh object. It paints strips of polygons that follow the mouse drag direction [see Fig. 15]. If you press **Shift** before starting the painting, 3ds Max paints from the closest existing edge. If you want to create polygon between two open edges, press **Alt** and then drag between the two open edges.

Surface: This tool paints a surface onto an object or grid. The size of the surface polygons are controlled by the **Minimum Distance** setting available in the expanded **PolyDraw** panel. The drop-down list associated with **Surface** has an option, **Quads**. When **Quads** is selected, the surface is made up of quads. When off, 3ds Max creates surface with triangles. To start the surface from an existing border edge, hold **Shift** before you start the drawing. It ensures that overlapping polygons are not created. To delete a polygon, click on it with the **Shift** held down; the associated isolated vertices are also deleted.

Branches: This tool creates multi-segmented extrusions from polygons [see Fig. 16]. This tool works only on the selected object and **Draw On** settings does not affect it. The extent of tapering of the branches is controlled by the **Branch Taper** setting available in the expanded **PolyDraw** panel. To create branches, drag the mouse pointer on the selected object, 3ds Max creates branches from the polygons closest to the mouse pointer. Press **Shift** to draw branches from all selected polygons. If you are at the **Polygon** level, click with **Ctrl** held down to select a polygon. You can also select/de-select additional polygons with **Shilft+Alt** held down.

Paint Deform Panel

The tools in this panel [see Fig. 17] give you ability to deform mesh geometry interactively in the viewport. These tools works similarly for at the **Object** level as well at the sub-object level, and are independent of any sub-object selection. To exit any tool, either click its button or **RMB** click in a viewport. Let's explore various deformation tools available in 3ds Max.

⬚ Shift/ ⬚ Shift Rotate/ ⬚ Shift Scale

These tools are used to move, rotate, or scale objects in the screen space [see Fig. 18]. These tools are like using the standard transformation tools with soft selection. However, with these tools no initial selection is required. You can revert to previous state by using the **Revert** ⬚ tool. However, this tool only works if you have used any other deform tool such as **Push/Pull**.

⬚ Push/Pull

This tool drags the vertices outward [see the left image in Fig. 19]. To move vertices inward, drag with the **Alt** held down [see the right image in Fig. 19]. When this tool is active you can use:

- **Ctrl** to revert to the previous saved state.
- **Shift** to relax the mesh.
- **Ctrl+Shift** to resize the brush
- **Shift+Alt** to change the strength of the brush.

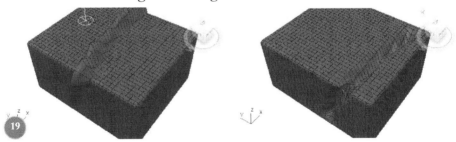

> ✎ *Note: The Paint Options panel*
> *When you use any deform tool except **Shift** tools, the floating **Paint Options** panel appears [see Fig. 20]. You can use the settings from this panel to control the behavior of the deform tools.*

Relax/Soften

This tool allows you to soften the corners [see Fig. 21]. With other brushes, you can soften a geometry with **Shift** held down.

Smudge

The **Smudge** tool is used to move the vertices [see Fig. 22]. It is somewhat similar to the **Shift** tool however it updates the effect continuously. Also, it does not use falloff.

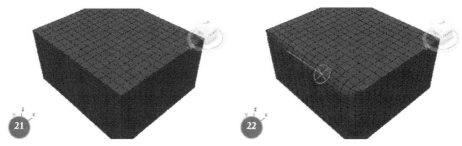

Flatten

This tool lets you flatten the concave and convex areas.

Pinch/Spread

You can use this tool to move vertices together or spread them apart. To spread, drag with the **Alt** held down.

Noise

You can use this tool to add convex noise to a surface [see Fig. 23]. To create concave noise, drag with **Alt** held down.

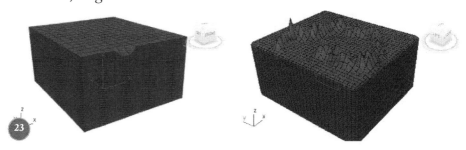

Exaggerate

This tool makes the features of the surface more pronounced by moving the convex areas outward and concave areas inward.

Constrain to Spline

Apart from the **Shift** tools, all other tools can use a spline as a path for mesh deformation. Create a spline and place it near the surface you want to deform [see the left image in Fig. 24]. Click **Pick** available below **Constrain to Spline** and then click on the spline in a viewport.

Make sure **Constrain to Spline** is active then pick a deform tool such as **Noise**. Now, when you paint on the object, the deform gizmo can only be moved along the spline. Drag the mouse pointer to create the deformation [see the right image in Fig. 24].

Defaults Panel

You can use this panel to save and load brush settings. The **Load All Brush Settings** option opens a dialog box that you can use to load brush settings from an existing file. The **Save All Brush Settings** option opens a dialog box that you can use to store brush settings to a file. The **Set Current Settings as Default** option saves the current brush settings as default.

Selection Tab

The **Selection** tab provides a wide array of tools that allow you to make sub-object selection such as you can select convex and concave areas, you can select the sub-object that face the camera, and so on. Let's explore the various panels available in the **Selection** tab.

Select Panel

The tools in this panel lets you select the sub-object based on the certain topologies. Table 7 summarizes the tools available in this panel.

Tool	Icon	Description
Tops		This tool selects the top of the extruded polygon. The selection depends on the active sub-object level. When the **Vertex, Edge,** or **Polygon** sub-object level is active, the vertices, edge outlines, or tops of the extruded polygons are selected. Fig. 25 shows the top of the extruded polygons selected.
Open		This tool selects all open sub-objects [see Fig. 26]. The final result depends on the active sub-object.
Hard		This tool is available at the **Edge** sub-object level. It selects all edges in a model whose faces do not share the same smoothing groups.
Non-Quads		This tool selects all non-quadrilateral polygons. This tool is available at **Polygon** sub-object level.

Table 7: The tools available in the **Select** panel

Table 7: The tools available in the **Select** panel

Tool	Icon	Description
Patterns	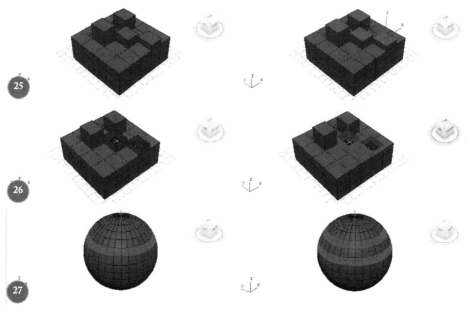	This tool allows you to grow the current selection based on the pattern you select from the **Pattern** drop-down list. The **Pattern 1** through **Pattern 8** options provide different selection patterns. Make a selection in the viewport and then experiment with various patterns. **Growlines** grows the selection with gaps of unselected lines [see Fig. 27]. **Checker** grows selection in from of a checker board pattern [see Fig. 28]. **Dots** grows the selection such that all sub-objects have gap between them [see Fig. 29]. **One Ring** grows a single polygon ring around the initial selection [see Fig. 30].
By Vertex	-	When you click a vertex using this tool, all sub-objects that use the clicked vertex are selected.
By Angle	-	When on and if you select a polygon, the neighboring polygons are also selected based on the value you set in the spinner available on the right of **By Angle**.
By Material ID	-	It opens the **Material ID** dialog box that you can use to set the material IDs. Also, you can select by ID and material name using this dialog box.
By Smoothing Group	-	It displays a dialog box that shows the current smoothing groups. To select polygon associated with a group, click the corresponding smoothing group.

25

26

27

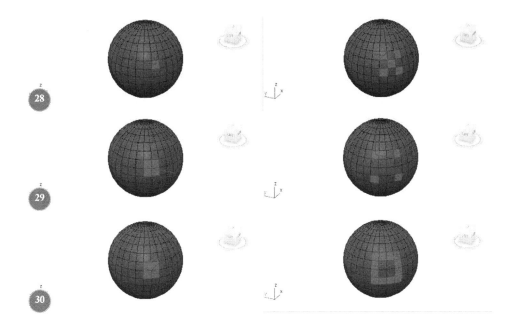

Stored Selection Panel

The options in this panel let you quickly and easily store and retrieve selections. You can also apply some basic operations between the stored selections. Table 8 summarizes the tools available in this panel.

Tool	Icon	Description
Table 8: The tools available in the **Stored Selection** panel		
Copy Store 1/ Copy Store 2		You can use these two buffers to place the current sub-object selection. When a buffer contains a selection, the associated button turns blue.
Paste Store 1/ Paste Store 2		These two tools restore the stored selection, clearing the existing selection. If you want to retain the current selection, click on these buttons with the **Shift** held down.
Add 1+2		It adds the two buffers and applies the selection at the current sub-object level.
Subtract 1-2		It selects non-overlapping area of **Store 1** and also clears both buffers.
Intersect		Selects the overlapping area of **Store 1** and **Store 2**.
Clear		Clears the stored selection.

Sets Panel

The tools in this panel gives you ability to copy and paste the named selection sets between objects. To use these tools, create named selection sets and then use the **Copy** and **Paste** tools from this panel to copy/paste selection from buffer.

By Surface Panel

The **Concave** 🔲 /**Convex** 🔲 tools allow you to select sub-objects in the concave or convex area of the mesh [see Fig. 31]. The spinner located next to the drop-down list allows you to specify the degree of concavity or convexity.

By Normal Panel

The tools in this panel let you select sub-objects based on their normal directions on the world axes. To make a selection, choose an axis and then set the value for the **Angle** parameter. You can invert the selection by clicking **Invert**. The selection shown in Fig. 32 is created by setting **Angle** to **87** and choosing the **Z** axis.

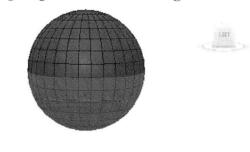

By Perspective Panel

The tools in this panel let you select sub-objects based on the extent they point toward the active view. To make a selection, define an angle using the **Angle** parameter and then click **Select** 🔲 [see the left image in Fig. 33]. If you click **Outline**, 3ds Max selects the outermost sub-objects [see the right image in Fig. 33].

By Random Panel

The tools in this panel select sub-objects at random number or percentage. Also, you can grow or shrink the current selection randomly. To make a selection, click **Number** # or **Percent** % to enable random selection by number or percentage and then click **Select** to make the selection from the current settings. The **Select Within Current Selection** 🔲 option in the **Select** drop-down list selects random sub-objects within the current selection [see Fig. 34]. **Random Grow** 🔲 and **Random Shrink** 🔲 grows or shrinks the selection randomly.

By Half Panel

These tools let you select the half of the mesh on the specified axis based on the area or volume. To select, choose an axis and then click **Select** ⤸ . To toggle the selection, click **Invert Axis** ◔.

By Pivot Distance Panel

You can use this tool to select the sub-objects based on their distance from the pivot. The spinner in this panel defines the distance. In Fig. 35, the selection is defined by setting spinner to **99.2%.**

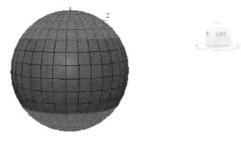

By View Panel

This feature allows you to select and grow sub-objects selection based on the current view. You can specify the distance using the **Grow From Perspective View** parameter.

By Symmetry Panel

You can use this feature to mirror the current sub-object selection on the specified local axis. This feature works on a symmetrical model. The center of the object is defined by the location of the pivot of the object.

By Color Panel

The options in this panel let you select vertices by color or illumination value. These options are available at only **Vertex** sub-object level. To select vertices, choose **Color** or **Illumination** from the drop-down list. Then, use the color swatch to specify a color. Next, click **Select** ⤸ to select the vertices.

By Numeric Panel

This feature allows you to select vertices by the number of connected edges or number of sides you specify. Fig. 36 shows the panel at the **Vertex** and **Polygon** levels, respectively. The

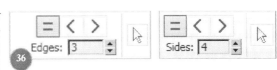

selection shown in Fig. 37 shows the selection made by specifying number of **Sides** to **4** at the **Polygon** level.

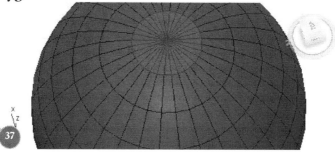

Object Paint Tab

The tools available in this tab [see Fig. 38] allow you to paint objects freehand anywhere in the scene or on the target objects. You can paint multiple objects in a specific order or randomly. The objects that you add by painting are not combined with other objects. You can use the **Fill** tool to fill an edge selection with the objects.

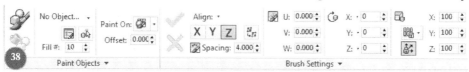

To understand the concept, create few primitives in the viewport and then create a teapot [see the left image in Fig. 39]. Ensure teapot is selected in a viewport and then click **Paint With Selected Object(s)** from the **Paint Objects** panel. Make sure **Scene** is selected from the **Paint On** drop-down list. Set **Spacing** to **15** and then freehand paint on the objects in the scene [see the right image in Fig. 39]. **RMB** click to exit the paint mode.

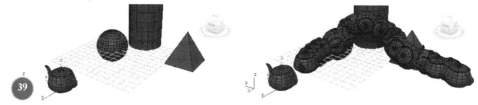

Caution: Exiting the paint mode
*You can adjust stroke after painting, therefore, do not **RMB** click to exit the paint mode until you are satisfied with the result.*

You can use the features in the **Object Paint** tab to make creative scenes. You can also use them to populate the scenes with, for example, characters or trees. I would recommend that you practice these tools and then integrate them in your workflow to create creative artwork.

Hands-on Exercises

Exercise 1: Creating a Desk

In this exercise, we will model a desk [see Fig. E1].

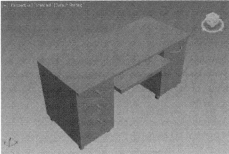

Table E1 summarizes the exercise.

Table E1	
Skill level	Intermediate
Time to complete	1 Hour
Topics	• Specifying the Units for the Exercise • Creating the Desk
Resources folder	**unit-dm5**
Units	**Metric - Centimeters**
Final file	**desk-finish.max**

Specifying the Units for the Exercise
Follow these steps:

1. From the **Customize** menu choose **Units Setup**. In the **Units Setup** dialog box that opens, select the **Metric** option from the **Display Unit Scale** group. Next, select **Centimeters** from the drop-down list located below the **Metric** option, if already not selected. Click **OK** to accept the change.

2. From the **File** menu, choose **Save** to open the **Save File As** dialog box. In the **File name** text box type **desk-finish.max** and then click **Save** to save the file.

Creating the Desk
Follow these steps:

1. In the **Create** panel, activate **Geometry**, then in the **Object Type** rollout, click **Box**. Create a box in the **Top** viewport. In the **Modify** panel > **Parameters** rollout, set **Length** to **60**, **Width** to **150**, and **Height** to **2.5**. Invoke the **Move** tool from the **Main** toolbar.

2. Set the **Transform Type-In** boxes to **0** in the **Status Bar** to place the box at the origin. Create another box in the **Top** viewport. In the **Modify** panel > **Parameters** rollout, set **Length** to **60**, **Width** to **40**, and **Height** to **62**. Align the two boxes [see Fig. E2]. Create copy the box that you have just created and then align it [see Fig. E3].

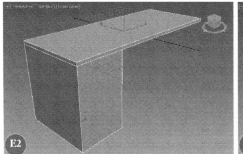
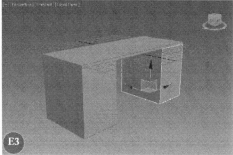

What next?
*Now, we will start using the tools and options available in the **Ribbon** to start shaping the desk. By default, the ribbon is minimized below the **Main** toolbar [see Fig. E4].*

3. Click **Show Full Ribbon** to display the full **Ribbon** [see Fig. E4]. You will notice that the tools in the **Polygon Modeling** panel are inactive because no polygon model exists in the scene [all objects are primitives at this stage]. To expand the **Polygon Modeling** panel and view all tools and options available in it, click **Polygon Modeling**. This action expands the panel and displays the tools available in it [see Fig. E5].

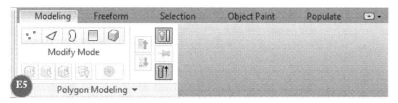

4. Select the top box. In the **Ribbon** > **Modeling** tab > **Polygon Modeling** panel, click **Convert to Poly** [refer to Fig. E6]. In the **Geometry (All)** panel, **Shift** click on **Attach**. In the **Attach List** dialog box that appears, select **Box002** and **Box003** using **Ctrl** and then click **Attach** to attach the selected boxes to the top box. Rename the unified geometry as **deskGeo**.

Tip: Opening settings of a tool
*If you want to open settings for any tool available in the **Ribbon**, **Shift** click on the tool.*

Note: How materials of the objects are combined

*When you attach objects to a poly object, the materials of the objects are combined. If the objects being attached have no material, they inherit the material of the poly object. If the poly object that you are attaching to doesn't have a material, it inherits material of the objects being attached. In case, when both objects have materials, the resulting material is a new **Muti/Sub-object** material that includes the input materials.*

5. In the **Ribbon > Modeling** tab > **Polygon Modeling** panel, click **Edge**. Select the edge as shown in Fig. E7 and then in the **Ribbon > Modeling** tab > **Modify Selection** panel, click **Ring**. In the **Ribbon > Modeling** tab > **Loops** panel, click **Connect**. An edge loop appears.

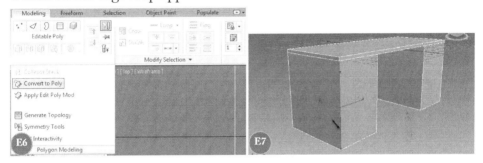

6. Select the edges shown in Fig. E8 and then connect them as done before [see Fig. E9]. Hold **Ctrl** and double-click on the edge loop that you created earlier to select them [see Fig. E10]. In the **Ribbon > Modeling** tab > **Edges** panel, **Shift** click on **Chamfer**. In the **Chamfer** caddy control, set **Edge Chamfer Amount** to **0.2** and then click **OK** [see Fig. E11].

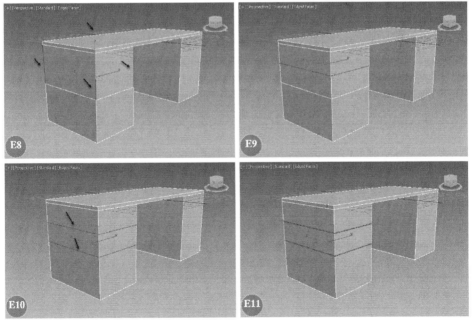

7. In the **Ribbon** > **Modeling** tab > **Polygon Modeling** panel, click **Polygon**. Select the polygons [see Fig. E12]. Invoke the **Move** tool from the **Main** toolbar. In the **Perspective** viewport, press **Shift** and then move the selected polygon slightly [about 1.2 units] outward in the negative Y direction. Release **Shift**. In the **Clone Part of Mesh** dialog box that appears, select the **Clone To Object** option. Now, type **drawerGeo** in the text box next to **Clone To Object** and click **OK**.

8. Ensure the **drawerGeo** is selected. From the **Modifier** list > **Object-Space Modifiers** section, choose **Shell**. In the **Parameters** rollout, set **Outer Amount** to **1.5**. Align the **drawerGeo** with the **deskGeo** [see Fig. E13]. Similarly, detach the polygon shown in Fig. E14.

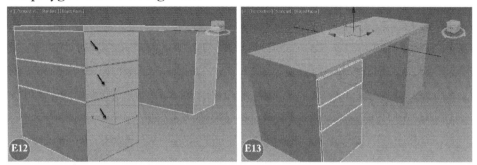

9. Name it as **drawerGeo1**, apply the **Shell** modifier and then align it with **deskGeo** [see Fig. E15]. Hide the drawer geometries from the scene using the **Scene Explorer**. Now, we don't need the edges that we created earlier to create drawer therefore we will remove them to clean the model. Select those four edge loops and then press **Ctrl+Spacebar** to delete them.

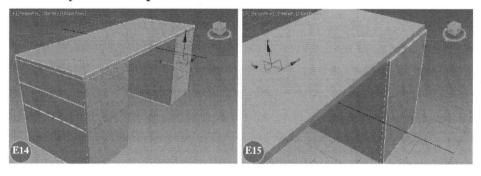

💡 *Tip: Removing Edges – Alternate Method*
*In the **Ribbon** > **Modeling** tab > **Polygon Modeling** panel, click **Edge**. In the **Ribbon** > **Modeling** tab > **Edit** panel, click **Swift Loop** to make it active. Press **Ctrl+Shift** and then click on the edges on the drawers. This action will remove the edges.*

*The **SwiftLoop** tool allows you to interactively place edges. As you move the cursor over the object surface, a real-time preview is shown indicating that where the loop will be created when you click.*

Following are some different features of this tool:

■ *Ctrl click to select an edge loop and activate the **Edge** sub-object level automatically.*
■ *Alt drag a selected edge to slide the edge loop between its bounding loops.*
*Ctrl+Alt drag is a same as the **Alt** drag. However, it also straighten out the edge loop, if necessary.*
■ *Ctrl+Shift click on a edge loop to remove it.*
■ *Shift click to insert a new loop and adjust it to the flow of the surrounding surface.*

10. Select **deskGeo** and activate the **Front** viewport. In the **Ribbon > Modeling** tab > **Polygon Modeling** panel, click **Edge**. In the **Ribbon > Modeling** tab > **Geometry (All)** panel, click **Slice Plane**. This action display a slice plane gizmo in the viewport and opens the **Slice Mode** panel. Adjust the position of the plane as shown in Fig. E16 and then click **Slice** on **Slice Mode** panel to subdivide the geometry [see Fig. E17].

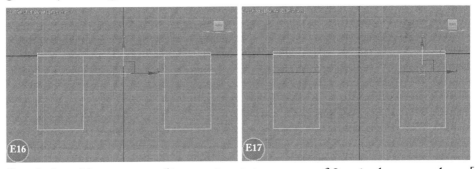

11. Similarly, add two more slices maintaining a gap of **2** units between them [see Fig. E18]. In the **Ribbon > Modeling** tab > **Polygon Modeling** panel, click **Polygon**. Select the polygons, refer to Fig. E19. In the **Ribbon > Modeling** tab > **Polygons** panel, **Shift** click **Extrude**. In the **Extrude's** caddy, set **Height** to **4** and click **OK**.

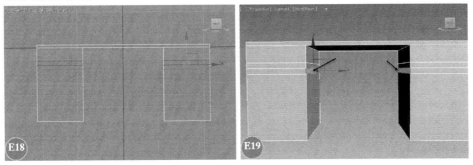

12. Select the polygons shown in Fig. E20. In the **Ribbon > Modeling** tab > **Geometry (All)** panel, click on **Detach**. In the **Detach** dialog box that appears, set **Detach as** to **sliderGeo**. Also, select the **Detach as Clone** check box and then click **OK**. Select **sliderGeo** and move it slightly toward the negative Y axis.

? What just happened?

*The **Detach** tool separates the selected sub-objects and associated polygons as new object or element[s]. When you click **Detach**, the **Detach** dialog box appears. Type the name of the new object in the **Detach as** text box and click **OK** to create the new object with the specified name. The selection is removed from the original object. You can select **Detach To Element** to make the detached sub-object selection part of the original object but it becomes a new element. Select **Detach as Clone** to detach the selection as copy of the original selection; the selection remains intact with the original object.*

13. In the **Ribbon > Modeling** tab > **Polygon Modeling** panel, click **Polygon**. In the **Ribbon > Modeling** tab > **Polygons** panel, click **Bridge** to create a bridge between the selected polygons [see Fig. E21].

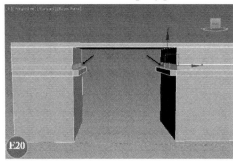
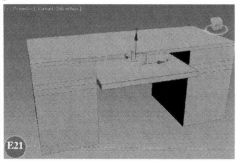

14. In the **Ribbon > Modeling** tab > **Polygon Modeling** panel, click **Border** and then select the border edges of **sliderGeo** [see Fig. E22]. In the **Ribbon > Modeling** tab > **Geometry (All)** panel, click on **Cap Poly** to cap the border edges.

15. Select **deskGeo** and then select the front polygon, refer to Fig. E23. Move it slightly toward the negative Y axis [see Fig. E23].

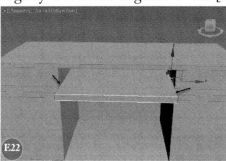
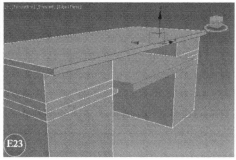

16. Ensure the **drawerGeo** and **drawerGeo1** are visible in the scene. In the **Create** panel, activate **Geometry**, then in the **Extended Primitives > Object Type** rollout, click **ChamferCyl**.

17. Create a cylinder in the **Top** viewport. In the **Modify** panel > **Parameters** rollout, set **Height** to **6**, **Radius** to **1.5**, and **Fillet** to **0.074**. Now, set **Height Segs** to **2**, **Fillet Segs** to **3**, and **Sides** to **18**. Align it with **drawerGeo** [see Fig. E24].

18. Select the cylinder and press **Alt+Q** to isolate it. In the **Ribbon > Modeling** tab > **Polygon Modeling** panel, click **Convert to Poly**. In the **Ribbon > Modeling** tab > **Modeling** panel, click **Edge**. Select the edge loop shown in Fig. E25.

19. In the **Ribbon > Modeling** tab > **Edges** panel, **Shift** click on **Chamfer**. In the **Chamfer's** caddy, set **Edge Chamfer Amount** to **0.1** and click **OK** [see Fig. E26]. In the **Ribbon > Modeling** tab > **Polygon Modeling** panel, **Ctrl** click **Polygon**. In the **Ribbon > Modeling** tab > **Modify Seelection** panel, click **Shrink** to select the polygons created using the chamfer edge operation [see Fig. E27].

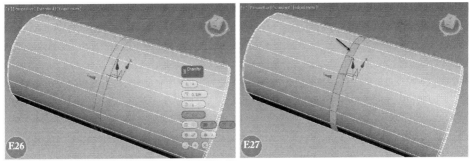

20. In the **Ribbon > Modeling** tab > **Polygons** panel, **Shift** click **Inset**. In the **Inset** caddy control, set **Amount** to **0.02** and click **OK** [see Fig. E28].

21. In the **Ribbon > Modeling** tab > **Polygons** panel, **Shift** click **Extrude**. In the **Extrude's** caddy, set **Extrusion Type** to **Local Normal** and **Height** to **-0.1**. Next, click **OK** [see Fig. E29]. Now, inset the selected polygon by **0.02** units.

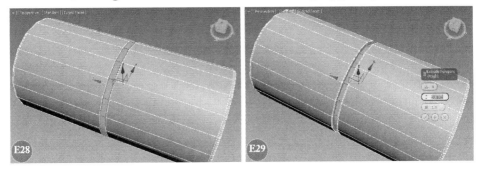

22. Now, select the edges that we created using the **Shift** and **Extrude** operations [see Fig. E30] and then scale them down by to **70%** [see Fig. E31]. In the **Ribbon > Modeling** tab > **Edit** panel, click **NURMS** to smooth the object. Choose **End Isolate** from the **Tools** menu and then create two more copies of knob and align them [see Fig. E32].

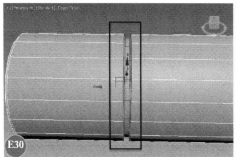

What just happened?

NURMS stands for Non-Uniform Rational Mesh Smooth. This tool allows you to smooth the objects using NURMS subdivision; the same method used by the MeshSmooth and TurboSmooth modifiers. When you click NURMS, the NURMS panel appears. The Iterations spinner in this panel specifies the number of iterations used to smooth the poly object.

Caution: Calculation Time

Specify the number of iterations carefully. It increases the number of vertices and polygons in the object. As a result, the calculation time can increase as much as four times for each iteration. The value in the Smoothness spinner parameters how sharp a corner must be before polygons are added to smooth it.

23. In the **Create** panel, activate **Geometry**, then on the **Extended Primitives > Object Type** rollout, click **ChamferBox**. Create a box in the **Top** viewport. In the **Modify** panel > **Parameters** rollout, set **Length** to 2, **Width** to 26.4, **Height** to 1.5, and **Fillet** to 0.05. Set **Width Segs** to 12.

24. From the **Modifier** list > **Object-Space Modifiers** section, choose **Bend**. In the **Parameters** rollout, set **Angle** to 152 and **Bend Axis** to X. Now, align the handle with the **drawerGeo1** [see Fig. E33].

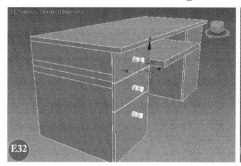
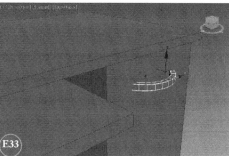

25. From the **Modifier** list > **Object-Space Modifiers** section, choose **Taper**. In the **Modify** panel > modifier stack display, expand **Taper** and click **Gizmo**. Invoke the **Scale** tool from the **Main** toolbar. Change the size of gizmo along the **x-axis** [see Fig. E34].

26. In the **Parameters** rollout, set **Amount** to **-1.1** and **Primary** to **Z**. Set **Effect** to **Y**. From the **Modifier** list > **Object-Space Modifiers** section, choose **TurboSmooth** to smooth the handle [see Fig. E35].

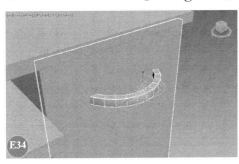 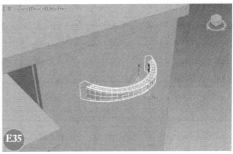

27. Convert **drawerGeo** and **drawerGeo1** to editable poly. Select **drawerGeo** and then in the **Ribbon** > **Modeling** tab > **Polygon Modeling** panel, click **Edge**. Press **Ctrl+A** to select all the edges of **drawerGeo**. In the **Ribbon** > **Modeling** tab > **Edges** panel, **Shift** click **Chamfer**.

28. In the **Chamfer Edges** caddy control, set **Chamfer Type** to **Quad Chamfer**, **Edge Chamfer Amount** to **0.07**, and click **OK**. Similarly, chamfer all edges of **drawerGeo1**, **sliderGeo**, and **deskGeo**.

29. In the **Create** panel, activate **Geometry**, then on the **Extended Primitives** > **Object Type** rollout, click **ChamferBox**. Create a box in the **Top** viewport. In the **Modify** panel > **Parameters** rollout, set **Length** to **4**, **Width** to **4**, **Height** to **8**, and **Fillet** to **0.353**. Set **Fillet Segs** to **2**. Ensure the **Length Segs**, **Width Segs**, and **Height Segs** are set to **1**.

30. Rename the box as **legGeo**. Next. align **legGeo** as shown in Fig. E36. Create seven more copies of **legGeo** and align them as shown in Fig. E37.

Exercise 2: Creating a USB Connector

In this exercise, we will model a USB connector [see Fig. E1].

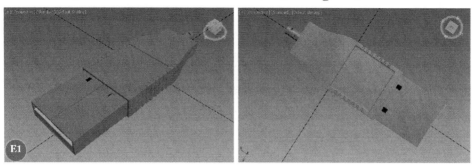

Table E2 summarizes the exercise.

Table E2	
Skill level	Intermediate
Time to complete	40 Minutes
Topics	• Specifying the Units for the Exercise • Creating the USB Connector
Resources folder	**unit-dm5**
Units	**Metric - Millimeters**
Final file	**usbconnector-finish.max**

Specifying the Units for the Exercise

Follow these steps:

1. From the **Customize** menu choose **Units Setup**. In the **Units Setup** dialog box that opens, select the **Metric** option from the **Display Unit Scale** group. Next, select **Millimeters** from the drop-down list located below the **Metric** option, if already not selected. Click **OK** to accept the change.

2. From the **File** menu, choose **Save** to open the **Save File As** dialog box. In the **File name** text box type **usbconnector-finish.max** and then click **Save** to save the file.

Creating the USB Connector

Follow these steps:

1. Create a box in the **Top** viewport. In the **Modify** panel > **Parameters** rollout, set **Length** to **15**, **Width** to **30**, **Height** to **5**, and **Width Segs** to **1**. Rename the box as **ucGeo**. Invoke the **Move** tool from the **Main** toolbar. Set the **Transform Type-In** boxes to **0** in the **Status Bar** to place the box at the origin.

2. In the **Ribbon > Modeling** tab > **Polygon Modeling** panel, click **Convert to Poly.** Activate the **Edge** sub-object level and then in the **Ribbon > Modeling** tab > **Edit** panel, click **SwiftLoop**. Create two loops [refer to Fig. E2] and then slide the loops toward right using **Alt**. Deactivate **SwiftLoop**.

3. Activate **Vertex** sub-object level and then adjust the shape of the connector using the **Move** and **Scale** tools [see Fig. E3]. Activate the **Polygon** sub-object level and then select the front polygon. In the **Ribbon > Modeling** tab > **Polygons** panel, **Shift** click **Inset**. In the **Inset** caddy control, set **Amount** to **0.5** and then click **OK** [see Fig. E4].

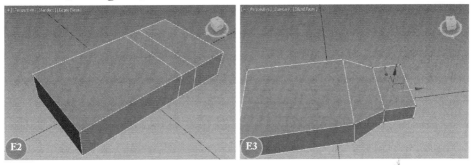

4. In the **Ribbon > Modeling** tab > **Polygons** panel, **Shift** click **Extrude**. In the **Extrude Polygons** caddy control, set **Amount** to **-8** and then click **OK** [see Fig. E5]. Activate **Edge** sub-object level and then select the edge shown in Fig. E6.

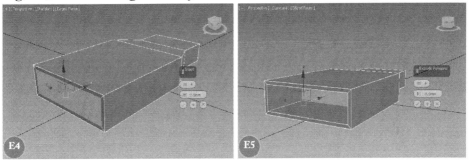

5. In the **Ribbon > Modeling** tab > **Modify Selection** panel, click **Ring**. In the **Ribbon > Modeling** tab > **Loops** panel, **Shift** click **Connect**. In the **Connect Edges** caddy control, set **Segments** to **2** and **Pinch** to **62** [see Fig. E7]. Click **OK**. Similarly, create two more edge loops [see Fig. E8].

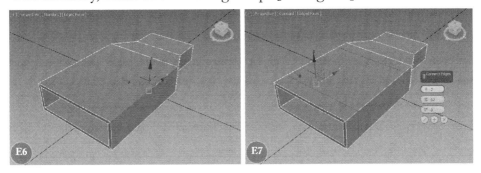

6. Activate the **Polygon** sub-object level and then select the polygon shown in Fig. E9. In the **Ribbon** > **Modeling** tab > **Polygons** panel, **Shift** click **Inset**. In the **Inset** caddy control, set **Amount** to **0.5** and then click **OK**. In the **Ribbon** > **Modeling** tab > **Polygons** panel, **Shift** click **Extrude**. In the **Extrude Polygons** caddy control, set **Amount** to **-0.3** and **then** click **OK** [see Fig. E10].

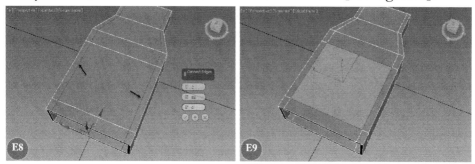

7. Activate the **Edge** sub-object level and then select the edge ring shown in Fig. E11. In the **Ribbon** > **Modeling** tab > **Loops** panel, **Shift** click **Connect**. In the **Connect Edges** caddy control, set **Segments** to **14** and **Pinch** to -25. Click **OK** [see Fig. E12].

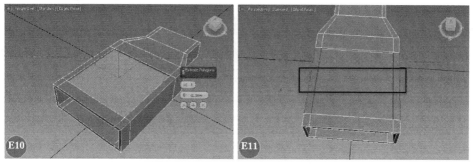

8. Activate **Polygon** sub-object level and then select every other polygon loop using the **Ctrl** and **Shift** [see Fig. E13].

9. Now, in the **Top** viewport, remove the polygons from the selection using **Alt** [see Fig. E14].

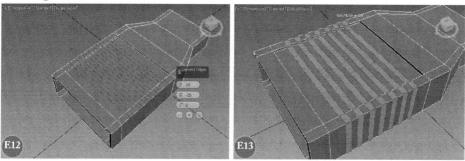

10. In the **Ribbon** > **Modeling** tab > **Polygons** panel, **Shift** click **Inset**. In the **Inset** caddy control, set **Amount** to **0.1** and then click **OK**. In the **Ribbon** > **Modeling** tab > **Polygons** panel, **Shift** click **Extrude**. In the **Extrude Polygons** caddy control, set **Extrusion Type** to **Local Normal** and **Amount** to **-0.2** and **then** click **OK** [see Fig. E15].

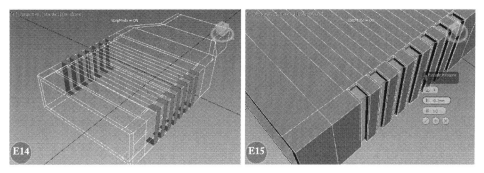

11. Activate **Edge** sub-object level and then on the **Ribbon > Modeling** tab > **Edit** panel, click **SwiftLoop**. Create edge loops around the sharp edges of the **ucGeo** [see Figs. E16 and E17].

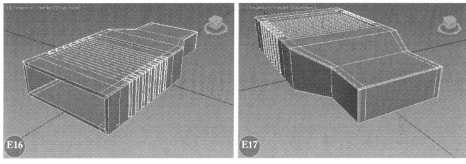

12. Now, insert an edge loop shown in Fig. E18. In the **Ribbon > Modeling** tab > **Edges** panel, **Shift** click **Chamfer**. In the **Chamfer** caddy, set **Edge Chamfer Amount** to **0.09** and **Connect Edge Segments** to **1**. Click **OK**.

13. Select the polygons created using the chamfer operation. In the **Ribbon > Modeling** tab > **Polygons** panel, **Shift** click **Extrude**. In the **Extrude Polygons** caddy, set **Amount** to **-0.04** and then click **OK** [see Fig. E19].

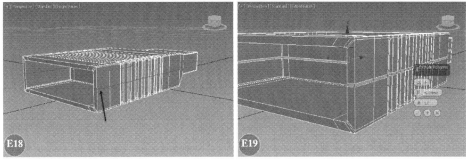

14. Create more edge loop using the **SwiftLoop** tool [see Fig. E20]. Similarly, add edge loops in the front of the connector [see Fig. 21]. From the **Object-Space Modifiers** section of the **Modifier** list, select **MeshSmooth**. In the **Subdivision Amount** rollout, change **Iterations** to **3** [see Fig. E22].

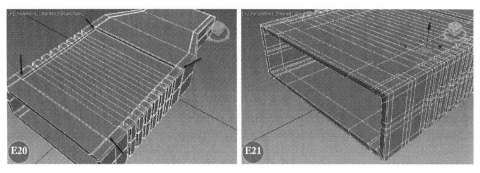

15. Create a box in the **Top** viewport. In the **Modify** panel > **Parameters** rollout, set **Length** to **14**, **Width** to **20**, **Height** to **4**, and **Width Segs** to **1**. Rename the cylinder as **cGeo**. In the **Ribbon** > **Modeling** tab > **Polygon Modeling** panel, click **Convert to Poly**.

16. Activate the **Polygon** sub-object level and then select the front polygon. In the **Ribbon** > **Modeling** tab > **Polygons** panel, **Shift** click **Inset**. In the **Inset** caddy control, set **Amount** to **0.5** and then click **OK** [see Fig. E23]. In the **Ribbon** > **Modeling** tab > **Polygons** panel, **Shift** click **Extrude**. In the **Extrude Polygons** caddy control, set **Amount** to **-6** and then click **OK** [see Fig. E24].

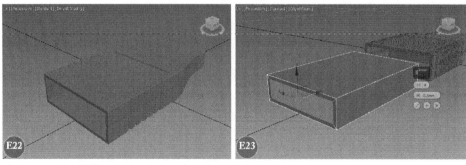

17. Activate the **Edge** sub-object level and then select the ring shown in Fig. E25. In the **Ribbon** > **Modeling** tab > **Loops** panel, **Shift** click **Connect**. In the **Connect Edges** caddy control, set **Segments** to **2** and **Pinch** to **-85**. Click **OK**.

18. Select the newly created polygons and in the **Ribbon** > **Modeling** tab > **Polygons** panel, **Shift** click **Extrude**. In the **Extrude Polygons** caddy control, set **Amount** to **-0.2**, **Type** to **Local Normal** and then click **OK** [see Fig. E26].

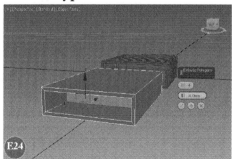 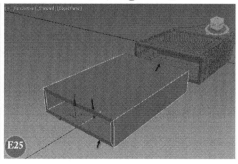

19. Activate the **Edge** sub-object level. Insert edge loops using **SwiftLoop** as shown in Fig. E27. Activate the **Polygon** sub-object level. Select the polygons shown in Fig. E28 and delete them using **Delete**.

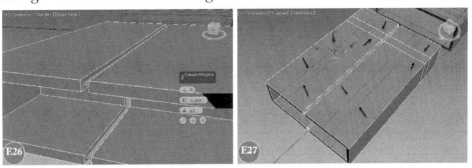

20. Activate the **Edge** sub-object level and select the outer edges shown in Fig. E29. In the **Ribbon > Modeling** tab > **Edges** panel, **Shift** click **Chamfer**. In the **Chamfer** caddy control, set **Chamfer Type** to **Quad Chamfer**, **Edge Chamfer Amount** to **0.06**, and **Connect Edge Segments** to **3**. Click **OK**.

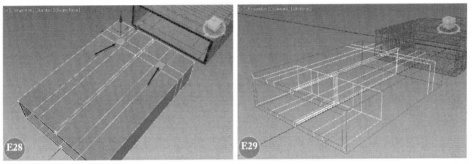

21. Select the edges that make up the holes and then on the **Ribbon > Modeling** tab > **Edges** panel, **Shift** click **Extrude**. In the **Extrude Edges** caddy control, set **Height** to **-0.1**, **Width** to **0**, and then click **OK**. Place the metal connector inside its case. If you find that the metal connector is large in size, you can adjust the shape by moving the vertices [see Fig. E30].

22. Now, create a new box primitive and then place inside the metal connector as shown in Fig. E31.

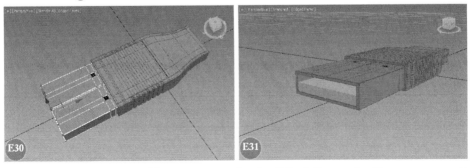

23. Create a cylinder in the **Top** viewport. In the **Modify** panel > **Parameters** rollout, set **Radius** to **2**, **Height** to **4.3**, and **Height Segments** to **5**. Align it with the USB connector.

24. In the **Ribbon** > **Modeling** tab > **Polygon Modeling** panel, click **Convert to Poly.** Activate **Polygon** sub-object level and then select the polygons shown in Fig. E32.

25. In the **Ribbon** > **Modeling** tab > **Polygons** panel, **Shift** click **Inset.** In the **Inset** caddy control, set **Amount** to **0.2** and then click **OK.** In the **Ribbon** > **Modeling** tab > **Polygons** panel, **Shift** click **Extrude.** In the **Extrude Polygons** caddy control, set **Amount** to **-0.5** and **then** click **OK** [see Fig. E33].

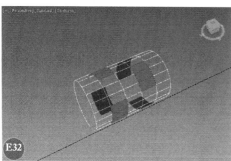 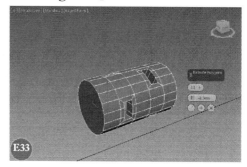

Exercise 3: Creating a Flash Drive

In this exercise, we will model a flash drive [see Fig. E1].

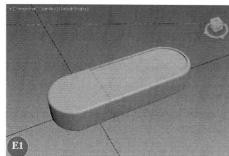 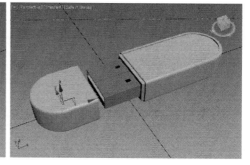

Table E3 summarizes the exercise.

Table E3	
Skill level	Intermediate
Time to complete	1 Hour
Topics	• Specifying the Units for the Exercise • Creating the Flash Drive
Resources folder	**unit-dm5**
Units	**Metric - Millimeters**
Final file	**flash-drive-finish.max**

Specifying the Units for the Exercise
Follow these steps:

1. From the **Customize** menu choose **Units Setup**. In the **Units Setup** dialog box that opens, select the **Metric** option from the **Display Unit Scale** group. Next, select **Millimeters** from the drop-down list located below the **Metric** option, if already not selected. Click **OK** to accept the change.

2. From the **File** menu, choose **Save** to open the **Save File As** dialog box. In the **File name** text box type **flash-drive-finish.max** and then click **Save** to save the file.

Creating the Flash Drive
Follow these steps:

1. Create a cylinder in the **Top** viewport. In the **Modify** panel > **Parameters** rollout, set **Radius** to **7.5**, **Height** to **7**, **Height Segments** to **1**, and **Sides** to **32**. Rename the cylinder as **usbGeo**. Invoke the **Move** tool from the **Main** toolbar. Set the **Transform Type-In** boxes to **0** on the **Status Bar** to place the cylinder at the origin. In the **Ribbon** > **Modeling** tab > **Polygon Modeling** panel, click **Convert to Poly**. Activate **Vertex** sub-object level and then select the vertices in the **Front** viewport [see Fig. E2].

2. In the **Top** viewport, move the selected vertices towards right along the x-axis about **25** units [see Fig. E3].

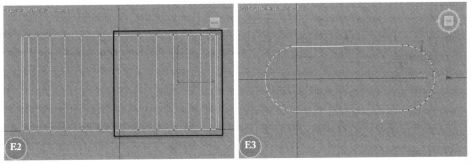

3. In the **Ribbon** > **Modeling** tab > **Geometry (All)** panel, click **Slice Plane**. This action will display a slice plane gizmo in the viewport and opens the **Slice Mode** panel. Adjust the position of the plane, as shown in Fig. E4, and then click **Slice** on **Slice Mode** panel to subdivide the geometry. In the **Ribbon** > **Modeling** tab > **Geometry (All)** panel, click **Slice Plane** to deactivate the slice plane feature.

4. Activate **Edge** sub-object level and then in the **Front** viewport, drag a selection window to select the edges [see Fig. E5].

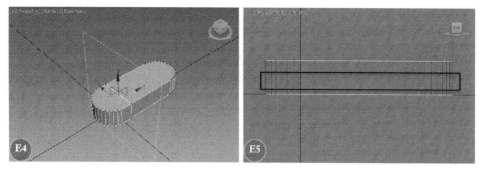

5. Press **Ctrl+I** to invert the selection. Remove the edges from the selection that we created using **Slice Plane**. In the **Ribbon** > **Modeling** tab > **Edges** panel, **Shift** click **Chamfer**. In the **Chamfer** caddy control, set **Edge Chamfer Amount** to **0.8** and **Connect Edge Segments** to **7** [see Fig. E6]. Click **OK**. Activate **Polygon** sub-object level and then select polygons [see Fig. E7].

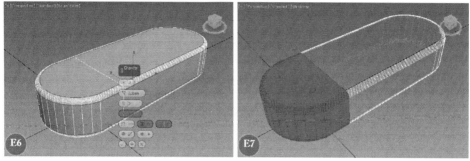

6. In the **Ribbon** > **Modeling** tab > **Geometry (All)** panel, click **Detach**. In the **Detach** dialog box that appears, type **capGeo** in the **Detach as** text box and then make sure that the **Detach to Element** and **Detach As Clone** checkboxes are clear. Now, click **OK**. Move the cap slightly towards left and then apply a **Shell** modifier to it. In the **Parameters** rollout, set **Inner Amount** to **0.4** and **Outer Amount** to **0**.

7. Activate the **Border** sub-object level for **usbGeo** and then make the border selection [see Fig. E8]. In the **Ribbon** > **Modeling** tab > **Geometry (All)** panel, click **Cap Poly** to create a polygon.

8. Activate the **Polygon** sub-object level and then select the newly created polygon. In the **Ribbon** > **Modeling** tab > **Polygons** panel, click **Shift** click **Inset**. In the **Inset** caddy control, set **Amount** to **0.5** and then click **OK**. In the **Ribbon** > **Modeling** tab > **Polygons** panel, **Shift** click **Extrude**. In the **Extrude Polygons** caddy control, set **Amount** to **0.8** and then click **OK** [see Fig. E9].

9. Activate the **Edge** sub-object level and then select the edge loops shown in Fig. E10. In the **Ribbon** > **Modeling** tab > **Edges** panel, **Shift** click **Chamfer**. In the **Chamfer** caddy control, set **Edge Chamfer Amount** to **0.1** and **Connect Edge Segments** to **4**. Click **OK** [see Fig. E11].

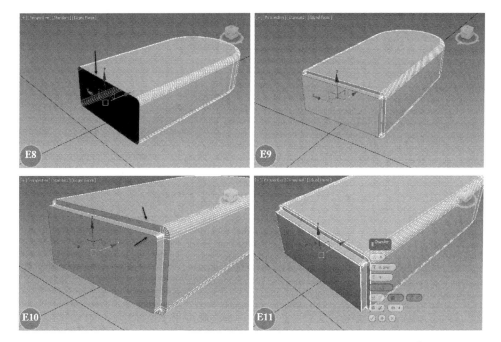

10. Activate the **Polygon** sub-object level and then select the top polygon of the **usbGeo** [see Fig. E12]. In the **Ribbon** > **Modeling** tab > **Polygons** panel, **Shift** click **Inset**. In the **Inset** caddy control, set **Amount** to **0.3** and **then** click **OK** [see Fig. E13].

11. In the **Ribbon** > **Modeling** tab > **Polygons** panel, **Shift** click **Extrude**. In the **Extrude Polygons** caddy control, set **Amount** to **-0.4** and **then** click **OK** [see Fig. E14].

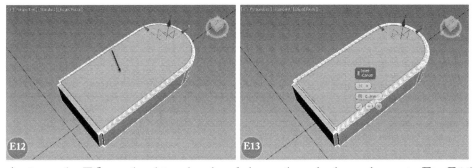

12. Activate the **Edge** sub-object level and then select the loop shown in Fig. E15. In the **Ribbon** > **Modeling** tab > **Edges** panel, **Shift** click **Chamfer**. In the **Chamfer** caddy control, set **Edge Chamfer Amount** to **0.4** and **Connect Edge Segments** to **3.** Click **OK** [see Fig. E16]. Now, create the USB connector as done in the previous exercise [see Fig. E17].

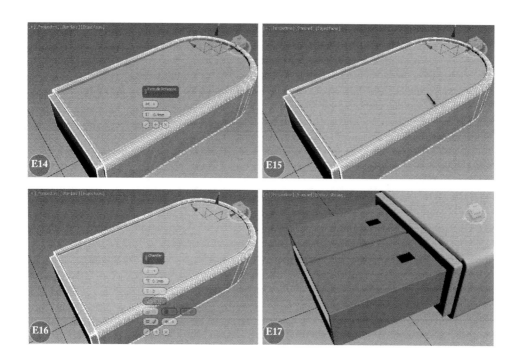

Quiz

Evaluate your skills to see how many questions you can answer correctly.

Multiple Choice
Answer the following questions:

1. Which the following panels is used to quickly sketch or edit a mesh on the grid or a surface?

   [A] PolyDraw   [B] SketchDraw
   [C] ObjectPaint   [D] None of the above

2. Which of the following keys is used to interactively change the conform brush's strength?

   [A] Ctrl+drag   [B] Alt+Drag
   [C] Shift+drag   [D] Ctrl+Shift+Drag

3. Which of the following tools is used to quickly layout the topology foundation for a mesh object?

   [A] Splines   [B] Stripes
   [C] Surface   [D] Branches

Fill in the Blanks
Fill in the blanks in each of the following statements:

1. The Graphite Modeling tools are available in the _____.

2. This _____ tool is used to remove the details from the model by drawing on it.

True of False
State whether each of the following is true or false:

1. When the **Step Build** tool is active, vertex ticks are not always visible in the viewport.

2. The options in the **Stored Selection Panel** let you quickly and easily store and retrieve selections.

Summary

The unit covered the following topics:

- Working with the **Graphite Modeling Tools**
- Selecting sub-objects
- Creating models using the tools available in the **Ribbon**

- Generate planar and 3d surfaces
- Paths and shapes for the loft components
- Generate extrusions
- Generate revolved surfaces
- Define motion path for animations

Unit DM6: Spine Modeling

A shape in 3ds Max is an object consists of one or more lines. These lines which can be 2D or 3D, are used to create components for other objects. 3ds Max provides two types of shape objects: **Splines** and **NURBS** curves. Most of the default shapes in 3ds Max are splines.

3ds Max provides thirteen basic spline objects, five extended spline objects, and two types of NURBS curves. You can use these objects in the following ways:

- Generate planar and 3d surfaces
- Paths and shapes for the loft components
- Generate extrusions
- Generate revolved surfaces
- Define motion path for animations

Apart from what mentioned above, you can also render the shape as is. When rendering is enabled for shapes, 3ds Max renders them using a circular or rectangular cross-section.

You can convert a basic spline or an extended spline to an editable spline object. This object offers a variety of parameters to create less regular and complex shapes. It allows you to edit the shape at the sub-object level. However, when you convert a spline to an **Editable Spline** object, you loose the parametric nature of the spline and cannot adjust the creation parameters. The **Editable Spline** object will be discussed later in this unit. You can use the **Edit Spline** modifier to retain the parametric nature of a primitive spline. This modifier matches all the capabilities of the **Editable Spline** object with some exceptions given next:

- The **Rendering** and **Interpolation** rollouts are not available when you are using the **Edit Spline** modifier.
- The direct vertex animation capabilities are not available.

It is recommended that you use the base **Editable Spline** object to edit the splines rather than store the changes in an **Edit Spline** modifier. The **Editable Spline** object is more reliable and efficient than the **Edit Spline** modifier.

Spline and Extended Splines Primitives

You can access the shape creation tools from the **Create** ➕ panel. Go to the **Create** panel and then click **Shapes** ⌕.

A drop-down list appears below the **Shapes** button with the entries: **Splines, NURBS Curves, Compound Shape, CFD, Max Creation Graph,** and **Extended Splines** [see Fig. 1].

Table 1 summarizes the available tools. You can also access these tools from the **Create** menu.

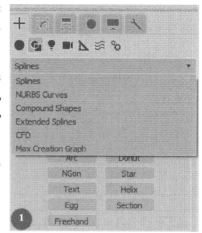

Table 1: The shapes tools available in 3ds Max	
Splines	**Line, Rectangle, Circle, Ellipse, Arc, Donut, NGon, Star, Text, Helix, Egg, Section,** and **Freehand**
NURBS Curves	**Point Curve** and **CV Curve**
Extended Splines	**WRectangle, Channel, Angle, Tee,** and **Wide Flange**

Spline Primitives
In this section, I will explain the basic spline primitives. Let's start with the **Line** spline.

Line Spline
A **Line** spline is a free-form spline that is made up of multiple segments. To create a line, go to the **Create** panel, click **Shapes,** and then click **Line** in the **Object Type** rollout. Notice that various rollouts appear in the **Create** panel. Choose the creation method from the **Creation Method** rollout. Click or drag in the viewport to create the first vertex [If you click, a **Corner** vertex is created otherwise a **Bezier** vertex will be created]. Now, click or drag to create additional points. To finish the creation method, do one of the following: either **RMB** click to create an open spline [see Fig. 2] or click on the first vertex and then choose **Yes** from the **Spline** message box that appears [see Fig. 3].

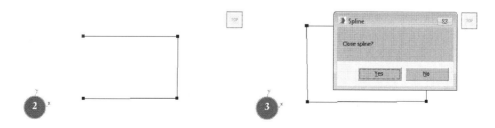

Tip: Constraining new points
Press and hold **Shift** *while creating splines to constrain new points to* **90** *degrees angle increments. Make sure that you are using the default initial type settings.*

Tip: Constraining new points to a custom angle increment
You can also constrain new points to a custom angle increment value. Select **Grids And Snaps** > **Grid And Snap Settings** *from the* **Tools** *menu. In the* **Grid and Snap Settings** *dialog box that appears, choose the* **Options** *panel and then set a value for the* **Angle** *spinner. Close the dialog box. Now, click* **Angle Snap Toggle** *in the* **Main** *toolbar. Press and hold* **Ctrl** *while creating new points to constrain them to the value you specified for the* **Angle** *spinner.*

Tip: Panning and orbiting while creating splines
If a spline requires two or more steps for its creation [such as **Line** *or* **Donut** *], you can pan and orbit the viewport between the creation steps.*

Note: Editable Spline object
3ds Max automatically converts a **Line** *spline to an editable spline object because it has no dimensions parameters. No need to convert it to an* **Editable Spline** *object or apply an* **Edit Spline** *modifier on it.*

Now, let's take a look at the various aspects/parameters associated with the **Line** spline. Many of them are common to most of the spline objects.

Combining Shapes While Creating Them

3ds Max allows you to combine shapes to create compound shapes. You can use this feature to create complex shapes. To create a compound shape, in the **Create** panel, clear the check box preceding the **Start New Shape** button and then begin creating shapes. Each spline that you create, added to the compound spline.

You can check whether all splines are part of a compound shape or not. Go to the **Modify** panel and then click **Editable Spline** in the modifier stack. You will notice that all splines are selected in the viewport [see Fig. 4].

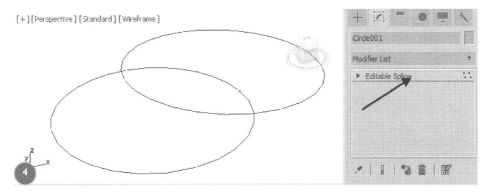

Caution: Parametric nature of splines
You cannot change creation parameters of a compound shape. For example, if you first create a circle, and then add a rectangle to create a compound shape, you cannot switch back and change the creation parameters of the circle.

Creation Method Rollout

The controls in this rollout allow you to specify what type of vertex that will be created when you click or drag vertices in the viewport. The creation method options for the **Line** spline are different from other spline primitives.

Table 2 summarizes the parameters available in the **Creation Method** rollout.

Table 2: Parameters in the **Creation Method** rollout of the **Line** spline

[Group]/ Parameter	Description
[Initial Type Group]	The parameters in this group set the type of vertex created when you click [not drag] a vertex location.
Corner	**Corner** creates sharp points and the spline created is linear to either side of the point.
Smooth	**Smooth** creates a smooth curve through the vertex that you can adjust manually. The curvature of the spline segment is controlled by the spacing of the vertices. Fig. 5 shows the splines created using the **Corner** and **Smooth** initial type options, respectively.
[Drag Type Group]	The parameters in this group define the type of vertex created when you drag a vertex location.
Corner, Smooth	The **Corner** and **Smooth** parameters work as discussed above.
Bezier	The **Bezier** parameter produces a smooth adjustable curve. The amount of curvature and direction of the curve are controlled by dragging the mouse at each vertex. You can manually change the smoothness or curvature by manipulating the vertex handles [refer right-most spline in Fig. 6].

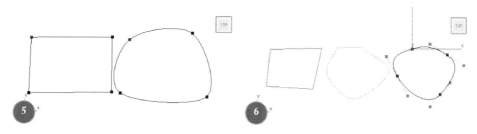

Keyboard Entry Rollout

You can use the **Keyboard Entry** rollout to precisely place vertices of a spline. To add a vertex, enter its coordinates in the **X**, **Y**, and **Z** spinners and then click **Add Point** to add a new point.

The subsequent points you insert will be added to the existing line until you click **Close** or **Finish**. **Close** closes the shape whereas **Finish** completes the line without closing it.

Rendering Rollout

The options in this rollout let you toggle the shape renderability in the viewports as well as in the rendered output. You can also use the options to generate the mapping coordinates and convert the mesh to an editable mesh or editable poly object. Table 3 summarizes the parameters available in the **Rendering** rollout.

Table 3: Parameters in the **Rendering** rollout of the **Line** spline	
Parameter	**Description**
Enable In Renderer	Select the **Enable In Renderer** check box to render the shape as 3D mesh using the **Radial** or **Rectangular** parameters set for the renderer. When the **Enable In Renderer** check box is selected, the **Renderer** option gets selected in this rollout. Now, you have two options for controlling the size of the mesh: **Radial** and **Rectangular**. **Radial** renders the shape with a circular cross section whereas **Rectangular** displays the mesh of the spline as a rectangle. Fig. 7 shows the spline shape with the circular cross section on rendering [**Thickness=2, Sides=12**]. Fig. 8 shows the mesh with the rectangular cross section [**Length=6, Width=2**].
Enable In Viewport, Use Viewport Settings	Select the **Enable In Viewport** check box to display the shape in the viewport as a 3D mesh with the circular or rectangular cross section [see Figs. 9 and 10]. Select **Use Viewport Settings** to display the mesh using the **Viewport** settings. When on, **Viewport** is activated and then you can use the **Viewport** settings to control the appearance of mesh of the spline in the viewport.
Generate Mapping Coords	Select **Generate Mapping Coords** to apply mapping coordinates to the spline mesh. 3ds Max generates coordinates in the **U** and **V** directions. The **U** coordinate wraps around the spline whereas the **V** coordinate is mapped along the length of the spline.
Real-World Map Size	The **Real-World Map Size** check box will only be available if you select **Generate Mapping Coords**. This parameter allows you to specify the actual width and height of a 2D texture map in the material editor.
Auto Smooth	**Auto Smooth** is turned on by default. The spline is automatically smoothed using the threshold value defined by the **Threshold** spinner available below **Auto Smooth**. This value is an angle measured in degrees.

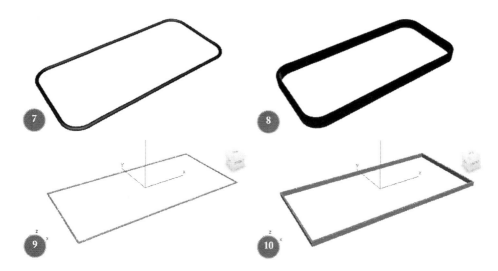

Radial and Rectangular Options: Now, let's have a look at the various parameters available for the radial and rectangular cross sections. Table 4 summarizes these parameters.

Table 4: Various parameters available for the radial and rectangular cross sections	
Parameter	**Description**
Thickness	Controls the diameter of the rendered spline mesh. Fig. 11 shows the splines rendered with the **Thickness** value set to **0.5** and **1**, respectively.
Sides	Controls the number of sides [or facets] of the mesh. Fig. 12 shows the splines rendered with the **Sides** value set to **4** and **62**, respectively.
Angle	Controls the orientation of the rendered cross section. Fig. 13 shows the splines rendered with the **Angle** value set to **0** and **60**, respectively.
Length	Controls the size of the cross section along the local Y-axis.
Width	Controls the size of the cross section along the local X-axis.
Aspect	Controls the aspect ratio of width to length. If the **Lock** button next to the spinner is active, adjusting length or width automatically adjusts the other to maintain the aspect ratio.

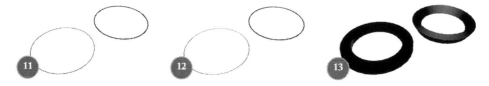

Interpolation Rollout

The parameters on this rollout allow you to adjust the smoothness of a curve. Each spline segment is made up of divisions called steps. Higher the number of steps, smoother the curve will be. By default, **Optimize** is turned on. When on, 3ds Max removes the steps that are not necessary. For example, 3ds Max will not add steps on the straight lines when **Optimize** is selected. When **Adaptive** is selected, the **Steps** parameter becomes inactive. It sets the number of steps for each spline to produce smooth looking result. Fig. 14 shows the wireframe view of the spline mesh created using the **Optimize** and **Adaptive** options, respectively.

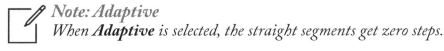

Note: Adaptive
*When **Adaptive** is selected, the straight segments get zero steps.*

Note: Creation Method Rollout
*Many spline shapes in 3ds Max allow you to use a creation method. You already know about the **Line** spline's creation methods. The **Text** and **Star** splines do not have a **Creation Method** rollout. Most of the spline primitives have the **Edge** and **Center** creation methods. If the **Edge** method is selected, the first click defines a point on the side or at a corner of the shape and then you drag a diameter or drag to a diagonal point. In the **Center** method, the first click defines the center of the shape and then you drag a corner point or radius.*

Rectangle Spline

It creates square or rectangular splines [see Fig. 15]. If you want to create a square spline, press and hold **Ctrl** while dragging in a viewport. To create a rectangular spline, first select a creation method and then drag the mouse pointer in a viewport to create a rectangle. Table 5 summarizes the parameters available in the **Parameters** rollout of the **Rectangular** spline:

Table 5: Parameters in the **Parameters** rollout of the **Rectangular** spline	
Parameters	**Description**
Length, Width	The **Length** and **Width** parameters specify the size of the rectangle along the **Y** and **X** axes, respectively.
Corner Radius	The **Corner Radius** parameter allows you to create rounded corners. See right-most spline in Fig. 15.

Circle Spline

It allows you to create close circular splines made up of four vertices [see Fig. 16]. To create a circular spline, first select the creation method and then drag the mouse pointer in a viewport to draw a circle. Table 6 summarizes the parameters available in the **Parameters** rollout of the **Circle** spline.

Table 6: Parameter in the **Parameters** rollout of the **Circle** spline	
Parameter	**Description**
Radius	The **Radius** parameter specifies the center to edge distance of the circle.

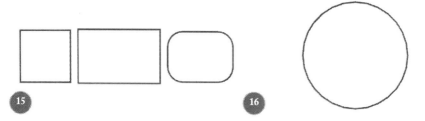

Ellipse Spline

You can use it to create circular or elliptical splines [see Fig. 17]. If you want to create a circular spline, press and hold **Ctrl** while dragging in the viewport. To create an elliptical spline, first select the creation method and then drag the mouse pointer in the viewport to draw the ellipse. Table 7 summarizes the parameters available in the **Parameters** rollout of the **Ellipse** spline:

Table 7: Parameters in the **Parameters** rollout of the **Ellipse** spline	
Parameters	**Description**
Length, Width	The **Length** and **Width** controls specify the size of the ellipse along the local **Y** and **Z** axes, respectively.
Outline, Thickness	The **Outline** check box lets you create an elliptical outline, see middle spline in Fig. 17. The **Thickness** parameter lets you specify the thickness of the ellipse.

Arc Spline

You can use the **Arc** spline to create open and closed partial circles made up of four vertices [see Fig. 18].

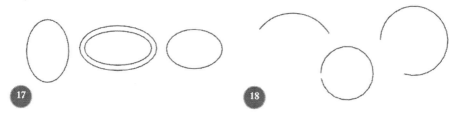

Creation Method Rollout

The **Arc** spline provides two methods for creating arcs: **End-End-Middle** and **Center-End-End**. To create an arc using the **End-End-Middle** method, make sure **End-End-Middle** is selected in the **Creation Method** rollout and then drag in the viewport to define the two ends of the arc. Now, release the mouse button. Next, move the mouse pointer up or down to specify the third point between the two end points.

To create an arc using the **Center-End-End** method, make sure **Center-End-End** is selected in the **Creation Method** rollout and then click to set the radial center of the arc. Drag the mouse pointer and click to specify the start point of the arc. Now, move the mouse and click to specify the other end of the arc. Table 8 summarizes the parameters available in the **Parameters** rollout of the **Arc** spline.

Table 8: Parameters in the **Parameters** rollout of the **Arc** spline	
Parameter	**Description**
Radius	**Radius** specifies the radius of the arc.
From, To	**From** specifies the location of the start point which is measured as angle from the local positive Y-axis. **To** specifies the location of the end point which is measured as angle from the local positive X-axis.
Pie Slice	When **Pie Slice** is on, it creates straight segments from the endpoints to the radial center which results in closed spline [see Fig. 19].
Reverse	When **Reverse** is on, the direction of the **Arc** spline is reversed.

Donut Spline

It creates the donut like shape of two concentric circles [see Fig. 20]. To create a **Donut** spline, first select a creation method. Drag the mouse pointer and then release the mouse button to define the first circle of the donut. Move the mouse pointer and then click to define the second concentric donut circle.

Table 9 summarizes the parameters available in the **Parameters** rollout of the **Donut** spline:

Table 9: Controls in the **Parameters** rollout of the **Donut** spline	
Parameters	**Description**
Radius 1, Radius 2	The **Radius 1** and **Radius 2** parameters specify the radius of the first and second circle, respectively.

NGon Spline

It creates flat sided splines with N number of sides and vertices [see Fig. 21]. To create an **NGon** spline, select a creation method and then drag the mouse pointer in a viewport. Release the mouse button to create the spline. Table 10 summarizes the parameters available in the **Parameters** rollout of the **NGon** spline.

Table 10: Controls in the **Parameters** rollout of the **NGon** spline

Parameters	Description
Radius, Inscribed, Circumscribed	The **Radius** parameter specifies the distance from the radial center to the edge of the NGon. If **Inscribed** is on [default], the distance is measured from the radial center to the corners. If **Circumscribed** is on, the distance is measured from the radial center to the side centers.
Sides	**Sides** specifies the number of sides which ranges from **3** to **100**.
Corner Radius	**Corner Radius** controls rounding applied to the corners of the NGon.
Circular	When **Circular** is on, 3ds Max creates a circular NGon which is equivalent to a circular spline but it may contain more than four vertices. The **Circle** spline creates a circular spline object with four control vertices.

Star Spline

It creates closed star-shaped splines with any number of points [see Fig. 22]. To create a **Star** spline, drag the mouse pointer and then release the mouse button to define the first radius. Move the mouse pointer and then click to define the second radius. The second radius can be less, equal, or greater than the first radius depending on how you moved the mouse pointer.

Table 11 summarizes the parameters available in the **Parameters** rollout of the **Star** spline.

Table 11: Parameters in the **Parameters** rollout of the **Star** spline

Parameters	Description
Radius 1, Radius 2	The **Radius 1** and **Radius 2** parameters specify the first set of vertices [created with the first drag] and second set of vertices, respectively.
Points	**Points** controls the number of points on the star. **Distortion** allows you to produce a sawtooth effect. This effect is generated by rotating **Radius 2** vertices about the center of the star.
Fillet Radius 1, Fillet Radius 2	**Fillet Radius 1** and **Fillet Radius 2** let you smooth the first and second set of vertices, respectively. The rounding is created by producing two **Bezier** vertices per point.

Text Spline

It creates splines in the shape of the text [see Fig. 23]. The text can be created using any **Windows** font [both **TrueType** and **OpenType**] installed on your system as well using the **Type 1 PostScript** font installed in the **Fonts** folder of the 3ds Max installation folder.

To create text, enter the text in the **Text** text box and then either click in a viewport to place the text or drag the mouse pointer to place the text and then release the mouse button. Table 12 summarizes the parameters available in the **Parameters** rollout of the **Text** spline.

Table 12: Parameters in the **Parameters** rollout of the **Text** spline	
Parameter	**Description**
Text Parameters	From this rollout, you can choose the font, font size, text alignment, kerning [distance between letters], and leading [distance between lines] for the text that you enter in the **Text** text box. The **Text** text box does not support word-wrap however you can paste multiple lines from the clipboard.

Helix Spline

It creates spiral like shapes [see Fig. 24]. To create a **Helix** spline, click and drag the mouse pointer to set the starting point as well as its starting radius [**Center** creation method] or diameter [**Edge** creation method]. Now, move the mouse pointer vertically and then click to define the height. Move the mouse pointer and then click to define the end radius. Table 13 summarizes the parameters available in the **Parameters** rollout of the **Helix** spline.

23 24

Table 13: Parameters in the **Parameters** rollout of the **Helix** spline	
Parameters	**Description**
Radius 1, Radius 2	The **Radius 1** and **Radius 2** parameters specify the radius of helix start and end, respectively. **Height** controls the height of the helix.
Turns	**Turns** specifies the number of turns in the helix.
Bias	**Bias** forces the turns in the helix to accumulate at the one end of the helix. Fig. 25 shows the rendered helix with **Bias** set to **-1, 0.2**, and **1**, respectively.
CC and CCW	**CC** and **CCW** specify whether helix should turn clockwise or counterclockwise.

Egg Spline

It creates an egg shaped spline [see Fig. 26]. To create an **Egg** spline, drag the mouse pointer vertically to define the initial dimension of the egg. Now, drag horizontally to change the orientation [angle] of the egg. Release the mouse button to compete the creation process. Table 14 summarizes the parameters available in the **Parameters** rollout of the **Egg** spline.

Table 14: Parameters in the **Parameters** rollout of the **Egg** spline

Parameter	Description
Length, Width	The **Length** and **Width** parameters specify the length and width of the egg along its long and short axes, respectively.
Outline, Thickness	When **Outline** is on, **Thickness** sets the distance between the main shape of the egg and its outline.
Angle	**Angle** specifies the angle of rotation around shape's local Z axis. When **Angle** is equal to **0**, the narrow end of the egg is at the top.

Section Spline

The **Section** spline is a special type of spline that lets you generate splines based on a cross-sectional slice through a geometry. To create a **Section** shape, click **Section** from the **Object Type** rollout and then drag a section plane in the viewport. Now, place and orient the plane in the viewport using transformation tools [see Fig. 27]. Notice a yellow line is displayed where the section intersects the mesh. Now, on the **Section Parameters** rollout, click **Create Shape**. In the **Name Section Shape** dialog box that appears, type the name for the spline and then click **OK**. Now, select the shape in the **Scene Explorer** and then move it away using the **Move** tool [see Fig. 28]. Table 15 summarizes the parameters available in the **Section Parameters** rollout of the **Section** spline.

Table 15: Parameters in the **Section Parameters** rollout of the **Section** spline

[Group]/ Parameter	Description
Create Shape	When you click this button, a shape is created based on the currently displayed intersection lines. The shape generated is an editable spline.
[Update]	The parameters in this group specify when the intersection line is updated.
When Section Moves	It updates the intersection line when you move or resize the section shape.
When Section Selected	It updates the intersection line when you select the section shape. Click **Update Section** to update the intersection.
Manually	It updates the intersection line only when you click **Update Section**.
[Section Events]	These parameters let you specify the extents of the cross section.
Infinite	When on, the selected plane is infinite in all directions [see Fig. 29].
Section Boundary	When on, the cross section is generated only for objects that are within or touched by the boundary of the section shape [see Fig. 30].
Off	No cross section is displayed or generated.
Color Swatch	You can use it to change the display color of the intersection.

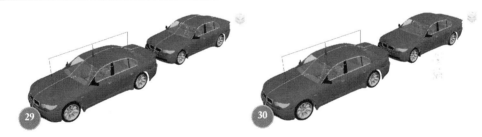

Section Size Rollout

The **Length** and **Width** parameters in the **Section Size** rollout control the size of the section rectangle.

Freehand Spline

You can use the **Freehand** spline to create hand-drawn splines directly in the viewport. You can use mouse or any other pointing device to draw the spline. You can also draw it on the selected objects in the viewport; it will automatically follow the contours. Table 16 summarizes the parameters available in the **Freehand Spline** rollout of the **Freehand** spline.

Table 16: Parameters in the **Freehand Spline** rollout of the **Freehand** spline

[Group]/ Parameter	Description
Show Knots	When on, the knots are displayed on the spline [see the right image in Fig. 31].
[Create Group]	
Granularity	Defines the number of cursor position samples taken before a knot is created.
Threshold	Defines how far the cursor must move before a knot is created. The higher the value you specify, the more the distance between the knots will be.
Constrain	When on, you can constrain the spline to the selected objects. To constrain the spline, select the objects in the viewport and then select **Constrain**. Selected objects will appear in the list box. You can pick additional objects using the **Pick Object** button. To clear the list, click **Clear**. Now, drag on the selected objects to constrain the spline [see Fig. 32].
[Options Group]	
Curved, Straight	You can use these settings to define whether the segments between the knots are curved or straight.
Closed	Select this check box to close the spline.
Normals	When on, 3ds Max shows the resulting normals of the constrained spline in the viewport [see the right image in Fig. 32].
Offset	You can use **Offset** to control the distance between the spline and the surface of the constraining object.
[Statistics Group]	
# of Splines	Displays the number of splines in the shape.
Orig Knots	Displays the number of knots automatically created while drawing the spline.
New Knots	Displays the new number of knots.

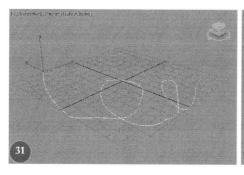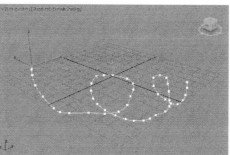

31

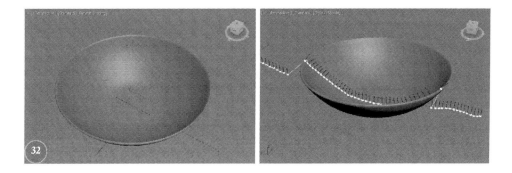

Extended Spline Primitives

In this section, I will explain the extended spline primitives. Let's start with the **WRectangle** spline.

WRectangle Spline

The **WRectangle** spline [walled rectangle] lets you create a closed shape from two concentric rectangles. Each rectangle is made up of four vertices [see Fig. 33]. To create a **WRectangle** spline, drag the mouse pointer in a viewport and then release the mouse button to define the outer rectangle. Move the mouse pointer and then click to define the inner rectangle.

Table 17 summarizes the parameters available in the **Parameters** rollout of the **WRectangle** spline.

Table 17: Parameters in the **Parameters** rollout of the **WRectangle** spline	
Parameters	**Description**
Length, Width	These parameters define the length and width of the **WRectangle** section, respectively.
Thickness	Controls the thickness of the **WRectangle** section.
Sync Corner Fillets	When on, the value specified for **Corner Radius 1** is used for both the interior and exterior corners.
Corner Radius 1	When **Sync Corner Fillets** is off, it controls the radius of the exterior corners.
Corner Radius 2	This parameter is only available when **Sync Corner Fillets** is off. It controls the radius of the interior corners.

Channel Spline

It creates a closed C shaped spline [see Fig. 34]. To create a **Channel** spline, drag the mouse pointer in a viewport and then release the mouse button to define the outer perimeter. Move the mouse pointer and then click to define the thickness of the walls of the channel. Table 18 summarizes the parameters available in the **Parameters** rollout of the **Channel** spline.

Parameter	Description
Length, Width	These parameters define the length and width of the channel section.
Thickness	Controls the thickness of the channel section.
Sync Corner Fillets	When on, the value specified for **Corner Radius 1** is used for both the interior and exterior corners.
Corner Radius 1	When **Sync Corner Fillets** is off, it controls the radius of the exterior corners.
Corner Radius 2	This parameter is only available when **Sync Corner Fillets** is off. It controls the radius of the interior corners.

Table 18: Parameters in the **Parameters** rollout of the **Channel** spline

Angle Spline

It creates a closed L shaped spline [see Fig. 35]. To create an **Angle** spline, drag the mouse pointer in a viewport and then release the mouse button to define the initial size of the angle. Move the mouse pointer and then click to define the thickness of the walls of the angle. Table 19 summarizes the parameters available in the **Parameters** rollout of the **WRectangle** spline.

34   35

Parameter	Description
Length, Width	These parameters define the height and width of the vertical and horizontal legs, respectively.
Thickness	Controls the thickness of the legs of the angle.
Sync Corner Fillets	When on, the value specified for **Corner Radius 1** controls the radius for both the vertical and horizontal legs.
Corner Radius 1	When **Sync Corner Fillets** is off, it controls the exterior radius between the vertical and horizontal legs of the spline.

Table 19: Parameters in the **Parameters** rollout of the **Angle** spline

Table 19: Parameters in the **Parameters** rollout of the **Angle** spline	
Parameter	**Description**
Corner Radius 2	This parameter is only available when **Sync Corner Fillets** is off. It controls the interior radius between the vertical and horizontal legs of the spline.
Edge Radii	Controls the interior radius at the outermost edges of the vertical and horizontal legs.

Tee Spline

It creates a closed T shaped spline [see Fig. 36]. To create a **Tee** spline, drag the mouse pointer in a viewport and then release the mouse button to define the initial size of the tee. Move the mouse pointer and then click to define the thickness of the walls of the tee. Table 20 summarizes the parameters available in the **Parameters** rollout of the **Tee** spline.

Table 20: Parameters in the **Parameters** rollout of the **Tee** spline	
Parameter	**Description**
Length, Width	These parameters define the height and width of the vertical web and flange crossing, respectively.
Thickness	Controls the thickness of the web and flange.
Corner Radius	Controls the radius of the two interior corners between the vertical web and horizontal flange.

Wide Flange Spline

It creates a closed I shaped spline [see Fig. 37]. To create a **Wide Flange** spline, drag the mouse pointer in a viewport and then release the mouse button to define the initial size of the wide flange. Move the mouse pointer and then click to define the thickness of the walls of the wide flange. Table 21 summarizes the parameters available in the **Parameters** rollout of the **Wide Flange** spline.

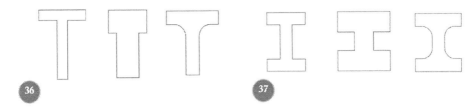

36   37

Table 21: Parameters in the **Parameters** rollout of the **Wide Flange** spline	
Parameter	**Description**
Length, Width	These controls define the height and width of the vertical web and horizontal flange crossing, respectively.
Thickness	Controls the thickness of the wide flenges.

Table 21: Parameters in the **Parameters** rollout of the **Wide Flange** spline	
Parameter	**Description**
Corner Radius	Controls the radius of the two interior corners between the vertical web and horizontal flanges.

Editing Splines

You can convert a spline object to an editable spline object. The editable spline object allows you to create complex shapes using the three sub-object levels that this object provides: **Vertex, Spline**, and **Segment**. The vertices define points and curve tangents. The segments connects vertices. The splines are made up of one or more connected segments.

You can convert a spline object into an **Editable Spline** object by using one of the following methods:

1. Select a spline in a viewport and then go to the **Modify** panel. Next, **RMB** click on the spline entry in the stack display and then choose **Editable Spline** from the pop up menu displayed [see Fig. 38].
2. Select a spline in a viewport and then **RMB** click. Choose **Transform** [in lower right quadrant] > **Convert To:** > **Convert to Editable Spline** [see Fig. 39].
3. Select a spline in a viewport and then apply the **Edit Spline** modifier to it.
4. Import a **.shp** file to the scene.
5. Merge a shape from a 3ds Max file.

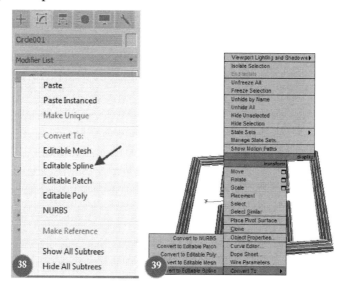

Selecting Sub-objects

You can select sub-objects using one of the following ways:

1. Expand the spline object's hierarchy from the stack display and then choose a sub-object level [see Fig. 40].
2. Click a selection button from the **Selection** rollout [see Fig. 40].
3. **RMB** click on a spline object in a viewport and then choose the sub-object level from the upper left quadrant of the **Quad** menu displayed [see Fig. 41].
4. Choose a selection or transform tool and then click on the sub-objects in a viewport using the standard selection techniques.

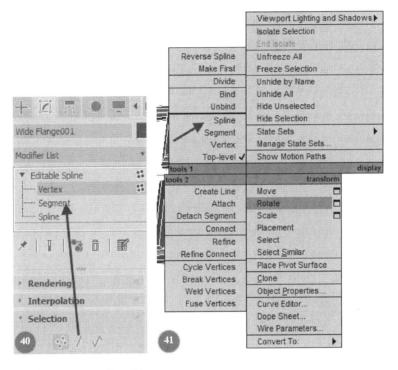

Note: Cloning sub-objects

*You can clone the sub-objects by first selecting them and then press and hold **Shift** while transforming them.*

Note: Adding and removing from the selection

*To select a segment, vertex, or spline, click it. To add to the sub-object selection, press and hold **Ctrl** and click. You can also drag a selection region to select a group of sub-objects. To subtract from the sub-object selection, press and hold **Alt** and click. You can also drag a selection region to deselect a group of sub-objects.*

Vertex Level

Vertices define points and curve tangents for a spline object. To select a vertex type, select vertex or vertices and then **RMB** click. Now, choose the required level from the upper left quadrant of the **Quad** menu [see Fig. 42]. Table 22 shows the list of vertex types available in 3ds Max.

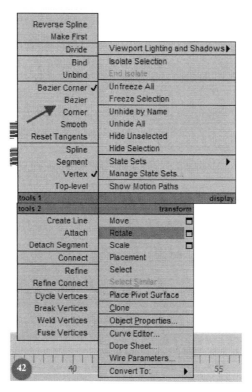

Table 22: The vertex types	
Type	**Description**
Corner	Creates non-adjustable vertices that generates sharp corners [see Fig. 43].
Bezier	Creates adjustable vertices with locked continuous tangent handles that produces a smooth curve. The curvature is determined by the direction and magnitude of the tangent handles [see Fig. 44]. You can adjust the tangent handles using the **Move** and **Rotate** tools.
Bezier Corner	Creates adjustable vertices with discontinuous tangent handles that produces a sharp corner [see Fig. 45]. The curvature is determined by the direction and magnitude of the tangent handles. You can adjust the tangent handles using the **Move** and **Rotate** tools.
Smooth	Creates non-adjustable vertices that generates smooth continuous curves. The curvature is determined by the spacing between the adjacent vertices [see Fig. 46].

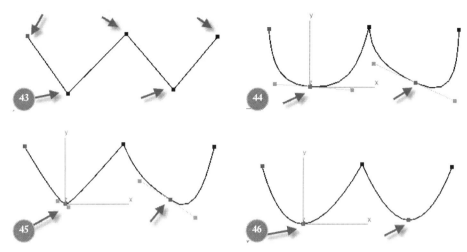

 Tip: Resetting tangents
*To reset the tangent position, **RMB** click on the vertex or vertices and then choose **Reset Tangents** from the upper left quadrant of the **Quad** menu.*

 Tip: Vertex types in the Quad menu
*If you are at the **Vertex** sub-object level, the vertex types are always displayed in the **Quad** menu. The mouse pointer doesn't have to be exactly over the vertices.*

Selection Rollout

The parameters in this rollout allow you to select sub-object levels of a spline, work with named selection sets and tangent handles, and display settings. Also, you can see information about the selected entities in this rollout.

At the top of the rollout, there are three buttons: **Vertex**, **Segment**, and **Spline**. These buttons let you select sub-object levels of a spline. The **Copy** and **Paste** parameters in the **Named Selections** rollout allow you to place selection into the copy buffer and paste selection from the copy buffer, respectively.

Generally, you can transform bezier handles of a single vertex in the viewport even if multiple vertices are selected. If you want to simultaneously transform bezier handles of multiple vertices, select the **Lock Handles** check box. When **Alike** is on, as you drag handle of an incoming or outgoing vector, all incoming and outgoing handles move simultaneously [except the broken tangents]. If you select the **All** parameter, any handle you move will affect all other handles regardless of whether they are broken.

 Tip: Breaking Tangents
*To break a tangent and move its handles independently, click on the tangent with **Shift** held down.*

Caution: Breaking Tangents
*To break a tangent, the **Alike** must be turned on.*

When the **Area Selection** check box is selected, you can define a radius in the associated spinner. When you click a vertex, all vertices that fall with in the specified radius of the clicked vertex will be selected. When the **Segment End** check box is selected, you can select a vertex by clicking on a point on the segment close to the vertex. You can add to the selection using **Ctrl**. The **Select By** button allows you to select vertices on the selected spline or segment. You need to first select a spline or segment using the **Spline** or **Segment** sub-object level and then you need to switch to the **Vertex** sub-object level. Click **Select By** to open the **Select By** dialog box. Now, click the desired button on the dialog box to select the vertices.

The **Show Vertex Numbers** check box toggles the display of vertex numbers in the viewport. The numbers are displayed next to the selected spline's vertices. If you select **Selected Only**, the vertex number only appears for the selected vertices.

Geometry Rollout

Now, let's explore the options available for editing the editable spline object at sub-object levels. These options are listed in the **Geometry** rollout.

New Vertex Type Group

The parameters in this group let you choose the type of tangency for vertices that are created when you clone segments or splines using the **Shift** key.

Caution: Scope
*These parameters have no effect on the tangency of the vertices created using tools such as **Create Line**, **Refine**, and so on. **Linear** sets linear tangency for the new vertices. **Smooth** sets smooth tangency. When on, the new overlapping vertices will be welded together. **Bezier Corner** sets the **Bezier** corner tangency.*

Note: Editable spline - object level
*The following parameters are also available at the editable spline object level: **New Vertex Type** group, **Create Line**, **Attach**, **Attach Mult.**, **Cross Section**, **Automatic Welding**, and **Insert**. This level is the one that is active when no sub-object level is selected.*

To use the **Connect Copy** feature, create a **Circle** spline and then convert it to editable spline. Activate the **Segment** sub-object level and then select the segments, as shown in the left image of Fig. 45. Select the **Connect** check box in the **Connect Copy** group. Now, invoke the **Scale** tool and then scale the segments outward with **Shift** held down. Max connects the newly created vertices with the original vertices [see the right image in Fig. 47].

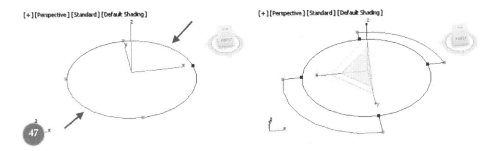

Create Line

Create Line adds more lines to the existing selected spline. The lines are separate splines but are part of the selected spline. To add another spline to the selected spline, select the existing spline and then create the new spline in the same way as you create the line spline.

Break

Break allows you to split a spline at the selected vertex or vertices. To split a spline, select one or more vertices and then click **Break**. Two overlapping vertices will be created at the break point. Use the **Move** tool to separate the vertices [see Fig. 48].

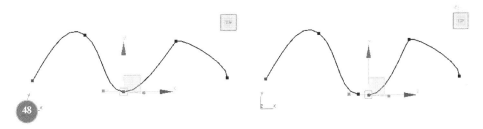

Attach

Attach attaches another spline object from the scene to the selected spline to create a compound shape. To attach a spline, select the spline and then click **Attach**. Now, hover the mouse pointer on the target spline. When the shape of the mouse pointer changes, click on the target spline to attach it to the selected spline. When you attach shapes, the materials assigned to the two objects are combined. Here's how:

- If the target object does not have a material assigned, it inherits the material from the selected object.
- If the selected object does not have a material assigned, it inherits the material from the target object.
- If both objects have materials, the **Attach Options** dialog box appears [see Fig. 49]. Select the desired options from the dialog box and then click **OK**. The resulting material will be a **Multi-Subobject** material.

Caution: Target shape's creation parameters
The target shape loses all its creation parameters. If there is any modifier stack attached to the target shape, it will be collapsed.

Attach Multiple

Attach Multiple lets you attach multiple shapes to a selected spline in a single operation. To understand this feature, select a spline object and then click **Attach Multiple**. Now, select the shapes in the **Attach Multiple** dialog box that appears [see Fig. 50] and click **OK** to attach the selected shapes.

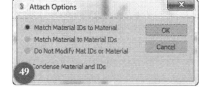

Note: Reorienting attached splines

*When **Reorient** is on, the attached splines are reoriented so that the local coordinate system of the attached splines is aligned with the selected spline.*

Cross Section

Cross Section allows you to create a spline cage out of cross sectional shapes. To create spline cage, make sure that all splines are attached. Click **Cross Section** and then click on the first spline, then second, and so on. **RMB** click to complete the process and create a cage [see Fig. 51].

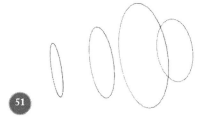

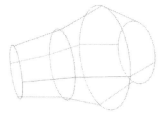

Tip: Keeping vertices together
*If you want to edit the spline cage, select **Area Selection** in the **Selection** rollout before selecting the vertices otherwise you would not be able to keep their position together.*

Refine

Refine adds vertices to the spline object without changing the curvature of the spline. To add vertices, click **Refine** and then hover the mouse pointer on the segments in a viewport. The shape of the mouse pointer changes on the eligible segments. Now, click to add a vertex. When you are done, click **Refine** again or press **RMB**.

If you click on an existing vertex, 3ds Max displays the **Refine & Connect** dialog box asking if you want to refine the vertex or connect to the vertex. If you choose **Connect Only**, a new vertex will not be created instead the clicked vertex will be connected to the existing vertex.

Caution: Connecting vertices
*You must select **Connect** before clicking **Refine**.*

The type of vertex created during the **Refine** operation is dependent on the bordering vertices of the segment:

- If bordering vertices are smooth, a vertex of **Smooth** type is created.
- If bordering vertices are of **Corner** type, a vertex of **Corner** type is created.
- If either of the bordering vertices are of a **Corner** or **Bezier Corner** type, a vertex of **Bezier Corner** type is created.
- If the bordering vertices do not fit in the above mentioned criterion, a vertex of **Bezier** type is created.

Connect: It creates a new spline sub-object by connecting the two vertices.

To understand functioning of **Connect**, create two straight lines in a viewport and attach them [see Fig. 52]. Select the **Vertex** sub-object level. Select **Connect**. Notice that there are some options that get activated in the **Refine** group. Now, click **Refine** and then click on the first segment. Now, click on the second segment [see Fig. 53], **RMB** click to create to connect two vertices [see Fig. 54].

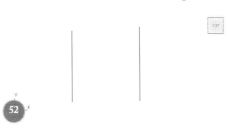

When **Linear** is on, the **Refine** operation creates straight lines using the vertices of the **Corner** type. When off, the created vertices are of **Smooth** type. **Closed** allows you to create closed splines by connecting the first and last vertices [see Fig. 55, numbers show clicking order].

When **Bind first** is on, it sets the first vertex created to be bound to the center of the selected segment [see Fig. 56]. **Bind last** sets the last vertex created to be bound to the center of the selected segment.

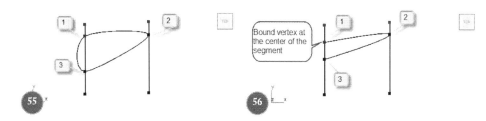

> ### Note: Bound vertices
> *Binding vertices helps in connecting splines when building a spline network for use with the **Surface** modifier. To distinguish the bound vertices from the standard vertices, 3ds Max makes them black. You cannot transform a bound vertex directly. However, you can move it by shifting the connected vertices. You can also change the type of the bound vertices from the upper left quadrant of the **Quad** menu.*

Automatic Welding

When on, the end vertex is welded automatically, if you move or place the vertex and the vertex fall within a distance specified using **Threshold Dist**.

> ### Note: Automatic welding
> *This feature is available at the object as well as at all the sub-object levels.*

Weld

Weld welds two end vertices or two adjacent vertices into a single vertex. To weld vertices, move the vertices close to each other and click **Weld**. If the vertices fall within a threshold defined by the spinner next to **Weld**, the selected vertices are welded to a single vertex [see Fig. 57].

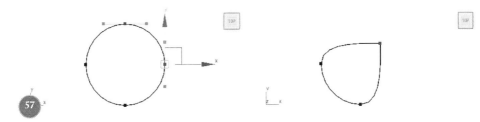

Connect

Connect connects two end vertices. To connect the vertices, click **Connect** and then drag the mouse pointer from one end vertex to another end vertex. It creates a linear segment by ignoring the tangent values of the end vertices. To connect the end points, click **Connect** and hover the cursor over one of the end vertex. When shape of the cursor changes, drag mouse pointer to the other end vertex to make the connection.

Insert

Insert lets you add one or more vertices creating additional segments in a spline. Click **Insert** and then click on the spline to attach the mouse pointer to the spline. Now, click to place the vertex; the spline gets attached with the mouse pointer. Now, continue clicking to create more vertices. **RMB** click to complete the operation. You are still in the insert mode, you can continue adding vertices on another segment or you can **RMB** click to exit. A single click creates a corner vertex whereas dragging the mouse pointer creates a bezier vertex.

Make First

It allows you to define which vertex in a spline is the first vertex. The first vertex in a spline is indicated by a small box around it. To make a vertex first vertex, select the vertex and then click **Make First**. If you are editing an open spline, the first vertex should be end point that is already not a first vertex. On closed spline, you can make any vertex first vertex. The first vertex has special significance in many operations in 3ds Max. Table 23 summarizes the importance of first vertex.

Table 23: First vertex use	
Use	**Description**
Loft Path	Indicates the start of the path [Level 0].
Loft Shape	Controls the initial skin alignment.
Path Constraint	Indicates the start of the path [indicates 0% on the location of the path].
Trajectory	Indicates the first position key.

Fuse

Fuse lets you move all selected vertices to their averaged center. To fuse the vertices, select them [first attach all splines] and then click **Fuse** to move the vertices to same location [see Fig. 58]. Note that the **Fuse** operation does not weld the vertices, it simply moves them to the same location.

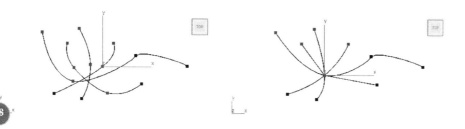

Cycle

Cycle allows you to select a specific vertex from the group of coincident vertices [vertices that shares the same location]. To select a specific vertex, select one or more vertices that share the same location, and then click **Cycle** repeatedly until you select the vertex you are looking for. Fuse two or three splines and then use **Cycle** to select the coincident vertices. Check the info about the selected vertex at the bottom of the **Selection** rollout.

CrossInsert

CrossInsert adds vertices at the intersection of two splines that are part of the same spline object. To add a vertex, click **CrossInsert** and then click at the intersection of the two splines. If the distance between the splines is within the threshold defined by the spinner next to **CrossInsert**, the vertices are added [they are not welded] to both splines [see Fig. 59].

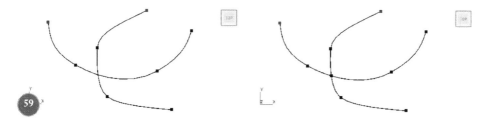

Fillet

Fillet lets you create the rounded corners by adding new control vertices. You can create rounded corners by dragging the mouse pointer in a viewport or by entering precise values in the spinner on the right of **Fillet**. To fillet the vertices, click **Fillet** and then drag the vertices in a viewport to add rounded corners [see Fig. 60]. As you drag with **Fillet**, the spinner on its right shows the fillet amount. You can continue dragging to add fillet to other vertices. To finish the operation, **RMB** click.

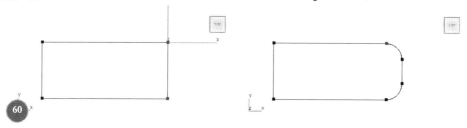

Chamfer

Chamfer chops off the selected vertices by creating segments connecting new vertices [see Fig. 61]. Like **Fillet** you can chamfer edges interactively or by entering precise values.

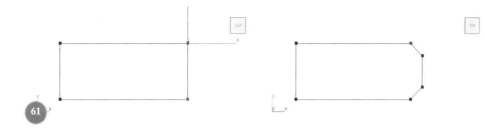

61

> *Note: Fillet/Chamfer functions*
> *Unlike the **Fillet/Chamfer** modifiers, you can apply these functions to any type of vertex. These modifiers only work with the **Corner** and **Bezier Corner** vertices.*

Tangent

The parameters available in this group let you copy paste vertex handles from one vertex to another. To copy tangent, select a vertex and then click **Copy**. Click on the tangent to copy tangent to the clipboard. Now, select another vertex, click **Paste**, and then click on the tangent of the vertex to paste the tangent [see Fig. 62]. When **Paste Length** is on, the length of the handle is also copied.

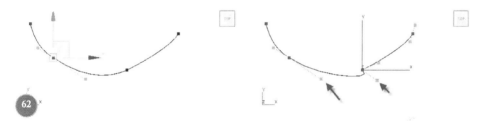

62

Hide

It allows you to hide the selected vertices and connected segments.

Unhide All

Unhide All allows you to unhide all hidden objects.

Bind/Unbind

Bind lets you create bound vertices. To create a bound vertex, click **Bind** and then drag from any end vertex to any segment expect the one connected to the vertex, a dashed line connects the vertex and the current mouse position. When the mouse is over an eligible segment, the pointer changes to a **Connect** symbol. When you release the mouse button, the vertex jumps to the center of the segment and bound to it. **Unbind** lets you disconnect the bind vertices.

Delete

Allows you to delete the selected vertices as well as one attached segment per deleted vertex.

Show selected segs

Lets you display the selected segments in red color at the **Vertex** sub-object level [see Fig. 63]. When off, the segments displayed in red only at **Segment** sub-object level.

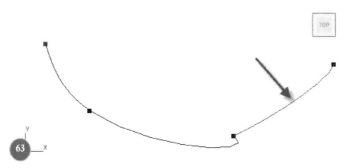

Segment Level

A segment is a part of spline between two vertices of the spline. You can select one or more segments by activating the **Segment** sub-object level. Once selected, you can transform them using the transformation tools.

Most of the parameters available for segments arc similar to those discussed in the **Vertex Level** group. The other parameters available at the segment sub-object level are discussed next.

Geometry Rollout

Divide

Divide subdivides the selected segment(s) by adding a number of vertices that are specified by using the spinner available on the right of this parameter. To subdivide a segment, select segment or segments of the spline. Now, specify the number of vertices and then click **Divide** [see Fig. 64]. The distance between the vertices is dependent on the curvature of the segment.

Delete

Deletes the selected segments from the spline [see Fig. 65].

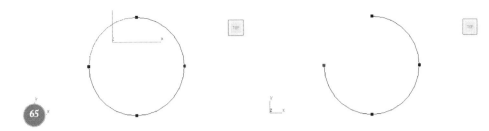

Detach

It lets you detach/copy selected segments from the spline. To detach segment or segments, select them and then click **Detach**. In the **Detach** dialog box that appears, type name in the **Detach as** text box and then click **OK**. The segment will be detached from the spline and new shape will be created [see Fig. 66].

There are some other parameters that can be used with the detach operation. Table 24 summarizes these options.

Table 24: The **Detach** options	
Parameter	**Description**
Same Shp	When on, **Reorient** gets deactivated. The detached segment remains part of the same spline. If **Copy** is also on, the detached segment is copied at the same location.
Reorient	When on, the detached segment copies the transformation values of the spline's creation local coordinate system.
Copy	Copies the selected segment without detaching it from the spline.

Surface Properties Rollout

The parameters in this layout allow you to apply different material IDs to spline segments. The material appears on the renderable shapes. To assign material ID to a segment or segments, select them and then enter the **ID** in the **Set ID** spinner. **Select ID** lets you select the segments corresponding to the material ID set in the spinner on the right of **Select ID**. The drop-down list below **Select ID** shows the name of the sub-materials, if you have applied **Multi-Subobject** material to the object. If you have applied a material other than the **Multi-Subobject** material, this drop-down list will be inactive.

When **Clear Selection** is on, selecting a new ID or material name deselects the previously selected segments or splines.

Changing Segment Properties

You can switch between the **Curve** or **Line** type for the selected segments. To change the type, select segments and then **RMB** click. Now, choose **Line** or **Curve** from the upper left quadrant of the **Quad** menu [see Fig. 67]. Fig. 68 shows a segment converted from the **Curve** type to the **Line** type.

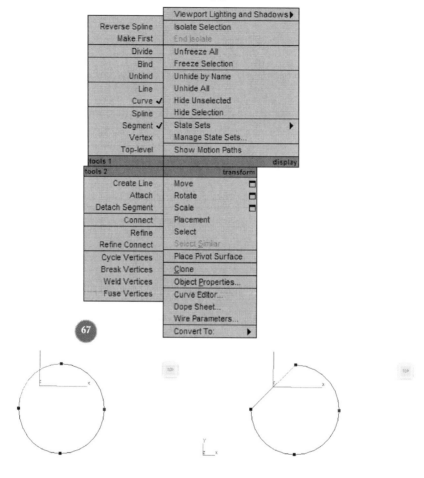

Spline Level

The **Spline** sub-object level allows you to select single spline or multiple splines in a single object. Once selected, you can transform them using the transformation tools. Most of the parameters available for segments are similar to those discussed in the **Vertex Level** and **Segment Level** sections. The other parameters available at the **Segment** sub-object level are discussed next.

Geometry Rollout
Connect Copy Group

Connect Copy works when you make a clone of the spline using **Shift**. You must select **Connect** before the cloning operation. When on, 3ds Max creates a new spline sub-object that connects the vertices of the original and cloned objects [see Fig. 69]. **Threshold** defines the distance that the soft selection uses during the **Connect Copy** operation.

Outline

Outline makes a copy of the spline. The copy offsets in all directions specified by the spinner on the right of **Outline**. You can also create an outline interactively by using the mouse. To create an outline, select one or more splines and then click **Outline**. Now, drag a spline to create outline [see Fig. 70]. When **Center** is on, the original spline and its outline moves away from an invisible center line by the distance specified by dragging operation or by the value specified for the spinner on the right of **Outline**.

Caution: Selecting splines
If there is one spline is in the scene, it is automatically selected for the outlining process. However, if you are using spinner to add outline, you must select it first.

Note: Open spline
If you are outlining an open spline, the outlining process creates a single closed spline [see Fig. 71].

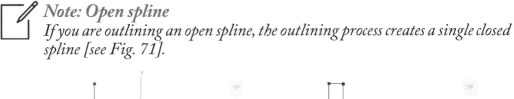

Boolean

Boolean combines two splines. It alters the first spline you select and deletes the other one. There are three types of **Boolean** operations available. Table 25 summarizes those operations.

Table 25: The boolean operations	
Operation	**Description**
Union	Combines two overlapping splines into a single spline. The overlapping portion is removed.
Subtraction	Subtracts the overlapping portion of the second spline from the first spline.
Intersection	Leaves the overlapping portions of the two splines.

To boolean splines, make sure both splines are part of a single spline object [use **Attach** to attach them]. Select a spline and then click **Union**, **Subtraction**, or **Intersection**. Now, click **Boolean**. Hover the mouse pointer on the second spline and then click when shape of the cursor changes to complete the operation [see Fig. 72].

Mirror
Mirror allows you to mirror splines horizontally, vertically, and diagonally. To mirror a spline, ensure it is selected and then click **Mirror Horizontally**, **Mirror Vertically**, or **Mirror Both**. Next, click **Mirror** to complete the operation [see Fig. 73].

If **Copy** is on, 3ds Max creates a mirror copy of the spline [see Fig. 74].

When **About Pivot** is on, 3ds Max mirrors the spline along its geometric center otherwise mirrors along the spline object's pivot point [see Fig. 75].

Trim

Trim allows you to clear the overlapping segments in a shape. The two splines must overlap each other and they should be part of the same spline object. To trim a spline, select the spline that will be used to trim the target spline. Click **Trim** and hover the cursor over the spline that you want to trim and then click when the shape of the cursor changes [see Fig. 76].

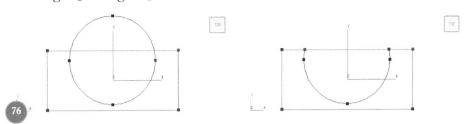

Extend

Extend allows you to extend an open spline. To extend spline, you need a segment that can extend to an intersecting segment of the spline. **Extend** does not work if intersection is not possible. To understand the **Extend** feature, create a circle and a line [see the left image in Fig. 77]. Convert the circle to an editable spline object and then attach it with the line. Select the **Spline** sub-object mode, click **Extend**. Now, click on the each end of the line to extend it to the circle [see the right image in Fig. 77]. When the **Infinite Bounds** check box is selected, 3ds Max treats open splines as infinite in length.

Explode

Explode breaks the segments of a selected spline and convert segments into separate splines or objects. There are two options available for the explode operation: **Splines** and **Objects**. If you choose **Objects**, the **Explode** dialog box appears. Type a name in the **Object Name** text box and click **OK**. Each successive object will use a name appended with an incremental three-digit number. For example, if you type name as **myShape** and click **OK**. The name of other objects will be: **myShape001**, **myShape002**, **myShape003**, and so on.

> *Note: Explode and Detach*
> **Explode** *is* **Detach** *on steroids.*

Changing the Spline Type

You can change the spline type from **Curve** to **Line** and visa-versa. To change type, select the spline and RMB click. Choose **Line** or **Curve** from the upper left quadrant of the **Quad** menu. Right image in Fig. 78 shows the spline object converted from **Curve** type into **Line** type.

Note: Checking self-intersecting splines

*You can use the **Shape Check** utility to check self-intersecting splines and NURBS curves. The self-intersecting shapes may produce unpredictable results when used in the loft, extrude, or lathed operations. To check intersection point, go to the **Utilities** panel and then click on **More** to open **Utilities** dialog box. Select **Shape Check** from the **Utilities** list and click **OK**. The **Shape Check** rollout appears in the **Utilities** panel. Click **Pick Object** and then click the spline or NURBS curve in a viewport. The red squares appear on the intersection points [see Fig. 79].*

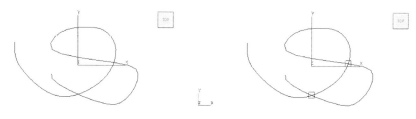

Hands-on Exercises

Exercise 1: Creating Bowling Pin and Ball
In this exercise, you will create model of the bowling pin and ball [see Fig. E1]. Table E1 summarizes the exercise.

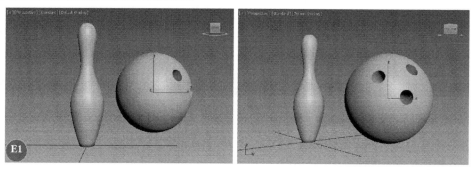

Table E1	
Skill level	Beginner
Time to complete	20 Minutes

Table E1	
Topics	• Specifying the Units for the Exercise • Creating the Bowling Pin • Creating the Ball
Resources folder	**unit-dm6**
Units	**Generic Units**
Final file	**pin-finish.max**

Specifying the Units for the Exercise

Follow these steps:

1. From the **Customize** menu choose **Units Setup**. In the **Units Setup** dialog box that appears, select **Generic Units** from the **Units Setup** dialog box. Click **OK** to accept the changes made.

2. From the **File** menu, choose **Save** to open the **Save File As** dialog box. In the **File name** text box type **pin-ball-finish.max** and then click **Save** to save the file.

Setting the Blueprint

Follow these steps:

1. Switch to the **Create** panel, click **Geometry**, then click **Plane**. In the **Front** viewport, create a plane. In the **Modify** panel > **Parameters** rollout, change **Length** to **100** and **Width** to **75**. Invoke the **Move** tool from the **Main** toolbar. Set the **Transform Type-In** boxes to **0** in the **Status Bar** to place the box at the origin [see Fig. E2]. Also, clear the **Real-World Map Size** check box, if not already clear.

2. Click **Material Editor** from the **Main** toolbar. Create a **Standard** material and apply it to the plane. Use the **pin-reference.jpeg** for the **Diffuse** map. RMB click on the material node and then choose **Show Shaded Material in the Viewport** option to display the image on the plane in the viewport. Select the **Bitmap** node and then in the **Parameter Editor** > **Coordinates** rollout, make sure **Use Real-World Scale** is off and **U Tiling** and **V Tiling** are set to **1** each. Change **V Offset** to **-0.043**. Select the material node and then in the **Parameter Editor** > **Blinn Basic Parameters** rollout, change **Opacity** to **50**.

3. In the **Front** viewport, change display mode to **Default Shading** [see Fig. E3]. RMB click on the plane and then choose **Object Properties** from the **Quad** menu. Select the **Freeze** check box from the **Interactivity** area and clear the **Show Frozen in Gray** check box from the **Display Properties** area. Click **OK**.

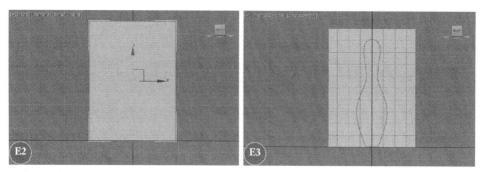

Creating the Bowling Pin

Follow these steps:

1. In the **Create** panel, click **Shapes**, and then click **Line**. Using the **Line** tool, create a half profile of the pin and then move the spline to the right [see Fig. E4]. In the **Modify** panel > **Selection** rollout, click **Vertex** to activate the vertex sub-object level.

2. Select all vertices except the first and last vertex and then **RMB** click; choose **Smooth** from the **Quad** menu > **tools 1** quadrant [see Fig. E5].

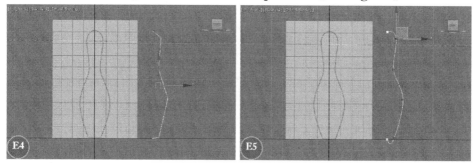

3. In the **Modify** panel > **Selection** rollout, click **Segment** to activate the segment sub-object level. Select the segment, as shown in Fig. E6. **RMB** click; choose **Line** from the **Quad** menu > **tools 1** quadrant. Now, align the bottom two points [see Fig. E7].

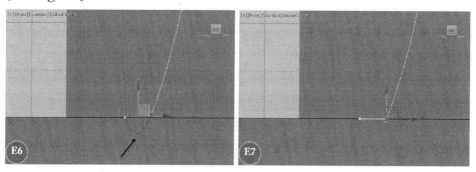

4. Move the line back on the profile and adjust the shape using the **Move** tool. Make sure that the start and end vertices are at same X position [see Fig. E8]. From the **Object-Space Modifiers** section of the **Modifier** list, select **Lathe**. In the **Modify** panel > **Parameters** rollout > **Align** group, click **Min**. Now, select

the **Weld Core** check box and change **Segments** to **32** [see Fig. E9]. Now, hide the plane using the **Scene Explorer** [see Fig. E10].

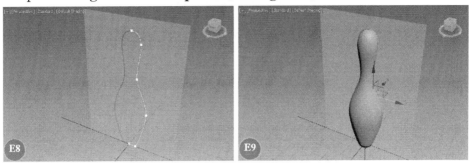

Creating the Ball
Follow these steps:

1. In the **Create** panel, click **Geometry**, and then in the **Object Type** rollout, click **Sphere**. In the **Perspective** viewport, create a sphere. Switch to the **Modify** panel and on the **Parameters** rollout, change **Radius** to **35** and **Segments** to **45**.

2. In the **Create** panel, click **Geometry**, and then in the **Object Type** rollout, click **Sphere**. Select the **AutoGrid** check box and then create **3** spheres on the surface of the sphere we just created [see Fig. E11]. Change radius of all small spheres to **5**.

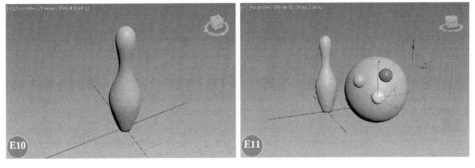

3. Change coordinate system to **Local** and then invoke the **Scale** tool. Now, scale the spheres about **350** units [see Fig. 12].

4. Select the bigger sphere. In the **Create** panel, click **Geometry**, and then choose **Compound Objects** from the drop-down list located below **Geometry**. Click **ProBoolean** and then make sure that **Subtraction** is selected in the **Parameters** rollout > **Operation** group. Click **Start Picking** and then click on small sphere one-be-one to create holes [see Fig. 13]. Click the **Start Picking** button again to finish the operation.

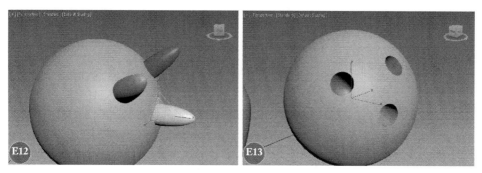

Exercise 2: Creating the Apple Logo

In this exercise, you will create 3D Apple logo [see Fig. E1].

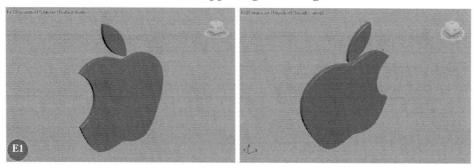

Table E2 summarizes the exercise.

Table E2	
Skill level	Basic
Time to complete	30 Minutes
Topics	• Getting Started • Creating the Logo
Resources folder	**unit-dm6**
Units	**Generic Units**
Final file	**logo-finish.max**

Getting Started

Follow these steps:

1. From the **Customize** menu choose **Units Setup**. In the **Units Setup** dialog box that opens, select the **Generic Units** option from the **Display Unit Scale** group.

2. Go to the **Create** panel, click **Geometry**, and then click **Plane**. In the **Front** viewport, create a plane. In the **Modify** panel > **Parameters** rollout, set **Length** to **180** and **Width** to **150**. Set **Length Segs** and **Width Segs** to **2** each. Also, clear the **Real-World Map Size** check box, if not already clear. Invoke the **Move** tool from the **Main** toolbar. Set the **Transform Type-In** boxes to **0** in the **Status Bar** to place the box at the origin.

3. Click **Material Editor** from the **Main** toolbar. Create a **Standard** material using the **Slate Material Editor** and apply it to the plane. Use the **apple-logo.jpg** for the **Diffuse** map. You need to select the **Show Shaded Material in Viewport** option for the material to display the image on the plane in the viewport.

4. Ensure in the **Coordinates** rollout of the bitmap, **Use Real-World Scale** is off and **U Tiling** and **V Tiling** are set to **1** each. Make sure the **Front** viewport is active and then press **G** to turn off the grid. Also, set the shading to **Default Shading** in the **Front** viewport. **RMB** click on the plane and then choose **Object Properties** from the **Quad** menu to open the **Object Properties** dialog box. In the **Interactivity** group of the dialog box, select the **Freeze** check box and in the **Display Properties** group, clear the **Show Frozen in Gray** check box. Next, click **OK** [see Fig. E2].

 What just happened?
Here, I've froze the object. Once you freeze the object, you won't be able to accidentally select or move it and it would be easy for you to trace the logo using splines.

Creating the Logo
Follow these steps:

1. Go to the **Create** panel, click **Shapes**, and then click **Line**. In the **Front** viewport, create a shape [see Fig. E3]. Ensure line is selected and then activate the **Vertex** mode from the **Modify** panel. Select all vertices except the first and last vertex and then **RMB** click; choose **Smooth** from the **Quad** menu > **tools 1** quadrant. Now, adjust the shape of the line according to the background image [see Fig. E4]. Make sure the X position of the two end vertices is same.

2. Activate the **Spline** level and select the spline in the viewport. Now, in the **Modify** panel > **Geometry** rollout, select the **Copy** check box and then click **Mirror**. Press **S** to activate the **Snap** toggle and then snap the copied spline with the original spline [see Fig. E5].

3. Weld the end vertices that you just snapped [see Fig. E6]. If required, adjust the shape of the spline to fit to the contours of the logo. Go to the **Create** panel, click **Shapes**, and then click **Circle**. Select **Edge** from the **Creation Method** rollout. Create a circle [see Fig. E7].

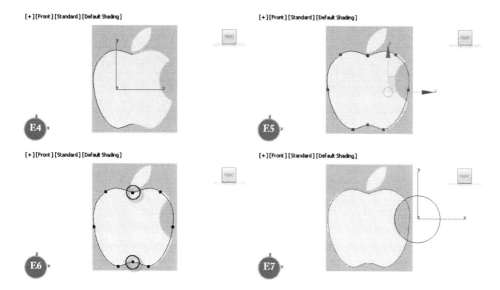

4. Select the profile curve of the logo and then in the **Create** panel, select **Shapes** and then select **Compound Shapes** from the drop-down list. Next, click **ShpBoolean**. In the **Boolean Parameters** rollout, click **Add Operands** and then select the **Circle** in the viewport. In the **Operands Parameters** rollout, click **Subtract** to subtract circle from the profile curve [see Fig. E8]. Create two circles for the upper part of the logo [see Fig. E9].

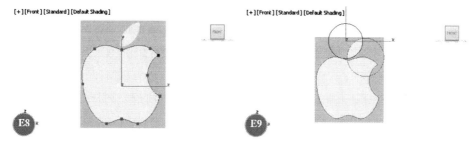

5. Create a **ShpBoolean** object and connect the two circles with it. In the **Operands Parameters** rollout, click **Intersect** to create the shape of the leaf [see Fig. E10].

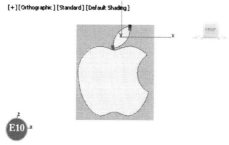

6. Convert the compound shape to editable spline and then attach them. Now, to make the unified spline smooth, in the **Modify** panel > **Interpolation** rollout, set **Steps** to **32**. Hide the plane object using the **Scene Explorer**.

7. From the **Modifier** list > **Object-Space Modifiers** section, choose **Bevel**. In the **Bevel Values** rollout, select the **Level 2** and **Level 3** checkboxes. Now, set **Start Outline** to **-0.5**, **Level 1 Height** to **0.5**, **Level 1 Outline** to **0.5**, **Level 2 Height** to **5**, **Level 2 Outline** to **0**, **Level 3 Height** to **0.5**, and **Level 3 Outline** to **-0.5**.

Exercise 3: Creating a Corkscrew

In this exercise, you will model a corkscrew using the **Helix** Spline and the **Loft** compound object [see Fig. E1].

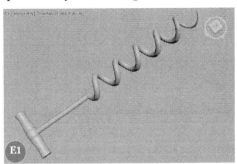 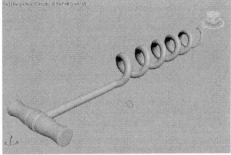

Table E3 summarizes the exercise.

Table E3	
Skill level	Beginner
Time to complete	15 Minutes
Topics	• Specifying the Units for the Exercise • Creating the Corkscrew
Resources folder	**unit-dm6**
Units	**Generic Units**
Final file	**corkscrew-finish.max**

Specifying the Units for the Exercise

From the **Customize** menu choose **Units Setup**. In the **Units Setup** dialog box that opens, select the **Generic Units** option from the **Display Unit Scale** group.

Creating the Corkscrew

Follow these steps:

1. Go to the **Create** panel, click **Shapes**, then click **Helix**. In the **Top** viewport, create a shape. In the **Modify** panel > **Parameters** rollout, set **Radius 1** to **8**, **Radius 2** to **8**, **Height** to **120**, and **Turns** to **5.5**. In the **Front** viewport, rotate it by **90** degrees around Y-axis [see Fig. E2].

2. **RMB** click on the helix and then choose **Convert To: > Convert to Editable Spline** from the **transform** quadrant of the **Quad** menu. In the **Modify** panel >

Selection rollout, click **Vertex** and then move the **first yellow** vertex toward left about **60** units in the **Front** viewport [see Fig. E3].

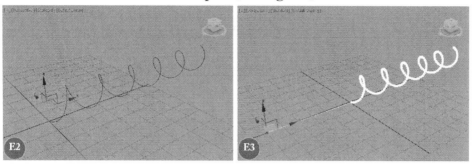

3. Apply the **Normalize Spline** modifier to the helix. In the **Modify** panel > **Parameters** rollout, set **Seg Length** to **5**. **RMB** click on the helix and then choose **Convert To:** > **Convert to Editable Spline** from the **transform** quadrant of the **Quad** menu.

 What just happened?
*You might have noticed that there were lots of vertices on the helix when I converted it into an editable spline. To reduce the number of vertices, I have applied the **Normalize Spline** modifier to the helix spline. This modifier adds new control points at regular intervals.*

4. Go to the **Create** panel, click **Shapes**, then click **Circle**. In the **Left** viewport, create a circle. In the **Modify** panel > **Parameters** rollout, set **Radius** to **2.5**. Select helix in a viewport. Go to the **Create** panel, click **Geometry** > **Compound Objects**, then click **Loft**. In the **Creation Method** rollout, click **Get Shape** and then click circle in a viewport to loft the circle along the helix [see Fig. E4].

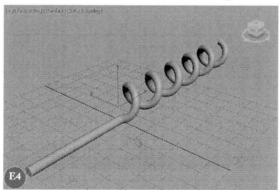

5. In the **Modify** panel > **Skin Parameters** rollout > **Options** group, set **Shape Steps** to **1** and **Path Steps** to **2**. In the **Modify** panel > **Deformations** rollout, click **Scale**. In the **Scale Deformation** dialog box that opens, click **Insert Corner Point** and then add a point below the **80** mark [see Fig. E5]. Now, click **Move Control Point** and move the end point downward [see Fig. E6] to scale the end area of the corkscrew [see Fig. E7]. Close the **Scale Deformation** dialog box.

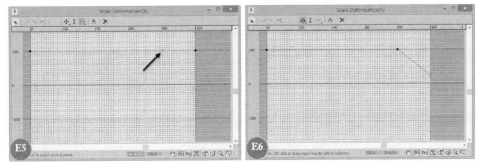

6. Go to the **Create** panel, click **Geometry** > **Standard Primitives**, then click the **Cylinder** button. In the **Front** viewport, create a cylinder. In the **Modify** panel > **Parameters** rollout, set **Radius** to **4.857**, **Height** to **43.771**, **Height Segments** to **6**, and **Sides** to **18**. Now, align the cylinder with the corkscrew [see Fig. E8].

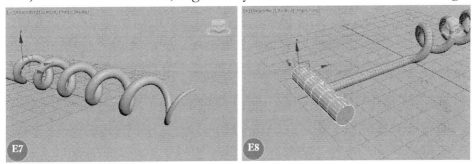

7. Convert cylinder into an editable poly object and then activate the **Edge** mode. Select the edges, as shown in Fig. E9. In the **Modify** panel > **Edit Edges** rollout, click the **Connect** > **Settings** button to open the **Connect Edges** caddy. Set **Segments** to **2**, **Pinch** to **-18**, and then click **OK** to connect the edges [see Fig. E10].

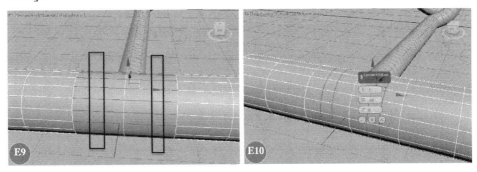

8. Select polygon loops, as shown in Fig. E11. Click the **Inset** > **Settings** button to open the **Inset** caddy. Set **Type** to **Group**, **Amount** to **0.31**, and then click **OK** [see Fig. E12].

9. Click the **Extrude** > **Settings** button to open the **Extrude Polygons** caddy. Set **Type** to **Local Normals**, **Height** to **-0.1**, and then click **Apply and Continue**. Now, set **Amount** to **-0.2** and then click **OK** [see Fig. E13]. Now, select the polygon loops, as shown in Fig. E14.

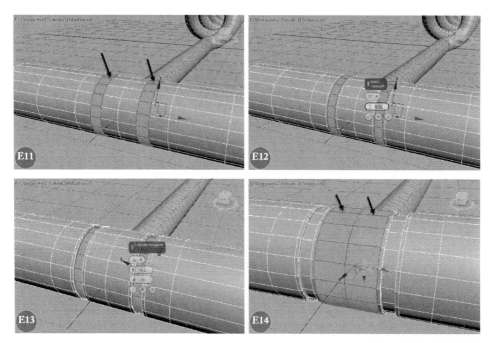

10. First extrude them by **0.4** units and then inset by **0.3** units [see Fig. E15]. Select the edge loops, as shown in Fig. E16 and then scale them down by **25%** using the **Select and Uniform Scale** tool [see Fig. E17].

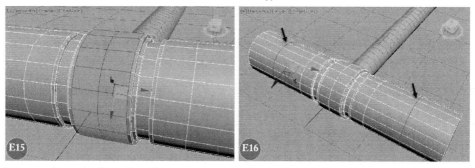

11. Now, select the border edges at both ends of the cylinder and then chamfer them [see Fig. E18]. Now, apply the **TurboSmooth** modifier to the cylinder.

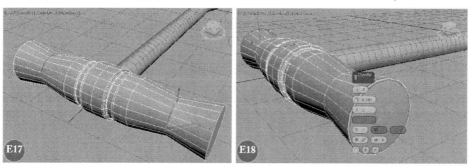

Exercise 4: Creating a Model of a Glass and Liquid

In this exercise, you will model a glass and liquid [see Fig. E1]. Table E4 summarizes the exercise.

Table E4	
Skill level	Intermediate
Time to complete	1 Hour
Topics	• Specifying the Units for the Exercise • Setting the Blueprint • Creating the Glass • Creating the Liquid
Resources folder	**unit-dm6**
Units	**Generic Units**
Final file	**glass-liquid-finish.max**

Specifying the Units for the Exercise

From the **Customize** menu choose **Units Setup**. In the **Units Setup** dialog box that opens, select the **Generic Units** option from the **Display Unit Scale** group.

Setting the Blueprint

Follow these steps:

1. Go to the **Create** panel, click **Geometry**, then click **Plane**. In the **Front** viewport, create a plane. In the **Modify** panel > **Parameters** rollout, set **Length** to **100** and **Width** to **75**. Also, clear the **Real-World Map Size** check box, if not already clear. Invoke the **Move** tool from the **Main** toolbar. Set the **Transform Type-In** boxes to **0** in the **Status Bar** to place the box at the origin.

2. Click **Material Editor** from the **Main** toolbar. Create a standard material using **Material Editor** and apply it to the plane.

3. Use the **glassRef.png** for the **Diffuse** map. You need to select the **Show Shaded Material in the Viewport** option for the material to display the image on the plane in the viewport. In the **Coordinates** rollout of the bitmap, make sure **Use Real-World Scale** is off and **U Tiling** and **V Tiling** are set to **1** each.

4. Make sure the **Front** viewport is active and then press **G** to turn off the grid. Also, change display mode to **Default Shading** [see Fig. E2]. **RMB** click on the plane and then choose **Object Properties** from the **Quad** menu. Select the **Freeze** check box from the **Interactivity** group and clear **Show Frozen in Gray** check box from the **Display Properties** group.

Creating The Glass
Follow these steps:

1. Go to the **Create** panel, click **Shapes**, then click **Line**. In the **Front** viewport, create a shape [see Fig. E3].

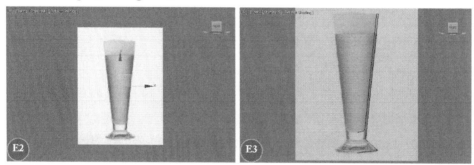

2. In the **Modify** panel > **Selection** rollout, click **Vertex**. In the **Modify** panel > **Geometry** rollout, click **Fillet**. Click and drag over the vertices to get the shape [see Fig. E4]. Make sure the **X** coordinate value for the selected vertices, shown in Fig. E5, is same.

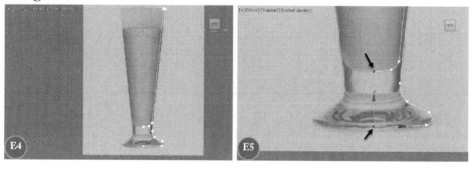

3. Make sure the profile of the curve is selected and then apply the **Lathe** modifier to it. In the **Modify** panel > **Parameters** rollout, click **Min** in the **Align** group. Set **Segments** to **32**. Now, select **Weld Core** [see Fig. E6]. Hide the plane and then rename the geometry as **glassGeo**.

Creating The Liquid
Follow these steps:

1. Select **glassGeo** and then on the **Ribbon** > **Polygon Modeling** panel, click **Convert to Poly**. Activate **Edge** sub-object level and then on the **Ribbon** > **Edit** panel, click **SwiftLoop**. Insert an edge loop as shown in Fig. E7. Click **SwiftLoop**

again to deactivate it. Activate **Polygon** sub-object level and then select the inner polygons shown in Fig. E8.

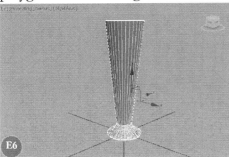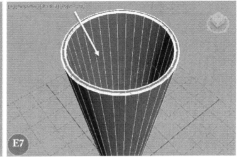

2. **Shift** drag the selected polygons to the right. In the **Clone Part of Mesh** dialog box that opens, select **Clone to Object** and then type **liquidGeo** as the name of the clone, and then click **OK** [see Fig. E9]. Make sure all polygons of **liquidGeo** are selected and then click **Flip** on the **Modify** panel > **Edit Polygons** rollout to flip the normals.

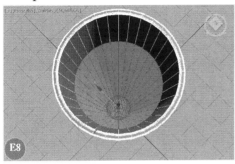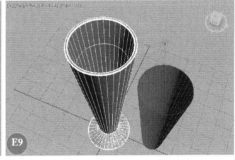

What just happened?
When we created liquidGeo using the Shift drag method, you would have noticed that the outer area of the geometry is appearing dark. It happens because of the wrong orientation of the surface normals. By flipping the polygons, normals are properly oriented now.

3. Select **liquidGeo** and then activate **Border** sub-object level. Now, select the border [see Fig. E10].

4. In the **Ribbon > Geometry (All)** panel, click **CapPoly**. Now, activate **Polygon** sub-object level and then select the cap polygon. In the **Ribbon > Polygons** panel, **Shift** click **Inset** . In the **Inset** caddy control, set **Amount** to **5** and then click **OK** [see Fig. E11].

5. In the **Ribbon > Polygon Modeling** panel, **Ctrl** click **Vertex**. In the **Ribbon > Vertices** panel, **Shift** click **Weld**. In the **Weld's** caddy, set **Weld Threshold** to **15** and then click **OK** [see Fig. E12] to weld the vertices. Activate the **Edge** sub-object level and then select the edge loop shown in Fig. E13.

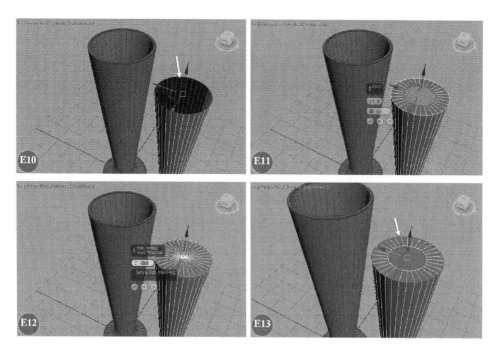

6. In the **Ribbon > Edges** panel, **Shift** click **Chamfer**. In the **Chamfer** caddy control, set **Edge Chamfer Amount** to **0.09** and **Connect Edge Segments** to **2** [see Fig. E14]. Click **OK**. Align the **glassGeo** and **liquidGeo** using the **Align** tool [see Fig. E15].

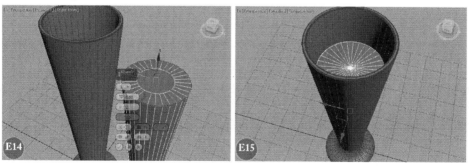

Exercise 5: Creating a Jug

In this exercise, we are going to create model of a jug using spline and polygon modeling techniques [see Fig. E1]. Table E5 summarizes the exercise.

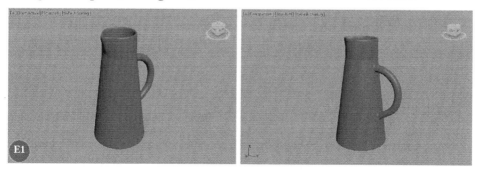

Table E5	
Skill Level	Intermediate
Time to Complete	30 Minutes
Topics	• Getting Ready • Creating Shape of the Jug Using Line and NGon Spline Primitive • Creating the Handle of the Jug Using Extrude Along Spline Feature • Refining the Model
Units	**Generic Units**
Resources folder	**unit-dm6**
Final file	**jug-finish.max**

Getting Ready

From the **Customize** menu choose **Units Setup**. In the **Units Setup** dialog box that opens, select the **Generic Units** option from the **Display Unit Scale** group.

Creating Shape of the Jug Using Line and NGon Spline Primitive

Follow these steps:

1. Activate the **Front** viewport. Go to the **Create** panel, click **Shapes**, and then ensure that **Splines** is selected in the drop-down list below the **Shapes** button. In the **Object Type** rollout, click **Line**. Expand the **Keyboard Entry** rollout, and then click **Add Point** to add a point at the origin. Now, set **Y** to **30** and then click **Add Point**. This action creates a line in the **Front** viewport [see Fig. E2]. This line will serve as path for the **Loft** tool. Click **Select Object** on the **Main** toolbar to deactivate the line tool.

2. In the **Object Type** rollout, click **NGon** and then create an **NGon** in the **Front** viewport. In the **Modify** panel > **Parameters** rollout, set **Radius** to **7**, and **Sides** to **26**. Select the **Circular** check box. Create four more copies of the **NGon**. The total number of **NGons** will be **5** [see Fig. E3]. Change the radius of the three right-most **NGons** to **4** [see Fig. E4].

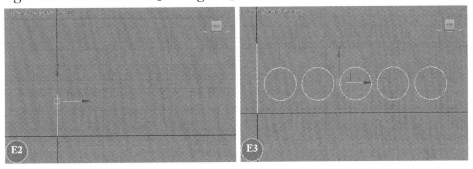

Why NGon is used instead of Circle?
*You can also use the **Circle** primitive to create the shapes for the jug but by default a **Circle** spline object just has four vertices. The **NGon** primitive we have used has **26** sides. As a result, a smooth surface will be created when we will loft the shapes along the path.*

3. The last **NGon** will be the spout of the jug. Select it and then covert into the **Editable Spline** object. Activate the **Vertex** sub-object level and then select the top four vertices as shown in Fig. E5.

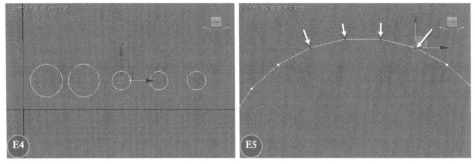

4. **RMB** click on the vertices and then choose **Corner** from the **tool1** quadrant of the **Quad** menu. Now, select the middle two vertices and move them using the **Select and Move** tool [see Fig. E6]. Ensure the vertices are still selected and them **RMB** click. In the **tool1** quadrant of the **Quad** menu, choose **Smooth** to make the shape of the spout [see Fig. E7]. If you want, you can fillet the other two corner vertices to create a smooth curve. Deactivate the **Vertex** sub-object level.

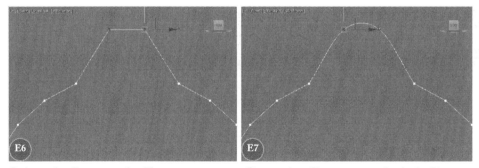

5. Select the **Line** in the **Front** viewport. Go to the **Create** panel, click **Geometry**, and then select **Compound Objects** in the drop-down list below the **Geometry** button. In the **Object Type** rollout, click **Loft**. In the **Path Parameters** rollout, ensure **Path** to set to **0** and click **Get Shape** button on the **Creation Method** rollout. Now, click on the first **NGon** that we have created. Set **Path** to **1** and then click **Get Shape**. Now, click on the second **NGon** in the **Front** viewport.

6. Similarly, pick the other three **NGons** with **Path** value set to **82, 85,** and **100,** respectively. This action creates the shape of the jug in the viewport [see Fig. E8].

7. In the **Modify** panel, clear **Cap End** check box from the **Skin Parameters > Capping** group. In the **Options** group, set **Shape Steps** to **0** and **Path Steps** to **3**. Select the **Linear Interpolation** check box. Now, delete all spline objects from the scene.

8. Add a **Shell** modifier to the stack and then set **Outer Amount** to **0.559** in the **Modify** panel > **Parameters** rollout [see Fig. E9].

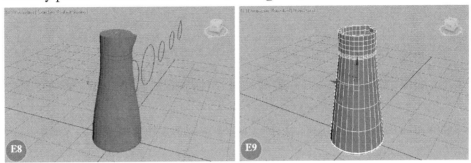

Creating the Handle of the Jug Using Extrude Along Spline Feature

Follow these steps:

1. Convert model to an **Editable Poly** object. Select all polygons and then in the **Modify** panel > **Polygon : Smoothing Groups** rollout, click **Auto Smooth**. Now, select the edges as shown in Fig. E10. In the **Ribbon > Loops** panel, click **Connect** with the **Shift** held down, the **Connect Edges** caddy appears in the viewport. Set **Segments** to **4** [see Fig. E11] and click **OK**.

2. In the **Left** viewport, create a shape as shown in Fig. E12. Now, select the vertices shown Fig. E13 and then click **Connect** from the **Modify** panel > **Edit Vertices** rollout to connect the vertices. Similarly, connect the other vertices diagonally [see Fig. 14].

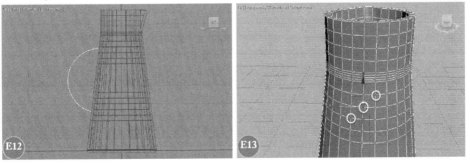

3. Select the center vertex and click **Chamfer > Settings** button on the **Modify** panel > **Edit Vertices** rollout. In the **Chamfer** caddy control, set **Amount** to **1.059** and click **OK** [see Fig. E15].

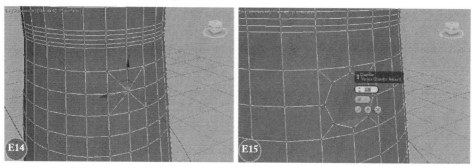

4. Select the edges, as shown in Fig. E16. In the **Ribbon > Loops** panel, click **Connect** with the **Shift** held down, the **Connect Edges** caddy appears in the viewport. Set **Segments** to **3** [see Fig. E17] and click **OK**. Similarly, connect other edges [see Fig. E18].

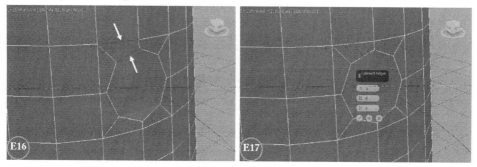

5. Select the vertices, as shown in Fig. E19 and then apply the **Spherify** modifier to round the shape [see Fig. 20]. Convert geometry to editable poly to bake the **Spherify** modifier. Select all polygons and then in the **Modify** panel > **Polygon : Smoothing Groups** rollout, click **Auto Smooth** [see Fig. 21].

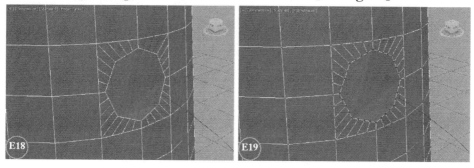

6. Convert geometry to editable poly. Similarly, create the round shape for the other part of the handle [see Fig. E22]. Convert geometry to editable poly. Select the polygon, as shown in Fig. E23 and then on the **Ribbon > Polygons** panel, click **Extrude on Spline** with the **Shift** held down, the **Extrude Along Spline** caddy control appears.

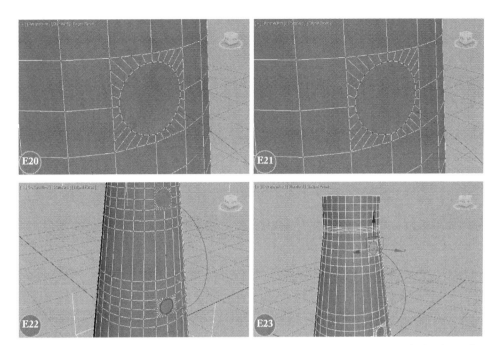

7. Click **Pick Spline** and then click on the curve in a viewport to extrude the selected polygon along the spline. In the **Extrude Along Spline** caddy, set the values as shown in Fig. E24 and then click **OK**.

8. Select the polygon shown in Fig. E25 and then bridge them [see Fig. E26]. In the **Ribbon > Edit** panel, click **NURMS** to display smooth model in the viewport. [see Fig. 27].

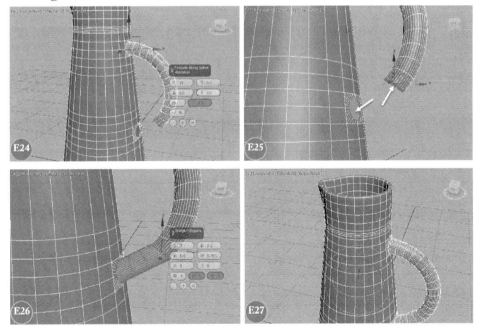

Quiz

Evaluate your skills to see how many questions you can answer correctly.

Multiple Choice
Answer the following questions:

1. Which of the following keys is used to constrain new points to 90 degrees angle increments while creating splines?

   [A] Shift   [B] Alt
   [C] Ctrl   [D] Shift+Alt

2. Which of the following is used to create splines in the shape of the text?

   [A] Text Object   [B] Text spline
   [C] Text   [D] All of the above

3. Which of the following keys is used to break a tangent and move its handles independently?

   [A] Alt   [B] Shift
   [C] Ctrl   [D] Shift+Alt

Fill in the Blanks
Fill in the blanks in each of the following statements:

1. 3ds Max provides two types of shape objects _____ and _____ curves.

2. You can use the _____ modifier to retain the parametric nature of a primitive spline.

3. The _____ and _____ rollouts are not available when you are use the **Edit Spline** modifier.

4. A _____ spline is a free-form spline that is made up of multiple segments.

5. The _____ spline is used to create spiral like shapes.

6. The _____ spline is a special type of spline that lets you generate splines based on a cross-sectional slice through a geometry objects.

7. To reset the tangent position, **RMB** click on the vertex or vertices and then choose _____ from the upper left quadrant of the **Quad** menu.

True of False
State whether each of the following is true or false:

1. 3ds Max allows you to combine shapes to create compound shapes.

2. You cannot change creation parameters of a compound shape.

3. You cannot clone the sub-objects by first selecting them and then pressing and holding **Shift** while transforming them.

4. The **Fuse** tool lets you move all selected vertices to their averaged center.

5. The **Fillet** tool lets you create the linear corners by adding new control vertices.

Summary

The unit covered the following topics:

- Generate planar and 3d surfaces
- Paths and shapes for the loft components
- Generate extrusions
- Generate revolved surfaces
- Define motion path for animations

- Using modifiers
- Stack display
- Object-Space modifiers vs World-Space modifiers
- How transform affects modifiers

Unit DM7: Modifiers

Modifiers in 3ds Max allow to sculpt or edit the objects without changing its base structure. For example, if you apply a **Taper** modifier to a cylinder, you will still be able to change its parametric properties such as **Radius** and **Height**. Modifiers can change the geometry of the objects as well as their properties. In other words, modifiers add more parameters to the objects.

Following are some points that you should remember about modifiers:

- When you apply modifiers to the objects, they are stored in a stack and displayed as a stack in the **Modify** panel. You can change the order of the modifiers in the stack to change the effect of the modifier. You can also collapse the stack to make the changes permanent.
- You can apply any number of modifiers to an object.
- When you delete a modifier, its effect on the object also vanishes.
- You can copy modifiers from one object to another.
- The order of the modifier in the stack determines the final effect. Each modifier in the stack affects the modifiers that are applied after it.
- You can apply modifiers to sub-object levels.
- You can toggle the effect of the modifiers from the stack display.

Object Space Modifiers Vs World Space Modifiers

Some modifiers that 3ds Max offers operate in the world-space. These modifiers use the world-space coordinates and are applied to the object after all object-space modifiers and transforms have been applied. You can apply the world-space modifiers like any other object-space modifier. A world-space modifier is indicated by either an asterisk of the text **WSM**.

On the other hand, the object-space modifiers affect the geometry of the object in local space. They use object's local coordinate system. The local coordinate system relates specifically to the selected object. Each object has its own local center and coordinate system. The local center and the coordinate system defines the object's local space. Unlike the world coordinate system, the directions of the object's axes [X, Y, and Z] depends on the current transform of the object.

Transform

Transform [move, rotate, and scale] are the most basic manipulations of the 3d objects. Unlike most of the modifiers, transforms are independent of internal structure of an object. The transformation values are stored in a matrix called **Transformation Matrix**. This matrix is applied to the entire object. The matrix is applied after all object-space modifiers have been applied but before the word-space modifiers.

Data Flow

Once you create an object and apply a modifier to it, 3ds Max evaluates the flow as per the table given below:

Order	Category	Modifiers/Transform/ Properties	Illustration
Table 1: The data flow			
1	Creation Parameters	Cylinder	
2	Object Modifiers	Bend, Taper	
3	Transforms	Rotate, Position, and Scale	
4	Space Warps	Ripple	
5	Object Properties	Checker Material	

Using Modifiers

You can access modifiers from the **Modifiers** menu, the **Modifier** list from the **Modify** panel, and from the applicable **Modifier Set** menu. To keep all modifiers organized, they are grouped in the **Modifiers** menu. The following table summarizes the options available in the **Modifiers** menu.

Table 2: The **Modifiers** menu overview	
Menu Item	**Sub-menu Items**
Selection Modifier	FFD Select, Mesh Select, Patch Select, Poly Select, Select By Channel, Spline Select, and Volume Select.
Patch/Spline Editing	Cross Section, Delete Patch, Delete Spline, Edit Patch, Edit Spline, Fillet/Chamfer, Lathe, Normalize Spline, Renderable Spline Modifier, Surface, Sweep, Trim/Extend, Optimize Spline, Spline Mirror, and Spline Relax.
Mesh Editing	Cap Holes, Chamfer, Delete Mesh, Edit Mesh, Edit Normals, Edit Poly, Extrude, Face Extrude, MultiRes, Normal Modifier, Optimize, ProOptimizer, Quadify Mesh, Smooth, STL Check, Symmetry, Tessellate, Vertex Paint, and Vertex Weld.
Conversion	Turn to Mesh, Turn to Patch, and Turn to Poly.
Animation	Attribute Holder, Flex, Linked XForm, Melt, Morpher, Patch Deform, Patch Deform (WSM), Path Deform, Spline Influence, Spline Morph, Spline Overlap, Path Deform (WSM), Skin, Skin Morph, Skin Wrap, Skin Wrap Patch, SpineIk Control, Surf Deform, and Surf Deform (WSM).
Cloth	Cloth, Garment Maker, and Welder.
Hair and Fur	Hair and Fur (WSM)
UV Coordinates	Camera Map, Camera Map (WSM), MapScaler (WSM), Projection, Unwrap UVW, UVW Map, UVW Mapping Add, UVW Mapping Clear, UVW and UVW XForm.
Cache Tools	Point Cache and Point Cache (WSM).
Subdivision Surfaces	Crease, CreaseSet, HSDS Modifier, MeshSmooth, OpenSubdiv, and TurboSmooth.
Free Form Deformers	FFD 2x2x2, FFD 3x3x3, FFD 4x4x4, FFD Box, and FFD Cylinder.
Parametric Deformers	Affect Region, Bend, Data Channel, Displace, Lattice, Mirror, Noise, Physique, Push, Preserve, Relax, Ripple, Shell, Slice, Skew, Stretch, Spherify, Squeeze, Twist, Taper, Substitute, XForm, and Wave.
Surface	Disp Approx, Displace Mesh (WSM), Material, and Material By Element.
NURBS Editing	Displace Approx, Surf Deform, and Surface Select.
Radiosity	Subdivide and Subdivide (WSM).
Cameras	Camera Correction.

Using the Modify Panel

To apply a modifier to an object, select the object in the scene and then go to the **Modify** panel. The name of the selected object appears on the top of the **Modify** panel. Apply a modifier to the object by using one of the following methods:

- Choose a modifier from the **Modifier** list available in the **Modify** panel. You can either use mouse to click on the **Modifier** or use the keyboard. For example, if you are looking for the **Mirror** modifier, type **mi**, the modifiers whose name start with **mi** [in this case the **Mirror** modifier only] appear in the **Modifier** list. Now, you can click on the **Modifier** or press **Enter** to apply it.
- Choose a modifier from the **Modifiers** menu.
- If the **Modifier** buttons are available in the on the **Modify** panel, click one of the buttons.

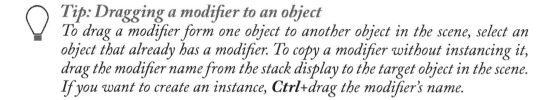

> *Tip: Dragging a modifier to an object*
> *To drag a modifier form one object to another object in the scene, select an object that already has a modifier. To copy a modifier without instancing it, drag the modifier name from the stack display to the target object in the scene. If you want to create an instance, **Ctrl**+drag the modifier's name.*

> *Tip: Modifier Instances*
> *When you create an instance of a modifier, its name appears in italics in the **Modify** panel indicating that the modifier is instanced.*

Using the Configure Modifier Sets Dialog box

When you click on the **Configure Modifier Sets** button in the **Modify** panel [below modifier stack], a menu is displayed. Choose **Show Buttons** from the menu to display the modifier buttons below the **Modifier** list. The buttons associated with the currently selected set will be displayed in the **Modify** panel. You can select various sets from the menu. Fig. 1 shows the buttons associated with the **Selection Modifiers** set.

When you choose the **Configure Modifier Sets** option from the menu, the **Configure Modifier Sets** dialog box appears [see Fig. 2]. This dialog box lets you create custom modifier and button sets for the **Modify** panel. To create a new set, specify the number of desired buttons using the **Total Buttons** option and then drag a modifier from the modifier list to a button.

You can also add a modifier by first highlighting the button and then double-clicking a modifier in the **Modifier** list. When you assign a modifier by double-clicking on its name, the highlight moves to the next button in the **Modifiers** group. Now, enter the name of the new set in the **Sets** edit field and then click **Save** to save the set.

Click **OK** from the **Configure Modifier Sets** dialog box to exit it. Similarly, you can modify an existing set.

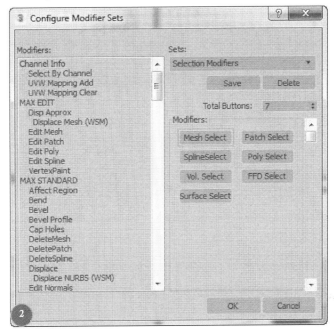

Using the Modifier Stack

The modifier stack [also referred to as just stack] is a list of modifiers that you apply to an object. The stack is evaluated from bottom to top. The first entry in the stack [from bottom] is always the object. The object-space modifiers appear above the object type. The world-space modifiers and space warps bound to the object are placed at the top.

You can use the stack in one of the following ways:

- Find a particular object and adjust its parameters using rollouts.
- Change the order of modifiers.
- Deactivate the effect of the modifier in the stack, viewport, or both.
- Select components [such as **Gizmo** or **Center**] of a modifier.
- Delete modifiers.

The buttons at the bottom of the stack allow you to manage the stack. Table 3 summarizes the functioning of these buttons.

Name	Icon	Description
Table 3: The buttons found below the modifier stack		
Pin Stack		It locks the stack and all parameters in the **Modify** panel to the selected object stack.
Show end result on/off toggle		When active, it shows the effect of the entire stack on the selected object. When inactive, shows the result up to the currently highlighted modifier.

Table 3: The buttons found below the modifier stack

Name	Icon	Description
Make unique		It makes an instanced object unique.
Remove modifier from the stack		It deletes the current modifier from the stack.
Configure Modifier Sets		When this button is clicked, a menu is displayed that lets you configure the modifier button sets.

Tip: Copying and pasting modifiers
*You can copy and paste modifiers between the objects. If you **RMB** click on a modifier; a popup menu appears. You can use the **Cut**, **Copy**, **Paste**, and **Paste Instanced** options from the menu to edit the stack.*

Caution: World-space modifiers
*While copy pasting the modifiers, ensure that you select the world-space and object-space modifiers separately. The **Cut**, **Copy**, and **Paste** options are disabled in the menu if you select both types of modifiers.*

Caution: Word-space modifiers
If you paste a word-space modifier in a section of object-space modifiers, the paste occurs at the top of the world-space section.

Collapsing the Stack

You can collapse the modifier stack of an editable object to merge the cumulative effect of the collapsed modifiers. You can collapse the modifier stack in one of the following situations:

- You have finished the model and you want to keep it as is.
- You want to discard animation tracks.
- You want to save the memory by simplifying the model.

In most of the cases, collapsing the entire modifier stack or part of the stack saves memory. However, some modifiers such as **Bevel** when collapsed increases the file size as well as the memory used.

Caution: Parametric nature of the objects

Once you collapse the modifier stack, you lose access to the parametric creation parameters of the object.

Tip: Preserving the original copy

*Before you collapse a stack, choose **Save As** > **Save Selected** from the **File** menu to preserve a copy of the original parametric object.*

3ds Max provides two options to collapse the stack: **Collapse To** and **Collapse All**. You can access these options by **RMB** clicking on the stack. The **Collapse To** option collapses the stack up to and including the chosen modifier to an editable object. You can still adjust the modifiers above the chosen modifier. The resultant object type depends on the uppermost modifier and the type of geometry it outputs. For example, if the uppermost modifier is **Edit Poly**, the resultant object will be an **Editable Poly** object. If no such modifier exists in the stack, the resultant object is an editable mesh. The **Collapse All** option collapses the entire stack. It does not affect any world-space bindings.

Exploring Modifiers

As already discussed, 3ds Max offers two types of modifiers: word-space modifiers and object-space modifiers. Let's explore these modifiers.

Word-Space Modifiers

The word-space modifiers act as object-specific space warps. They use world-space rather than object-space. When you apply a world-space modifier to the an object, it appears at the top of the modifier stack. The world-space modifiers are discussed next.

Hair and Fur (WSM)

This modifier is the engine of the **Hair and Fur** feature in 3ds Max. You can apply this modifier to either a mesh object or a spline object. If you apply it to splines, the hair grows between the splines. When you select an object on which you have applied this modifier, hair is displayed in the viewport. You cannot select the fur itself in the viewport. However, you can select hair guides using the **Guides** sub-object level.

 Note: Hair in the viewports
*The hair only renders in the **Perspective** or **Camera** viewport. If you try to render an orthographic viewport, 3ds Max presents a warning that says that the hair will not appear in the render.*

Camera Map (WSM)

This modifier is similar to the **Camera Map** modifier. It is used to apply the **UVW** mapping coordinates to the object based on a specified camera. It causes the object to blend with the background if you apply same map to the object as you apply to the scene environment. To apply a **Camera Map** modifier, create a scene with a camera and one or more objects. Ensure that the object that you want to map is visible to the camera in the scene. Apply the **Camera Map** modifier and then click **Pick Camera** from the **Camera Mapping** rollout and click on the camera in a viewport. Now, you need to apply a map to the background.

Press **8** to open the **Environment & Effects** window. Assign a map using the **Environment Map** button. Now, open the material editor and drag the map from the **Environment and Effects** dialog box to the material editor, choose **Instance** from the dialog box that appears and then click **OK**. Set the tiling in the **Coordinates** rollout, if required.

Apply a material to the object in the scene and then assign the map you just created to the **Diffuse** component of the material. To create the render shown in Fig. 3, I have applied a **Checker** map to both the environment and the object. Notice that the **Checker** map on the object matches the background but the shading effect of the material makes the object visible. To blend the object completely in the background, set the **Specular Level** and **Glossiness** of the material to **0**. Also, turn off the **Self Illumination** color and set the **Self Illumination** to **100**. Now, take a render using the camera that you have assigned to the modifier [see Fig. 4]. Also, refer to **camera-wsm.max**.

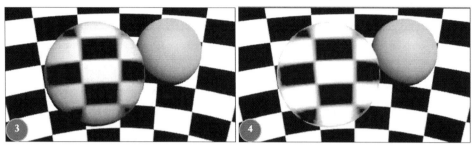

Displace Mesh (WSM)

This modifier allows you to see the effect of the **Displacement** mapping on editable mesh objects in the viewports. Also, you can see the effect of the **Displacement** mapping if you have applied a **Disp Approx** modifier to an object. This is useful when you want to visualize the effect of **Displacement** mapping in the viewports especially when you have animated the **Displacement** map or when you want to create an editable mesh from the displaced geometry in the scene.

To understand the functioning of this modifier, create a **Plane** primitive with **Length**, **Width**, **Length Segs**, and **Width Segs** values set to **150, 150, 50,** and **50**, respectively. Apply the **Disp Approx** modifier to the plane. Open the material editor and apply the **Standard** material to the plane. Connect the **Noise** map to the **Displacement** slot of the material. Adjust the properties of the **Noise** map, if required. Now, add the **Displace Mesh (WSM)** modifier to the stack. The effect of the **Displacement** map appears in the viewport [see Fig. 5]. Also, refer to **displace-mesh-wsm.max**.

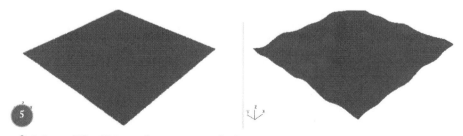

✎ *Note: The Disp Approx modifier*
If you are applying displacement to an editable mesh object, you don't need to apply this modifier in order to see the displacement effect in the viewport.

If you have changed parameters of the map [the **Noise** map in this case], click **Update Mesh** on the **Displacement Approx** rollout to update the mesh in the viewports. When **Subdivision Displacement** is on [you need to select the **Custom Settings** check box first], this modifier uses the settings that you specify in the **Subdivision Method** group of the rollout. You can also use the presets available in the **Subdivision Presets** group of the rollout. If **Subdivision Displacement** is off, this modifier applies the map by moving the vertices just as the **Displace** modifier does.

MapScalar (WSM)

This modifier is used to maintain the scale of a map that is applied to the object. In other words, it lets you resize the geometry without changing the scale of the map. Create a box and set its **Length**, **Width**, and **Height** to **70** each. Create a **Standard** material with a **Checker** map connected to its **Diffuse** slot. Apply the material to the box. Add the **MapScalar(WSM)** modifier to the stack. In the **Parameters** rollout of the modifier, set scale and offset values using the **Scale**, **U Offset**, and **V Offset** parameters. Now, resize the box using the **Scale** tool. You will notice that the scale of the map does not change regardless of how the geometry is scaled [see Fig. 6]. Also, refer to **maxscaler-wsm.max**.

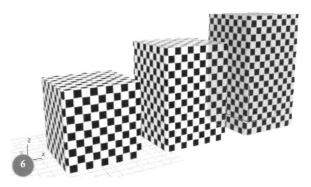

Patch Deform (WSM)

This modifier allows you to deform an object based on the contours of a patch object.

Point Cache (WSM)

This modifier allows you to store the modifier and sub-object animation to a disk file in your HDD. This file records changes in the vertex positions. When animation is played back, this file is used instead of the modifier keyframes. This modifier is useful when computation for vertex animation slows down the system and playback. This modifier is also useful in cloth animations.

Subdivide (WSM)

This modifier is similar to the object-space **Subdivide** modifier. However, in the world-space version, the size limit is on for the mesh after it is transformed into world-space coordinates.

Surface Mapper (WSM)

This modifier takes a map assigned to the **NURBS** surface and then projects it onto the modified objects. It is useful in applying a single map to a group of surface sub-objects within the same **NURBS** model.

Create a **Point Surf** NURBS object and a teapot in the scene [see the left image in Fig. 7]. Create a **Standard** material and connect a **Checker** map to the **Diffuse** component of the material. Apply the material to both the **NURBS** object and teapot. Select the **Teapot** in a viewport and then add the **Surface Mapper (WSM)** modifier to the stack of the **Teapot**. In the **Parameters** rollout of the **Modify** panel, click **Pick NURBS Surface** and then click on the **NURBS** object in a viewport. The **NURBS** object projects the map onto the **Teapot** [see the right image in Fig. 7]. Also, refer to **surface-mapper-wsm.max**.

SurfDeform (WSM)

The functioning of this modifier is same as of the **PathDeform (WSM)** modifier, except that it uses a **NURBS Point** or **CV** surface instead of a curve.

PathDeform (WSM)

The **PathDeform** modifier deforms an object based on a shape, spline, or NURBS curve. This modifier works the same as the object-space **PathDeform** modifier. Create a line and a cone in the scene [see Fig. 8]. Apply the **PathDeform (WSM)** modifier to the cone. In the **Modify** panel > **Parameters** rollout, click on the **Pick Path** button and then click the line in the viewport. Now, click **Move to Path** button to snap the cone to the line [see Fig. 9].

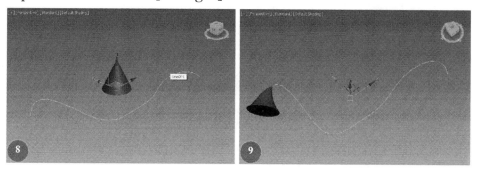

Adjust the **Stretch** spinner to stretch the cone along the line [see Fig. 10]. Adjust the **Height Segments** spinner of the cone object to smooth the stretch. You can also use the radius parameters to adjust the shape [see Fig. 11]. Now, if you want to create a growing vine like animation, you can animate the **Stretch** parameter. Also, refer to **pathdeform-wsm.max**.

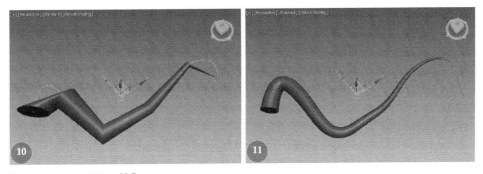

Object-Space Modifiers

The object-space modifiers affect the geometry in the local space. These modifiers are discussed next:

Affect Region

This modifier is a surface modeling tool. It work well with at the **Vertex** sub-object level. You can use it to create a bubble or indentation in the surface. When you add this modifier to stack, it assigns an arrow like gizmo to the object that you can use in the viewport to alter the geometry. The parameters in the **Parameters** rollout allow you to numerically control the shape of the deformation [see Fig. 12]. Also, refer to **affect-region-osm.max**.

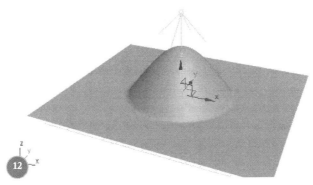

Attribute Holder

This modifier allows you to hold custom attributes for the objects in the **Modify** panel. It is an empty modifier to which you can add the custom attributes. It is a stripped down version of the **Parameter Collector** dialog box. It can collect only the custom attributes and appears in the **Modify** panel instead of a floating dialog box.

Create a **Cylinder** primitive in the scene with the **Radius** and **Height** parameters set to **10** and **100**, respectively. Add the **Bend** modifier to the stack followed by the **Attribute Holder** modifier. Ensure that the **Attribute Holder** modifier is highlighted in the stack. Choose **Parameter Editor** from the **Animation** menu to open the **Parameter Editor** dialog box. Alternatively, you can press **Alt+1**.

In this dialog box, set **Add to Type** to **Selected Object's Current Modifier**, **Parameter Type** to **Float**, **UI Type** to **Slider**, and **Name** to **Cylinder Height** [see Fig. 13]. Click **Add** from the **Attribute** Rollout, the **Cylinder Height** parameter appears in the **Modify Panel** > **Custom Attributes** rollout [see Fig. 14].

Click **Add** on the **Attribute** rollout of the **Parameter Editor** dialog box. Set **Add to Type** to **Selected Object's Current Modifier**, **Parameter Type** to **Integer**, **UI Type** to **Spinner**, and **Name** to **Cylinder H Segments**. In the **Integer UI Options** rollout, set **Range > From** and **Range > To** to **1** and **60**, respectively. Similarly, add two more float spinners with the name **Bend Angle**, and **Bend Direction**, respectively [see Fig. 15]. Close the **Parameter Editor** dialog box.

Press **Alt+5** to open the **Parameter Wiring** dialog box. In the left pane of the dialog box, choose **Objects > Cylinder001 > Modified Object > Cylinder (Object) > Height**. In the right pane, choose **Objects > Cylinder001 > Modified Object > Attribute Holder > Custom_Attributes > Cylinder Height**. Now, click **Two-way connection** followed by **Connect** to create a connection between the selected attributes [see Fig. 16]. The label on the **Connect** button changes to **Update**. Similarly, connect the **Cylinder (Object) > Height Segments**, **Bend > Angle**, and **Bend > Direction** parameters from the left pane to **Cylinder H Segs**, **Bend Angle**, and **Bend Direction**, respectively, parameters of the right pane [see Fig. 17]. Close the **Parameter Wiring** dialog box.

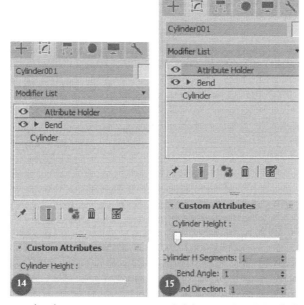

Now, experiment with the parameters available in the **Modify** panel > **Custom Attributes** rollout of the **Attribute Holder** modifier [see Fig. 18]. Also, refer to **attribute-holder-osm.max**.

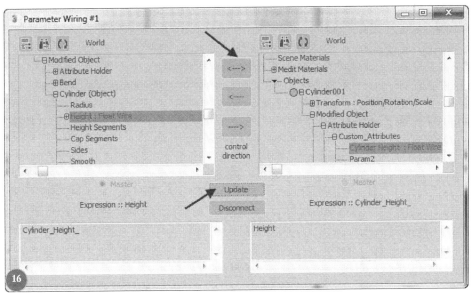

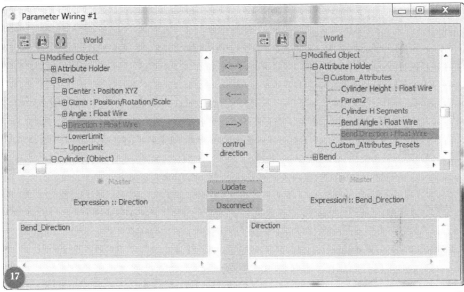

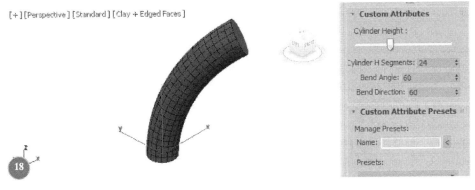

Bend

You can use this modifier to create a uniform 360 degree bend on a geometry about a single axis. You can limit bend to a section of the geometry as well as you can control the bend angle and direction.

To bend an object, add the **Bend** modifier to the stack. In the **Parameters** rollout of the modifier, set **Angle** and **Direction** in the **Bend** group to specify the angle to bend from the vertical plane and direction of the bend relative to the horizontal plane, respectively. Specify the axis to be bent from the **Bend Axis** group. To limit the bend effect to a particular area of the object, select the **Limit Effect** check box and then specify the limit using the **Upper Limit** and **Lower Limit** parameters [see Fig. 19].

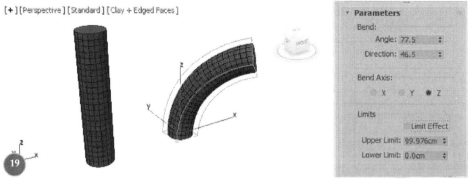

This modifier offers two sub-objects. You can change the effect of the modifier using the **Gizmo** sub-object by transforming or animating it [see Fig. 20]. You can translate or animate the **Center** sub-object to change the shape of the **Gizmo** resulting in the change of the bend effect [see Fig. 21].

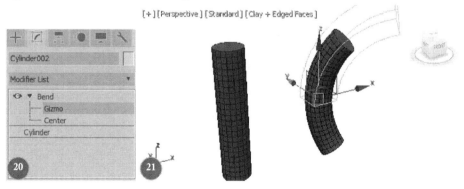

Bevel

This modifier allows you to extrude spline shapes into 3D objects and then applies a flat or round bevel on the edges. You can control the beveling from the **Bevel Values** rollout of the modifier. Create a **Text** spline and then add a **Bevel** modifier to the stack. Adjust the parameters in the **Parameters** and **Bevel Values** rollouts of the modifier [see Fig. 22]. Also, refer to **bevel-osm.max**.

Bevel Profile

This modifier is another version of the **Bevel** modifier but it extrudes a shape using a path or profile [beveling profile]. Create a shape and profile curve and then apply the **Bevel Profile** modifier to the shape's stack.

Create a **Text** object and a **Helix** object. Select the **Text** object and add **Bevel Profile** to the stack. In the **Modify** panel > **Parameters** rollout > **Bevel Profile** group, select the **Classic** option. Now, in the **Classic** rollout, click **Pick Profile** and then click the **Helix** object in a viewport to create bevel [see Fig. 23]. Also, refer to **bevel-profile-osm.max**.

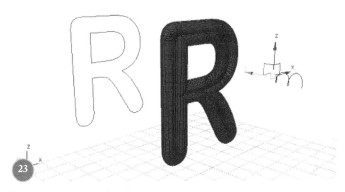

> *Note: Improved method*
> *There is another method that you can use to bevel a shape using a profile, it's called **Improved** method. To use this method, select the **Improved** option from the **Parameters** rollout > **Bevel Profile** group and then open the **Bevel Profile Editor** by clicking on the **Bevel Profile Editor** button. Now, create a profile for the bevel using this editor. Also, refer to **bevel-profile-osm-2.max**.*

Camera Map

This modifier is the object-space version of the **Camera Map (WSM)** modifier. It assigns the planar mapping coordinates based on the current frame and a specified camera. This behavior is different from the **Camera Map (WSM)** modifier which updates the coordinates at every frame.

Cap Holes

This modifier build faces on the holes in a mesh. This modifier works well with the planar holes, however, it does a reasonable job when applied to non-planar holes [see Fig. 24].

Cross Section

This modifier creates a skin across multiple various shaped splines by connecting the vertices of the 3D splines. The result is another spline object to which you can apply the **Surface** modifier to create a patch surface. These two modifiers sometimes also referred to as **Surface Tools**.

Create an **Arc** object in the scene and convert it to **Editable** spline. Now, create three more copies of the **Arc** object and change their shape using the **Scale** tool [see the left image in Fig. 25]. Attach all splines to form a single spline object. Add the **Cross Section** modifier to form a combined spline [see the middle image in Fig. 25]. Now, add the **Surface** modifier to the stack to create skin [see the right image in Fig. 25]. Also, refer to **cross-section-osm.max**.

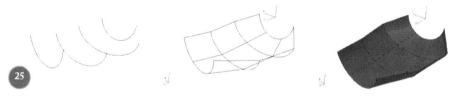

To change the shape, edit the combined spline at sub-objects level. The output of the **Surface** modifier is a patch surface. Therefore, you can add the **Edit Patch** modifier to the stack and edit the surface using the patch edit parameters.

Data Channel

The **Data Channel** modifier is used to automate complex modeling operations. You can feed mesh data through a series of parameters to create variety of effects that dynamically update in the viewport.

Delete Mesh

This modifier allows you to parametrically delete sub-object selection based on faces, vertices, edges, and objects. Create a **Teapot** object and then add the **Poly Select** modifier to the stack. Select the polygons as shown in the left image of Fig. 26. Add a **Delete Mesh** modifier to delete the selected faces [see the right image in Fig. 26].

 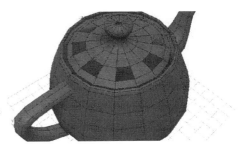

Delete Patch

It provides parametric deletion based on the patch sub-object selection. The possible choices are vertices, edges, patches, and elements.

Delete Spline

It provides parametric deletion based on the **Spline** sub-object selection. The possible choices are vertices, segments, and splines. Create a **Line** object. Add the **Spline Select** modifier to the stack and then select a segment. Now, add the **Delete Spline** modifier to the stack to delete the selected segment [see Fig. 27].

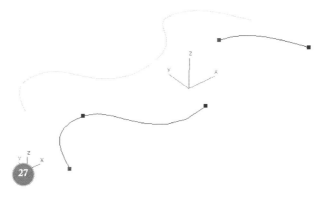

Displace Approx
See the **Displace Mesh Modifier (WSM)**.

Displace

This modifier pushes the object's geometry to reshape it using a map or bitmap texture. This modifier allows you to apply the effect using two methods:

- Apply the effect directly onto the object using the **Strength** and **Decay** values.
- Apply the effect using the grayscale values of a bitmap image.

You can use this modifier to simulate magnetic push like effect by animating its gizmos. The four gizmos provided by this modifier are: **Planar, Cylindrical, Spherical,** and **Shrink Wrap**. These gizmos are used to distribute the force specified by the **Strength** and **Decay** values.

Create a **Plane** primitive with **30** length and width segments. Add a **Displace** modifier to the stack and then set **Strength** to **-100** and **Decay** to **-0.66** in the **Parameters** rollout of the modifier. Choose **Spherical** from the **Map** group of the rollout and then select **Gizmo** sub-object from the stack. Now, use the **Move** tool to see the effect of this modifier [see the left image in Fig. 28]. Also, refer to **displace-osm-1 .max**. You can also use a bitmap or map to produce this effect. Click **None** associated with the **Map** parameter in the **Image** group to open **Material/Map Browser**. Double-click on **Noise** to select this map. Select **Planar** from the **Map** group and then set **Strength** to **38**; the effect of the modifier is displayed in the viewport [see the right image in Fig. 28]. Also, refer to **displace-osm-2 .max**.

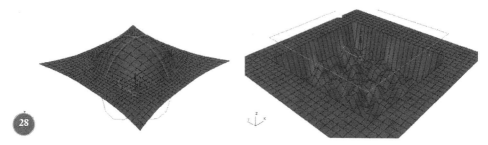

To change the parameters of the **Noise** map, drag the **Map** button to the material editor. Choose **Instance** from the dialog box displayed. Now, double-click on the map node to view its properties. Change the properties as per your requirement.

Edit Mesh
The **Edit Mesh** modifier has all the capabilities of the **Editable Mesh** object except that you cannot animate sub-objects.

Edit Normals
You can use this modifier to procedurally and interactively change the vertex normals of an object. This modifier is specifically used when you intend to output the meshes for the game and 3D rendering engines that support specified normals. The orientation of the vertex normals affects how light is reflected by the neighboring surfaces. By default in 3ds Max, rules of real-world physics are followed in which the angle of reflection is equal to the angle of incidence. However, using this modifier, you can set the angle of reflection as required.

Edit Patch
The **Edit Patch** modifier has all the capabilities of the **Editable Patch** object except that you cannot animate sub-objects.

Edit Poly
The **Edit Poly** modifier has all the capabilities of the **Editable Poly** object except **Vertex Color** information, **Subdivision Surface** rollout, **Weight** and **Crease** settings, and **Subdivision Displacement** rollout. This modifier lets you animate sub-object transforms and parameters.

Edit Spline

The **Edit Spline** modifier has all the capabilities of the **Editable Spline** object. The **Rendering** and **Interpolation** rollouts are not available for this modifier. Also, you cannot create direct vertex animation using this modifier.

Extrude

This modifier allows you to add depth to a shape object. It also makes the shape object parametric. Create a **Rectangle** shape object and covert it to editable spline. Create an outline and apply **Extrude** modifier to the spline object. In the **Parameters** rollout, specify a value for the **Amount** parameter to set the depth of extrusion [see Fig. 29]. Specify a value for the **Segments** parameter to set the segments that will be created for the extruded object.

You can use the **Cap Start** and **Cap End** parameters to generate a flat surface over the start and end of the extruded object [see Fig. 29]. The parameters in the **Output** group let you choose the output mesh type when stack is collapsed. The available options are **Patch**, **Mesh**, and **NURBS**.

Face Extrude

This modifier extrudes the faces along their normals [see Fig. 30]. There are many differences between the **Face Extrude** function and the **Face Extrude** modifier. The one big difference is that all parameters of this modifier are animatable.

FFD

FFD stands for **Free-Form** deformation. You can use these modifiers in a variety of ways. You can use it to create bulge in a mesh, animate dancing cars, and so on. When you apply a **FFD** modifier such as **FFD 2x2x2**, **FFD 3x3x3**, or **FFD 4x4x4**, it surrounds the selected geometry with a lattice. You can transform the lattice and use its control points to adjust the shape of the geometry [see Fig. 31].

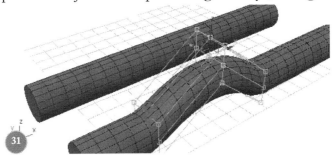

Each modifier provides a different lattice resolution [**2x2x2**, **3x3x3**, and **4x4x4**]. For example, a **4x4x4** resolution produces a lattice with four control points across each of its dimensions resulting in **12** points in each side of the lattice.

There are three sub-objects available with this modifier. At the **Control Points** sub-object level, you can select the control points of the lattice and then change the shape of the underlying geometry by transforming them. At the **Lattice** sub-object level, you can transform the lattice box separately from the geometry. At **Set Volume** level, the color of the lattice control points turns green. You can select and manipulate the points without affecting the underlying geometry. You should use this level to set the initial state of the lattice.

 Note: The FFD(box) and FFD(cyl) modifiers
*You can use the **FFD(box)** and **FFD(cyl)** modifiers to create box-shaped or cylinder-shaped FFD lattices. These modifiers are also available as space warps.*

Fillet/Chamfer

This modifier lets you fillet or chamfer corner vertices between linear segments of the shape objects. This modifier rounds corners where the segments meet by adding new control vertices. It also bevels the corners. This modifier works on the splines at the sub-object level. It does not work between two independent shape objects.

Create a **Star** shape object in the scene, convert it to editable spline, and add the **Fillet/Chamfer** modifier to the stack. Now, at the **Vertex** sub-object level of the modifier, select the vertices that you want to affect and then specify the desired settings in the **Edit Vertex** rollout to generate different shapes [see Fig. 32].

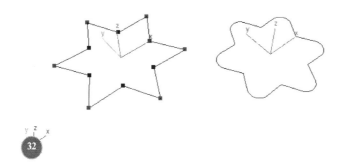

Flex

This modifier creates virtual springs between vertices of an object thus simulating a soft body dynamics behavior. You can control the stiffness and stretching of the springs. You can also control the sway of the springs that is how much the spring angle changes in relation with the movement of the springs. This modifier works with NURBS, patches, polygon and mesh objects, shapes, FFD space warps, and any plug-in-based object types that can be deformed.

HSDS

HSDS stands for **Hierarchical SubDivision Surfaces**. This modifier implements the Hierarchical SubDivision Surfaces. You can use this modifier to as a finishing tool for subdivision surfaces.

Lathe

You can use the **Lathe** modifier to rotate a shape or NURBS curve about a specified axis. Create a **Shape** object [see the left image in Fig. 33] and add the **Lathe** modifier to the stack. In the **Parameters** rollout of the modifier, ensure that **Degrees** is set to **360** to create a full 360 degrees lathe. Specify the segments for the lathe object using the **Segments** parameter. Click **Y** in the direction group to set the **Y** axis as the axis of revolution relative to the pivot point of the object. Click **Min** from the **Align** group to align the axis of revolution to the minimum extent of the shape. The right image in Fig. 29 shows the full lathe object.

You can select the **Weld Core** check box to weld vertices that lie on the axis of revolution. This modifiers also presents the **Axis** sub-object. At this level, you can transform and animate the axis of revolution.

Lattice

This modifier allows you to create renderable structure from a geometry. It can be thought of an alternative method to create wireframe effect. It gives you options to create joints, struts, or both. Fig. 34 shows a sphere with joints, struts, and both join and struts, respectively.

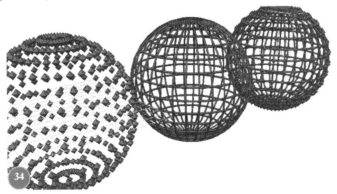

Linked XForm

This modifier links the transform of any object or sub-object selection to another object. The other object is called the control object. The transforms of the control object are passed onto the object or sub-object selection.

Create a **Sphere** and a **Cone** primitive in the scene. The cone will be the control object. Now, select sphere and add **Linked XForm** modifier to the stack. In the **Parameters** rollout, click **Pick Control Object** and then click on the cone in a viewport. Now, when you transform [move, scale, or rotate] the cone, the sphere will also receive the transforms. Refer to **linked-xform-osm.max**.

Delete the modifier from the stack and convert sphere to **Editable Poly**. At **Vertex** sub-object level, select some vertices [see the left image in Fig. 35]. Link **Cone** to vertices as discussed above. Now, when you move the cone, the selected vertices will also receive the transform. Refer to **linked-xform-osm-2.max**.

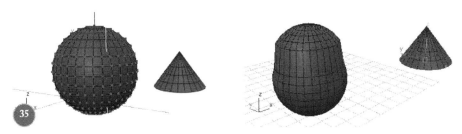

MapScalar
See the **MapScalar Modifier (WSM)** modifier.

Material
This modifier allows you to animate or change the assignment of the existing material IDs on an object.

MaterialByElement
This modifier allows you to apply different material IDs to objects containing multiple elements. You can apply IDs at random or you can use a formula. Select **Random Distribution** from the **Parameters** rollout to assign the material IDs to different elements at random. The **ID Count** parameter lets you assign the minimum number of materials IDs to be assigned. Select **List Frequency** to define a percentage of each [up to eight] of the material IDs.

Melt
This modifier allows you to create realistic melting effect on all types of objects, including editable patches and NURBS objects. It also works on the sub-object selections passed up the stack. Create a cylinder with enough sub-divisions and then apply the **Melt** modifier to it. In the **Melt** group of the **Parameters** rollout, specify the strength of the melt using the **Amount** parameter. The **% of Melt** parameter in the **Spread** group lets you specify the spread of the melt [see Fig. 36].

The parameters in the **Solidity** group determine the center of the melted object. There are several presets available in this group that you can use to specify the solidity of the object. If you want to specify a custom solidity, select **Custom** from this group. This modifier has two sub-objects, **Gizmo** and **Center**. You can transform and animate these two sub-objects to change the effect of the melt.

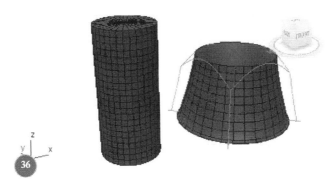

Mesh Select

This modifier provides a superset of the selection functions available in the **Edit Mesh** modifier. It allows you to pass the sub-object selection up the stack to other subsequent modifier.

MeshSmooth

This modifier allows you to smooth the geometry by subdividing it. You can use this modifier to produce a **Non-Uniform Rational MeshSmooth** object, **NURMS** in short. A **NURMS** objects is similar to the **NURBS** object in which you set different weights for vertices [see Fig. 37]. You can farther alter the geometry by modifying the edge weight.

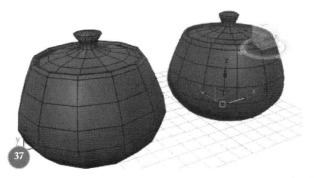

You can choose the desired method from the **Subdivision Method** drop-down list of the **Subdivision Method** rollout. The available methods are: **NURMS**, **Classic**, and **Quad Output**. The **Iterations** parameter in the **Subdivision Amount** rollout lets you specify the number of times you want to subdivide the mesh.

Mirror

This modifier allows you to parametrically mirror an object or a sub-object selection [see Fig. 38]. Apply this modifier to the stack and then select the axis or axis pair from the **Mirror Axis** group of the **Parameters** rollout. If you want to create a copy of the object, select the **Copy** check box and then specify the offset distance using the **Offset** parameter.

Tip: Modeling a character
*When you have created one side of a character and you want to mirror the other side, use the **Symmetry** modifier instead of the **Mirror** modifier as the **Symmetry** modifier allows you to weld the seam which results in a better looking model.*

Morpher

You can use this modifier to change the shape of the mesh, patch, or **NURBS** model. Morphing is generally used for lip-sync and facial expressions. This modifier also allows you to morph splines and world-space **FFDs**. Also, you can morph from one shape to another using this modifier.

MultiRes

This modifier reduces the number of polygons in a mesh to improve the rendering time [see Fig. 39]. You can also reduce the number of vertices and polygons using the **Optimize** modifier. However, this modifier has certain advantages over the **Optimize** modifier such as it is faster and lets you specify exact percentage for reduction. You can also specify the vertex count for reductions.

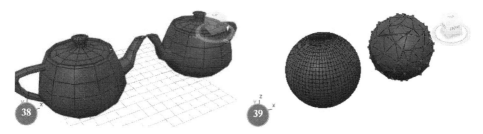

To reduce the polygons, apply this modifier to the stack. In the **Generation Parameters** group of the **MultiRes Parameters** rollout, click **Generate** to initialize the modifier. In the **Resolution** group, specify a value for the **Vert Percent** or **Vert Count** to reduce the polygons.

Noise

This modifier alters the position of the vertices of an object along any combination of three axes [see Fig. 40]. You can use it to create random variations in the shape of the object. You can also animate the change in shape of the mesh. Add the modifier to the stack and then in the **Strength** group of the **Parameters** rollout, set the strength using the **X, Y,** and **Z** parameters. Select the **Fractal** check box from the **Noise** group to produce a fractal like effect [see Fig. 41]. When you select this check box, the **Roughness** and **Iterations** parameters appear in the rollout. You can use these parameters to determine the extent of the fractal variation and number of iteration used by the modifier, respectively.

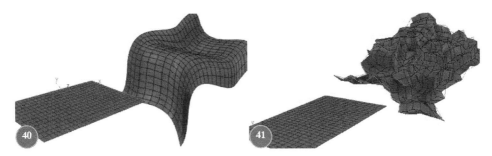

Normal

This modifier allows you to unify or flip the normals of an object without first converting it to an **Edit Mesh** modifier. Select the **Unify Normals** check box in the **Parameters** rollout to unify the normals so that they all point in the same direction, usually outward. Select the **Flip Normals** check box to reverse the direction of all surface normals.

Normalize Spline

You can use this modifier to add new control points at regular interval in a spline [see Fig. 42]. This is useful in normalizing the spline that you will use with the motion paths. The **Set Length** parameter in the **Parameters** rollout lets you set the length of the spline segments. 3ds Max uses this control to set the vertices at the regular intervals.

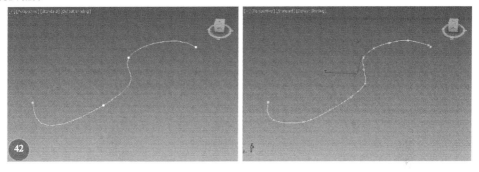

Optimize

See the **MultiRes Modifier**.

Patch Select

This modifier provides a superset of selection functions available in the **Edit Patch** modifier.

Patch Deform

See the **PatchDeform Modifier (WSM)** modifier.

PathDeform

See the **PathDeform Modifier (WSM)** modifier.

Point Cache

See the **Point Cache Modifier (WSM)** modifier.

Poly Select

This modifier provides a superset of selection functions available in the **Edit Poly** modifier.

Preserve

When you push and pull vertices to model a surface, the edges of the mesh get stretched that results in an irregular geometry. This modifier allows you to retain [as much as possible] the original length of the edge thus producing a cleaner mesh.

Projection

This modifier is generally used for producing normal bumps maps. Apply this modifier to the low-resolution object and then pick a high resolution object as the source of the projected normals.

Projection Holder

This modifier appears when the **Project Mapping** feature of the **Projection** modifier is used. It contains data generated by the **Project Mapping** feature such as the **UVW** mapping data.

ProOptimizer

This modifier allows you to interactively reduce the number of vertices in a model while preserving the original appearance/features of the model such as material, mapping, and vertex color information. When this modifier is used, the memory requirement for a model are reduced. You can optimize a model using one of the following two methods:

- You can use the **ProOptimizer** modifier to interactively optimize the model.
- You can use the **Batch ProOptimizer** utility to optimize multiple scenes at one go. When you use this utility, you can optimize the meshes before you import them to save the time.

Push

This modifier allows you to push the selected vertices inward or outward along the average vertex normals to create an inflation like effect [see Fig. 43].

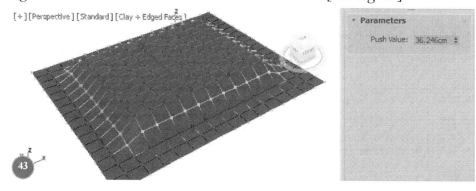

Quadify Mesh

You can use this modifier to convert object structure to quadrilateral polygons using the relative size that you specify. This modifier helps you to create mesh with rounded model with help of the **Smooth** modifier.

Relax

This modifier allows you to reduce the surface tension by moving the vertices closer to or away from their neighbors. This results in smooth object, however, the model appears little smaller than the un-relaxed model.

> *Note: Neighboring Vertex*
> *A neighboring vertex is the vertex that shares a visible edge with the current vertex.*

Renderable Spline

This modifier makes a spline object renderable without needing to convert it to an **Editable Spline** object. It also allows you to apply same rending properties to multiple splines. This modifier is useful when you link an AutoCAD drawing.

Ripple

You can use this modifier to create a ripple effect on the geometry [see Fig. 44]. You can use its **Gizmo** sub-object to change the ripple effect.

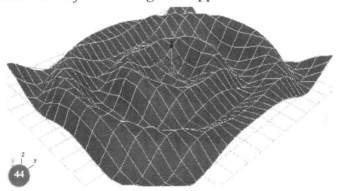

> *Note: The Ripple space warp*
> *The **Ripple** space warp has the same features as the **Ripple** modifier. However, you can apply the **Ripple** space warp to a large number of objects.*

Select By Channel

This modifier is used with the **Channel Info** utility. When you save a vertex selection into a sub-component using the **Channel Info** utility, you can use this modifier to quickly access the selection.

Shell

This modifier allows you to give thickness to an object by creating extra set of faces on the opposite direction of the existing faces [see Fig. 45]. You can specify the offset distances using the **Inner Amount** and **Outer Amount** parameters available in the **Parameters** rollout.

Skew

This modifier can be used to create a uniform offset in an object's geometry [see Fig. 46]. You can control and direction of the skew on any of three axes. You can also limit the skew effect by selecting the **Limit Effect** check box and then using the **Upper Limit** and **Lower Limit** parameters.

Skin Modifier

This modifier is a skeleton deformation tool that allows you to deform one object with another object. You can deform the **Mesh**, **Patch**, and **NURBS** objects using the bones, splines, and other objects.

Skin Morph

This modifier allows you to use a bone's rotation to drive the deformation of the mesh object. This modifier is used with other modifiers such as **Skin** and **Physique**.

Skin Wrap

You can use this modifier to deform an object with another object. Although, you can use this modifier in a variety of ways but its primary use is to animate a high-resolution object mesh with help of a low-resolution mesh.

Skin Wrap Patch

This modifier allows you to deform a mesh object with help of a patch object. Each point on the patch object influences a surrounding volume of points on the mesh object.

Slice

You can use this modifier to slice though selected objects or sub-objects using a cutting plane. Its functioning is similar to the **Slice** function of the **Editable Mesh** object. However, it does not require to be an **Editable Poly** or **Editable Mesh** object. You can also animate the position and rotation of the slicing plane.

Smooth

You can smooth a faceted geometry using this modifier. It eliminates the faceting by grouping the faces into smoothing groups. It smoothens the faces based on the angle of adjacent faces.

Spherify

This modifier distorts an object into a spherical shape [see Fig. 47]. The end result is dependent on the topology of the object.

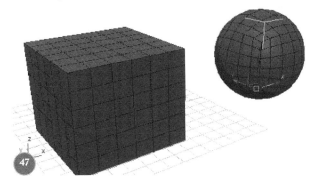

Spline IK Control

The basic use of this modifier is to prepare a spline or **NURBS** curve for use with the **Spline IK Solver**. When this modifier is applied to a spline object, you can transform its vertices without needing to access the **Vertex** sub-object level. It places knots [control points] at each vertex and then you can manipulate the knots to change the shape of the spline.

Spline Influence Modifier

This modifier creates a soft selection of the spline knots. The selection is shown in the viewport as a color gradient ranging from red to blue. The red color represents completely selected knots whereas the blue color represents the un-selected knots.

Spline Mirror Modifier

Similar to the **Symmetry** modifier, this modifier duplicates a spline along a specified axis. Available normals are also duplicated.

Spline Morph Modifier

You can use this modifier to morph between splines using either a progressive or blended method.

Spline Overlap Modifier

This modifier allows you to detect self-overlapping splines and adjusts the displacement of the intersection elements.

Spline Relax Modifier

This modifier relaxes knot positions and/or handles resulting in the smooth out splines.

Spline Select

This modifier is a superset of the selection functions found in the **Edit Spline** modifier. It passes a sub-object selection up the stack to other modifiers.

Squeeze

The modifier lets you create a squeezing [create bulge] effect on the objects [see Fig. 48]. The vertices closest to the object's pivot point move inward. The squeeze operation is applied around the **Squeeze** gizmo's local Z axis.

STL Check

This modifier checks if the object is correct for exporting to an **STL** file format. **STL** [**stereolithography**] files are used by the specialized machines to create prototype models based on the supplied **STL** file. The **STL** file must have a complete and closed surface.

Stretch

The **Stretch Modifier** allows you to create traditional squash and stretch effects that are used in animations [see Fig. 49]. This modifier applies a scale effect along a specified axis and opposite scale along the two remaining minor axes.

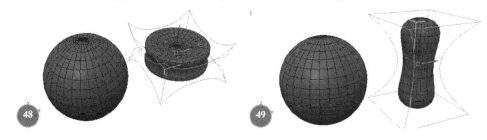

Subdivide Modifier

See the **Subdivide Modifier (WSM)** modifier.

Substitute

This modifier allows you to replace one or more objects with other objects in a viewport or at the render time. The substitute object can be instanced in the current scene or can be referenced from an external file. This modifier is useful for the designers who use 2D shapes in their AutoCAD drawings. When they link the AutoCAD drawing to 3ds Max, they want to see how the object will look like in their design. This modifier allows them to achieve that objective.

Surface

See the **Cross Section** modifier.

Surface Select

This modifier allows you to add a **NURBS** sub-object selection in the stack. Then, you can modify the selected sub-objects. It can select any kind of NURBS sub-objects except imports.

SurfDeform

See the **SurfDeform Modifier (WSM)** modifier.

Sweep

You can use this modifier to extrude a cross section along an underlying spline or **NURBS** curve path. It provides a number of pre-made cross sections such as angles, channels, wide flenges, and so on [see Fig. 50]. You can also use a custom spline or NURBS curve as custom sections.

Symmetry

See the **Mirror** modifier.

Taper

This modifier creates tapered contours by scaling both ends of an object's geometry [see Fig. 51]. It scales up one end and scales down the other end. You can also limit the taper effect.

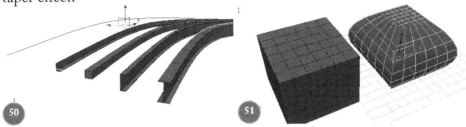

Tessellate

This modifier is used to subdivide the faces of a mesh [see Fig. 52]. It is useful in smoothing the curved surface and creating additional geometry for other modifiers to act on. The **Tension** parameter in the **Parameters** rollout allows you to add convexity or concavity to the subdivided surface.

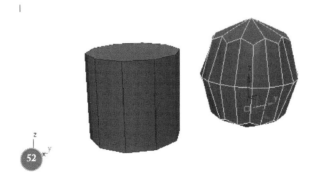

Trim/Extend

This modifier is used to clean up the overlapping or open splines in a multi-spline shape. To trim you need the intersecting splines. If the section intersects at both ends, the entire section will be deleted by this modifier up to the two intersections. To extend, you need an open spline.

TurboSmooth

This modifier is like the **MeshSmooth** modifier with the following differences:

- **TurboSmooth** is faster and memory efficient than the **MeshSmooth** modifier.
- **TurboSmooth** uses a single subdivision method, NURMS. It has no sub-object levels and outputs a triangle-mesh object.

Turn To Mesh Modifier/ Turn To Patch Modifier/ Turn To Poly Modifier

These modifiers allow you to apply the object conversions in the modifier stack. When you apply general purpose modifiers, these modifiers give you ability to explicitly control the output type of the object before hand.

Twist

This modifier creates a twisting effect on the surface of an object [see Fig. 53]. You can control the angle of twist as well as you can limit the effect of the **Twist** modifier. When you add this modifier to the stack, its gizmo is placed at the pivot point of the object and the gizmo lines up with the local axis of the object.

UVW Mapping Modifiers

These modifiers are used to control the texture mapping. You can use them to manage UV coordinates and to apply materials to the objects.

UVW Map

Use this modifier to control how mapped and procedural materials appear on the surface of the object. The mapping coordinates defines how bitmaps are projected onto an object.

UVW Mapping Add

This modifier is added to the object's modifier stack when you add a channel in the **Channel Info** utility.

UVW Mapping Clear

This modifier is added to the object's modifier stack when you clear a channel with the **Channel Info** utility.

UVW Mapping Paste

This modifier is added to the object's modifier stack when you paste a channel with the **Channel Info** utility.

UVW XForm

You can use this modifier to adjust the tiling and offset in existing UVW coordinates. If you have an object with complex UVW coordinates already applied, you can apply this modifier to adjust those coordinates farther.

Vertex Weld

This modifier works similar to the **Weld** feature in an **Editable Poly** and similar objects. You can use this modifier to combine the vertices that lies within a specified distance from each other.

VertexPaint

This modifier allows you to paint vertex colors onto an object. The amount of color that 3ds Max applies to the vertex depends on the distance of the vertex from the position of the cursor on the face. You can also paint vertex alpha and illumination values as well.

Volume Select

This modifier lets you make a sub-object selection of vertices or faces. You can use a cylinder-shaped or sphere shaped gizmo, or an object in the scene to define the volume of the selection area to which you can then apply other modifiers.

Wave

This modifier creates a wave like effect [see Fig. 54]. You can use the standard **Gizmo** and **Center** sub-objects to change the wave effect. This modifier is similar to the **Wave** space warp which is useful when you want to create a wave effect on the large number of objects.

XForm

This modifier is used to apply transformations to the objects. You can use it to animate the transformations of a sub-object selection. Also, you can transform an object at any point in the stack.

Chamfer Modifier

The **Chamfer** modifier is used to procedurally add edges to specific parts of an object. This modifier can be used to generate quadrilateral output. You can apply this modifier at all sub-objects levels and it is typically used to round off the edges [see Fig. 55]. The options in the **Presets** group can be used to load and save chamfer presets. The options in the **Mitering** drop-down list allow you to select a method for joining corners when multiple edges connect to the same vertex. Fig. 56 shows the **Quad**, **Uniform**, and **Tri** methods, respectively.

 Tip: Rounding off edges
If you mainly want to round off sharp edges and corners, you should consider using **OpenSubdiv** modifier.

Hands-on Exercises

Exercise 1: Creating a Microphone

In this exercise, we will create a microphone [see Fig. E1]. Table E1 summarizes the exercise.

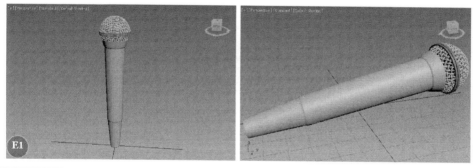

Table E1	
Skill level	Intermediate
Time to complete	40 Minutes
Topics	• Specifying the Units for the Exercise • Creating the Microphone
Resources folder	**unit-dm7**
Units	**Generic Units**
Final file	**microphone-finish.max**

Specifying the Units for the Exercise
Follow these steps:

1. From the **Customize** menu choose **Units Setup**. In the **Units Setup** dialog box that appears, select **Generic Units** from the **Units Setup** dialog box. Click **OK** to accept the changes made.

2. From the **File** menu, choose **Save** to open the **Save File As** dialog box. In the **File name** text box type **microphone-finish.max** and then click **Save** to save the file.

Creating the Microphone
Follow these steps:

1. In the **Create** panel, click **Geometry**, and then in the **Object Type** rollout, click **Plane**. In the **Perspective** viewport, create a plane. Switch to the **Modify** panel and then in the **Parameters** rollout, change **Length** to **50**, **Width** to **50**, **Length Segs** to **30**, and **Width Segs** to **30**. Place the plane at the origin.

2. **RMB** click on the plane and then choose **transform** quadrant > **Convert To:** > **Convert to Editable Poly**. In the **Modify** panel > **Selection** rollout, click **Edge** to activate the edge sub-object level.

3. Select the edge, as shown in Fig. E2 and then in the **Modify** panel > **Selection** rollout, click **Ring** followed by **Loop** to make the selection [see Fig. E3].

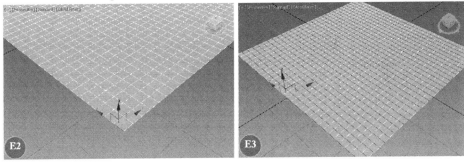

What next?
Now, we will create a shape from the selected edges. Next, we will use different modifiers to create metal grid pattern for the mic.

4. In the **Edit Edges** rollout, click **Create Shape From Selection** to create the shape [see Fig. E4]. Delete **Plane**.

5. In the **Modify** panel > **Selection** rollout, click **Vertex** to activate the vertex sub-object level. Now, select every alternative row of vertices in the **Left** viewport, as shown in Fig. E5. Move the selected vertices by **0.4** unit in the **+Y** direction

[see Fig. E6]. Invert the selection by pressing **Ctrl+I** and then move the vertices by **0.4** unit in the **-Y** direction [see Fig. E7].

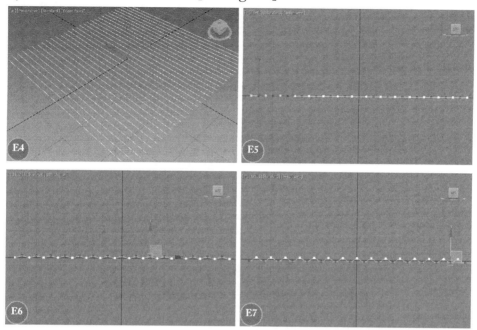

6. In the **Modify** panel > **Selection** rollout, click **Spline** to activate the spline sub-object level. Select alternate splines, as shown in Fig. E8. From the **Object-Space Modifiers** section of the **Modifier** list, select **Mirror**. In the **Parameters** layout, change **Mirror Axis** to **Z** [see Fig. E9]. Now, convert spline to **Editable Spline**.

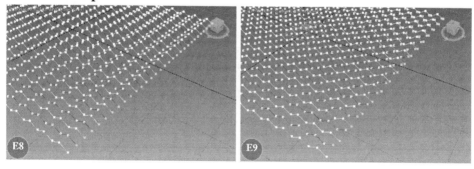

7. In the **Object** level, create a copy of the shape using **Shift** and the **Rotate** tool by rotating it **90** degrees. Make sure the newly created spline is selected and then from the **Object-Space Modifiers** section of the **Modifier** list, select **Mirror**. In the **Parameters** layout, change **Mirror Axis** to **Z** [see Fig. E10]. Convert shape to **Editable Spline**.

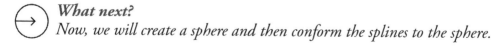
  What next?
  Now, we will create a sphere and then conform the splines to the sphere.

8. In the **Create** panel, click **Geometry**, and then in the **Object Type** rollout, click **Sphere**. In the **Perspective** viewport, create a sphere. Switch to the **Modify** panel

and then in the **Parameters** rollout, change **Radius** to **12**, **Segments** to **60**, and **Hemisphere** to **0.5**. Also, select the **Squash** check box. Place the sphere at the origin.

9. Convert sphere to editable poly and delete the bottom faces [see Fig. E11]. From the **Object-Space Modifiers** section of the **Modifier** list, select **XForm**. Now, using the **Scale** tool, scale down the **Sphere** using the **XForm** gizmo [see Fig. E12]. Make sure you are at the **Object** level before scaling the sphere.

10. Attach the two spline objects using the **Attach** function and then select the new spline. From the **Object-Space Modifiers** section of the **Modifier** list, select **Skin Wrap**. In the **Parameters** rollout, click **Add** and then click on the **Sphere** the viewport. Now, select sphere and then turn off the **XForm** modifier.

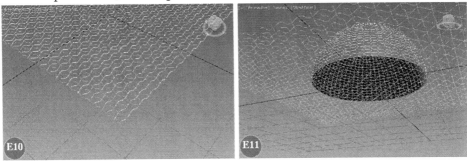

11. Select **Spline** and then select **Skin Wrap** modifier in the **Modify** panel. In the **Parameters** rollout, select the **Weight All Points** check box. Change **Fallloff** to **2**, **Distance Infl** to **10**, and **Face Limit** to **30**. Select the **Blend To Base Mesh** check box and then change **Bend Distance** to **200** [see Fig. E13].

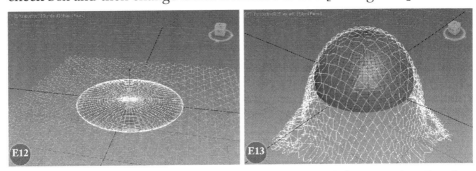

12. From the **Object-Space Modifiers** section of the **Modifier** list, select **Renderable Spline**. In the **Parameters** rollout, select the **Enable In Renderer** and **Enable In Viewport** checkboxes, if not already selected. Change **Thickness** to **1**, **Sides** to **6**, and **Threshold** to **180** [see Fig. E14].

13. From the **Object-Space Modifiers** section of the **Modifier** list, select **Symmetry**. In the **Parameters** rollout, change **Mirror Axis** to **Z** [see Fig. E15].

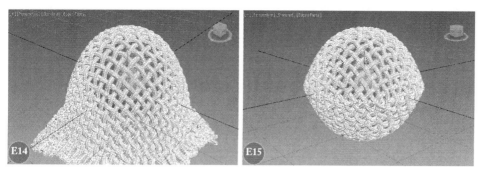

14. In the **Create** panel, click **Geometry**, and then in the **Object Type** rollout, click **Tube**. In the **Parameters** rollout, change **Radius 1** to **14.7**, **Radius** to **13.86**, **Height** to **1.208**, and **Sides** to **42**. Now, align the tube, as shown in Fig. E16. From the **Object-Space Modifiers** section of the **Modifier** list, select **Mirror**. In the **Parameters** rollout, change **Mirror Axis** to **Z** and **Offset** to **-0.31**. Also, select the **Copy** check box [see Fig. E17].

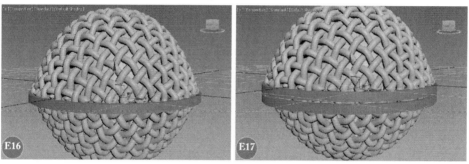

15. From the **Object-Space Modifiers** section of the **Modifier** list, select **Chamfer**. In the **Parameters** rollout, change **Amount** to **0.06** [see Fig. E18].

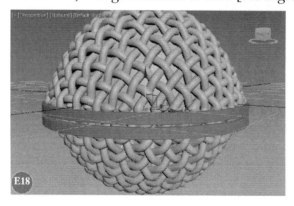

16. Select **Sphere** and then from the **Object-Space Modifiers** section of the **Modifier** list, select **Taper**. In the **Parameters** rollout, change **Amount** to **0.01** and **Curve** to **0.3**.

17. Using the **Line** tool, create a shape, as shown in Fig. E19. Now, smooth the vertices of the line using the **Fillet** function. From the **Object-Space Modifiers** section of the **Modifier** list, select **Lathe**. In the **Modify** panel > **Parameters**

rollout > **Align** group, click **Min**. Now, select the **Weld Core** check box and change **Segments** to **32** [see Fig. E1].

Exercise 2: Creating a Model of a Building

In this exercise, we will model a building using various modifiers [see Figs. E1 through E4]. Table E2 summarizes the exercise.

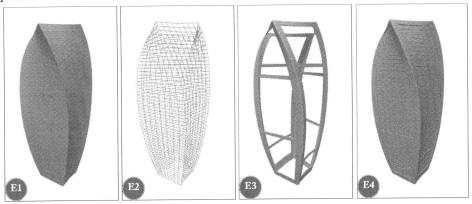

Table E2	
Skill level	Intermediate
Time to complete	45 Minutes
Topics	• Specifying the Units for the Exercise • Creating the Tower • Creating the Mullions • Creating the Outer Shell
Resources folder	**unit-dm7**
Units	**Metric - Meters**
Final file	**building-finish.max**

Specifying the Units for the Exercise

Follow these steps:

1. From the **Customize** menu choose **Units Setup**. In the **Units Setup** dialog box that opens, select the **Metric** option from the **Display Unit Scale** group. Next,

select **Meters** from the drop-down list located below the **Metric** option, if already not selected. Click **OK** to accept the change.

2. From the **File** menu, choose **Save** to open the **Save File As** dialog box. In the **File name** text box type **building-finish.max** and then click **Save** to save the file.

Creating the Tower

Follow these steps:

1. In the **Create** panel, click **Geometry**, and then in the **Object Type** rollout, click **Box**. In the **Perspective** viewport, drag out a box of any size. Go to the **Modify** panel, and in the **Parameters** rollout, set **Length** to **80**, **Width** to **80**, and **Height** to **400**. Also, set **Length Segs** to **8**, **Width Segs** to **8**, and **Height Segs** to **50** [see Fig. E5]. Place the box at the origin.

2. Change the name of the object to **Tower**. Now, you will apply various modifiers to create distinct building shape. From the **Object-Space Modifiers** section of the **Modifier** list, select **Taper**. In the **Taper** group of the **Parameters** rollout, set **Amount** to **0.35** and curve to **2.04**. The building bulges out [see Fig. E6].

3. From the **Object-Space Modifiers** section of the **Modifier** list, select **Bend**. In the **Bend** group of the **Parameters** rollout, set **Angle** to **27.5** and **Bend Axis** to **Y**. The building bends along the Y axis [see Fig. E7]. From the **Object-Space Modifiers** section of the **Modifier** list, select **Twist**. In the **Twist** group of the **Parameters** rollout, set **Angle** to **45.5** and **Bias** to **93.5**. The building twists along the Z axis [see Fig. E8].

Creating the Mullions

Follow these steps:

1. Select **Tower** in the **Scene Explorer** and then **RMB** click on it. From the **Quad** menu that opens, choose **Clone** to open the **Clone Options** dialog box. Select **Reference** from the **Object** group. Next, type **Mullions** in the **Name** text box and the click **OK**.

2. In the **Scene Explorer**, click **Tower's** bulb icon to hide it. Select **Mullions** and then go to the **Modify** panel. From the **Object-Space Modifiers** section of the **Modifier** list, select **Edit Poly**. In the **Selection** rollout, click **Polygon** and then select the center polygons [see Fig. E9]. Click **Grow** thrice in the **Selection** rollout to select all top polygons of the building [see Fig. E10].

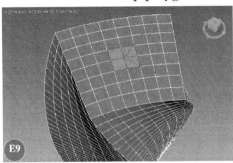 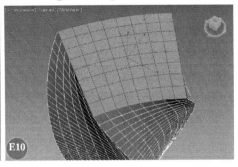

3. Delete the selected polygons by pressing **Delete**. Similarly, delete the bottom polygons. From the **Object-Space Modifiers** section of the **Modifier** list, select **Lattice**. In the **Struts** group of the **Parameters** rollout, set **Radius** to **0.5**, and **Sides** to **5**. Also, select **Smooth**.

Creating the Outer Shell

Follow these steps:

1. In the **Scene Explorer**, click the **Mullions's** bulb icon to hide it. Select **Tower** and create a clone with the name **Shell**. Make sure to select **Reference** from the **Object group** in the **Clone Options** dialog box.

2. Make sure **Tower** and **Mullions** are not visible in the scene and **Shell** is visible in the scene. Select the top and bottom polygons of **Shell** and delete them as done earlier. Also, turn off the **Twist**, **Bend**, and **Taper** modifiers.

3. In the **Selection** rollout, make sure the **Ignore Backfacing** check box is clear. In the **Front** viewport, select polygons [see Fig. E11]. Press **Delete** to remove the selected polygons. Similarly, remove polygons from the other remaining two sides. Use a different pattern for these sides [see Fig. E12].

4. In the **Selection** rollout, click **Edge** and then select the four corner edges [see Fig. E13]. Now, click **Loop** to select the loops. In the **Edit Edges** rollout, click **Chamfer > Settings** to open the **Chamfer** caddy control. Set **Amount** to **1.636** and **Segments** to **5** [see Fig. E14]. Click **OK**.

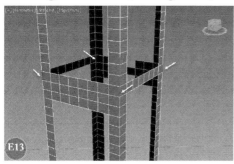
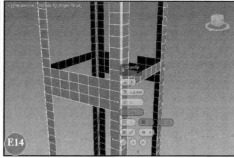

5. From the **Object-Space Modifiers** section of the **Modifier** list, select **Shell**. In the **Parameters** rollout, set **Outer Amount** to **2.0** [see Fig. E15]. Now turn on the **Twist, Taper,** and **Bend** Modifiers. Turn on the **Tower** and **Mullions** from the **Scene Explorer**. Assign colors of your choice to **Tower, Shell,** and **Mullions** [see Fig. E16]. Now, create different version of the building by modifying the parameters of the modifiers [see Fig. E17].

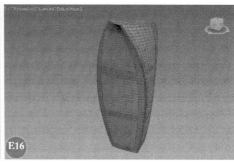

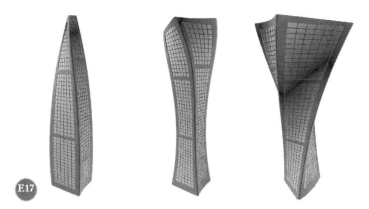

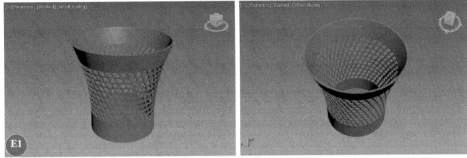

Exercise 3: Creating a Model of a Paper Basket

In this exercise, you will model a melted waste paper basket using various modifiers [see Fig. E1]. Table E3 summarizes the exercise.

Table E3	
Skill level	Beginner
Time to complete	35 Minutes
Topics	• Specifying the Units for the Exercise • Creating the Basket
Resources folder	**unit-dm7**
Units	**Metric - Centimeters**
Final file	**basket-finish.max**

Specifying the Units for the Exercise

Follow these steps:

1. From the **Customize** menu choose **Units Setup**. In the **Units Setup** dialog box that opens, select the **Metric** option from the **Display Unit Scale** group. Next, select **Centimeters** from the drop-down list located below the **Metric** option, if already not selected. Click **OK** to accept the change.

2. From the **File** menu, choose **Save** to open the **Save File As** dialog box. In the **File name** text box type **basket-finish.max** and then click **Save** to save the file.

Creating the Basket

Follow these steps:

1. In the **Create** panel, click **Geometry,** and then in the **Object Type** rollout, click **Cylinder.** In the **Perspective** viewport, drag out a cylinder of any size. Go to the **Modify** panel, and on the **Parameters** rollout, set **Radius** to **14.5** and **Height** to **30.** Also, set **Height Segments** to **12** and **Sides** to **40** [see Fig. E2].

2. From the **Object-Space Modifiers** section of the **Modifier List,** select **Edit Poly.** In the **Selection** rollout, click **Vertex** and then select top row of vertices of the cylinder in the **Front** viewport. **RMB** click on the **Select and Move** button on the **Main** toolbar.

3. In the **Offset:Screen** group of the **Move Transform Type-In** dialog box that opens, set **Y** to **5** and then press **Enter** to move the vertices by **5** units in the **Y** direction [see Fig. E3].Select all the vertices except the bottom row and move them by **6** units in the **Y** direction [see Fig. E4].

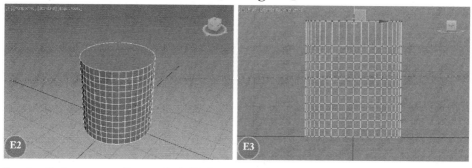

4. In the **Selection** rollout, click **Polygon** and then select all the middle polygons [see Fig. E5]. In the **Edit Polygons** rollout, click **Inset > Settings.** In the **Inset** caddy control, select **By Polygon** for **Type.** Now, set amount to **0.3** and click **OK** to inset the selected polygons [see Fig. E6]. Delete the polygons.

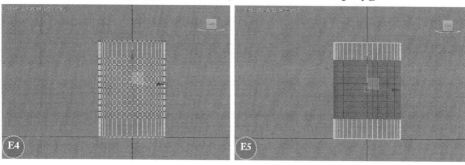

5. Select the top cap polygon and delete it as well [see Fig. E7]. From the **Object-Space Modifiers** section of the **Modifier** list, select **Shell.** In the **Parameters** rollout, set **Outer Amount** to **0.5.**

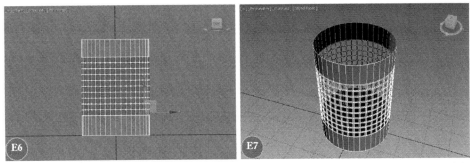

6. From the **Object-Space Modifiers** section of the **Modifier** list, select **Taper**. In the **Parameters** layout, set **Amount** to **0.44** and **Curve** to **-0.7**. From the **Object-Space Modifiers** section of the **Modifier List**, select **Twist**. In the **Parameters** layout, set **Angle** to **66.5**.

Exercise 4: Creating a Rope

In this exercise, we will create a rope [see Fig. E1]. Table E4 summarizes the exercise.

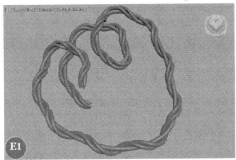
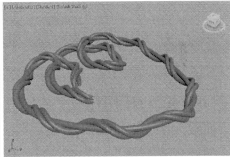

Table E4	
Skill level	Beginner
Time to complete	40 Minutes
Topics	• Specifying the Units for the Exercise • Creating the Rope
Resources folder	**unit-dm7**
Units	**Generic Units**
Final file	**rope-finish.max**

Specifying the Units for the Exercise

Follow these steps:

1. From **Customize** menu choose **Units Setup**. In the **Units Setup** dialog box that appears, select **Generic Units** from the **Units Setup** dialog box. Click **OK** to accept the changes made.

2. From the **File** menu, choose **Save** to open the **Save File As** dialog box. In the **File name** text box type **rope-finish.max** and then click **Save** to save the file.

Creating the Rope
Follow these steps:

1. In the **Create** panel, click **Shapes,** and then click **Freehand.** Using the **Freehand** tool, create a spline [see Fig. E2]. You can also open the **rope-curve-start.max** file, if you want to follow along.

2. Make sure the spline is selected. From the **Object-Space Modifiers** section of the **Modifier List,** select **Spline Relax.** In the **Modify** panel > **Relax** rollout, change **Amount** to **1** and **Iterations** to **7** [see Fig. E3].

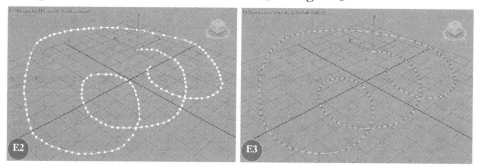

3. From the **Object-Space Modifiers** section of the **Modifier** list, select **Optimize Spline.** In the **Modify** panel > **Optimize Spline** rollout > **Reduce Knots** group, change **By %** to **10** [see Fig. E4].

4. From the **Object-Space Modifiers** section of the **Modifier** list, select **Renderable Spline.** In the **Modify** panel > **Parameters** rollout, select **Enable in Renderer** and **Enable in Viewport** check boxes, if not already selected. Now, change **Thickness** to **2** [see Fig. E5].

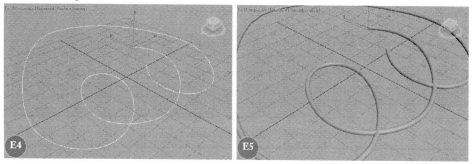

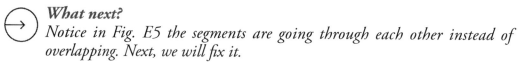

What next?
Notice in Fig. E5 the segments are going through each other instead of overlapping. Next, we will fix it.

5. From the **Object-Space Modifiers** section of the **Modifier List,** select **Spline Overlap.** In the **Modify** panel > **Overlap** rollout, change **Thickness** to **1.584** [see Fig. E6].

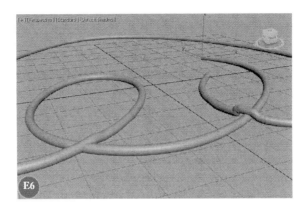

E6

What next?

Notice in Fig. E6, the overlapping of segments is not clean because of the irregular distribution of the knots. Let's fix that.

6. Add the **Normalize Spline** modifier above the **Renderable Spline** in the stack [see Fig. E7]. In the **Modify** panel > **Parameter** rollout > **Normalize By** group, change **Seg Length** to **4.683** [see Fig. E8].

E7

7. Select the **Renderable Spline** modifier in the stack and then in the **Parameters** rollout > **Capping Options** group, select the **Quad Cap** check box and then change **Segments** to **5** and **Sphere** to **1** [see Fig. E9]. Also, ensure that the **Twist Correction** check box is selected.

E8

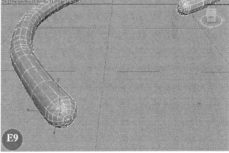

E9

8. In the modifier stack, turn off the **Renderable Spline** modifier. From the **Object-Space Modifiers** section of the **Modifier** list, select **Noise**. In the **Modify** panel > **Parameters** rollout > **Noise** group, change **Scale** to **10**. In the **Strength** group, change **Z** to **50** [see Fig. 10].

What just happened?

*Here, the **Noise** modifier modulating the position of the knots and as you can see in Fig. E10, the **Noise** modifier is affecting whole spline. If you want to affect a part of the spline, you need to use the influencers.*

9. In the **Create** panel, click **Helpers,** and then click **Influence.** Click-drag in the viewport to create the gizmo. In the **Modify** panel > **Parameters** rollout, change **Near** and **Far** to **31** and **42,** respectively [see Fig. E11].

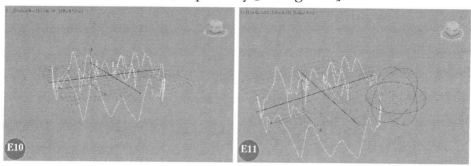

10. Select the spline. From the **Object-Space Modifiers** section of the **Modifier** list, select **Spline Influence.** In the **Modify** panel > **Influence Parameters** rollout, click **Pick** and then click on the gizmo in the viewport. Also, change **Falloff Type** to **Smooth.**

11. Move the **Noise** modifier at the top of the stack. If you now move the influencer in the viewport, you will notice the knots are being affected only inside the area of the influencer [see Fig. E12]. Turn on the **Renderable Spline** modifier in the stack display [see Fig. E13].

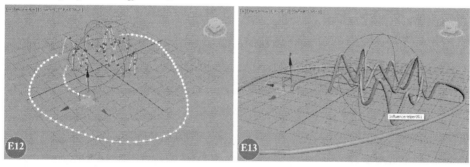

12. Turn off the **Renderable Spline** modifier in the stack display. In the **Create** panel, click **Geometry,** and then in the **Object Type** rollout, click **Cylinder.** In the **Perspective** viewport, create a cylinder. Switch to the **Modify** panel and on the **Parameters** rollout, change **Radius** to **2** and **Height** to **500,** and **Height Segments** to **35** [see Fig. E14]. Create two more copies of the cylinder and then align them as shown in Fig. E15.

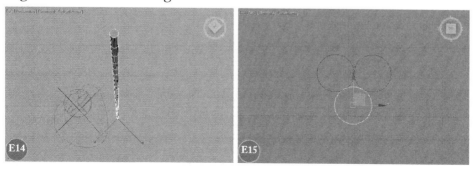

13. Convert one of the cylinders to editable poly and then attach the remaining two cylinders using the **Attach** function.

14. From the **Object-Space Modifiers** section of the **Modifier** list, select **Path Deform**. In the **Modify** panel > **PathDeform** rollout, click **None** and then click the spline in the viewport. Change **Stretch** to **1.827** and then in the **Rotation** group, change **Twist** to **3000** [see Fig. E16]. Turn off **Noise** from the spline's modifier stack. Now, change the **Stretch** value according to the length spline.

15. From the **Object-Space Modifiers** section of the **Modifier** list, select **TurboSmooth**. Place the **TurboSmooth** modifier below the **Path Deform** modifier. In the **TurboSmooth** rollout, change **Iterations** to **2** [see Fig. E17].

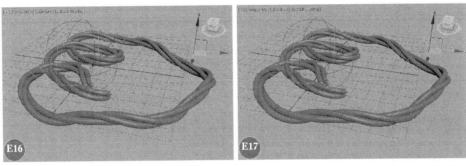

16. Select spline and then select the **Spline Overlap** modifier in the stack display. In the **Overlap** rollout, adjust the **Thickness** value as per your requirement [see Fig. E18].

17. In the **Modify** panel > **Path Deform** modifier > **Path Deform** rollout > **Rotation** group, change **Twist** to **5569** [see Fig. E19].

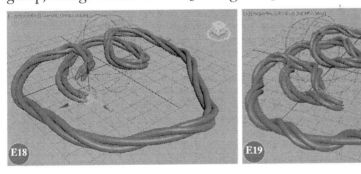

Quiz

Evaluate your skills to see how many questions you can answer correctly.

Multiple Choice
Answer the following questions:

1. Which of the following keys is used to create an instance of a modifier?

   [A] Shift   [B] Alt
   [C] Ctrl   [D] Shift+Alt

2. Which of the following modifiers is used to add depth to a shape object?

   [A] Edit Spline   [B] Extrude
   [C] Chamfer   [D] All of the above

Fill in the Blanks
Fill in the blanks in each of the following statements:

1. OSM and WSM stand for _____ and _____.

2. The transformation values are stored in a matrix called _____.

3. The hair only renders in the _____ or _____ viewports.

True of False
State whether each of the following is true or false:

1. You can copy and paste modifiers between the object.

2. The **Fillet/Chamfer** modifier lets you fillet or chamfer corner vertices between linear segments of the shape objects.

Summary
The unit covered the following topics:

- Using modifiers
- Stack display
- Object-Space modifiers vs World-Space modifiers
- How transform affects modifiers

Unit DMB: Bonus Hands-on Exercises [Modeling]

Exercises - Modeling

Exercise 1: Creating a Serving Bowl

In this exercise, we will create model of a bowl [see Fig. E1]. Table E1 summarizes the exercise.

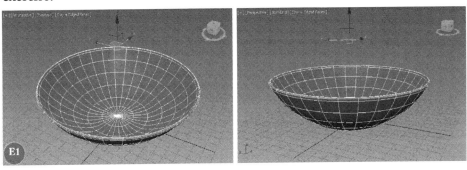

Table E1	
Skill level	Beginner
Time to complete	20 Minutes
Topics	• Specifying the Units for the Exercise • Creating the Bowl
Resources folder	**unit-dmb**
Units	**Metric - Centimeters**
Final file	**bowl-finish.max**

Specifying the Units for the Exercise
Follow these steps:

1. From the **Customize** menu choose **Units Setup**. In the **Units Setup** dialog box that appears, select **Metric** from the **Display Unit Scale** group. Next, choose **Centimeters** from the drop-down list located below **Metric**. Click **System Unit Setup** to open the **System Unit Setup** dialog box and then make sure **1 Unit** is equal to the **1 Centimeters** [see Fig. E2]. Click **OK** and then click **OK** in the **Units Setup** dialog box.

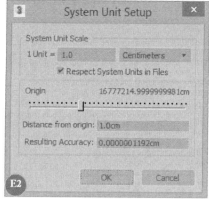

2. **RMB** click on any snap toggle button in the **Main** toolbar. In the **Grid and Snap Settings** dialog box that opens, choose the **Home Grid** panel and then set **Grid Spacing** to **3**, **Major Lines every Nth Grid Line** to **4**, and **Perspective View Grid Extent** to **10**. Close the **Grid and Snap Settings** dialog box. From the **File** menu, choose **Save** to open the **Save File As** dialog box. In the **File name** text box type **bowl-finish.max** and then click **Save** to save the file.

Creating the Bowl
Follow these steps:

1. In the **Create** panel, click **Geometry**, and then in the **Object Type** rollout, click **Sphere**. In the **Perspective** viewport, create a sphere. Switch to **Modify** panel and on the **Parameters** rollout, change **Radius** to **26**.

2. **RMB** click on the sphere and then choose **transform** quadrant > **Convert To:** > **Convert to Editable Poly**. In the **Modify** panel > **Selection** rollout, click **Polygon** to activate the polygon sub-object level.

3. In the **Front** viewport, select the polygons, as shown in Fig. E3 and then press **Delete** to delete the selected polygons [see Fig. E4]. In the **Modify** panel > **Selection** rollout, click **Vertex** to activate the vertex sub-object level and then select the vertices, as shown in Fig. E5.

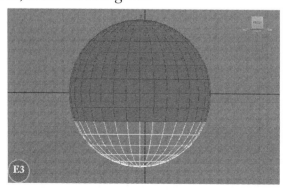

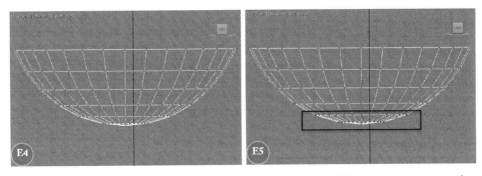

4. In the **Modify** panel > **Edit Geometry** rollout, click **Z** button corresponding to the **Make Planer** parameter to make the selected vertices coplanar [see Fig. E6]. Press **Ctrl+A** to select all vertices and then slightly scale them down along the negative **Y** axis using the **Scale** tool [see Fig. E7]. Press **6** to switch to the **Object** mode and then place the bowl at the origin. Fig. E8 shows the bowl at the origin.

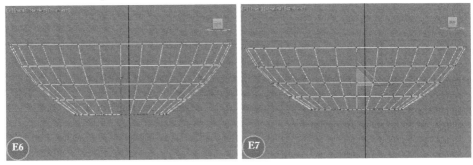

What next?
*If you look at Fig. E8, the surface of the bowl is paper thin. To give it some volume, we will use the **Shell** modifier.*

5. From the **Object-Space Modifiers** section of the **Modifier** list, select **Shell**. In the **Parameters** layout, change **Outer Amount** to **0.7** and **Segments** to **2** [see Fig. E9]. From the **Object-Space Modifiers** section of the **Modifier** list, select **Edit Poly**.

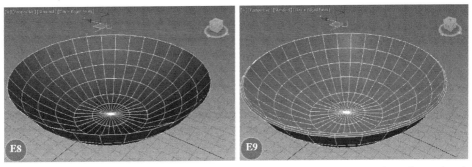

6. In the **Modify** panel > **Selection** rollout, click **Edge** to activate the edge sub-object level and then select the newly added segment [see Fig. E10]. Move it slightly up using the **Move** tool.

7. Select the outer edge loops, as shown in Fig. E11. In the **Modify** panel > **Edit Edges** rollout, click **Chamfer** > **Settings** to open the **Chamfer** caddy control. In the caddy control, change **Amount** to **0.13** and then click **OK** [see Fig. E12].

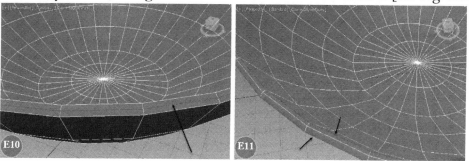

8. From the **Object-Space Modifiers** section of the **Modifier** list, select **MeshSmooth** [see Fig. E13].

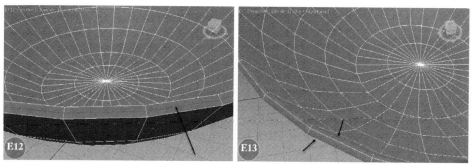

Exercise 2: Creating a Plate

In this exercise, you will create model of a plate [see Fig. E1]. Table E2 summarizes the exercise.

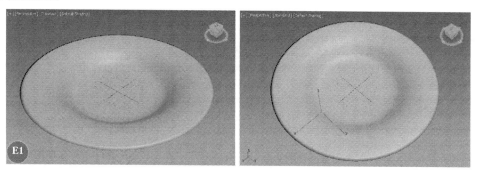

Table E2	
Skill level	Beginner
Time to complete	20 Minutes
Topics	• Specifying the Units for the Exercise • Creating the Plate
Resources folder	**unit-dmb**
Units	**Generic Units**
Final file	**plate-finish.max**

Specifying the Units for the Exercise
Follow these steps:

1. From the **Customize** menu choose **Units Setup**. In the **Units Setup** dialog box that appears, select **Generic Units** from the **Units Setup** dialog box. Click **OK** to accept the changes made.

2. From the **File** menu, choose **Save** to open the **Save File As** dialog box. In the **File name** text box type **plate-finish.max** and then click **Save** to save the file.

Creating the Plate
Follow these steps:

1. Enable 2D snapping from the **Main** toolbar. In the **Create** panel, click **Shapes,** and then click **Line**. In the **Front** viewport, create a shape [see Fig. E2].

2. From the **Object-Space Modifiers** section of the **Modifier** list, select **Lathe**. In the **Modify** panel > **Parameters** rollout > **Align** group, click **Min** [see Fig. E3]. Now, select the **Weld Core** check box and change **Segments** to **32** [see Fig. E4].

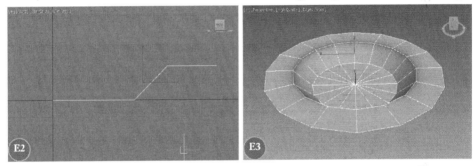

3. From the **Object-Space Modifiers** section of the **Modifier** list, select **Shell**. In the **Parameters** layout, change **Outer Amount** to **2**. From the **Object-Space Modifiers** section of the **Modifier List**, select **Edit Poly**.

4. In the **Modify** panel > **Selection** rollout, click **Edge** to activate the edge sub-object level. Now, select the edge loop, as shown in Fig. E5. In the **Modify** panel > **Edit Edges** rollout, click **Chamfer** > **Settings** to open the **Chamfer** caddy control. In the caddy control, change **Amount** to **4.5** and then click **OK** [see Fig. E6].

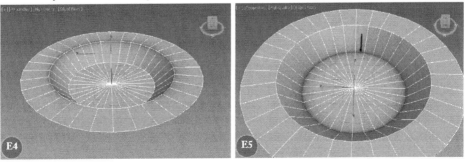

5. Press **6** to switch to the **Object** level. From the **Object-Space Modifiers** section of the **Modifier** list, select **MeshSmooth** [see Fig. E7].

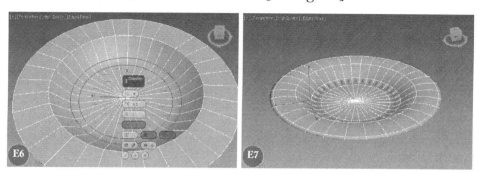

Exercise 3: Creating a Braided Cable

In this exercise, we will create a braided cable [see Fig. E1]. Table E3 summarizes the exercise.

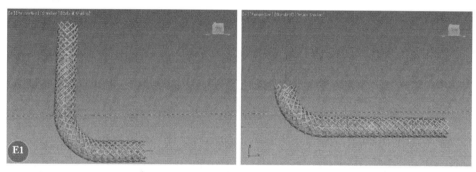

Table E3	
Skill level	Intermediate
Time to complete	40 Minutes
Topics	• Specifying the Units for the Exercise • Creating the Cable
Resources folder	**unit-dmb**
Units	**Generic Units**
Final file	**braided-cable-finish.max**

Specifying the Units for the Exercise

Follow these steps:

1. From the **Customize** menu choose **Units Setup**. In the **Units Setup** dialog box that appears, select **Generic Units** from the **Units Setup** dialog box. Click **OK** to accept the changes made.

2. From the **File** menu, choose **Save** to open the **Save File As** dialog box. In the **File name** text box type **braided-cable-finish.max** and then click **Save** to save the file.

Creating the Cable

Follow these steps:

1. In the **Create** panel, click **Shapes**, and then click **Rectangle**. In the **Front** viewport, create a rectangle and then place it at the origin. In the **Modify** panel > **Parameters** rollout, change **Length** to **30** and **Width** to **30**. Now, align the rectangle, as shown in Fig. E2.

2. **RMB** click on the rectangle and then choose **transform** quadrant > **Convert To:** > **Convert to Editable Spline**. Create a copy of the rectangle using **Shift** and snap the end vertices [see Fig. E3].

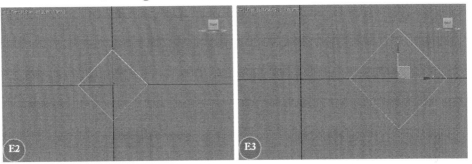

3. Select one of the rectangles and then in the **Modify** panel > **Geometry** rollout, click **Attach** and then click on the other rectangle to attach the rectangles. In the **Modify** panel > **Selection** rollout, click **Segment** to activate the segment sub-object level. Now, select and delete segments, refer to Fig. E4.

4. Select the segments, refer to Fig. E5 and then in the **Modify** panel > **Geometry** rollout, click **Detach** to open the **Detach** dialog box. In this dialog box, type **RightShape** in the **Detach as** text box and then click **OK**. Now, rename the remaining shape as **LeftShape**.

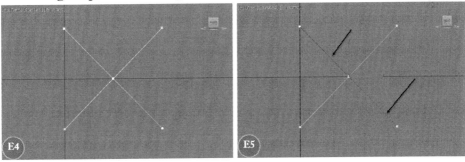

5. Select **LeftShape**, in the **Modify** panel > **Selection** rollout, click **Vertex** to activate the vertex sub-object level. Select the center vertices and then in the **Modify** panel > **Geometry** rollout, click **Weld** to weld the vertices. Repeat the process for **RightShape**. Place the shape at the origin [see Fig. E6].

6. In the **Perspective** viewport, move the spline by **63** units along the **+Y** axis and then select **Use Transform Coordinate Center** from the **Use Center** flyout [see

Fig. E7]. Choose **Array** from the **Tools** menu to open the **Array** dialog box. Set the values as shown in Fig. E8, Fig. E9 shows the result.

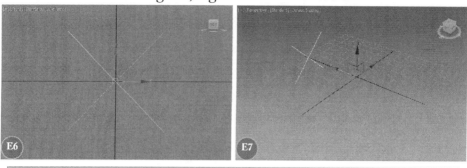

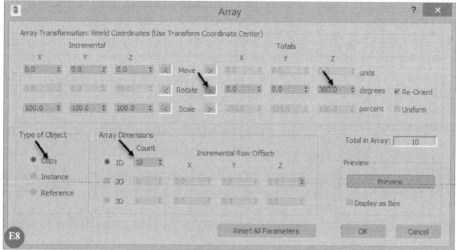

7. Select **LeftShape** and then in the **Modify** panel > **Geometry** rollout, click **Attach Mult** to open the **Attach Multiple** dialog box. Select all left shapes and then click **Attach**. Similarly, repeat the process for the right shapes.

8. Select **LeftShape** and then in the **Modify** panel > **Selection** rollout, click **Vertex** to activate the vertex sub-object level. Select **Use Transform Coordinate Center** from the **Use Center** flyout. Select the center vertices [see Fig. E9] and then scale them by **94%** [see Fig. E10]. Now, press **Ctrl+I** to invert the selection and then scale them by **104%**.

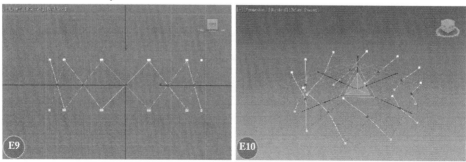

9. Select **RightShape**. Scale the center vertices by **104%** and rest of the vertices by **94%** [see Fig. E11]. Now, attach **LeftShape** and **RightShape** as done earlier. Now, weld the top and bottom vertices [see Fig. E12].

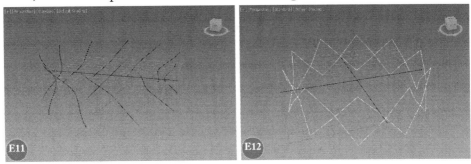

10. In the **Front** viewport create **30** copies of the spline using **Shift** and then attach them [see Fig. E13].

11. From the **Object-Space Modifiers** section of the **Modifier** list, select **Sweep**. In the **Modify** panel > **Selection Type** rollout, change **Built-In Section** to **Pipe**. In the **Parameters** group, change **Radius** to **5.229** and **Thickness** to **0.21** [see Fig. E14].

12. Move the pivot point at the bottom of the cable [see Fig. E15].

13. Create a line using the **Line** tool and rename it as **Path** [see Fig. E16]. Select the cable and then from the **World-Space Modifiers** section of the **Modifier** list, select **Path Deform**.

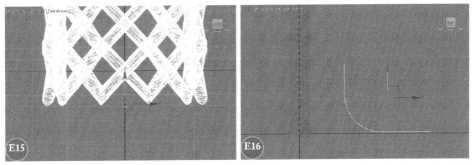

14. In the **Modify** panel > **Parameters** rollout, click **Pick Path** and then click **Path** in the viewport. Now, in the **Path Deform Axis** group, change axis to **Y**. In the **Path Deform** group, change **Percent** to **38.5** [see Fig. E17].

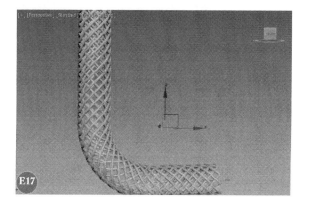

Exercise 4: Creating a Chair

In this exercises, you will create model of a chair, as shown in Fig. E1.

E1

Table E4.1 summarizes the exercise.

Table E4.1	
Skill level	Intermediate
Time to complete	40 Minutes
Topics	• Getting Started • Creating the Frame of the Chair • Creating Seats of the Chair
Resources folder	**unit-dmb**
Units	**Decimal Inches**
Final file	**chair-finish.max**

Getting Ready

Start a new scene in 3ds Max and set units to **Decimal Inches**.

Creating Frame of the Chair
Follow these steps:

1. Go to the **Create** panel, click **Shapes** and then click **Line**. Expand the **Keyboard Entry** rollout and then set **X, Y,** and **Z** to **9.886, -10.75,** and **0.086**, respectively. Click **Add Point** to create the 1st point. Similarly create other points using the values given in Table E4.2. After entering the values shown in the table, click **Finish**; the line appears in the viewports [see Fig. E2].

Table E4.2 - Coordinates for creating points			
Point	X	Y	Z
1st	9.886"	-10.75"	0.086"
2nd	-9.836"	-10.75"	0.086"
3rd	-9.836"	-10.75"	14.834"
4th	6.285"	-10.75"	14.834"
5th	9.886"	-10.75"	27.011"

2. In the **Modify** panel > **Rendering** rollout, select the **Enable In Renderer** and **Enable In Viewport** checkboxes. Now, set **Thickness** to **0.9** and **Sides** to **14**. Make sure **Line001** is selected and then create a copy of the line by **Shift** dragging it about **21** units along the **Y** axis [see Fig. E3].

[+][Perspective][Standard][Default Shading]   [+][Perspective][Standard][Default Shading]

E2   E3

3. Select **Line001** and then in the **Modify** panel > **Geometry** rollout, click **Attach**. Now, click **Line002** in the viewport to attach the two lines. Turn on **Vertex** snapping from the **Main** toolbar. Activate the **Vertex** sub-object level and then click **Create Line** from the **Geometry** rollout.

4. Drag from one vertex to another to create a line [see Fig. E4]. Click **Yes** when prompted to weld the vertices. Click on **Create Line** to deactivate it. Disable snapping. Select all vertices and then **RMB** click. Choose **Bezier Corner** from the **tool1** quadrant of the **Quad** menu.

5. Select the vertices [see Fig. E5] and then click **Weld** from the **Geometry** rollout to weld the vertices. Now, select the vertices shown in Fig. E6. In the **Geometry** rollout, type **1.5** in the field located next to **Fillet** parameter and then press **Enter** to fillet the vertices [see Fig. E7].

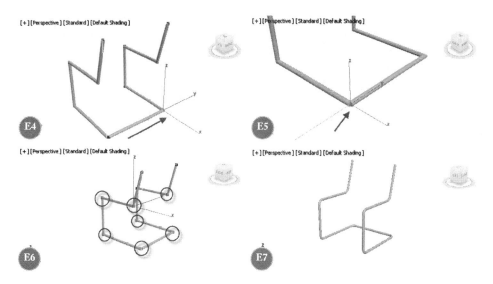

6. In the **Create** panel, click **Geometry** and then in the **Object Type** rollout, click **Tube**. Create a tube in the viewport. Go to the **Modify** panel and then in the **Parameters** rollout, set **Radius 1** to **0.641**, **Radius 2** to **0.429**, and **Height** to **2.133**. Also, set **Sides** to **32**. Align the tube with the frame [see Fig. E8]. Create a copy of the tube and then align it with the other side of the frame.

Creating Seats of the Chair

Follow these steps:

1. In the **Create** panel, click **Geometry** and then in the **Object Type** rollout, click **Box**. Create a box in the **Top** viewport. Go to the **Modify** panel and then in the **Parameters** rollout, set **Length** to **24.283**, **Width** to **14.152**, and **Height** to **2.988**. Set **Length Segs**, **Width Segs**, and **Height Segs** to **4, 4**, and **3**, respectively. Align the box, as shown in Fig. E9. From the **Modifier List > Object-Space Modifiers** section, choose **Turbosmooth**. In the **Parameters** rollout, set **Iterations** to **2**.

2. Now, we'll create piping for the seat. Convert the object to editable poly. Activate the **Edge** mode and select the edge loops [see Fig. E10]. In the **Modify** panel > **Edit Edges** rollout, click **Create Shape From Selection** to open the **Create Shape** dialog box. Click **OK** to close the dialog box and create the shape.

3. Select **Shape001** and then in **Modify** panel > **Rendering** rollout, set **Thickness** to **0.2** [see Fig. E11]. Select **Box001** and then in **Modify** panel > **Edit Geometry** rollout, click **Attach**. Click on **Shape001** to combine the two objects.

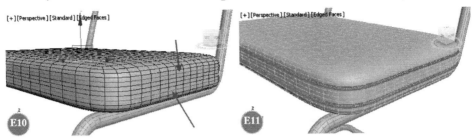

4. From the **Modifier** list > **Object-Space Modifiers** section, choose **FFD 3x3x3**. Activate the **Control Points** sub-object level and select the middle control points. Move the points downwards to create a bend in the seat [see Fig. E12]. Convert the stack to the editable poly. Now, create a copy of the seat and then rotate/scale to create the back support [see Fig. E13].

Tip: Aligning back seat
*To easily align [rotate] the back support with the frame, move the pivot point at the bottom of the back support. Also, use the **Local** coordinate system.*

Exercise 5: Creating a Lamp

In this exercise, you will create a model of a lamp [see Fig. E1]. Table E5 summarizes the exercise.

Table E5	
Skill level	Intermediate
Time to complete	40 Minutes
Topics	• Getting Started • Creating the Lamp
Resources folder	**unit-dmb**
Units	**Generic Units**
Final file	**lamp-finish.max**

Getting Ready

Start a new scene in 3ds Max and set units to **Generic Units**.

Creating the Lamp

Follow these steps:

1. In the **Create** panel, click **Geometry,** and then in the **Extended Primitives >
Object Type** rollout, click **Hedra**. Create a hydra in the viewport. Go to the
Modify panel and then on the **Parameters** rollout > **Family** group, select **Dodec/
Icos**. In the **Family Parameters** group, set **P** and **Q** to **0.32** and **0.35**, respectively.
Set **Radius** to **40** [see Fig. E2]. Convert hedra to editable poly. Activate the
Polygon mode and select the polygon shown in Fig. E3.

2. In the **Ribbon > Modeling** tab > **Modify Selection** panel, click **Similar** [see
Fig. E4] to select the polygon similar to the selected polygon [see Fig. E5]. Press
Delete to delete the selected polygons. Press **Ctrl+A** to select all polygons.

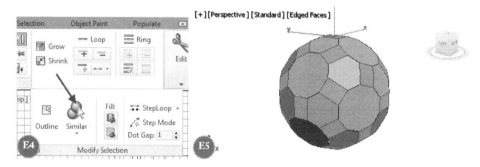

3. Click **Settings** on the right of **Extrude** in the **Modify** panel > **Edit Polygons** rollout. In the **Extrude Polygon** caddy control, set extrude **Type** to **Local Normal** and **Height** to **10** and click **Apply and Continue**. Now, click **OK** [see Fig. E6]. In the **Modify** panel > **Selection** rollout, click **Grow**. Press **Ctrl+I** to invert the selection and then press **Delete** to delete the polygons. Select all polygons and then in the **Modify** panel > **Polygon: Smoothing Groups** rollout, click **Auto Smooth** to smooth the polygon [see Fig. E7].

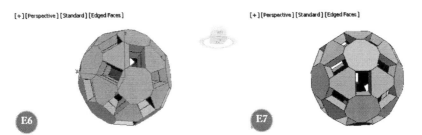

4. Activate the **Edge** mode and then select the edges, as shown in Fig. E8. In the **Ribbon** > **Modeling** tab > **Modify Selection** panel, click **Similar**. Click **Settings** on the right of **Chamfer** in the **Modify** panel > **Edit Edges** rollout. In the **Chamfer's** caddy, set **Chamfer Type** to **Quad Chamfer**, **Edge Chamfer Amount** to **0.294**, and **Connect Edge Segments** to **1**. Click **OK**.

5. Select the **Element** mode and click on the hedra in the viewport. In the **Ribbon** > **Modeling** tab > **Subdivision** panel, click **Tessellate** [see Fig. E9]. Activate the **Edge** mode and then select the edges shown in Fig. E10. In the **Ribbon** > **Modeling** tab > **Modify Selection** panel, click **Similar**. In the **Modify** panel > **Edit Edges** rollout, click **Create Shape From Selection** to open the **Create Shape** dialog box. Click **OK** to create the shape [see Fig. E11].

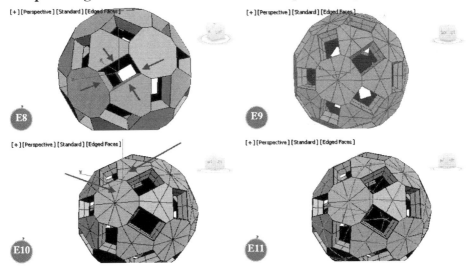

6. Select **Shape001**. In the **Modify** panel > **Rendering** rollout, select the **Enable In Renderer** and **Enable In Viewport** checkboxes. Now, set **Thickness** to **0.9** and **Sides** to **14**. Select **Hedra001** and then in the **Modifier List** > **Object-Space Modifiers** section, choose **Turbosmooth**. In the **Parameters**

rollout, set **Iterations** to **2** [see Fig. E12]. Select **Shape001** and **Hedra001**. Group them with the name **Lamp**.

[+][Perspective][Standard][Default Shading]

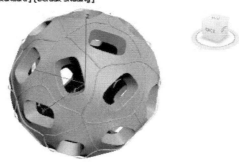

7. Now, create the stand for the lamp and align it with the stand.

Exercise 6: Creating a Waste Bin

In this exercise, you will create a model of a waste bin [see Fig. E1]. Table E6 summarizes the exercise.

Table E6	
Skill level	Intermediate
Time to complete	50 Minutes
Topics	• Getting Started • Creating the Waste Bin
Resources folder	**unit-dmb**
Units	**Decimal Inches**
Final file	**bin-finish.max**

Getting Ready
Start a new scene in 3ds Max and set units to **Decimal Inches**.

Creating the Waste Bin
Follow these steps:

1. In the **Create** panel, click **Geometry** and then in the **Object Type** rollout, click **Cylinder**. Create a cylinder in the **Top** viewport. Go to the **Modify** panel and then in the **Parameters** rollout, set **Radius** to **15**, **Height** to **45**, **Sides** to **50**, and

Height Segments to **30**. Convert cylinder to editable poly. Activate the **Polygon** mode, select the top polygon and then delete it [see Fig. E2].

2. Select the top and bottom polygon loops [see Fig. E3] and then click **Settings** on the right of **Extrude** in the **Modify** panel > **Edit Polygons** rollout. In the **Extrude Polygons** caddy control, set **Type** to **Local Normal** and **Height** to **1.2** and click **OK**.

3. Ensure the newly created polygons are still selected and then click **Settings** on the right of **Bevel** in the **Modify** panel > **Edit Polygons** rollout. In the **Bevel** caddy control, set **Type** to **Local Normal**, **Height** to **0.6**, **Outline** to **-0.9333**. Click **OK** [see Fig. E4].

4. Select every alternate column of polygons using **Shift**, see Fig. E5. Now, using the **Alt** key, remove polygons form the selection [see Fig. E6]. Click **Settings** on the right of **Extrude** in the **Modify** panel > **Edit Polygons** rollout. In the **Extrude Polygons** caddy control, set **Type** to **Local Normal** and **Height** to **-0.5** and click **OK**.

5. From the **Modifier** list > **Object-Space Modifiers** section, choose **Shell**. In the **Modify** panel > **Parameters** rollout, set **Outer Amount** to **0.15** [see Fig. E7]. Now, apply a **TurboSmooth** modifier to the cylinder. Now, we'll create lid for the waste bin.

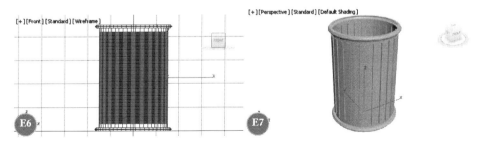

6. In the **Create** panel, click **Geometry** and then in the **Object Type** rollout, click **Cylinder**. Create a cylinder in the **Top** viewport. Go to the **Modify** panel and

then in the **Parameters** rollout, set **Radius** to **17**, **Height** to **2**, **Sides** to **50**, and **Height Segments** to **1**.

7. Convert cylinder to the editable poly object. Activate the **Polygon** mode and select the bottom polygon [see Fig. E8], and then click **Settings** on the right of **Inset** in the **Modify** panel > **Edit Polygons** rollout. In the **Inset Polygons** caddy control, set **Amount** to **1** and click **OK** [see Fig. E9].

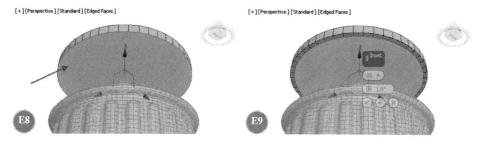

8. Click **Settings** on the right of **Extrude** in the **Modify** panel > **Edit Polygons** rollout. In the **Extrude Polygons** caddy control, set **Type** to **Local Normal** and **Height** to **-1** and click **OK** [see Fig. E10]. Now, align the lid with the bin.

9. Select the outer edges [refer to Fig. E11] of lid and then chamfer them. Refer to Fig. E12 for chamfer settings. Select the top polygon of the lid and then click **Settings** on the right of **Inset** in the **Modify** panel > **Edit Polygons** rollout. In the **Inset** caddy control, set **Amount** to **9** and click **OK**. Make sure the polygon is still selected and then move it slightly upwards [see Fig. E13]. Let's now create handle for the lid.

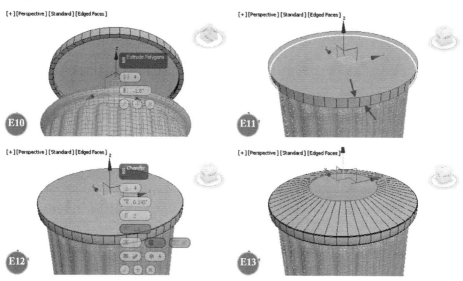

10. In the **Create** panel, click **Geometry** and then in the **Object Type** rollout, click **Torus**. Create a torus in the **Top** viewport. Go to the **Modify** panel and then on the **Parameters** rollout, set **Radius 1** to **4.64**, **Radius 2** to **0.84**, **Segments** to **50**, and **Sides** to **18**. Also, select the **Slice On** check box and then set **Slice From** and **Slice To** to **90**, and **270**, respectively. Now, align the torus at the center of the lid [see Fig. E14].

[+] [Perspective] [Standard] [Edged Faces]

Exercise 7: Creating a Bottle

In this exercise, you will create a bottle using the **Loft** compound object [see Fig. E1]. Table E7 summarizes the exercise.

Table E7	
Skill level	Intermediate
Time to complete	45 Minutes
Topics	• Getting Started • Creating the Bottle
Resources folder	**unit-dmb**
Units	**Generic Units**
Final file	**bottle-finish.max**

Getting Ready

Follow these steps:

1. Go to the **Create** panel, click **Geometry**, and then click **Plane**. In the **Front** viewport, create a plane. In the **Modify** panel > **Parameters** rollout, set **Length** to **180**, **Width** to **150**, **Length Segs** to **2**, and **Width Segs** to **2**. Invoke the **Move** tool from the **Main** toolbar. Set the **Transform Type-In** boxes to **0** in the **Status Bar** to place the box at the origin.

2. Click **Material Editor** from the **Main** toolbar. Create a standard material and then apply it to the plane. Use the **whiskey.jpg** for the **Diffuse** map. You need to select the **Show Shaded Material in Viewport** option for the material to display the image on the plane in the viewport.

373   **3ds Max 2020**

3. Ensure in the **Coordinates** rollout of the bitmap, **Use Real-World Scale** is off and **U Tiling** and **V Tiling** are set to **1** each. Make sure the **Front** viewport is active and then press **G** to turn off the grid. Also, set the shading to **Default Shading** in the **Front** viewport.

4. **RMB** click on the plane and then choose **Object Properties** from the **Quad** menu to open the **Object Properties** dialog box. In the **Interactivity** group of the dialog box, select the **Freeze** check box and in the **Display Properties** group, clear the **Show Frozen in Gray** check box [see Fig. E2].

Creating the Bottle
Follow these steps:

1. Go to the **Create** panel, click **Shapes**, and then click **Line**. In the **Front** viewport, create a shape [see Fig. E3] that is aligned with the vertical center of the bottle [create the first point at the bottom of the bottle]. You can create line anywhere in the scene but placing it at the center of the bottle will help you in the modeling process.

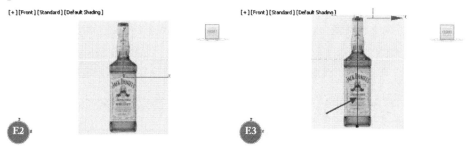

2. Go to the **Create** panel, click **Geometry**, and then click **Rectangle**. Create a rectangle in the **Top** viewport. In the **Modify** panel > **Parameters** rollout, set **Length** to **40**, **Width** to **40**, and **Corner Radius** to **8**. Go to the **Create** panel, click **Geometry**, and then click **Circle**. Create a circle in the **Top** viewport. In the **Modify** panel > **Parameters** rollout, set **Radius** to **7.5** [see Fig. E4].

3. Ensure the line is selected in and then click **Loft** on **Create** panel > **Geometry** > **Compound Objects** > **Object Type** rollout. Click **Get Shape** on the **Creation Method** rollout and then click the rectangle in the viewport to create the lofted object. In the **Path Parameters** rollout, set **Path** to **100**. Click **Get Shape** on the **Creation Method** rollout and then click the circle in the viewport to create the basic shape of the bottle [see Fig. E5].

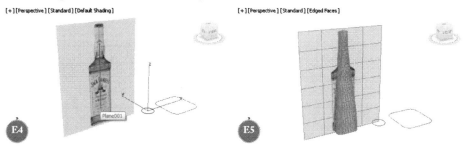

4. **RMB** click on the lofted objects and choose **Object Properties** from the **Quad** menu to open the **Object Properties** dialog box. In the **Display Properties** group of the dialog box, select the **See-Through** check box. Click **OK** to close the dialog box.

What just happened?
Notice in Fig. E5, the image is obscured by the lofted object. Here, I have enabled the x-ray mode for the object so that we can see through it.

5. Enable the **Shape** sub-object level of the **Loft** object from the **Modify** panel and then select the rectangle shape on the loft object. Create a copy of the shape using **Shift+Drag** operation. Now, uniformly scale the copied rectangle so that it fits in the profile of the bottle [see Fig. E6]. Repeat the process until you get a rough shape using the copies of rectangle and circle [see Fig. E7].

6. Now, hide the plane geometry and turn off the x-ray mode [see Fig. E8] from the **Object Properties** dialog box. Make sure bottle is selected and then in **Modify** panel > **Skin Parameters** rollout, clear the **Cap End** check box. From the **Modifier** list > **Object-Space Modifiers** section, choose **Shell**. In the **Parameters** rollout, set **Outer Amount** to **0** and **Inner Amount** to **1**. If you render the geometry, you would see that facets are appearing on the bottle. Let's fix it.

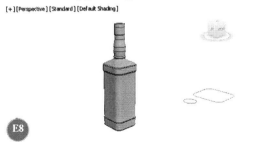

7. From the **Modifier** list > **Object-Space Modifiers** section, choose **Smooth**. In the **Parameters** rollout, select the **Auto Smooth** check box to smooth the geometry.

What just happened?
*Here, I've applied the **Smooth** modifier to eliminate the facets on geometry by grouping faces into smoothing groups. Faces in the same smoothing group appear as a smooth surface when you render the geometry.*

Exercise 8: Creating a Chair

In this exercise, you will create a chair using the spline and polygon modeling techniques [see Fig. E1]. Table E8 summarizes the exercise.

 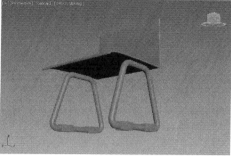

Table E8	
Skill level	Intermediate
Time to complete	45 Minutes
Topics	• Getting Started • Creating the Chair
Resources folder	**unit-dmb**
Units	**Decimal Inches**
Final file	**chair1-finish.max**

Getting Ready

We'll first create a box that will work like a template that will help us in the modeling process. Follow these steps:

1. In the **Create** panel, click **Geometry** and then in the **Object Type** rollout, click **Box**. Create a box in the **Top** viewport.

2. Go to the **Modify** panel and then in the **Parameters** rollout, set **Length** to **20**, **Width** to **20**, and **Height** to **30**. Set **Length Segs**, **Width Segs**, and **Height Segs** to **1**, **4**, and **2**, respectively. Set the **Transform Type-In** boxes in the **Status Bar** to **0** to place the box at the origin [see Fig. E2].

Creating the Chair

Follow these steps:

1. Activate the **Front** viewport and enable snapping [**Vertex**] by pressing **S**. Go to the **Create** panel, click **Shapes**, and then click **Rectangle**. In the **Front** viewport, create a shape [see Fig. E3]. Convert rectangle to editable spline. Activate the **Vertex** level and then press **Ctrl+A** to select all vertices. **RMB** click and then choose **Corner** from **Quad** menu > **tool1** quadrant. Now, move the top vertices as shown in Fig. E4.

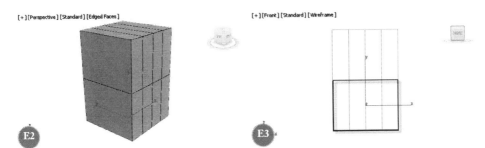

2. Press **Ctrl+A** to select all vertices and then on the **Modify** panel > **Geometry** rollout, enter **2** [type 2 and then press **Enter**] in the **Fillet** field to fillet all the vertices [see Fig. E5]. In the **Modify** panel > **Rendering** rollout, select the **Enable In Renderer** and **Enable In Viewport** checkboxes. Now, set **Thickness** to **1.5**. Turn off snapping.

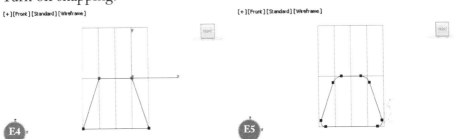

3. In the **Create** panel, click **Geometry** and then in the **Extended Primitives** > **Object Type** rollout, click **ChamferBox**. Create a box in the **Top** viewport. Go to the **Modify** panel and then on the **Parameters** rollout, set **Length** to **1.9**, **Width** to **4.02**, **Height** to **1.9**, and **Fillet** to **0.045**. Set **Length Segs**, **Width Segs**, **Height Segs** and **Fillet Segs** to **1, 1, 1**, and **3**, respectively. Align it with the base of the chair [see Fig. E6]. Create a copy of the box and then align, as shown in Fig. E7.

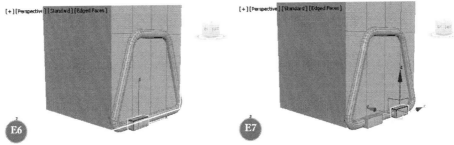

4. Select the line and the two chamfer boxes. Click **Mirror** in the **Main** toolbar. In the **Mirror** dialog box that appears, set the values shown in Fig. E8 and click **OK** to accept the value and create copy of the selected geometry [see Fig. E9]. Hide **Box001**.

5. In the **Create** panel, click **Geometry** and then in the **Object Type** rollout, click **Plane**. Create a plane in the **Top** viewport. In the **Modify** panel > **Parameters**

rollout, set **Length, Width, Length Segs**, and **Width Segs** to **23, 20, 1**, and **1**, respectively. Align it with the base [see Fig. E10]. Convert the plane to editable poly.

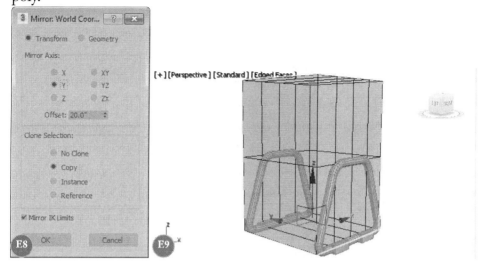

6. Active the **Edge** mode and select the back edge [refer to Fig. E11]. Now, extrude the edge upward by **15** units [see Fig. E12] using **Shift**+drag. Similarly, extrude the front edge [see Fig. E13]. Now, select the middle edge. Click **Settings** on the right of **Chamfer** in the **Modify** panel > **Edit Edges** rollout.

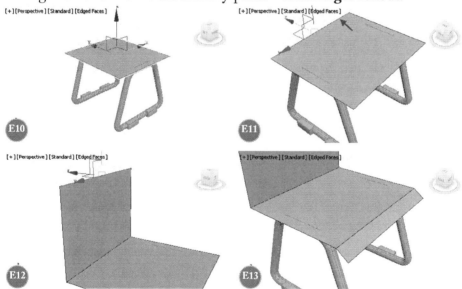

7. In the **Chamfer** caddy control, set **Type** to **Standard Chamfer, Edge Chamfer Amount** to **1.5**, and **Connect Edge Segments** to **4**. Click **OK** [see Fig. E14]. Now, create edges as shown in Fig. E15 using the **Swift Loop** tool.

8. From the **Modifier** list > **Object-Space Modifiers** section, choose **Shell**. In the **Modify** panel > **Parameters** group, set **Outer Amount** to **0.53**. From the **Modifier** list > **Object-Space Modifiers** section, choose **Turbosmooth**. In the **Modify** panel > **Parameters** group, set **Iterations** to **2**.

E14
E15

Exercise 9: Creating an Exterior Scene

In this exercise, you will model an exterior scene using various modeling techniques [see Fig. E1]. Table E9 summarizes the exercise.

E1

Table E9	
Skill level	Intermediate
Time to complete	60 Minutes
Topics	• Getting Started • Creating the Scene
Resources folder	**unit-dmb**
Units	**Meters**
Final file	**ext-finish.max**

Getting Ready

Start a new scene in 3ds Max and set units to **Meters**.

Creating the Scene

Follow these steps:

1. In the **Create** panel, click **Geometry** and then in the **Object Type** rollout, click **Box**. Create a box in the **Top** viewport. Go to the **Modify** panel and then in the **Parameters** rollout, set **Length** to **20**, **Width** to **60**, and **Height** to **8**. Create another box and then set its **Length** to **14**, **Width** to **52**, and **Height** to **8**. Also, set **Length Segs**, **Width Segs**, and **Height Segs** to **4**, **14**, and **1**, respectively. Now, align the boxes [see Fig. E2].

2. Select the **Box001** in a viewport and then convert it to **Editable Poly**. Activate the **Edge** mode and then connect the edges [see Fig. E3]. Activate the **Polygon** mode and then inset the front two faces [see Fig. E4]. Now, extrude the faces by -5 units [see Fig. E5].

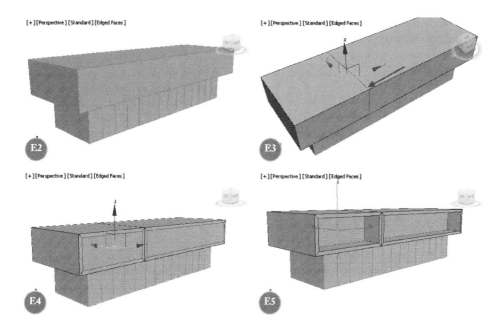

3. Create a box and then set its **Length** to **4.61**, **Width** to **0.602**, and **Height** to **6.827**. Also, set **Length Segs**, **Width Segs**, and **Height Segs** to **1** each. Now, align the box [see Fig. E6]. You might need to adjust the height of the cube as per the inset amount you have specified. Create instances of the box using **Shift** dragging [see Fig. E7].

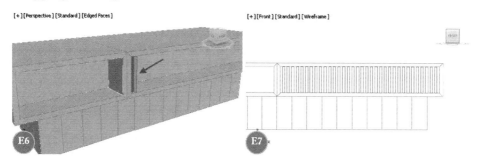

4. Select **Box002** and convert it to **Editable Poly**. Select the polygon shown in Fig. E8. Now, inset the polygons by **0.22** units [see Fig. E9]. Now, extrude the polygons by **-0.25** units. Make sure the polygons are still selected and then enter **glassSelection** in the **Named Selection Sets** field in the **Main** toolbar.

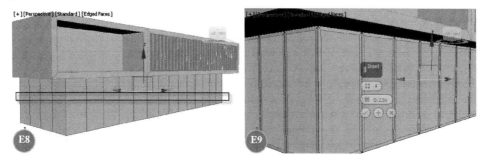

5. Create a **Plane** primitive and then set its **Length** and **Width** to **600**, and **800**, respectively. Align the plane as shown in Fig. E10. Create a box with **Length** to **36**, **Width** to **71**, and **Height** to **0.2**. Also, set **Length Segs**, **Width Segs**, and **Height Segs** to **1** each. Align it as shown in Fig. E11. Also, align the plane below it.

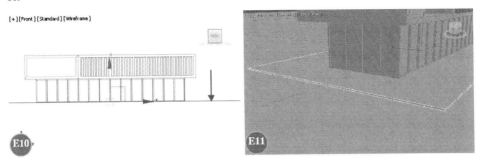

6. Create a **Rectangle** spline in the viewport and then set its **Length, Width**, and **Corner Radius** to **12, 48**, and **4**, respectively. Apply the **Extrude** modifier to it and then set **Amount** to **0.4**. Align the rectangle, as shown in Fig. E12.

7. Now, create a light pole using the spline and polygon modeling techniques. Create an instance of the pole and align [see Fig. E13]. Create doors for the building [see Fig. E14]. Now, create a logo using the **TextPlus** primitive [see Fig. E15].

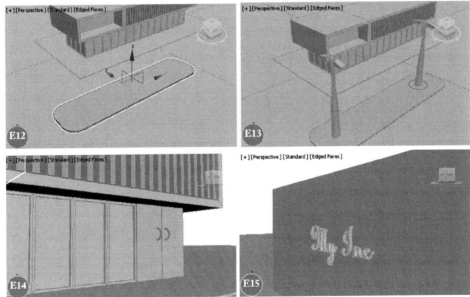

This page is intentionally left blank

Unit DMP: Practice Activities [Modeling]

Practice Activities

Activity 1: Creating a Road Side Sign

Create a road side sign, as shown in Fig. A1, using the **Box, Pyramid,** and **Box** primitives.

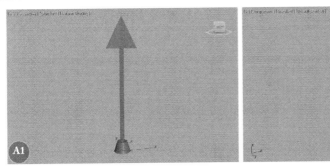

Activity 2: Creating a Robo Model

Create a robot model, as shown in Fig. A2, using the **Standard** primitives.

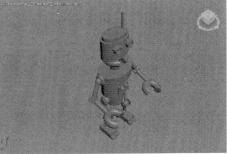

Hints:

- *The primitives used in the model shown in Fig. A2 are:* **Box, Sphere, Cylinder, Pyramid, Cone, Torus,** *and* **Pipe**.
- *The fingers are created using* **Torus** *primitives. Select* **Slice On** *in the* **Parameters** *rollout of torus to create opening in the torus.*

- Use the **Auto Grid** and **Select and Place** features of 3ds Max to align and place body parts.
- Create one leg and then use the **Mirror** tool to create a copy on the other side. Apply same concept on eyes and hands. Create a group before applying the **Mirror** tool.
- Create layers for different parts in **Layer Explorer**. For example, keep all geometries that make hand in the hands layer, and so on.
- Try to use various features of the **Scene Explorer**.

Activity 3: Creating a Coffee Table

Create the coffee table model [see Fig. A3] using the **Box** primitive.

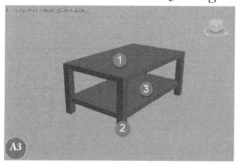 

Dimensions:
1: *Length=35.433", Width=21.654", Height=1.5"*
2: *Length=34.037", Width=20.8", Height=1.5"*
3: *Length=2", Width=2", Height=13.78"*

Activity 4: Creating a 8-Drawer Dresser

Create the 8-drawer model [see Fig. A4] using the **Box** primitive. Create the knobs using the **Sphere** and **Cylinder** primitives.

Dimensions:
1: *Length=65", Width=21", Height=1.5"*
2: *Length=2", Width=2", Height=35"*
3: *Length=60.997", Width=18.251", Height=30"*
4: *Length=27.225", Width=19.15", Height=11"*
5: *Length=27.225", Width=19.15", Height=7"*
6: *Length=12.871", Width=19.15", Height=5"*

Activity 5: Creating a Foot Stool

Create the foot stool model [see Fig. A5] using the **ChamferCyl** primitive.

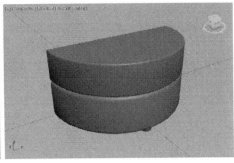

Dimensions:
1: *Radius=14", Height=5.91", Fillet=0.32", Sides=24, and Fillet Segs=3*
2: *Radius=14", Height=7.5", Fillet=0.74", Sides=24, and Fillet Segs=3*
3: *Radius=1.104", Height=2.238", Fillet=0.276", and Fillet Segs=3*

Hint:
*Check **Slice On** for the cylinders and set **Slice To** to **–180**. Apply the **Taper** modifier to the legs of the stool.*

Activity 6: Creating a Sofa

Create the sofa model [see Fig. A6] using the **Chamfer Box** primitive. Assume the dimensions.

Activity 7: Creating a Wine Glass

Create the wine glass model [see the left image in Fig. A7] using the **Line** primitive.

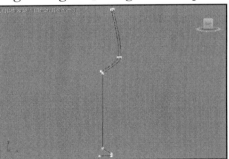

Hint:

*Create a shape [see the right image in Fig. A8] and the use the **Lathe** modifier to create the glass.*

Activity 8: Creating a Glass Rack

Create a model of a glass rack using the **Rectangle** spline, the **ChamferCyl** primitive, and the **Extrude** modifier [see the left image in Fig. A8].

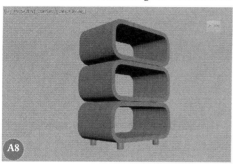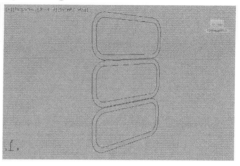

Hint:

*Create a **Rectangle** spline, convert it to editable spline, give it some outline, and then apply the **Extrude** modifier [see the right image in Fig. A8].*

- Compact Material Editor
- Slate Material Editor

Unit DT1: Material Editors

A material editor is a window that allows you to create and edit materials as well as to assign them to the objects in the scene. A material in 3ds Max defines how light is reflected and transmitted by the objects in a scene.

3ds Max offers two material editors, **Compact Material Editor** and **Slate Material Editor**. These editors offer a variety of functions and features that allow you to design realistic looking surfaces in 3ds Max. To open an editor, choose **Compact** 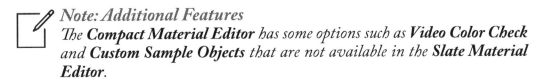 or **Slate** option from the **Material Editor** flyout on the **Main** toolbar. You can also open an editor by choosing **Compact Material Editor** or **Slate Material Editor** from the **Rendering** menu > **Material Editor** sub-menu.

Compact Material Editor

This was the only material editor available prior to the 2011 release of 3ds Max. It is comparatively a small window [see Fig. 1] than the **Slate Material Editor** window and allows you to quickly preview the material. If you are assigning materials that have already been designed, this material editor is the preferred choice.

> *Note: Additional Features*
> *The **Compact Material Editor** has some options such as **Video Color Check** and **Custom Sample Objects** that are not available in the **Slate Material Editor**.*

The **Compact Material Editor's** interface consists of menu bar at the top [see Fig. 1], sample slots below the menu bar, and toolbars at the bottom and right of the sample slots. Now onwards, I will refer to these toolbars as horizontal and vertical toolbar, respectively. The interface also consists of many rollouts. The content on these rollouts depends on the active material slot and the type of material it hosts.

> *Note: Switching Editors*
> *If you want to switch to the **Slate Material Editor**, choose **Slate Material Editor** from the editor's **Modes** menu.*

Sample Slots

The sample slots allow you to preview material and maps. By default, six sample slots appear in the editor. You can increase the number of slots by choosing **Cycle 3x2, 5x3, 6x4 Sample Slots** from the editor's **Options** menu. This option cycles through the 3x2, 5x3, and 6x4 slots arrangement. To make a sample slot active, click on the sample slot. The active sample slot appears with a white border around it.

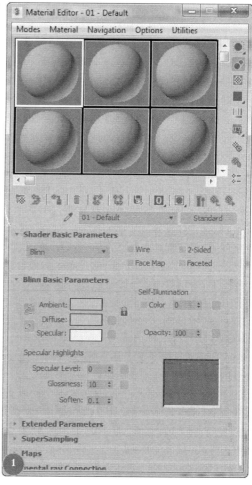

 Caution: Maximum number of sample slots
*The **Compact Material Editor** allows you to edit up to **24** materials at a time. However, the scene can contain an unlimited numbers of materials. When you finish a material and apply it to the objects in the scene, you can use the slot occupied by that material to design the next material.*

By default, material appears on a sphere geometry in a sample slot. You can change the sphere to cylinder or cube by choosing the desired option from the **Sample Type** flyout. This flyout is the first entry in the editor's vertical toolbar. To view a magnified version of the sample slot in a floating window, double-click on it. You can resize the window to change the magnification level of the sample slot.

Hot and Cool Materials

A sample slot is considered to be hot if it is assigned to one or more surfaces in the scene. When you use the editor to adjust properties of a hot material, the changes are reflected in the viewport at the same time. The corners of a sample slot indicates whether the material is hot or not. Given below are the possibilities:

- **No triangle:** The material is not used in the scene.
- **Outlined white triangle:** The material is hot and the changes you make to it will change the material displayed in the scene.
- **Solid white triangle:** The material is not only hot but it is also applied to the currently selected object in the scene.

Notice the three sample slots in Fig. 2 that show three possibilities: a hot material applied to the currently selected, a hot material is applied to the scene but not on the currently selected object, and a cool material which is active but not assigned to scene, respectively.

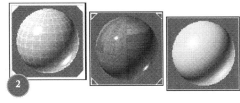

If you want to make a hot material cool, click **Make Material Copy** ⬚ from the horizontal toolbar. You can have the same material with the same name in multiple slots but only one slot can be hot. However, you can have more than one hot sample slots as long as each sample slot has a different material.

✎ Note: *Dragging a material*
If you drag a material to copy it from one sample slot to another, the destination slot will be cool whereas the original slot remains hot.

When you **RMB** click on a sample slot, a context menu appears. Table 1 summarizes the options available in this menu.

Table 1: Sample slot context menu	
Option	**Description**
Drag/Copy	This is active by default. When active, dragging a sample slot copies the material from one sample slot to another.
Drag/Rotate	When you select this option, dragging the sample slot rotates the sample geometry in the slot. This is useful in visualizing the map in the slot.
Reset Rotation	Resets the sample slot's rotation.
Render Map	Opens the **Render Map** dialog box that allows you to render the current map. You can create an **AVI** file if the map is animated.
Options	Opens the material editor's options.
Magnify	Generates a magnified view of the current sample slot.
Select By Material	Selects objects based on the material in the sample slot.
Highlight Assets in ATS dialog box	This option is typically used for the bitmap textures. It opens the **Asset Tracking** dialog box with the assets highlighted.
Sample Windows Options	You can use one of these options to change the number of slots displayed in the material editor.

By default, the **Standard** material is displayed when you select a sample slot. If you want to use the **Standard** material, you can choose the desired shading model from the drop-down list available in the **Shader Basic Parameters** rollout of the editor and then assign colors or maps to the various components of the material. For example, if you want to assign a map to the **Diffuse** component of the material, click on the button located at the right of the **Diffuse** color swatch to open the **Material/Map Browser** which is a modeless dialog box. From the browser, select the map from the **Maps > General/Scanline/Environment/OSL** rollout and then click **OK**.

Tip: Material/Map Browser
You can also double-click on a map to select it and close the browser.

For example, if you want to apply a checker map, double-click on the **Checker** map from the **Maps > General** rollout of the browser. Once you select the map, 3ds Max shows rollouts in the editor that you can use to edit the properties of the map. To go back to the parent level, click **Go To Parent** ▨ from the horizontal toolbar.

You can also copy map from one component to another component. For example, if you have applied a map to the **Diffuse** component of the material and you want to copy it to **Opacity** component. Drag the **Diffuse's** button onto the **Opacity's** button, the **Copy (Instance) Map** dialog box appears. Select the desired option from the **Method** group and then click **OK** to create an instance, a copy, or just to swap the materials from one slot to another.

Note: Other materials
*If you want to use any other material apart from the **Standard** material, click on **Type** button [labelled as **Standard**] to open the **Material/Map Browser**. Double-click on the desired material from the **Materials > General/Scanline** rollout; the **Replace Material** dialog box appears with options to discard the old material or keep the old material as a sub-material. Choose the desired option and then click **OK**. The label **Standard** on the button will be replaced by the type of the new material. For example, if you have chosen **Blend**, the **Standard** label will be replaced by the **Blend** label.*

By default, 3ds Max gives a name to each material [01 - **Default, 02 - Default,** and so on]. The name appears below the horizontal toolbar. If you want to change the name, edit the name in the field. The name field only displays **16** characters but the material name can be longer than **16** characters.

If the material you want to change is present in the scene but is not displayed in any of the sample slots, you can get it directly from the scene. To do this, select the object in the scene and click a sample slot to make it active. From the horizontal toolbar, click **Get Material** ▨ to open the **Material/Map Browser**. Find the scene material in the **Scene Materials** rollout and then double-click on the name of the material. You can also drag the material name to the sample slot. When you get a material from the scene, it is initially a hot material.

To apply a material to an object[s] in the scene, drag the sample slot that contains the material to the object[s] in the scene. If there is only one object selected in the scene, the material is immediately applied to that object. If there are more than one objects selected, 3ds Max prompts you to choose whether to apply the material to the single object or to the whole selection. You can also apply material to the selection by clicking **Assign Material To Selection** on the horizontal toolbar. Once you apply material to objects in the scene, click **Show Shaded Material in Viewport** on the horizontal toolbar to view the material on the objects in the scene.

Tip: Hot material
When you apply a material to an object, the material becomes a hot material.

Tip: Removing material from an object
To remove a material from an object, select the object and then execute the following command from the MAXScript Listener: $.material=undefined.

Note: Selecting objects that have the same material applied
*From the vertical toolbar, click **Select By Material**. This button will not be available unless the active sample slot contains a material that is applied to the objects in the scene. The **Select Objects** dialog box appears. Those objects onto which the material has been applied appear highlighted in the dialog box. Click **Select** to select the objects in the scene.*

You can also save a material to the library. A material library helps you in organizing materials. You can use a material from a library in another scene, if required. To save a material to the library, on the horizontal toolbar, click **Put To Library**, the **Put To Library** dialog box appears. In this dialog box, change the name of the material or leave as is. Click **OK** to save the material. The material is saved in the currently opened library. If no library is open, a new library is created. You can save this library as a file using the **Material/Map Browser** parameters.

To get a material from the library, click **Get Material** to open the **Material/Map Browser**. Now, open a library group. In the list of the materials in the library, double-click on the name of the material that you intend to use. The material you choose from the library replaces the material in the active sample slot.

Material/Map Browser

The **Material/Map Browser** [see Fig. 3] allows you to choose a material or map. When you click the **Type** button or any button on the **Compact Material Editor**, a modal version of the **Material/Map Browser** opens.

Note: Slate Material Editor
*In the **Slate Material Editor**, the **Material/Map Browser** appears as a panel and always visible.*

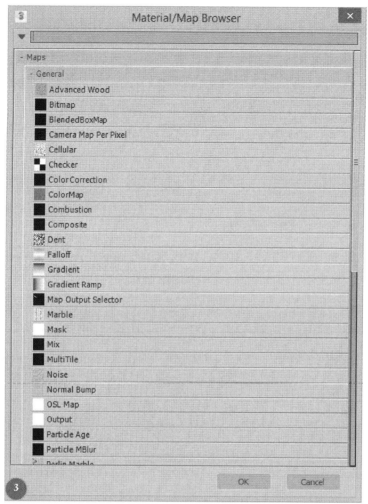

At the top-left corner of the browser, the **Material/Map Browser Options** button ▼ is available. When you click this button, a menu is displayed from where you can set various options for the **Material/Map Browser**. The **Search by Name** field on the right of the button allows you to filter the maps and materials in the browser. For example, if you type **grad** in the field, the maps and materials will be displayed below the field whose names start with the characters **grad** [see Fig. 4].

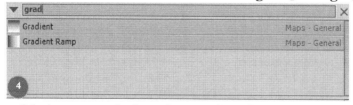

The main part of the browser is the list of materials and maps arranged in the rollouts [groups]. You can collapse or expand these groups.

Caution: Materials and maps in the Material/Map Browser
*By default, the **Material/Map Browser** only displays those maps and materials that are compatible with the active renderer.*

Note: Material/Map Browser's contextual menu
*When you **RMB** click on the header of a rollout, a context menu appears [see Fig. 5]. This menu shows the general options related to that particular group.*

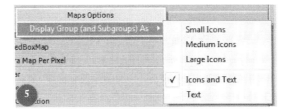

Material Explorer

The **Material Explorer** [see Fig. 6] allows you to browse and manage all materials in a scene. You can open the explorer from the **Rendering** menu. You can also open it as an extended viewport. To do this, choose **Material Explorer** from the **Point-Of-View (POV) Viewport** label menu > **Extended Viewports**.

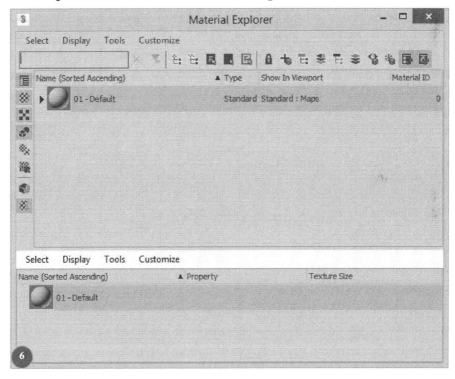

The **Compact Material Editor** lets you set the properties of the materials but there is limitations on number of materials it can display at a time. However, with the **Material Explorer**, you can browse all the materials in the scene. You can also see the objects onto which the materials are applied, you can change the material assignment, and manage materials in other ways.

Slate Material Editor

The **Slate Material Editor** is little complex than the **Compact Material Editor**. In this editor, the entities are displayed in form of nodes that you can wire together to create material trees. If you are working on a large scene with lots of materials, this editor is the preferred choice. The powerful search function provided by this editor lets you find materials in a complex scene easily.

I mostly use the **Slate Material Editor** because its interface [see Fig. 7] is more intuitive when it comes to designing materials. I have marked various components of the interface with numbers in Fig. 7. Table 2 summarizes the **Slate Material Editor's** interface.

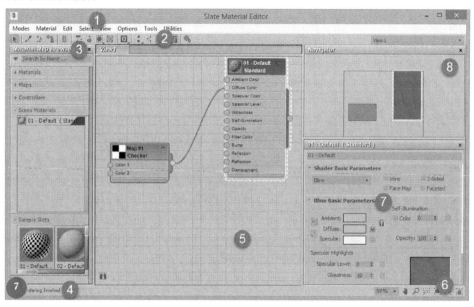

Table 2: The **Slate Material Editor's** interface overview	
Number	Description
1	Menu bar
2	Toolbar
3	Material/Map Browser
4	Status
5	Active View
6	View navigation
7	Parameter Editor
8	Navigator

There are three main visual elements of the **Slate Material Editor: Material/Map Browser, Active View,** and **Parameter Editor.** The **Active View** is the area where you create material trees and make connections between nodes using wires. The

Parameter Editor is the area where you adjust settings of maps and materials. You can float the components of the editor such as the **Material/Map Browser**, or the **Parameter Editor** [except view]. For example, to float the **Material/Map Browser**, double-click on its title. To dock it back to the editor, again double-click on its title.

Note: Preview window
By default, each material's preview window opens as a floating window. When you dock a material preview window, it docks to the upper-left area of the editor.

When you add materials or maps in the **Slate Material Editor**, they appear as nodes [see the left image in Fig. 8] in the active view.

You can then connect these nodes using wires to make material trees. A node has several components, here's is a quick rundown.

- The title bar of the node shows name of the material or map, material or map type, and a small preview icon of the material or map.
- Below the title bar the component of the material or map appears. By default, 3ds Max shows only those components that you can map.
- On the left side of each component, circular slots [marked as 1 in the right image of Fig. 8] are available for input. You can use these sockets to wire maps to the node.
- On the right of the node, a circular slot [marked as 2 in the right image of Fig. 8] is used for the output.

You can collapse a node to hide its slots. To do this, click on the minus sign [marked as 1 in Fig. 9] available on the upper right corner of the node. To resize a node horizontally, drag the diagonal lines available on the bottom-right of the node [marked as 2 in Fig. 9].

When you resize a node horizontally, it is easier to read the name of the slots. To change the preview icon size, double-click on the preview. To reduce the size, double-click again. When a node's parameters are displayed in th **Parameter Editor**, 3ds Max shows a dashed border around the node in the active view [see Fig. 10].

To create a new material, drag the material from the **Material/ Map Browser** to the active view, 3ds Max places a node for the material in the active view. It is a good habit to change the name of the material immediately. It will make your life easier if you are working on a complex scene with tons of materials. To rename a material, **RMB** click on it and then choose **Rename**. In the **Rename** dialog box, change the name of the material and click **OK**. To change the properties of the material, double-click the node in the active view and then change the properties from the **Parameter Editor**.

 Tip: Renaming materials
The name of a material can contain special characters,
numbers, and spaces.

To get a material from the scene, click **Pick Material from Object** ![icon] from the toolbar. Now, click on the object in a viewport to get the material. To apply a material to an object in the scene, drag the output socket of the node and then drop the wire on an object in the scene. As you drag the mouse in a viewport, a tooltip appears below the mouse pointer showing the name of the object. You can apply the material even if the object is not selected. If there is only one object selected in the scene, the material is immediately applied to that object. If there are more than one objects in the scene, 3ds Max prompts you to choose whether to apply the material to the single object or to the whole selection. You can also apply material to the selection by clicking **Assign Material To Selection** ![icon] on the toolbar.

To make a copy of the existing material, drag the material from the **Material/Map Browser > Scene Materials** group (or any library) to the active View. The **Instance (Copy)** dialog box appears. Select **Instance** or **Copy** from this dialog box and click **OK**. To duplicate a node in the active view, select the node[s] that you want to duplicate and then drag the node[s] with the **Shift** held down.

To select the objects onto which you have applied the same material, in the active view, select the node and then click **Select By Material** ![icon] from the toolbar. 3ds Max opens the **Select Objects** dialog box with the objects highlighted. Click **Select** to select the highlighted objects.

Selecting, Moving, and Laying Out Nodes
To select a node, ensure the **Select Tool** ![icon] [hotkey S] is active, and then click on the node. To select multiple nodes, click on the nodes with the **Ctrl** held down. If you want to remove nodes from the selection, click on the nodes with **Alt** held down. To select all nodes, press **Ctrl+A**. To invert the selection, press **Ctrl+I**. To select none of the nodes, press **Ctrl+D**. To select children, press **Ctrl+C**. To select a node tree, press **Ctrl+T**. These functions are also accessible from the **Select** menu of the editor.

Note: Selected node
When a node is selected in the view, a white border appears around it. Also, the background including the title bar is darker. When node is not selected, the border appears gray and background is lighter.

Tip: Deselecting nodes
*To deselect nodes, click on the blank area of the view using the **Select Tool*** ▶.

To move a node, drag it in the active view. To create clone of a node, drag it with the **Shift** held down. If you drag a node with **Ctrl+Shift** held down, 3ds Max clones the node and all its children. These methods also work on multiple selections.

If you want to move a node and its children, click **Move Children** ⊞ from the toolbar and drag a node. You can toggle this feature temporarily without clicking **Move Children** by moving the node with **Ctrl+Alt** held down. This feature can be accessed from the editor's **Options** menu. You can click the **Hide Unused Nodeslots** ⊞ option from the toolbar to hide the unused ports on the selected material.

The layout buttons on the toolbar allow you to arrange nodes in the active view. The **Layout All - Vertical** ⊞, and **Layout All - Horizontal** ⊞ buttons on the toolbar allow you to arrange nodes in an automatic layout along the vertical or horizontal axis in the active view, respectively. These options are also available in the editor's **View** menu. The **Layout Children** button allows you to automatically layout the children of the selected node.

If you select **Show Shaded Material In Viewport** ⊞ from the toolbar for a material, a red diagonal shape appears on the node in the active view [see the left image in Fig. 11]. **Navigator** also shows a red diagonal shape to indicate this [see the middle image in Fig. 11]. This shape also appears in the **Scene Materials** rollout of the **Material/Map Browser** [see the right image in Fig. 11].

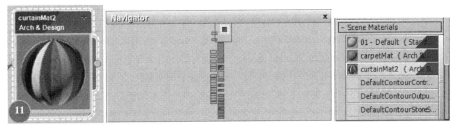

Previewing Materials

The **Preview** window [see Fig. 12] of the editor allows you to visualize how material or map will appear in the scene. The main part of the window is a rendering of the material or map. You can resize this window like you resize any other window in 3ds max that is, by dragging its corners. Making a window larger helps you in visualizing the materia. However, larger previews take longer to render. To open this window, **RMB** click on a node and then choose **Open Preview Window** from the context menu.

To close a window, click X on the upper-right corner of the window. By default, a sphere is displayed as a sample geometry in the window. If you want to change this geometry, choose **Cylinder** or **Box** from the context menu > **Preview Object Type** sub-menu. You can open any number of **Preview** windows in the editor. You can use the drop-down list available at the bottom of the **Preview** window allows you to switch the previews in a single window.

 Caution: Preview window
*When open a new scene, the **Preview** window remains open. However, it may not correspond to any material. I recommend that you close all **Preview** windows before creating a new scene. The previews are not saved with the scene.*

When the **Auto** check box is selected in the **Preview** window, 3ds Max automatically renders the preview again when you make any changes to the properties of a material or map. When this check box is clear, the **Update** button becomes active. The render will be displayed only when you click **Update**. The **Show End Result** toggle available on the right of **Update** allows you to control when the **Preview** window displays a map. When off , the **Preview** window shows the map itself. When on, the **Preview** window shows the end result that is, the final result of the node.

Wiring Nodes

As you already know, wires are used to connect material or map components. To understand the wiring process, from the **Material/Map Browser** > **Materials** rollout > **General** rollout, drag **Standard** to the active view to create a **Standard** material node. Similarly, drag **Checker** from the **Material/Map Browser** > **Maps** rollout > **General** rollout to the active view to create a **Checker** node [see the left image in Fig. 13]. Click-drag the **Standard** material's **Diffuse Color** socket, a wire appears. Now, drop the wire on the output socket of the **Checker** node to make a connection [see the right image in Fig. 13]. You can also connect in reverse. Also, you can connect the output socket of the **Checker** node to the **Diffuse Color** slot of the **Standard** material.

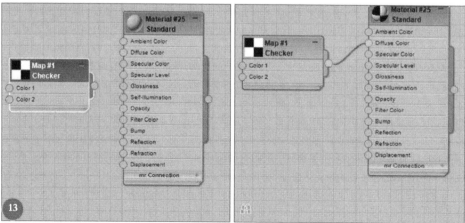

Now, drag and the **Standard** material's **Bump** socket to the blank area, a popup menu appears [see the left image in Fig. 14], choose **Standard** > **Noise** from the menu to insert a **Noise** node and make connection between the **Noise** node and **Bump** socket of the **Standard** material [see the right image in Fig. 14].

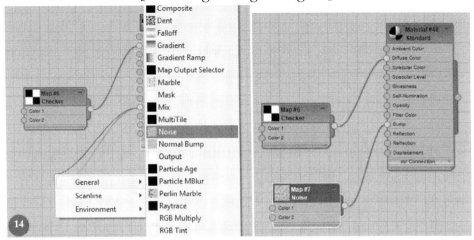

You can also connect a map directly to a socket without first dragging to the active view. To do this, drag the **Falloff** map from the **Material/Map Browser** > **Maps** rollout > **General** rollout to the **Reflection** socket of the **Standard** material. When the socket turns green, release the mouse to make the connection [see Fig. 15]. Another way to connect a node to a socket is to double-click on a socket to open the **Material/Map Browser**. Now, select the desired map or material from the browser. You can also drag a wire on the title bar of a node. A popup menu appears [see Fig. 16] that allows you to select component to wire.

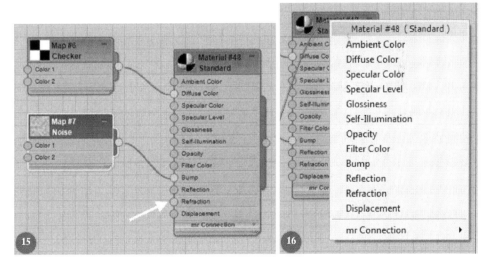

To delete a connection [wire], select the wire; the selected wire appears in white. Now, press **Delete**. You can also drag away a wire from a socket where it has been connected to terminate the connection. To replace one map with another, drag from the new map's output socket to the output socket of the original map.

To insert a node into a connection, drag the node from the **Material/Map Browser** and then drop it on the wire. You can also drag from one of the node's input sockets to the wire to insert the node. If a node is lying on the active view and you want to insert it, drop the node on the wire with **Ctrl** held down. To disconnect an inserted node, drag the node with **Alt** held down.

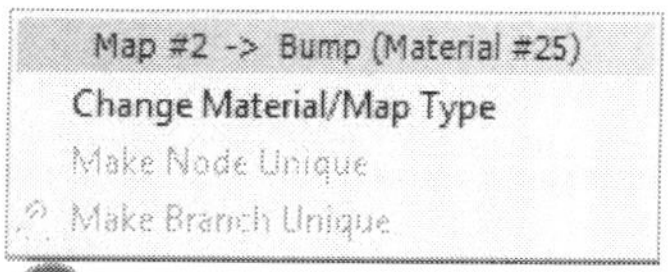

When you **RMB** click on a wire, a context menu appears [see Fig. 17].Choose **Change Material/Map Type** to open the **Material/Map Browser** and then choose a different type for the material or map. This option always affects the child node. The **Make Node Unique** option makes the child unique if the child node is instanced. The **Make Branch Unique** makes the child unique, as well as duplicates children of the child if the child node is instanced.

Views

The active view is the main area of the **Slate Material Editor** where all action takes place. Navigating an active view is similar to the navigating a scene in 3ds Max. To pan the view, drag with **MMB**. If you **MMB** drag with **Ctrl+Alt** held down, 3ds max zooms the view. You can also zoom by scrolling the mouse wheel. The navigational tools are also available at the bottom-right corner of the editor's interface. Table 3 summarized these controls.

Table 3: Slate Material Editor navigational controls		
Control	**Hotkey[s]**	**Menu**
Zoom percentage drop-down list	None	
Pan Tool	Ctrl+P	View > Pan Tool
Zoom Tool	Alt+Z	View > Zoom Tool
Zoom Region Tool	Ctrl+W	View > Zoom Region Tool
Zoom Extents	Ctrl+Alt+Z	View > Zoom Extents
Zoom Extents Selected	Z	Zoom Extents Selected
Pan to Selected	Alt+P	View > Pan to Selected

If you are working on a complex scene, you might face difficulties locating nodes in the active view. You can use the search function of the editor to locate the nodes in the scene. Make a habit of renaming the nodes as you create them so that you can find the nodes using their names. To search a node, click the **Search For Nodes** button available on the bottom-left corner of the active view, 3ds Max expands the search tool. Type the name of the node in the search field and press **Enter** to locate the node and zoom on the node in the active view.

By default, **Navigator** appears on the upper-right corner of the **Slate Material Editor**. This window is most useful when you have lots of material trees displayed in the active view. This window shows a map of the active view. The red rectangle in the navigator shows the border of the active view. If you drag the rectangle, 3ds max changes the focus of the view.

Named Views

If you are working on a complex scene, you can create named views to organize materials in a scene. You can create any number of views in the editor and then make one of them the active view. When you open the editor in a new scene, a single view is displayed with the name **View1**. To manage views, **RMB** click on one of the tabs and then choose the desired options from the context menu displayed [see Fig. 18].

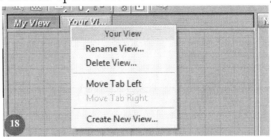

To cycle through the tabs, use the **Ctrl+Tab** hotkeys. You can also select a view from the drop-down list available above **Navigator**. To move a tree from one view to another, **RMB** click on the node and then choose **Move Tree to View > Name of the View** from the context menu.

Quiz

Evaluate your skills to see how many questions you can answer correctly.

Multiple Choice
Answer the following questions:

1. Which of the following keys is used to invoke the **Select Tool** in the **Slate Material Editor**?

   [A] K   [B] H
   [C] S   [D] N

2. Which of the following hotkeys is used to invoke **Zoom Tool**?

   [A] Ctrl+Z   [B] Shift+Z
   [C] Alt+Z   [D] Ctrl+Shift+Z

Fill in the Blanks

Fill in the blanks in each of the following statements:

1. When the _____ check box is selected in the **Preview** window, 3ds Max automatically renders the preview again when you make any changes to the properties of a material or map.

2. To delete a connection [wire], select the wire and then press _____.

3. To cycle through the tabs in the **Active View**, use the _____ hotkeys.

True or False

State whether each of the following is true or false:

1. The **Compact Material Editor** allows you to edit up to **36** materials at a time.

2. A sample slot in the **Compact Material Editor** is considered to be hot if it is assigned to one or more surfaces in the scene.

3. In the **Compact Material Editor**, if you drag a material to copy it from one sample slot to another, the destination slot will be cool whereas the original slot remains hot.

Summary

The unit covered the following topics:

- Compact Material Editor
- Slate Material Editor

- Standard materials
- Standard maps

Unit DT2: Standard Materials and Maps

Standard Materials are non-photometric materials. Do not use these materials if you plan to create physically accurate lighting models. However, these materials are suitable for games, films, and animation. In this unit, we are going to look at the standard materials and maps.

General/Scanline Materials

Let's explore the **Scanline** materials.

Standard Material

A surface having a single color reflects many other colors such as ambient, diffuse, and specular. The **Standard** materials use a four-color model to simulate the reflected colors from a surface. However, there may be variations depending on the shader by the ambient light only. The **Diffuse** color appears on the surface when the lights falls directly on it. The term **Diffuse** is used because light is reflected in various directions. The **Specular** color appears in the highlights. Highlights are reflection of light sources on the surface.

Generally, shiny surfaces have specular highlights where the viewing angle is equal to the angle of incident. Metallic surfaces show another type of highlights called glancing highlights. The glancing highlights have a high angle of incidence. Some surfaces in the real-world are highly reflective. To model such surfaces, you can use a reflection map or use raytracing. **Filter Color** is the color transmitted through an object. **Filter Color** will only be visible, if **Opacity** is less than **100** percent.

The three color components blend at the edge of their respective regions. The blend of the **Diffuse** and **Ambient** components is controlled by the shader. However, you can control the blending by using the **Standard** material's highlight parameters.

To create a **Standard** material, press **M** to open the **Slate Material Editor**. In the **Material/Map Browser** > **Materials** > **General** > **Scanline** rollout, double-click **Standard** to add a standard material node to the active view. Fig. 1 shows the **Standard** material's interface. If you double-click on the material node, its attributes appear in various rollouts in the **Parameter Editor**. The parameters in these rollouts change according to the shader type chosen from the **Shader Basic Parameters** rollout [see Fig. 2].

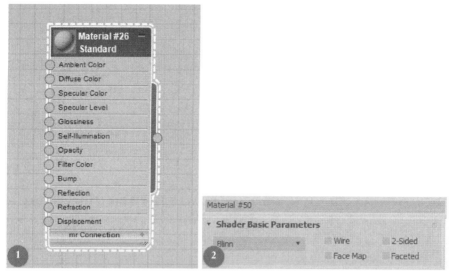

The parameters in this rollout let you choose the type of shader to use with the **Standard** material. **Wire** lets you render the material in the wireframe mode [see Fig. 3]. You can change the size of the wire using the **Size** parameter in the material's **Extended Parameters** rollout. Fig. 4 shows the render with **Size** set to **2. 2-Sided** allows you to make a 2-sided material. When you select this option, 3ds Max applies material to the both sides of the selected faces.

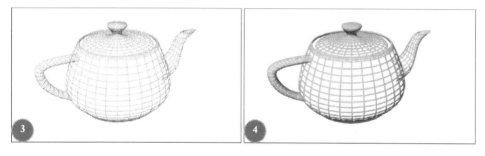

> ✎ *Note: One-sided faces*
> *In 3ds Max, faces are one-sided. The front side is the side with the surface normals. The back side of the faces is invisible to the renderer. If you see this other side from the back, the faces will appear to be missing.*

The **Face Map** parameter allows you to apply the material to the faces of the geometry. If material is a mapped material, it requires no mapping coordinates and automatically applied to each face. Figs. 5 and 6 show the render with the **Face Map** check box enabled and disabled, respectively. The **Faceted** parameter renders each face of the surface as if it were flat [see Fig. 7].

Tip: Rendering both sides of a face
There are two ways to render both sides of a face. Either you can select the
Force 2-Sided *check box in the* **Render Setup** *window >* **Common** *panel >*
Options *group or apply a two sided material to the faces.*

The **Shader** drop-down list located at the extreme left of the rollout lets you choose a shader for the material. Here's is the quick rundown to the various material shaders:

Phong Shader

You can use this shader to produce realistic highlights for shiny and regular surfaces. This shader produces strong circular highlights. This shader can accurately render bump, opacity, shininess, specular, and reflection maps. When you select the **Phong** shader, the **Phong Shader Parameters** rollout appears in the material's **Parameter Editor** [see Fig. 8].

Phong Shader Parameters Rollout

The parameters in this rollout let you set the color of the material, shininess, and transparency of the material. The **Ambient, Diffuse,** and **Specular** parameters let you set the colors for ambient, diffuse, and specular color components, respectively. To change a color component, click on the color swatch and then use the **Color Selector** to change the values of the color component. You can also copy one color component to another by dragging the source color swatch to the target color swatch. In the **Copy or Swap Colors** dialog box that appears, click the **Swap** or **Copy** button. Click **Cancel** to cancel the operation. You can lock or unlock two color components using the **Lock** button [see Fig. 9].

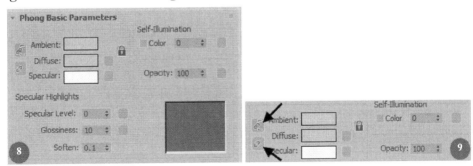

The buttons located on the right of color swatches can be used to apply texture maps to the respective color components. On clicking these buttons, the **Material/Map Browser** appears that allows you to select a map for the color component. If you want to apply different maps to the **Ambient** and **Diffuse** components, click on the **Lock** button located to the right of these components [see Fig. 10].

Self-Illumination Group: You can use the parameters in this group to make the material self-illuminated. The illusion of self-illumination is created by replacing shadows with the diffuse color. There are two ways to enable self-illumination in 3ds Max. Either you can select the check box located in this group and use a self-illumination color or use the spinner.

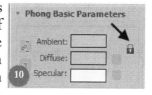

 Note: Self-illuminated materials
Self-illuminated materials do not show shadows cast onto them. Also, they are unaffected by the lights in the scene.

Opacity Group: You can use the parameter in this group, to make a material opaque, transparent, or translucent. To change the opacity of the material, change opacity to a value less than 100%. If you want to use a map for controlling opacity, click the **Opacity** map button.

Specular Highlight Group: The **Phong**, **Blinn**, and **Oren-Nayar-Blinn** shaders produce circular highlights and share same highlight parameters. The **Blinn** and **Oren-Nayar-Blinn** shaders produce soft and round highlights than the **Phong** shader. You can use the **Specular Level** parameter to increase or decrease the strength of a highlight. As you change the value for this parameter, the **Highlight** curve and the highlight in the preview changes. The shape of this curve affects the blending between the specular and diffuse color components of the material. If the curve is steeper, there will be less blending and the edge of the specular highlight will be sharper. To increase or decrease the size of the highlight, change the value for **Glossiness**. **Soften** softens the specular highlights especially those formed by the glancing light.

Extended Parameters Rollout

The **Extender Parameters** rollout [see Fig. 11] is same for all shaders except the **Strauss** and **Translucent** shaders. The parameters in this rollout allow you to control the transparency and reflection settings. Also, it has parameters for adjusting the wireframe rendering.

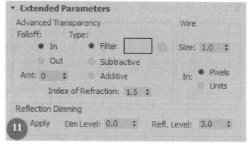

Advanced Transparency Group: These parameters do not appear for the **Translucent** shader. **Falloff** allows you to set the falloff and its extent. **In** increases transparency towards the inside of the object [like glass bottle] whereas **Out** increases transparency towards the outside of the object [like clouds]. **Amt** lets you adjust the amount of transparency at the outside or inside extreme.

The **Type** parameters let you specify how transparency is applied. The **Filter** color swatch computes a filter color that it multiplies with the color behind the transparent surface. The **Subtractive** option subtracts from the color behind the transparent surface. The **Additive** option adds to the color behind the transparent surface. **Index of Refraction** allows you to set the index of refraction used by the refraction map and raytracing.

Reflection Dimming Group: This group does not appear for the **Strauss** shader. These parameters dim the reflection in the shadows. Select the **Apply** check box to enable reflection dimming. **Dim Level** controls the amount of dimming that takes place in shadow. **Refl. Level** affects the intensity of the reflection that is not in shadow.

SuperSampling Rollout

The **SuperSampling** rollout [see Fig. 12] is used by the **Architectural, Raytrace, Standard,** and **Ink 'n Paint** materials to improve the quality of the rendered image. It performs an additional antialiasing pass on the material thus resulting in more render time. By default, a single **SuperSampling** method is applied to all materials in the scene.

Caution: Super Sampling and Scanline Renderer
*If you turn off **Antialiasing** in the default **Scanline Renderer** dialog box > **Renderer** panel > **Scanline Renderer** rollout, **SuperSampling** settings are ignored.*

Maps Rollout: The **Maps** rollout [see Fig. 13] is available for all materials. The parameters in this rollout allow you to assign maps to various components of a material. To assign a map to a component, click the corresponding map button. Now, choose the desired map option from the **Material/Map Browser** that opens.

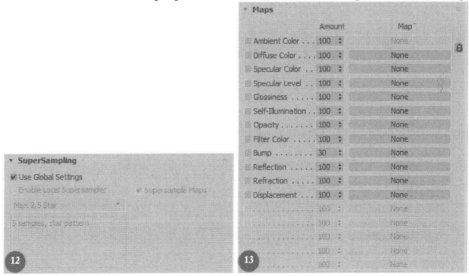

Blinn Shader

This is the default shader. It produces rounder, softer highlights than the **Phong** shader. The **Blinn** and **Phong** shaders have the same basic parameters.

Metal Shader

You can use the **Metal** shader to create metallic surfaces and a variety of organic-looking materials. The metal material calculates its specular color automatically. The output specular color depends on the diffuse color of the material and the color of the light.

This shader produces distinctive highlights. Like the **Phong** shader, **Specular Level** still controls intensity. However, **Glossiness** affects both the intensity and size of the specular highlights. Fig. 14 shows the parameters in the **Metal Basic Parameters** rollout.

Oren-Nayar-Blinn Shader

This shader is a variant of the **Blinn** shader and can be used to model matte surfaces such as fabric. It has two additional parameters to model a surface with the matte look: **Diffuse Level** and **Roughness**.

The **Diffuse Level** parameter in the **Oren-Nayar-Blinn Basic Parameters** rollout > **Advanced Diffuse** group [see Fig. 15] controls the brightness of the diffuse component of the material. It allows you to make the material lighter or darker. **Roughness** allows you to control the rate at which the diffuse component blends into the ambient component.

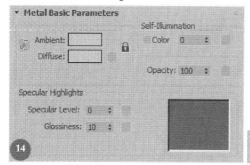

> *Note: Roughness Parameter*
> *The **Roughness** parameter is available only with the **Oren-Nayar-Blinn** and **Multi-Level** shaders, and with the **Physical** material.*

> *Note: Diffuse Level parameter*
> *The **Blinn, Metal, Phong,** and **Strauss** shaders do not have the **Diffuse Level** parameter.*

Strauss Shader

This shader is a simpler version of the **Metal** shader. It can be used to model the metallic surfaces.

Strauss Basic Parameters Rollout: The **Color** parameter [see Fig. 16] lets you specify the color of the material. The **Strauss** shader automatically calculates the ambient and specular color components. **Glossiness** controls the size and intensity of the specular highlights. On increasing the value for this parameter, the highlight gets smaller and the material appears shiner. The **Metalness** parameter adjusts the metalness of the surface. The effect of this parameter is more prominent when you increase the **Glossiness** value. **Opacity** sets the transparency of the material.

Anisotropic Shader

You can use this shader to create surfaces with elliptical, anisotropic highlights. This shader is suitable for modeling the hair, glass, or brushed metal surfaces. The **Diffuse Level** parameter is similar to that of the **Oren-Nayar-Blinn** shader and the basic parameters are similar to that of the **Blinn** or **Phong** shading, except the **Specular Highlights** parameters.

Anisotropic Basic Parameters rollout > **Specular Highlight** group: The **Specular Level** [Fig. 17] parameter sets the intensity of the specular highlights. On increasing the value for this parameter, the highlight goes brighter. **Glossiness** controls the size of the specular highlights. **Anisotropy** controls the anisotropy or shape of the highlight. **Orientation** controls the orientation of the highlight. This value is measured in degrees.

Multi-Layer Shader

This shader is similar to the **Anisotropic** shader. However, it allows you to layer two sets of specular highlights. The highlights are layered that allows you to create complex highlights. Fig. 18 shows the two specular layers in the **Multi-Layer Basic Parameters** rollout.

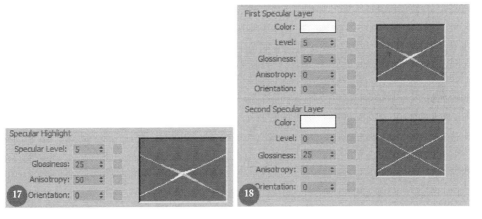

Translucent Shader

This shader is similar to the **Blinn** shader but allows you set the translucency of the material. A translucent object not only allows light to pass through but it also scatters light within.

Translucent Basic Parameters rollout > **Translucency** group: The **Translucent Clr** parameter [see Fig. 19] sets the translucency color that is the color of the light scattered

within the material. This color is different from the **Filter** color which is the color transmitted through transparent or semi-transparent material such as glass. The **Opacity** parameter sets the opacity or transparency of the material.

Raytrace Material

This material is an advanced surface-shading material. It supports the same diffuse surface shading that a **Standard** material supports.

However, it also supports fog, color density, translucency, fluorescence, and other special effects. This material is capable of creating fully raytraced reflections and refractions. Fig. 20 shows the **Raytrace** material's interface.

Architectural Material

The properties of this material [see Fig. 21] create realistic looking images when used with Photometric lights and **Radiosity**. Therefore, you should use this material when you are looking for high level of accuracy. If you don't need high details this material produces, use the **Standard** material or any other material.

When you create a new **Architectural** material, you can choose from a wide variety of templates that are built into this material. You can use these templates as starting point for the shading model you wish to create. You can choose template from the drop-down list available in the **Templates** rollout.

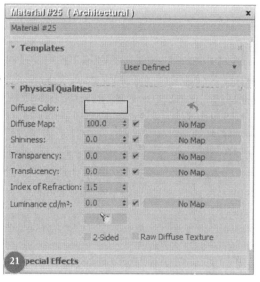

Advanced Lighting Override Material

You can use this material to directly control the radiosity properties of a material. You can use this material directly. It is a always a supplement to the base material [see Fig. 22]. This material has no effect on the ordinary renderings. It is used with the **Radiosity** and **Light Tracing** solutions.

This material has two primary usages:

* Adjusting properties of a material used in a **Radiosity** or **Light Tracing** solution.
* Contributing energy to the **Radiosity** solution with self-illuminating objects.

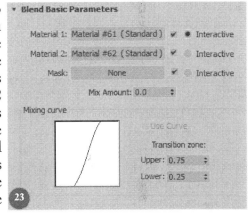

General Materials

Let's explore the **General** materials.

Blend Material

The **Blend** material allows you to mix two materials on a single side of the surface. You can use the **Mix Amount** parameter [see Fig. 23] to control the way two materials are blended together. You can also animate this parameter. The **Material 1** and **Material 2** parameters let you assign the two materials to be blended. You can also use the corresponding check boxes to turn material on or off. The **Interactive** option specifies which of the materials or mask map will be displayed in the viewport by the interactive renderer.

The **Mask** parameter lets you assign a map as mask. The lighter and darker areas on the mask map control the degree of blending. The lighter areas display more of the **Material 1** whereas the darker areas show more of **Material 2**. The **Mix Amount** parameter controls the proportion of blend in degrees. A value of **0** means only **Material 1** will be visible on the surface whereas a value of **100** means **Material 2** will be visible on the surface.

When you assign a mask map for blending, you can use the mixing curve to affect the blending. You can use the parameters in the **Transition Zone** group to adjust the level of the **Upper** and **Lower** limits.

> *Note: Interactive renderer and the Blend material*
> *Only one map can be displayed in the viewports when using the interactive renderer.*

Note: Blend Material and Noise Map

*The **Mix Amount** parameter is not available when you use mask to blend the material. Using a **Noise** map as mixing map can produce naturally looking surfaces.*

Double Sided Material

The **Double Sided** material lets you assign two different materials to the front and back surfaces of an object. The **Facing Material** and **Back Material** parameters [see Fig. 24] allow you to specify the material for the front and back faces, respectively. The **Translucency** parameter allows you to blend

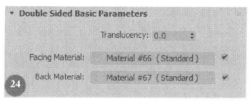

the two materials. There will be no blending of the materials if **Translucency** is set to **0**. At a value of **100**, the outer material will be visible on the inner faces and the inner material will be visible on the outer faces.

Composite Material

This material can be used to composite up to ten materials. The materials are composited from top to bottom. The maps can be combined using additive opacity, subtractive opacity, or using an amount value. The **Base Material** parameter [see Fig. 25] allows you to set the base material. The default base material is the **Standard** material.

The **Mat.1** to **Mat.9** parameters are used to specify the materials that you want to composite. Each material parameter has an array of buttons called **ASM** buttons. These buttons control how the material is composited.

The **A** button allows you to use the additive opacity. The colors in the materials are summed based on the opacity. The **S** button allows you to use the subtractive opacity. The **M** button is used to mix the materials using a value. You can enter the value in the spinner located next to the **M** button. When the **M** button is active, amount ranges from **0** to **100**. When amount is **0**, no compositing happens and the material below is not visible. If the amount is **100**, the material below is visible.

Tip: Composite Material v Composite Map

*If you want to achieve a result by combining maps instead of combining materials, use the **Composite** map that provides greater control.*

Morpher Material

The **Morpher** material is used with the **Morpher** modifier. For example, when a character raises his eyebrows, you can use this material to display wrinkles on his forehead. You can blend the materials the same way you morph the geometry using the channel spinners of the **Morpher** modifier.

Multi/Sub-Object Material

The **Multi/Sub-Object** material allows you to assign materials at the sub-object level. The number field on the left of the **Set Number** button [see Fig. 26] shows the number of sub-materials contained in the **Multi/Sub-Object** material. You can use the **Set Number** button to set the number of sub-materials that make up the material. The **Add** button allows you to a new sub-material to the list. Use the **Delete** button to remove currently chosen sub-material from the list. The **ID, Name,** and **Sub-Material** parameters allow you to sort the list based on the material id, name, and sub-material, respectively. To assign materials to the sub-objects, select the object and assign the **Multi/sub-Object** material to it. Apply a **Mesh Select** modifier to the

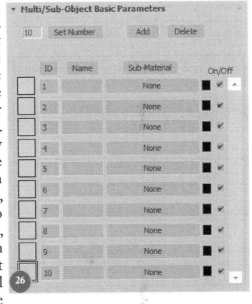

object. Activate the **Face** sub-object level. Now, select the faces to which you will assign the material. Apply a **Material** modifier and then set the material ID value to the number of the sub-material you need to assign.

Shellac Material

Shellac material allows you to mix two materials by superimposing one over the other. The superimposed material is known as the **Shellac** material. The **Base Material** parameter [Fig. 27] lets you choose or edit the base sub-material. The **Shellac Material** parameter lets you choose or edit the **Shellac** material. The **Shellac Color Blend**

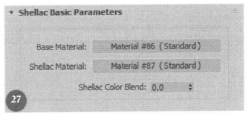

parameter adjusts the amount of color mixing. The default value for this parameter is **0**. Hence, the **Shellac** material has no effect on the surface. There is no upper limit for this parameter. Higher values overload the colors of the **Shellac** material. You can also animate this parameter.

Top/Bottom Material

This material lets you assign two different materials to the top and bottom portions of an object. You can also blend the two materials. The top faces of an object are those faces whose normals point up. The bottom faces have the normals down. You can control the boundary between the top and bottom using the parameters available in the **Coordinates** group [see Fig. 28].

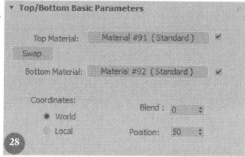

The **World** option lets you specify the direction according to the world coordinates of the scene. If you rotate the object, the boundary between the top and bottom faces remains in place. The **Local** option allows you to control the direction using the local coordinate system.

You can specify the top and bottom materials using the **Top Material** and **Bottom Material** parameters, respectively. The **Swap** button allows you to swap the materials. You can blend the edge between the top and bottom materials using the **Blend** parameter. The value for this parameter ranges from **0** to **100**. If you set **Blend** to **0**, there will be a sharp line between the top and bottom materials. At **100**, the two materials tint each other.

The **Position** parameter allows you to specify the location where the division between the two materials will occur. The value for this parameter ranges from **0** to **100**. If you set **Position** to **0**, only top material will be displayed. At **100**, only bottom material will be displayed.

Matte/Shadow Material

The **Matte/Shadow** material is used to make whole objects or any set of faces into matte object. The matte objects reveal the background color or the environment map. A matte object is invisible but it blocks any geometry behind it however it does not block the background. The matte objects can also receive shadows. The shadows cast on the matte object are applied to the alpha channel. To properly generate shadows on a matte object, clear the **Opaque Alpha** check box and then select the **Affect Alpha** check box.

Ink 'n Paint Material

The **Ink 'n Paint** material is used to create cartoons effects. This material produces shading with inked borders.

DirectX Shader Material

It is a special material that allows you to shade objects in the viewport using DirectX (Direct3D) shaders. When you use this material, materials in the viewport more accurately represent how they will look on some other software or hardware device.

Tip: Quicksilver Hardware Renderer
*You can use the **Quicksilver Hardware Renderer** to render **DirectX Shader** materials.*

XRef Material

This material lets you use a material applied to an object in another 3ds Max scene file. This material is typically used with the XRef objects. You can also use the **Override Material** rollout to assign a local material to the XRef'd object.

Physical Material

Physical material allows you to model shading effects of the real-world materials with ease. This material is the layered material that gives you ability to efficiently use the physically-based workflows. This material is compatible with the **ART** renderer.

General/Scanline Maps

Maps allow you to improve the appearance of the materials. They also help you to enhance the realism of the materials. You can use maps in a variety of ways, you can use them to create environments, to create image planes for modeling, to create projections from light, and so on. You can use the **Material/Map Browser** to load a map or create a map of a particular type. A map can be used to design different elements of a material such as reflection, refraction, bump, and so on.

Maps and Mapping Coordinates

When you apply a map to any object, the object must have mapping coordinates applied. These coordinates are specified in terms of the UVW axes local to the object. Most of the objects in 3ds Max have the **Generate Mapping Coordinates** option. When on, 3ds Max generates default mapping coordinates.

UVW Mapping Coordinate Channels

Each object in 3ds Max can have **99** UVW mapping coordinates. The default mapping is always assigned the number **1**. The **UVW Map** modifier can send coordinates to any of these **99** channels.

3ds Max gives you ability to generate the mapping coordinates in different ways:

- The **Generate Mapping Coords** option is available for most of the primitives. This option provides a projection appropriate to the shape of the object type.
- Apply the **Unwrap UVW** modifier. This modifier comes with some useful tools that you can use to edit mapping coordinates.
- Apply the **UVW Map** modifier. This modifier allows you to set a projection type from several projection types it provides.

Given below is the quick rundown to the projection types:

- **Box projection:** It places a duplicate of the map image on each of the six sides of a box.

- **Cylindrical projection:** This wraps the image around the sides of the object. The duplicate images are also projected onto the end caps.

- **Spherical projection:** This projection type wraps the map image around a sphere and gather the image at the top and bottom.

- **Shrink-wrap projection:** This type is like the spherical projection but creates one singularity instead of two.

- Use special mapping coordinates. For example, the **Loft** object provides built-in mapping coordinates.
- Use a **Surface Mapper** modifier. This modifier uses a map assigned to a NURBS surface and projects it onto the object(s).

Given below is a quick rundown to the cases when you can apply a map and you don't need mapping coordinates:

- Reflection, Refraction, and Environment maps.
- 3D Procedural maps: **Noise** and **Marble**.
- Face-mapped materials.

Tip: UVW Remove utility
*The **UVW Remove** utility removes mapping coordinates or materials from the currently selected objects. The path to the utility is as follows: **Utilities** panel > **Utilities** rollout > **More** button > **Utilities** dialog box > **UVW Remove**. You can also remove material from objects using the **UVW Remove** utility.*

Real-World Mapping

The real-world mapping is an alternative mapping method that you can use in 3ds Max. This type of mapping considers the correct scaling of the texture mapped materials applied to the geometry in the scene.

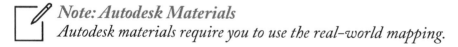
Note: Autodesk Materials
Autodesk materials require you to use the real-world mapping.

In order to apply the real-world mapping correctly, two requirements must be met. First, the correct style of UV texture coordinates must be assigned to the geometry. In other words, the size of the UV space should correspond to the size of the geometry. To address this issue, the **Real-World Map Size** check box is added to the many rollouts in 3ds Max [see Fig. 29].

The second requirement is available in the **Coordinates** rollout of the material editor, the **Use Real-World Scale** check box. When this check box is selected, **U/V** changes to **Width/Height** and **Tiling** changes to **Size** [see Fig. 30].

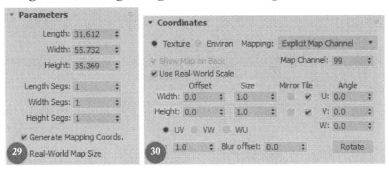

Tip: The Real-World Map Size check box
*You can turn on the **Real-World Map Size** feature by default from the **Preferences** dialog box by using the **Use Real-World Texture Coordinates** check box. This check box is available in the **Texture Coordinates** group of the **General** panel.*

Output Rollout

The options in this rollout [see Fig. 31] are responsible for setting the internal parameters of a map. These options can be used to determine the rendered appearance of the map. Most of the parameters in this rollout are for the color output.

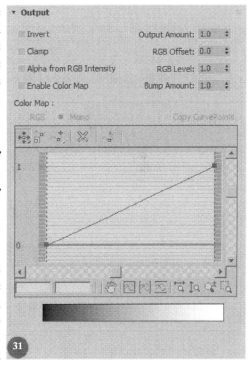

 Note: Output rollout
*These parameters do not affect the bump maps except the **Invert** toggle, which reverses the direction of the bumps and bump amount.*

2D Maps

The 2D maps are two-dimensional images that are mapped to the surface of the geometric objects. You can also use them to create environment maps. The **Bitmap** is the simplest type 2D maps. 3ds Max also allows you to create 2D maps procedurally.

Coordinates Rollout

The **Coordinates** rollout shown in Fig. 30 allows you to adjust coordinate parameters to move a map relative to the surface of the object. This rollout also allows you to set tiling and mirroring of the texture pattern. The repetition of the texture pattern on the surface of an object is known as tiling. The mirroring is a form of tiling in which 3ds Max repeats the map and then flips the repeated map.

In this rollout, there are two options that you can use to control the mapping type. These options are **Texture** and **Environ**. The **Texture** type applies texture as a map to the surface. The **Environ** type uses map as an environment map. For both of these options, you can select the types of coordinates from the **Mapping** drop-down list.

Given below is the list of options available in the **Mapping** drop-down list:

- **Explicit Map Channel:** It uses any map channel from **1** to **99**. When you select this option, **Map Channel** becomes active.
- **Vertex Color Channel:** This option uses assigned vertex colors as a channel.
- **Planar from Object XYZ:** This option uses planar mapping based on the object's local coordinates.
- **Planar from World XYZ:** This option uses planar mapping based on the scene's world coordinates.
- **Spherical Environment/Cylindrical Environment/Shrink-wrap Environment:** These options project the map into the scene as if it were mapped to an invisible object in the background.
- **Screen:** This option projects a map as a flat backdrop in the scene.

Noise Rollout

You can add a random noise to the appearance of the material using the parameters available in this rollout [see Fig. 32]. These parameters modify the mapping of pixels by applying a fractal noise function.

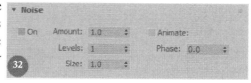

Bitmap Map

This map is the simplest type of map available in 3ds Max. This map is useful for creating many type of materials from wood to skin. If you want to create an animated material, you can use an animation or video file with this map. When you select this map, the **Select Bitmap Image File** dialog box opens. Navigate to the location where the bitmap file is stored and then click **Open** to select the file.

Tip: Bitmap and Windows Explorer
*You can also create a bitmap node by dragging a supported bitmap file from the **Windows Explorer** to the **Slate Material Editor**.*

Tip: Viewport Canvas
*The **Viewport Canvas** feature allows you create a bitmap on the fly by painting directly onto the surface of the object. To open the canvas, choose **Viewport Canvas** from the **Tools** menu.*

Checker Map

This map is a procedural texture that applies a two-color checkerboard pattern [see Fig. 33]. The default colors used to produce the pattern are black and white. You can also change these colors with map and it's true for all color components of the other maps.

 Tip: Swapping colors
*You can swap colors by dragging one color swatch over another and then choosing **Swap** from the popup menu that appears.*

Camera Map Per Pixel Map

This map allows you to project a map from the direction of a particular camera. It is useful when you are working on a matte painting. Fig. 34 shows the **Marble** map projected on the teapot using the camera [see Fig. 35]. Fig. 36 shows the node network [refer to the **camera-map.max** file].

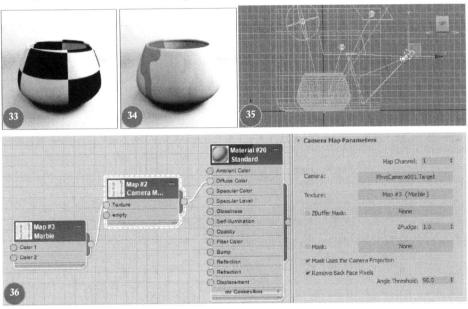

 Note: Two maps with the same name
If a map with the same name exists in two places, only one map is loaded to save the loading time. If you have two maps with different contents but with the same name, only the first map encountered by 3ds Max appears in the scene.

 Caution: Camera Map Per Pixel Map
This map cannot be used with the animated objects or animated textures.

Gradient Map

This map type allows you to create a gradient that shades from one color to another. Fig. 37 shows the shift from one color to another. In Fig. 37, the red, green, and blue colors are used for the gradient. Fig. 38 shows the result when the fractal noise is applied to the gradient. Fig. 39 shows the node network.

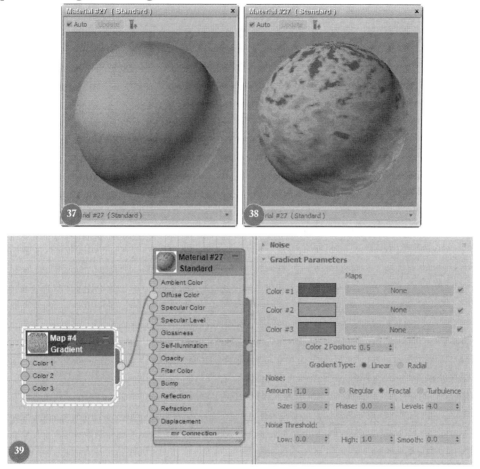

Gradient Ramp Map

This map is similar to the **Gradient** map. Like the **Gradient** map, it shades from one color to another, however, you can use any number of colors [see Fig. 40]. Also, you have additional parameters to create a complex customized ramp. Fig. 41 shows the node network used to produce the result shown in Fig. 40. Refer to the **gradient-ramp.max** file.

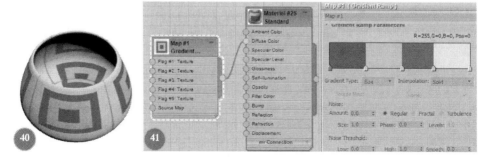

Normal Bump Map

This map allows you to connect a texture-baked normal map to a material. Fig. 42 shows the bump on the surface created using the **Normal Bump** map. Fig. 43 shows the node network. Refer to the **normal-bump.max** file.

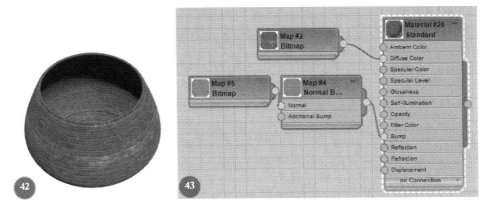

Substance Map

This map is used with the **Substance** parametric textures. These textures are resolution-independent 2D textures and use less memory. Therefore, they are useful for exporting to the game engines via the **Algorithmic Substance Air** middleware.

Swirl Map

This map is 2D procedural map that can be used to simulate swirls [see Fig. 44].

Tiles Map

You can use this map to create a brick or stacked tiling of colors or maps. A number of commonly used architectural brick patterns are available with this map. Fig. 45 shows render with the **English Bond** type applied. Refer to the **tiles.max** file.

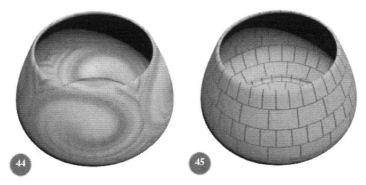

Vector Map

Using this map, you can apply a vector-based graphics, including animation as textures. You also use **AutoCAD Pattern** (PAT) files, **Adobe Illustrator** (AI) files, **Portable Document** (PDF) files, and **Scalable Vector Graphics** (SVG) files [see Fig. 46].

Vector Displacement Map

This map allows you to displace the meshes in three directions whereas the traditional method permits displacement only along the surface normals.

3D Maps

3D maps are patterns generated by 3ds Max in 3D space. Let's have a look at various 3D maps.

Cellular Map

You can use this map to generate a variety of visual effects such as mosaic tiling, pebbled surfaces, and even ocean surfaces [see Fig. 47].

Dent Map

This map generates a procedural map using a fractal noise algorithm. The effect that this produces depends on the map type chosen.

Falloff Map

The **Falloff** map generates a value from white to black based on the angular falloff of the face normals. Fig. 48 shows the **Falloff** map applied to the geometry with the **Falloff** type set to **Fresnel**.

Marble Map

You can use this map to create a marble texture with the colored veins against [see Fig. 49] a color background.

Noise Map

This map allows to create a noise map that creates the random perturbation of a surface based on the interaction of two colors or materials. Fig. 50 shows the **Noise** map with the **Noise Type** set to **Fractal**.

Particle Age Map

This map is used with the particle systems. This map changes the color of the particles based on their age.

Particle MBlur Map

This map can be used to alter the opacity of the leading and trailing ends of particles based on their rate of motion.

Perlin Marble Map

This map is like the **Marble** map. However, it generates a marble pattern using the **Perlin Turbulence** algorithm.

Smoke Map

You can use this map [see Fig. 51] to create animated opacity maps to simulate the effects of smoke in a beam of light, or other cloudy, flowing effects.

Speckle Map

This map [see Fig. 52] can be used to create granite-like and other patterned surfaces.

Splat Map

This map can be used to create patterns similar to the spattered paint [see Fig. 53].

Stucco Map

You can use this map [see Fig. 54] as a bump to create the effect like a stuccoed surface.

Waves Map

You can use this map as both bump or diffuse map [see Fig. 55]. This map is used to create watery or wavy effects.

Wood Map

This map creates a wavy grain like wood pattern [see Fig. 56]. You can control the direction, thickness, and complexity of the grain.

Advanced Wood

The **Advanced Wood** map is used to generate realistic 3d wood textures. This map appears in the browser if the current active renderer supports it. Use this map with the **Physical** material to get good results. There are number of wood presets available with this map. You can select the presets from the **Presets** rollout in the **Parameter Editor**.

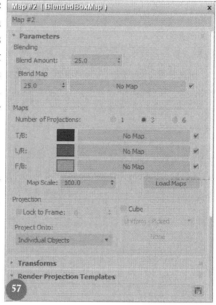

BlendedBoxMap

The **BlendedBoxMap** map allows you to simplify the process of blending projected texture maps. As a result, you can easily customize the maps and the output. Fig. 57 shows the map's interface.

This map appears in the browser if the current active renderer supports it. This map is very useful in cases when you want to box-project a texture onto an object such a dirt texture [refer to Fig. 58 and the **BlendedBoxMap.max** file]. This map projects images from three 90 degrees directions. You can project 1, 3, or 6 different maps for every side of the projection box.

Compositor Maps

These maps are specifically designed for compositing colors and maps. Let's have a look at these maps.

Composite Map

You can use this map to layer other maps atop each other using the alpha channel and other methods.

Mask Map

This map can be used to view one material through another on the surface.

Mix Map

With this map, you can combine two colors or materials on a single side of the surface. You can also animate the **Mix Amount** parameter to control how two maps are blended together over time.

RGB Multiply Map

This map combines two maps by multiplying their RGB values. This map is generally used as a **Bump** map.

Color Modifiers Maps

These maps change the color of the pixels in a material. Let's have a look:

Color Correction Map

This map allows you to modify color of a map using various tools. This map uses a stack-based method.

Output Map

You can use this map to apply output settings to the procedural maps such as **Checker** or **Marble**.

RGB Tint Map

This map adjusts the three color channels in an image.

Vertex Color Map

In 3ds Max, you can assign vertex colors using the **VertexPaint** modifier, the **Assign Vertex Colors** utility, or the vertex controls for an editable mesh, editable patch, or editable poly. This map makes any vertex coloring applied to an object available for rendering.

Reflection and Refraction Maps

These maps are used to create reflections and refractions. Here's is a quick rundown.

Flat Mirror Map

This map produces a material that reflects surroundings when it is applied to the co-planer faces. It is assigned to the **Reflection** map of the material.

Raytrace Map

This map allows you to create fully raytraced reflections and refractions. The reflections/refractions generated by this map are more accurate than the **Reflect/Refract** map.

Reflect/Refract Map

You can use this map to create a reflective or refractive surface. To create reflection, assign this map type to the **Reflection** map. To create refraction, apply it to the **Refraction** map.

Thin Wall Refraction Map

This map can be used to simulate a surface as if it is part of a surface through a plate of glass.

Other Maps

Here's is a quick rundown.

Shape Map

You can use this map to create resolution independent graphical textures that you can animate. This map uses splines to apply textures to the selected object. The results can be fully animated. You can set outlines, fill colors as well as the map boundaries. You can change the shape of the spline even after applying it to the object in the scene. Also, all adjustment to the shape can be keyframed. As a result, you can animate the textures. The functioning of this map is demonstrated in an hands-on exercise later in the unit.

Text Map

Like splines, you can also create textures using text. You can create creative textures using the **Text Map** and all adjustments can be animated. The functioning of this map is demonstrated in an hands-on exercise later in the unit.

TextureObjMask

This texture map allows you to control the textures using a primitive control object [plane, box, or sphere]. You can use the box or sphere primitive to control inside/outside color. The plan primitive allows you to control above/below color. The functioning of this map is demonstrated in an hands-on exercise later in the unit.

ColorMap

This map allows you to create solid color swatches and bitmaps. You can easily create and instance solid color swatches that allow you to maintain consistency and accuracy of color choices. You can also use a bitmap as an input and adjust gamma and gain.

Combustion

You can use this map to interactively create maps using Autodesk Combustion and 3ds Max simultaneously. When you paint a map in combustion, the material automatically updated in 3ds Max [in material editor and shaded viewports].

 Caution: Combustion
This map works only if Autodesk Combustion is installed on your system. 3ds Max is only available for Windows, as a result, you can not use this map on a Macintosh system.

Map Output Selector

This map is used with the multi-output map such as **Substance**. It tells 3ds Max which output to use. This map is automatically inserted when you assign an output of multi-output **Substance** map to input of a material.

MultiTile

This texture allows you to implement support for UDIM, Z-Brush, and Mudbox compatible multi-tile textures. ZBrush is the default value.

Hands-on Exercises

Exercise 1: Shading an outdoor Scene

In this exercise, we are going to apply materials and textures to an outdoor scene [see Fig. E1].

Table E1 summarizes the exercise.

Table E1	
Topics	• Getting Ready • Shading the Scene
Skill level	Intermediate
Resources folder	**unit-dt2**
Start file	**ext-start.max**
Final file	**ext-finish.max**
Time to complete	30 Minutes

Getting Ready

Make sure the **ext-start** is open in 3ds Max.

Shading the Scene

Follow these steps:

1. Select **wall-geo** in the **Scene Explorer** and then press **M** to open the **Slate Material Editor**. Drag **Standard** from the **Material/Map Browser** > **Maps** > **Scanline** rollout to active view.

2. Rename the material as **wall-mat**. RMB click on the **wall-mat** node and then choose **Assign Material to Selection**. Again, RMB click and then choose **Show Shaded Material in Viewport**.

3. In the active view, drag the **Diffuse Color** socket onto the empty area and release the mouse button. Choose **General** > **Bitmap** from the popup menu. In the **Select Bitmap Image File** dialog box that opens, select **red-brick.png** and then click **Open** to make a connection between the **Diffuse Color** socket and bitmap.

4. Double-click on the **Bitmap** node and then in the **Parameter Editor** > **Coordinates** rollout, change **U Tiling** and **V Tiling** to **4**. Similarly, connect the **Bump** socket to the **red-brick-gray.png** and change **Tiling** to **4**. Notice in the viewport the map is displayed on the wall [see Fig. E2].

5. Ensure **wall-geo** is selected in the **Scene Explorer** and then go to **Modify** panel and add the **UVW Map** modifier to the stack. Select the modifier's **Gizmo** and scale the texture so that the size of the bricks appear in right proportions [see Fig. E3].

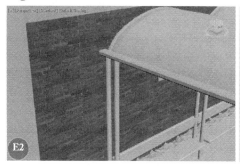 

6. Select **floor-geo** in the **Scene Explorer** and then in the **Slate Material Editor**, drag **Standard** from the **Material/Map Browser** > **Maps** > **Scanline** rollout to the active view. Rename the material as **road-mat**. RMB click on the **road-mat** node and then choose **Assign Material to Selection**. Again, RMB click and then choose **Show Shaded Material in Viewport**.

7. In the active view, drag the **Diffuse Color** socket onto the empty area and release the mouse button. Choose **General > Bitmap** from the popup menu. In the **Select Bitmap Image File** dialog box that opens, select **road.jpg** and then click **Open** to make a connection between the **Diffuse Color** socket and texture.

⊙→ *What next?*
*Notice in the viewport, the texture appears on the **floor-geo** [see Fig. E4]. Now, we need to change the direction of the yellow line. We will do so by using the **UVW Map** modifier.*

8. Ensure **floor-geo** is selected in the **Scene Explorer** and then go to **Modify** panel and add the **UVW Map** modifier to the stack. Select the modifier's **Gizmo** and rotate it by **90** degrees by using the **Rotate** tool. You can also use the **Move** tool to position the texture on the geometry [see Fig. E5].

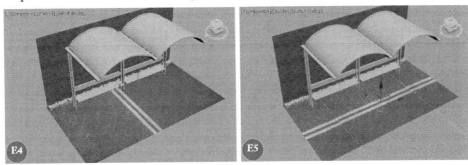

⊙→ *What next?*
*Now, we will apply the material to billboard. We will use the **Multi/Subobject** material. The **ID 1** has been assigned to the screen component of the board whereas rest of the geometry is held by **ID 2**.*

9. Select **billBoard-geo** in the **Scene Explorer** and then add a **Multi/Subobject** node to the active view. Rename the material as **billboard-mat**. In the **Parameter Editor > Multi/Sub-Object Basic Parameters** rollout, click **Set Number**. Now, in the **Set Number of Materials** dialog box, change **Number of Materials** parameter to **2** and click **OK**. RMB click on the **billboard-mat** node and then choose **Assign Material to Selection**.

10. Drag the **1** socket to the empty area of the view and then choose **Materials > Scanline > Standard** from the popup menu. Connect the **Standard's** materials **Diffuse Color** socket to the **honda.jpg**. Connect another **Standard** material to the **2** socket of the **billboard-mat**.

11. In the **Parameter Editor > Blinn Basic Parameters rollout > Specular Highlight** group of the **Standard** material that you connected to port **2**, change **Specular Level** and **Glossiness** to **92** and **33**, respectively. Also, change **Diffuse** color to RGB **[20, 20, 20]**. The material appears on the **billBoard-geo** in the viewport [see Fig. E6]. You need to enable **Show Shaded Material in Viewport** for the two **Standard** materials.

12. Create two **Standard** materials and assign dark gray and yellow colors to them. Now, apply these materials to alternate brick from the **brick-grp** group [see Fig. E7].

13. Create a **Standard** material and then rename it as **metal-mat**. In the **Parameter Editor > metal-mat > Blinn Basic Parameters** rollout, click the **Diffuse** color swatch. In the **Color Selector : Diffuse Color** dialog box, change **Value** to **12** and then click **OK**. In the **Specular Highlights** group, change **Specular Level** to **150** and **Glossiness** to **80**.

14. In the **Maps** rollout, change **Reflection** to **90** and then click the **Reflection** map button. In the **Material/Map Browser** that appears, double-click on **Raytrace** in the **Maps > General** rollout.

15. In the **Scene Explorer**, select **bsGeo11, bsGeo12, bsGeo15, bsGeo16, bsGeo18, bsGeo19, bsGeo20, bsGeo22, bsGeo23, bsGeo24, bsGeo26**, and **bsGeo27**. Assign the **metal-mat** material to the selected objects [see Fig. E8]. Also, assign **metal-mat** material to **bsGeo3** and **bsGeo6**.

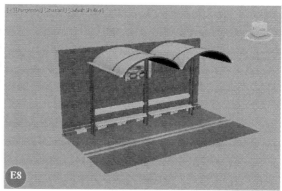

16. In the **Scene Explorer**, select **bsGeo04, bsGeo05, bsGeo07**, and **bsGeo08**. In the **Slate Material Editor**, drag **Standard** from the **Material/Map Browser > Maps > Scanline** rollout to the active view. Rename the material as **wood-mat**.

17. **RMB** click on the **wood-mat** node and then choose **Assign Material to Selection**. Again, **RMB** click and then choose **Show Shaded Material in Viewport**. In the active view, drag the **Diffuse Color** socket onto the empty area and release the mouse button. Choose **General > Advanced Wood** from the popup menu; a popup menu is displayed. Select the **Diffuse Color** option from the popup menu to make the connection.

18. In the **Parameter Editor** > **Advanced Wood** > **Presets** rollout, select **3D Cherry - Glossy** from the **Presets** drop-down list. The wood texture is displayed in the viewport [see Fig. E9].

19. In the **Scene Explorer**, select **bsGeo21**, and **bsGeo25**. In the **Slate Material Editor**, drag **Standard** from the **Material/Map Browser** > **Maps** > **Scanline** rollout to the active view. Rename the material as **roof-mat**.

20. **RMB** click on the **roof-mat** node and then choose **Assign Material to Selection**. Again, **RMB** click and then choose **Show Shaded Material in Viewport**. In the **Parameter Editor** > **roof-mat** > **Blinn Basic Parameters** rollout, change **Diffuse** to **RGB [23, 241, 12]** and then change **Opacity** to **25**. Fig. E10 shows the roof material in the viewport.

Exercise 2: Creating the Gold Material

In this exercise, we are going to create the gold material [see Fig. E1].

Table E2 summarizes the exercise.

Table E2	
Topics	• Getting Ready • Creating the Gold Material
Skill level	Beginner
Time to complete	10 Minutes

Table E2	
Resources folder	**unit-dt2**
Start file	**shader-ball.max**
Final file	**gold-finish.max**

Getting Ready
Open the **shader-ball.max** file in 3ds Max.

Creating the Gold Material
Follow these steps:

1. Press **M** to open the **Slate Material Editor**. In the **Material/Map Browser > Materials > Scanline** rollout, drag the **Standard** material to the active view. Rename the material as **gold-mat**.

2. Apply the material to **sample-geo-1, sample-geo-2**, and **sample-geo-3**. In the **Parameter Editor > gold-mat > Shader Basic Parameters** rollout, choose **Multi-Layer** from the drop-down list. In the **Multi-Layer Basic Parameters** rollout, set **Diffuse** to **RGB [148, 70, 0]** and then set **Diffuse Level** to **25**. Render the scene [see Fig. E2].

 What next?
Now, we will add specularity and reflection to add the detail.

3. In the **First Specular Layer** group, set **Color** to **RGB [247, 227, 10]**. Set **Level** to **114**, **Glossiness** to **32**, **Anisotropy** to **82**, and **Orientation** to **90**.

4. In the **Second Specular Layer** group, set **Color** to **RGB [192, 77, 8]**. Set **Level** to **114**, **Glossiness** to **32**, **Anisotropy** to **82**, and **Orientation** to **90**. Render the scene [see Fig. E3].

5. In the **Maps** rollout, click **Reflection** map button. In the **Material/Map Browser** that appears, double-click **Falloff**. In the **Parameter Editor** > **Falloff** > **Falloff Parameters** rollout, click the **Swap Colors/Maps** button. Also, change **Falloff Type** to **Fresnel**.

6. Click the white swatch map button and then in the **Material/Map Browser** that appears, double-click **Raytrace** in the **Maps** > **General** rollout. In the **Parameter Editor** > **Raytrace** > **Raytracer Parameters** rollout, select **Reflection** from the **Trace Mode** group. Render the scene [see Fig. E4].

7. In the **Falloff** > **Mix Curve** rollout, RMB click on the first point and then choose **Bezier-Corner** from the context menu [see Fig. E5]. Similarly, convert second point to **Bezier-Corner** and change the shape of the curve as shown in Fig. E6.

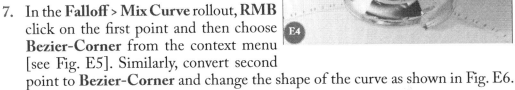

8. Render the scene to view the final result.

Exercise 3: Creating the Copper Material

In this exercise, we are going to create the copper material [see Fig. E1].

Table E3 summarizes the exercise.

Table E3	
Topics	• Getting Ready • Creating the Copper Material
Skill level	Beginner
Time to complete	10 Minutes
Resources folder	**unit-dt2**
Start file	**gold-finish.max**
Final file	**copper-finish.max**

Getting Ready

Make sure the **gold-finish.max** file that you created in the previous exercise is open in 3ds Max.

Creating the Copper Material

Follow these steps:

1. Press **M** to open the **Slate Material Editor**, if not already open. Create a copy of the **gold-mat** node by shift dragging it [see Fig. E2].

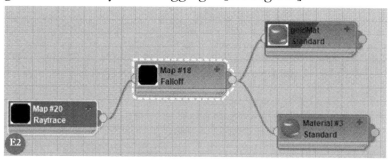

2. Rename the node as **copper-mat** and then apply it to **sample-geo-1**, **sample-geo-2**, and **sample-geo-3**. In the **Multi-Layer Basic Parameters** rollout, change **Diffuse** to RGB [88, 28, 9].

3. In the **Parameter Editor > First Specular Layer** group, change **Color** to RGB [177, 75, 44]. In the **Second Specular Layer** group, change **Color** to RGB [255, 123, 82]. Render the scene.

Exercise 4: Creating the Brass Material

In this exercise, we are going to create the brass material [see Fig. E1]. Table E4 summarizes the exercise.

Table E4		
Topics	• Getting Ready • Creating the Brass Material	
Skill level	Beginner	
Time to complete	10 Minutes	
Resources folder	**unit-dt2**	
Start file	**copper-finish.max**	
Final file	**brass-finish.max**	

Getting Ready
Make sure the **copper-finish.max** file that you created in the previous exercise is open in 3ds Max.

Creating the Brass Material
Follow these steps:

1. Press **M** to open the **Slate Material Editor**, if not already open. Create a copy of the **copper-mat** node by **Shift** dragging it. Rename the node as **brass-mat** and then apply it to **sample-geo-1, sample-geo-2**, and **sample-geo-3**.

2. In the **Multi-Layer Basic Parameters** rollout, change **Diffuse** to RGB [49, 38, 14]. In the **First Specular Layer** group, change **Color** to RGB [212, 154, 30]. In the **Second Specular Layer** group, change **Color** to RGB [174, 98, 61]. Render the scene [see Fig. E1].

Exercise 5: Creating the Chrome Material
In this exercise, we are going to create the chrome material [see Fig. E1]. Table E5 summarizes the exercise.

Table E5	
Topics	• Getting Ready • Creating the Chrome Material
Skill level	Beginner
Time to complete	10 Minutes
Resources folder	**unit-dt2**
Start file	**shader-ball.max**
Final file	**chrome-finish.max**

Getting Ready

Make sure the **shader-ball.max** is open in 3ds Max.

Creating the Chrome Material

Follow these steps:

1. Press **M** to open the **Slate Material Editor**. In the **Material/Map/Browser > Materials > Scanline** rollout, drag the **Standard** material to the active view. Rename the material as **chrome-mat**. Apply the material to **sample-geo-1, sample-geo-2,** and **sample-geo-3**.

2. In the **Parameter Editor > chrome-mat > Blinn Basic Parameters** rollout, click the **Diffuse** color swatch. In the **Color Selector : Diffuse Color** dialog box, change **Value** to 12 and then click **OK**. In the **Specular Highlights** group, change **Specular Level** to 150 and **Glossiness** to 80.

3. In the **Maps** rollout, change **Reflection** to 90 and then click the **Reflection** map button. In the **Material/Map Browser** that appears, double-click on **Raytrace**. In the **Raytrace** map > **Raytracer Parameters** rollout> **Background** group, click **None**.

4. In the **Material/Map Browser** that appears, double-click **Bitmap**. In the **Select Bitmap Image File** dialog box that appears, select **ref-map.jpeg**. Render the scene.

Exercise 6: Creating the Brushed Aluminum Material

In this exercise, we are going to create the brushed aluminum material using Photoshop and 3ds Max [see Fig. E1].

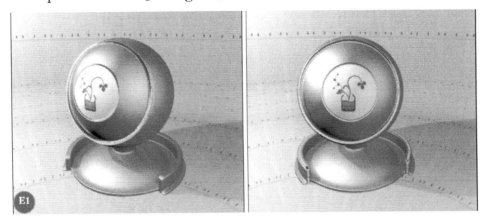

Table E6 summarizes the exercise.

Table E6	
Topics	• Getting Ready • Creating the Brushed Aluminum Material
Skill level	Beginner
Time to complete	15 Minutes
Resources folder	**unit-dt2**
Start file	**shader-ball.max**
Final file	**alluminium-finish.max**

Getting Ready

Make sure the **shader-ball.max** file is open in 3ds Max.

Creating the Brushed Aluminum Material

Follow these steps:

1. Start Photoshop. Create a **1000 x 1000 px** document and fill it with **50%** gray color. Choose **Noise > Add Noise** from the **Filter** menu and then change the parameters as shown in Fig. E2 and then click **OK**.

2. Choose **Blur > Motion Blur** from the **Filter** menu and then change the parameters as shown in Fig. E3 and then click **OK**.

3. Choose **Adjustments > Brightness\Contrast** from the **Image** menu and then change the parameters as shown in Fig. E4 and then click **OK**. Save the document as **scratch.jpg**.

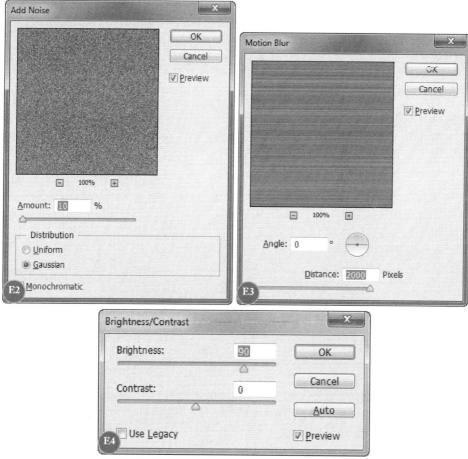

4. Switch to 3ds Max and then press **M** to open the **Slate Material Editor**. In the **Material/Map Browser > Materials > Scanline** rollout, drag the **Standard** material to the active view. Rename the material as **bal-mat**. Apply the material to **sample-geo-1**, **sample-geo-2**, and **sample-geo-3**.

5. In the **Parameter Editor > bal-mat > Shader Basic Parameters** rollout, select **Oren-Nayar-Blinn** from the drop-down list. In the **Parameter Editor > bal-mat > Oren-Nayar-Blinn Basic Parameters** rollout, click **Ambient** color swatch. In the **Color Selector : Ambient Color** dialog box, change **Value** to **84** and click **OK**. Render the scene [see Fig. E5].

6. Unlock the **Ambient** and **Diffuse** map components of the material. Click the **Diffuse** map button and then in the **Material/Map Browser** that appears, double-click **Mix**. In the **Parameter Editor > Mix** map, change **Color 1** to the value **127** and assign **scratch.jpg** to **Color 2** using the **Bitmap** map. Set **Mix Amount** to **72**. Render the scene [see Fig. E6].

7. In the **bal-mat** > **Oren-Nayar-Blinn Basic Parameters** rollout > **Advanced Diffuse** group, change **Diffuse Level** to 81, and **Roughness** to 80. Now, render the scene [see Fig. E7].

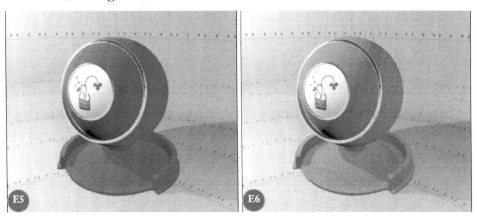

8. In the **Parameter Editor** > **bal-mat** > **Oren-Nayar-Blinn Basic Parameters** rollout > **Specular Highlight** group, change **Specular Level** to 156, **Glossiness** to 13, and **Soften** to 0.48. Now, render the scene [see Fig. E8].

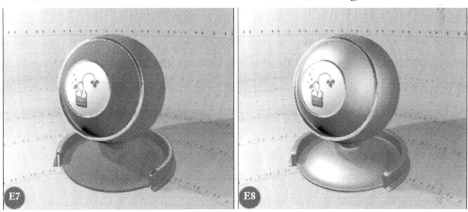

9. In the **Parameter Editor** > **scratch.jpg** > **Output** rollout, change **Output Amount** to 0.6. Render the scene.

Exercise 7: Creating the Denim Fabric Material

In this exercise, we will create the denim fabric material [see Fig. E1] using Photoshop and 3ds Max. Table E7 summarizes the exercise.

Table E7	
Topics	• Getting Ready • Creating the Denim Fabric Material
Skill level	Beginner
Time to complete	15 Minutes
Resources folder	**unit-dt2**

Table E7	
Start file	shader-ball.max
Final file	denim-finish.max

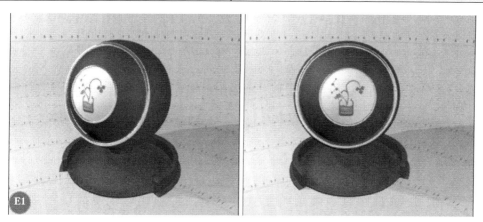

Getting Ready

Make sure the **shader-ball.max** is open in 3ds Max.

Creating the Denim Fabric Material

Follow these steps:

1. Start Photoshop. Create a **1000 x 1000 px** document and fill it with **RGB [41, 67, 102]** color. Create a new layer and fill it with **50%** gray. Press **D** to switch to the default colors.

2. Choose **Filter Gallery> Sketch > Halftone Pattern** from the **Filter** menu and then change the parameters as shown in Fig. E2 and then click **OK**. Choose **Pixelate > Mezzotint** from the **Filter** menu and then change the parameters as shown in Fig. E3 and then click **OK**.

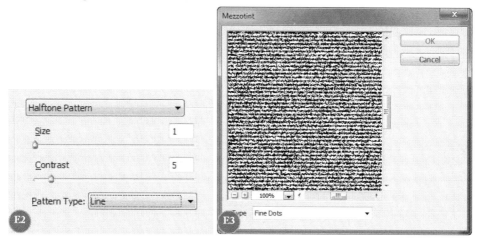

3. Duplicate the layer and rotate and scale the duplicate layer [see Fig. E4]. Choose **Blur > Gaussian Blur** from the **Filter** menu and then apply a blur of radius **1**. Set blending mode to **Multiply**. Also, change the blending mode of the middle layer [Layer 1] to **Softlight** [Fig. E5]. Save the file as **denim-febric.jpg**.

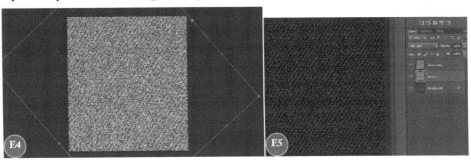

4. Choose **Flatten Image** from the **Layer** menu to flatten the image. Now, press **Ctrl+Shift+U** to desaturate the image and then save it as **denim-febric-bump.jpg**.

5. Switch to 3ds Max, press **M** to open the **Slate Material Editor**. In the **Material/ Map Browser > Materials > Scanline** rollout, drag the **Standard** material to the active view. Rename the material as **denim-mat**. Apply the material to **sample-geo-1, sample-geo-2,** and **sample-geo-3**.

6. In the **Parameter Editor > denim-mat > Shader Basic Parameters** rollout, choose **Oren-Nayar-Blinn** from the drop-down list. In the **Parameter Editor > denim-mat > Oren-Nayar-Blinn Basic Parameters** rollout, click **Ambient** color swatch. In the **Color Selector : Ambient Color** dialog box, change **RGB** to **50, 53,** and **57** and click **OK**.

7. Unlock the **Ambient** and **Diffuse** map components of the material. Click on the **Diffuse** map button and then on the **Material/Map Browser** that appears, double-click **Bitmap**. Assign **denim-febric.jpg**. In the **denim-mat > Oren-Nayar-Blinn Basic Parameters** rollout > **Advanced Diffuse** group, change **Diffuse Level** to **250** and **Roughness** to **75**. Now, render the scene [see Fig. E6].

8. In the **Parameter Editor > denim-mat > Oren-Nayar-Blinn Basic Parameters** rollout > **Specular Highlight** group, change **Specular Level** to **7**, and **Glossiness** to **10**. Render the scene [see Fig. E7]. In the **Maps** rollout, ensure **Bump** is set to **28%** and then click on the **Bump** map button.

9. In the **Material/Map Browser** that appears, double-click **Bitmap**. In the **Select Bitmap Image File** dialog box that appears, select **denim-febric-bump.jpg**. Render the scene.

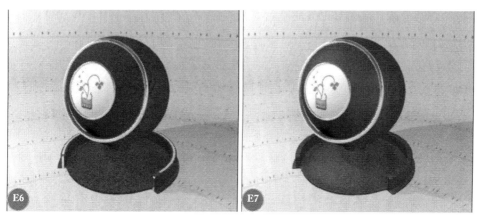

Exercise 8: Creating the Microscopic Material

In this exercise, we will create a microscopic material [see Fig. E1]. The following material(s) and map(s) are used in this exercise: **Standard, Mix, Falloff,** and **Noise.**

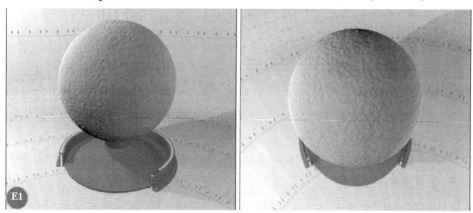

Table E8 summarizes the exercise.

Table E8	
Topics	• Getting Ready • Creating the Microscopic Material
Skill level	Intermediate
Resources folder	**unit-dt2**
Start file	**micro-start.max**
Final file	**micro-finish.max**
Time to complete	20 Minutes

Getting Ready

Make sure **micro-start.max** is open in 3ds Max.

Creating the Microscopic Material

Follow these steps:

1. Press **M** to open the **Slate Material Editor** and then create a new **Standard** material and assign it to the **sph-geo** in the scene. Rename the material as **micro-mat**. Connect the **Falloff** map to the **micro-mat's Diffuse** port.

2. In the **Parameter Editor** > **Falloff** map > **Falloff Parameters** rollout > **Front:Side** group, change first color swatch to **RGB [20, 20, 20]** and make sure that the second color swatch to white. Ensure **Falloff Type** is set to **Perpendicular/Parallel** and **Falloff Direction** is set to **Viewing Direction (Camera Z-Axis)** [see Fig. E2]. Also, change the **Mix Curve** to as shown in Fig. E3. Now, we will create two **Noise** maps and mix them using the **Mix** map.

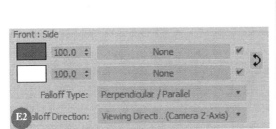
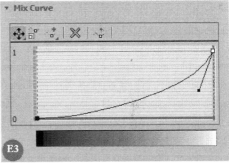

3. Connect a **Mix** map to the **micro-mat's Bump** port. In the **Parameter Editor** > **Mix** map > **Mix Parameters** rollout, change **Mix Amount** to **37.8**. In the **Slate Material Editor**, connect two **Noise** maps, one each to the **Color 1** and **Color 2** ports. For the **Color 1** > **Noise** map use the settings shown in Fig. E4. Fig. E5 shows the **Noise** map settings connected to **Color 2**. Fig. E6 shows the node network.

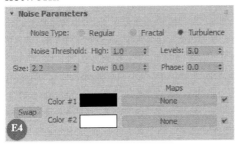
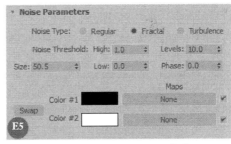

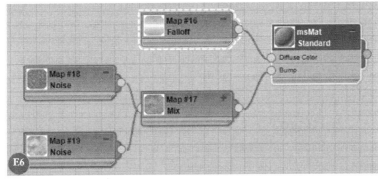

4. Now, render the scene. Notice that the output is little bit on the darker side. To address this, in the **Parameter Editor > Falloff** map > **Falloff Parameters** rollout > **Front:Side** group, change first color swatch to **RGB [80, 80, 80]**. Render the scene.

Exercise 9: Creating Material for a Volleyball

In this exercise, we will apply texture to a volleyball [see Fig. E1]. The right image in Fig. E1 shows the reference whereas the left image shows the rendered output. The following material(s) and map(s) are used in this exercise: **Multi/Sub-Object, Standard**, and **Noise**.

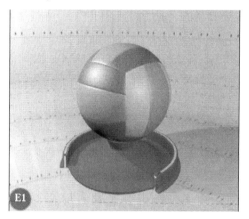 

Table E9 summarizes the exercise.

Table E9	
Topics	• Getting Ready • Creating Material for a Volleyball
Skill level	Intermediate
Resources folder	**unit-dt2**
Start file	**vb-start.max**
Final file	**vb-finish.max**
Time to complete	15 Minutes

Getting Ready
Make sure the **vb-start.max** is open in 3ds Max.

Creating Material for a Volleyball
Follow these steps:

1. Select the **volleyball-geo** in any viewport and then go to the **Modify** panel. In the **Selection** rollout, click **Element** and then select the elements that make the yellow part of the volleyball [see Fig. E2]. See the right image in Fig. E1 for reference.

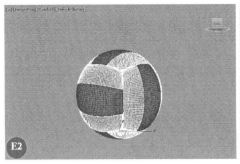
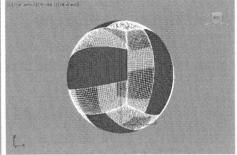

2. In the **Modify panel > Polygon: Material IDs** rollout, change **Set ID** to **1** [see Fig. E3]. Similarly, select the blue and white elements and assign them ID **2** and **3**, respectively.

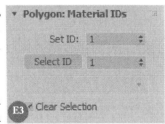

3. Press **M** to open the **Slate Material Editor** and then create a new **Multi/Sub-object** material and assign it to the **volleyball-geo** in the scene. Rename the material as **vb-mat**. In the **Parameter Editor > vb-mat > Multi/Sub-Object Parameters** rollout, click **Set Number** and then change **Number of Materials** to **3** in the dialog box that appears. Next, click **OK**.

4. In the **Slate Material Editor**, connect a **Standard** material to the port **1** of the **vb-mat**. In the **Parameter Editor > Blinn Basic Parameter** rollout, change the **Diffuse** component to **RGB [242, 140, 8]**. In the **Specular Highlights** group, change **Specular Level** to **71** and **Glossiness** to **28**.

5. Connect a **Noise** map to the **Bump** port of the **Standard** material. Set **Bump** to **2%**. In the **Parameter Editor > Noise > Noise Parameters** rollout, change **Noise Type** to **Turbulence**, **Levels** to **9**, and **Size** to **0.5**.

6. In the **Slate Material Editor**, select the **Standard** material and **Noise** map. Now, create a copy of the selected nodes using **SHIFT**. Connect the new Standard material to the port **2** of the **vb-mat**. Similarly, create another copy and connect it to port **3**. Fig. E4 shows the node network.

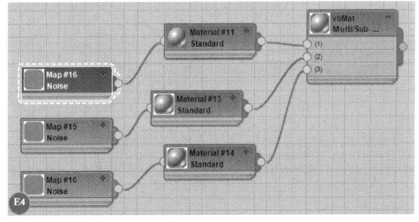

7. Set **Diffuse** components of the material connected to the port **2** and **3** to **RGB [11, 91, 229]** and **RGB [236, 236, 230]**, respectively. Now, render the scene.

Exercise 10: Creating Material for a Water Tunnel

In this exercise, we will apply texture to a water tunnel [see Fig. E1]. The following material(s) and map(s) are used in this exercise: **Raytrace, Standard, Mix,** and **Noise.**

Table E10 summarizes the exercise.

Table E10	
Topics	• Getting Ready • Creating Material for a Water Tunnel
Skill level	Intermediate
Resources folder	**unit-dt2**
Start file	**tunnel-start.max**
Final file	**tunnel-finish.max**
Time to complete	30 Minutes

Getting Ready
Make sure the **tunnel-start.max** is open in 3ds Max.

Creating Material for a Water Tunnel
Follow these steps:

1. Press **M** to open the **Slate Material Editor** and then create a new **Raytrace** material and assign it to the **water-geo** in the scene. Rename the material as **water-mat.**

2. In the **Parameter Editor > Raytrace Basic Parameter** rollout, change **Diffuse** to black. Set **Transparency** to **RGB [146, 175, 223]**. Set **Reflect** to **RGB [178, 178, 178]**. In the **Specular Highlight** group, change **Specular Level** to **161** and **Glossiness** to **29**. Connect a **Noise** map to the **Bump** port of the **water-mat** material. Use the default values for the **Noise** map. Render the scene [Fig. E2].

3. In the **Slate Material Editor**, create a new **Standard** material and assign it to the **cave-geo** in the scene. Rename the material as **cave-mat**. Connect a **Mix** map to the **Diffuse** port of the **cave-mat**. Connect a **Noise** map to the **Color 1** port of the **Mix** map. In the **Noise Parameters** rollout, change **Noise Type** to **Turbulence**, **Levels** to **10**, **Size** to **31.7**. Set **Color 1** to RGB [132, 77, 6] and **Color 2** to RGB [154, 100, 79].

4. Connect a **Noise** map to the **Color 2** port of the **Mix** map. In the **Noise Parameters** rollout, change **Noise Type** to **Turbulence**, **Levels** to **10**, **Size** to **72**. Set **Color 1** to RGB [212, 84, 45] and **Color 2** to RGB [181, 99, 54].

5. In the **Parameter Editor** > **Mix Parameters** rollout, change **Mix Amount** to **40**. In the **Mixing curve** group, select the **Use Curve** check box and then change **Upper** to **0.6** and **Lower** to **0.53**. Render the [Fig. E3].

6. Connect a **Mix** map to the **Displacement** port of the **cave-mat**. Set **Displacement** to **25%** in the **Maps** rollout. Connect a **Noise** map to the **Color 1** port of the **Mix** map. In the **Noise Parameters** rollout, change **Noise Type** to **Turbulence**, **Levels** to **8.4** and **Size** to **21.2**.

7. Connect a **Noise** map to the **Color 2** port of the **Mix** map. In the **Noise Parameters** rollout, change **Noise Type** to **Turbulence**, **Levels** to **10**, **Size** to **81.5**. In the **Parameter Editor** > **Mix Parameters** rollout, change **Mix Amount** to **18.4**. Select **cave-geo** in the scene and then apply **Disp Approx** modifier to it. Render the scene.

8. Similarly, create a material for the **floor-geo**. If you want to see the values I have used, open **tunnel-finish.max** and check the **floor-mat** material.

Exercise 11: Creating Rusted Metal Texture

In this exercise, we will create a rusted metal texture [see Fig. E1]. The following material(s) and map(s) are used in this exercise: **Standard, Composite, Bitmap, Color Correction**, and **Noise**. Table E11 summarizes the exercise.

Table E11	
Topics	• Getting Ready • Creating Rusted Metal Texture
Skill level	Beginner
Resources folder	**unit-dt2**
Start file	**shader-ball.max**
Final File	**rust-fiinish**
Time to complete	20 Minutes

Getting Ready

Make sure the **shader-ball.max** is open in 3ds Max.

Creating Rusted Metal Texture

Follow these steps:

1. Press **M** to open the **Slate Material Editor**. In the **Material/Map Browser >
   Materials > Scanline** rollout, double-click on **Standard** to add a **Standard** material
   to the active view. Rename the material as **rust-mat** and apply it to **sample-geo-1**,
   sample-geo-2, and **sample-geo-3**.

2. Connect a **Composite** map to the **rust-map's Diffuse Color** port. Now, connect
   rust.jpg to the **Composite** map's **Layer 1** port [see Fig. E2].

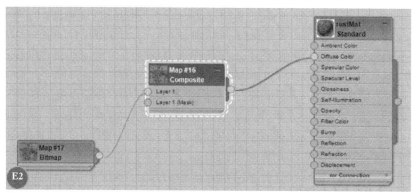

3. In the **Parameter Editor** > **Composite** map > **Composite Layers** > **Layer 1** rollout, click **Add a New Layer** button to add a new layer [see Fig. E3]. Notice that a new port with the name **Layer 2** has been added to the **Composite** map node in the active view.

4. Connect **rust-paint.jpg** to the **Composite** map's **Layer 2** port. In the **Parameter Editor** > **Composite** map > **Composite Layers** > **Layer 2** rollout, change **Opacity** to **10%** and blend mode to **Color Dodge** [see Fig. E4]. Render the scene [see Fig. E5].

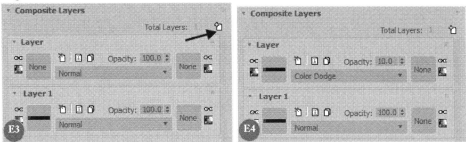

5. Connect **scratches-mask.jpg** to the **Composite** map's **Layer 2 (Mask)** port using a **Bitmap** map. Now, select the **Invert** check box from the **Bitmap**'s **Output** rollout. Render the scene [see Fig. E6].

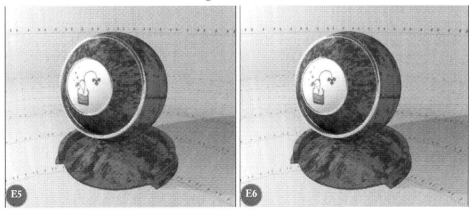

6. In the **Slate Material Editor**'s active view, create copy of the **Bitmap** node connected to the **Composite** map's **Layer 2 (Mask)** node using **Shift**. Connect the duplicate node to the **Bump** node of **rust-mat**. In the **Parameter Editor** > **rust-mat** > **Maps** rollout, change bump map's strength to **10%** and then render the scene.

Exercise 12: Working with the ShapeMap

In this exercise, we will create a resolution independent map using **ShapeMap**. Table E12 summarizes the exercise.

Table E12	
Topics	• Getting Ready • Working with ShapeMap

Table E12	
Skill level	Beginner
Resources folder	**unit-dt2**
Start file	**shape-start.max**
Final file	**shape-finish.max**
Time to complete	20 Minutes

Getting Ready

Open **shape-start.max** in 3ds Max.

Working with the ShapeMap

Follow these steps:

1. Press **M** to open the **Slate Material Editor** and then from the **Material/Map Browser > Materials > Scanline** rollout, drag **Standard** to the active view. Connect the **ShapeMap** map to the **Diffuse Color** slot of the material.

2. Select the plane in the viewport. **RMB** click on the material node and then choose **Assign Material to Selection**. Again, **RMB** click and then choose **Show Shaded Material in Viewport**. Notice only standard logo is displayed in the viewport at this moment [see Fig. E1].

3. In the **Parameter Editor > ShapeMap > Shape Parameters** rollout, click **None** and then click the apple logo spline in any viewport. The shape is now displayed on the plane in the viewport [see Fig. E2].

4. In the **Closed Shapes** group, select the **Render Outline** check box. In the **Outlines** group, change **Width** to 5.

5. Set **Fill Color, Line Color, Background Color** to RGB [141, 141, 141], RGB [252, 255, 0], and RGB [156, 188, 247], respectively. In the **Map Boundary** group, select **Manual** and then change **Width** and **Height** to 537 and 300, respectively. The logo is now centered on the plane [see Fig. E3].

6. Render the scene [see Fig. E4]. Now, if zoom in on an area of the logo and then render, you would notice that you will still get a high resolution output [see Fig. E5].

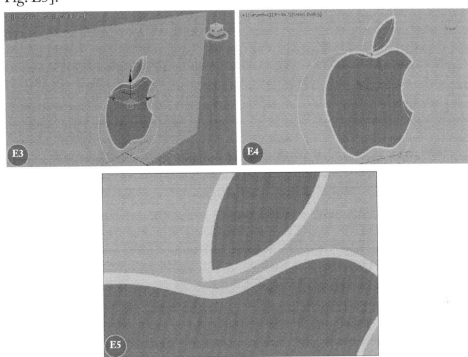

Exercise 13: Working with Text Map

In this exercise, we will create a resolution independent map using **Text Map**. Table E13 summarizes the exercise.

Table E13	
Topics	• Getting Ready • Working with Text Map
Skill level	Beginner
Resources folder	**unit-dt2**
Start file	**text-start.max**
Final file	**text-finish.max**
Time to complete	20 Minutes

Getting Ready
Open **text-start.max** in 3ds Max.

Working with the Text Map

Follow these steps:

1. Press **M** to open the **Slate Material Editor** and then from the **Material/Map Browser** > **Materials** > **Scanline** rollout, drag **Standard** to the active view. Connect the **TextMap** map to the **Diffuse Color** slot of the material. Select the plane in the viewport. **RMB** click on the material node and then choose **Assign Material to Selection**. Again, **RMB** click and then choose **Show Shaded Material in Viewport**. Notice only standard logo is displayed in the viewport at this moment [see Fig. E1].

2. In the **Parameter Editor** > **Text Map** > **Text Parameters** rollout, click **None** and then click the **TextPlus** object in any viewport. The text is now displayed on the plane in the viewport [see Fig. E2]. In the **Characters** group, select the **Render Outline** check box. In the **Outlines** group, change **Width** to 5.

3. Set **Fill Color, Line Color, Background Color** to RGB [141, 141, 141], RGB [252, 255, 0], and RGB [156, 188, 247], respectively. In the **Map Boundary** group, select **Manual** and then change **Width** and **Height** to **500** and **200**, respectively. The text is now centered on the plane [see Fig. E3].

4. Render the scene [see Fig. E4]. Now, if zoom in on an area of the text and then render, you would notice that you will still get a high resolution output [see Fig. E5].

Exercise 14: Working with TextureObjMask Map

In this exercise, we will create a resolution independent map using the **TextureObjMask** map. Table E14 summarizes the exercise.

Table E14	
Topics	• Getting Ready • Working with TextureObjMask Map
Skill level	Beginner
Resources folder	**unit-dt2**
Start file	**tom-start.max**
Final file	**tom-finish.max**
Time to complete	20 Minutes

Getting Ready
Open **tbm-start.max** in 3ds Max.

Working with the TextureObjMask Map
Follow these steps:

1. Press **M** to open the **Slate Material Editor** and then drag **TextureObjMask** to the active view from the **Material/Map Browser > Maps > General** rollout. In the **Parameter Editor > TextureObjMask > Parameters** rollout, click **Control Object**'s **None** button and then click on the sphere in a viewport to make it the control object.

2. Drag the **Cellular** and **Noise** maps to the active view the **Material/Map Browser > Maps > General** rollout. Change the color as desired and then connect the **Cellular** map to the **Texture1** [outside texture] port of the **TextureObjMask** and the **Noise** map to the **Texture2** [inside texture] port [see Fig. E1]. In the **Parameter Editor > TextureObjMask > Parameters** rollout, change **Transition Range** to **125**.

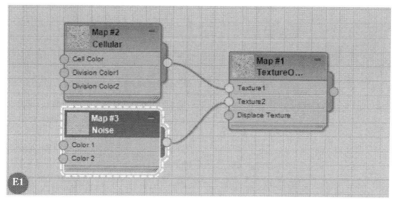

3. Create a **Standard** material and connect its **Diffuse Color** port to the **TextureObjMask.** Select the plane in a viewport and **RMB** click on the material node and then choose **Assign Material to Selection.** Again, **RMB** click and then choose **Show Shaded Material in Viewport.** Render the scene [see Fig. E2]. Notice that the sphere is masking the plane rendering. Create another **Standard** material and change its **Opacity** to 35. Render the scene [see Fig. E3].

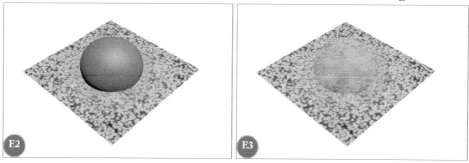

Quiz

Evaluate your skills to see how many questions you can answer correctly.

Multiple Choice
Answer the following questions:

1. Which of the following shading models is used to create realistic highlights for shiny and regular surfaces?

    [A] Phong   [B] Blinn
    [C] Metal   [D] Strauss

2. Which of the following shading models is used to create surfaces with elliptical, anisotropic highlights?

    [A] Phong   [B] Blinn
    [C] Metal   [D] Oren-Nayar-Blinn

Fill in the Blanks

Fill in the blanks in each of the following statements:

1. The option in the _____ rollout are used by the **Architectural, Raytrace, Standard,** and **Ink 'n Paint** materials to improve the quality of the rendered image.

2. You can use the _____ shader to create realistic-looking metallic surfaces and a variety of organic-looking materials.

3. The _____ shader is a variant of the **Blinn** shader and can be used to model matte surfaces such as fabric.

4. The _____ material allows you to mix two materials on a single side of the surface.

5. The _____ material is used with the **Morpher** modifier.

6. The _____ material allows you to assign materials at the sub-object level.

7. The _____ material lets you assign two different materials to the top and bottom portions of an object.

8. The _____ material is used to make whole objects or any set of faces into matte objects.

9. The _____ material is used to create cartoons effects. This material produces shading with inked borders.

10. The _____ utility removes mapping coordinates or materials from the currently selected objects.

True or False

State whether each of the following is true or false:

1. Self-illuminated materials do not show shadows cast onto them. Also, they are unaffected by the lights in the scene.

2. The **Roughness** parameter is available only with the **Oren-Nayar-Blinn** and **Multi-Level** shaders, and with the **Physical** material.

3. The **Multi-Layer Shader** has three layers of specular highlights.

4. You can not use the **Quicksilver Hardware Renderer** to render **DirectX Shader** materials.

5. This **XRef** material lets you use a material applied to an object in another 3ds Max scene file.

Summary
The unit covered the following topics:

- General/Scanline materials
- General maps

- Autodesk materials
- Physical material

Unit DT3: Physical and Autodesk Materials

The Autodesk materials are only visible in the **Material/Map Browser** if the active renderer is **ART** or **Quicksilver Hardware** renderer. The **Physical** material is physically-based material and it is compatible with both the **ART** and **Arnold** renderers. Autodesk materials are used to model commonly used surfaces in the construction, design, and the environment. These materials correspond to the materials found in other Autodesk products such as **Autodesk AutoCAD**, **Revit** and **Autodesk Inventor**. So, if you work between these applications, you can share surface and material information among them.

Autodesk Materials

Autodesk materials work best when you use them with physically accurate lights such as photometric lights in a scene, modeled in the real-world units. Many of the Autodesk materials use **Autodesk Bitmaps**. **Autodesk Bitmap** is a simple bitmap type. This bitmap type always uses the real-world mapping coordinates. Therefore, if you have applied the **UVW Map** modifier to any geometry, make sure you enable **Real-World Map Size** in the **Parameters** rollout. You can also change the default bitmap assignment.

Caution: Autodesk Bitmap compatibility
*3ds Max allows you to disconnect a bitmap, or replace it with another map. However, if you disconnect **Autodesk Bitmap** in other application such as **Autodesk AutoCAD**, you won't be able to read the Autodesk material. If you are using other applications, make sure that you do not replace the bitmap with a map that only 3ds Max understands.*

Caution: Autodesk Material Library
*If you uninstall or remove Autodesk material library, the materials will no longer will be available for other Autodesk products such as **AutoCAD**, **Revit**, or **Inventor**.*

Autodesk Ceramic

You can use this material to model the glazed ceramic material including porcelain. Figs. 1 and 2 show the **Ceramic** and **Porcelain** types, respectively.

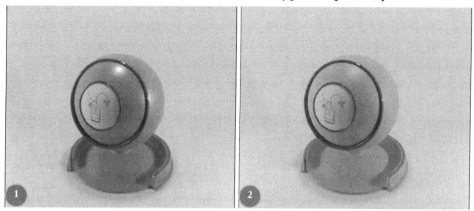

Autodesk Concrete

This material allows you to model the concrete material [see Figs. 3 and 4]. The **Sealant** parameter in the **Concrete** rollout controls the reflectiveness of the surface. **None** does not affect the surface finish. **Epoxy** adds a reflective coating on the surface whereas **Acrylic** adds a matte reflective coating. Refer to **auto-mat-concrete.max**.

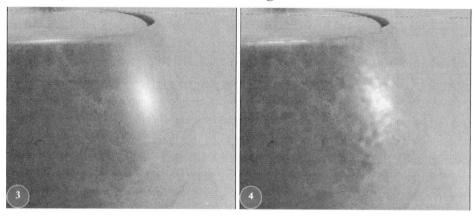

Autodesk Generic

This material provides a generic interface for creating a custom appearance. You can convert an Autodesk material to the **Autodesk Generic** material by **RMB** clicking on the node in the active view of the **Slate Material Editor** and then choosing **Copy as Generic** from the popup menu.

Autodesk Glazing

This material allows you to model a thin and transparent material such as glazing in windows and doors. The **Color** parameter in the **Glazing** rollout lets you choose the color for the sheet of glass. Fig. 5 shows the teapot rendered with **Blue Green** color applied to it.

Autodesk Harwood

This material is used the model the appearance of a wood. The **Stain** parameter in the **Wood** rollout allows you to choose a stain to add to the base harwood pattern. Fig. 6 shows the wood material with **Stain** set to **None**. Refer to **auto-mat-harwood.max**.

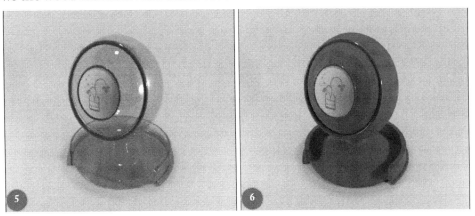

The **Finish** parameter lets you choose the surface finish of the harwood. **Unfinished** is the default option [see Fig. 6]. The other options available are: **Semi-Gloss Varnish** [see Fig. 7], and **Satin Varnish** [see Fig. 8].

Autodesk Masonry/CMU

This material can be used to model masonry or concrete masonry units [**CMUs**], see Fig. 9. Refer to **auto-mat-masonry.max**.

Autodesk Metal

You can use this material to model various metallic surfaces. The **Type** parameter in the **Metal** rollout lets you choose the type of material you want to create. These materials define the base color and texture of the material. Fig. 10 show the brass material. The **Finish** parameter lets you choose the surface finish for the surface. Figs. 10 and 11 show the brass material with the **Polished** and **Brushed** finish, respectively.

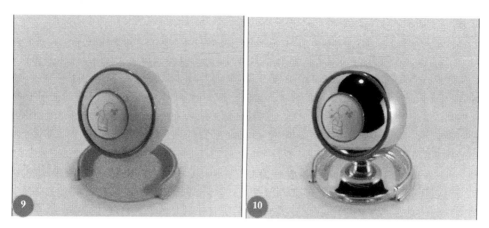

Autodesk Metallic Paint

This material allows you to model a metallic paint surface such as paint of a car [see Fig. 12].

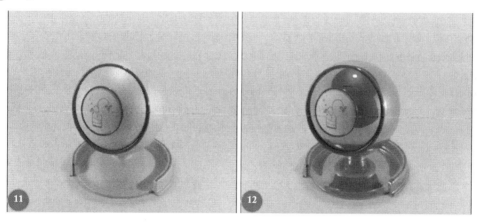

Autodesk Mirror

This material lets you model a mirror material [see Fig. 13]. Refer to **auto-mat-mirror.max**.

Autodesk Plastic/Vinyl

This material allows you to model the surfaces that have a synthetic appearance such as plastic or vinyl [see Figs. 14 and 15].

Autodesk Solid Glass

This material allows you to model the appearance of the solid glass [see Fig. 16].

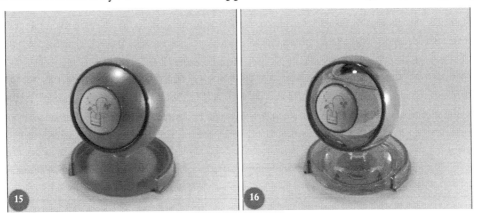

Autodesk Stone

You can use this material to create the appearance of the stone [see Figs. 17 and 18]. The **Type** parameter in the **Finish Bumps** rollout lets you specify the bump pattern. Available options are: **Polished Granite, Stone Wall, Glossy Marble,** and **Custom**.

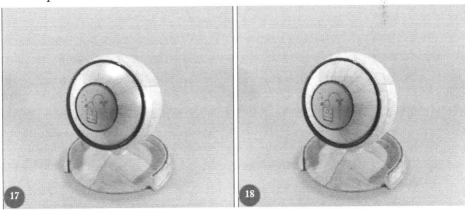

Autodesk Wall Paint

This material can be used to model the appearance of a painted surface such as paint on the walls of a room. The **Application** parameter in the **Wall Paint** rollout lets you choose the texture method. In other words, you can control how paint is applied on the surface. **Roller** is the default method. Other two methods are **Brush** and **Spray**.

Autodesk Water

This material can be used to model appearance of a water surface [see Fig. 19]. The **Type** parameter in the **Water** rollout lets you choose the scale and texture of the water. The available options are **Swimming Pool, Generic Reflecting Pool, Generic Stream/ River, Generic Pond/Lake,** and **Generic Sea/Ocean.** The **Color** parameter lets you specify the color of the water. This option is only available for **Generic Stream/ River, Pond/Lake,** and **Sea/Ocean.**

The following options are available for adjusting the color of the water: **Tropical, Algae/Green, Murky/Brown, Generic Reflecting Pool, Generic Stream/River, Generic Pond/Lake, Generic Sea/Ocean,** and **Custom.**

Physical Material

The **Physical** material allows you to model shading effects of the real-world materials with ease. This material is the layered material that gives you ability to efficiently use the physically-based workflows. This material is compatible with **ART** and **Arnold** renderers. Do not use the legacy **Scanline** renderer with it as **Scanline** renderer shows just the approximation of the shader and does not support many crucial features.

This material is comprised of the following:

- A base layer that represents a diffuse color or colored metallic reflections. There can be an optional clear-coat layer at the top. The clear-coat layer stays at the top of all layers and reduces energy based on how much energy it reflects and transparency color of the coating.
- Transparency layer
- Sub-surface scattering/translucency layer
- Emission [self-illumination] layer. This layer does not participate in the energy conversation and adds energy.

According to the energy conservation model of this material, the sum of various shading components can not exceed 100%. One exception is emission, in this case, energy is added. The energy calculation is based on the weight parameters instead of color parameters. This material ensures that the light does not amplify. When the **Metalness** parameter of the material is set to 1, the material is opaque. It does not produce any diffuse, transparency, or sub-surface scattering effects.

Physical Material comes with number of presets that you can use as a quick starting point. You can select the presets from the **Presets** rollout of the material. The **Material mode** drop-down list also available in the **Presets** rollout, lets you choose a mode. The two available modes are **Standard** and **Advanced.** The **Advanced** mode is the superset of the **Standard** mode with hidden parameters. In most of the cases, the parameters in the **Standard** mode are sufficient to make physically plausible materials. Some of the advanced parameters are: **Reflection Color** and **Weight, Diffuse Roughness,** and parameters in the **Advanced Reflectance Parameters** rollout.

Hands-on Exercises

Exercise 1: Creating Glossy Varnished Wood

In this exercise, we will create a varnished glossy wood material using the **Physical** material [see Fig. E1].

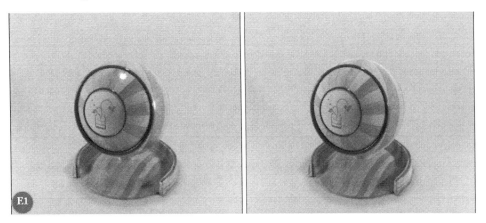

Table E1 summarizes the exercise.

Table E1	
Topics	• Getting Ready • Creating the Material
Skill level	Intermediate
Resources folder	**unit-dt3**
Start file	**physical-start.max**
Final file	**warnish-finish.max**
Time to complete	20 Minutes

Getting Ready
Open **physical-start.max**.

Creating the Material
Follow these steps:

1. Open the **Slate Material Editor**. Double-click on **physical-mat** in the active view. In the **Parameter Editor > Presets** rollout, select **Standard** from the **Material mode** drop-down list, if not already selected.

2. In the **Basic Parameters** rollout > **Base Color and Reflections** group, click the **Base Color**'s button. In the **Material/Map Browser > Maps > General** rollout, double-click **Bitmap**. In the **Select Bitmap Image File** dialog box, choose **wooden-plank-1.jpeg**. Also, set **Override** to **2.2** in the **Gamma** group. Click **Open** and render the scene [see Fig. E2].

What next?

Notice the render in Fig. E2, the wood is highly reflective, we need to add some roughness to the reflection and transparency components.

3. Set **Roughness** to **0.9** and then render the scene[see Fig. E3].

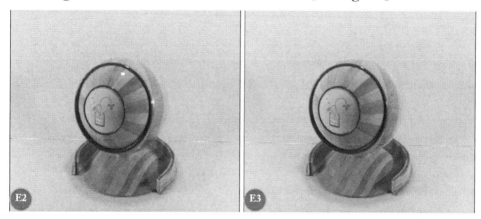

What just happened?

*Notice that by specifying a value of **0.9** for the **Roughness** parameter, the material has lost its gloss and looks very flat. **Glossiness** is the effectively the inverse of the roughness. If you enable the **Inv** option corresponding to the **Roughness** parameter, it will yield glossy material. The **Roughness** parameter lets you control the roughness of the material. A higher **Roughness** value yields a blurrier result. You can lower the **Roughness** value to make the mirror like material.*

4. Enable the **Inv** option and then set **IOR** to **1.7**.

Note: The IOR parameter

*The **IOR** parameter controls the index of refraction level of the material. It defines how much rays bend when they enter a medium. It also affects the angular dependency of the reflectivity.*

5. In the **Anisotropy** rollout, select **Map channel** and then set channel to **1**. Set **Anisotropy** and **Rotation** to **0.4**, and **0.3**, respectively. Render the scene.

✏️ *Note: The Anisotropy parameter*
*The **Anisotropy** parameter controls the U–direction roughness in relation to the V–direction roughness. The **Rotation** parameter controls the anisotropy angle. This parameter ranges from **0** to **1** which represents one full revolution. The **Auto** option automatically orients the anisotropy whereas the **Map channel** option orients the anisotropy based on a given texture space.*

→ *What next?*
*Now, we will create a bump map using the **Noise** map.*

6. Drag the **Noise** map to the active view from the **Material/Map Browser**. In the **Parameter Editor** > **Noise** map > **Coordinates** rollout, set **Source** to **Explicit Map Channel** and ensure **Map Channel** is set to 1. Set **Tiling U, V,** and **W** to **0.5, 200,** and **100**, respectively.

7. In the **Noise Parameters** rollout, set **Size** to **0.2** [see Fig. E4]. Set **Color #1** to RGB[180, 180, 180]. Drag the **Mix** map to the active view. Connect **Noise** map to the **Color 1** port of the **Mix** map and **Bitmap** to the **Color 2** port. Connect the **Mix** map to the **Bump Map** port of **physical-mat** [see Fig. E5].

8. Drag and drop the **Color Correction** map from the **Material/Map Browser** to the wire connecting the **Bitmap** and **Mix** nodes. Now, in the **Parameter Editor** > **Color Correction** > **Color** group, change **Saturation** to -100.

9. In the **Parameter Editor** > **Mix** map > **Mix Parameters** rollout, set **Mix Amount** to **30**. Render the scene [see Fig. E1].

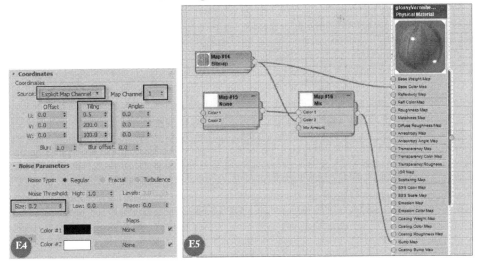

Now, if you want to create a less glossy satin varnished wood material, you need to lower down the reflection **Roughness** and **IOR** values. Check the **warnish-fiinish-2. max** file for the satin varnished material.

Exercise 2: Creating Glass Materials

In this exercise, we will create a glass materials using the **Physical** material [see Fig. E1].

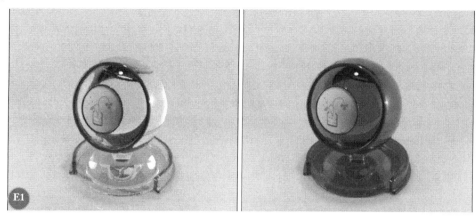

Table E2 summarizes the exercise.

Table E2	
Topics	• Getting Ready • Creating the Materials
Skill level	Intermediate
Resources folder	**unit-dt3**
Start file	**physical-start.max**
Final file	**glass-finish.max**
Time to complete	20 Minutes

Getting Ready
Open **physical-start.max**.

Creating the Materials
Follow these steps:

1. Open the **Slate Material Editor**. Double-click on **physical-mat** in the active view. In the **Parameter Editor > Presets** rollout, select **Advanced** from the **Material mode** drop-down list.

> *Note: Physical material modes*
> *There are two types of modes available for the **Physical** material: **Standard** and **Advanced**. When you choose the **Standard** mode, you get access to the parameters that you can use to create most physically plausible materials. The **Advanced** mode gives you access to advanced reflection, roughness, and weight parameters. You can use these parameters to create advanced materials.*

2. In the **Parameter Editor > Basic Parameters** rollout > **Base Color** group, set **Base Color** weight to **0**. The material turns black. In the **Transparency** group, set the **Transparency Weight** to **1** to make the glass completely transparent. In the **Reflections** group, set **IOR** to **1.7**. Render the scene [see Fig. E2].

> ✎ *Note: IOR parameter*
> *The* **IOR** *value sets the index of refraction level. It controls how much rays bend when entering in a medium.*

3. Select the **Thin-walled** check box and render the scene [see Fig. E3]. Clear the **Thin-walled** check box.

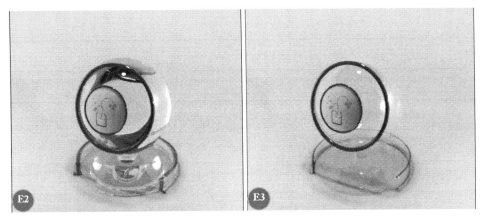

> ✎ *Note: Thin-Walled check box*
> *When this check box is selected, the object is considered to be made out of an infinitely thin transparent shell. This shell is not reflective. Also, the transparency depth is disabled and the sub-surface scattering is replaced by translucency.*

> → *What next?*
> *Now, we will create tinted glass by specifying a color for* **Transparency** *and specifying a depth.*

4. In the **Transparency** group, set color to red and then set **Depth** to **0.05** and render the scene [see Fig. E4].

5. In the **Transparency** group, set **weight** to **0.85** and render the scene [see Fig. E5].

> → *Note: Sub-Surface Scattering*
> *You can create some interesting effects by using sub-surface scattering option. In the* **Sub-Surface Scattering** *group, set color to yellow and render the scene. Notice that there is no change in the color of the glass. As discussed earlier, the sum of various shading components can not exceed* **100%**, *therefore, you need to reduce weight of other parameters to see the effect of sub-surface scattering.*

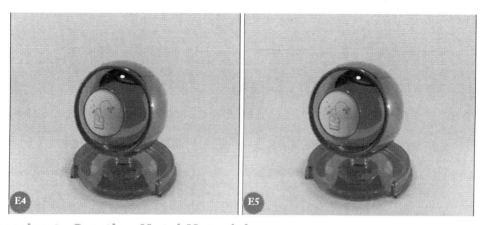

Exercise 3: Creating Metal Materials

In this exercise, we will create metal materials using the **Physical** material [see Fig. E1].

Table E3 summarizes the exercise.

Table E3	
Topics	• Getting Ready • Creating the Materials
Skill level	Intermediate
Resources folder	**unit-dt3**
Start file	**physical-start.max**
Final file	**metal-finish.max**
Time to complete	20 Minutes

Getting Ready

Open the **physical-start.max** file.

Creating the Materials

Follow these steps:

1. Open the **Slate Material Editor**. Double-click on **physical-mat** in the active view. In the **Parameter Editor** > **Presets** rollout, select **Advanced** from the **Material mode** drop-down list.

 What next
First, we will create highly reflective material.

2. In the **Parameter Editor** > **Basic Parameters** rollout > **Base Color** group, set **Base Color** weight to **0**. In the **Reflections** group, set **IOR** to 48 and then render the scene [see Fig. E2].

 What just happened?
The reflection in the material is coming from the gray background. If you want more reflections in the metal, use a reflection map.

 What next?
Now, if you want to create a material like aluminium, blur the reflections by adding some roughness to the metal.

3. In the **Reflections** group, set **Roughness** to **0.3** and then render the scene [see Fig. E3]. You can make the metal darker by darkening the **Reflection** color. Set it to medium gray and render the scene [see Fig. E4].

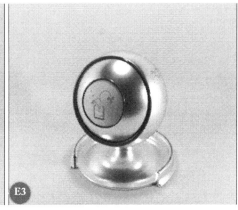

Note: IOR and Metalness parameters
*If you want to add of the weight of the base color to the material, it will have no effect because of the high **IOR** value. If you use low **IOR** value, you loose the metal look. To compensate for this, you can use the **Metalness** parameter. If you set **Metalness** to **1**, you do not see the base layer, just the colored reflections.*

4. In the **Parameter Editor** > **Basic Parameters** rollout > **Base Color** group, set base color to **RGB [0.82, 0.416, and 0.099]** and weight to **0.3**. In the **Reflections** group, set reflection color to **RGB [0.584, 0.584, 0.584]**, weight to **0.7**, **Roughness** to **0.3**, **Metalness** to **0.5**, and **IOR** to **6**. Render the scene [see Fig. E5].

Quiz

Evaluate your skills to see how many questions you can answer correctly.

Multiple Choice
Answer the following questions:

1. Which of the following renderers supports **Autodesk** materials?

   [A] Quicksilver Hardware   [B] ART
   [C] A and B   [D] None of these

2. Which of the following options is available in the **Material mode** drop-down list of the **Physical** material?

   [A] Standard   [B] Advanced
   [C] A and B   [D] None of these

Fill in the Blanks
Fill in the blanks in each of the following statements:

1. The **Physical** material is physically-based material and it is compatible with both the _____ and _____ renderers.

2. According to the energy conservation model of the **Physical** material, the sum of various shading components can not exceed _____ %.

3. The _____ parameter controls relative measurement of the color of the corresponding component.

4. The _____ parameter controls the index of refraction level of the material.

5. The _____ parameter controls the U-direction roughness in relation to the V-direction roughness.

True or False
State whether each of the following is true or false:

1. **Autodesk Bitmap** always uses the real-world mapping coordinates.

2. The **Scanline** renderer shows just the approximation of the **Physical** material and does not support many crucial features.

3. When the **Metalness** parameter of the **Physical** material is set to **1**, the material becomes transparent.

Summary

The unit covered the following topics:

- Autodesk materials
- Physical material

Unit DTB: Bonus Hands-on Exercises [Texturing]

Exercises

Exercise 1: Creating Balloon Material

In this exercise, we will create a balloon shader using the **Shellac** material, see Fig. E1.

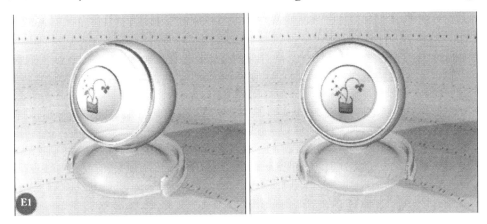

Table E1 summarizes the exercise.

Table E1	
Skill level	Intermediate
Time to complete	20 Minutes
Topics	• Getting Ready • Creating the Material
Resources folder	**unit-dtb**
Start file	**shader-ball.max**
Final file	**balloon-finish.max**

Getting Ready

Open the **shader-ball.max** file.

Creating the Material

Follow these steps:

1. Open the **Slate Material Editor** and then drag the **Shellac** material to the active view. Rename the material as **balloon-mat**. Apply material to **sample-geo1**, **sample-geo-2**, and **sample-geo-3**.

2. Rename the material connected to the **Shellac Mat** slot as **gloss-mat**. Similarly, rename the material connected to the **Base Material** slot as **color-fall-off-mat**.

 What next?
First, we will create the glossy material and then we will model translucency for the material.

3. In the **Parameter Editor** > **gloss-mat** > **Blinn Basic Parameters** rollout, set **Diffuse** to red color. In the **Specular Highlights** group, set **Specular Level** and **Glossiness** to **225** and **70**, respectively. In the **Parameter Editor** > **balloon-mat** > **Shellac Basic Parameters** rollout, set **Shellac Color Blend** to **30**.

4. In the **Parameter Editor** > **color-fall-off-mat** > **Shader Basic Parameters** rollout, select **Translucent Shader** from the drop-down list. Now, in the **Translucent Basic Parameters** rollout, set **Diffuse** and **Specular** to RGB [246, 14, 14] and RGB [235, 255, 141], respectively.

5. In the **Specular Highlights** group, set **Specular Level** and **Glossiness** to **99** and **22**, respectively. Render the scene [see Fig. E2]. Notice that we have created a glossy red material.

 What next?
Now, we will add translucency to the material.

6. In the **Translucency** group, set **Translucent Clr, Filter Color**, and **Opacity** to RGB [250, 143, 143], RGB [221, 198, 148], and **30**, respectively. Render the scene [see Fig. E3].

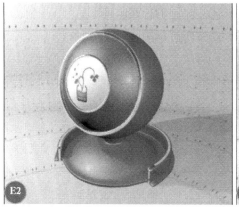
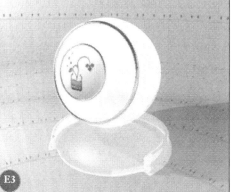

What just happened?
Notice that 3ds Max has added translucency to the material but we need to control the opacity as well the translucency based on the viewing angle.

7. Connect the **Falloff** map to the **Opacity** slot of **color-fall-off-mat**. Create a copy of the **Falloff** map using **Shift** and then connect it to **Translucent Color** port. Render the scene [see Fig. E4].

8. In the **Property Editor** > **Falloff** map [connected to the **Translucent Color** port] > **Falloff Parameters** rollout, set the first and second color swatches to **RGB** [230, 87, 77] and **RGB** [55, 6, 7], respectively. Render the scene [see Fig. E5].

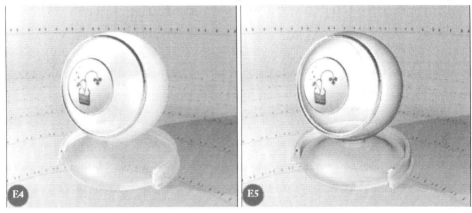

Exercise 2: Creating Concrete Asphalt Material
In this exercise, we will create the concrete asphalt material [see Fig. E1].

Table E2 summarizes the exercise.

Table E2	
Skill level	Beginner
Time to complete	15 Minutes

Table E2	
Topics	• Getting Ready • Creating the Material
Resources folder	**unit-dtb**
Start file	**shader-ball.max**
Final file	**asphalt-finish.max**

Getting Ready
Open the **shader-ball.max** file.

Creating the Material
Follow these steps:

1. Open the **Slate Material Editor** and then drag the **Standard** material to the active view. Rename the material as **asphalt-mat**. Apply material to **sample-geo1**, **sample-geo-2**, and **sample-geo-3**.

2. In the **Parameter Editor > asphalt-mat > Blinn Basic Parameters** rollout, set **Ambient** to RGB [25, 25, 25]. In the **Specular Highlights** group, set **Specular Level** and **Glossiness** to **48** and **23**, respectively.

3. Connect **asphalt.bmp** to the **Diffuse Color** port of **asphalt-mat**. Create copies of the bitmap node using **Shift** and connect them to **Specular Color, Specular Level**, and **Bump** ports.

4. Render the scene [see Fig. E1].

Exercise 3: Creating Eyeball Material
In this exercises, we will create material for an eyeball, see Fig. E1.

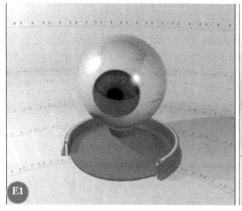

Table E3 summarizes the exercise.

Table E3	
Skill level	Beginner
Time to complete	15 Minutes
Topics	• Getting Ready • Creating the Material
Resources folder	**unit-dtb**
Start file	**eye-start.max**
Final file	**eye-finish.max**

Getting Ready

Open the **eye-start.max** file.

Creating the Material

Follow these steps:

1. Open the **Slate Material Editor** and then drag the **Raytrace** material to the active view. Rename the material as **eyeball-mat**. Apply material to **eye-geo** in the scene.

2. In the **Parameter Editor > eyeball-mat > Raytrace Basic Parameters** rollout, set **Index of Refl** to **1.6**. In the **Specular Highlight** group, set **Specular Level** and **Glossiness** to **225** and **60**, respectively. Connect **eyeball.jpg** to the **Diffuse** port of **eyeball-mat**.

> *Note: Texture Courtesy*
> *http://oliverwolfson.com/eye-texture*

3. Render the scene [see Fig. E2]. Notice that we need to fix the UV mapping. Make sure **eye-geo** is selected in the scene and then from the **Object-Space Modifiers** section of the **Modifier** list, select **UVW Map**. In the **Modify** panel > **Parameters** rollout, make sure **Planer** is selected. Render the scene [see Fig. E3].

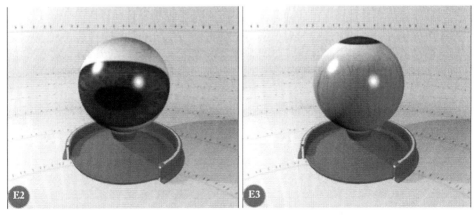

4. In the stack display, select **UVW Map** > **Gizmo** and then rotate it by **90** degrees. Render the scene [see Fig. E4].

5. Connect a **Falloff** map to the **Reflect** port of **eyeball-mat**. In the **Parameter Editor** > **Falloff Parameters** rollout, set **Falloff Type** to **Fresnel**. Render the scene [see Fig. E5].

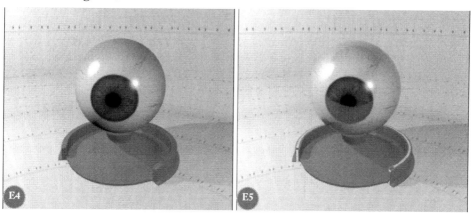

Exercise 4: Creating Water Material

In this exercise, we will create the water material, see Fig. E1.

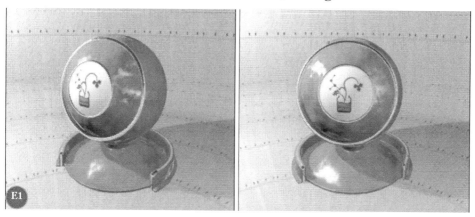

Table E4 summarizes the exercise.

Table E4	
Skill level	Beginner
Time to complete	15 Minutes
Topics	• Getting Ready • Creating the Material
Resources folder	**unit-dtb**
Start file	**shader-ball.max**
Final file	**water-finish.max**

Getting Ready
Open the **water-start.max** file.

Creating the Material
Follow these steps:

1. Open the **Slate Material Editor** and then drag the **Standard** material to the active view. Rename the material as **water-mat**. Apply material to **sample-geo1**, **sample-geo-2**, and **sample-geo-3**.

2. In the **Parameter Editor > water-mat > Shader Basic Parameters** rollout, select **Anisotropic** from the drop-down list. In the **Anisotropic Basic Parameters** rollout, unlock the **Ambient** and **Diffuse** color swatches. Set **Ambient** to **RGB [12, 12, 12]**, **Diffuse** to **RGB [85, 127, 157]**, and **Specular** to **RGB [160, 178, 190]**. Render the scene [see Fig. E2].

3. In the **Specular Highlight** group, set **Specular Level, Glossiness,** and **Anisotropy** to **160, 55,** and **60,** respectively. Connect the **Noise** map to the **Bump** port of **water-mat**. In the **Noise** map > **Noise Parameters** rollout, set **Noise Type** to **Fractal, Levels** to **9,** and **Size** to **18**. Render the scene [see Fig. E3].

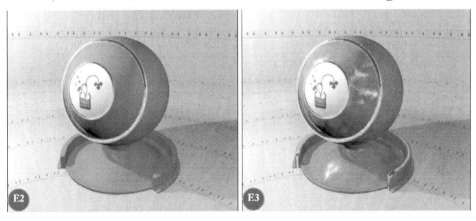

4. Connect the **Mask** map to the **Reflection** slot of **water-mat**. Connect **lakerem.jpg** to the **Map** port of the **Mask** map. In the **Parameter Editor > lakerem.jpg > Coordinates** rollout, select **Environ** and then set **Mapping** to **Spherical Environment**. Render the scene [see Fig. E4].

5. Connect **Falloff** map to the **Mask** port of the **Mask** map. In the **Property Editor > Falloff** map > **Falloff Parameters** rollout, set **Falloff Type** to **Fresnel**. Render the scene [see Fig. E5].

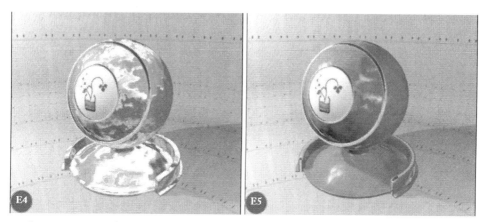

Exercise 5: Creating X-Ray Material

In this exercises, we will create the X-Ray material, see Fig. E1.

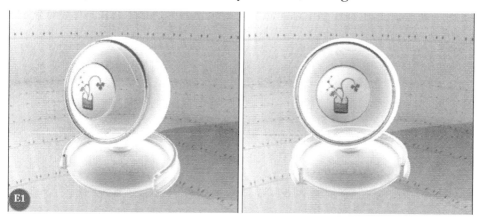

Table E5 summarizes the exercise.

Table E5	
Skill level	Intermediate
Time to complete	15 Minutes
Topics	• Getting Ready • Creating the Material
Resources folder	**unit-dtb**
Start file	**shader-ball.max**
Final file	**xray-finish.max**

Getting Ready

Open the **shader-ball.max** file.

Creating the Material
Follow these steps:

1. Open the **Slate Material Editor** and then drag the **Standard** material to the active view. Rename the material as **xray-mat**. Apply material to **sample-geo1**, **sample-geo-2**, and **sample-geo-3**.

2. In the **Parameter Editor** > **xray-mat** > **Blinn Basic Parameters** rollout, set **Specular Level** and **Glossiness** to **0** and **15**, respectively.

3. Connect the **Falloff** map to the **Diffuse Color** port of the **xray-mat**. In the **Property Editor** > **Falloff** map > **Mix Curve** rollout, shape the curve as shown in Fig. E2. Render the scene [see Fig. E3].

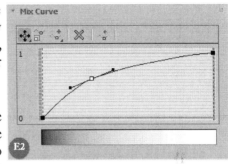

4. Connect the existing **Falloff** map to the **Self-illumination** port. Render the scene [see Fig. E4]. Connect the **Falloff** map to the **Opacity** slot of **xray-mat**. Render the scene [see Fig. E1].

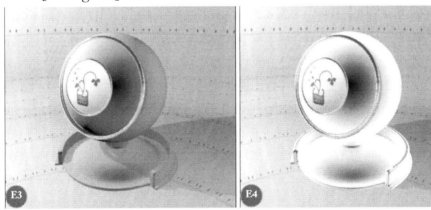

Exercise 6: Texturing a Cardboard Box
In this exercise, we will texture a cardboard box [see Fig. E1] using the **UV Editor**. Table E6 summarizes the exercise.

Table E6	
Skill level	Intermediate
Time to complete	20 Minutes
Topics	• Getting Ready • Texturing the Cardboard Box
Resources folder	**unit-dtb**
Final file	**cardboard-finish.max**

Getting Ready

Reset 3ds Max. Set units to **Generic Units** and then create a box with the **Length, Height,** and **Width** set to **190** each.

Texturing the Cardboard Box

Follow these steps:

1. Ensure the box is selected in a viewport and then go to **Modify** panel. Add the **Unwrap UVW** modifier to the stack.

 Note: Unwrap UVW Modifier

*This modifier allows you to assign texturing coordinates to the objects and sub-object selections. You can edit the coordinates using various tools. You can use this modifier on **Mesh, Patch, Polygon, HSDS,** and **NURBS** meshes. This modifier gives you access to the **Edit UVWs** window which is a texture coordinate editor. You can also use it along with the **UVW Map** modifier. This is required when you want to use a mapping method that is not available [such as **Shrink Wrap**] with the **Unwrap UVW** modifier.*

 Note: UVW Map Modifier

*The **UVW Map** modifier controls how mapped and procedural textures appear on the surface of the geometry. UVW mapping coordinates are used to project bitmaps onto an object. This coordinate system is similar to the XYZ coordinate system. The **U** and **V** axes of a bitmap correspond to the **X** and **Y** axes whereas the **W** axis corresponds to the **Z** axis. Generally, the **W** axis is used with the procedural maps.*

2. Click **Polygon** ▢ on the **Selection** panel and then press **Ctrl+A** to select all polygons. In the **Projection** rollout, click **Box Map** ▣ and then click again to deactivate.

? *What just happened?*
*Here, I have activated the **Polygon** selection mode and then selected all polygons. Then, I have applied box mapping to the selected polygons. Box mapping is best suited for the box shaped objects. When you apply this mapping, 3ds Max maps each polygon to the side of the box gizmo that most closely matches the orientation.*

3. In the **Edit UVs** rollout, click **Open UV Editor** to open the **Edit UVWs** window. Choose **Unfold Mapping** from the **Mapping** menu of the window; the **Unfold Mapping** dialog box appears. Click **OK** to accept the default settings and to unfold UVs [see Fig. E2].

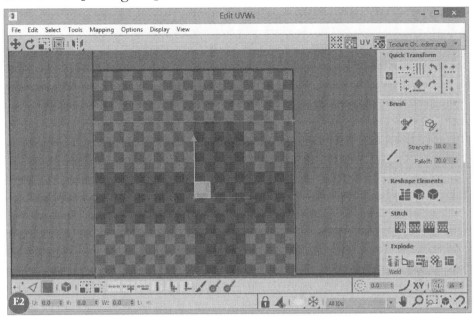

What just happened?

*Here, I have applied the unfold mapping function to the selected polygons. This function removes UV clutter and ensures that polygons do not overlap. This function is available only in the **Polygon** selection mode.*

4. Choose **Pick Texture** from the drop-down list located on the top-right corner of the **Edit UVWs** window to open the **Material/Map Browser**. In the browser, double-click on **Bitmap** in the **Maps > General** rollout. In the **Select Bitmap Image File** dialog box, select **cardboard_texture.png** and click **Open**. The **cardboard_texture.png** appears in the **Edit UVWs** window [see Fig. E3].

What just happened?

*The **Pick Texture** option allows you to place a map or bitmap in the editor's view. You can then use that map or bitmap as a reference for moving UVs.*

5. Click **Vertex** from the bottom-left corner of the **Edit UVWs** window to activate the **Vertex** selection mode. Notice that all the vertices are selected. If they are not selected, press **Ctrl+A** to select them. Ensure **Move Selected Subobject** is active from the **Edit UVWs** window's toolbar and then align all UVs to the background texture [see Fig. E4]. Press and hold **Shift** while dragging to constrain the movement.

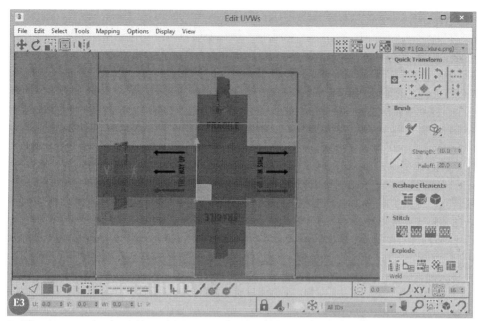

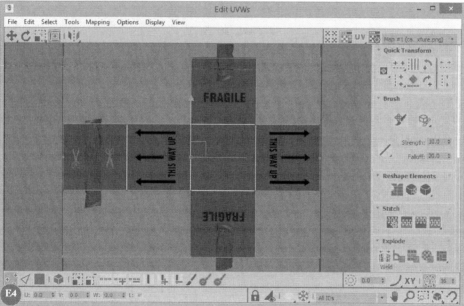

6. Individually select group of vertices and fine tune the alignment with the background texture [see Fig. E5]. You can also select vertices in a viewport. Close the **Edit UVWs** window.

Tip: *Aligning UVs horizontally or vertically*
*If the UVs are not in a straight line, you can use **Align Horizontally to Pivot*** 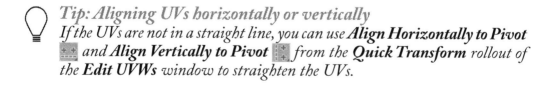 *and **Align Vertically to Pivot*** *from the **Quick Transform** rollout of the **Edit UVWs** window to straighten the UVs.*

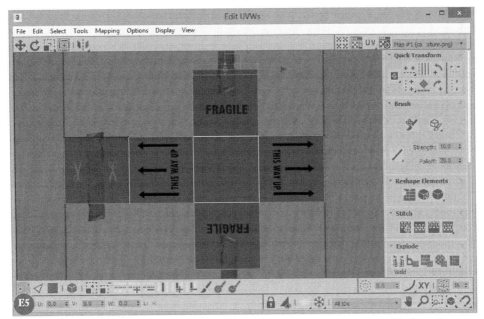

7. Press **M** to open the **Slate Material Editor**. In the **Material/Map Browser** > **Materials** rollout > **Scanline** rollout, double-click **Standard** to add it to the active view and then assign it to the box in the scene. Rename the material as **box-mat**.

8. Connect **cardboard_texture.png** texture to the **Diffuse Color** slot of the material. **RMB** click on **box-mat** node and choose **Show Shaded Material in Viewport** from the menu to display the texture in the viewport.

Exercise 7: Texturing a Dice

In this exercise, we will texture a dice [see Fig. E1] using the **UV Editor**. We will export the UVs template to the Photoshop and then use Photoshop to create the texture. We will then import the texture back into 3ds Max and then apply it to the dice geometry. Table E7 summarizes the exercise.

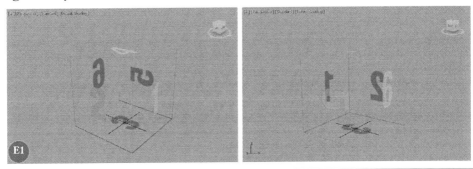

Table E7	
Skill level	Intermediate
Time to complete	20 Minutes

Table E7	
Topics	• Getting Ready • Texturing the Dice
Resources folder	**unit-dtb**
Final file	**dice-finish.max**

Getting Ready

Reset 3ds Max. Set units to **Generic Units** and then create a box with the **Length, Height**, and **Width** set to **190** each.

Texturing the Dice

Follow these steps:

1. Ensure the box is selected in a viewport and then go to the **Modify** panel. Add the **Unwrap UVW** modifier to the stack. Click **Polygon** ▣ on the **Selection** panel and then press **Ctrl+A** to select all polygons. In the **Projection** rollout, click **Box Map** 📦 and then click again to deactivate.

2. In the **Edit UVs** rollout, click **Open UV Editor** to open the **Edit UVWs** window. Choose **Unfold Mapping** from the **Mapping** menu of the window; the **Unfold Mapping** dialog box appears. Click **OK** to accept the default settings and unfold UVs.

3. Choose **Render UVW Template** from the **Tools** menu to open the **Render UVs** dialog box. In this dialog box, click **Render UV Template**; the **Render Map** window appears. Click **Save Image** on the window's toolbar to open the **Save Image** dialog box. Type **dice-template** in the **File name** field and choose **PNG Image File** from the **Save as type** drop-down list.

4. Click **Save** to save the template. Click **OK** from the **PNG Configuration** dialog. Now, close all windows and dialog boxes. Open **dice_template.png** in **Photoshop**. **Layer 0** appears in the **Layers** panel. Create a new layer below **Layer 0** and fill it with **black** [see Fig. E2].

5. Using the **Photoshop** tools and features create dice texture according to the dice template. I am putting simple numbers to identify the faces of the dice [see Fig. E3]. You should go ahead and create a nice looking dice texture for your dice model.

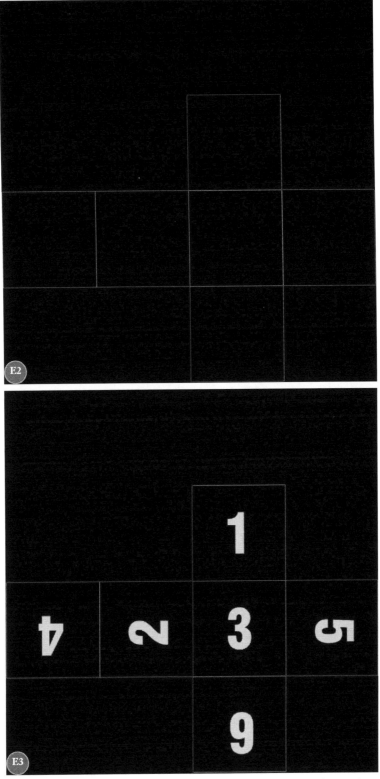

6. Turn off the black layer and the template layer. Save the **Photoshop** document as **dice-texture.png**.

7. In 3ds Max, apply a **Standard** material to the box. Set **Diffuse Color** to **red**. Connect **dice-texture.png** to the **Diffuse Color** and **Opacity** ports of the material's node. Render the scene.

8. In the **Parameter Editor > Bitmap > Bitmap Parameters** rollout, select the **None (Opaque)** check box from the **Alpha Source** group. Render the scene.

- Basic lighting concepts
- Creating and placing lights
- 3ds Max lights
- Light linking
- Shadows

Unit DL1: Standard Lighting

To achieve professional-quality, realistic renders in 3ds Max, you need to master the art of lighting. Lights play an important role in the visual process. They shape the world we see. The trick to simulate realistic looking light effects is to observe the world around us. The lights you create in a scene, illuminate other objects in the scene. The material applied to the objects simulates color and texture. The reasons to add the light objects to the scene are as follows:

- They improve the illumination of the scene.
- They enhance the realism of the scene through realistic lighting effects.
- They give depth to the scene by casting shadows.
- They enhance the scene by projecting maps onto the scene.
- They also help in modeling light sources such as headlights of a car.
- They create lights using files from manufactures [such as IES files].

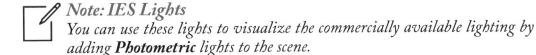

Note: IES Lights
You can use these lights to visualize the commercially available lighting by adding **Photometric** *lights to the scene.*

Standard Lights

The standard lights in 3ds Max are computer based lights that simulate lights such as lamps and bulbs. Unlike the **Photometric** lights, these lights do not have the physically-based intensity values. To create a light, in the **Create** panel, click **Lights**. Choose **Standard** from the drop-down list available below **Lights** and then in the **Object Type** rollout, click the type of light you want to create. Now, click on a viewport to create the light. The creation method in the viewport depends on the type of light you have chosen. For example, if a light has target, you need to click-drag to set the target.

Whenever you create a light in the scene, the default lighting is turned off. It will be restored when you delete all lights from the scene. Like all objects in 3ds Max, lights have name, and color. You can set these options from the **Name and Color** rollout.

Now, let's explore the standard lights.

Target Spotlight

The target spotlight casts a focused beam of light. You can use this light to simulate flashlight, a follow spot on a stage, or the headlights of the car. To create a target spotlight, click **Target Spot** from the **Object Type** rollout. Now, drag in a viewport to place the light. The initial point of the drag defines the location of the spotlight whereas the point at which you release the mouse defines the location of the target. In Fig. 1, I have marked light with **1** and its target with **2**.

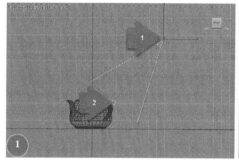 

> ✎ *Note: Light and its target*
> *When you create a light that has a target, two objects will appear in the **Scene***
> ***Explorer**: light object and its target. The target name has an extension **.target**.*
> *For example, if you create a spot light in the scene, the name of the light and*
> *its target will be as follows: **Spot001** and **Spot001.Target**. When you rename*
> *a light, its target object will be automatically renamed accordingly. However,*
> *remember that renaming a target object does not rename its parent light.*

> ✎ *Note: Free Spotlight*
> ***Free Spotlight** is similar to **Target Spotlight** except the difference that it has*
> *no target. You can move and rotate **Free Spotlight** to aim in any direction.*

To adjust the target, select it in a viewport or in the **Scene Explorer** and then move the target using the **Move** tool. The spotlight is always aimed at its target. The distance of the target from the light does not affect the attenuation or brightness of the light.

You can also change a viewport to a light view so that the viewport shows the light's point of view. This feature is immensely helpful in placing the lights accurately. To change a viewport to a light view, click or RMB click on POV label in the viewport. Now, choose **Lights** > **Name** of the light from the menu. Fig. 2 shows the point of view of the light that was shown in Fig. 1. Refer to **target-spot.max**. You can change the properties of the spot light from the rollouts available in the **Modify** panel. Let's explore the parameters available in these rollouts.

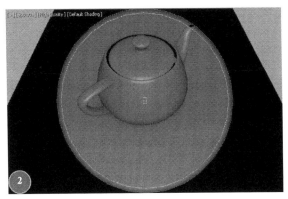

General Parameters Rollout

This rollout is displayed for the **Standard** lights. The parameters in this rollout allow you to turn light on or off, exclude or include objects in the scene, and change the type of light. You can also toggle the shadow casting from this rollout.

To turn a light on or off, use the **On** check box in this rollout. The drop-down list on the right of the **On** check box lets you switch between the light types. When the **Targeted** check box is selected, the light is targeted. When selected, the distance between the light and its target is displayed on the right of this check box.

To toggle shadow casting, use the **On** check box in the **Shadows** group. Select the **Use Global Settings** check box to use the global settings for shadows that are cast by this light. The shadow parameters defined by the light are shared with all the lights of same class. When this check box is clear, the shadow parameters are specific to that light. The drop-down list in the **Shadows** group lets you choose the algorithm to be used by the light to cast shadows. The following table summarizes various algorithms.

Table 1: The shadow generating algorithms	
Algorithm	**Description**
Shadow Map	Shadow map is a bitmap that is generated during a pre-rendering pass of the scene. This map doesn't show the color cast by transparent or translucent objects. A shadow map can produce soft-edged shadows that cannot be generated by a ray-traced shadow [see Fig. 3]. Also, depth map shadows take less time to render than the ray-traced shadows. You can change the shadow map options from the **Shadows Parameters** and **Shadow Map Param** rollouts.

Table 1: The shadow generating algorithms	
Algorithm	**Description**
Ray-Traced Shadows Adv. Ray-Traced Shadows	The **Ray-traced shadows** [see Fig. 4] are more accurate than the shadow-mapped shadows and are generated by tracing the path of the rays sampled from a light source. They create better results for the transparent or translucent objects. Only ray-traced shadows can generate shadows for wireframed objects. The **Adv. Ray-Traced Shadows** are same as ray-traced shadows, however they provide anti-aliasing parameters to fine tune the shadows.
Area Shadows	This algorithm simulates shadows generated by a light with area of volume. You can change volume type from the drop-down list available in the **Basic Options** group of the **Area Shadows** rollout. Fig. 5 shows the shadows generated by using the **Box Light** volume.

 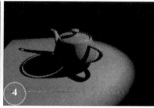 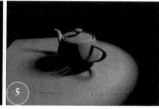

 Tip: Transparent and translucent objects
If you want convincing looking shadow results for the transparent and translucent objects, use raytraced or advance raytraced shadows.

 Tip: Preventing an object from casting shadows
*You can prevent an object from casting shadows in the scene, to do this, select the object and then **RMB** click. Choose **Object Properties** from the **Quad** menu and then clear the **Cast Shadows** check box from the **Rendering Control** group of the **Object Properties** dialog box.*

You can also exclude the selected object from the effects of the lights. This feature is very useful when you want a light to lit specific objects in the scene. Click **Exclude** to open the **Exclude/Include** dialog box [see Fig. 6].

Now, select the objects that you want to affect from the **Scene Objects** group of the dialog box. Select **Include** or **Exclude** from the right of the dialog box. Now, click >> to add the selected object to the right pane of the dialog box. You can click << to move objects from right pane to the left pane. You have three options to control the effect: **Illumination**, **Shadow Casting**, and **Both**. You can use these options to exclude/include illumination, shadows, or both. Now, click **OK** to close the dialog box and include/exclude objects with the light.

Intensity/Color/Attenuation Rollout

The parameters in this rollout let you set the color and intensity of the light. Also, you can define the attenuation of the light. The **Multiplier** parameter amplifies the power of the light. You can use negative values to reduce the illumination. High **Multiplier** values wash out the colors whereas the negative values darkens the objects. The color swatch next to the **Multiplier** parameter lets you select a color to be cast by the light.

Tip: Flashing light on and off
*Animate the **Multiplier** value to **0** [0 and 1] in repeated keyframes and then assign step tangent to **Multiplier**'s graph.*

The parameters in the **Decay** group let you control the light's intensity over distance. The following table summarizes the options available in the **Type** drop-down list.

Table 2: Decay types	
Type	**Description**
None	No decay is applied [see the left image in Fig. 7]. The light retains its full strength.
Inverse	It applies inverse decay [see the middle image in Fig. 7]. The formula used to calculate decay is **luminance=R0/R. R0** is the radial source of the light. **R** is the radial distance of the illuminated surface from **R0**.
Inverse Square	It applies inverse-square decay [see the right image in Fig. 7]. The formula used is **(R0/R)2**. This decay type is used by **Photometric** lights and it is the real-world decay of the light. Also, refer to **light-decay.max**.

If you don't use the attenuation settings [discussed next], the **Start** parameter sets the distance at which the light begins to decay. You can use the **Show** check box to display the decay range in the viewports. For spotlights, the decay range appears as lens-shaped section of the cone [see the left image in Fig. 8]. For directional light, it appears as circular section of the cone [see the middle image in Fig. 8]. For omni lights and spot or directional lights with **Overshoot** turned on, the range appears as a sphere [see the right image in Fig. 8].

Attenuation is the effect of the light diminishing over distance. **Far Attenuation** controls the distance at which the light drops off to zero. The **Near Attenuation** value controls the distance at which the light fades in. You can turn on the attenuation from the **Near Attenuation** and **Far Attenuation** groups of the **Intensity/Color/Attenuation** rollout by using the **Use** parameter. The **Start** and **End** parameters in these groups define the attenuation distances.

When you set the **Far Attenuation** value, the light intensity remains at the value specified by **Multiplier** up to the distance specified by **Start** and then drops off to zero at the distance specified by **End**. When you set the **Near Attenuation** value, the light intensity remains zero up to the distance specified by **Start** and then from the **Start** to the distance specified by the **End**, the light intensity increases. Beyond **End**, the light intensity remains at the value specified by **Multiplier**.

Spotlight Parameters Rollout

The parameters in this rollout controls the hotspot and falloff properties of the spotlight. The **Show Cone** check box displays the cone in the viewport. The cone is always visible when a light is selected. This check box allows you to show the cone even if the light is not selected. When the **Overshoot** check box is selected, the light casts light in all directions [not just within the cone] but the shadows and projections appear within the cone. The **Hotspot/Beam** and **Falloff/Field** parameters control the angle of the light's cone and light's falloff, respectively.

The **Circle** and **Rectangle** parameters define the shape of the falloff and hotspot areas. The **Aspect** parameter controls the aspect ratio of the rectangular light beam. The **Bitmap Fit** button lets you specify the aspect ratio as per the supplied bitmap.

Advanced Effects Rollout

The parameters in this rollout define how light affects the surfaces. Also, you can create projector lights. The **Contrast** parameter adjusts the ambient and diffuse areas of the surface. The default value is zero for this parameter that creates normal contrast. The **Soften Diff Edge** parameter softens the edge between the diffuse and ambient components. The **Diffuse** check box when selected, affects the **Diffuse** properties of an object's surface. Similarly, the **Specular** and **Ambient Only** checkboxes can be used to affect the specular and ambient components, respectively.

The parameters in the **Projector Map** group let you make a light a projector. To create a projector light, open the material editor and then create a map. Drag the map from material editor to the **None** button in the **Projector Map** group. Select **Instance** from the dialog box that appears and click **OK**. The name of the map appears as button's label. Notice in Fig. 9, I have used a **Cellular** map to project it on the teapot using a spotlight.

Atmospheres and Effects Rollout

You can use this rollout to assign, delete, and edit parameters for various atmospheric and rendering effects associated with the light. For example, to create the volume fog effect, click **Add** to open the **Add Atmosphere or Effect** dialog box. Select **Volume Light** from the list and then click **OK** to close the dialog box. In the **Atmospheres and Effects** rollout, select **Volume Light** and then click **Setup** to open the **Environments and Effects** dialog box. Now, you can adjust the parameters from the **Atmosphere** rollout. Render the scene to see the effect. Notice in Fig. 10, I have projected the **Cellular** map and then added volume effect to it. Refer to **advanced-effects.max**.

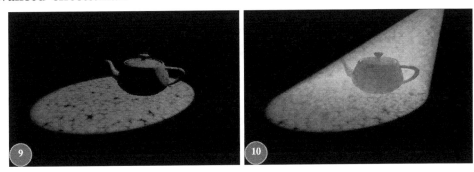

Shadow Parameters Rollout

The parameters in this rollout are displayed for all light types expect **Skylight**. You can use these parameters to define the shadow color and other general shadow properties. Use the **Color** swatch to change the color of the shadows. You can also animate the shadow color. **Dens** controls the density [darkness] of the shadows. You can also assign negative values to **Dens** that allows you to simulate the reflected light. Select the **Map** check box to assign a map to the shadows using the button available on its right. The process to add the map is the same as discussed with the projector light. Fig. 11 shows the **Dent** map applied to the shadows. When the **Light Affects Shadow Color** check box is selected, the color of the light blends with the color of the shadow. Refer to **shadow-map. max**.

Select the **On** check box in the **Atmosphere Shadows** group to allow atmospheric effects to cast shadows as light passes through them. The **Opacity** parameter defines the opacity of the atmospheric shadows whereas the **Color Amount** parameter defines the amount of atmosphere color bleed into the shadows.

Shadow Map Params Rollout

This rollout is displayed when you choose the **Shadow Map** method for generating shadows. The **Bias** parameter moves the shadow toward or away from the shadow-casting objects. Fig. 12 shows the render with **Bias** set to 1 and 5, respectively. Refer to **shadow-bias.max**.

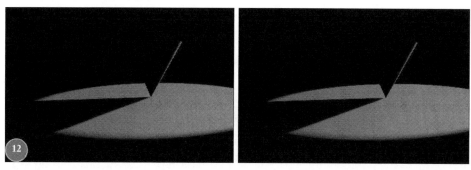

The **Size** parameter defines the size of the shadow map in square pixel computed for the light. The higher the value of **Size**, the more detailed the map will be. The **Sample Range** parameter controls how much area in the shadow is averaged. This settings affects the edges of the shadow. On increasing this value, 3ds Max blends the shadow edges and removes the granularity from the shadow.

The **Absolute Map Bias** check box works with the **Bias** parameter. If you specify a low value for **Bias**, the shadows can leak and if you specify a too high value, the shadow might detach from the object. Setting an extreme value in either case might result in no shadows at all. This behavior depends on the **Absolute Map Bias** check box. When this check box is clear, **Bias** is calculated based on the scene extents and then it is normalized to one. This outputs similar results regardless of the size of the scene. When check box is selected, the **Bias** value is treated in 3ds Max scene units and the result is dependent on the size of the scene.

When the **2 Sided Shadow** check box is selected, back faces are not ignored when calculating shadows. Fig. 13 shows the render of the teapot when the **2 Sided Shadows** option turned on and off, respectively.

The type of renderer you choose will also affect your choice of shadow algorithm used. The **Quicksilver Hardware** renderer always casts shadow-mapped shadows. The following table summarizes the pro and cons of each shadow type:

Table 3: Shadow types comparison		
Type	**Pros**	**Cons**
Advanced Ray-Traced	Supports opacity and transparency. It uses less memory than the raytraced shadows. This type is recommended for complex scenes with lots of light.	It is slower than the shadow map and computed at every frame. It does not support soft shadows.
Area	Supports opacity and transparency and uses very less RAM. It supports different format for area shadows.	It is slower than the shadow map and computed at every frame.
Shadow Map	Fastest shadow type. It produces soft shadows. It is computed once if there is no animated object present in the scene.	Uses a lot of RAM and does not support objects with transparency and opacity maps.
Ray-Traced	Supports transparency and opacity mapping. It is computed once if there is no animated object present in the scene.	It does not support soft shadows. It is slower than the shadows maps.

Ray Traced Shadow Params Rollout

This rollout is displayed when you choose the **Ray Traced Shadows** method for generating shadows. The **Ray Bias** parameter moves the shadow toward or away from the shadow casting object. The **Max Quadtree Depth** parameter sets the depth of Quadtree used by the raytracer. The higher the value you specify for this control, the more enhanced the results will be. However, you will be taxed on the render time.

> *Note: Quadtree*
> *Quadtree is the data structure used by the raytracer. It represents scene from the point of the view of the light. The root node of the Quadtree contains all*

*visible objects in the scene. If there are too many objects available in the scene, four more nodes [leaf nodes] are generated to hold these objects. This process continues adoptively until each node has a small number of objects and Quadtree depth limit is achieved. The maximum size of a **Quadtree** is the square of two to the power of the maximum Quadtree depth. For example, at the depth of 7, the total number of leaf nodes generated will be 27 * 27=128 * 128=16384.*

Caution: Omni light and Quadtree
*An omni light can generate up to ten **Quadtrees**, therefore, if you are using raytraced shadows, it will use more memory and render time.*

Adv. Ray Traced Params Rollout

The parameters in this rollout allow you to control the advanced raytraced shadows. These shadows are similar to the raytraced shadows, however, they give you more control. The drop-down list in the **Basic Options** group allows you to select type of raytracing. The **Simple** type casts a single ray of light towards the surface. No antialiasing is performed when you select this type.

Shadow Integrity defines the number of rays cast from an illuminated surface. This parameter is not available if raytracing mode is **Simple**. **Shadow Quality** defines the secondary rays cast from the illuminated surface. This parameter is not available when type is set to **Simple** or **1-Pass Antialias**. **Shadow Spread** defines the radius in pixels to blur the antialias edge. This parameter is not available when mode is set to **Simple**. **Shadow Bias** controls the minimum distance from the point being shaded that an object must be to cast a shadow. If you increase the blur value, you should also increase the bias value to compensate. The **Jitter Amount** parameter breaks the regular pattern of the rays and add randomness to the ray positions.

Area Shadows Rollout

This rollout is displayed when you choose the **Area Shadows** method for generating shadows. You need to define the dimensions of the virtual light to fake an area shadow. You can choose the type of fake light from the drop-down list available in the **Basic Options** group of the rollout. The dimensions can be set from the **Area Light Dimensions** group of the rollout.

Tip: Rendering area lights
*If you are using area lights, try to match the dimension of the light with the parameters in the **Area Light Dimensions** group.*

Optimizations Rollout

This rollout contains additional parameters for fine tuning advanced raytraced and area shadows. When the **On** check box in the **Transparent Shadows** area is selected, the transparent surfaces will cast a colored shadow, otherwise, all shadows are black. **Antialiasing Threshold** defines the maximum color difference allowed between transparent object samples, before the antialiasing is triggered. On increasing the value of the color, the shadow becomes less sensitive to aliasing artifacts and rendering speed will also improve.

When the **Supersampled Material** check box is selected, while shading a supersampled material only pass 1 is used during 2-pass antialiasing. When the **Reflect/Refract** check box is selected, only pass 1 is used during 2-pass antialiasing. If these two checkboxes are disabled, render time can increase without resulting in a better quality image.

The **Skip Coplanar Faces** check box in the **Coplanar Face Culling** group prevents faces from shadowing each other in curved surfaces. The angle between the adjacent faces is controlled by the **Threshold** parameter.

Target Directional Light

This light is used to simulate a distant light source [see Fig. 14] that casts parallel light rays in a single direction [like the Sun]. These lights are generally used to simulate sunlight. Like the **Target Spotlight**, it has a target object to aim the light. When you create a **Target Directional** light, the **Directional Parameters** rollout appears in the **Modify** panel. You can use the parameters to define the shape of the light. These parameters are similar to those described in the **Target Spotlight** group.

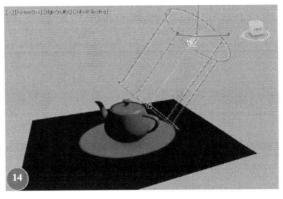

 Note: Free Directional Light
*The **Free Directional** light is similar to the **Target Directional** light except the difference that it has no target. You can move and rotate the **Free Directional** light to aim in any direction.*

Omni Light

An **Omni** light casts rays in all directions from a single source like a light bulb. These lights are specifically used for creating fill lighting or simulating point source lights.

Skylight

When you use this light, it models a sky as a dome above the scene. You can use this light to model daylight. You can also use a map to model the sky. When you add a **Sky** light to the scene, the **Skylight Parameters** rollout appears in the **Modify** panel.

The **On** check box allows you to turn light on or off. The **Multiplier** parameter controls the power of the light. The parameters in the **Sky Color** group let you set the color of the sky. Select the **Use Scene Environment** radio button to color the light using the environment color set in the **Environment** dialog box. The **Sky Color** parameter lets you set a color tint for the sky. You can also assign a map using the **Map** check box. Use HDR files such as **OpenEXR** for best results.

Select the **Cast Shadows** check box in the **Render** group to cause the **Skylight** to cast shadows. Fig. 15 show a teapot rendered with a skylight when the **Cast Shadows** check box is selected. The **Rays Per Sample** parameter allows you to set the number of rays used to calculate the skylight falling on a point in question. The **Ray Bias** parameter defines the closest distance at which objects can cast shadows on a given point in the scene.

Note: Radiosity and Light Tracer
*The **Cast Shadows** check box has no effect when you are using **Radiosity** or **Light Tracer**. Also, the **Sky** light does not cast shadows in the **ActiveShader** rendering.*

Note: Render group
*The parameters in this group are not available if you are not using the **Scanline** renderer or **Light Tracer** is active.*

Tip: Skylight and Light Tracer
*There are many methods in 3ds Max to model the skylight. For best results, use **Skylight** with **Light Tracer**.*

Note: Light Tracer
***Light Tracer** is a lighting plugin that is used to generate soft-edged shadows in a brightly lit scene such as outdoor scenes. It is typically used with the **Sky** light. It does not attempt to create a physically accurate lighting and it is easy to setup.*

Note: Radiosity
*It is a rendering technique used to calculate the indirect light in a scene. It calculates the inter-reflections of the diffuse light and then illuminates the scene. You can find the **Light Tracer** and **Radiosity** options in the **Advanced Lighting** panel of the **Render Setup** window.*

Hands-On Exercises

Exercise 1: Illuminating an Outdoor Scene

In this exercise, we are going to illuminate an outdoor scene using the **Standard** lights. We will also use **Light Tracer** to enhance the scene [see Fig. E1].

Table E1 summarizes the exercise.

Table E1	
Skill level	Beginner
Time to complete	45 Minutes
Topics	• Getting Ready • Adding Lights to the scene • Enabling the **Light Tracer** plugin
Resources folder	**unit-dl1**
Start file	**outdoor-start.max**
Final File	**outdoor-finish.max**

Getting Ready
Open the **outdoor-start.max** file in 3ds Max.

Adding Lights to the Scene
You will first add a directional light to simulate the light coming from the Sun and then the **Skylight** light to model the light coming from the sky. Follow these steps:

1. In the **Create** panel, click **Lights** and, then select **Standard** from the drop-down list available below **Lights**. In the **Object Type** rollout, click **Target Direct** and then in the **Left** viewport click on the upper-left area of the viewport to place the light and then drag toward the ladder to aim the light. Now, release the mouse button to set the aim [see Fig. E2].

2. In the **Modify** panel > **General Parameters** rollout, select the **On** check box from the **Shadows** group and then select **Adv. Ray Traced** option from the drop-down list in this group. In the **Directional Parameters** rollout, set **Hotspot/Beam** to

17.58 so that the directional light covers the whole scene [see Fig. E3]. Ensure the **Perspective** view is active and then press **C** to activate the **Camera** view. Render the scene [see Fig. E4].

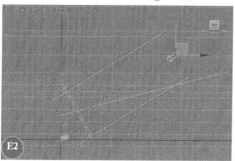

What next?

*Now, we will add a **Skylight** light to the scene. This light will provide the sky light and also it will create nice contact shadows. But, before we add **Skylight**, let's turn off the directional light so that we can see what effect the **Skylight** produces.*

3. In the **General Parameters** rollout, clear the **On** check box in the **Light Type** group. In the **Create** panel > **Object Type** rollout, click **Skylight** and then click anywhere in the scene to place the **Skylight** in the scene.

 Note: Skylight

*The position of the **Skylight** does not affect the way it illuminates the scene therefore you can place light anywhere in the scene.*

4. Render the scene. You will notice that 3ds Max rendered a washed out image [see Fig. E5]. Let's adjust some parameters to get the effect correct.

5. In the **Modify** panel > **Skylight Parameters** rollout, set **Multiplier** to **0.3**, **Sky Color** to light blue color: **RGB [189, 192, 201]**. In the **Render** group, select the **Cast Shadows** check box and then set **Rays per Sample** to **10**. Render the scene [see Fig. E6]. Notice that now we have got better result.

6. Select the directional light from the **Scene Explorer** and then turn it back on. In the **Intensity/Color/Attenuation** rollout, set color to a warm color: **RGB [255, 234, 197]**. Render the scene [see Fig. E7]; notice the render is looking much better now after both the lights in the scene illuminate the objects in it.

7. In the **Shadow Parameters** rollout, select the **Light Affects Shadow Color** check box. Render the scene.

Enabling Light Tracer

Follow these steps:

1. Open the **Render Setup** window and then go to **Advanced Lighting** panel. Select **Light Tracer** from the drop-down list available in the **Select Advanced Lighting** rollout. Notice that the **Parameters** rollout appears in the panel. You can use the parameters available in this rollout to control the effect of the **Light Tracer** plugin.

2. In the **General Settings** group, set **Rays /Sample** to **500**, **Filter Size** to **0.7**, and **Bounces** to **1**. Now, render the scene to see the final render [see Fig. E8].

→ *What next?*
*Next, save the render as a **16 bit TIF** file and farther refine the render in Photoshop. As you have seen, **Light Tracer** allows you to create soft-shadows and also helps in producing a smooth render. Table E1.1 summarizes **Light Tracer** parameters.*

Table E1.1: The **Light Tracer** parameters	
Parameter	**Description**
Global Multiplier	It defines the overall lighting level.
Object Mult.	It defines the level of the light reflected by the objects in the scene. The effect of this parameter is more pronounced when **Bounces** is set to a value of **2** or higher.
Sky Lights	It scales the intensity of the skylights.
Color Bleed	Defines the color bleed that happens when light is inter-reflected among the scene objects.

Table E1.1: The **Light Tracer** parameters	
Parameter	**Description**
Rays/Sample	Defines the number of rays per sample used by **Light Tracer**. Increasing this value produces smooth results at a cost of render time.
Color Filter	It filter all the light falling on the object. Change color to apply a tint to the scene.
Filter Size	The filter size used to reduce the noise.
Extra Ambient	When you set a color for this parameter [other than black], **Light Tracer** adds that extra color to the ambient.
Ray Bias	It controls the position of the bounced light effects.
Bounces	Defines the number of time a ray bounces. On increasing its value, the color bleed also increases in the scene. Higher the value, more light will flow in the scene, and better result **Light Tracer** will produce at a cost of render time.
Cone Angle	It controls the angle used for regathering.
Volumes	When this check box is selected, **Light Tracer** multiplies the amount of light it gathers from the volumetric lighting effects.

The parameters in the **Adaptive Undersampling** group let you speed up your renderings. These parameters allow you to specify the settings to reduce the number of light samples taken. **Light Tracer** initially takes samples from a grid superimposed on the pixels of the scene. When it finds enough contrast between the samples, it subdivides that region and takes farther samples, down to a minimum area specified by the **Subdivide Down To** parameter.

If you are rendering a complex scene, **Light Tracer** can slow down the rendering. For test renderings or a quick preview, given below are some tips:

- To generate a quick render, lower the values for the **Rays/Sample** and **Filter Size** parameters.
- Use **Adaptive Undersampling** to create a quick preview. Set the **Initial Sample Spacing** and the **Subdivide Down To** parameters to the same value and then lower the **Rays/Sample** value and set **Bounces** to 0.
- If there are some objects in the scene that have negligible impact on the scene, disable **Light Tracing** for these objects from the **Object Properties** dialog box.
- To increase the amount of color bleeding, adjust the values of the **Bounces** and **Color Bleed** parameters.
- If there are glass objects in the scene, increase the value for the **Bounces** parameter.
- If **Skylight** is the main light in the scene and you need specular highlights, create a directional light parallel to the **Skylight**. Enable shadows for the light and clear the **Diffuse** check box in the **Advanced Effects** rollout

of the light. In the render shown in Fig. E9, I have cleared the **Diffuse** check box for the directional light to create an overcast sky like effect [see **outdoor-overcast.max**].

💡 *Tip: Using map with Skylight*
*If you are using a map for the skylight, ensure that you completely blur the image in a program like Photoshop. You can blur the map beyond recognition and **Light Tracer** will still fetch the info required for gathering light. Blurring the image helps in reducing the render time. In the render shown in Fig. E10, I have completely blurred the image and then applied it to **Skylight**. I have also set the contribution of the map to **30%** using the parameter on the right of the **Map** check box in the **Skylight Parameters** rollout [see **outdoor-blurred-Sky.max**].*

Exercise 2: Quickly Rendering an Architectural Plan

Sometimes, you need to send a quick draft render to your clients to check the CG assets and other related information in an architectural plan. Once approved, you can then proceed to produce the high quality render in **VRay** or **Arnold**. In this exercise, we are going to render an architectural plan using the **Standard** lights and the **Light Tracer** plugin [see Fig. E1]. To speed up the rendering, I have not placed any models in the scene except the walls.

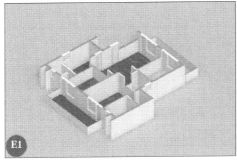 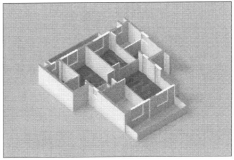

Table E2 summarizes the exercise.

Table E2	
Skill level	Intermediate
Time to complete	30 Minutes

Table E2	
Topics	• Getting Ready • Illuminating the Plan
Resources folder	**unit-dl1**
Start file	**plan-start.max**
Final file	**plan-finish.max**

Getting Ready
Open the **plan-start.max** file in 3ds Max.

Illuminating the Plan
Follow these steps:

1. Add a **Skylight** to the scene and then in the **Modify** panel > **Skylight Parameters** rollout, set **Multiplier** to **0.5** and **Sky Color** to RGB [184, 184, 255]. Select the **Cast Shadows** check box in the **Render** group and then set **Rays per sample** to **10**.

2. In the **Top** viewport, create a **Target Direct** light aiming toward the **Camera's** target. Now, in the **Left** viewport move the light up. You can use the following values for placing the light and its target: **Light** [11825, -7069, 76], and **Target** [11889, -7097, 0].

3. Change the parameters of the directional light in the **Modify** panel, refer to Table E2.1. Fig. E2 shows the light in the scene. Now, make sure the **Camera** view is active and then render the scene [see Fig. E3].

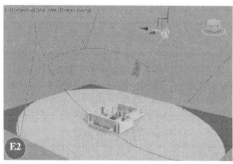
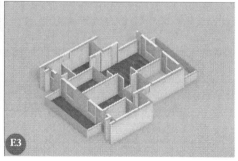

Table E2.1: The parameters of **Target Light**	
Rollout	**Values**
General Parameters > Shadows	Select the **On** check box. Select **Adv. Ray Traced** shadows type.
Directional Parameters	Hotspot/Beam: **72**
Intensity/Color/ Attenuation	Multiplier: **1.5**, Color: RGB [255, 242, 198].

Table E2.1: The parameters of **Target Light**	
Rollout	**Values**
Shadow Parameters	Dens: **0.5**. Select the **Light Affects Shadow Color** check box.
Adv. Ray Traced Params	Shadow Integrity: **10**, Shadow Quality: **5**, Shadow Spread: **20**, and Jitter Amount: **0.8**

4. Enable **Light Tracer** from the **Render Setup** window > **Advanced Lighting** panel.

5. Adjust **Light Tracer**'s parameters using the values shown in Table E2.2 and then render the scene.

Table E2.2: The parameters of **Light Tracer**	
Rollout	**Values**
Parameters	Global Multiplier: **1.2**, Rays/Sample: **500**, Bounces: **2**
Parameters > Adaptive Undersampling	Initial Sampling Spacing: **32x32**

Note: Direct Light and Light Tracer
*Experiment with various parameters of **Target Direct** and **Light Tracer** to achieve different results.*

Exercise 3: Illuminating a Night Scene

In this exercise, we will illuminate the same scene that we used in **Exercise 1** but here we will simulate night lighting by using the **Target Spot** and **Omni** lights [see Fig. E1].

Table E3 summarizes the exercise.

Table E3	
Skill level	Intermediate
Time to complete	30 Minutes

Table E3	
Topics	• Getting Ready • Illuminating the Scene
Resources folder	**unit-dl1**
Start file	**ext-night-start.max**
Final file	**ext-night-finish.max**

Getting Ready

Open the **ext-night-start.max** file in 3ds Max.

Illuminating the Scene

Follow these steps:

1. Create a **Target Spot** light in the **Front** viewport and then align it [see Fig. E2]. Now, select **Spot001** in the **Scene Explorer**. In the **Front** viewport, drag the light with **Shift** held down along the X direction to the other light fixture on the left.

2. In the **Clone Options** dialog box that appears, select **Instance** from the **Object** group and then click **OK** to create a clone of the selected light. Now, align the cloned light with the fixture [see Fig. E3].

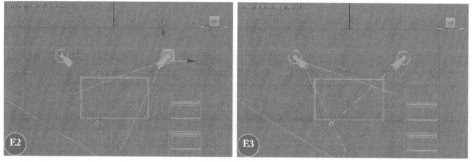

You can also use the values shown in Table E3.1 to position the spot lights.

Table E3.1: The transform values for spot lights	
Object	**XYZ Values**
Spot001	**39.991, -6.159, 116.401**
Spot001.Target	**-20.628, -6.159, 58.77**
Spot002	**-38.549, -6.159, 116.401**
Spot002.Target	**8.85, -6.159, 58.77**

3. Render the scene [see Fig. E4].

*You will notice [see Fig. E4] that spot lights are illuminating the road as well. We need to confine the illumination to the billboard only. For that, we will use the **Attenuation** settings.*

4. Ensure one of the spot lights is selected and then in the **Modify** panel > **Spotlight Parameters** rollout, set **Hotspot/Beam** to **43.7** and **Falloff/Field** to **67**. In the **Intensity/Color/Attenuation** > **Far Attenuation** group, select the **Use** and **Show** checkboxes and then set **End** to **116**. Now, render the scene to see the area the spotlights are illuminating [see Fig. E5].

5. Add an **Omni** light to the scene and place it at the following location [XYZ]: **38.169, -103.246, 117.664**. Change the parameters of the **Omni** light using the values shown in Table E3.2 and then render the scene.

Table E3.2: The parameters of the **Omni** light	
Rollout	**Values**
General Parameters > Shadows	Select the **On** check box. Select **Adv. Ray Traced** shadows type.
Intensity/Color/ Attenuation	Multiplier: **0.1**, Color: **RGB [173, 175, 208]**.
Shadow Parameters	Select the **Light Affects Shadow Color** check box.
Adv. Ray Traced Params	Shadow Integrity: **10**, Shadow Quality: **5**, Shadow Spread: **10**, and Jitter Amount: **0.7**

6. In the **Modify** panel > **Intensity/Color/Attenuation** rollout of spot light, set **Multiplier** to **2** to make the area illuminated by the spot lights brighter. Render the scene to view the result.

Quiz

Evaluate your skills to see how many questions you can answer correctly.

Multiple Choice
Answer the following questions:

1. Which of the following options are available for controlling the decay of the light?

   [A] **None**   [B] **Inverse**
   [C] **Inverse Square**   [D] All of the above

2. Which of the following algorithms are available for controlling shadows?

   [A] **Ray-Traced**   [B] **Area**
   [C] **Shadow Map**   [D] All of the above

Fill in the Blanks
Fill in the blanks in each of the following statements:

1. _____ is a bitmap that is generated during a pre-rendering pass of the scene.

2. _____ shadows are more accurate than the shadow-mapped shadows and are generated by tracing the path of the rays sampled from a light source.

3. The _____ formula is used to calculate the **Inverse** decay type.

4. The _____ check box displays the cone of a spot light in the viewport.

5. The _____ parameter moves the shadow toward or away from the shadow casting object.

6. An _____ light casts rays in all directions from a single source like a light bulb.

True or False
State whether each of the following is true or false:

1. **Standard** lights have physically-based intensity values.

2. The color that you set for the light from the **Name and Color** rollout only changes the color of the light geometry in the scene. It has no effect on the color cast by the light.

3. When you delete all light objects from the scene, 3ds Max uses the default lighting for illuminating the scene.

4. The **Free Spotlight** is similar to the **Target Spotlight** except the difference that it has no target.

5. Only ray-traced shadows can generate shadows for the wireframed objects.

6. You cannot prevent an object from casting shadows in the scene.

7. When the **Overshoot** check box is selected for a spot light, the spot light casts light in all directions [not just within the cone] but the shadows and projections appear within the cone.

Summary
This unit covered the following topics:

- Basic lighting concepts
- Creating and placing lights
- 3ds Max lights
- Light linking
- Shadows

This page is intentionally left blank

- Photometric light types: **Target Light** and **Free Light**
- Color temperatures
- Shadow generating shapes
- Exposure controls

Unit DL2: Photometric Lights

Photometric lights allow you to accurately define the lighting model for your scene. They use the light energy [photometric values, real-world light measurement values] to create lights that follow the real-world scenarios. You can create lighting models using various distribution and color characteristics. You can also import photometric light files [provided by the light manufactures] into 3ds Max. In this unit, you will learn about photometric lights that 3ds Max offers.

Target Light

Target Light has a target sub-object that you can use to aim the light. When you create **Target Light** in a viewport, 3ds Max automatically adds a **Look At Controller** to it. The target object of the light is assigned as **Look At Target**. You can use the **Motion** panel of the **Command** panel to assign any object as the **Look At Target**.

 Note: Light and its target
*When you create a light that has a target, two objects will appear in the **Scene Explorer**: the light object and its target. The target name has an extension **.target**. For example, if you create first **Target Light** in the scene, the name of the light and its target will be as follows: **TPhotometricLight001** and **TPhotometricLight001.Target**.*

When you rename a light, its target object will be automatically renamed accordingly. However, remember that renaming a target object does not rename its parent light.

Whenever you create a photometric light, a message box appears, recommending that the **Logarithmic Exposure Control** to be enabled. Exposure controls are plug-in components that are used to adjust the output levels and color range of a rendering as if you are adjusting the film exposure [tone mapping]. These controls are useful if you are rendering a scene with **Radiosity** or the **HDR** imagery. It is especially useful for compensating for the limited dynamic range of the computer displays. The following table summarizes the exposure controls available in 3ds Max.

Table 1: Exposure controls	
Control	**Description**
Automatic Exposure Control	This control enhances some lighting effects that would otherwise be too dim to see. It builds a histogram to give good color separation across the entire dynamic range of rendering. Do not use this control in animation because it causes the animation to flicker. This happens because different histograms are generated for each frame.
Linear Exposure Control	It uses the average brightness of the scene to map physical values to RGB values. This is best suitable for scene with fairly low dynamic range.
Logarithmic Exposure Control	It uses brightness and contrast to map physical values to RGB values. This control is best suitable for scenes with a very high dynamic range. Also, it is best suited for animation as it does not generate histograms. If you're rendering to texture, use **Logarithmic Exposure Control**, not the **Automatic** or **Linear** control.
Physical Camera Exposure Control	It sets exposure for **Physical** cameras, using an **Exposure Value** and a color-response curve.
Pseudo Color Exposure Control	It is a lighting analysis tool that provides an intuitive way of visualizing and evaluating the lighting levels in the scenes.

To create a target light, in the **Create** panel, click **Lights** and then choose **Photometric** from the drop-down list [see Fig. 1]. Click **Target Light** in the **Object Type** rollout. Click **Yes** from the **Photometric Light Creation** message box and then click-drag in a viewport to set the location of the light. The initial point drag of the mouse pointer defines the location of the light whereas the last drag point defines the position of the target. Now, you can use the **Move** tool to farther refine the position of the light and its target. Adjust the parameters of the light from the rollouts in the **Command** panel. Several of the rollouts for the photometric

lights are the same as those for the standard lights but there are some key parameters that are different. Let's now explore these parameters.

Template Rollout

This rollout [see Fig. 2] allows you to choose a light preset among a variety of preset light types. When you choose a template from this rollout, the parameters in other rollouts updated that you can use to fine-tune the settings of the light.

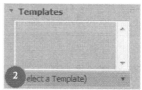

The following presets are available in the **Template** rollout:

(Bulb Lights)
- 40 Watt (W) Bulb
- 60W Bulb
- 75W Bulb
- 100W Bulb

(Halogen Lights)
- Halogen Spotlight
- 21W Halogen Bulb
- 35W Halogen Bulb
- 50W Halogen Bulb
- 75W Halogen Bulb
- 80W Halogen Bulb
- 100W Halogen Bulb

(Recessed Lights)

- Recessed 75W Lamp (web)
- Recessed 75W Wallwash (web)
- Recessed 250W Wallwash (web)

(Fluorescent Lights)
- 4 ft. Pendant Fluorescent (web)
- 4 ft. Cove Fluorescent (web)

(Other Lights)
- Street 400W Lamp (web)
- Stadium 1000W Lamp (web)

General Parameters Rollout

The parameters in this rollout are similar to that of the standard lights that we saw in **Unit DL1** except the **Light Distribution (Type)** group. The drop-down list in this group lets you choose the type of the light distribution model. The model defines the method of how a photometric light is distributed. Let's explore these types.

- **Uniform Spherical:** This type casts lights in all directions [see Fig. 3] like the standard **Omni** light. The **Uniform Spherical** distribution is represented by a small sphere in the viewports. The position of the sphere indicates whether the distribution is spherical or hemispherical.

- **Uniform Diffuse:** This type casts diffuse light in one hemisphere [as if a light is positioned along a wall] only according to the **Lambert's** cosine law [see Fig. 4].

- **Spotlight:** This type casts a focused beam of light [see Fig. 5] like a flashlight or a car's headlights. The beam angle of the light defines the main strength of the beam whereas the field angle defines the spill of the light.

- **Photometric Web:** A photometric web is based on a geometric web that represents the light intensity distribution of a light source [see Fig. 5]. The distribution information is stored in a photometric data file [that can be obtained from the light's manufacturer] in the **IES** format using the **IES LM-63-1991** standard file format.

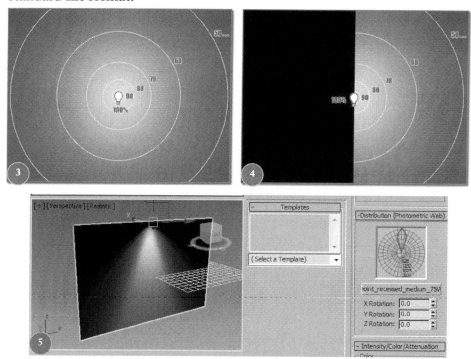

Intensity/Color/Attenuation Rollout

This rollout [see Fig. 6] lets you set the color and intensity of the light. You can also set attenuation form this rollout.

Color Group

The first drop-down list in this group allows you to pick a common lamp specification. Given below are the options available:

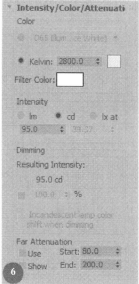

- D50 Illuminant (Reference White)
- D65 Illuminant (Reference White) (the default)
- Fluorescent (Cool White)
- Fluorescent (Daylight)
- Fluorescent (Lite White)
- Fluorescent (Warm White)
- Fluorescent (White)
- Halogen
- Halogen (Cool)
- Halogen (Warm)
- HID Ceramic Metal Halide (Cool)

- HID Ceramic Metal Halide (Warm)
- HID High Pressure Sodium
- HID Low Pressure Sodium
- HID Mercury
- HID Phosphor Mercury
- HID Quartz Metal Halide
- HID Quartz Metal Halide (Cool)
- HID Quartz Metal Halide (Warm)
- HID Xenon
- Incandescent filament lamp

Note: HID
HID *stands for high-intensity discharge.*

Note: D65 Illuminant (Reference White)
This default option in the drop-down list approximates a mid day Sun in western or northern Europe. ***D65*** *is a white value defined by the* ***Comission Internationale de l'Éclairage (CIE)***, *the* ***International Lighting Commission***.

Fig. 7 shows the render with the **D50 Illuminant (Reference White)**, **Fluorescent (Cool White)**, and **HID High Pressure Sodium**, respectively.

In addition to the list of lights, you can specify a color based on the temperature expressed in **Kelvin**. The **Kelvin** option allows you to set the color of the light by adjusting the color temperature spinners located next to it. The associated color appears on the color swatch on the right of the spinner. **Filter Color** allows you to simulate the effect of a color filter placed in front of the light source. The color temperature defines a color in terms of degree **Kelvin [K]**. The following table summarizes the color temperature for some common types of lights:

Table 2: Color temperatures		
Light Source	**Temperature [K]**	**Hue**
Overcast daylight	6000	130
Noontime sunlight	5000	58
White fluorescent	4000	27
Tungsten/halogen lamp	3300	20
Incandescent lamp (100 to 200 W)	2900	16

Table 2: Color temperatures		
Light Source	**Temperature [K]**	**Hue**
Incandescent lamp (25 W)	2500	12
Sunlight at sunset or sunrise	2000	7
Candle flame	1750	5

Intensity Group

There are three parameters in this group: **lm** [lumen], **cd** [candela], and **lx at** [lux]. These parameters define the strength or brightness of the lights in physically based quantities. **Lumen** measures the overall output [luminous flux] power of the light. A **100 watt** bulb has about **1750 lm** luminous flux. **Candela** measures the maximum luminous intensity of the light, generally along the direction of the aim. A **100 watt** bulb has about intensity of **139 cd**. **Lux** measures the illumination caused by the light shining on a surface at a certain distance in the direction of the source. **Lux** is the international scene unit which is equivalent to **1 lumen per square meter**. To specify the illuminate of the light first enter the **lx** value in the first spinner and then enter **distance** in the second.

Dimming Group

The **Resulting Intensity** label shows the intensity caused by the dimming. It uses the same units that you have defined in the **Intensity** group. Select the **Dimming Percentage** check box to control the dimming of the light. At **100%**, the light has full intensity. When the **Incandescent lamp color shift when dimming** check box is selected, the light simulate an incandescent light. The color of the light turns more yellowish as it is dimmed.

Shape/Area Shadows Rollout

You can use the parameters in this rollout [see Fig. 8] to choose the light shape used for generating shadows. Let's explore the parameters.

Emit Light From (Shape) Group

The drop-down list in this group allows you to choose the shadow generating shape for the light. When you choose a shadow generating shape other than **Point**, the parameters appear in the **Emit Light From (Shape)** group to control the dimensions of the shape. Also, the **Shadow Samples** parameter appears in the **Rendering** group of the rollout.

The following table summarizes the shapes.

Table 3: The shadow generating shapes	
Shape	**Description**
Point	Calculates shadows as if the light were emitted from a point like a light bulb. It has no other parameters.

Table 3: The shadow generating shapes	
Shape	**Description**
Line	Calculates shadows as if the light were emitted from a line like a fluorescent tube. This shape has a **Length** parameter.
Rectangle	Calculates shadows as if the light were emitted from a rectangular area like a bank of fluorescent lights. This shape has the **Length** and **Width** parameters.
Disc	Calculates shadows as if the light were emitted from a disc like the light out of the top of a shaded lamp. This shape has the **Radius** parameter.
Sphere	Calculates shadows as if the light were emitted from a sphere like a Chinese lantern. This shape has the **Radius** parameter.
Cylinder	Calculates shadows as if the light were emitted from a cylinder. This shape has the **Length** and **Radius** parameters.

Rendering Group

When the **Light Shape Visible in Rendering** check box is selected, the shape is visible in the renderings as a self-illuminated glowing shape. When this check box is clear, no shape is rendered. The **Shadow Samples** parameter sets the overall quality of the shadows for the lights that have an area. If render is grainy, increase the value for the **Shadow Samples** parameter. This parameter does not appear for the **Point** shadow shape.

Distribution (Photometric File) Rollout

This rollout appears [see Fig. 9] when you create or select a light with the **Photometric Web** distribution. You can use the parameters in this rollout to select a photometric web file and adjust its settings. After you choose a photometric file, the thumbnail [also referred to as **Web Diagram**] shows a schematic diagram of the distribution pattern of the light [refer to Fig. 5].

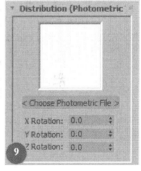

The bright red outline shows the beam of the light. In some web diagrams, you will see a darker red outline that shows the field which is less bright than the beam. Click the **Choose Photometric File** button to select a file to use as a photometric web. The file can be in one of the following formats: **IES**, **LTLI**, or **CIBSE**. Once you select the file, this button displays the name of the file. The X **Rotation**, Y **Rotation**, and Z **Rotation** parameters rotate the web about the X, Y, and Z axis, respectively.

Distribution (Spotlight) Rollout

This rollout appears [see Fig. 10] when you select or create a photometric light with the **Spotlight** distribution. The parameters in this rollout control hotspots and falloff of the spotlights. Use the **Hotspot/Beam** and **Falloff/Field**

parameters to increase or decrease the size of the beam angle and field angle regions, respectively. The **Cone visible in viewport when unselected** check box toggles the display of the cone on and off.

Free Light

The **Free Light** is similar to **Target Light** except it has no target sub-object.

Quiz

Evaluate your skills to see how many questions you can answer correctly.

Multiple Choice
Answer the following questions:

1. Which of the following exposure controls is used with the **Photometric** lights?

   [A] Linear Exposure Control   [B] Logarithmic Exposure Control
   [C] Physical Camera Exposure Control [D] All of the above

2. Which of the following light distribution models are available for the **Photometric** lights?

   [A] Uniform Spherical   [B] Uniform Diffuse
   [C] Photometric Web   [D] All of the above

3. Which of the following file types can be used to assign web diagrams to the **Photometric** lights?

   [A] IES   [B] CIBSE
   [C] LTLI   [D] All of the above

Fill in the Blanks
Fill in the blanks in each of the following statements:

1. When you create **Target Light** in a viewport, 3ds Max automatically adds a _____ to it.

2. _____ controls are plug-in components that are used to adjust the output levels and color range of a rendering as if you are adjusting the film exposure [tone mapping].

3. _____ stands for high-intensity discharge.

True or False
State whether each of the following is true or false:

1. **Physical Camera Exposure Control** sets exposure for **Physical** cameras, using an **Exposure Value** and a color-response curve.

2. The **Resulting Intensity** label shows the intensity caused by the dimming.

Summary

This units covered the following topics:

- Photometric light types: **Target Light** and **Free Light**
- Color temperatures
- Shadow generating shapes
- Exposure controls

- Sunlight and Daylight Systems
- Positioning the Compass
- Choosing a location
- Sun Positioner and Physical Sky

Unit DL3: Sunlight and Daylight Systems

The sunlight and daylight systems are the built for simulating external lighting based on the Sun. These systems follow the geographically correct angle and movement of the Sun over the earth at a given location and are suitable for shadow study for the proposed or existing structures. Using these systems, you can animate date and time, latitude, longitude, **North Direction** [rotational direction of the compass rose], and **Orbital Scale** [the distance of the Sun from the ground plane].

Using the Sunlight and Daylight Systems

The legacy **Sunlight** and **Daylight** systems are similar in how they are used [they have similar interface] but there are some differences:

- **Sunlight** uses a directional light.
- **Daylight** combines **Sunlight** and **Skylight**. The **Sunlight** component can be one of the following: **IES Sun** light or a standard light [a target direct light]. The **Skylight** component can be one of the following: **IES Sky** light or a **Skylight**.

> ✎ *Note: Standard and Photometric Lights*
> *The **IES Sun** and **IES Sky** lights are photometric lights. You can use them if you are rendering a scene using **Radiosity** and exposure control. The **Standard** lights and **Skylight** are non-photometric. You can use them if you are using standard lighting or you are using light tracing.*

You can access the **Sunlight** and **Daylight** systems from the **System** panel of the **Command** panel. To create either of these systems, go to the **Create** panel and then click **Systems** [see Fig. 1]. In the **Object Type** rollout, click **Sunlight** or **Daylight** and drag the mouse pointer in a viewport [should be a **Top**, **Perspective**, or **Camera** view].

A compass helper object appears on the grid. Click again to create a **Direct** light representing the Sun and drag to set its height above the ground plane. Fig. 2 shows the compass created using the **Daylight** system.

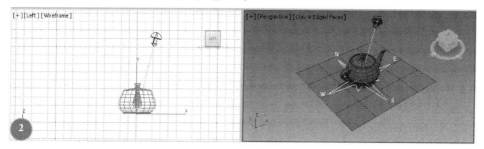

When you first create a **Daylight** system, the **Daylight System Creation** message box appears [see Fig. 3], recommending to enable the **Logarithmic Exposure Control** for external light. Click **Yes** to enable the exposure control.

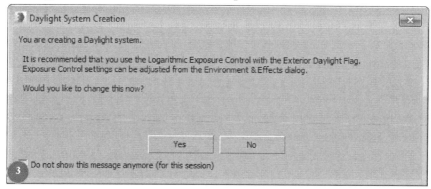

Upon creation, you will have two objects in the scene. The compass rose, which is a helper object and provides the world directions for the Sun. The light itself which is child of the compass and is always targeted at the center of the compass rose. If you have created a **Daylight** system, you can choose the type of sunlight and skylight from the **Modify** panel. The **Sunlight** drop-down list lets you choose **IES Sun** or **Standard** (directional). The **Skylight** drop-down list lets you choose **IES Sky** or **Skylight**. You can also choose **<No Sunlight>** or **<No Skylight>** from the drop-down lists.

The parameters for adjusting the geographic location of the Sun can be accessed from the **Motion** panel of the **Command** panel. The default time is noon whereas the default date and time is dependent on the settings of the computer you are using. The default location is **San Francisco, CA**.

Once you create a **Daylight** system, the parameters appear in the **Modify** panel. Let's explore the parameters that are unique to the **Daylight** system:

Daylight Parameters Rollout

The parameters in this rollout [see Fig. 4] lets you define the Sun object of the **Daylight** system. You can use these parameters to set the behavior of the sunlight and skylight. The **Sunlight** drop-down list lets you choose the sunlight for your scene. The **Active** check box lets you toggle the sunlight on and off.

The parameters in the **Position** group let you define the correct geographical angle of the Sun. The **Manual** parameter lets you manually adjust the location of the daylight. The **Date, Time and Location** parameter uses the geographically correct angle and movement of the Sun over the earth at a given location. The **Weather Data File** parameter allows you to derive the angle and intensity of the Sun from a weather data (**EPW**) file.

When you choose the **Weather Data File** option and then click **Setup**, 3ds Max opens the **Configure Weather Data** dialog box. You can choose which weather data you want the daylight system to use. When you choose the **Manual** or **Date, Time And Location** parameter, clicking on **Setup** button opens the **Motion** panel [see Fig. 5] from where you can set the time, location, and site of your daylight system.

Control Parameters Rollout

This rollout appears in the **Motion** panel. The **Azimuth** and **Altitude** parameters display the azimuth and altitude of the Sun. **Azimuth** is the compass direction [**North=0, East=90**] of the Sun in degrees. **Altitude** is the height [**Sunrise/Sunset=0**] of the Sun above the horizon in degrees. The parameters in the **Time** group let you define the time, date, and time zone. When the **Daylight Savings Time** check box is selected, 3ds Max calculates daylight savings by adjusting azimuth and altitude during the summer months.

The parameters in **Location** group let you define location of your scene in the world. You can manually enter location based on the latitude and longitude. You can also specify location by using the **Geographic Location** dialog box which appears [see Fig. 6] when you click **Get Location**. You can define the longitude and latitude values by selecting a location on the map or from a list of cities. The **North Direction** parameter defines the rotational direction of the compass rose in the scene. By default, north direction is **0**. The **Orbital Scale** parameter in the **Site** group defines the distance of the Sun from the compass rose. The distance of Sun from the compass rose has no effect on the accuracy of the sunlight.

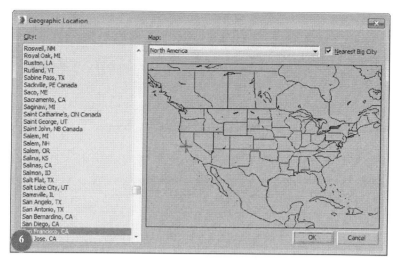

Using Sun Positioner and Physical Sky

Like the **Daylight** and **Sunlight** systems, the **Sun Positioner** and the **Physical Sky** system provides the light follows the geographically correct angle and movement of the Sun over the earth at a given location. However, the **Sun Positioner** and the **Physical Sky** system provides intuitive workflow compared to these legacy systems. The component of the legacy systems are scattered all over the interface. For example, the legacy systems are located in the **System** panel of the **Command** panel whereas the location settings are found in the **Motion** panel of the **Command** panel.

The **Sun Positioner/Physical Sky** system is found in the **Light** panel. Once you position the Sun object in the scene, you can adjust the exposure controls from the **Environment and Effects** window. You can open this window by pressing **8**. The shading parameters can be adjusted from the **Scene Materials** rollout of the **Slate Material Editor** [see Fig. 7].

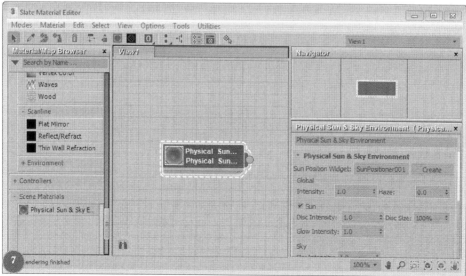

Hands-on Exercise

Exercise 1: Shadow Pattern Study

In this exercise, we will create an animated shadow pattern for shadow study according to the position of the Sun. Fig. E1 shows the render at frame **25** and **200**, respectively.

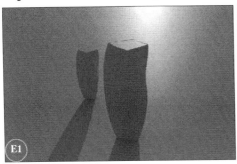

The following table summarizes the exercise:

Table E1	
Topics in this exercise	• Getting Ready • Creating the Gold Material
Skill level	Intermediate
Resources folder	**unit-dl3**
Start file	**shadow-study-start.max**
Final file	**shadow-study-finish.max**
Time to complete	25 Minutes

Getting Ready
Open the **shadow-study-start.max** file in 3ds Max.

Creating the Gold Material
Follow these steps:

1. In the **Create** panel, click **Lights**, and then select **Photometric** from the drop-down list available below **Lights**. In the **Object Type** rollout, click **Sun Positioner** and then create a **Sun Positioner** object in the scene [see Fig. E2].

2. Choose the **Time Configuration** button ⚙ from the timeline to open the **Time Configuration** dialog box. In this dialog box, set **End Time** to **500** and then click **OK**.

3. Make sure the **SunPositioner001** object is selected and time slider is at frame **0**. Switch to the **Modify** panel. In the **Display** rollout, set **Radius** to **0.987** and **North Offset** to **100**. In the **Sun** group, set **Distance** to **555.74**. Fig. E3 shows the **SunPositioner001** object in the scene.

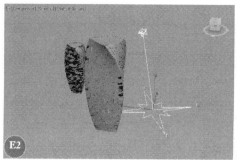
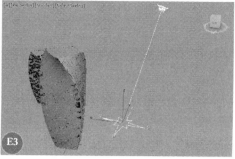

> *Note: Default position of the Sun*
> *The **SunPositioner001** object uses **San Francisco, CA** as the default location. If you want to change the location, click on **San Francisco, CA** from the **Location on Earth** group of the **Sun Position** rollout to open the **Geographic Location** dialog box. Now, you can choose desired location from this dialog box.*

4. In the **Date & Time** group, clear the **Use Date Range** check box and then set **Time** to 7. Toggle on the **Auto Key** mode Auto Key from the timeline. Drag the time slide to frame **500**.

5. In the **Date & Time** group of the **Sun Position** rollout, set **Time** to **18**. Toggle off the **Auto Key** mode and then click the **Play Animation** button ▶ to view the animation of the Sun. Now, render the sequence to see the shadow pattern.

Quiz

Evaluate your skills to see how many questions you can answer correctly.

Fill in the Blanks
Fill in the blanks in each of the following statements:

1. _____ uses a directional light to simulate the Sun.

2. You can access the **Sunlight** and **Daylight** systems from the _____ panel of the **Command** panel.

3. If you have created a _____ system, you can choose the type of sunlight and skylight from the **Modify** panel.

4. The _____ system provides intuitive workflow than the legacy **Daylight** and **Sunlight** systems for the geographically correct angle and movement of the Sun over the earth at a given location.

Summary

This unit covered the following:

- Sunlight and Daylight Systems
- Positioning the Compass
- Choosing a location
- Sun Positioner and Physical Sky

This page is intentionally left blank

- Why Arnold is different?
- What's wrong with the biased algorithms?
- What are the advantages of being physically-based?
- Studio Lighting
- Sampling and Ray Depth

Unit DA1: Introduction to Arnold

Arnold developed by Solid Angle [wholly owned subsidiary of Autodesk Inc] is an advanced cross-platform rendering library [API]. Today, it is used by various studios in film, gaming, animation, and broadcast industries across the globe. This unit introduces you to the **MAXtoA** plugin. **MAXtoA** is a plugin for Autodesk 3ds Max which provides a bridge to the Arnold rendering system from within the standard 3ds Max interface.

Arnold was designed to easily adapt to the existing pipelines. It can be extended and customized by writing new shaders, cameras, filters, custom ray types, user-defined geometric data, and so on. The primary goal of the Arnold engine is to provide a complete solution as primary render engine for animation and visual effects projects. However, you can also use it as:

- A ray server for the traditional scanline renderers.
- A tool for creating lightmaps for video games.
- An interactive rendering tool.

 Why Arnold is different?
Here's a quick rundown:

- *It uses highly optimized algorithms to make the most effective use of the computer hardware.*
- *It is physically-based, highly optimized, and photo-realistic.*
- *Its architecture is highly customizable. You can extend and customize it by writing your own shaders, cameras, filters, and so on.*
- *It uses physically-based Monte Carlo ray/path tracing engine thus eliminating the possibility of artifacts [generally produced by the photon mapping and final gather algorithms] produced by the caching algorithms.*
- *It is designed to simplify the production pipeline and renders complex images demanded by VFX studios efficiently.*

- *It is used to bake the lighting data to produce lightmaps for video games.*
- *It is used to as an interactive rendering and relighting tool.*

 What's wrong with photon mapping or final gather?
To speed up the rendering, these methods attempt to cache the data that can be sampled later. As a result, they consume large amounts of memory and introduce bias into the sampling thus producing artifacts. Also, as a user, they require you to understand the details of how these methods work in order to speed up the rendering without affecting the quality. The worse part of all this is that the settings for these methods get affected by other things in the scene. Arnold allows you to spent time on other aspects of the scene such as modeling, animating, and lighting and it takes care of the rendering.

 Why physically-based?
The advantage is that artists can work in a physically accurate and high-range dynamic workflow. It also ensures that other aspects of rendering are not broken.

 Note: Downloading plugin
*The **MAXtoA** plugin is automatically installed when you install 3ds Max 2020. However, if a new version is available, you can download it from the Arnold's website:*
***https://www.arnoldrenderer.com/arnold/arnold-for-3dsmax/** and then install it.*

Studio Lighting

Before moving farther, let's first create a photographic lighting studio setup that we will use to render all kinds of objects.

Follow these steps:

1. From the **Customize** menu choose **Units Setup**. In the **Units Setup** dialog box that appears, select the **Metric** radio button from the **Display Unit Scale** group. Next, select **Centimeters** from the drop-down list located below **Metric** and then click **OK** to accept the changes.

2. From the **File** menu, choose **Save** to open the **Save File As** dialog box. In the **File name** field type **studio-lighting.max** and then click **Save** to save the file.

3. In the **Create** panel, click **Geometry**, and then in the **Object Type** rollout, click **Plane**. In the **Perspective** viewport, create a plane. Switch to the **Modify** panel and then on the **Parameters** rollout, change **Length** to **334**, **Width** to **181**, **Length Segs** to **1**, and **Width Segs** to **1** [see Fig. 1].

4. Convert plane to editable poly and then rename it as **BG**. In the **Modify** panel > **Selection** rollout, click **Edge** to activate the edge sub-object level. Now, select the edge, as shown in Fig. 2. Extrude the edge, as shown in Fig. 3 using **Shift** and the **Move** tool.

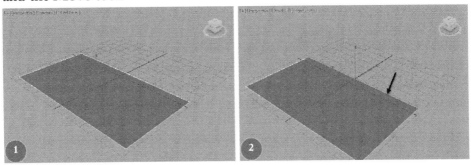

5. Select the middle edge and then in the **Modify** panel > **Edit Edges** rollout, click **Chamfer** > **Settings** to open the **Chamfer** caddy control. In the caddy control, change **Edge Chamfer Amount** to **18** and **Connect Edge Segments** to **4** [see Fig. 4].

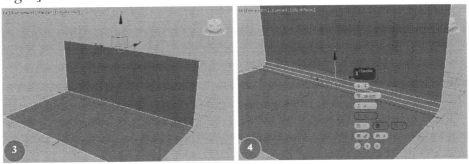

6. In the **Create** panel, click **Geometry**, and then in the **Object Type** rollout, click **Plane**. In the **Front** viewport, create a plane. Switch to the **Modify** panel and then in the **Parameters** rollout, change **Length** to **132**, **Width** to **175**, **Length Segs** to **1**, and **Width Segs** to **1**. Now, align the plane [see Fig. 5]. Create a copy of the plane and then align it on the right [see Fig. 6].

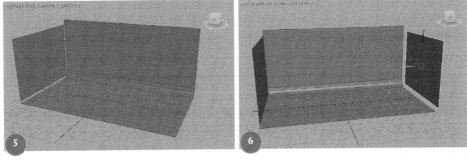

7. Rename the planes as **sidePlane1** and **sidePlane2**, respectively. Group all three planes and name it **Studio**.

8. In the **Create** panel, click **Geometry**, and then in the **Object Type** rollout, click **Sphere**. In the **Perspective** viewport, create a sphere. Switch to **Modify** panel and then in the **Parameters** rollout, change **Radius** to **30** and **Segments** to **64** [see Fig. 7].

9. In the **Create** panel, click **Cameras**, and then in the **Object Type** rollout, click **Physical**. Create a camera in the **Top** viewport [see Fig. 8]. Press **C** to make the camera active and then press **Shift+F** to show safe frames [see Fig. 9]. Now, adjust the camera's view [see Fig. 10].

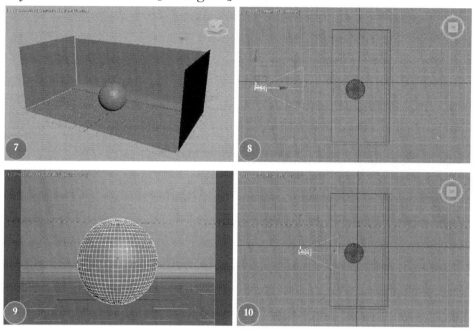

10. Press **F10** to open the **Render Setup** window. In this window, change **Target** to **ActiveShade Mode** and **Renderer** to **Arnold**. In the **Common** panel > **Output Size** group, change **Width** and **Height** to as per your requirements. I recommend that you use low resolution settings for test renders. Close the **Render Setup** window.

11. In the **Create** panel, click **Lights**, and then select **Arnold** from the drop-down list available below **Lights**. In the **Object Type** rollout, click **Arnold Light**. Create a light and then align it [see Fig. 11]. In the **Modify** panel > **Shape** rollout, change **Quad X** and **Quad Y** to **120** and **100**, respectively [see Fig. 12].

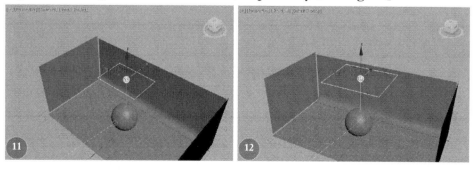

12. Press **M** to open the **Slate Material Editor**. Drag **Standard Surface** to active view from the **Material/Map Browser > Materials > Arnold > Surface** rollout. Rename the material as **matBG**. Apply the material to **Studio** in the scene. In **Parameter Editor > Specular** rollout, change specular strength to **0** [see Fig. 13].

13. Create a new **Standard Surface** and then rename it as **matObject**. Assign it to the sphere in the scene.

14. Click **ActiveShade** on the **Main** toolbar or press **Shift+Q** to render the scene. Notice in Fig. 14 that render is dark; to fix this either we can increase the **Intensity** or **Exposure** control in the **Modify** panel > **Color/Intensity** rollout > **Intensity** group or we can adjust the camera exposure and f-stop settings. In the **Modify** panel > **Color/Intensity** rollout, change **Exposure** to **9**. Render the scene[see Fig. 15].

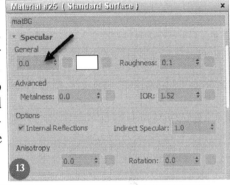

15. Create two more quads lights and align them [see Fig. 16]. Render the scene [see Fig. 17. Notice in Fig. 17 that there is some noise in the render, we will fix it later. Save the scene.

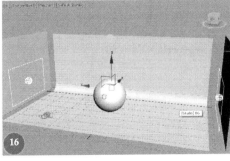

16. Rename lights as **leftLight**, **topLight**, and **rightLight**, respectively. Change **Exposure** setting to **8** for all three lights.

17. Select **leftLight** and then in the **Modify** panel > **Color/Intensity** rollout > **Color** group, select the **Kelvin** radio button and then enter **4000** in the spinner. Similarly, use **12000** as temperature for right light. Render the scene.

Sampling

Arnold is a raytracing renderer. Sampling and ray depth are one of the most important settings for the **Arnold** raytracer. In order to produce a rendered image, Arnold needs to know color value of each pixel. To do so, Arnold fires a number of rays from the camera and then they hit objects in the scene. When rays hit something in the scene, they calculate the information about the surface and return it for processing. This process is called sampling.

The **Sampling** and **Ray Depth** settings are available in the **Render Setup** window > **Arnold Renderer** panel > **Sampling and Ray Depth** rollout [see Fig. 18]. These settings control the sampling [image quality] of the rendered images. Increasing the sample rate removes the noise from the rendered images but at the expense of the increased render time.

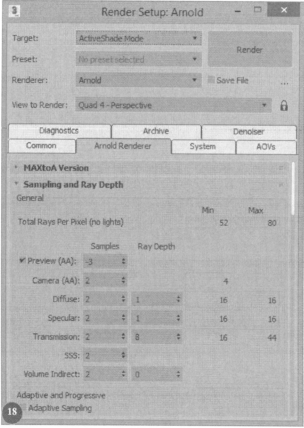

The actual number of samples is the square root of the specified value. For example, if you specify **Camera (AA)** samples as **3** [AA=anti-aliasing], it means that **3x3=9** samples will be used by Arnold for anti-aliasing. If you specify a value of **2** for the **Diffuse > Samples**, it means that **2x2=4** samples will be used for global illumination. The same is true for other settings as well.

The **Camera (AA)** setting can be considered global multiplier for all other components: **Diffuse, Specular, Transmission, SSS,** and **Volume Indirect** because for these components sampling rates are expressed for each **Camera (AA)** sample.

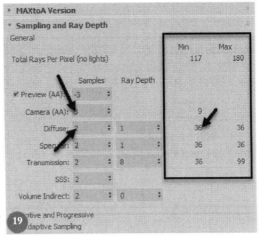

For example, if you specify **Camera (AA)** value as **3** and **Diffuse** as **2**, the total number of samples per pixel used will be 36 [(3*3)x(2*2)]. Refer to Fig. 19.

Let's now discuss various sampling components:

Preview (AA) Samples

It controls the super-sampling value for previews. It affects the quick first frame before the actual super-sampling starts. The default value for this setting is **-3**. Negative values sub-sample the render therefore allowing faster feedback in the render window.

Camera AA Samples

As discussed earlier, the **Camera (AA)** parameter is global multiplier for all other components. The higher the value you specify for this setting, the better the anti-aliasing quality, and the longer render time will be. In general, use a value of **4** for medium quality, **8** for high quality, and **16** for ultra high quality.

> ✎ Note: Motion blur and depth–of–field
> The quality of the motion blur and depth–of–field effects can be improved by increasing the value of the **Camera (AA)** setting.

Open **studio-lighting-01.max**. Press **F10** to open the **Render Setup** window. In the **Arnold Renderer** panel > **Sampling and Ray Depth** rollout, change **Camera (AA), Diffuse, Specular, Transmission, SSS,** and **Volume Indirect** samples to **1** each. Render the scene [see Fig. 20]. Notice that there is lots of noise in the render because we have only used **1** ray-per-pixel.

Now, in the **Render Setup** window, change **Camera (AA)** to **5**. Render the scene [see Fig. 21]. Notice that we are now able to remove substantial amount of noise from the render because of the higher number of AA rays [5*5=25 rays-per-pixel].

In practice, you will not be using the **Camera (AA)** setting to increase or decrease the quality of the render without paying any attention to other available ray types and the origin of the noise. Close the file.

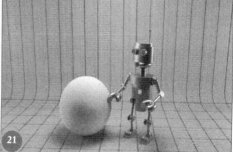

Diffuse Samples

This setting controls the number of rays fired when computing the reflected indirect-radiance. When this value is greater than zero, the camera rays intersecting with the diffuse surfaces fire indirect diffuse rays. The diffuse rays are fired in random directions within a hemispherical spread. The noise is introduced when there are insufficient rays to resolve the range of values from the environment. You can increase **Diffuse** samples value to reduce the indirect diffuse noise and improve quality. Fig. 22 is from Arnold website which shows how diffuse rays are propagated in the Arnold render.

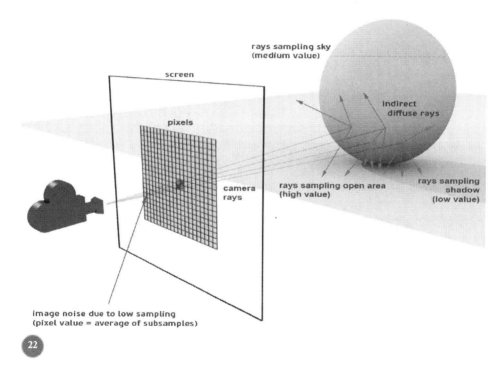

Open **studio-lighting-04.max**. Press **F10** to open the **Render Setup** window. In the **Arnold Renderer** panel > **Sampling and Ray Depth** rollout, change **Diffuse** > **Samples** to 0 and then render the scene [see Fig. 23]. Notice in Fig. 23 that there is no indirect lighting or global illumination in the scene. The render is only showing the effect of the direct lighting.

In the **Render Setup** window > **AOVs** panel, click **Add AOV File** and then expand **builtin** option in the list. Now, select **diffuse_direct** and **diffuse_indirect** using **Ctrl** and then click **Add** to add the diffuse AOV channels. Render the scene. Fig. 24 shows the **diffuse_direct** channel and Fig. 25 shows the **diffuse_indirect** channel. The render is black because we have set **Diffuse > Samples** to **0**.

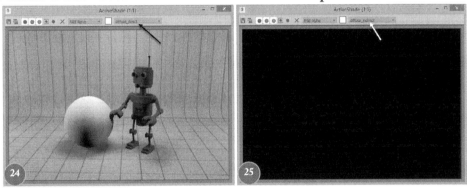

Change **Diffuse > Samples** to **1** and then render the scene; Fig. 26 shows the **diffuse_indirect** channel. The most common cause of noise in a render is due to indirect diffuse noise. It will be more visible in the shadowed areas. Now, we know that the noise in Fig. 26 is indirect diffuse noise Therefore, instead of raising the value of **Camera (AA)** samples, we will raise **Diffuse > Samples** samples.

Change **Diffuse > Samples** to **5** and render the scene; Fig. 27 shows the **diffuse_indirect** channel. If you compare Fig. 27 with Fig. 26, you will notice that we have quite cleaner result now. Fig. 28 shows the resulting RGBA channel.

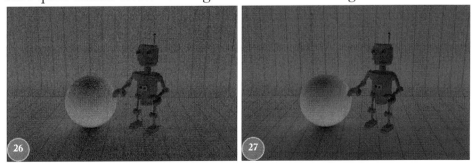

Specular Samples

This setting controls the number of rays fired when computing the reflected indirect-radiance integrated over the hemisphere weighted by a specular BRDF. Fig. 29 from Arnold's website shows how specular rays are propagated in the Arnold render.

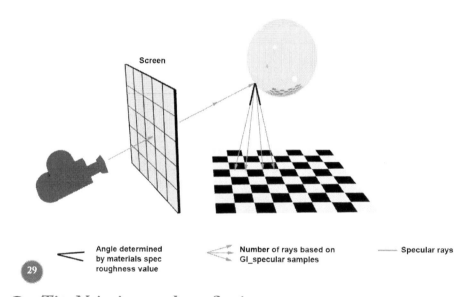

| Angle determined by materials spec roughness value | Number of rays based on GI_specular samples | Specular rays |

Tip: Noise in specular reflections
*Change the number of **Specular** > **Samples** to **0** and **Specular** > **Ray Depth** to*
***0**. If noise disappears in the render then the noise is due to specular reflections.*

Open **studio-lighting-02.max**. Press **F10** to open the **Render Setup** window. In the **AOVs** panel, click **Add AOV Channel(s) to this EXR file** and then add the **specular_direct** and **specular_indirect** AOVs from the **builtin** group. In the **Arnold Renderer** panel > **Sampling and Ray Depth** rollout, change **Camera (AA)**, **Diffuse**, **Transmission**, **SSS**, and **Volume Indirect** samples to 1 each.

Change **Specular** > **Samples** to **0** and then render the scene. As expected, the **specular_indirect** channel will render black because there are no samples to calculate indirect specular component. Fig. 30 shows the **specular_direct** channel. Notice in

Fig. 30 that the sphere at the left is not appearing in the render because the material applied to it has no specularity. Change **Camera (AA)** and **Specular** samples to **2** and **5**, respectively. Render the scene; Figs. 31 and 32 show the **specular_direct** and **specular_indirect** channels, respectively.

To improve the **specular_direct** pass, we need to increase the light samples. Select **leftLight** and then in the **Modify** panel > **Rendering** rollout, change **Samples** to 4. Repeat the process for other two lights and then render the scene. Fig. 33 shows the improved **specular_direct** pass. Close the file.

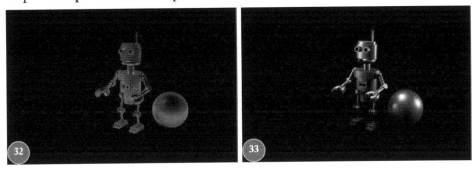

Transmission Samples

This setting controls the number of samples used to simulate the microfacet-based transmission evaluations.

Tip: Noise in transmission
*Change the number of **Transmission** samples to **0** and **Transmission** **Ray Depth** to **0**. If noise disappears in the render then the noise is due to transmission.*

Open **studio-lighting-03.max**. Press **F10** to open the **Render Setup** window. Render the scene [see Fig. 34]. In the **Arnold Renderer** panel > **Sampling and Ray Depth** rollout, change **Camera (AA)**, **Diffuse**, **Specular**, and **Transmission** to 4, 3, 3, and 5, respectively. Render the scene [see Fig. 35].

SSS [Sub Surface Scattering] Samples

This setting controls the number of lighting samples [direct and indirect] that will be taken to estimate lighting within a radius of the point being shaded to compute sub-surface scattering. The higher the values you specify, the cleaner the result be, and the longer the render time will be.

 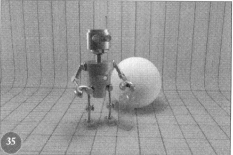

This settings is used to control the number of rays fired to compute the indirect lighting of the volume.

Ray Depth

The **Ray Depth** settings corresponding to the **Diffuse, Specular, Transmission,** and **Volume Indirect** samples allow you to configure settings that limit the ray recursion based on ray type. The higher the value you specify, the longer the render time will be. The different ray depth options are discussed next.

Diffuse

The **Diffuse > Ray Depth** parameter controls the diffuse depth bounces. If you set **Diffuse > Ray Depth** to 0, there will be no diffuse illumination in the scene. On increasing the depth, there will be more bounced light in the scene, which can be especially noticeable in the interior scenes. Figs. 36, 37, and 38 show the render with **Diffuse Ray > Depth** set to 0, 1, and 2, respectively. Also, refer to **diffuse-rays.max**.

Specular

The **Specular > Ray Depth** parameter allows you to define the maximum number of times a ray can be glossily reflected. Figs. 39, 40, and 41 show the render with **Specular > Ray Depth** set to 0, 1, and 2, respectively. Also, refer to **specular-rays.max**.

Transmission

The **Transmission > Ray Depth** parameter allows you to define the maximum number of times a ray can be refracted. If there are many refractive surfaces in the scene, you may require to use higher ray depth value. Fig. 42 shows the ray depth required for a glass surface with double-sided thickness. Figs. 43, 44, and 45 show the render with **Transmission > Ray Depth** set to **4**, **8**, and **16**, respectively. Also, refer to **transmission-rays.max**.

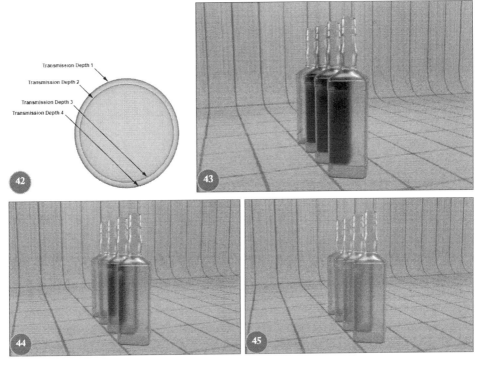

Note: Depth Limits

The options in the **Sampling and Ray Depth** *rollout >* **Depth Limits** *group allow you to set the depth limits for the rays. The* **Ray Limit Total** *parameter specifies the total recursion depth of any ray in the scene. The total rays should be less than equal to the sum of the* **Diffuse**, **Transmission**, *and* **Specular** *rays.*

The **Transparency Depth** *parameter specifies number of allowed transparency hits. When you raise this value, it allows Arnold to pass more rays through the transparent surfaces. Figs. 46, 47, and 48 show the render with* **Transparency Depth** *set to* **1**, **5**, *and* **14**, *respectively. Also, refer to* **t–depth.max**. *There are six boxes in this scene overlapping each other. The opacity is created using the material's* **Opacity (Cutout)** *parameter. This parameter is available in the* **Special Features** *rollout of the material.*

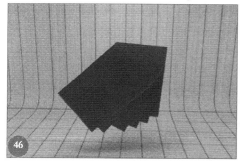 

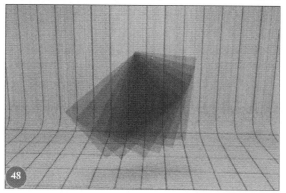

What Low Light Threshold does?

Raising the value of the **Low Light Threshold** *parameter allows to speed up the rendering by not tracing a shadow ray for light samples who contribution is below a certain threshold value. Figs. 49 and 50 shows render with the* **Low Light Threshold** *value set to* **0.13** *and* **0.01**, *respectively. Also, refer to the* **llt.max** *file.*

Volume Indirect

The **Volume Indirect** setting defines the number of multiple scattering bounces within a volume. This is specially useful in rendering large volumes of clouds. Fig. 51 shows the render with the **Volume Indirect** value set to **0** [the default value] and **5**, respectively.

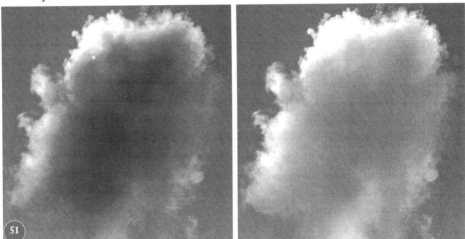

Quiz

Fill in the Blanks
Fill in the blanks in each of the following statements:

1. Arnold uses the physically-based _____ ray/path tracing engine thus eliminating the possibility of artifacts produced by the caching algorithms.

2. The advantage of using physically-based workflow is that artists can work in a physically accurate and _____ dynamic workflow.

3. Arnold is a _____ renderer. _____ and _____ are one of the most important settings for the Arnold raytracer.

4. The _____ samples parameter is global multiplier for all other components.

5. The _____ samples setting controls the number of rays fired when computing the reflected indirect-radiance.

6. The _____ samples setting controls the number of samples used to simulate the microfacet-based transmission evaluations.

7. The _____ parameter allows you to define the maximum number of times a ray can be glossily reflected.

8. The _____ control allows you to define the maximum number of times a ray can be refracted.

True or False
State whether each of the following is true or false:

1. Arnold developed by Solid Angle [a wholly owned subsidiary of Autodesk Inc] is an advanced cross-platform rendering API library.

2. The photon mapping or final gather methods consume large amounts of memory and introduce bias into the sampling thus producing artifacts.

3. Increasing the sample rate does not remove the noise from the rendered images.

4. The **Camera (AA) Samples** value controls the quality of anti-aliasing.

5. The **Specular > Samples** setting defines the number of rays fired when computing the reflected indirect-radiance integrated over the hemisphere weighted by a specular BRDF.

6. The **Diffuse > Samples** setting defines the diffuse depth bounces.

Summary
The unit covered the following topics:

- Why Arnold is different?
- What's wrong with the biased algorithms?
- What are the advantages of being physically-based?
- Studio Lighting
- Sampling and Ray Depth

- Arnold lights
- Limitations of the Arnold lights
- Light filters
- Fog shader
- Atmospheric Volume shader

Unit DA2: Arnold Lights

To achieve professional-quality, realistic renders in 3ds Max, you need to master the art of lighting. Lights play an important role in the visual process. They shape the world we see. The trick to simulate realistic looking light effects is to observe the world around us. The lights you create, illuminate other objects in the scene. The material applied to the objects simulates color and texture.

To access Arnold lights, in the **Create** panel, click **Lights**, and then select **Arnold** from the drop-down list available below **Lights** [see Fig. 1]. Now, click **Arnold Light** in the **Object Type** rollout; the **Name and Color, General, Shape, Color/Intensity, Rendering, Shadow, Contribution**, and **AOV** rollouts will be displayed.

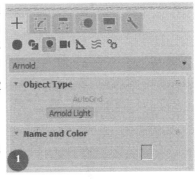

Now, click-drag in a viewport to create a light in the scene.

There are some limitations when using the 3ds Max's **Photometric** lights with Arnold. Here's is the quick rundown of the features not supported by Arnold:

- Some of the light shapes do not support the **Spherical** distribution.
- Only raytraced shadows are supported, rest of the settings are ignored by Arnold.
- The **Exclude/Include** feature is not supported.
- Incandescent lamp-color shift is not supported.
- The light shape is not visible to the camera rays.
- Shadow parameters are not supported.
- The legacy **Atmosphere and Effects** are not supported.

Caution: Exposure Control
*The **Physical Scale** value in the **Environment and Effects** window >*
***Exposure Control** > **Physical Scale** group influences the rendering with*
Arnold lights. In order to get the correct intensity, you need to disable or
*adjust the **Physical Scale** value to get the expected intensity [refer to Fig. 2].*

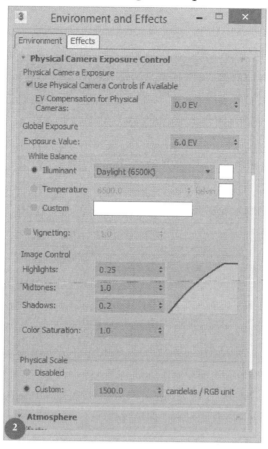

Caution: Constant light decay
The constant light decay feature is not supported in Arnold. However, the
***Quad** and **Disk** area lights have a **Spread** parameter that you can use to*
*mimic constant falloff. Similarly, the **Spotlight** type has a **Lens Radius***
parameter that you can use along with a low angle to mimic the constant
falloff. Another workaround to get constant falloff is to use the distant/
directional lighting.

Quad Light

The **Quad** light type simulates light from an area source [refer to Fig. 3]. The source can be defined as a quadrilateral specified using four vertices. The following rollouts appear for this light type.

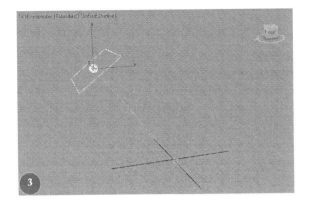

General

The **On** check box is used to toggle the light on/off [refer to Fig. 4]. By default, the **Targeted** check box is selected. As a result, the light will have target object that you can use to point light towards an object. The **Targ. Dist** parameter controls the distance between the light and its target object.

Shape

The options in the **Type** drop-down list are used to select the light type [refer to Fig. 5]. The default light is **Quad**. Other options available are: **Point, Distant, Spot, Quad, Disc, Cylinder, Skydome, Photometric,** and **Mesh**.

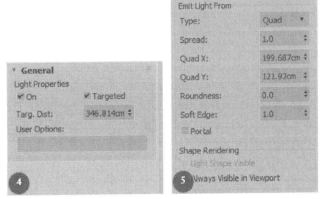

The **Spread** parameter controls the focus of the light in the direction along the normal. The default value for this parameters is **1**. As a result, a diffuse emission of the light is produced. A value of **0** produces a focused laser beam type of emission. The images in Fig. 6 show the render with the **Spread** value set to **0.2, 0.5,** and **1,** respectively. Refer to **spread.max**.

Caution: Noise
*Keep in mind that the low **Spread** values produce more noise than the higher values.*

The **Quad X** and **Quad** Y parameters control the four corner points of the quadrilateral. The **Roundness** parameter allows you to change the shape of the light from square [value=0, default] to disc [value=1]. The images in Fig. 7 show the shape of the light with **Roundness** is set to **0, 0.5,** and **1,** respectively. Refer to **roundness.max**.

The **Soft Edge** parameter controls the smooth falloff for the edges of the light shape. This parameter works similar to the penumbra angle of spot lights. The images in Fig. 8 show the falloff with **Soft Edge** is set to **1, 0.5,** and **0,** respectively. Refer to **soft-edge.max**.

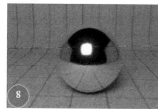

When you select the **Portal** check box, the light object does not generate any illumination and the light object becomes a light portal. You can use portals with **Skydome** lights to reduce noise in interior scenes. In such scenarios, light portals are used to guide the skydome light sampling instead of emitting light. In order to guide the samples, light portal must be placed to cover all windows, doors, and other openings through which the skydome light comes into the scene.

When the **Light Shape Visible** check box is selected, the shape of the light is visible as a self-illuminated object in the render. This option is only available for the **Skydome** type. On selecting the **Always Visible in Viewport** check box, the shape of the light will be visible in the viewport even if light is de-selected.

Color/Intensity
The **Color** parameter controls the color emitted by the light. The are some presets available for the light color. You can select them from the **Preset** drop-down list. You can use the **Kelvin** parameter to specify the light temperature using Kelvin values. The middle and right images in Fig. 9 show the render with **Kelvin** value set to **4000** and **12000,** respectively.

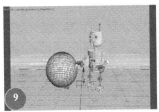  

The **Texture** parameter can be used to apply a map to the light that will set its color. Fig. 10 shows the render when I connected a HDR map to the **Texture** parameter. Also, refer to the **light-texture.max**. The **Filter Color** parameter allows you to select a color that will be added to the main color of the light.

The **Intensity** parameter controls the brightness of the light source by multiplying the color. The **Exposure** parameter is a f-stop value which multiplies the intensity by $2^{Exposure}$. Therefore, increasing the **Exposure** value by **1** will result in the double the amount of light emitted. The following formula is used for the total amount of light emitted: **Color * Intensity * $2^{Exposure}$**

You can get the same output by either modifying the **Intensity** or **Exposure** value. For example, if you set **Color** to white, **Intensity** to **2**, and **Exposure** to **3**; the output will be **16** [**1** * **2** * **2³**]. You can get same output by setting **Intensity** to **16** and **Exposure** to **0** to get output as **16** [**1*16* 2⁰**]. The **Res. Intensity** label displays the output computed using **Intensity** and **Exposure**.

When the **Normalize Energy** check box is selected, you can control the softness of the shadows changing the size/radius of the light without affecting the amount of emitted light. If you clear this check box, the amount of emitted light is proportional to the surface area of the light.

The images in Fig. 11 show the output with the **Normalize Energy** check box selected and cleared, respectively. The size of the **Quad** light used is **30x30**, refer to **normalize-energy.max**. The images in Fig. 12 show the output with size of the **Quad** light set to **50x50** and **200x200**, respectively. Notice the difference in the softness of the shadows. The **Normalize Energy** check box is cleared in this case.

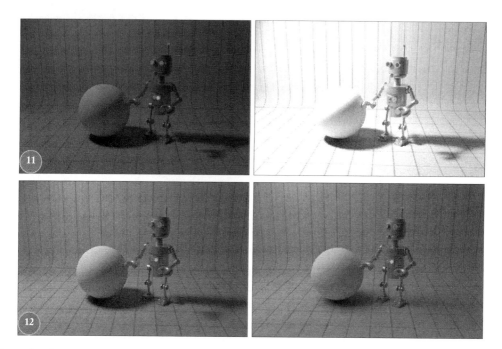

Rendering

The **Samples** parameter controls the quality of the noise in specular highlights and soft shadows. The higher the value you specify, the lower the noise, and the longer it will take to render. The number of shadow rays sent to the light are equal to the square of the value you specify for the **Samples** parameter multiplied by the **AA** samples. The images in Fig 13 show the render with **Samples** set to 1 and 4, respectively. The **Volume Samples** parameter controls the number of samples used to integrate the in-scattering from direct light. Like the **Samples** parameter, it is also a squired value.

Shadow

The **Cast Shadows** and **Atmospheric Shadows** check boxes allow you enable or disable the computation of the shadow cast from the light and volumetric shadows, respectively. The **Atmospheric Shadows** parameter is not available for the **Distance** and **Skydome** light types.

The **Color** parameter defines the intensity of each color channel for shadows. The **Density** parameter defines the density of strength of the shadows. Normally, you would use a value of **1** which is the default value. The images in Fig. 14 show the strength of shadow with **Density** set to **0, 0.5,** and **1,** respectively.

Contribution

The **Diffuse, Specular, Transmission, SSS,** and **Volume** parameters control the per-light scaling of the diffuse, specular, transparency, sub-surface scattering, and volume components. To produce physically accurate results, the value should be **1** for the contribution. The **Indirect** parameter defines the relative energy loss/gain at each bounce. This parameter should be left at **1** for physically accurate results.

The **Max. Bounces** parameter defines the maximum number of time the energy from the light is allowed to bounce in the scene. A value of **0** will disable global illumination in the scene. This parameter works along with the global ray depth defined in the **Render Setup** window therefore the maximum value of **999** is a theoretical maximum. In practice, the actual ray depth limits are much lower.

When the **Affect Viewport** check box is selected, the light will be used for lighting the scene in the viewport.

> *Note: Other light types*
> *Now, let's explore other light types available in Arnold. The common light parameters have already been discussed in the **Quad Light** section. Following sections describe additional parameters.*

Point Light

The **Point** light type [see Fig. 15] simulates light from a point like a light bulb. Although, the name of the light is **Point** for historical reasons but in practice, a point light is an emissive sphere. The **Radius** parameter defines the radius of the light's spherical radius. If you specify a value of **0** for this parameter then it becomes a true point light with no physical size and it will cast sharp shadows, see Fig. 16.

Distant Light

This light is used to simulate light coming from a distant light source. It is often used to model sunlight. The **Angle** parameter defines the angular size of the Sun. Non-zero values produces realistic looking soft shadows. For example, if you use a value of **1** or **2**, this light will produce slightly soft shadows like produced by hazy sunshine. Higher values like **6** produce much softer shadows.

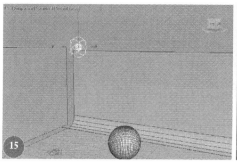

Spot Light

The **Spot** light [see Fig. 17] simulates light from a spot light. You can use this light to simulate flashlight, a follow spot on a stage, or the headlights of the car.

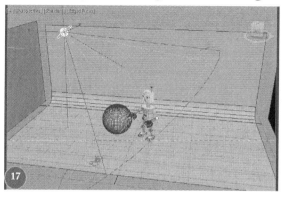

If you set **Radius** to **0**, the cone of light will emanate from a notional point source. With non-zero values, the light source will behave like a spherical source. The radius of the sphere is controlled by the **Radius** parameter. The images in Fig. 18 show the render with **Radius** set to **0, 2,** and **6,** respectively.

The **Cone Angle** parameter defines the cone angle in degrees. No light can be simulated outside this cone. The **Lens Radius** parameter controls the position of the vertex of the cone. If you specify a value of **0** for the **Cone Angle** parameter, the position of the light coincides with the vertex of the cone.

If value is non-zero, the light comes from a virtual position that falls behind the specified position of the light. The images in Fig. 19 show the output when **Lens Radius** is set to **0, 1,** and **2,** respectively.

The **Penumbra Angle** parameter is measured in degrees from the outer edge of the cone towards the spot light's axis. In the area defined by this parameter, the light's intensity smoothly falls off to zero at the cone's edge.

You can use the **Aspect Ratio** parameter to simulate theater lights such as PAR cans that produce elliptical cross sections. The default aspect ratio of **1** produces circular cross-section. The images in Fig. 20 shows the cross sections with **Aspect Ratio** set to **0.1, 0.3**, and **1**, respectively. Refer to **spot-aspect.max**.

The **Roundness** parameter controls the roundness of the shape of the spot light. The images in Fig. 21 shows the cross sections with **Roundness** set to **0, 0.5**, and **1**, respectively.

Disc Light

The **Disc** light [see Fig. 22] is used to simulate light from a circular area source. The source will always be circular. The **Radius** parameter controls the radius of the disk.

Cylinder Light

The **Cylinder** light [see Fig. 23] is used to simulate light coming from the tube shape objects. The **Radius** parameter is used to increase or decrease the cylindrical light size. The higher the value you specify for this parameter, the larger the area size, and the softer the area shadows will be. The **Height** parameter is used to scale the height of the light.

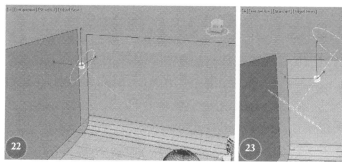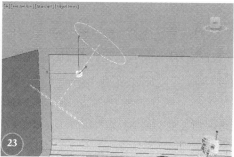

Skydome Light

The **Skydome** light allows you to simulate light coming from a hemisphere or dome above the scene. You can also this light with HDR images to simulate image-based lighting. It is specifically used for rendering exterior scenes.

 Caution: Interior scenes
*This light specifically suitable for exterior lighting and is represented by a dome above the scene. In interior scenes, most of the trace rays will hit an object. As a result, there will be noise in the render. You can reduce noise by using light portals when using the **Skydome** lighting.*

 Note: Environment
*When you add an **Environment** map, **Skydome** light is automatically enabled. As a result, no extra light creation is required. You can specify the environment settings from the **Render Setup** window > **Arnold Renderer** rollout > **Environment, Background & Atmosphere** rollout.*

The **Resolution** parameter controls the details of reflections on the skydome. For the accurate results, match this value with the resolution of the HDR image. However, in many cases, you can lower the value without a noticeable loss of detail in reflections. The higher the value you specify for this parameter, the longer it will take to precompute the importance table for the light. As a result, scene startup time will increase.

The options in the **Format** drop-down list allow you to select the type of map being connected. The available options are: **Lat-long, Mirrored Ball,** and **Angular.** The options in the **Portal** drop-down list allow you to define how **Skydome** lights interacts with the light portals. The following three options are available:

- **Off:** This option disables the portals.
- **Interior Only:** It blocks any light placed outside portals for interior only scenes.
- **Interior/Exterior:** This option lets light outside portals through for mixed interior and exterior scenes.

Tip: Transparent background
*By default, the skydome lights are visible in the background. If you lower the contribution of the camera rays, you will make them invisible. You can lower the contribution by changing the value of the **Camera** parameter in the **Contribution** rollout.*

Caution: Atmosphere Volume shader
*The **Skydome** light doesn't work with the **Atmosphere Volume** shader. You must use regular lights that have a precise location and size, and the inverse-square decay enabled.*

Mesh Light

The **Mesh** light can be used in situations where the conventional light shapes are not suffice. Some effects such as neon lighting can be achieved more easily with the **Mesh** light. To assign a geometry to the **Mesh** light, click **None** in the **Shape** rollout > **Emit Light From** group and then click on the geometry in the viewport.

Caution: NURBS Surfaces
*At present, NURBS surfaces do not work with the **Mesh** lights.*

Caution: Mesh lights and camera rays
*At present, the mesh light is not visible to camera rays. A workaround is create a **Standard Surface** shader and then in the **Parameter Editor** > **Emission** rollout, change emission value to **1**. In the **Base** rollout, change base color strength to **0**. Now, apply this material to the geometry. This workaround will give the impression is that the geometry is incandescent.*

Photometric Light

The **Photometric** lights use data measured from the real-wold lights often provided by the manufacturers themselves. You can import IES profiles from the companies like **Osram** and **Philips**. These companies provide accurate intensity and spread data. To assign a IES file to the light, make sure the light is selected and then in the **Modify** panel > **Shape** rollout, click the browse button corresponding to the **File** parameter and then select the file using the **Select File** dialog box. Refer to Figs. 24, 25, and **photo-light.max**.

Caution: IES Files
*Some of the light manufactures put extra text at the beginning of IES files. If you are facing difficulties in rendering an IES file, open it in a text editor such as **Notepad**. If there is extra text at the beginning, delete it. The file should typically start with **TILT=NONE**.*

Light Filters

Light filters in Arnold are arbitrary shaders that you can use to modify the output of the light based on its distance, position, and other factors. In Arnold for 3ds Max, these filters are available as modifiers. These filters will only be available if you select an Arnold light. The Arnold light filters are discussed next:

Arnold Barn Doors Filter

Barn doors are used in theatrical and film lighting. These are opaque moving panel attached to the sides of the light opening. You can use these doors with Arnold's **Spot** light. When you apply **Arnold Barn Doors Filter** to a **Spot** light, you can access four flaps [**Top, Bottom, Left,** and **Right**] from the **Modify** panel > **Barn Doors** rollout. Each flap has three groups of parameters [**Top, Bottom,** and **Edge**] that you can use to precisely position flaps. Fox example, you can use the **Top Left, Top Right,** and **Top Edge** to control the left corner of the top flap, right corner of top flap, and edge softness of the top flap, respectively. Refer to Figs. 26 and 27.

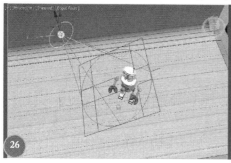
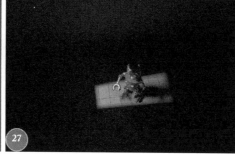

Arnold Gobo Filter

Gobo filters [or cookies] are used in theatrical and film lighting. A gobo is a thin sheet of metal with holes to break up the light beam into an irregular pattern. To apply gobo to a **Spot** light, select it and then from the **Object-Space Modifiers** section of the **Modifier** list, select **Arnold Gobo Filter**. In the **Modify** panel > **Gobo** rollout, assign a map using the **Color** button in the **Slide Map** group and then render the scene to see the effect [refer to Fig. 28 and **gobo-filter.max**]. Any texture map or procedural shader can be projected through the light.

The options in the **Filter** Mode drop-down list allow you to control the blending equation by which the slide map of the gobo is combined with the light's output. **blend** is the default option [refer to Fig. 28]. The images in Fig. 29 show the output with **Filter Mode** to set to **replace, add**, and **mix**, respectively.

The **Density** parameter controls the density of the gobo. The higher the value you specify, the more opaque the gobo will be. The images in Fig. 30 show the output with **Density** set to **0, 0.5**, and **0.75**, respectively.

The **Offset** parameter allows you to offset the direction of the texture map. The **Scale S** and **Scale T** parameters are used to scale the map in the S and T directions, respectively. The **Wrap S** and **Wrap T** parameters control how the texture map is repeated in the S and T directions, respectively.

Arnold Blocker Filter

Arnold Blocker Filter is a flexible filter that allows you to artificially mask the light beams without adding additional geometry thus giving the artistic freedom. There are four types are blockers available: **box, sphere, plane**, and **cylinder**. You can select the blockers from the **Type** drop-down list available in the **Blocker** rollout > **Properties** group. Fig. 31 shows the **box** blocker in action [also, refer to **blocker.max**].

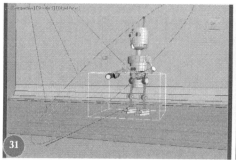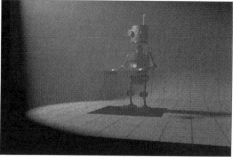

You can control the position, scale, and rotation of the blocker using the parameters available in the **Position, Rotation**, and **Scale** groups of the **Blocker** rollout. You can also mask the effect by connecting a texture map with the filter using the parameters available in the **Shader** group. Unlike gobos, you can position a shadow independently of the light transform using **Arnold Blocker Filter** and it works with all lights. Gobos also contribute to the illumination in the scene. However, the shader mask only works if you set **Type** to **box**.

Arnold Decay Filter

By default, all Arnold lights have physically-based falloff. However, if you want to adjust falloff manually, you can use **Arnold Decay Filter**. It allows you to adjust both near and far attenuations. The images in Fig. 32 show the effect of the filter. Also, refer to the **decay-filtcr.max**.

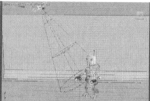

Hands-on Exercises

Exercise 1: Working with the Mesh Light
In this exercise, we are going to work with the mesh light [see Fig. E1].

Table E1 summarizes the exercise.

Table E1	
Topics	• Getting Ready • Working with the Mesh Light
Skill level	Beginner
Time to complete	20 Minutes
Resources folder	**unit-da2**
Start file	**mesh-light-start.max**
Final file	**mesh-light-finish.max**

Getting Ready

Open **mesh-light-start.max**.

Working with the Mesh Light

Follow these steps:

1. In the **Create** panel, click **Lights**, and then select **Arnold** from the drop-down list below **Lights**. Now, in the **Object Type** rollout, click **Arnold Light**, and then create a light in the scene.

2. Switch to the **Modify** panel and then in the **Shape** rollout, change **Type** to **Mesh**. Click the **None** button and then click on **Mesh01** in the viewport. Render the scene [see Fig. E2].

What just happened?
*Here, we have made **Mesh01** emit light in the scene but as you can see in Fig. E2 that light source itself is not visible.*

What next?
*At present, there are no parameters available to make the light source visible using the **Modify** panel. A workaround is to create an emissive **Standard Surface** Arnold material and apply it to the light mesh in the scene.*

3. Press **M** to open the **Slate Material Editor**. In the **Material/Map Browser > Materials > Arnold > Surface** rollout, drag **Standard Surface** to the active view. In the **Parameter Editor > Base** rollout, set base color strength to **0**. In the **Emission** rollout, set emission strength to **1**. Assign the material to **Mesh01** in the scene.

4. Select light in the scene and then in the **Modify** panel > **Rendering** rollout, change **Samples** to **4**. Render the scene [see Fig. E3].

What next?
*Notice in Fig. E3 that the emissive material is contributing to the diffuse lighting. We need to disable GI bounces for the mesh as the **Mesh** light is already emitting light.*

5. Select **Mesh01** and then from the **Object-Space Modifiers** section of the **Modifier** list, select **Arnold Properties**. In the **Modify** panel > **General Properties** rollout, select the **Visibility** check box and clear the **Diffuse Reflections** check box. Render the scene [see Fig. E4].

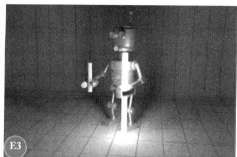

6. Convert **Mesh02** to a mesh light, as discussed above. Render the scene [see Fig. E5].

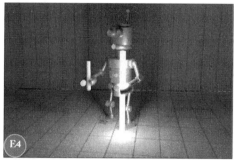

7. Press **F10** to open the **Render Setup** window. In the **Arnold Renderer** panel > **Sampling and Ray Depth** rollout, change **Camera (AA)**, **Diffuse**, and **Specular** samples to **4**, **6**, and **4**, respectively. Render the scene [see Fig. E6].

8. Now, adjust the **Exposure** value to get the output you are looking for.

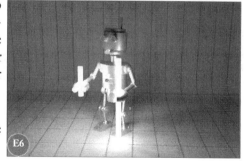

Exercise 2: Working with the Barn Doors Filter
In this exercise, we are going to work with **Arnold Barn Doors Filter** [see Fig. E1].

Table E2 summarizes the exercise.

Table E2	
Topics	• Getting Ready • Working with the Barn Doors Filter
Skill level	Beginner
Time to complete	20 Minutes
Resources folder	**unit-da2**
Start file	**barn-doors-start.max**
Final file	**barn-doors-finish.max**

Getting Ready
Open **barn-doors-start.max**.

Working with the Barn Doors Filter
Follow these steps:

1. Select **topLight** and then from the **Object-Space Modifiers** section of the **Modifier** list, select **Arnold Barn Doors Filter**. The barn doors flaps are represented by the blue wireframe at the bottom of the **Spot** light's cone [see Fig. E2].

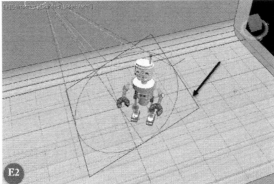

2. In the **Modify** panel > **Barns Doors** rollout > **Top** group, change **Left** to **0.2**.

What just happened?
*By increasing the value of **Top > Left**, we have clipped the effect of the light using the top flap from the left side. Refer to Figs. E3 and E4.*

What next?
*Now, we will increase the **Top > Right** value to match it with the left value. We will also increase the **Top > Edge** value to soften the effect of the barn doors.*

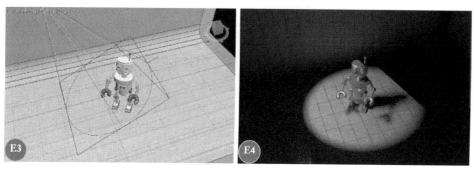

3. In the **Modify** panel > **Barns Doors** rollout > **Top** group, change **Right** to **0.2** and **Edge** to **0.05** [see Figs. E5 and E6].

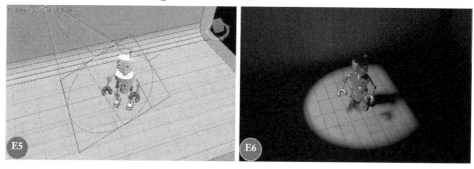

4. Repeat the process for the **Bottom** flap. To match the **Bottom** values with the **Top** values, change **Bottom** > **Left** and **Bottom** > **Right** to **0.8** each [1-0.2=0.8]. Refer to Figs. E7 and E8.

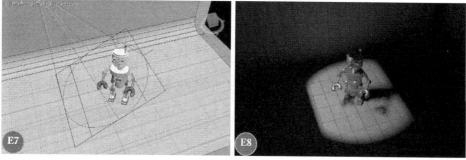

5. In the **Modify** panel > **Barns Doors** rollout > **Left** group, change **Top, Bottom** and **Edge** to **0.2, 0.2**, and **0.05**, respectively.

6. In the **Modify** panel > **Barns Doors** rollout > **Right** group, change **Top, Bottom** and **Edge** to **0.8, 0.8**, and **0.05**, respectively [see Figs. E9 and E10].

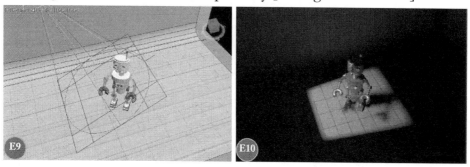

Exercise 3: Working with the Skydome Light

In this exercise, we will illuminate an interior scene using the **Skydome** light [see Fig. E1].

Table E3 summarizes the exercise.

Table E3	
Topics	• Getting Ready • Illuminating the Interior Using the Skydome Light • Illuminating the Interior Using Quad Lights
Skill level	Beginner
Time to complete	30 Minutes
Resources folder	**unit-da2**
Start file	**interior-start.max**
Final file	**interior-finish.max** **interior-finish-02.max**

Getting Ready

Open **interior-start.max**. This scene is taken from the Arnold's website. You can download this file and other scene files from the following page:

https://docs.arnoldrenderer.com/display/A5AF3DSUG/Learning+Scenes

Illuminating the Interior Using the Skydome Light

Follow these steps:

1. In the **Create** panel, click **Lights**, and then select **Arnold** from the drop-down list below **Lights**. Now, in the **Object Type** rollout, click **Arnold Light**, and then change **Type** to **Skydome**. Now, click in the viewport to create a light.

2. Select light in the scene and then in the **Modify** panel > **Color/Intensity** rollout > **Intensity** group, change **Intensity** to **1.3** and **Exposure** to **1**. In the **Rendering** rollout, change **Samples** to **4**. Render the scene [see Fig. E2].

3. In the **Shape** rollout > **Shape Rendering** group, select the **Light Shape Visible** check box. Render the scene [see Fig. E3].

What next?
*Notice In Fig. E3 that there is lots of noise in the render. Now, we will create three portal lights to guide the **Skydome** samples to the interior to reduce the noise.*

4. In the **Shape** rollout, change **Portal Mode** to **Interior** Only.

5. In the **Create** panel, click **Lights**, and then select **Arnold** from the drop-down list below **Lights**. Now, in the **Object Type** rollout, click **Arnold Light**, and then change **Type** to **Quad**. In the **Top** viewport, create the light [see Fig. E4].

6. In the **Modify** panel > **Shape** rollout, change **Quad X** and **Quad Y** to **2341** and **1902**, respectively. Now, align the light [see Fig. E5]. Also, select the **Portal** check box. Create two more instances of the light and align them [see Fig. E6].

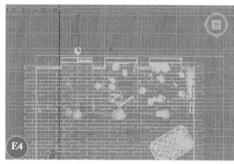
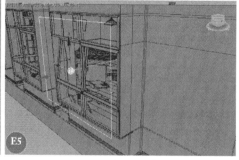

7. Select **Skydome** in the scene and then in the **Modify** panel > **Color/Intensity** rollout > **Intensity** group, change **Intensity** to **0.5** and **Exposure** to **0.8**. Render the scene [see Fig. E7].

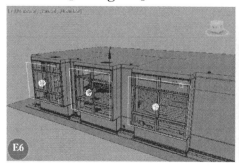

8. In the **Create** panel, click **Lights**, and then select **Arnold** from the drop-down list below **Lights**. Now, in the **Object Type** rollout, click **Arnold Light**, and then change **Type** to **Distant**. In the **Left** viewport, create the light [see Fig. E8].

9. In the **Modify** panel > **Color/Intensity** rollout > **Color** group, select the **Kelvin** radio button and then change **Kelvin** value to **4500**. In the **Rendering** rollout, change **Samples** to **4**. Render the scene[see Fig. E9].

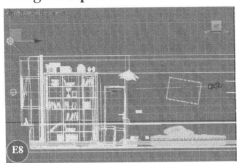 

10. Press **F10** to open the **Render Setup** window. In the **Arnold Renderer** panel > **Sampling and Ray Depth** rollout, change **Camera (AA)** and **Diffuse** samples to **5** and **6**, respectively. Also, change **Diffuse** > **Ray Depth** to **2**. Render the scene [see Fig. E10].

Illuminating the Interior Using Quad Lights
Follow these steps:

1. Press **F10** to open the **Render Setup** window. In the **Arnold Renderer** panel > **Sampling and Ray Depth** rollout, change **Camera (AA)** and **Diffuse Samples** to **3** and **2**, respectively. Also, change **Diffuse** > **Ray Depth** to **1**.

2. Select the **Skydome** light and then in the **Modify** panel > **Contribution** rollout, change **Diffuse, Specular, Transmission, SSS, Indirect**, and **Volume** to **0**. Render the scene [see Fig. E11]. In the **Shape** rollout, change **Portal Mode** to **Off**.

What just happened?
*By adjusting the contribution values, I have ensured that **Skydome** will be visible to the camera but will not contribute to indirect illumination.*

3. Select one of the portal lights and then in the **Shape** rollout, clear the **Portal** check box. Repeat process for other portal lights as well. In the **Modify** panel > **Color/Intensity** rollout > **Intensity** group, change **Intensity** to **2** and **Exposure** to **16**. Render the scene [see Fig. E12].

4. Press **F10** to open the **Render Setup** window. In the **Arnold Renderer** panel > **Sampling and Ray Depth** rollout, change **Camera (AA)** and **Diffuse** samples to **5** and **6**, respectively. Also, change **Diffuse** > **Ray Depth** to **2**. Render the scene [see Fig. E13].

Exercise 4: Working with the Image Based Lighting

In this exercise, we will illuminate an exterior scene using the **Skydome** light [see Fig. E1].

Table E4 summarizes the exercise.

Table E4	
Topics	• Getting Ready • Illuminating the Scene Using Image-Based Lighting
Skill level	Beginner
Time to complete	30 Minutes
Resources folder	**unit-da2**
Start file	**ibl-start.max**
Final file	**ibl-finish.max**

Getting Ready

Open **ibl-start.max**. This scene is taken from the Arnold's website. You can download this file and other scene files from the following page:

https://docs.arnoldrenderer.com/display/A5AF3DSUG/Learning+Scenes

Illuminating the Scene Using Image-Based Lighting

Follow these steps:

1. Press **8** to open the **Environment and Effects** window. In the **Physical Camera Exposure Control** rollout, clear the **Use Physical Camera Controls if Available** check box and then in the **Global Exposure** group, change **Exposure Value** to 13.

2. Press **F10** to open the **Render Setup** window. Change **Target** to **ActiveShade Mode** and **Renderer** to **Arnold**. Close the dialog box and then press **Shift+Q** to render the scene [see Fig. E2].

 What just happened?
*Here, I have set **Exposure Value** to 13 which is good setting for a daylight scene. We got dark render because there is no light in the scene and all illumination is coming from the default light.*

3. In the **Create** panel, click **Lights**, and then select **Arnold** from the drop-down list below **Lights**. Now, in the **Object Type** rollout, click **Arnold Light**, and then change **Type** to **Skydome**. Now, create the light in the **Perspective** view.

4. Render the scene; you will notice that the render is too bright [see Fig. E3]. Now, we will decrease the light's exposure to fix it.

5. Make sure light is selected and then in the **Modify** panel > **Color/Intensity** rollout > **Intensity** group, change **Exposure** to 5. In the **Rendering** rollout, change **Samples** to 4. Render the scene [see Fig. E4].

6. In the **Shape** rollout > **Shape Rendering** group, select the **Light Shape Visible** check box, if not already selected. In the **Color/Intensity** rollout, select the **Texture** radio button and then click **No Map** to open the **Material/Map Browser**. In the **Maps** > **General** rollout, double-click on **Bitmap** to open the **Select Bitmap Image File** dialog box. Double click on **sky.exr** to open the **OpenEXR Configuration** dialog box. Click **OK**.

7. Render the scene [see Fig. E5].

> **What Next?**
> *Notice in Fig. E5 that the orientation of the sky is not correct. Next, we will fix it.*

8. Make sure that light is selected and then in the **Modify** panel > **Shape** rollout, change **Format** to **LatLong** and **Resolution** to **2000**. Also, rotate the light to get the desired view of the sky. Render the scene [see Fig. E6].

9. Make sure light is selected and then in the **Modify** panel > **Color/Intensity** rollout > **Intensity** group, change **Exposure** to 6. Render the scene [see Fig. E7].

> **What just happened?**
> *Notice in Fig. E7 that by increasing the light's **Exposure** value, the sky is not at the correct exposure level. However, the diffuse illumination looks fine. Now, we will fix sky by using the **Contribution** values.*

10. In the **Modify** panel > **Color/Intensity** rollout > **Intensity** group, change **Exposure** to 7. In the **Contribution** rollout, change **Camera** and **Specular** to 0.25 each. Render the scene [see Fig. E8].

11. Press **F10** to open the **Render Setup** window. In the **Arnold Renderer** panel > **Sampling and Ray Depth** rollout, change **Camera (AA)** and **Diffuse** samples to **5** and **6**, respectively. Render the scene.

Exercise 5: Working with Physical Sky

In this exercise, we will illuminate an exterior scene using **Physical Sky** [see Fig. E1].

Table E5 summarizes the exercise.

Table E5	
Topics	• Getting Ready • Illuminating the Scene
Skill level	Beginner
Time to complete	30 Minutes
Resources folder	**unit-da2**
Start file	**psky-start.max**
Final file	**psky-finish.max**

Getting Ready

Open **psky-start.max**. This scene is taken from the Arnold's website. You can download this file and other scene files from the following page:

https://docs.arnoldrenderer.com/display/A5AF3DSUG/Learning+Scenes

Illuminating the Scene
Follow these steps:

1. Press **F10** to open the **Render Setup** window. Change **Target** to **ActiveShade Mode** and **Renderer** to **Arnold**. Close the window.

2. Press **8** to open the **Environment and Effects** window. In the **Physical Camera Exposure Control** rollout, clear the **Use Physical Camera Controls if Available** check box and then in the **Global Exposure** group, change **Exposure Value** to **13**.

3. In the **Common Parameters** rollout, click **Environment Map > None** button to open the **Material/Map Browser**. In the **Maps > Arnold > Environment** rollout, double-click **Physical Sky**. Render the scene [see Fig. E2].

> *Note: Physical Sky*
> *The **Physical Sky** shader allows you to implement the **Hosek-Wilkie** sky radiance model in 3ds Max. You can connect it into the 3ds Max's environment or to the **Color** input of the Arnold light. At present, this shader is invisible to **GI Diffuse** and **Specular** rays therefore if you want to use it as a light source, you must attach it to the **Skydome** light.*

4. Press **M** to open the **Slate Material Editor** and then drag the **Physical Sky** map from the **Environment and Effects** window into the active view of the material editor as an **Instance**.

5. In the **Parameter Editor > Physical Sky > Parameters** rollout, change **Intensity** to **200**. Render the scene [see Fig. E3].

> *Parameter: Intensity*
> *The **Intensity** parameter value is a scalar multiplier for the sky radiance. This value is similar to the **Sky Tint** value. The difference is that **Sky Tint** uses RGB values whereas it uses scalar values [easier to adjust].*

6. Change **X Axis** to [1, 0, 0], **Y Axis** to [0, 0, 1], and **Z Axis** to [0, 1, 0]. Render the scene [see Fig. E4]. Change **Azimuth** to **215** and **Elevation** to **30**. Render the scene [see Fig. E5]. Change **Sun Size** to **4**.

Parameters: Elevation and Azimuth

*This shader uses polar coordinate system. **Elevation** [sunrise to sunset – measured north to east] has an angle between **0** to **180** degrees whereas the **Azimuth** has an angle [angle of the Sun around horizon] between **0** to **360** degrees.*

Parameter: Sun Size

*The **Sun Size** parameter controls the size of the visible Sun disk. The default value **0.51** is the solid angle of the Sun as seen from the earth. You can increase the size of the disk for artistic purposes. Increasing the value of the **Sun Size** parameter will create softer shadows.*

7. Click on the **Ground Albedo** color swatch to open the **Color Selector** dialog box. Enter **0.5** in the **Value** spinner and click **OK**.

Parameter: Ground Albedo

*This parameter controls the amount of light reflected from earth's surface back into atmosphere. You can use a **RGB** value between **0** to **1** for this parameter.*

8. Change **Azimuth, Elevation, Sun Size, Intensity**, and **Turbidity** to 360, 12, 4, 100, and 1.5, respectively.

Parameter: Turbidity

*This parameter determines the amount of aerosol content [dust, moisture, ice, and fog] of the air. This value [range **1** to **10**] affects the color of the Sun and sky. Given below is a quick rundown of the values you can use:*

2: Produces a very clear, arctic–like sky.
3: A clear sky in a temperature climate [default value].
6: A sky on a warm–moist day.
10: A slightly hazy day.

9. Press **F10** to open the **Render Setup** window. In the **Arnold Renderer** panel > **Sampling and Ray Depth** rollout, change **Camera (AA)** and **Diffuse** samples to **4** and **3**, respectively. Render the scene.

Caution: Fireflies

*Fireflies can appear in the render if you have glass surfaces in the scene and you are using the **Physical Sky** shader to illuminate the scene. This artifacts is caused by the bright Sun disc connected to the background. A workaround is to connect a different **Physical Sky** shader to **Background** that has the **Enable Sun** parameter disabled.*

Exercise 6: Working with the Fog Shader
In this exercise, we will use the **Fog** shader to create the fog in the scene [see Fig. E1].

Table E6 summarizes the exercise.

Table E6		
Topics	• Getting Ready • Creating the Fog	
Skill level	Beginner	
Time to complete	30 Minutes	
Resources folder	**unit-da2**	
Start file	**fog-start.max**	
Final file	**fog-finish.max**	

Getting Ready
Open **fog-start.max**. This scene is taken from the Arnold's website. You can download this file and other scene files from the following page:

https://docs.arnoldrenderer.com/display/A5AF3DSUG/Learning+Scenes

Creating the Fog
Follow these steps:

1. Press **F10** to open the **Render Setup** window. In the **Arnold Renderer** tab > **Environment, Background & Atmosphere** rollout > **Atmosphere** group, click the **No Mat** button to open the **Material/Map Browser**.

2. In the **Materials** > **Arnold** > **Atmosphere** rollout, double-click on **Fog**.

Note: Fog Shader
*The **Fog** shader is used in the outdoor environments. It allows you to create effect of light scattering which causes the distant objects to appear in low contrast.*

3. Open the **Slate Material Editor** and drag **Fog** material from the **Render Setup** window to the material editor's active view as an **Instance**. Render the scene [see Fig. E2].

4. In the **Parameter Editor** > **Fog** > **Parameters** rollout, click on the **Color** swatch to open the **Color Selector** dialog box. In this dialog box, set **Hue, Sat,** and **Value** to **0, 0, 0.8**, respectively. Render the scene [see Fig. E3].

Parameter: Color
*The **Color** parameter allows you to set the color of the fog. It is recommended that you use unsaturated values for best results.*

5. Change **Distance** to **0.06** and then render the scene [see Fig. E4]. Change **Height** to **15** and then render the scene [see Fig. E5].

Parameters: Distance and Height
*The **Distance** parameter controls the density of the fog. An exponential distribution is used for the density. The higher the value you specify for this parameter, the denser the fog will be. The **Height** parameter changes the rate of exponential decay along the direction axis. The direction axis is controlled by the **Direction** parameter.*

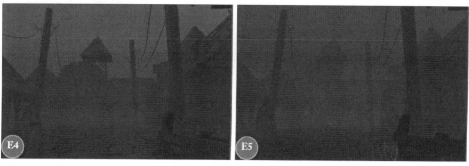

6. Change **Origin** to **[0, 0, -10]** and make sure **Direction** is set to **[0, 0, 1]**. Render the scene.

Parameter: Origin
*The **Origin** parameter controls the starting point for the fog along the direction axis. The direction axis is controlled by the **Direction** parameter.*

Exercise 7: Working with the Atmosphere Volume Shader

In this exercise, we will use the **Atmosphere Volume** shader to create the atmospheric volume in the scene [see Fig. E1].

Table E7 summarizes the exercise.

Table E7	
Topics	• Getting Ready • Creating the Volume
Skill level	Beginner
Time to complete	30 Minutes
Resources folder	**unit-da2**
Start file	**vol-start.max**
Final file	**vol-finish.max**

Getting Ready

Open **vol-start.max**.

Creating the Volume
Follow these steps:

1. Press **F10** to open the **Render Setup** window. In the **Arnold Renderer** tab > **Environment, Background & Atmosphere** rollout > **Atmosphere** group, click the **No Mat** button to open the **Material/Map Browser**.

2. In the **Materials > Arnold > Atmosphere** rollout, double-click on **Atmosphere Volume**.

    > *Note: Atmosphere Volume shader*
    > *You can use the **Atmosphere Volume** shader to simulate light scattered by a thin, uniform atmosphere. This shader is scene–wide volume shader meaning that it will affect all eligible lights in the scene. This shader works with only the **Point**, **Spot**, and **Quad** lights.*

3. Open the **Slate Material Editor** and drag **Atmosphere Volume** from the **Render Setup** window to the material editor's active view as an **Instance**.

4. In the **Parameter Editor > Atmosphere Volume > Parameters** rollout, change **Density** to **0.02**. Render the scene [see Fig. E2].

5. Click on the **Density Color** swatch to open the **Color Selector** dialog box. In this dialog box, set **Hue**, **Sat**, and **Value** to **0.6, 0.3, 0.8**, respectively. Render the scene [see Fig. E3].

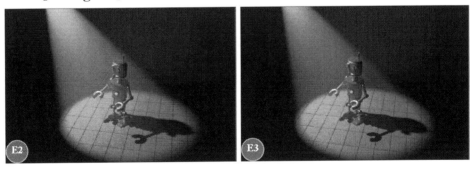

> *Parameters: Density and Density Color*
> *The **Density** parameter controls the density of the atmospheric volume. The **Density Color** value is multiplied with the value of the **Density** parameter. For example, if you set **Density Color** to red, the red light will be scattered.*

6. Change **Attenuation, Eccentricity**, and **Samples** to **0.01, 0.7**, and **8**, respectively. Render the scene.

Parameters: Attenuation, Attenuation Color, Eccentricity, and Samples

The **Attenuation** *parameter controls the rate at which the rays of lights in a scattering medium are extinguished and how much light coming from the background is blocked. The higher the value you specify, the shorter the light travels in the medium. The* **Attenuation Color** *value is multiplied with the value of the* **Attenuation** *parameter. For example, if you set* **Attenuation Color** *to red, the red light will be attenuated.*

The **Eccentricity** *parameter is the* **Henyey-Greenstein** *anisotropy coefficient which ranges from* **-1** *to* **1** *[**full back-scatter** to **full forward-scatter**]. The default value of this parameter is* **0**, *which uniformly scatters light in all directions. The positive values bias the scattering in the direction of the light [forward-scatter] whereas the negative values bias the scattering towards the light [backward-scatter]. When you change the* **Eccentricity** *value, the effect generated by light depends on whether the camera is looking toward the light or away from the light. The* **Samples** *parameter defines the quality of the scattering effect.*

 Contribution Parameters

The **Affect Camera**, **Affect Diffuse**, *and* **Affect Reflection** *parameters allow you to control the contribution of the camera rays, diffuse GI rays, and reflection rays, respectively. Non-zero values slow down the rendering speed because the GI rays now need to also do volume calculations.*

 Note: Maps

You can also use maps to affect the scattering effect. You can assign maps from the **Parameter Editor** > **Maps** *rollout of the* **Atmospheric Volume** *shader. For example, you can connect Arnold's* **Noise** *map to the* **Maps** > **Density Color** *parameter to break uniformity in the scattering effect.*

Quiz

Multiple Choice
Answer the following questions:

1. Which of the following light types is not available in Arnold?

   [A] Quad   [B] Circle
   [C] Cylinder   [D] Mesh

2. Which of the following filters is available in Arnold?

   [A] Arnold Barns Door   [B] Arnold Gobo
   [C] Arnold Blocker   [D] All of these

Fill in the Blanks
Fill in the blanks in each of the following statements:

1. The _____ light type simulates light from an area source.

2. The _____ parameter controls the focus of the light in the direction along the normal.

3. The _____ and _____ parameters control the four corner points of the quadrilateral of a **Quad** light.

4. The _____, _____, _____, and _____ parameters control the per-light scaling of the diffuse, specular, sub-surface scattering, and volume components.

5. The _____ shader allows you to implement the **Hosek-Wilkie** sky radiance model in 3ds Max.

True or False
State whether each of the following is true or false:

1. Light portals are used to guide the skydome light sampling instead of emitting light.

2. When the **Light Shape Visible** check box is selected, the shape of the light is visible as a self-illuminated object in the render.

3. You cannot use the **Temperature** parameter to specify light temperature using **Kelvin** values.

4. The following formula is used for the total amount of light emitted: **Color * Intensity * $2^{Exposure}$**

5. The **Ground Albedo** parameter controls the amount of light reflected from atmosphere into earth's surface.

Summary
The unit covered the following topics:

- Arnold lights
- Limitations of the Arnold lights
- Light filters
- Fog shader
- Atmospheric Volume shader

- Shaders
- Materials
- Subdivision and displacement mapping
- Legacy 3ds Max maps

Unit DA3: Arnold Shaders and Materials

Arnold supports most of the legacy 3ds Maps such as **Gradient, Noise,** and so on using a feature that calls native C++ maps [not materials]. This feature uses a special Arnold adapter shader.

In order to enable the legacy maps, you need to enable the **Legacy 3ds Max Support** option. To do this, press **F10** to open the **Render Setup** window. Make sure that Arnold is the active renderer. In the **System** tab of the window, select the **Legacy 3ds Max support** check box.

Caution: Legacy 3ds Max support
*Note that this feature only works within **MAXtoA**, it is not supported in the exported **.ASS** files. In some cases, there might be stability issue with **ActiveShade**.*

Here's the list of some of the limitations when using legacy maps with 3ds Max:

- The legacy feature only works within **MAXtoA** because when you use legacy maps, native 3ds Max code is called.
- Since native 3ds Max code is called, you cannot export these maps to an Arnold Scene Source file.
- Everything upstream to a shader must be a 3ds Max shader. Therefore, you cannot use an Arnold shader as input to a 3ds Max shader.
- Every legacy 3ds Max map is not guaranteed to work with Arnold.

Note: Viewport Shaders
*If you use **OSL** maps with **Arnold Surface** shaders, the texture displayed in the viewport will not match the texture displayed in the rendered output because Arnold shaders do not support shader fragments. As a result, the texture are baked before displaying the viewport.*

Caution: ActiveShade
*When **ActiveShade** is running, material previews in the material editor are not rendered because only one render session can be active in Arnold.*

 Note: Third-Party Shaders
*Any third-party shader compiled for the current version of Arnold for Windows will work in Arnold. You need to copy the **DLL/MTD/OSL** files to **Plugins/MAXtoA** folder of your 3ds Max installation. Once you copy the files, restart 3ds Max; the shaders will appear in the **Material/Map Browser**.*

Tip: V-Ray Materials
*You can covert **V-Ray** Materials to **Arnold** materials. A workaround is that you convert V-Ray materials to Autodesk's **Physical** material using the **Universal Material Converter** utility.*

*Then, you can render the **Physical** material within Arnold. This utility can be accessed from the following page: https://www.3dstudio.nl/webshop/product/1-universal-material-converter*

 Note: Supported 3ds Max materials
*The Autodesk's **Physical** material is supported by Arnold. Behind the scenes, 3ds Max translates the material to Arnold's **Standard Surface** material. However, not all features are supported by Arnold. Few material management materials such as **Multi/Sub-Object**, **Blend**, and **Double Sided** as well as pass-through features such as **Direct X Shader**, **Shell Material**, and **XRef** material are supported by Arnold.*

*Other native materials are not supported in Arnold and will render black. If you want to work with some old scenes, use the **Scene Converter** utility to upgrade materials to the **Physical** material.*

Math Shader

Mix Shader

You can use the **Mix Shader** to blend two materials. This shader is available in the **Material/Map Browser > Materials > Arnold > Math** rollout. You need to use two shaders of the same type such as the **Standard Surface** shader with the **Mix Shader**.

To get the output of the **Mix Shader**, connect two shaders of same type to the **shader1** and **shader2** ports. Then, change the blend mode using the **Mode** drop-down list. The **Mix** parameter controls the mix weight [the blending between shaders]. You can also use a map to mix the two shaders using the **Mix** parameter available in the **Maps** rollout. The left image in Fig. 1 shows **shader1**, the middle image shows **shader2**, and the right image shows the output of the **Mix** node. The blending output in Fig. 1

was generated by setting **Mode** to **blend** and specifying a weight of **0.3** for the **Mix** parameter. Also, refer to the **mix-shader.max**.

The left image in Fig. 2 shows the weight map that is used to get the result shown in the right image. Refer to **mix-shader-weight.max**.

Surface Shaders

Car Paint Shader

The **Car Paint** shader is a simple shader useful for creating car paint materials quickly. Its a layer shader with three layers: **Base**, **Specular**, and clear **Coat**. These layers work similarly to those in the **Standard Surface** shader. However, there are some unique attributes available for the **Car Paint** shader for controlling color ramps and falloff. Also, you can easily add flakes to the specular layer.

In the **Base** rollout, the **Base**, **Base Color**, and **Base Roughness** parameters define the weight, color, and roughness of the primer layer, respectively. The images in Fig. 3 show the result with **Base** set to **0**, **0.5**, and **1**. Also, refer to **car-paint.max**.

In the **Specular** rollout, the **Specular** parameter controls the weight of the base coat color. The **Specular Color** parameter defines the color of the specular reflection. It is used to tint the highlight from the base coat layer. The **Specular IOR** parameter controls the index of refraction of the base coat. The **Specular Roughness** parameter controls the glossiness of the base coat layer. The images in Fig. 4 show the result with **Specular IOR** set to **1.5**, **3**, and **6**. Also, refer to **car-paint-specular.max**.

The **Specular Flip Flop** parameter modulates the specular reflection from the base coat depending on the viewing angle. You can connect a **Ramp Rgb** map to this parameter to get the color variation. The images in Fig. 5 show the result with and without the ramp map. Fig. 6 shows the ramp. Also, refer to **car-paint-flipflop.max**.

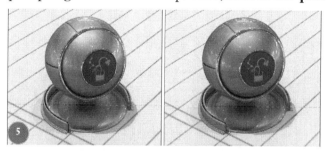

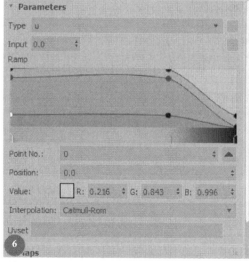

The **Specular Light Facing** parameter modulates the base coat specular color of the area facing the light source. The **Specular Falloff** parameter controls the falloff rate of the light facing color. By specifying a value of **1** for the **Specular Falloff** parameter disables the effect of the **Specular Light Facing** color. The **Flake Color** parameter in the **Flakes** rollout allows you to tint the specular highlight from flakes. The **Flake Density** parameter controls the density of flakes. If you a specify a value of **1** for this parameter, the surface will be fully covered with flakes. There will be no flakes if you specify a value of **0** for this parameter. The **Normal Randomize** parameter randomizes the orientation of the flakes. Fig. 7 shows the result with **Flake Density** and **Normal Randomize** parameters set to **0.2** and **1**, respectively. Also, refer to **car-paint-flakes.max**.

The attributes in the **Coat** rollout let you coat the material. The **Coat, Coat Color, Coat Roughness,** and **Coat IOR** parameters control the coat weight, color of the coating layer's transparency, glossiness of the specular reflections, and fresnel reflectivity of the material, respectively.

Lambert Shader

The **Lambert** shader outputs a simple RGB color using the **Simple Lambertian** reflectance model. The **Diffuse, Color,** and **Opacity** parameters control the diffuse weight, diffuse color, and opacity of the material, respectively.

Layer Shader

The **Layer Shader** allows you to mix up to eight shaders together. The **Enable** check box is used to enable or disable the layer. You can rename the layer using the **Name** parameter. The **Input [1-8]** expect a surface shader as input. The **Mix [1-8]** parameter control the blending between the input shaders. The right image in Fig. 8 shows the blending of two surface shaders, the left and middle images show the materials that are blended using the **Layer** shader. Refer to **layer-shader.max**.

Matte Shader

The **Matte** shader allows you to create holdout effects by rendering alpha as **0**. The right image in Fig. 9 shows the result when the **Matte** shader was applied to the sphere on the left. The right image shows the resulting alpha channel. Refer to **matte-shader.max**.

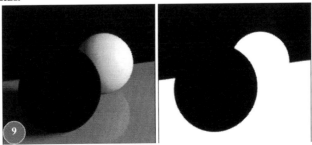

Standard Hair Shader

The **Standard Hair** shader is a physically-based shader that you can use to render hair and fur. This shader is based on the **d'Eon** model for specular and **Zinke** model for the diffuse component. This shader is designed to work with the curve shape node of Arnold and doesn't work on other type of shapes. The **Lambert** shader also work with curves but cannot accurately simulate hair scattering.

To apply this shader, create a **Standard Hair** shader node in the material editor and then select the object. Apply the **Hair and Fur (WSM)** modifier to the object. In the **Modify** panel > **Hair and Fur (WSM)** modifier > **Custom** rollout, select the **Apply Shader** check box and connect the **Standard Hair** node.

The intended workflow to connect textures to hair is to set **Melanin** to **0** and then connect texture to the **Base Color** parameter. You can leave **Diffuse** at **0**. In this case, the **Base Color** parameter will affect the secondary specular and transmission components. For accurate results, it is recommended that you don't use the scattering and specular tints parameters found in the **Tint** rollout. These parameters provide antistatic control and therefore are not physically accurate.

The **Base** parameter defines the brightness of the hair, its the multiplier of the base color. The images in Fig. 10 show the result with **Base** set to **0.02**, **0.5** and **1**. The **Base Color** was set to RGB [**0.0, 0.141, 0.859**]. Refer to **base-hair.max**.

The **Base Color** parameter defines the color of the hair. This color is absorbed by hair which gives hair its color as light scatters around. You can also connect a texture map to **Base Color** to get variation in the hair color.

 Caution: Bright colored hair
For blond and bright colored hair, a higher number of specular bounces are required to get accurate results.

 Tip: Human hair
To resemble the appearance of the human hair, it is recommended that you leave ***Base Color*** *as pure white and use the* ***Melanin*** *controls to get the plausible colors.*

The **Melanin** parameter lets you control the natural hair colors. It controls the amount of melanin in the hair. You can use a value of **0.2, 0.5**, and **1** for red, brown, and black hair, respectively.

The images in Fig. 11 show the result with **Melanin** set to **0.2, 0.5** and **1**. The **Base Color** was set to pure white and **Melanin Redness** was set to **0.5**. Refer to **base-melanin.max**.

 Tip: Generating hair color using a texture map
*If you want to control hair color using a texture, use a value of **0** for the* ***Melanin*** *parameter and then connect the texture to the* ***Base Color*** *parameter.*

The images in Fig. 12 show the result when texture maps were connected to the ***Base Color*** *parameter and* ***Melanin*** *was set to **0**. Refer to* ***base-color-maps.max***. *The images in Fig. 13 show the maps.*

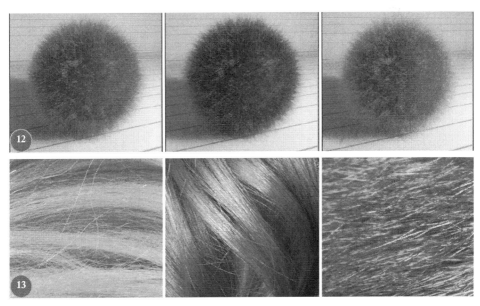

The **Melanin Redness** defines the redness of the hair. The higher the value you specify for this parameter, the more the proportion of the red **pheomelanin** [found in red hair] will be used relative to the amount of brown **eumelanin**. The **Melanin Randomize** parameter randomizes the amount of melanin in hair fibers.

The **Roughness** parameter in the **Specular** rollout defines the roughness of the hair specular reflections and transmission. Lower values generate sharper and brighter specular highlights whereas higher values generate softer highlights. The images in Fig. 14 show the result with **Roughness** set to **0.2, 0.5** and **1**. Refer to **hair-roughness.max**.

Each fiber of hair is modeled as a dielectric cylinder in Arnold. This fiber reflects and absorbs light depending on the value of the **IOR** parameter. Lower **IOR** values produce strong forward scattering whereas the higher values produce stronger reflection. Fig. 15 show the result with **IOR** set to **1.3, 1.55** and **3**. Refer to **hair-ior.max**.

The **Shift** parameter controls the angle of hair fiber. It shifts the primary and secondary specular reflections away from the prefect mirror detection. For human hair, use a value between **0** and **10** degrees. For synthetic hair, use a value of **0** since the surface of the fiber is smooth. The following table summarizes some of the suggested values.

Table 1: Suggested values for the **Shift** parameter	
Fiber	**Value**
Piedmont	2.8
Light brown European	2.9
Dark brown European	3.0
Indian	3.7
Japanese	3.6
Chinese	3.6
African-American	2.3

Rest of the parameters in **Tint, Diffuse**, and **Emission** rollouts provide additional artistic control but are not required to achieve realistic results.

Note: The Hair & Fur render effect
*To render hair in 3ds Max, the scene must contain a **Hair and Fur** effect. The render effect is automatically added to the scene the first time you apply the **Hair And Fur** modifier to an object. You can access the **Hair and Fur** effect from the **Environment and Effects** window > **Effects** panel [see Fig. 16]. In order to render hair using Arnold, change **Hairs** to **mr prim** from the **Hair and Fur** rollout [refer to Fig. 16] of the **Environment and Effects** window.*

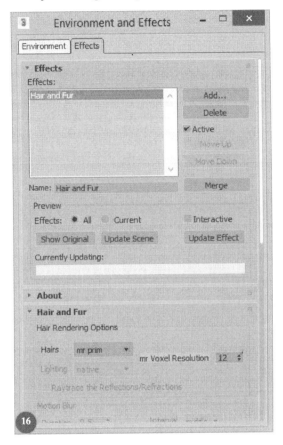

Standard Surface Shader

The **Standard Surface** shader is a physically-accurate shader that you can use to model many types of materials. This material has many layers:

- Diffuse layer
- Specular layer for materials like metals
- Specular transmission layer for materials like glass
- SSS layer for skin
- Thin scattering layer for water and ice materials
- A second layer for specular coat
- A layer for light emission.

By changing few parameters [given below], you can create different materials:

- **Metalness:** Gold, Silver, Iron, and Car Paint
- **Transmission:** Glass, Water, Honey, and Soap Bubble
- **Subsurface:** Skin, Marble, Wax, Paper, and Leaves
- **Thin Walled:** Paper, Leaves, and Soap Bubble

Note: Energy Conversion
*Arnold's **Standard Surface** shader is energy conversing by default. In other words, the amount of light leaving does not exceed the amount of incoming light.*

Caution: Layer weights and colors
*If you use layer weights and colors with the value greater than **1**, the energy conservation is broken. It is recommended that you don't use such weights or colors because it may lead to increased noise in the render and poor rendering time.*

Caution: Surface normal direction
When rendering diffuse surfaces, make sure that the normals are facing in the right direction to get the predictable results.

The **Standard Surface** shader has lots of parameters. These parameters are grouped under different rollouts. Let's explore these parameters.

Base Parameters

Base Color Group

The first spinner in the **Base, Specular, Transmission, Subsurface, Coat, Sheen, Thin Film,** and **Emission** rollouts is the weight of the corresponding component. The **Base Weight** parameter [default is **0.8**] defines the weight of the base color. The images in Fig. 17 show the output when **Base Weight** set to **0**, **0.5**, and **1**.

The **Base Color** parameter defines the base diffuse color. It controls how bright the surface is when lit directly with a white light source with **100%** intensity. The images in Fig. 18 show the output when **Base Color** is set to red, green, and blue. You can also connect maps to the **Base Color** parameter. The images in Fig. 19 show the output with diffuse file textures connected to **Base Color**.

The base component of the shader follows the **Oren-Nayar** reflection model with surface roughness. The **Roughness** parameter allows you to create roughness on the surface. A value of **0** is equal to a **Lambert** reflection, higher values result in rougher surfaces such as concrete, sand, and so on. The images in Fig. 20 show the output with **Roughness** set to **0, 0.5,** and **1**.

Advanced Group

The **Enable Caustics** check box controls whether the specular or transmission bounces behind diffuse bounces are enabled or not. This check box is not selected by default because caustics can be noisy.

> *Caution: Caustics*
> *You should take care before selecting the check box because Arnold will need a high number of **Diffuse** samples to achieve a clean result.*

The **Indirect Diffuse** parameter traces a ray against the background/environment when the maximum GI depth [reflection/refraction] is met and return the color of the background/environment in that direction. If you assign a value of **0** to this parameter, the path is terminated and returns black when the maximum GI depth [reflection/refraction] is met.

Specular Parameters

General Group

The **Specular Weight** parameter defines the brightness of the specular highlights. The images in Fig. 21 show the output with **Specular Weight** set to **0, 0.5,** and **1**.

The **Specular Color** parameter tints the color of the reflections. You should only use **Specular Color** for certain type of metals. Non-metallic surfaces do not have a colored specular component. The images in Fig. 22 show the output with **Specular Color** set to red and blue.

The **Roughness** parameter controls the glossiness of the specular reflections. The lower the value you specify, the sharper the reflection. The images in Fig. 23 show the output with **Roughness** set to **0.1**, **0.4**, and **0.6**. You can also use a grayscale map to get the variation in specular highlights. The rougher the surface becomes, the more the reflected light will be blurred.

Note: Roughness

*The **Roughness** parameter affects both specular reflection and refraction. If you need additional roughness for refraction, you can use the **Extra Roughness** parameter in the **Transmission** rollout > **Advanced** group. If you need to layer the components, you can use the **Coat** layer to create a rough reflection layer over a sharp refraction.*

The **IOR** parameter is used to define the fresnel reflectivity of the material. This value defines the balance between reflections on surfaces facing the viewer and on surface edges. The images in Fig. 24 show the output with **IOR** set to **1**, **1.52**, and **5**.

Caution: Normals
When rendering reflective surfaces, it is very important that the normals are facing in the right direction. Also, it is equally important when rendering single-sided surfaces. The normals should face the outward direction. This is extremely important when rendering surfaces with double-sided thickness, such as glass.

Note: Rendering refraction
*If you see any black where there should be refraction then you may need to increase the **Transmission** > **Ray Depth** value. The default value is **8** which is sufficient in most of the cases. You can change the **Transmission** > **Ray Depth** value from the **Render Setup** window > **Arnold Renderer** tab > **Sampling and Ray Depth** rollout.*

The **Metalness** parameter allows you to model a metallic surface. It uses fully specular reflection and complex fresnel. If you want to create prefect sharp mirror-like reflections, set **Metalness** to **1**. The images in Fig. 25 show the output with **Metalness** set to **0, 0.5**, and **1**. The following values were used:

Base Weight: 0.8, **Base Color:** 0.944, 0.776, 0.373
Specular Weight: 0.2, **Specular Color:** 0.998, 0.981, 0.751

The metal appearance is controlled by the **Base Color** and **Specular Color** parameters. The **Base Color** parameter controls the facing color whereas the **Specular Color** parameter controls the edge tint.

Note: IOR and Metalness
*You should normally use **IOR** for materials like plastic, glass, or skin [dielectric fresnel] and **Metalness** for metals [conductive fresnel with Complex IOR]. Using a very high **IOR** value can look quite similar to **Metalness**. The **Metalness** is easy to control as it ranges from **0** to **1**.*

Tip: PBR metalness map
*If you use **Substance Painter**, you can create a metalness map from it and connect it to the **Metalness** parameter.*

Options Group
If you clear the **Internal Reflections** check box, Arnold will disable indirect specular and mirror perfect reflection computations when ray refraction depth is bigger than

0. The **Indirect Specular** parameter controls the amount of specularity received from the indirect sources. It scales the indirect specular component. If you use any value other than **1**, the material will not follow energy preservation.

Anisotropy Group

The **Specular Anisotropy** value reflects the light with a directional bias and causes the material to be rougher or glossier in certain directions. The higher the value you specify, the more pronounced the anisotropic reflectance will be. The images in Fig. 26 show the output with **Specular Anisotropy** set to **0, 0.5**, and **1**. Refer to the **anisotropy.max** file.

 Caution: Faceting in specular highlights
*You may notice faceting appear in the specular highlights [see the left image in Fig. 27]. To fix it, you can enable smooth subdivision tangents. Also, this requires a subdivision iteration of at least **1** in the geometry. To fix faceting, select the geometry and then from the **Object–Space Modifiers** section of the **Modifier** list, select **Arnold Properties**. In the **Subdivision** rollout, select the **Enable** check box and change **Iterations** to 2. Also, in the **UV Smoothing** group, select the **Smooth Tangents** check box. Refer to right image in Fig. 11 and the **anisotropic-faceting.max** file.*

The **Rotation** parameter changes the orientation of the anisotropy in the UV space. At **0**, there is not rotation, while at **1** the anisotropy effect is rotated by **180** degrees. The images in Fig. 28 show the output with **Rotation** set to **0.3, 0.7**, and **0.9**. Refer to the **anisotropic-rotation.max** file.

Transmission Parameters
General Group

The **Transmission Weight** parameter allows light to scatter through the surface for refractive materials such as glass or water. The images in Fig. 29 show the output with **Transmission Weight** set to **0, 0.5**, and **1**. Refer to the **trans-weight.max** file.

Note: Refraction and the Skydome light
*The **Skydome** light has some limitation when rendering refractive surfaces. In the **trans-weight.max** file, I have used the HDR image in the **Environment Map** slot of the **Environment and Effects** window. You need to adjust the **Global Exposure** value accordingly.*

Caution: Refraction > Ray Depth
*If you see the black color where there should be transparency in the render then you may need to increase the **Transmission > Ray Depth** value in the **Render Setup** window > **Sampling and Ray Depth** rollout.*

The **Transmission Color** parameter controls the transmission color. The longer the light travels inside a medium, the more it gets affected by the transmission color. In other words, the red glass appears dark red as light travels through thicker parts. It is recommended that you use low saturation colors with this parameter.

Caution: Transmission Color
*The **Transmission Color** parameter will only work for the single-sided geometries, if the **Thin-Walled** check box is selected in the **General** group.*

The **Depth** parameter controls the absorption and scattering of the rays. The higher the value you specify for this parameter, the less the light absorption and scattering will be. The images in Fig. 30 show the output with **Transmission Color** set to red and **Depth** set to **0, 3**, and **7**. Refer to the **trans-depth.max** file.

Caution: The Depth parameter

*The **Depth** parameter is scene scale dependent. The transmittance and absorption will depend on the scale of the object. For smaller objects, you need to set a quite a low value for the **Depth** parameter. If you cannot see anything, you may need to check the size of your scene.*

The **Thin-Walled** parameter allows you to simulate translucency effect on single sided geometries. You get the effect of a translucent object being lit from behind. This parameter is ideal for thin-sided object such as bubbles. If you use this parameter with thick objects, the thickness may render incorrectly. The images in Fig. 31 show the output with **Thin-Walled** disabled and enabled. Refer to the **trans-thin-walled.max**.

You can also use the **Thin-Walled** parameter to create effect of light passing through the back of the sheet of a paper. To create this effect, change **Transmission Weight** to **0**, select the **Thin-Walled** check box and then in the **Subsurface** rollout, specify a value for the **Subsurface Weight** parameter.

The images in Fig. 32 show the output with **Subsurface Weight** set to **0**, **0.5**, and **1**. Refer to **trans-paper.max**.

The **Exit to Background** parameter traces a ray against the background/environment when the maximum GI reflection/refraction depth is met. Then, it returns the color that is visible in the ray direction. When the parameter is disabled, the ray path is terminated and returns black color on termination of the path. The images in Fig. 33 show the output with **Exit to Background** disabled and enabled. Refer to the **trans-exit-bg.max** file. In this file, a value of **3** was used for **Transmission > Ray Depth**.

Advanced Group

You can create blurry reflections/refractions using the specular **Roughness** parameter [see the left image in Fig. 34]. However, if you want to create blurry refraction with the clear reflections, you can use the **Extra Roughness** parameter. It allows you to add some additional blurriness to refraction [see the right image in Fig. 34].

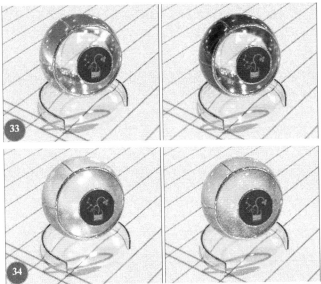

This parameter ranges from **0** [no roughness] to **1**. Refer to **trans-er.max**. In this file, values of **0.05** and **0.3** are used for the specular **Roughness** and **Extra Roughness** parameters, respectively. For the left image, a value of **0.25** is used for the **Roughness** parameter.

The **Dispersion Abbe** parameter defines the **Abbe** number of the material. The **Abbe** number defines how much the **IOR** varies across wavelength. This parameter is especially useful for gemstones such as diamond.

If the **Transmit AOVs** check box is selected, transmission will pass though the AOVs. In this case, if the background is transparent, the transmissive surface becomes transparent and then you can composite the render over another background.

Scatter Group

The scatter **Color** parameter allows you model surface of any liquid that is thick such as honey or a deep body of water. You can also use it to create materials like ice, or milky glass [see Fig. 35]. The **Anisotropy** parameter controls the directional bias of the scattering. Positive values bias the effect forwards [in the direction of the light] whereas negative values backward [towards the light]. Refer to **trans-scatter.max**.

Subsurface Parameters

Sub-Surface Scattering or SSS allows you to simulate the effect of the light entering an object and scattering beneath its surface. When you enable SSS, not all light gets reflected from the surface, some of it penetrates below the surface of the illuminated object.

Then, some of the scattered light come back out of the surface and becomes visible to the camera. The SSS effect is necessary for simulating surfaces like marble, skin, leaves, was, milk, and so on. SSS is also important when replicating materials such as plastics. Arnold calculates SSS using the brute-force raytracing method.

 Caution: Normals
Make sure the normals are facing in the correct direction, otherwise, you will get undesired results.

The **Subsurface Weight** parameter blends between the diffuse and sub-surface scattering. If you specify a value of **0** for weight, there will be only lambert. If you set value to **1**, there will be only SSS.

In most cases, you will use a value of **1** [full SSS]. The **Subsurface Color** parameter defines the color that determines the effect of sub-surface scattering. The images in Fig. 36 show the output with **Subsurface Weight** is set to **0, 0.5**, and **1**. Refer to the **sss-weight.max** file. The images in Fig. 37 show the output when **Subsurface Color** set to red, green, and blue.

The **Scale** parameter controls the distance that light travels under the surface before reflecting back. This parameter is multiplier that multiplies the SSS radius color. The images in Fig. 38 show the output with **Scale** set to **0.5, 1**, and **2**. Refer to **sss-scale.max**.

The **Radius** parameter controls the distance upto which the light can scatter below the surface. The higher the value you specify for the **Radius** parameter, the smoother the appearance of the scattering effect will be. The lighter the **Subsurface Color**, the more the light will be scattered. A value of **0** produces no scattering effect. The images in Fig. 39 show the output with **Radius** set to **0.25, 0.5,** and **1**. Refer to **sss-radius.max**.

There are three methods available for tracing: **diffusion, randomwalk** and **randomwalk_v2**. You can select one of the methods from the **Type** drop-down list. The **diffusion** method is the default method. Unlike the **diffusion** method, the **randomwalk** method actually traces below the surface with a real random walk and makes no assumptions about the geometry being locally flat. It takes into account the anisotropic scattering like the brute-force volume rendering and produces much better results around concavities and small details. The images in Fig. 40 show the output with **Type** set to **diffusion** and **randomwalk**. Refer to file **sss-type.max**.

The **Anisotropy** parameter defines the **Henyey-Greenstein** anisotropy coefficient between **-1** to **1**. The default value is **0** which scatters light evenly in all directions.

Positive values bias the scattering effect forwards [in the direction of the light] while negative values bias the scattering backward [toward the light]. The images in Fig. 41 show the output with **Anisotropy** set to **-0.7, 0**, and **0.7**.

 Caution: The Anisotropy parameter
*Note that this parameter only works with the **randomwalk** method.*

Emission Parameters

The options in the **Emission** rollout are used to give the appearance that the material is emitting incandescent light. Note that a **Mesh** light works better in a situation where you need an object to cast realistic looking ray-traced shadows. The **Emission Weight** parameter controls the amount of emitted light. The **Emission Color** parameter defines the emitted color.

Coat Parameters
Clearcoat Group

The **Coat Weight** parameter controls weight of the coat layer. The coat layer simulates a dielectric material which absorbs light and therefore tints all the transmitted light. The **Coat Color** parameter controls the color of the coating layer's transparency. In most of the cases, the **Coat Color** parameter should be set to white. However, you can use it for artistic control.

The left image in Fig. 42 shows material with specular **Roughness** set to **0.4**. The image in the right shows the blue **Coat Color** which acts as a clear coat layer with the **Roughness** value of **0.1**, tinting the specular reflection underneath. Refer to **coat-color.max**.

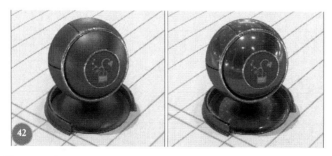

The images in Fig. 43 show the output with **Coat Weight** set to **0, 0.5**, and **1** [Coat Color: RGB **0.937, 0.329, 0**]. A value of **5** was used for the specular **IOR** parameter.

Caution: Coat layer and Fresnel
*When a low roughness coat is combined on the top of the high roughness specular component, the sharp coat will disappear at the center due to **Fresnel**.*

The **Roughness** parameter defines the glossiness of the specular reflections. The lower the value, the sharper the reflections. You can connect a map with this parameter to get variations in the coat highlight. The images in Fig. 44 show the output with **Roughness** set to **0.1**, **0.5**, and **1**.

The **Coat Normal (Bump)** parameter controls the Fresnel blending of the coat over the base. You can also use this parameter to create a bumpy coat layer over a smoother base.

For example, you can create a rain effect, flakes on the car paint, or carbon fiber shader. You can also use it to create oily, wet surfaces.

Fig. 45 shows the output when a **Cellular** map is used with the **Coat Normal (Bump)** parameter. Refer to **coat-normal.max**.

The **IOR** parameter controls the fresnel reflectivity of the material. The images in Fig. 46 show the output with **IOR** set to **3**, **5**, and **7**. Notice in Fig. 46 that IOR defines the balance between reflections on surfaces facing the viewer and on surface edges, the reflection intensity on the front side changes a lot. Refer to **coat-ior.max**.

Affect Underlying Group

The parameters in this group allow you to create effects like varnished wood. In the real-world, when a material is coated, there is a certain amount of internal reflections on the inside of the coating. As a result, light bounces onto the surface multiple times before escaping and enhances the color of the material. The right image in Fig. 47 shows the result with the underlying **Color** set to **0** and **1**.

The **Roughness** parameter causes the roughness of the coating to have an effect on the roughness of the underlaying layer. As a result, a blurring effect is created that is seen through the top layer.

Sheen Parameters

The parameters in the **Sheen** rollout allow you to create an energy-conserving sheen layer that can use used to simulate micro-fiber and cloth like surfaces such as velvet and satin. You can also use it for leaves, fruits, and for the peach fuzz on the face.

The sheen layer is layer onto the diffuse component and its weight is defined by the **Sheen Weight** parameter. The images in Fig. 48 show the output with **Sheen Weight** set to **0, 0.1**, and **0.25**. Refer to **sheen-weight.max**.

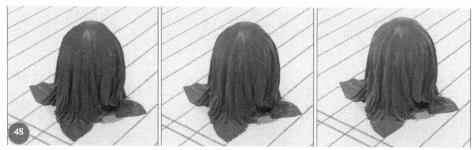

The **Sheen Color** parameter tints the color of the sheen contribution whereas the **Roughness** parameter controls how much the micro-fibers diverge from the surface normal direction. The images in Fig. 49 show the output with **Sheen Color** set to **[1, 0.918, 0]**, **[1, 0.235, 0]** and **[1, 1, 1]**. The **[0, 0.134, 0.417]** color was used as **Base Color**. Refer to **sheen-color.max**. The images in Fig. 50 show the output with **Roughness** set to **0.1**, **0.3**, and **0.6**. Refer to **sheen-roughness.max**.

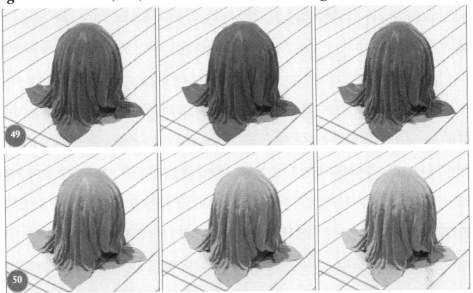

Thin Film Parameters

The parameters in this rollout are used to simulate effect of a thin film interface on a surface. You can use it to create effects like multi-tone car paint, burnt chrome, film on the bubbles, reflective coating on a beetle, and so on.

The **Thickness** parameter controls the actual thickness of the film between the specified min **[0]** and max **[2000]** thickness. The thin film layer affects the specular, transmission, and coat layers. The images in Fig. 51 show the output with **Thickness** set to **300**, **400**, and **550**. Refer to **tfilm-thicness.max**.

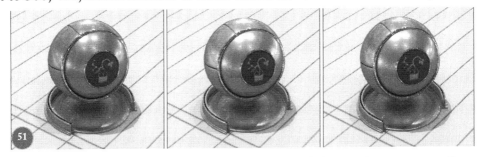

The **IOR** parameter defines the refractive index of the medium surrounding the material. Normally, you want to set it to **1** for air. The images in Fig. 52 show the output with **IOR** set to **1.5**, **2**, and **3**. Refer to **tfilm-ior.max**.

Special Features Parameters

The **Opacity (Cutout)** parameter controls the degree to which light is not allowed to travel through it. This parameter affects the whole shader. You can use this parameter for retaining the shadow definition of an object, while making the object itself invisible to the camera. You can connect a normal map usually exported from Mudbox or ZBrush to the **Normal (Bump)** parameter. If the tangent map is available [on which the normal map relies] and exported from your sculpting tool, you can connect it to the **Tangents** parameter.

Two Sided Shader

The **Two Sided** shader applies two shader on either side of a double-sided surface. The **Back Material** and **Front Material** parameters are used to input shader for the back and front surfaces, respectively [see Fig. 53].

Volume Shader

Standard Volume

The **Standard Volume** shader is physically-based volume shader. Using this shader, you can independently control volume density, scatter color, and transparent color. The blackbody emission is used to render fire and explosions directly from physics simulations.

Caution: Rendering
In volume rendering, the shader network is called many times per ray. Therefore, it is recommended to keep the volume shading network as lean as possible.

To use the **Standard Volume** shader, you need a volumetric model. To do so, in the **Create** panel, click **Geometry**, and then select **Arnold** from the drop-down list. Now, in the **Object Type** rollout, click **Volume**, and then drag in the viewport to create the **Volume** object.

Now, in the **Modify** panel, assign the volumetric file path using the **VDB File Path** parameter; the **Load Volume** dialog box will be displayed. Select a file; the **Select VDB Grid to use** dialog box will be displayed. Select the grids as per your requirements. In this dialog box, if you select the **Set up a default Standard Volume shader** check box, the **Standard Volume** shader will be automatically assigned to the volumetric model. If you don't select this check box, you need to manually assign the shader to the volumetric model. Now, click **OK** to accept the changes.

> *Note: Volumetric models courtesy*
> *The volumetric models used in this book are downloaded from* **OpenVDB**'s *website:* ***http://www.openvdb.org/download***.

The **Density** parameter in the **Density** rollout, defines the density of the volume. Higher values generate thick volumes. This parameter acts as a multiplier on the density channel. If no density channel is available, you can connect a shader like the volume sample or a procedural texture. The images in Fig. 54 show the result with **Density** set to **0.1**, **0.25**, and **1**. Also, refer to **volume-density.max**. The **Density >** **Channel** parameter allows to read the density channel from the volume object.

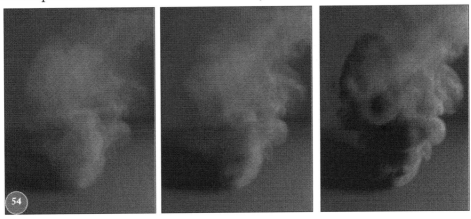

The **Scatter** parameter in the **Scattering** rollout defines the brightness of the volume under illumination. This value is the ratio of the light scattered [not absorbed]. You need to use a value from the range **0** to **1** for energy conservation.

The **Scatter Color** parameter controls the color of the volume under illumination. The **Channel** parameter read the scatter channel from the volume object. It is a multiplier on **Scatter Color**. The images in Fig. 55 show the result with **Scatter Color** set to three different colors: RGB **[0.969, 0.635, 0.455]**, RGB**[0.169, 0.11, 0.122]**, and RGB **[0.072, 0.068, 0.069]**. Also, refer to **volume-scatter-color.max**.

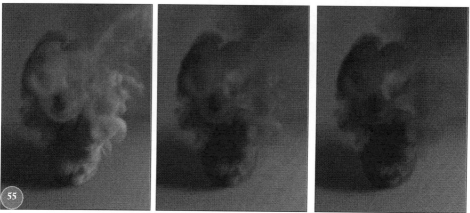

The **Anisotropy** parameter controls the directional bias, or anisotropy of the scattering effect. The default value of **0** scatters light evenly in all directions. It is recommended that you don't use values above **0.95** and below **-0.95** because these value will produce scattering that is so directional that it will not be visible from most of the angles.

The images in Fig. 56 show the result with **Anisotropy** set to **-0.78**, **0**, and **0.78**. Also, refer to **volume-density.max**.

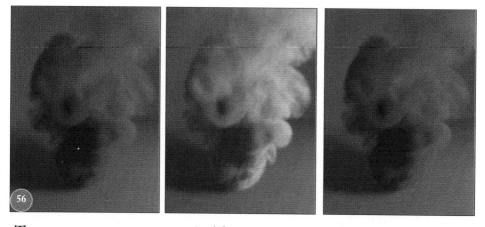

The **Transparency** parameter in the **Transparency** rollout is an additional control for altering density of the volume. It is used to tint the color of the volume shadows and objects seen through the volume.

The **Depth** parameter defines the depth into the volume at which the transparent color is realized. The **Depth > Channel** parameter read the transparency channel from the volume object. It is multiplier on **Transparency**.

The images in Fig. 57 show the result with **Transparency** set to three different colors: RGB [**1, 0.3, 0.1**], RGB[**0.8, 0.9, 1**], and RGB [**0.898, 0.914, 0.914**]. A value of **0.3** was used for the **Depth** parameter. Also, refer to **volume-transparency-color.max**.

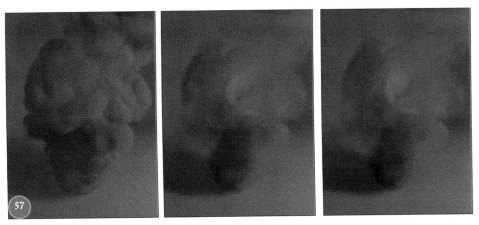

The parameters in the **Emission** rollout are used to control the emission of light. The emission algorithm you can select from the **Mode** drop-down list. Given below is a quick summary:

- **none:** No light is emitted
- **channel:** Emits light using a specified emission channel
- **density:** Emits light using the density channel
- **blackbody:** Emits color and intensity based on temperature, for rendering fire and explosions

The images in Fig. 58 show the result when **Mode** is set to **none, channel** [the **heat** channel was used], **density**, and **blackbody**. Also, refer to **emission-volume.max**.

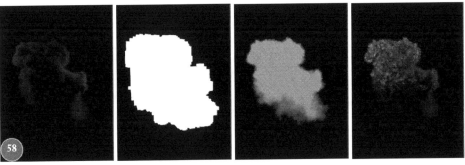

The **Emission** parameter defines the rate at which a volume emits light. If a density, blackbody, or emission channel is used for emission, this parameter acts as a multiplier to decrease or increase the emission. If no such channel is used, you can use a shader like volume sample or procedural texture and connect it to this parameter to control where light is emitted. The **Emission Color** parameter is used to tint the emission.

The **Temperature** parameter in the **Blackbody** rollout is used as a multiplier for the blackbody temperature. Alternatively, you can use a shader like volume sample or procedural texture and connect it to this parameter to control the temperature of the blackbody. The images in Fig. 59 show the result with **Temperature** set to **0.5**, **0.78**, and **1**.

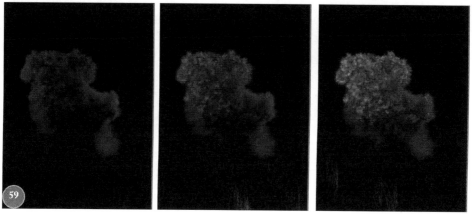

The **Channel** parameter is used to read the temperature channel. The **Kelvin** parameter is used as a multiplier for the temperature. The **Blackbody Intensity** parameter controls the intensity of the blackbody emission.

Utility Shaders

Map to Material Shader

The **Map to Material** shader can be used to assign the map shaders [**Curvature** map, **Utility** map, and so on] that you cannot apply directly to the objects in the scene. Refer to Fig. 60 and **map-to-material.max**. Fig. 60 shows the output of the **Curvature** map using the **Map to Material** shader.

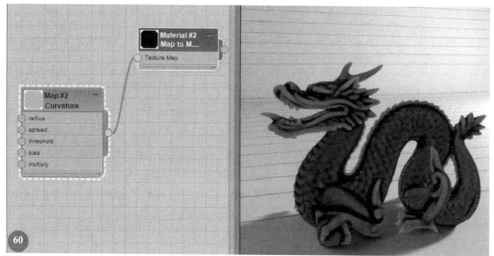

Passthrough Shader

The **Passthrough** shader has **22** inputs: **eval1** to **eval20, Passthrough, and Normal**. When a shading network is connected to the **Passthrough** shader, the shader connected to the **Passthrough** port is evaluated first and passed as-is to output. This shader is used with AOVs.

Ray Switch Shader

Ray Switch Shader is used to evaluate different shader trees per ray. This feature gives you more artistic control. You can control the camera, shadow, diffuse reflection, diffuse transmission, specular reflection, specular transmission, and volume rays using this shader. For example, if you want to give different appearance to an area which is behind a glass object, connect an input shader to the **Specular Transmission** parameter of the **Ray Switch** shader [see Fig. 61]. Also, refer to **ray-switch-shader.max**.

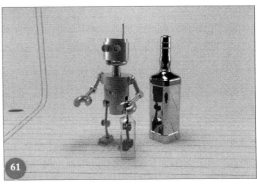

Switch Shader

Switch Shader is used to switch between different shader. There are **20** ports [**input0** to **input19**] available on the **Switch Shader** node. You can make a shader active by entering its index number in the **Index** field. For example, if you want to make **input2** active, enter **1** in the **Index** field. Refer to **switch-shader.max**.

Trace Set

You can use the **Trace Set** shader to tag the rays so that it hit or avoid tagged objects. This feature may be removed in a future version of Arnold.

AOV Shaders

The AOV Shaders allows you to write float, int or color data to custom AOVs. You can use these nodes to create custom AOVs.

Subdivisions and Displacement Mapping

The displacement and subdivision mapping settings can be accessed via the **Arnold Properties** modifier [see Fig. 62]. Each rollout has one or more **Enable** checkboxes [see Fig. 63] that you can use to override the defaults on just the part you want to control. If you collapse the stack the modifier will remain.

Subdivision

Before we discuss the displacement mapping, lets first have a look at subdivision settings. Select the **Enable** check box in the **Subdivision** rollout to enable subdivision settings. The options in the **Type** drop-down list allow you select the subdivision algorithm. The **None** option renders the mesh as is. The **Linear** option adds vertices at the center of the each face. The **Catmull-Clark** option creates smooth surface using quadrilateral faces. The images in Fig. 64 show the result with **Type** set to **None, Linear,** and **Catmull-Clark.** Refer to **subd-type.max**.

Tip: Wireframe render
The wireframe you see in Fig. 64 is created by connecting the Arnold's **Wireframe** *utility to the* **base_color** *port of the* **Standard Surface** *shader. Refer to* **subd-type.max**.

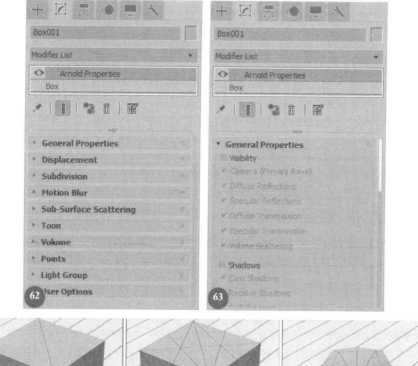

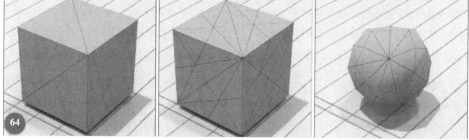

The **Iterations** parameter defines the maximum number of subdivision rounds applied to the mesh. The images in Fig. 65 show the result with **Type** set to **Catmull-Clark** and **Iterations** set to **1, 2,** and **3**.

Caution: Number of polygons
Each subdivision iteration quadruples the number of polygons.

The **Metric** parameter controls the amount of error between a given subdivision level and the limit surface.

- **Flatness:** You can use it when the curvature of the mesh in pixels is the feature used to choose the adaptive subdivision level.
- **Edge Length:** When the length of the polygonal edges in pixels is used.
- **Automatic:** This option uses **Flatness** when no displacement is applied. It uses **Edge Length** when a displacement map is applied to the mesh.

The **Error** parameter defines the maximum allowable difference in pixels between the adoptively chosen subdivision level and the "limit" subdivided surface. The options in the **Space** drop-down allow you to define the subdivision space. The adaptive subdivision in the raster space does not work well when the **Raster** space is used. Using the **Object** space ensures that all instances will subdivide properly.

The parameters in **UV Smoothing** group are useful for anisotropic shaders to get distortion free anisotropic highlights. If you notice faceting in the anisotropic highlights, use the **Smooth Tangents** check box.

 Caution: The Smooth Tangents parameter and memory consumption
*When you use **Smooth Tangents**, there will be memory overhead [approx. **100** extra bytes per vertex per keyframe].*

Displacement
Unlike bump maps, the displacement maps alter the geometry. As a result, correct silhouette, and self-shadowing effects are generated. You can use it to add the surface details that would take lots of time using the regular modeling methods. The displacement mapping occurs in two ways:

- The Float, RGB & RGBA inputs displace geometry along the normal.
- The vector input displaces geometry along the vector.

 Caution: Number of polygons
Make sure that your base geometry have sufficient numbers of polygons in order to get the predictable results. Also, ensure that you use highest quality texture maps for the displacement mapping.

 Tip: .tx files
*Arnold works well with high resolution maps as long as you process the maps using the **maketx** utility. This utility convert textures to .tx files. The .tx files are mipmapped tiles files.*

In Arnold, displacement settings affect object on a per-object basis. It is useful when you want to use the same map for two different results. To enable displacement feature, select the **Enable** check box in the **Displacement** rollout. To use a texture map, select the **Use Map** check box in the **Displacement Map** group and then drag texture from the material editor to the **No Map** button.

The **Height** parameter controls the amount of displacement. You can enter a negative or a positive value for this parameter. This parameter only affects the normal displacement. The images in Fig. 66 show the result with **Height** set to **0**, **1**, and **5**. Refer to **disp.max**.

The **Zero** parameter defines a floating point value which shifts the displacement map. It defines the value of the displacement map that is considered zero displacement. The **Bounds Pad** parameter is used to extend the bounding box of the mesh to include any additional displacement coming from the shader.

When the **Enable** check box is selected in the **Autobump** group, Arnold puts the high frequencies of a displacement map into the bump attribute. As a result, you don't need high subdivision iteration value. This check box is selected by default.

Caution: UV Coordinates
The autobump algorithm needs UV coordinates to compute the surface tangents. Therefore, make sure that the mesh has a UV set applied to it.

On changing the subdivision type to **Catmull-Clark** or **Linear** and increasing the iteration value will improve the displacement quality. However, be careful when increasing the value because each iteration quadruples the geometry.

Hands-on Exercises

Exercise 1: Creating the Copper Material

In this exercise, we will create the copper material using the **Standard Surface** material. Fig. E1 shows the rendered output.

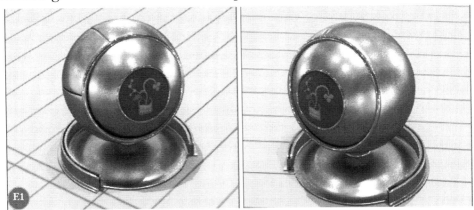

Table E1 summarizes the exercise.

Table E1	
Difficulty level	Intermediate
Estimated time to complete	15 Minutes
Topics	• Getting Started • Creating the Material
Resources folder	**unit-da3**
Start file	**shader-ball-01.max**
Final file	**copper-material-finish.max**

Getting Started
Open **shader-ball-01.max** in 3ds Max and make sure the **Physical** camera is active.

Creating the Material
Follow these steps:

1. Open the **Slate Material Editor** and then double-click on **sample-mat** swatch.

2. In the **Parameter Editor > Base** rollout > **Base Color** group, change **Base Weight** to **1** and **Base Color** to RGB [**0.926, 0.721, 0.504**], see Fig. E2. In the **Specular** rollout > **General** group, change **Specular Color** to RGB [**0.996, 0.957, 0.823**], see Fig. E3.

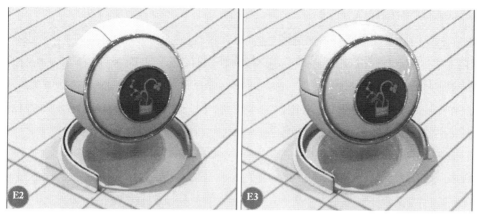

3. In the **Specular** rollout > **Advanced** group, change **Metalness** to **1** [see Fig. E4]. In the **Specular** rollout > **General** group, change **Roughness** to **0.15** [see Fig. E5].

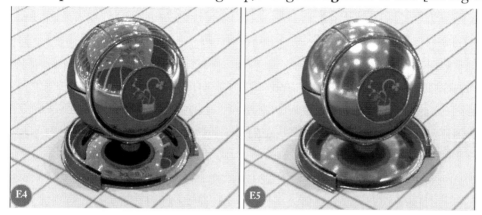

4. In the **Slate Material Editor**, double-click on the **sample-mat** node > **specular-roughness** port to open the **Material/Map Browser**. Double-click on **Bitmap** in the **Maps** > **General** rollout. In the **Select Bitmap Image File** dialog box, double-click on **dirt-a.png** to select it [see Fig. E6].

5. In the **Parameter Editor** > **dirt-a.png** bitmap > **Output** rollout, select the **Invert** check box followed by the **Enable Color Map** check box. Now, change the color map, as shown in Fig. E7. Fig. E8 shows the render.

6. In the **Slate Material Editor**, double-click on the **sample-mat** node > **normal** port to open the **Material/Map Browser**. Double-click on **Bump2D** in the **Maps** > **Arnold** > **Bump** rollout.

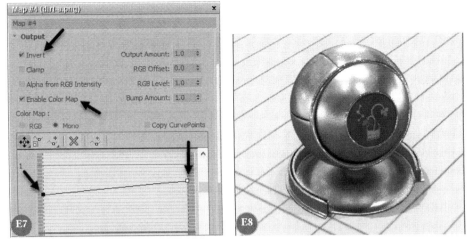

7. In the **Slate Material Editor**, connect output of the **dirt-a.png** bitmap with the **bump_map** port of the **Bump 2D** node [see Fig. E9].

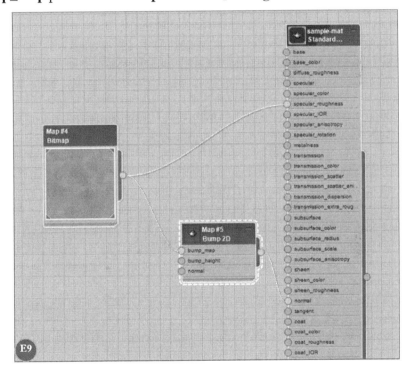

8. In the **Parameter Editor > Bump 2D > Parameters** rollout, change **Bump Height** to **0.05**. Render the scene.

Exercise 2: Creating the Honey Material

In this exercise, we will create the honey material using the transmission component of the **Standard Surface** material. Fig. E1 shows the rendered output.

Table E2 summarizes the exercise.

Table E2	
Difficulty level	Intermediate
Estimated time to complete	30 Minutes
Topics	• Getting Started • Creating the Material
Resources folder	**unit-da3**
Start file	**dragon-transmission.max**
Final file	**honey-finish.max**

Getting Started

Open **dragon-transmission.max** in 3ds Max and make sure the **Physical** camera is active.

Creating the Material

Follow these steps:

1. Open the **Slate Material Editor** and then double-click on **sample-mat** swatch.

2. In the **Parameter Editor > Base** rollout > **Base Color** group, change **Base Weight** to **0**.

3. In the **Specular** rollout > **Advanced** group, change **IOR** to **1.48**. In the **Transmission** rollout > **General** group, change **Transmission Weight** to **1** and then change **Transmission Color** to RGB [**0.647, 0.257, 0.028**] and **Depth** to **0.5** [see Fig. E2].

4. In the **Transmission** rollout > **Scatter** group, change **Color** to RGB [**0.647**, **0.41**, **0.27**], see Fig. E3. In the **Specular** rollout > **General** group, change **Roughness** to **0.25**.

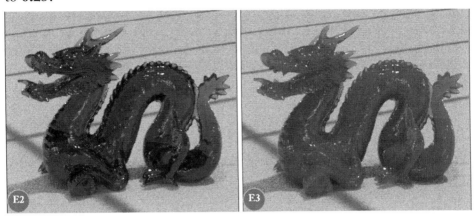

Exercise 3: Creating the Chocolate Material

In this exercise, we will create the chocolate material using the transmission component of the **Standard Surface** material. Fig. E1 shows the rendered output.

Table E3 summarizes the exercise.

Table E3	
Difficulty level	Intermediate
Estimated time to complete	30 Minutes
Topics	• Getting Started • Creating the Material
Resources folder	**unit-da3**
Start file	**dragon-transmission.max**
Final file	**chocolate-finish.max**

Getting Started

Open **dragon-transmission.max** in 3ds Max and make sure the **Physical** camera is active.

Creating the Material

Follow these steps:

1. Open the **Slate Material Editor** and then double-click on **sample-mat** swatch.

2. In the **Parameter Editor > Base** rollout > **Base Color** group, change **Base Weight** to **0**.

3. In the **Transmission** rollout > **General** group, change **Transmission Weight** to **1** and then change **Transmission Color** to RGB [**2, 0.799, 0.705**] and **Depth** to **0.15** [see Fig. E2].

4. In the **Transmission** rollout > **Scatter** group, change **Color** to RGB [**0.878, 0.208, 0**], see Fig. E3.

5. In the **Advanced** rollout, change **Extra Roughness** to **0.3**. In the **Specular** rollout > **General** group, change **Roughness** to **0.15**.

Exercise 4: Creating the Car Paint Material

In this exercise, we will create the car paint material using the **Standard Surface** material. Fig. E1 shows the rendered output. Table E4 summarizes the exercise.

Table E4	
Difficulty level	Intermediate
Estimated time to complete	30 Minutes
Topics	• Getting Started • Creating the Material
Resources folder	**unit-da3**

Table E4	
Start file	**shader-ball-01.max**
Final file	**car-paint-finish.max**

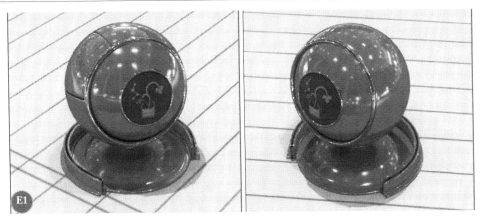

Getting Started

Open the **shader-ball-01.max** in 3ds Max and make sure the **Physical** camera is active.

Creating the Material

Follow these steps:

1. Open the **Slate Material Editor** and then double-click on **sample-mat** swatch.

2. In the **Parameter Editor > Base** rollout > **Base Color** group, change **Base Weight** to **0.7** and **Base Color** to RGB [**0.044, 0.326, 0.604**].

3. In the **Specular** rollout > **General** group, change **Specular Weight** to **1** and **Specular Color** to RGB [**0.101, 0.996, 0.079**]. In the **General** group, change **Roughness** to **0.1**. In the **Advanced** group, change **IOR** to **5**, see Fig. E2.

4. In the **Coat** rollout, change **Coat Weight** to **1**. In the **Affect Underlying** group, change **Color** to **0.2**, see Fig. E3.

5. In the **Thin Film** rollout, change **Thickness** to **500**.

Exercise 5: Creating the Wax Material

In this exercise, we will create the wax material using the **Standard Surface** material. Fig. E1 shows the rendered output.

Table E5 summarizes the exercise.

Table E5	
Difficulty level	Intermediate
Estimated time to complete	30 Minutes
Topics	• Getting Started • Creating the Material
Resources folder	**unit-da3**
Start file	**sss-studio.max**
Final file	**wax-finish.max**

Getting Started

Open **ssss-studio.max** in 3ds Max and make sure the **Physical** camera is active.

Creating the Material

Follow these steps:

1. Open the **Slate Material Editor** and then double-click on **sample-mat** swatch.

2. In the **Parameter Editor** > **Base** rollout > **Base Color** group, change **Base Weight** to **0.7** and **Base Color** to RGB [**0.439, 0.011, 0.422**]. Also, change **Roughness** to **0.4**, see Fig. E2.

3. In the **Specular** rollout > **General** group, change **Roughness** to **0.4**. In the **Specular** rollout > **Advanced** group, change **IOR** to **1.67**, see Fig. E3.

4. In the **Subsurface** rollout, change **Subsurface Weight** to **1**, **Subsurface Color** to RGB [**0.439, 0.174, 0.428**], and **Scale** to **0.7**, see Fig. E4.

5. Change **Radius X, Y**, and **Z** to **0.4** each, see Fig. E5. Change **Type** to **randomwalk**.

Exercise 6: Studio Automotive Rendering

In this exercise, we will render an automobile style shot. Fig. E1 shows the rendered output.

Table E6 summarizes the exercise.

Table E6	
Difficulty level	Advanced
Estimated time to complete	40 Minutes
Topics	• Getting Started • Adding Light • Creating Material for the Floor • Creating Material for the Reflector • Creating Material for the Car's Body
Resources folder	**unit-da3**
Start file	**auto-start.max**
Final file	**auto-finish.max**

Getting Started
Open **auto-start.max** in 3ds Max and make sure the **Physical** camera is active.

Adding Light
Follow these steps:

1. In the **Create** panel, click **Lights**, and then select **Arnold** from the drop-down list below **Lights**. Now, in the **Object Type** rollout, click **Arnold Light**, and then change **Type** to **Quad**. Now, click-drag in the **Front** viewport to create a light [see Fig. E2].

2. In the **Modify** panel > **Shape** rollout, change **Quad X** and **Quad Y** to **1.952** and **2.857**, respectively. Now, align the light [see Fig. E3]. Render the scene [see Fig. E4].

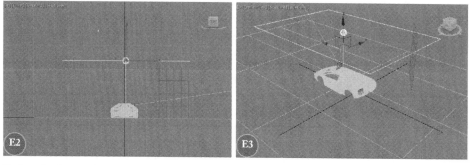

3. Select light in the scene and then in the **Modify** panel > **Color/Intensity** rollout > **Intensity** group, change **Intensity** to **5** and **Exposure** to **10**. In the **Rendering** rollout, change **Samples** to **4**. Render the scene [see Fig. E5].

Creating Material for the Floor
Follow these steps:

1. Open the **Slate Material Editor** and then create a **Standard Surface** shader node in the active view. Rename the shader as **mat-floor** and apply it to **floor-geo**. Create a **Ramp Rgb** node from **Maps > Arnold > Texture** rollout to the active view. Connect the **Ramp Rgb** node to the **base_color** port of **mat-floor**.

2. In the **Parameter Editor > mat-floor > Base** rollout, change **Base Color Weight** to **0.3**. In the **Specular** rollout, change **Roughness** to **0.4**. Render the scene [see Fig. E6]. Now, change the ramp for the **Ramp Rgb** node, as shown in Fig. E7.

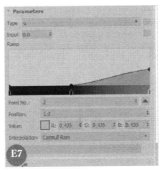

3. Render the scene [see Fig. E8].

Creating Material for the Reflector
Follow these steps:

1. In the **Slate Material Editor** and create a **Standard Surface** shader node in the active view. Rename the shader as **mat-ref** and apply it to **ref-plane-geo**.

2. In the **Parameter Editor > mat-ref > Base** rollout, change **Base Color Weight** to **0**. In the **Emission** rollout, change **Emission Weight** to **1**.

Creating Material for the Car's Body

Follow these steps:

1. Add a **Car Paint** shader node to the active view and then rename it as **mat-car-body**. Now, apply it to **car-body**.

2. In the **Base** rollout, change **Base** to **0.2**, **Base Color** to RGB [**0.016, 0.031, 0.216**], and **Base Roughness** to **0.3**. Render the scene [see Fig. E9].

3. In the **Specular** rollout, change **Specular Color** to RGB [**0.216, 0.843, 0.996**], **Specular Roughness** to **0.5**, and **Specular IOR** to **6.0**. Render the scene [see Fig. E10].

What next?
*Now, we will use a **Ramp Rgb** node to modulate the specular reflection from the base coat depending on the viewing angle.*

4. Add a **Ramp Rgb** map node to the active view and connect it to the **specular_flip_flop** port of the **mat-car-body** node. Now, change the ramp, as shown in Fig. 11. Use the following two colors: RGB [**55, 215, 254**] and RGB [**4, 8, 55**]. Render the scene [see Fig. E12].

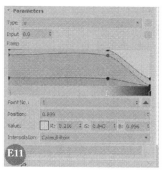

What next?
*Now, we will assign a color to modulate the base coat specular color of the area facing the light source using the **Specular Light Facing** parameter.*

5. In the **mat-car-body** > **Specular** rollout, change **Specular Light Facing** to RGB [**0.722, 0, 0.957**] and **Specular Falloff** to **0.07**. Render the scene [see Fig. E13].

What next?
Now, we will add flakes to the car paint.

6. Copy the **Specular Color** parameter's color value from the **Specular** rollout and then paste it on the color swatch of **Flake Color** parameter in the **Flakes** rollout.

7. In the active view, connect the **Ramp Rgb** node connected to the **specular_flip_flop** port to the **flake_flip_flop** port. Change **Flake Density** to **0.02** and **Normal Randomize** to **0.2**. Render the scene [see Fig. E14].

What next?
Let's now adjust the intensity of the light.

What just happened?
Notice the blown highlights on the hood of the car in Fig. E14. We can reduce the effect by adjusting the exposure of the light. As a result, the overall illumination of the scene will be reduced, which is what we don't want. We can get the same effect by reducing the specular contribution of the light. Also, we need to reduce weight of the emission of the reflective plane. Let's do it.

8. Select light and then in the **Modify** panel > **Contribution** rollout, change **Specular** to **0.5** and then render the scene [see Fig. E15].

9. In the **mat-ref** shader > **Parameter Editor** > **Emission** rollout, change **Emission Weight** to **0.5**. Render the scene [see Fig. E16].

10. Press **F10** to open the **Render Setup** window. In the **Arnold Renderer** panel > **Sampling and Ray Depth** rollout, change **Camera (AA)**, **Diffuse**, and **Specular** samples to **5**, **6**, and **4** respectively. Also, change **Ray Depth** > **Diffuse** to **2**. Render the scene [see Fig. E17].

Quiz

Multiple Choice
Answer the following questions:

1. Which of the following materials are supported by Arnold?

   [A] Multi/Sub-Object   [B] Shell
   [C] Arch & Design   [D] All of these

2. Which of the following parameters allow light to scatter through the surface for refractive materials such as glass or water?

   [A] Transmission Weight   [B] Transparency
   [C] Transmission Roughness   [D] None of these

3. Which of the following shaders allows you to mix up to eight shaders together?

   [A] Mix   [B] Blend
   [C] Layer   [D] Top Bottom

4. Which of the following layers is not available in the **Car Paint** Shader?

   [A] Base   [B] Specular
   [C] Coat   [D] Base Color

Fill in the Blanks
Fill in the blanks in each of the following statements:

1. When _____ is running, material previews in the material editor are not rendered because only one render session can be active in Arnold.

2. Arnold's _____ shader is energy conversing by default.

3. The _____ parameter defines the base diffuse color of the **Standard Surface** shader.

4. The base component of the **Standard Surface** shader follows the _____ reflection model with surface roughness.

5. The _____ parameter is used to define the fresnel reflectivity of the material.

6. The transmission _____ parameter is scene scale dependent.

7. The _____ effect is necessary for simulating surfaces like marble, skin, leaves, was, and milk.

8. In the SSS layer, the _____ parameter controls the distance upto which the light can scatter below the surface.

9. In SSS layer, there are two methods available for tracing: _____ and _____ .

10. The coat layer simulates a _____ material which absorbs light and therefore tints all the transmitted light.

11. The _____ parameter controls the index of refraction of the base coat of the **Car Paint** shader.

12. The _____ parameter in the _____ rollout allows you to tint the specular highlight from flakes.

13. The _____ shader allows you to mix up to eight shaders together.

14. The _____ shader allows you to create holdout effects by rendering alpha as **0**.

15. To resemble the appearance of the human hair, it is recommended that you leave _____ as pure white and use the _____ controls to get the plausible colors.

16. To render hair in 3ds Max, the scene must contain a _____ effect.

True or False
State whether each of the following is true or false:

1. Arnold does not support most of the legacy 3ds Maps.

2. If you use **OSL** maps with the Arnold's **Standard Surface** shader, the texture displayed in the viewport will not match the texture displayed in the rendered output.

3. The **Indirect Diffuse** parameter traces a ray against the background/environment when the maximum GI depth [reflection/refraction] is met and return the color of the background/environment in that direction.

4. The **Thin-Walled** parameter allows you to simulate translucency effect on single sided geometries.

5. The lighter the **Subsurface Color**, the less the light will be scattered.

6. In the SSS layer, the **Anisotropy** parameter works only with the diffusion type.

7. When a low roughness coat is combined on the top of high roughness specular component, the sharp coat will disappear at the center due to Fresnel.

8. In the **Thin Film** layer, the **IOR** parameter defines the refractive index of the medium surrounding the material.

9. In the **Car Paint** shader, if you a specify a value of **0** for the **Flake Density** parameter, the surface will be fully covered with flakes.

10. For the blond and bright colored hair, a higher number of specular bounces are required to get accurate results.

11. The **Melanin** parameter lets you control the natural hair colors.

12. The **Two Sided** shader applies two shaders on either side of a double-sided surface.

13. The **Standard Volume** shader is physically-based volume shader.

14. Each subdivision iteration quadruples the number of polygons.

Summary

The unit covered the following topics:

- Shaders
- Materials
- Subdivision and displacement mapping
- Legacy 3ds Max maps

Unit DAP: Practice Activities [Arnold]

Practice Activities

Activity 1: Creating Metals

Create the Aluminium, Gold, Iron, and Nickel materials using the **Standard Surface** shader. Refer to Figs. A1 through A4.

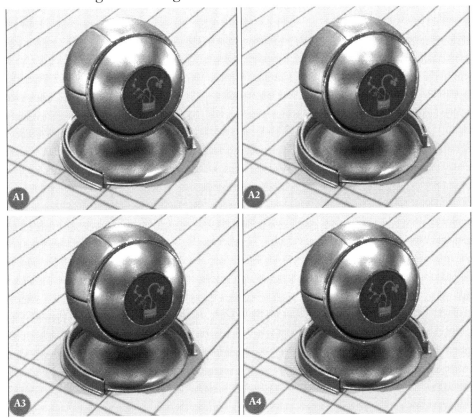

Use the following values for the **Base Color** and **Specular Color** parameters.

Aluminium:	*0.912, 0.914, 0.920*	*0.970, 0.979, 0.988*
Gold:	*0.944, 0.776, 0.373*	*0.998, 0.981, 0.751*
Iron:	*0.531, 0.512, 0.496*	*0.571, 0.540, 0.586*
Nickel:	*0.649, 0.610, 0.541*	*0.797, 0.801, 0.789*

Activity 2: Creating the Chrome Material

Create the chrome material using the **Standard Surface** shader [see Fig. A5].

Hint:
Use the white color for both the **Base Color** and **Specular Color** parameters.

Activity 3: Creating the Glass Material

Create the glass material using the **Standard Surface** shader [see Fig. A6]. Use the **glass-mat-start.max** file.

Hint:
Work on the transmission color and depth to achieve the result.

Activity 4: Creating the Car Paint Material

Create the car paint material using the **Standard Surface** shader [see Figs. A7 and A8].

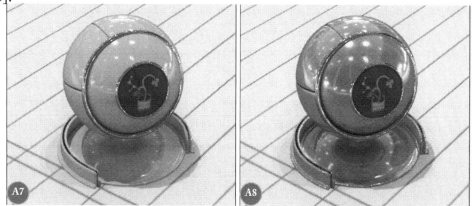

Appendix DMA: Quiz Answers [Modeling]

Multiple Choice
1. A, 2. B, 3. D, 4. A, 5. B

Fill in the Blanks
1. Ctrl+N, 2. RMB, 3. Reset, 4.Ctrl+H, Alt+Ctrl+F, 5. Ctrl+A, 6. W, E, R,
7. Alt+Home, 8. Ctrl+D, 9. -, =, 10. J, 11. F3, 12. F4

True/False
1. T, 2. T, 3. T, 4. F, 5. T, 6. T, 7. T

Unit DM2: Introduction to 3ds Max - II

Multiple Choice
1. C, 2. A, 3. C, 4. B

Fill in the Blanks
1. Clone, Edit, Ctrl+V, 2. Spacing Tool, 3. Reference, 4. Select and Manipulate,
5. Shift+A, 6. Normal

True/False
1. F, 2. T, 3. F, 4. T, 5. T, 6. T

Unit DM3 - Geometric Primitives and Architectural Objects

Fill in the Blanks
1. Tetra, Octa, Icosa, 2. Ctrl, 3. Ace Templates.mat

True/False
1. T, 2. T, 3. T

Unit DM4: Polygon Modeling

Multiple Choice
1. B, 2. A, 3. D, 4. B

Fill in the Blanks
1. Vertex, Edge, Border, Polygon, Element, 2. triangular, 3. Edit Poly, 4. 1, 5, 6, 5. Attach, 6. Delete, Backspace

True/False
1. T, 2. T, 3. F

Unit DM5: Graphite Modeling Tools

Multiple Choice
1. A, 2. A, 3.B

Fill in the Blanks
1. Ribbon, 2. Optimize

True/False
1. T, 2. T

Unit DM6: Spline Modeling

Multiple Choice
1. A, 2. B, 3. B

Fill in the Blanks
1, Splines, NURBS, 2. Edit Spline, 3. Rendering, Interpolation, 4. Line, 5. Helix, 6. Section, 7. Reset Tangents

True/False
1. T, 2. T, 3. F, 4. T, 5. F

Unit DM7: Modifiers

Multiple Choice
1. C, 2. B

Fill in the Blanks
1. Object Space Modifiers, World Space Modifiers, 2. Transformation Matrix, 3. Perspective, Camera

True/False
1. T, 2. T

Appendix DTA: Quiz Answers [Texturing]

Unit DT1 - Material Editors

Multiple Choice
1. C, 2. C

Fill in the Blanks
1. Auto, 2. Delete, 3. Ctrl+Tab

True/False
1. F, 2. T, 3. T

Unit DT2 - Standard Materials and Maps

Multiple Choice
1. A, 2. D

Fill in the Blanks
1. SuperSampling, 2. Metal, 3. Oren-Nayar-Blinn, 4. Blend, 5. Morpher, 6. Multi/Sub-Object, 7. Top/Bottom, 8. Matte/Shadow, 9. Ink 'n Paint, 10. UVW Remove

True/False
1. T, 2. T, 3. F, 4. F, 5. T

Multiple Choice
1. C, 2. C

Fill in the Blanks
1. ART, Arnold, 2. 100, 3. weight, 4. IOR, 5. Anisotropy

True/False
1. T, 2. T, 3. F

Appendix DLA: Quiz Answers [Lighting]

Multiple Choice
1. D, 2. D

Fill in the Blanks
1. Shadow Map, 2. Ray-traced, 3. luminance=R0/R, 4. Show Cone, 5. Ray Bias, 6. Omni

True/False
1. F, 2. T, 3. T, 4. T, 5. F, 6. F, 7. T

Multiple Choice
1. B, 2. D, 3. D

Fill in the Blanks
1. Look At Controller, 2. Exposure, 3. HID

True/False
1. T, 2. T

Fill in the Blanks

1. Sunlight, **2.** System, **3.** Daylight, **4.** Sun Positioner

Appendix DAA: Quiz Answers [Arnold]

Unit DA1 - Introduction to Arnold

Fill in the Blanks
1. Monte Carlo, 2. high-range, 3. raytracing, Sampling, Ray Depth, 4. Camera (AA),
5. Diffuse, 6. Transmission, 7. Specular Ray Depth, 8. Transmission Ray Depth

True/False
1. T, 2. T, 3. F, 4. T, 5. T, 6. F

Unit DA2 - Arnold Lights

Multiple Choice
1. B, 2. D

Fill in the Blanks
1. Quad, 2. Spread, 3. Quad X, Quad Y, 4. Diffuse, Specular, SSS, Volume, 5. Physical Sky

True/False
1. T, 2. T, 3. F, 4. T, 5. T

Unit DA3 - Arnold Shaders and Materials

Multiple Choice
1. A, B, 2. A, 3. C, 4. D

Fill in the Blanks
1. ActiveShade, 2. Standard Surface, 3. Base Color, 4. Oren-Nayar, 5. IOR, 6. Depth, 7. SSS, 8. Radius, 9. diffusion, randomwalk, 10. dielectric, 11. Specular IOR, 12. Flake Color, Flakes, 13. Layer, 14. Matte, 15. Base Color, Melanin, 16. Hair and Fur

True/False
1. F, 2. T, 3. T, 4. T, 5. F, 6. F, 7. T, 8. T, 9. F, 10. T, 11. T, 12. T, 13. T, 14. T

This page is intentionally left blank

Index

This page is intentionally left blank

Other Publications by
PADEXI ACADEMY

*Visit **www.padexi.academy** to know more about the books, eBooks, and video courses published by PADEXI ACADEMY.*

Cinema 4D

- MAXON Cinema 4D R20: Modeling Essentials
- MAXON Cinema 4D R20: A Detailed Guide to Texturing, Lighting, and Rendering
- MAXON Cinema 4D R20: A Detailed Guide to Modeling, Texturing, Lighting, Rendering, and Animation
- MAXON Cinema 4D R20: A Detailed Guide to XPresso
- Exploring 3D Modeling with Cinema 4D R19
- Exploring MoGraph with Cinema 4D R19
- Exploring XPresso With Cinema 4D R19

3ds Max

- Autodesk 3ds Max 2020: Modeling Essentials
- Autodesk 3ds Max 2019: A Detailed Guide to Arnold Renderer
- Autodesk 3ds Max 2019: A Detailed Guide to Modeling, Texturing, Lighting, and Rendering
- Autodesk 3ds Max 2019: Arnold Essentials
- Exploring 3D Modeling with 3ds Max 2019
- MAXON Cinema 4D R20 and Autodesk 3ds Max 2019: Modeling Essentials

Photoshop

- Exploring Filters With Photoshop CC 2017

Coming Soon:

- Autodesk 3ds Max 2020: A Detailed Guide to Arnold Renderer
- MAXON Cinema 4D R20: A Detailed Guide to MoGraph
- MAXON Cinema 4D R20: A Detailed Guide to Dynamics

Printed in Poland
by Amazon Fulfillment
Poland Sp. z o.o., Wrocław